WITH A FEW GUNS

The Royal Regiment of Canadian Artillery in Afghanistan

Volume I

2002-2006

PRAISE FOR WITH A FEW GUNS

Gunners see the world as targets, and this well-written and massively researched book hits them all — the Taliban, the allies, NDHQ, the policy makers, the bureaucrats, and the politicians. This volume covers Canada's role in Afghanistan through Operation Medusa in 2006 and describes in detail the artillery's role — its difficulties and its triumphs — in a sometimes bewildering and always dangerous environment. Gunners will love it. Others should study it.

—J.L. Granatstein, author of Canada's Army:
Waging War and Keeping the Peace, 3rd edition (2020)

In Britain if you say "Gunners" some people will think you are talking about the Arsenal Football Club. In Canada if you say "Gunners" too many people will say, "What?" Well, you should know who Gunners are and this book will make it very clear, not only why you should know, but also why what you learn will make you damn proud.

—Peter Mansbridge

What our Canadian Gunners achieved "with a few guns," in a very challenging environment, is quite remarkable and made an incredible difference in the war effort in Afghanistan. The Taliban were having a devastating and deadly impact on CAF and NATO troops. Much of that impact was neutralized when our gunners showed.

As readers can see in this book, the Canadian Artillery adapted quickly and effectively to changing equipment, technology and tactical roles in a very complex challenging battlefield. They did essentially what they have always done throughout the history of Canada; they adapted, demonstrated outstanding ingenuity and agility in the field and most importantly got the job done. This is a story of the professionalism, dedication, resilience, fighting spirit, and courage of our Gunners and those with whom they served. "With a Few Guns" reminds us of the need to learn from our past, but also how proud we should all be of the members of our armed forces and their families. They made me proud when I had the privilege to serve as Minister of National Defence, and I shall forever be proud of and grateful to our Gunners. This book tells you why.

—The Hon Peter MacKay PC KC
Minister of National Defence 2007- 2013

This book records an important chapter of our country's distinguished and honourable military history that Canadians should celebrate. We sent men and women to Afghanistan at the behest of the United Nations, NATO, and our allies. This is a story of how our Canadian artillery met and often exceeded our allies' expectations. It should make us all proud.

—The Honourable John P. Manley, PC OC Minister of Foreign Affairs 2000 – 2002, Deputy Prime Minister 2002 – 2003

Napoleon said, "It is with guns that one makes war." Canada ignored that basic truth in the 'Decade of Darkness' and had to claw its way back to war-making in the opening years of its long and bitter conflict in Afghanistan.

Wolf Riedel's "With A Few Guns" tells the story of that renaissance in this comprehensive and compelling book. Essential reading for planners, policy makers and Canadians interested in how "can do" personnel overcome the perils of negligence and modern war.

—Marc Milner, PhD, Professor Emeritus, University of New Brunswick

With a Few Guns tells the important story of how Canada's gunners rendered critical and heroic service, out of all proportion to their numbers, in Afghanistan during 2002-2006. Riedel has captured their story with accuracy and grace. This volume is sure to be a go-to source for future historians of the war.

—Douglas Delaney CD, BA, MA, PhD, FRHistS, Professor, The Royal Military College of Canada

WITH A FEW GUNS

The Royal Regiment of Canadian Artillery in Afghanistan

Volume I

2002-2006

BY

Brian Reid
Wolf Riedel &
Mark Zuehlke

DOUBLE‡DAGGER

DEDICATION

With A Few Guns is dedicated to the greater family of the Royal Regiment of Canadian Artillery—from those who served with distinction in the face of danger in Afghanistan, to those who trained and supported them to become mission-ready, and especially to those who kept the rest of the family together at home.

In memory of "Reid B.A of the RCA" (1939-2023) and his dedicated service to the Guns, his sage advice and his literary prowess in recording parts of the Canadian Army's rich history.

The opinions expressed in this book are those of the authors and/or the cited sources. They do not purport to reflect the opinions or views of the Department of National Defence or the Canadian Armed Forces.

Library and Archives Canada Cataloguing in Publication
Reid, Brian, author
Riedel, Wolf, author
Zuehlke, Mark, author
With a Few Guns / B. Reid, W. Riedel & M. Zuehlke

A selection of photos have been used courtesy of the Department of National Defence, and other rights holders as captioned. Cover image credited to Stephen Gallagher. Maps are copyrighted by and used courtesy of C. Stuart Daniel.

Issued in print and electronic formats.
ISBN: 978-1-990644-86-3 (paperback)
ISBN: 978-1-990644-87-0 (ebook)

Cover Design: Pablo Javier Herrera
Interior Design: Winston A. Prescott

Double Dagger Books Ltd.
Toronto, Ontario, Canada
www.doubledagger.ca

TABLE OF CONTENTS

GLOSSARY

1 RCHA – 1st Regiment, Royal Canadian Horse Artillery
2 RCHA – 2nd Regiment, Royal Canadian Horse Artillery
4 AD Regt - 4th Air Defence Regiment, RCA
5 RALC – 5e Régiment d'artillerie légère du Canada
ASCC – airspace coordination centre
FAC - forward air controller
FOB – forward operating base
FOO – forward observation officer
FSCC – fire support coordination centre
IED – improvised explosive device
ISAF – International Security Assistance Force
ISTAR - intelligence, surveillance, target acquisition, and reconnaissance
JTAC - joint terminal attack controller
KAF – Kandahar Airfield
LAV – light armoured vehicle
NATO – North Atlantic Treaty Organization
PB – patrol base
PRT – provincial reconstruction team
QRF – quick reaction force
RCAS – Royal Canadian Artillery School
Recce – reconnaissance
RPG – rocket propelled grenade
STA – surveillance and target acquisition
TACC – target acquisition coordination centre
UAV – unmanned aerial vehicle
UN – United Nations

FOREWORD

Canada has a significant history in war, both at home and later as a valued friend and ally in a variety of alliance and coalition structures, culminating in the titanic struggles of the two world wars. Millions of Canadians served both in uniform and in the production of the instruments of war, and hundreds of thousands paid the price in blood. As a direct result of the tragedies of the Second World War and the existential threat of nuclear holocaust between the United States and the Soviet Union, Canada was at the forefront in helping create various organizations to share the burdens and responsibilities for collective defence and keeping the peace at the global (the UN in 1945), regional (NATO in 1949) and local levels (NORAD in 1958). Underlying all of this was the relatively common determination to invest in military deterrence capabilities which, though expensive, were appreciated as being far less costly than a war. For the first few decades Canada was a key influencer, mainly due to a robust military capability that was effective and made valued contributions to a long list of deterrence, peacekeeping, and peacemaking missions around the world.

The tragedy of the 9/11 attacks on the United States was the immediate trigger which led Canada to Afghanistan. Shocked and enraged, the Americans made it very clear that Canada was expected to help, as per our long-standing treaty obligations under both NATO and NORAD. An attack on one was an attack on all. Under enormous pressure from our neighbor and largest trading partner to contribute significant military forces to the ongoing U.S. - led coalition war in Iraq or Afghanistan, Prime Minister Chrétien opted for Afghanistan.

What this really meant is that for the first time since the Second World War, Canada's government did not have a choice about sending the Canadian Armed Forces (CAF) into harm's way, at least not if our single, most important relationship with the U.S. was to survive intact. This was to be a 'come as you are' mission against a cunning and ruthless foe, with almost no time to prepare. From the Canadian perspective, the immediate problem was that for decades the political attention and support to the CAF had been reduced to the extent that money for the required people, sophisticated equipment, and training were in short supply. In the relentless pursuit of voter-pleasing social programs, various governments and the supporting bureaucracy had grown used to seeing the budget of the Department of National Defence as discretionary spending. They had gambled that the U.S. would always protect us, that modern equipment would not be needed, or that Canada could simply choose not to take part. They were wrong. And the rest is history.

With a Few Guns is focused on the contributions to the Afghanistan mission by the men and women of the Royal Regiment of Canadian Artillery, one of the largest and oldest of the Canadian Army's regimental families that traces their lineage back to pre-Confederation. All regiments have at their core the importance of maintaining the regimental family as a healthy, growing and dedicated institution that Canadians can be proud of and what younger Canadians want to join. Stories of those who prepared, deployed and fought for Canada are a cornerstone of our regimental traditions.

This book's perspective is varied and deeply personal, and mainly about gunners. It is set within the strategic context of why Canada was in Afghanistan, what Canada tried to do as part of the larger coalition of nations, how they were trained and equipped, who was there and how they went about trying to get things done at both the operational and tactical levels. The narrative is historical in its flow, with dozens of individual stories from gunners and those they supported within the combined arms team woven together not only in battles fought, but amongst all who contributed. The purpose of these stories is to capture what it was like, what happened, what went well, what we could do better and the actions/reactions of those under enormous pressure in a very complicated and chaotic environment.

As time wore on and the Afghan mission evolved to increasing levels of both complexity and combat, a key lesson for the wider army community and a reminder for all gunners is that the artillery is much more than just delivering fires where needed. It's also about the command and control of fires from all sources be they land, sea, air and space, and being able to influence not only when to shoot, but when not to; the use of cutting edge technologies to better inform the intelligence systems to contribute to the coordination of air defense and target acquisition systems; of incorporating increasingly sophisticated sensors such as loiter drone or unmanned aerial vehicles that can not only kill, but can help the individual platoons and sections find the immediate dangers behind the next house; and the incorporation of new or allied systems of long range precision fires into the overall plan, an asset which has greatly extended the area of influence and the battle space of all land formations.

The bottom line is that the gunners of Canada both regular and reserve, full time and part time, responded in a magnificent fashion to the life and death challenges of the Afghanistan mission, and did amazing things as a valued member of the combined arms team. They helped re-establish Canada's reputation as soldiers who can make thing happen in the midst of chaos; who can worry about helping farmers repair their roads while using cutting edge technologies to find and destroy those who were seeking to kill the weak and the innocent, soldiers who can help rally troops from several nations to do really hard things where lives would be taken, and lost.

Let's think about the current global context and what the immediate future might hold for the Canadian Armed Forces. Russia has recently invaded Ukraine (again) with a large conventional army causing shock waves felt around the world, with over 500,000 dead and hundreds of billions spent on people, equipment and shattered infrastructure. China is now Russia's not so quiet partner, and increasingly vocal about 'reintegrating' Taiwan while being very aggressive throughout the Indo-Pacific region. Surrounded by dangers, fear, and uncertainty, the world is starting to divide between those who support the U.S led coalition, or that of the China/Russia entente. Most nations are becoming very focused on trying to quickly acquire significant new defence capabilities to deter and defend against the predators, though Canada lags far behind most NATO nations. It is increasingly probable that Canada's troops will be sent into harm's way in the not-too-distant future, and it is hoped that *With a Few Guns* may help better inform them on what it was like, what worked and what they need to change as they face the threats of their future.

Ubique.

Lieutenant-General (Retd) Andrew B. Leslie, PC, CMM, MSC, MSM, CD

AUTHOR'S NOTE

One should start off by clearly stating what "With A Few Guns" is and what it isn't. The two volumes which will make up this book are not the "official history" of the Canadian artillery in Afghanistan, nor are they intended to be a critical study of the events and circumstances of the times. As authors, we did not initially have access to any classified documents which would be required to make a full and accurate record of what happened there. What this book is, is a narrative provided by the gunners, and others, who were there and told us of what they saw through their own eyes and of what they experienced in preparing for and during their deployments in theatre. These we put into context with the events at the time with other unclassified or open source materials.

We fully appreciate that there are other recollections and remembrances of those days. Some will differ from the experiences recounted here. That's only human nature when people observe events from different points of view and try to recollect them some ten to twenty years after the fact. In fairness, we tried to interview as many participants and research as many accounts as possible in order to obtain as balanced a view of events that happened in times of extreme stress and great personal risk.

We know that we missed many stories. Some that we reached out to considered what most of us would view as dramatic and dangerous activities as being nothing out of the ordinary; as simply doing their job, and certainly nothing worth bothering the general public with. Others simply couldn't participate. For them the ghosts of Afghanistan are still very real. It was obvious during some of the interviews that post-traumatic stress is still a factor in their lives. In other cases that wasn't obvious until we were receiving feedback on draft chapters we had provided to them for review for accuracy. We urge anyone with symptoms and who are not already undergoing professional treatment to seek assistance.[1] As of the time of writing such assistance is available for serving members, veterans and their families at 1 (800) 268-7708.

---

[1] An overview of Post-traumatic Stress issues can be found at the Veterans Affairs Canada site at https://www.veterans.gc.ca/eng/health-support/mental-health-and-wellness/understanding-mental-health/ptsd-warstress

We are grateful, in general, to all who served, and in particular, to all who participated and came forward to share their recollections.

Underlying the stories of individual gunners who participated in what has become Canada's longest war, are several recurring themes: the role of army transformation and its impact on the structure and capabilities of the artillery; the shift in focus from massed artillery to precision fire from individual batteries formed from composite troops; the role of the instructors in gunnery, master gunners, assistant instructors in gunnery and the Royal Canadian Artillery School as gatekeepers of the artillery's corporate knowledge; the state of the regiment's equipment from time to time; the revival of surveillance and target acquisition artillery with the corresponding demise of air defence artillery; the importance of artillery coordination cells; the transformation of Canadian forward air controllers into joint terminal attack controllers; the deployment rotation system and managed readiness; and the changing nature of the enemy and of policy directions including the use of artillery in counterinsurgency operations with its tensions between security operations and reconstruction efforts.

Dr. Sean Maloney, in his "Note from the Author" of his three-volume set "The Canadian Army in Afghanistan," calls for other authors to "expand, enhance, correct, or even contradict" his work.[2] Unfortunately his books only reached us after the manuscript of Volume I was complete and being readied for the publisher. It did, however, serve as a very timely gunner's "double check" on the chronology of events. "With A Few Guns" is the Canadian artillery's contribution to expand and enhance the army's story.

Volume 1 of "With A Few Guns" deals with the transformation of the artillery from a Cold War establishment to one suitable to providing support in failed state scenarios. It starts with the first few steps in that transition and ends in the midst of a full-on war. Volume 2 will take up the story in 2007. At the end of Volume 2 we will need to answer the question of where the transformed Canadian artillery stands in light of its mission in Latvia and the large-scale, high intensity operations currently ongoing in Ukraine.

While "With a Few Guns" was never intended to be a "lessons learned" account, many of those at the strategic, operational, tactical and personal levels pop out. More importantly, the stories of the resilience and dedication of gunners, and the respect that they earned under tremendously challenging conditions is the greatest lesson we all have re-learned. Many times during the years in Afghanistan the gunners would hear that age-old expression – "Thank God the Guns!"

Wolf Riedel
Southwest Ontario, September, 2023

---

[2] Sean M. Maloney, *The Canadian Army in Afghanistan Volume 1: A Nation Under Fire, 2001-2006.* Ottawa: Army Publication Office, 2022., xvi.

INTRODUCTION

WINTERS IN SHILO, MANITOBA CAN BE BRUTAL AT TIMES. It has temperatures that stay far below zero and cold winds that can cut through a person like a knife. Snowfalls as late as April are common and ones in May are not unheard of. The first few days of March 2006 had been like that, cold ... windy ... a bit of snow, but they hadn't been the worst of days as far as the weather went. They would, however, be days that would test the soul of the little military community that calls Shilo home.

It had been a tough day for Debbie Gallagher and it was about to become a lot tougher as she stood in front of the door of one the base's private married quarters. Debbie's husband, Steve, commanded A Battery of the 1st Regiment, Royal Canadian Horse Artillery (1 RCHA) which had been deployed to Kandahar, Afghanistan a mere month prior. Canadian gunners had been to Afghanistan before: once in the immediate aftermath of 9/11 and then again, starting in 2003 for several years in Kabul. There had been a few Canadian casualties during those tours but none from the artillery. This new deployment to Kandahar, however, was rumoured to be the one that would really challenge the mettle of Canada's small military family.

After learning that the battery would be deploying, Debbie and Steve had gone to Colorado Springs to meet with an American army wife and husband that they had become good friends with while living in Gagetown, New Brunswick. Debbie had gone there to learn about what needed to be done to prepare herself and, more importantly, the families of their soon to be deployed members. Her friend told her how the Americans handled things. It quickly became clear to Debbie that Canada had none of that; that no one in Canada, "was talking about it. No one was saying that, you know, this is war; and this is, this is going to be ugly. People are going to die ...and nobody was talking about it."[1]

Debbie and Steve immediately resolved to set things in motion to create a network in Shilo that would be there to support the families while the battery was overseas. With the help of several of the other spouses they formed a team and created plans to support each other, to support their deployed members and to be ready in case the worst should happen. Their motto was "Nobody sits and worries at home alone."

One of the team's efforts was the creation of a newsletter to circulate to the soldiers' families. Doreen Savage from Gaspé, Quebec, mother of Gunner[2] Janie Duguay, who was on her first operational deployment, stressed the importance of that connection. For her it provided an opportunity of contact with the military and reinforced the fact that there was no need for her to be alone and worry; that they were not alone even if they felt like they were.[3]

It was that planning and her role on that team that had brought Debbie to that door on that cold day. It had started with a request to meet with one of the spouses in the network who needed to talk. The spouse had said to Debbie,

> *I don't know what to do with the guilt...You know how we all know that if you get through six o'clock, chances are we're going to be okay. Well, I woke up early and went to the kitchen and didn't turn on the light ... and I saw the cars pull on the street. I saw a man in uniform and the padre get out and I went over to the phone and I sat in a fetal position on the floor and watched the clock until six thirty and then I realized they weren't going to ring my doorbell; they rang the neighbour's.[4]*

The fatality had been a member of the 2nd Battalion, Princess Patricia's Canadian Light Infantry whose wife and children were new to Shilo and whose own families lived far away. Debbie quickly agreed to help and so,

> *I called our girls and we went that night with cots and pillows and beds and food and made sure that everyone was going to be okay...When I came to the door, a little girl was coming down the stairs, and it was a little girl from the school so, of course she knew me, and she said: 'Mrs Gallagher. My daddy went to heaven today. He's a hero. Can you help me tie my bathrobe?' And I did. And she wrapped her little arms around my legs and then she said: 'Did you bring cookies?' So we went and we had a cookie.[5]*

It wouldn't be long before the Regiment would have its own losses. On April 22nd, Bombardier Myles Mansell, a reservist from the 5th (British Columbia) Field Artillery Regiment, RCA from Victoria, British Columbia and Lieutenant William Turner, a reservist who had been with the 20th and 11th Field Artillery Regiments, RCA from Edmonton, Alberta and Guelph, Ontario, both serving with the Kandahar provincial reconstruction team, would be its first sons to die. They, along with two other soldiers, died when their vehicle struck by an improvised explosive device in Gumbad village Kandahar Province, Afghanistan.

Just a few weeks later, on May 17th, A Battery's own Captain Nichola Goddard, operating as Call Sign Golf 13[6]—a forward observation officer—would be the Regiment's first ever daughter to die in combat when her light armoured vehicle was hit by several rocket propelled grenades in Pashmul village, Kandahar Province near what would soon gain infamy as the "white school."

When you strip away the uniforms and the customs and traditions, what is left of a Regiment is that it is a family. It has its share of overbearing big brothers, thoughtful sisters, crazy uncles, perhaps a solid dad, definitely a caring mother and a whole bunch of diverse kids and their wives and husbands. Families might squabble sometimes, but deep down there is a solid bond. Woe to the neighbour—be they one from another unit, or worse yet, someone from outside the army—who tries to do wrong to a member of that family.

All of the Canadian artillery is one family, one regiment—strangely enough it's one made up of a number of regiments, currently four from the regular force and sixteen from the reserve force.[7] They all share the same uniform and cap badge and are all units of the 'Regiment'—the Royal Regiment of Canadian Artillery. That's hard to explain to an outsider sometimes.

The story of how the Royal Regiment came to be in that remote and often dusty place is a long one. Even more so is the story that followed their arrival. This is that story. A story of Canada's artillery after the events of that fateful day on September 11th, 2001 when a fanatical terrorist organization brought down two high-rise office towers in New York City, damaged the Pentagon and killed many more innocent civilians in a fourth plane crash near Shanksville, Pennsylvania. It's the story of how thousands of Canadian gunners, both regular force and reserve force, answered the call and fought their first combat actions since the Korean War (1950-1953).

It's the story of the gunner family, as told by them. It's the story of who they were and what they accomplished in Afghanistan ... with only a few guns.

PROLOGUE:
ARTILLERY FOR THE NEW MILLENNIUM

IN ORDER TO UNDERSTAND THE CHALLENGES that Canadian gunners faced in Afghanistan, one must first take a look at the state of Canada's artillery, and its army, at the turn of the 21st Century. That in itself requires a brief examination of their roles during the preceding half century that started at the end of the Second World War.

The story of Canadian artillery is one of cycles; cycles which come with periods of extreme highs and dismal lows. The high points come in times of war when everyone recognizes the comfort that well-placed rounds of high explosive in fire for effect[1] can bring to cure the troubles facing the pinned-down infantryman. Unsurprisingly, the lows come during lengthy periods of peace where the government and the leadership of the military give more priority on how to save a dollar than on what is necessary to keep a vital combat capability viable during times of austerity.

These cycles have been with the Canadian artillery throughout its history. Canada's full-time permanent force, or permanent active militia, before the start of the First World War, held a mere two field batteries[2] and five garrison artillery[3] companies. Its part-time non-permanent active militia had 24 field batteries and 21 garrison artillery batteries and companies. By war's end, there were 78 full-time batteries of field, siege, trench mortar, and anti-aircraft artillery.[4]

Peacetime converted the bulk of that force back to a reserve status. By the start of the Second World War, the full-time component mustered only three field batteries, one medium battery, three heavy coastal batteries, and one air defence battery. The part-time component, on the other hand, contained 160 field, medium, heavy, anti-aircraft, and searchlight batteries. It was a force designed for mobilization. When war came, the army topped-up the part-time batteries with new recruits so that by 1945 the First Canadian Army in Europe alone consisted of 117 field, medium, heavy, anti-tank, anti-aircraft, rocket, and survey batteries.[5] Starting in 1940 there had been several name changes for both components, but the structure of a full-time and a part-time force essentially remained.

Thereafter, the post-war cycle again took hold. Peace-time reorganization drew the full-time force down to only seven batteries of field, medium, anti-tank, and anti-aircraft artillery while the army demobilized, disbanded, or returned the remaining units to the part-time force.

The quantity and quality of the guns and related equipment held by Canada's artillery also ebbed and flowed with times of war and peace, as did the number of gunners that manned them.

Cycles.

The Korean War and the concurrent stand-off with the Soviets in Europe reversed the peace versus war/full-time versus part-time rhythm. Canada gradually turned its funding towards a larger full-time standing army whose designation settled into the current "regular force". The government spent less attention and committed fewer resources to the shrinking and under-equipped part-time component, which would eventually continue under the title "reserve force".

Only a single brigade group with a single artillery regiment deployed during each of the three rotations of the Korean War starting in 1951, yet with the growing Soviet threat in Europe, the regular force grew. By the mid 1960s, the army had four full-time brigade groups with four field artillery regiments totaling between 16 to 20 field batteries, two light air defence batteries—which were eventually converted to surface-to-surface nuclear missile batteries—and varying numbers of locating batteries. Equipment ranged during this period from 81mm, 4.2 inch and 120mm mortars, 105mm M2A2[6] and L5 Pack howitzers, 155mm M1A1 towed and M109 self-propelled howitzers, a variety of anti-aircraft guns and to Honest John nuclear missile launchers.

Conversely, the many and varied post-war reserve force artillery regiments devolved over time to 22 regiments with 71 lightly manned and lightly equipped field batteries.[7] One point stood out, however: while not fully equipped, the reserve artillery during this time used many of the same howitzers, vehicles and radios as their regular force counterparts. This provided the ability to not only quickly reinforce the regular force with augmentees who were already trained on the equipment, but in the event of an emergency, it also permitted the artillery to expand its size with additional, equipped batteries. That ability to grow the army, regretfully, was about to change.

A form of stability reigned from the 1960s through the 1990s. Yes, there were force reductions and task and equipment changes as budgets fluctuated. Prime Minister

Pierre Trudeau came into office and brought forth an agenda in April of 1969, in part, calling for the withdrawal from Europe. A program to divest the Centurion tank fleet brought rapid intervention by key European leaders in 1972 who made it clear that access to European trade depended on Canada's continuing defence commitment to Europe. Trudeau listened and acted. The resulting spending programs not only brought about the purchase of the Leopard tanks to replace the Centurions, but also the acquisition of the CF18, the Aurora, the Canadian Patrol Frigate and other major weapon systems.[8] The rebirth of the air defence trade grew out of this period as well. Thus, there had been a cycle of reinvigoration within one of decline and as a result, the Canadian army's underlying doctrine and organization continued to focus, in large part, on the Soviet threat in Europe. It was also developing a small, but politically favoured, side business in United Nations (UN) peacekeeping.

The regular force settled into two broad capabilities: a tracked, armoured force oriented towards Europe—typified for the artillery by the 155mm M109 self-propelled howitzers—and a light, air portable force in Canada, typified by 105mm L5 pack howitzers. The reserve force slowly lost its mobilization role to only become augmentees of the regular force. It continued to be equipped with 1950s era 105mm C1 howitzers, which, while capable of operational use, were more and more seen merely as training guns.

From 1981 to just before the fall of the Soviet Union in 1991, Canada committed itself to supplying two brigade groups to the North Atlantic Treaty Organization (NATO). 4 Canadian Mechanized Brigade Group, garrisoned full-time in Germany, was the tactical reserve to NATO's Central Army Group. 5e Groupe-brigade mécanisé du Canada garrisoned in Valcartier, Quebec provided the Canadian Air-Sea Transportable Brigade Group to NATO's northern flank in Norway as a follow-up force to 2 Canadian Mechanized Brigade Group's battle group-size[9] commitment to the Allied Command Europe Mobile Force (Land).

Doctrinally, Canada oriented its army at the Soviet threat. Even the two lighter brigades designated for the "Defence of Canada" were now equipped with light wheeled armoured vehicles, general purpose and trained very much like their heavier counterparts.

Doctrine is often debated, and it changes from time to time. For the Americans in Europe during this period it encompassed "active defence", flirted with "manoeuvrism" and, beginning in the 1980s, settled on the more comprehensive "AirLand Battle."[10] It was during this time that Lieutenant-General Charles Belzile set Canada's army, then known as Mobile Command, on the road towards a divisional structure. Units and equipment were upgraded to suit the formation. The Rendezvous series of division-level exercises trained and tested the army in its primary role and made it clear to everyone what was expected of them.[11]

Not everything worked to plan. Mobile Command designed Exercise BRAVE LION for 1986 to test the efficacy of deploying 5ᵉ Groupe-brigade mécanisé du Canada to Norway. It essentially failed.[12] The brigade was re-tasked to reinforce 4 Canadian Mechanized Brigade Group within Central Army Group under the newly reformed 1ˢᵗ Canadian Division. The division had a forward command element in Germany and had formed the 1ˢᵗ Canadian Division Artillery Brigade Headquarters and Signals Squadron to command and control the artillery resources allocated to the division.

The main takeaway coming out of this era was that doctrine is more than just "a mindset"; a more comprehensive approach of "cognitive, procedural, organizational, material, and moral components" in doctrine was argued for.[13] Belzile had given the army not just the doctrinal mindset but the organization, the tools, the teaching and training, and the psychological foundation that defined its role. Canada's army knew what it was, knew what was required of it, and for the most part, had the equipment to do it with. The army also knew what the role of the artillery was and organized it and equipped it, both field and air defence, to fulfill that role.

And then the Soviets fell apart and went home. They left behind a rusting-out East German army and a Yugoslavia whose fragmentation into its ethnic constituent parts devolved to open warfare by mid-1990.

Canada, for its part, sought a peace dividend. From 1989 to 1995 the Deputy Minister of National Defence opposed and undermined any attempts to refurbish the army's heavy components.[14]

Paradoxically, Canada's government, while routinely cutting budgets, started committing its army—which for all intents and purposes had spent the Cold War operating out of garrisons—even in Europe—to a continuing stream of one expeditionary deployment after another.

Canada became involved in peace stabilizations in the fragmented countries of the Balkans even before 4 Canadian Mechanized Brigade Group was fully withdrawn from Germany and disbanded in 1993. Starting with the April 1992 entry of the 1ᵉ Battalion, Royal 22ᵉ Régiment battle group—known as CANBAT within the United Nations Protection Force—under Operation HARMONY and other complementary operations,[15] one Canadian contingent after another had maintained a presence in the region.[16] For the infantry, the disbandment of 4 Canadian Mechanized Brigade Group meant the eventual reorganization into six mechanized and three light 10/90 battalions in Canada.[17]

And then there was the 1992-3 mission to Somalia. Somalia not only consumed resources while ongoing but ended up with the dissolution of the Canadian Airborne Regiment. The investigation into the beating death of a captive Somali teenager, Shidane Arone, at the hands of Canadian soldiers, created a crisis in confidence on the part of the government and the public as to the military and, in particular, the military's leadership. The redistribution of the Airborne's three commandos to their parent regiments facilitated the end of the 10/90 experiment and the three light battalions becoming full regular force units.

There had been an on-again, off-again airborne capability within the Canadian artillery since the Second World War when three small parachute qualified forward observation units were formed. An airborne gun capability came in 1949 with the formation of 1st Light Battery (Para), Royal Canadian Artillery armed with 75mm M1A1 pack howitzers. It remained in service until 1956 but the capability was revived in 1968 with the formation of the 105mm L5 howitzer and 81mm mortar equipped 1st Airborne Battery, Royal Canadian Artillery. In 1977, when the Airborne Regiment moved to Petawawa as part of the Special Service Force, the parachute role was taken up by E Battery (Para), 2 RCHA until it converted to M109 self-propelled howitzers in 1993/4. Thereafter individuals in forward observation officer (FOO) and forward air controller (FAC) parties were parachute qualified to support the parachute companies established in each of the three regular force light infantry battalions.

The continued, and unending, commitment in the Balkans had given rise to two concepts which would very much influence the army's, and thereby the artillery's, force structure and readiness methodology in the new century.

The first was the army's transition from a Cold War army focus to one more in tune with operations other than war. That is not to say that the Cold War army was not capable of other missions. It quite clearly was, as shown by the multitude of United Nations (UN) missions undertaken by it. A prime example was the lengthy battalion-sized commitment to the UN Force in Cyprus.

Canada's army during the Cold War was what one could call a "fully balanced army"; one trained for everything up to thermonuclear war with a peer, yet able to provide disaster relief and peacekeeping service.[18] Thereafter, starting during what some refer to as the Canadian military's Decade of Darkness,[19] the army was gradually restructured.

Readiness, or perhaps more accurately, the method of creating and measuring operational readiness, had never been an issue with the Cold War army as the Somalia Inquiry pointed out.[20] Canada's Cold War army was kept at a high level of readiness by training at up to the divisional level through its annual training cycles. In addition, the army maintained 4 Canadian Mechanized Brigade Group in Germany at a higher level of capabilities than the rest of the force.

By 1997, not long after the Somalia Inquiry had been brought to a halt, the army knew that it had lost its way. The high tempo of operations had impeded training; atrophy had impacted its foundation; its vision for strategic planning, capability development and doctrinal design was weak; and it was perpetually caught up in managing crises.[21]

There had been great debate in the late 1990s about the process for the army's development. In 1998, the then commander of the 1st Canadian Division and the Army Training Authority, Major-General Mike Jeffery, a gunner, had been advocating for a Three Army/Three Horizon transformation model. This, however, did not gain universal acceptance. The then Chief of the Land Staff resisted army transformation. It wouldn't be until 2000, when Jeffery himself became Chief of the Land Staff, that it was finally accepted and the army took steps to formulate a strategy based on growing the army through three phases over some 20-plus years.[22] These evolved into the "Advancing with Purpose" change agenda.[23]

Foremost was the need to address the severe resource restraints that the army was under. As it stood only a fraction of the army's units had sufficient funding to even carry out a battalion level exercise each year. Change was needed to properly understand the limitations that the army worked under and to maximize its limited resources. The army would develop an army training and operations framework in 2001 supported by a managed readiness system in 2002 and the whole fleet management of equipment. This was to be phased in over five years. The objective was to prioritize training and equipping for those elements of the army designated for deployment.[24]

In effect, these steps, taken at the turn of the century. formalized a system whereby the army was divided into three parts based on its three regular force brigade groups. The brigades and their equipment rotated from a state of low readiness to one of high readiness in three annual phases. Added to this was a system of readiness evaluation.[25] Managed readiness would define what personnel and what equipment was needed and at what level. With this, the Cold War army's focus on the brigade group and the division was slipping away in favour of a formalized force structure based on battle group deployments, notwithstanding that the government's defence papers still called for a full mechanized brigade group to be deployed on 90 days' notice.[26]

The managed readiness system was intended to ensure that the army could meet its essential readiness requirements when faced with a high tempo and limited resources. Concurrently it was also designed to address the army's shortage of manpower; frequently referred to as "lacking boots on the ground" or "hollowness."[27]

Difficulties in meeting regular force manpower commitments during the late 1990s had resulted in an ever-increasing need for reserve force volunteers. On Operation PALLADIUM in the Balkans, the going rate was between 15 to 20% of the contingent being reservists.[28] The 2nd Battalion, Princess Patricia's Canadian Light Infantry battle group's rifle companies, which fought under the United Nations Protection Force in the Medak Pocket in 1993, had between 50 to 80%

reserve augmentation.[29] Infantry units were preserving their core rifle company competencies often at the expense of reducing or zero-manning their mortar, pioneer and anti armour platoons.[30] More and more, the regular army was clamoring for more person-years to help fill its holes while searching its existing establishments for spare people for higher priority tasks.

General Jeffery's restructure laid the groundwork for functioning within the reality of reduced funding, but did not translate into a change of the fundamental structure of the army or the artillery in particular. Initially there was no plan to divest tanks, nor self-propelled artillery nor air defence capabilities.[31] That would change with time.

While the army's developing transformation plan was causing both stress and uncertainty amongst gunners, the organization and equipment of the artillery had changed little since 1997 when it introduced the light French 105mm GIAT LG1 into its inventory. The 3rd Regiment, Royal Canadian Horse Artillery (3 RCHA) had been reduced to nil strength upon the repatriation of 4 Canadian Mechanized Brigade Group a few years prior. The 1st Regiment, Royal Canadian Horse Artillery (1 RCHA) had replaced it in Shilo as the 1 Canadian Mechanized Brigade Group's direct support regiment. Each of 1 RCHA, 2nd Regiment, Royal Canadian Horse Artillery (2 RCHA) and the 5e Régiment d'artillerie légère du Canada (5 RALC) had two six-gun M109A4+ batteries to support their respective brigade group's two mechanized battalions, and one six-gun LG1 battery to support their brigade's light battalion.

As the Twentieth Century came to a close, 5 RALC's Batterie X was preparing to return from Rotation 5 of Operation PALLADIUM in Bosnia while 1 RCHA was preparing to deploy A Battery as an LG1 battery on Roto 6. It would be the first such operational deployment of guns since the Korean War. Meanwhile, C Battery was preparing to deploy there as an infantry company with the 3rd Battalion, Princess Patricia's Canadian Light Infantry. B Battery would deploy to replace A Battery on Rotation 7.

Thirty-four reserve force gun batteries—organized into 15 field regiments—and two independent batteries, each of which was equipped with approximately four 105mm C3[32] howitzers, stood to augment their regular force counterparts.

Besides the field guns, the artillery also provided an air defence capability in 2000. 4th Air Defence Regiment, RCA (4 AD Regt) was formed under the Very Low Level Air Defence Project on November 27th, 1987 in Lahr Germany with three batteries: 127, 128 and 129 Air Defence Batteries.

The pre-existing 128 and 129 Airfield Air Defence Batteries had converted from Boffins—naval versions of the 40mm Bofors anti-aircraft gun—and British

Blowpipe air defence missiles to eight Oerlikon Skyguard fire control radars, sixteen twin 35mm Oerlikon GDF-005 air defence gun systems and eight Oerlikon/Martin Marietta Air Defence Anti Tank System (ADATS) using laser-beam-riding guided missiles mounted on M113 tracked armoured personnel carrier variants.

127 Air Defence Battery, tasked to work with 4 Canadian Mechanized Brigade Group, had twelve ADATS while a fourth battery in Canada, 119 Air Defence Battery, was also equipped with ADATS. Concurrently, all other existing air defence batteries and troops, which since the 1970s had been part of the three regular force regiments in Canada, were reduced to nil strength. With the dissolution of 4 Canadian Mechanized Brigade Group in Lahr in 1992, 4 AD Regt was reduced to nil strength as well.

4 AD Regt was reactivated in 1996 as a total force[33] regiment with 128 Air Defence Battery in Moncton, NB and 119 Air Defence Battery and 210 Workshop in Gagetown, New Brunswick.[34] Five total force air defence batteries were stood up by converting reserve force field units and equipping them with Thales shoulder-launched Javelin S-15 Surface to Air Missiles: 1st Air Defence Regiment, RCA in Pembroke, Ontario (two batteries); 18th Air Defence Regiment, RCA in Lethbridge, Alberta (two batteries); and 58e Batterie antiaérienne, part of 6e Régiment d'artillerie de campagne, ARC in Levis, Quebec. These five batteries were tasked to augment 4 AD Regt with a total of three Javelin troops. In total, some 475 regular force gunners and some 430 reservists equipped with a mixture of Skyguard, ADATS, 35mm Oerlikons and Javelin missiles made up the artillery's air defence branch.[35]

Of particular significance is that 4 AD Regt also contained three brigade group level airspace coordination centres (ASCC) whose role was to deconflict airspace as between aircraft and ground based munitions within a brigade group's area of operations.

Supporting all Canadian gunners until 1970 was the Royal Canadian School of Artillery in Shilo, Manitoba which thereafter became the Royal Canadian Artillery School (RCAS) in Gagetown, New Brunswick. Its various batteries and departments supported everything from gunnery to maintenance to doctrine and tactics. For some time, it had provided only limited support to the field previously known as locating artillery. At this time the term "locating artillery" was changing to "surveillance and target acquisition" (STA).

While the artillery's field and air defence components had been decimated over the last half century, its locating arm had been utterly destroyed.

Finding and engaging enemy guns—counter-battery tasks—has been one role of the artillery since it was first invented. At first guns dueled in direct view of each other from hilltops or battlements but as guns became more sophisticated and could engage targets they couldn't see, counter-battery activities also became more complex. Starting with hot air balloons, observers would rise up into the sky to see over the horizon and find and engage enemy guns. In the First World War, observers in airplanes augmented and then replaced balloons as air observation posts.

That war also introduced sound ranging—the techniques of using a series of microphones—to pinpoint the location from which a gun was firing. When the electronic age arrived with the Second World War, radars were tasked with locating mortar, and subsequently gun positions by the arc that their projectiles traced through the sky. These three methods, aerial observation, sound ranging and radar, formed the artillery's three staple counter-battery sensor systems.

To increase accuracy, guns and sensors were assisted by artillery survey systems that accurately located the sensors, and thereby the targets, and the responding guns to a common geographic grid. Another component, an artillery intelligence role, processed information from the sensors and other sources into an appropriate response from the guns. These then—aerial observation, radars, sound ranging, survey and artillery intelligence—are the key components of surveillance and target acquisition (STA) artillery.[36]

After the Second World War, the various wartime counter-battery agencies were placed into one reserve force locating regiment, a regular force locating battery, a divisional air observation flight, and into the survey sections of each regular force artillery regiment. Both the locating regiment and the battery eventually disappeared to the supplementary order of battle in the 1960s. The air observation flight remained as detachments of the regular force artillery regiments but which on unification, together with other army aviation resources, transferred into Royal Canadian Air Force (RCAF) light observation helicopter flights under the army's 10th Tactical Air Group.

By the early 1970s, the locating trade had died out, except for small pockets of surveyors in the regiments and a small cell within the RCAS. A few AN/MPQ-501 counter mortar radars had been retained for a while with 1 RCHA in Germany but by the end of the century they too were long gone. From time to time, experimentation had taken place to develop unmanned aerial vehicles (UAV) but these too were now relegated mostly to history.

By 1996, the RCAF and army, having retired the heavy lift CH-47 Chinooks a few years earlier for budget reasons, sought to replace its CH-135 Twin Huey utility transport helicopters with forty new ones. The government of the day decided that they would also retire the CH-136 Kiowa light observation helicopters and replace all of the tactical helicopter fleet with the CH-146 Griffon multi-role utility helicopter. This aircraft has been criticized as unsuitable for any of the roles assigned to it primarily because it is underpowered for its utility and heavy transport role and too large for its reconnaissance (recce) role.[37]

With the loss of the Kiowas the artillery aerial observation and armoured aerial recce functions all but disappeared. Just as important, with the replacement of the L5, the CH-135 and the CH-47 made airmobile operations involving the LG1 and CH-146 very difficult even though short lifts were possible. The LG1 is simply too heavy for the Griffon.[38]

The regimental survey sections continued to hang on but they would also disappear following the general adoption of newer technology such as global positioning and the gun laying and positioning system. As the new millennium dawned, the locating branch of the artillery had shrunk from some 450 gunners during the 1960s to being zero-manned by the year 2000. What was left of the corporate knowledge for the employment of STA resided in just 11 gunners roaming the halls of building J7 of the RCAS.[39]

While other countries had been investing in both STA personnel and their equipment—particularly UAVs and radars—the Canadian army's interest was low; or perhaps it would be more accurate to say that it wasn't prepared to make it a high enough priority to spend immediate money on.

The reasons for this were varied. A common argument for the lack of interest related to the organizational structure of the Canadian army as a whole. At the time, STA was generally more of a divisional resource than a brigade group one and in order to spend money on a divisional resource, one needed to have a division. While Canada had between three and five equipped and manned regular force formations over the years, its commitment to having an organized and functioning divisional headquarters and divisional support troops had varied over the years since the Second World War. For most of these years the headquarters was either at nil strength or only lightly manned. Others reject this argument as fallacious. Lieutenant-General Mike Jeffery had been an instructor-in-gunnery at the school for three years. His view on the decades-long demise of STA was that,

> *It was a professionally short sighted and intellectually dishonest approach by senior officers who saw the priority as almost exclusively kinetic capability and didn't want capital program competition. The fact that the army was blind in an age where information was the key to operational success cannot be excused by reliance on an antiquated doctrinal organization argument. The challenge the army faced was realizing a doctrine which ensured it could put capable and effective forces into operations that possessed all of the critical functions irrespective of size. Officers could not accept that a decade of experience in the Balkans focused on Battle Group size operations could be the future and that [division] operations, while still possible, were unlikely*

in the short term. And even if they were required such capability could not be achieved short of mobilization and major capability development. Thus I don't believe it is a "fair" argument.[40]

Suffice it to say that in the latter part of the Twentieth Century the Canadian artillery's STA capability was, for all intents and purposes, dead. To keep some currency, every second year the RCAS sent an instructor in gunnery and an assistant instructor in gunnery to attend the British annual Gunnery Career Course at the Royal School of Artillery in Larkhill. Attendance kept at least a tiny part of the Canadian artillery's head in the game, if not its hand.

That, in a nutshell, is the environment that the Royal Regiment of Canadian Artillery existed in and the resources that it had to work with as the century ended. While the army struggled with its continuing commitments in the Balkans, the gunners worried about what the artillery's future would be under army transformation. Precision munitions delivered by air power were becoming the preferred fire power solution. The M109s and air defence had the least hope for the future. Light guns and mortars seemed to be where everyone would end up. No one expected that within two years the government would call on them to go to war. When that call came, the Regiment answered it, and answered it well, but it would have to reinvent itself and did not come out the same way as it had gone in.

The coming decade would teach, or perhaps remind, everyone of some vital lessons. Foremost amongst those is that neither guns nor gunners—and especially their more esoteric sub-specialties—can be produced in a hurry. A critical mass is needed at all times to retain expertise and proficiency. When peace appears to reign, leaders, both political and military, too often forget that true deterrence needs to be backed up by a credible force and not one lacking key capabilities. To be effective, deterrence must present a force sufficient to convince a potential aggressor that there is little likelihood of military success.[41]

Canada's army would go into Afghanistan more or less structured for a mechanized battlefield but one which needed fine tuning to work. Despite the hardships and dangers of Afghanistan, the environment would be permissive enough to allow the army, and the artillery, the opportunity to evolve without the risk of annihilation. The guns would prove their worth as a combat arm that can deliver vital effects for their manoeuvre elements; the gunners, both regular and reserve, would prove their flexibility in being able to step up and adapt to new equipment and new environments; and the artillery's system of instructors in gunnery, assistant instructors in gunnery and technical staff would show themselves as being vital gatekeepers of the artillery's corporate knowledge.

Paradoxically, while Canada's war in Afghanistan would have some very positive outcomes for the Regiment it would also have some very negative consequences. These would continue to plague the artillery, and hence the army, long after the guns had come home. A former commander of Mobile Command, Lieutenant-General Charles Belzile in discussing planning for mobilization and expansion of the army, expressed the view that the army thought in terms of small forces and didn't have any plans for expanding the force in an emergency.[42] The army has tied itself to a few towed howitzer and stopped thinking of the artillery as a guaranteed, all-weather delivery system of massed fires. Instead, it thinks in individual rounds of precision fire delivered by single guns or a small two-gun troop. That, perhaps reflects the attitudes towards collateral damage that were reinforced in Afghanistan. The roll of reservists is as mere augmentees to existing regular force units and on the limited amounts of regular force equipment. Any "big" thinking that the army might do is naturally constrained by what can be accomplished in the face of political limitations set by successive governments who have not faced up to international reality.[43] The war ongoing in the Ukraine, at the time of the writing of this book, is challenging, or should challenge, that line of thinking.

The Regiment would prove in Afghanistan that an army previously trained and equipped for high-intensity warfare can, in time, fine-tune itself downward for asymmetric operations. The challenging question that needs to be examined at the conclusion of these books is: can Canada's artillery, structured for small-scale, asymmetric operations, be restructured back to high-intensity peer conflict? One where it can offer a credible threat to modern adversaries. Is that, however, merely a question of additional resources and capabilities that the government is prepared to commit, or should the army be more proactive in achieving higher levels of readiness for high intensity combat from the resources already available to it? Canada's potential opponents are changing. They are magnitudes better equipped and trained than the ones faced in Afghanistan. Will the army have the time to adapt once it realizes that it must do so?

Those, however, are questions for the future. What follows is the tale of how Canadian gunners at the turn of the century met the challenge of going to war for the first time in a half century and how they became what they are today.

1

PREPARING FOR WAR

AFGHANISTAN: In a land where everything—the dirt, the splintered scree, the rocks, even the miserable, scruffy clumps of leafless, knee-high brush—came in shades of tan, green-clad soldiers stood out as dark splotches on the hillside. One of those, C Battery's Bombardier[1] Ryan Herbert, as the detachment's Number 3,[2] knelt to the right of his 81mm mortar. He held a high explosive mortar bomb at the mouth of its tube with his right hand and faced his Number 1. Sergeant Kevin "K.T." Johnson watched the Number 2, Gunner Marc LaBonte, look through the sight and make a final, minuscule adjustment with the cross levelling hand-wheel and then lean away.

"Fire!"

Herbert released the bomb into the tube and bent his upper body down below the muzzle as he slid his hand down to the cooling fins to feel for the vibration of the propelling charge detonating. The bomb slid down one and one quarter metres before hitting the firing pin and arcing away across the ridge to impact, several kilometres away, on a suspected Taliban position in a crevasse on the ridge's far side. Other rounds would follow.

The fire mission had come down at 0821 hours on March 15th, 2002 on a mountain ridge called Tergul Ghar but known to everyone in the coalition as either the "Whale" or "Whale Back." It was on the west side of the Shah-i-Kot Valley. Across the valley stood a mountain—Takur Ghar—attached to an even greater and more rugged ridge. For the last two weeks, this valley had been the centre of a deadly battle between the remnants of al-Qaeda and the Taliban, and a combined force of Americans, allied Afghan militia, and various other coalition forces including Canadian snipers and special forces. The battle's opening phase had resulted in the deaths of eight Americans, seven of them on the top of Takur Ghar.

The terrain was rough and unforgiving. A few hundred metres below, but still roughly two and one half kilometres above sea level, was the floor of the valley. It was covered by a web of seasonal mountain stream beds connecting clusters of villages and hundreds of fields and individual farm compounds. Takur Ghar, at just over three thousand metres above sea level, was still capped with snow. Here the air was thin and the nights were freezing cold.

From where Herbert crouched, he could clearly see across the valley to the mountain where so many had died in a vain attempt to rescue a US Navy SEAL.[3] When he stood up at the edge of the position and looked across the valley, he could just make out the first of the two Chinook helicopters that had crashed during that operation. The second Chinook, unseen, was still on top of the mountain. It was said that between 500 and 800 of the enemy had died here. Many of their bodies were in hastily dug graves, or remain unburied, still waiting to be found.

While the rounds Herbert had just fired had been the first high explosive rounds fired in anger by Canadian artillery since the Korean War, they had not been the first operational rounds fired. That had been the month prior on the night of February 21st at Kandahar Airfield (KAF), where the four tubes had fired illumination missions near the scruffy airfield's perimeter.

What had brought 40 gunners from C Battery of the 1st Regiment, Royal Canadian Horse Artillery (1 RCHA) in Shilo, Manitoba to this place? And why with mortars?

Part of the answer was that C Battery was in the right place at the right time.

The morning of Tuesday, September 11th, 2001 had started off normally like any other weekday. Everywhere, Canadian gunners were going to work. One of them, Lieutenant-General Mike Jeffery, a former commanding officer of the 3rd Regiment, Royal Canadian Horse Artillery (3 RCHA) and now the Chief of the Land Staff,[4] had just returned from a meeting with a committee on Parliament Hill. As he walked into his office, which was one of the few on the Executive Floor with a television, he found it jammed with staff officers watching the events in New York. He stood there and watched as the second aircraft hit the World Trade Center. The fact that it was two planes and not just one told him that this was a conspiracy of some sort. Jeffery recalls, "A very quick discussion with my chief of staff. Talking with a brigadier-general with the sort of background that he had, I didn't have to tell him a lot. He knew intuitively where I was and that this is all about readiness. We need to figure out exactly where we are and what we can do and how quickly we can do it."[5]

The images of the terrorist attacks on the World Trade Center and the Pentagon were being flashed around the world in real time. At Oslo's international airport, a reconnaissance (recce) party from Edmonton's 3rd Battalion, Princess Patricia's Canadian Light Infantry battle group, watched their world turn upside down. They were in Europe as part of the preparations for two major exercises scheduled for later that year in Norway. Their aim would be to practice the battle group in its high readiness role as the Canadian army's Immediate Reaction Force (Land). With them was Major "Ranger" Fred Wolanski, the battery commander of C Battery, 1 RCHA, the battalion's affiliated battery.

Wolanski recalled that Lieutenant-Colonel Pat Stogran, the commanding officer of the 3rd Battalion, seemed preoccupied by something else, "[he] just wasn't into it and seemed to have something on his mind as there were several urgent calls home."[6]

The 3rd Battalion was one of Canada's three regular force light infantry battalions. The remaining six battalions were mechanized and, at the time, were in the process of converting from the tracked M113 armoured personnel carriers and the six-wheeled armoured vehicles general purpose to the new, eight-wheeled light armoured vehicle (LAV). The 1st and 2nd Battalions had only just received their new vehicles the year before. There were unsubstantiated rumours that the light battalions were on their way out under the army's transformation plan.

Rumours or not, the battalion certainly faced challenges, particularly in the number of its personnel. All three rifle companies were under-strength and, at one point, the mortar platoon was broken up and distributed amongst them. With the immediate reaction tasking, however, came a renewed energy and intensive training cycle which kept the battalion's members busy.[7]

Bombardier Herbert had been with several members of the battalion on an exchange trip to the United Kingdom on September 11th. He notes that, "We kind of figured at that point that we're the pointy end of the stick. We're the ones that were training up for anything that could possibly happen. So when we did get back to Canada, we didn't necessarily know what assets were going to come from 1 RCHA."[8]

Herbert's uncertainty was universal. It would be many months, with many discarded courses of action, before matters finally settled on a plan. In Ottawa, the Deputy Chief of Defence Staff[9] hunkered down with the intelligence staff while he and the Chief of Defence Staff were burning up the phone lines internationally, especially to the Americans, to get a handle on what was going on.[10]

On September 12th, The North Atlantic Treaty Organization's (NATO) North Atlantic Council convened and, for the first time in the alliance's history, provisionally invoked Article 5 of the North Atlantic Treaty of 1949 to identify 9/11 as an attack on one, and hence an attack on all of its members.[11] In Ottawa, both the Armed Forces Council and the Defence Management Committee[12] were meeting to take stock of the situation. Jeffery was of the view that if you are facing the unknown, then you need to get ready for the unknown, which includes putting money into the "readiness bucket".[13]

Things proceeded slowly, as no one had a contingency plan prepared for this type of situation. While countries debated what they could do, they waited for the Americans to take the lead. On September 17th, President George W. Bush of the United States identified Osama bin Laden as the responsible terrorist leader and on the 20th announced the War on Terror. With bin Laden and his al-Qaeda organization's identification, the focus turned to bin Laden's sanctuary in Afghanistan.

On September 20th as well, the first public sign of Canadian military support came through. Art Eggleton, the Minister of National Defence, authorized any personnel serving on exchange postings with foreign nations engaging in the War on Terror to deploy with their host countries.

The lead combatant command for the Americans would be US Central Command at MacDill Air Force Base in Tampa, Florida. Its staff immediately started planning a major, multi-phase campaign and worked at getting all the key building blocks in place. Not only would they mobilize ground and air forces, but also dispatch naval forces and, in conjunction with their Department of State, make arrangements with foreign countries in the region to host staging bases and lines of communication.

Afghanistan is a landlocked country of approximately 652,000 square kilometres in area–roughly the size of the Province of Alberta. Its terrain varies from broad dusty deserts and plains to rugged and inhospitable mountains. Summers are blisteringly hot in the south and the winters are freezing cold, especially in the mountains. Less than ten percent of its lands are arable and these generally lie along the many river valleys which are fed by spring runoff from the mountains.

Its population is of varied ethnicity and is mostly tribal in nature. It adheres to the Muslim religion and to a variety of social codes with Pashtunwali predominant in the south and east.

Since Afghanistan lies at the crossroads of South Asia and Central Asia, its history has been steeped in turbulence from even before Alexander the Great's occupation of 330 BCE, to the Soviet Union's invasion during the period 1979-1989, and its own civil wars thereafter.[14] For a time, its capital city, Kabul, had been a modern cosmopolitan city in the post-Second World War era when the country had good relations with both the West and the Soviets.

A communist coup in 1978, followed by the decade-long Afghan-Soviet War, followed by a civil war and the ascendancy of the ultra-conservative Taliban, had left a country dominated by warlords and a diverse agriculture industry with a significant reliance on opium production. By 2001, the primarily Pashtun-based Taliban dominated 90% of the country, leaving a small corner in the northeast to a group of warlords called the Northern Alliance.

Al-Qaeda had set up its base near the southern city of Kandahar in 1996 as guests of the Taliban. Under the Pashtunwali code of Melmastia—hospitality and protection for all guests—the Taliban had developed a symbiotic relationship with the terrorist group. 9/11 wasn't about to change that.[15]

Starting with Security Council Resolution 1368, the United Nations (UN) would pass several resolutions condemning the terrorist act, condemning terrorism and confirming a nation's right to self defence.[16] NATO formally invoked Article 5 on October 4th.[17]

Prime Minister Chrétien announced on the 7th that Canada would commit military forces to the war. The next day, Operation APOLLO officially began. Commodore Jean-Pierre Thiffault would be the commander of Joint Task Force Southwest Asia with his national command element headquartered with US Central Command. Central Command's relatively small headquarters at the time was entirely inadequate and its parking lot quickly sprouted a sub-division of temporary buildings to accommodate the many national contingents and the command's ballooning staff.

Canada's commitment would be 2,000 personnel, including six ships, six aircraft, and elements from Joint Task Force 2.

The same day, October 7th, the US started its bombing campaign of Afghanistan. In the meantime, the American army's 5th Special Forces Group (Airborne)[18] from Fort Campbell, Kentucky, supported by elements of the 10th Mountain Division from Fort Drum, New York, started flying into Karshi-Khanabad Air Base in Uzbekistan to organize and group with the anti-Taliban forces of the Northern Alliance. On October 19th, Operational Detachment Alpha 595 put their boots on the ground in Afghanistan.[19] Covert Tier 1 special operators from the US Joint Special Operations Command and even the Central Intelligence Agency also deployed under a variety of task force names to conduct special recce and direct action missions.

Canada, in the meantime, was searching for a mission for its ground forces. It was clear that an American conventional force would follow the special operations forces into Afghanistan. They would not be alone. A number of European countries were eying the formation of a force to take over the capital region of Kabul. Their agenda included stabilizing the capital so that humanitarian aid could be rendered to what was a populace desperately ravaged and disadvantaged under Taliban rule. This force would eventually be called the International Security Assistance Force (ISAF) established by United Nations Resolution 1386 on December 20th.[20]

Canada's Liberal government badly wanted to take part in ISAF.[21] The British, who were organizing and would initially lead the force, wanted no part of Canada in it.

The official excuse was that it was to be a Europeans-only organization. General Rick Hillier, at the time the Deputy Chief of Land Staff, was of the view that the refusal came as a result of the British believing that Canada was no longer a war-fighting country and could not be relied upon when things got tough.[22] The British experience with the moribund Canadian command structure in Yugoslavia was that it would take days or even weeks to approve a mission. Canada's risk-averse micromanagement of operations now stood in the way of the government's ambitions.[23]

The British also wanted someone to lead a follow-on mission–something Canada, with its commitments in Bosnia, was not prepared to do.[24] The Turks were, and just like that, Canada would not be part of ISAF.[25] That message had not gotten down to the troops in the gun park. 1 RCHA had been hearing rumours that C Battery would deploy in the civil-military cooperation role.[26]

Whatever discussions might have been going on between US Central Command and the Chief of Defence Staff, they were not ones that Jeffery was privy to. He recollects,

> *Then suddenly, seemingly out of nowhere, came this idea, "We'd like you to send us a battle group." It had to be a fairly light battle group because everybody going in on Operation ENDURING FREEDOM was being done on very light scales. Everything was being deployed by air, so it had to be relatively light. And, low and behold, we very quickly saw ourselves with an approved mission to send a light infantry battalion. The understanding was that we wouldn't necessarily replace it [at the end of its deployment].[27]*

The official announcement came quickly. Minister of Defence Art Eggleton announced on November 6th that Canada would send ground troops to Afghanistan. A few days later he stated that the tour would be for six months.[28]

There were still issues to solve; what manner of indirect fire support would the battle group take with them, and who would supply it?

If you'd have asked a gunner, he would have said: "guns, of course." Ones manned by gunners. That wasn't to be for many reasons. Prime amongst those was that there just wasn't airlift for that even though every two hours a plane was landing in Kyrgyzstan carrying everything required to support the special forces already there and the conventional forces flowing in behind.[29]

The American conventional force would end up being led by elements of the headquarters of the 10th Mountain Division now designated as Combined Joint Task Force MOUNTAIN with two understrength light infantry brigades: Fort Drum's 2nd Brigade, 10th Mountain Division called Task Force COMMANDO, and Fort Campbell's 3rd Brigade, 101st Airborne Division called Task Force RAKKASAN.

RAKKASAN was deployed at KAF, where it would have two light infantry battalions: its own 2nd Battalion, 187th Infantry Regiment and a Canadian one. Another of its battalions, the 1st of the 187th, was operating further north. 10th Mountain Division had brought its 1st Battalion, 87th Infantry Regiment, which had been doing airfield security in Kyrgyzstan, but was now operating out of Bagram and Kabul.

These two brigade headquarters and their three battalions had brought no artillery, just 81mm and 120mm mortars. In an interview, Major-General Franklin Hagenbeck, commander of the 10th Mountain Division, was of the view that artillery was unnecessary and that the job could be done by mortars and the myriad of close air support available. In his view, the lack of guns was not a contentious issue.[30]

Others disagreed. Captain Joshua Mitchell, an American gunner clearly felt that not bringing guns was a mistake. He later pointed to the problems experienced on Operation ANACONDA in the Shah-i-Kot as proof that mortars and air support alone were insufficient.[31]

A recce by Lieutenant-Colonel Stogran and his principal staff resulted in the battalion's configuration being like that of the Americans. After negotiations, a four-tube mortar group, not even a full platoon, is what it would be.[32]

The manning of those mortars was an issue and equally convoluted. The Canadian army was transforming from a Cold War force to one more oriented towards the anticipated future missions; a strategically and operationally mobile and agile medium-weight force.[33] In the course of this, every element within the army had to justify its institutional relevance. Transformation would require additional person-years in some places and demand reductions in others. Indirect fire support—both mortars and guns—was one of those challenging areas. The faith the Americans placed in precision munitions delivered by air power was not theirs alone. The same views were prevalent in other countries, including Canada, where a push was on to reduce ground-based indirect fire support.[34]

There simply weren't enough person-years to operate both nine mortar platoons and three field artillery regiments; some hard choices had to be made. The long-range plan under the nascent "Advancing With Purpose" reforms called for a lighter force where the artillery would be able to deploy three mortar batteries, two light howitzer batteries—all at tiered readiness—and three medium batteries at low readiness. While some gunners may have felt trepidation over the loss of three batteries of M109s for three of mortars, not all felt that way. Major Tim Young, at the time the Chief Instructor in Gunnery at the Royal Canadian Artillery School (RCAS) recalls a briefing by Lieutenant-General Jeffery on the subject,

> One of the key parts that I remember from that is having the mortar role, taking the light mortar role from the infantry, and then what that made to us. To me, it was pretty simple, because it's just another gun platform with a

sight. And I trained in E Battery with the L5, and we put the 81-millimetre mortar right off the left trail, and we could fire both at once. Coordinate illumination was better with the mortar, and then you could fire the howitzer, which would give you a better punch.[35]

These guns and mortars would support six mechanized and three light infantry battalions, an armoured regiment and two recce regiments.[36] With that came plans to reduce the infantry battalions' mortar and pioneer platoons to nil strength.

In Shilo, the rumour mill was operating flat out. About all that the troops knew was that some deployment options were being considered for C Battery. The first potential tasking as a 16-person civil-military cooperation detachment was set out on November 16th. This gave way in short order to a battery commander's detachment and two forward observation officer (FOO) detachments. Finally, and notwithstanding that mortars were not yet making their way from the infantry battalions to the artillery regiments, the order went out that 1 RCHA would support Operation APOLLO with a battery commander's detachment, a fire support coordination centre, two FOO detachments, a mortar fire control team and a four-tube mortar group.[37] Thus, in the third week of November, Lieutenant-Colonel Bob Chamberlain, the commanding officer of 1 RCHA, directed Fred Wolanski to retrain his people to operate mortars.[38]

The decision was not a welcome one amongst many in the infantry. Already smarting from the army reducing battalion mortar and pioneer platoons to nil strength in order to bolster manning elsewhere, they resented, in particular, that some of their people would miss out on the first wartime operation in a half a century. It wasn't just the 3rd Battalion that would be missing out. Their personnel shortages had already demanded a redistribution of their personnel to beef up A and B Companies. The 2nd Battalion from Shilo was tasked to provide C Company and the 1st Battalion was initially earmarked to provide the mortar platoon.[39] Many in the battalion would view the gunners throughout the tour as "job thieves."[40]

The problem wouldn't end there. While the battery commander and the FOOs would do the job that they normally do with the infantry, the battalion would assign a mortar-trained infantry captain and warrant officer to take command of the mortar line. It went so far that around St. Barbara's Day, the infantry captain called Wolanski and informed him that he was coming out to Shilo to train "his mortar platoon". That situation was resolved in a quick commanding officer to commanding officer telephone discussion and the trip was called off albeit that the mortars' infantry captain and his warrant officer would still have command of the mortar line in theatre.[41] It would not be a happy marriage.

Regardless, the battery threw itself into hard training for the month of December.

1 RCHA acquired the mortars and ancillary equipment. Wolanski's experience in mortar operations as a former airborne gunner, two weeks of dry training, and a short live fire exercise on the -30°C wind-swept, arctic-like plains of Shilo had the battery ready to go.

Having confidence in his peoples' gunnery instincts, Major Wolanski knew keenly that the most challenging aspect of this deployment would be the physical demands put on dismounted troops accustomed to functioning in a mounted role. In his view, "dismounted mortar exercises are the hardest bag-drive you can do."[42]

Vehicle transport would be limited at best, so it was decided to operate on very light scales, with the primary mode of transport being the long-suffering human back. And suffer they would. Man-packing dismantled mortars and two or three mortar bombs, a loaded rucksack, personal weapon with ammunition, rations and water, and maybe a manpack radio meant that each soldier was humping nearly their own body weight. This resulted in a decision to opt for the simplest means of computation of firing data for the mortars: a prismatic compass to orient the tubes, tabular firing tables, and Convergence, Position and Fuze Correction Graphs to produce the bearing and range to the targets. It wasn't fancy, and it wasn't very precise, but it would work. Indirect Fire Control Computing Systems in the form of laptop computers—ordinarily used in the command post to calculate firing data— were also taken along but not relied on due to the difficulty of charging batteries when deployed on dismounted operations.[43]

The equipment state was less favourable for the FOOs especially when employed as forward air controllers (FAC). First, the battery had only two qualified and current FACs on strength. The equipment status was no better. Among the "don't haves" was the LTM 91 Laser Target Marker to guide GBU 12 500 lb Mk82 laser-guided bombs onto their targets. In Shilo, the battery was told they would receive their target markers in Edmonton; in Edmonton the word was that they "would get them in theatre"; and in Afghanistan, they learned that there were none available.

The Canadian mix of three different radios of limited capability was decidedly inferior to the American PRC 117 radio, an "all-singing, all-dancing" set that could operate with army units, fast air, helicopters, and SATCOM as required. Inadequate communications capability played a large part in the initial American reluctance to allow Canadians to control aircraft.

Finally, while laser target pointers/illuminators, spotting scopes, and Vector binoculars were not available within the artillery, they could be obtained from the 3rd Battalion in Edmonton. The artillery's deficiency was a known one within the Directorate of Land Requirements 2[44] at the time but did not have a high enough funding priority for acquisition.[45] The Vector was particularly useful, being lightweight, durable, and equipped with both a magnetic compass and an eye-safe laser range finder. Not only that, but when connected to a global positioning system device, it could produce ten-figure grid references almost instantaneously. It was the perfect device for FOOs and FACs but not issued to them while being available to infantry recce platoons.

Trained and more or less equipped, the battery merely waited for the word to go. Major Wolanski admits that one of his most memorable personal challenges was telling his guys just days before going on Christmas leave that they would be going to war in January with no plan yet in place for redeployment. The battery then went on Christmas leave and waited for the order to go. That order came in January. It scheduled them to fly to Edmonton on January 29th. C Battery showed up, but the aircraft didn't. Instead, they went to Edmonton by bus.

Things were even worse in Edmonton. There were some equipment shortfalls to be made good here. They weren't. The USAF had sent three C-5 Galaxies to fly the battle group to Germany. Only one was initially serviceable, which caused several aborted starts. Eventually, one plane left on February 5th. Among others, it took out the command group, including the battery commander. Another aircraft left on the 9th. It took A Company and Captain David Grebstad and his G32[46] FOO detachment to Frankfurt, where they changed planes to USAF C-17 Globemasters for the last leg to Kandahar. One of the C-17s experienced a problematic refueling boom while air-to-air refueling causing a return to Germany for maintenance. B Company and Captain Tyler Kennedy and his G31 FOO party would be on the ground by the 12th, but C Company, with the battery's gun position officer, Lieutenant Mark Batten, stayed back until air transport became available for them to finally arrive on March 9th.

INTO THE FIGHT

KANDAHAR AIRFIELD (KAF) WAS AN EYE OPENER for most. Sergeant Donnie "Homer" Simpson, the forward observation officer (FOO) technician for G31, has a clear recollection of their flight and arrival. For him the first "We're not in Kansas anymore, Toto" moment came on the C-17, as it was bucking behind a tanker being air-to-air refueled. The second came about an hour before landing as warrant officers started breaking open crates of live ammunition and distributing it to the troops. "When I say 'busted out' the [ammunition] that means everything. We were filling [magazines], uncasing grenades and putting them in our pouches. Everything. M72s [light anti-tank weapons] were coming out ... It was a real gut-check moment."[1]

Warrant Officer Dave Poss, the troop sergeant major, recalls:

> We got off our plane loaded for bear ... We were on [operations] as soon as we hit the tarmac. We were moved to a staging area which was just a rundown part of [the airfield] ... It was just a blown up airfield ... There were literally—when we hit the runway with the C-17—it was pavement and then 500-pound bomb craters with dirt patches over them ... Then we got dragged through this austere place and that's where we spent the night ... The airfield was littered with Russian planes and helicopters and dried out little huts and stuff. It was like a little town that had all been blown to pieces. It was like landing on the surface of the moon.[2]

Sergeant Simpson also recalls that, "by the time the last guy got in the building, that C-17 was gone. They didn't fuel them. Whatever cargo, whatever personnel that they had on board those planes, it was a dump and run thing."[3]

Inside the building, an officer gave them a quick briefing starting with, "Stay in your fucking lane. There are special operations units here from across the world. You do not need to worry about what they are doing."[4]

G32's Captain David Grebstad and Sergeant Dennis Goodland had come in on the previous chalk and met the new arrivals. They brought them through ankle deep moon dust to the battery's lines, a group of four-man tents in the middle of a dirt field. Here they were told to bed down and to get some sleep.

Breakfast was the only fresh meal of the day. C-130 Hercules would fly it in and deliver it by backing their rear ramps up to approximately ten kitchen trailers aligned along the edge of the tarmac.[5] Lunch and supper for the first three months were boil-in-a-bag individual meal packs.

The mortar group received a pleasant surprise early on when Captain Lisa Smid arrived at KAF. Lisa was deploying as the second-in-command of the National Command and Control System Signals Squadron. She had previously served as the regimental signals officer for the 1st Regiment, Royal Canadian Horse Artillery (1 RCHA) where she had married a gunner, Captain Ryan Smid.[6] Lisa had picked up Kentucky Fried Chicken in Dubai for the boys while inbound. Lundrigan recalls, "It was probably, to this day, one of the most well received, nicest things that we ever got over there."[7]

Their bivouac area was not the most scenic part of the airfield, but it certainly qualified as the most odiferous. Just off the southwestern end of the runways is what some maps politely described as a "filtration field". In truth, it's a massive, above ground septic pond which would, over the next ten years, acquire almost legendary

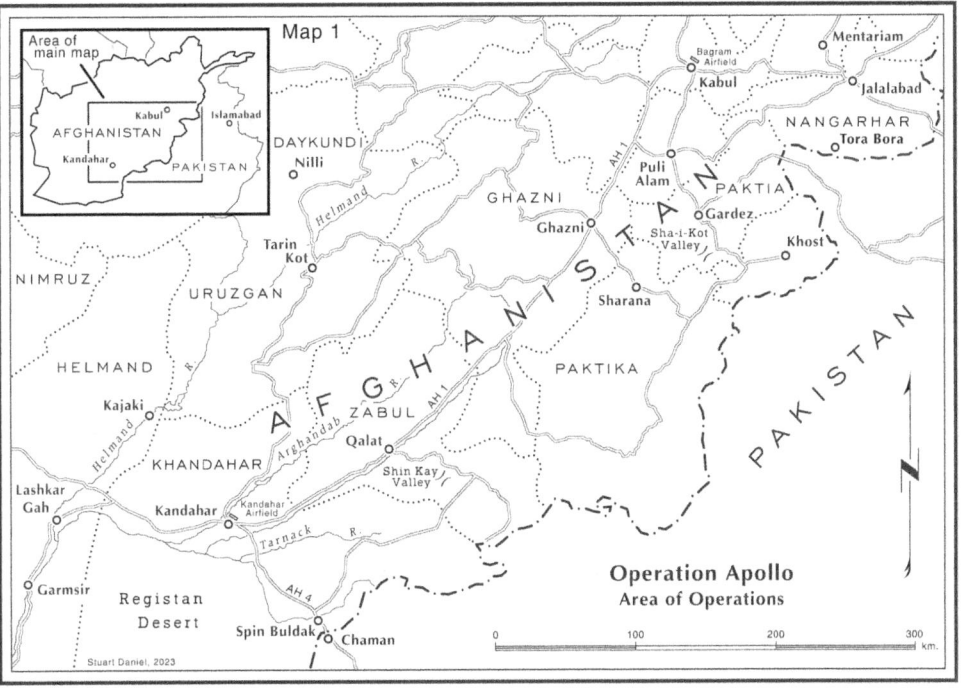

status as the "Poo Pond". To enrich the smell, there was a garbage dump nearby and several burn barrels used daily for burning additional human waste in diesel fuel. This came from a vast number of field expedient "three-man and ten-man shitters"— nothing as sophisticated as a "Blue Rocket" portable toilet. Those, and a septic truck to empty them, would come later.

The Canadians joined Task Force RAKKASAN. From the start, the reception by the US forces was very positive and welcoming. They appreciated their allies' presence. It confirmed they were not in this alone. There were other forces at the airfield, mostly US Air Force, a US Marine Corps infantry battalion from Naval Expeditionary Task Force 58, and special operations forces from several other countries, including the highly secret Delta Force and the Canadians of Joint Task Force 2.

Ottawa had given the battle group four missions: provide perimeter security for the airfield; conduct offensive operations on order; conduct sensitive site exploitation; and facilitate humanitarian aid if and when it arrives in theatre.[8]

Colonel Francis Wiercinski, the commander of Task Force RAKKASAN, wasted no time putting the battle group to work on perimeter security. For the gunners, this meant deploying to battle positions as soon as each contingent arrived. By February 12th, C Battery would deploy two observation posts and two mortar base plate positions on the airfield's perimeter as part of Operation VIGILANT.

G31's Captain Tyler Kennedy, Sergeant Donnie Simpson, and Bombardiers Donnie Bishop and Troy Roach would man the flat roof of a building towards the northern end of the airfield as part of A Company's WHITE SECTOR. Their continual presence, looking over the edge of the roof, would earn them the nicknames "The Gargoyles" and "Gargoyle 31."[9]

B Company was assigned BLACK SECTOR at the southern end of the airfield. Here G32's Captain Dave Grebstad, Sergeant Dennis Goodland, Master Bombardier Todd Buchanan, and Bombardier Derek Baylis at first occupied a flimsy bunker made of sandbags left by the previous US Marine Corps occupants. Part of their arcs of observation included the bombed-out rubble of Tarnak Farms, the abandoned al-Qaeda base.

G33, the battery's mortar fire controller detachment, staffed by Sergeant Pete Carmichael, Master Bombardier Mike Soper, Bombardier Mark Fiander and Gunner Jamie Murphy were destined for C Company. As it had not arrived yet, they would initially stay with the engineers.

G39, with Warrant Officer Joe Moore, Sergeant Ken Hood and Bombardier Pat Coté, operated the battle group's fire support coordination centre (FSCC) within the battle group's tactical operations centre.

By this time, the rather strange configuration that the battalion had imposed on the battery had taken hold. The mortar line, broken into two sections of two mortars each—Call Signs 52 and 53—was now part of the battalion's combat support company and under the command of an infantry captain and warrant officer. They appeared less than thrilled with their charges. Besides the attitude that in taking over the mortars, the gunners were "job thieves", there were also disagreements about the gunners' mortar procedures.

The infantry, understandably, adhered to the infantry way of doing things while the gunners had adapted the mortar to being just another gun using artillery gun-line procedures. A case in point was the gunners' preference for deploying the group in a diamond formation, which produced a very useful fall of shot in any direction without having to make individual adjustments for each mortar. The mortars' infantry leadership wanted a straight mortar line because that's what their doctrine and range safety practices set out. Warrant Officer Dave Poss, the gunners' own mortar platoon warrant officer, smoothed out many of these issues.

Major Wolanski was of the view that the imposed infantry leadership had little understanding of the FSCC function, other than controlling the fire of the battalion mortars. As such, they added little value to the battery. He again protested their attachment to the commanding officer, but was overruled. This situation persisted until June by which time, the battery had experienced mutual hardships with the battle group, and the gunners had proven they could soldier just as well as everyone else. At that point they would go from being "job thieves" with mild neglect, like "we were stray dogs or an unwelcome guest", to acceptance by the battle group's infantry.[10]

Like the observers, Wolanski deployed the mortars to separate ends of the airfield, primarily because of their limited range. The runway itself is close to four kilometres long, which was a challenge for mortars with a range of only five kilometres.

Warrant Officer Dave Poss and Sergeants Wayne Lundrigan and Dave Strickland's detachments, as call sign 52, took over the positions in the southwest while Sergeant Kevin Johnson and Master Bombardier Gilbert Caron's two detachments, as call sign 53, occupied the position in the northeast. Not only did they take over the positions, but also the Americans' ammunition. Canadian ammunition would not arrive for some time.[11]

Once deployed, the battle group joined in the planned operational rotations with the brigade's American battalions: a month defending the airfield, a month prepping for operations, and a month on active operations.

Foremost was clearing up the rudimentary mortar positions left by their American predecessors and digging-in with proper defences. Right from the start, other challenges arose: orientation and maps–or rather, the lack of either.

The deployment had come so quickly that the Canadian Forces' Mapping and

Charting Establishment had not had the time to react and did not provide the mission with a means of determining both fixation and orientation. Concerning fixation, one thing that was available in small numbers were old Soviet maps which not only labelled everything in the Russian Cyrillic alphabet, but also had several different grid line overlays. That might be adequate for some uses, but gunners prefer to be a bit more precise.[12] There was a second, related problem. The light scales of equipment had resulted in the decision to orient the mortars using prismatic compasses, but nowhere was there a way of confirming the right magnetic declination to correct from magnetic north to grid north. Mapping and Charting Establishment personnel would usually achieve this by setting up a calibration point from which individuals could calibrate all their individual devices. If such a point existed at KAF, no one had told the Canadians about it.

Solutions would, however, be forthcoming. Serendipitously, Captain Tyler Kennedy ran into a USAF officer who was about to fly back, and who had a map that he was prepared to leave behind. With this, Kennedy, Poss and Simpson could produce maps of the airfield area through taking air photos and overlaying them with a common grid system.[13] That only produced a handful of maps–just good enough to get a round into the area of the target.

Orientation was even more fortuitous. On the airfield was a Delta Force detachment with 120mm mortars and a gun laying and positioning system.[14] This was a device which had not yet been issued within the Canadian Forces, but fortunately for the battery, Dennis Goodland had been involved in the trials of it at the Royal Canadian Artillery School (RCAS). He knew what it was and how to use it. Goodland: "I set it up, the [gun laying and positioning system], and oriented [it] and basically, for all intents and purposes; it became a survey point ... That's how we calibrated our compasses and the whole works."[15]

Controlling aircraft was a problem as well. On February 9th, Major Wolanski met with Lieutenant-Colonel Bartsch, the commander of Task Force K-BAR's[16] air support operations squadron, to organize forward air controller (FAC) training for his FOO parties. The battery only had two qualified and current controllers. He soon discovered that the Americans insisted on additional training and evaluations for the Canadians before they would allow them to control American aircraft. Part of this was because the Canadian FAC course was not fully recognized by the Americans. In addition, there was also the lack of laser designators and PRC 117 radios.[17]

The battery was now in a combat zone, and treated it as such. FOOs maintained a continuous watch over their zones of observation, and with their company commanders, conducted defensive fire planning. A battle group defensive fire target list, including final protective fire, was prepared, the basic load of ammunition was issued down to each tube, and dry practice missions were conducted to polish command post and detachment skills.

The Canadians experienced the first Taliban attack on the airfield on February 15th, a matter of days after they occupied their battle positions. The response was unique, in more ways than just being the first operational engagement by Canadian FOOs for a very long time. Each of Kennedy's G31 and Grebstad's G32, in that order, fired an illuminating mission using the two 120mm mortars of Delta Force. Indirect fire support at the airfield was controlled by the Americans' fire direction center which went by the call sign, "Steel Control 1."[18]

Illumination was fired again on February 21st, this time with all three observers firing at least one mission each and, for the first time, using the Canadian tubes of both call signs 52 and 53. It had been raining for days, and in places there was as much as 300 millimetres of water. The Americans had engaged the Taliban outside the airfield perimeter and had called for illumination missions. As the order to fire the first round was given, Bombardier Ryan Herbert dropped the bomb down the tube of Johnson's mortar, and as per the drill, bent down to avoid the muzzle blast. When the primer struck the firing pin and the mortar base plate rebounded in the sludge, he got a big mouth full of muck. Gunner LaBonte handed him another round and stated, with a straight face, "it's two rounds fire for effect!" then promptly backed away so he wouldn't get splashed.[19]

In due course, the battery also conducted live fire training at Tarnak Farm, the nearby training ranges.

Tarnak had been al-Qaeda's home base in Kandahar from 1998 to 2001. It served them as an advanced operational training camp, including for the use of poisons and explosives.[20] It was widely believed to have been where bin Laden planned the 9/11 attacks. The Americans had bombed it into rubble in the immediate aftermath. It may have been poetic justice, but the Americans converted it into a live-fire training area in 2001 after they had moved into the area.

The minor Taliban attacks had never really ceased but neither did they ever develop into a large threat throughout the duration of the deployment. Wolanski described harassing fire from Taliban rockets and mortars as fairly common. There also had been several incursions into the perimeter that had resulted in firefights. When it became the turn of the battalion to take over the line, Lieutenant-Colonel Stogran asked for and received permission to apply a "Canadian touch" to the control of no-man's-land. He deployed the reconnaissance (recce) elements outside the wire with the local Afghan militia who were working for the coalition. They patrolled and manned checkpoints in the area surrounding the airfield. With Canadian Coyote surveillance vehicles providing 24/7 early warning, and the recce platoon and the Afghans controlling the ground, the security environment changed virtually overnight. The terrorists went underground and resorted to launching ineffective rocket attacks from hastily constructed earth and rock ramps and to planting mines on previously cleared routes.[21]

These attacks, however, would establish two glaring technical issues.

The first was the lack of any artillery target acquisition resources. Both rocket and mortar firing positions are relatively easy to pinpoint using counter mortar radars. Canada had none, and the Americans had not deployed any of theirs.

The first time that there was a rocket attack after the battery's arrival was on February 23rd. The Americans inquired whether the battlegroup had anyone capable of doing crater analysis. Wolanski put his hand up and said he would use the 50-minute lecture he had received on his instructor in gunnery course. He recalls,

> So I literally went out with tent pegs and 550 cord, paracord, and my compass and went out with the [Afghan] guys and did crater analysis of the craters.

> Ideally, the theory goes, it's just like triangulation with navigation ... you want three points. I only had two points. Two impact points ... So I put in the tent pegs; tied the string to the tent pegs; did a back bearing ... Where the two points intersected on my map, I say to the [recce] platoon commander, "We need to go here.".... Within 600 metres we found the launch sites thanks to the [Afghans].

> I found bits of the rockets...and the [Afghans] commander takes us to their [ammunition] compound and he shows me one of the rockets...so it's a 107[mm] Chinese rocket. I bring one of those back to the camp. I'm a gunner. I know you can't fire it unless you electrically fire it. Nothing's going to happen, it's not going to explode, but the [individuals who saw the rocket] went fucking crazy, lost their fucking minds that I brought this thing back.[22]

The Taliban had simply aimed it with a pile of rocks underneath it and fired it with a car battery. In response to the threat, the Americans brought in an AN/TPQ 36 Firefinder counter mortar radar to the airfield.[23]

The second issue was range. Older Chinese and Soviet 107mm and 122mm rockets easily out-ranged the 81mm mortar, albeit that their accuracy was terrible with the Taliban's expedient launch systems. Even with the radar, counter-battery fire would be problematic because of the range involved and the time lag in getting clearance from Bagram to engage.[24]

Things had quieted down in Afghanistan prior to the Canadians' arrival. The Taliban and al-Qaeda were on the run even though the allies had missed their big chance in the Battle of Tora Bora the previous December. As the winter dragged on and more conventional forces started becoming active in Afghanistan, commanders looked to using them to augment the highly successful special operations forces and Northern Alliance operations. To an extent, shaping the ground for humanitarian operations was also becoming an objective.

One geographic area drawing the attention of the intelligence agencies was located some 400 kilometres northeast of KAF in Paktia province. Intelligence believed the survivors of Tora Bora were concentrating in the Shah-i-Kot valley. Estimates put their number anywhere between the 50 and 1,000 mark. Such intelligence also predicted that if seriously challenged, the enemy would not stand and fight.[25]

A lesson that had come out of Tora Bora was that the Americans couldn't fully rely on their Afghan allies. The Afghans would often run their own game. Combined Joint Task Force MOUNTAIN believed that the lack of American conventional forces had allowed enemy leaders to exfiltrate from Tora Bora through the Afghan militia cordon.[26]

Planning for what would become Operation ANACONDA ran throughout the month of January and into February. The plan had several moving parts. Tier 1 Special Forces from both Delta, the Naval Special Warfare Development Group (more popularly known as SEAL Team 6), and from several allied nations would insert a few days before the operation, tasked with special recce.

The main assault force into the valley would be two Afghan militia forces sweeping around both ends of a large ridge feature nicknamed the "Whale" with their US Green Beret advisers, while the better part of two infantry battalions, the 2nd of the 187th Infantry to the north and the 1st of the 87th Infantry to the south, would air assault into a string of helicopter landing zones quaintly named alphabetically for the wives of some of the planning staff (from Landing Zone AMY to Landing Zone HEATHER) along the eastern edge of the valley. Their role would be to block escape from the valley into the mountains. A third battalion, the 1st of the 187th Infantry, would remain uncommitted as the operation's reserve.

A further outer cordon of teams from several American and allied special forces task forces, including Canada's Joint Task Force 2, would deploy to cover obvious ratlines into and out of the valley. While the Canadian battle group, as a whole, was uncommitted, the .50 calibre McMillan Tac-50 sniper rifles of their sniper section had caught the attention of Task Force RAKKASAN's leaders, and they deployed the Canadian snipers to work with the Americans to clear the valley.

The plan principally relied on air and aviation support, including fast air, attack helicopters, bombers, and AC-130 gunships—a variant of the venerable four-engine Hercules transport aircraft whose on-board armament included an M102 105mm cannon. The Americans planned to take a few mortars in, but the initial air assault only had one 120mm mortar included.

The Tier 1 special recce forces started their infiltration on February 27th and quickly reported a large al-Qaeda force. The conventional force itself was delayed by bad weather but eventually went in during the early morning hours of March 2nd.

Problems developed before dawn with the road move of the Afghan militia. A friendly fire incident from an AC-130 caused their first casualties, killing one American Green Beret and wounding several other personnel. This effectively put the Afghan militia into stasis for the next several days.

While the first helicopter assault wave achieved surprise and took only moderate fire, the enemy quickly rallied and put up very effective air defence using both heavy 12.7mm DShK machine guns and volleys of rocket-propelled grenades. These were so effective that only two of the second wave of Chinook helicopters could land. The forces which had managed to land came under heavy attack from all sides, including dug-in and sheltered mortar positions all along the mountains.

In the valley, the fight grew desperate for the 1st of the 87th, which was taking many wounded from both mortar and small arms fire. They responded with their single 120mm mortar, attack helicopters and bombers. Their sole mortar was struck twice, the second time knocking it out of action. Al-Qaeda's 82mm mortars were their most effective weapon, and in their dug-in positions, were hard to knock out even with bombs.

That night, Task Force RAKKASAN ordered the 1st of the 187th Infantry to reinforce the north via a heliborne insertion. Their flights departed around noon on the 3rd but were warned off that their landing zone was hot. Running low on fuel, they turned off to Khost to refuel ... except for two Chinooks, carrying one company, who did not get the order to turn back but inserted their troops safely. There had been talk of reinforcing the 1st of the 87th as well, but eventually the brigade made the decision to pull it out overnight with its 26 wounded, and take it back to Bagram to reconstitute for future operations.

In the early hours of March 4th, an attempt to insert a SEAL team on the top of Takur Ghar went disastrously wrong. The Chinook attempting to land the team came under effective fire causing it to abort its mission, but one member of the team fell off the ramp onto the mountainside. He survived the fall. The Chinook itself made it to the base of the mountain, where it crash landed without further casualties. A second Chinook successfully dropped off a different SEAL team at another location and managed to fly off safely, albeit under fire.

The special forces then attempted to rescue the downed SEAL with a quick reaction force (QRF) using a two-Chinook insertion of US Army Rangers at the top of the mountain. Circumstances caused the first Chinook to land in a hot landing zone where it was promptly shot down, with its surviving members engaged in a life-and-death firefight supported by gunships, jets, bombers, and Predator unmanned aerial vehicles (UAV). The second Chinook eventually landed at an offset landing zone, dropping off a ground force which would later reach the peak and secure the mountain top. Later that night, aircraft landed to remove the dead and wounded, and their rescuers. In all, seven Americans had died on Takur Ghar.

It was obvious at this point that al-Qaeda was not running away. They stood their ground and stood it hard. In fact, fighters were coming from outside the area to reinforce the valley. They were engaged by the special forces picket line using air power. The task now turned to a deliberate clearing of the eastern slopes overlooking the valley, using the 1st and 2nd Battalions of the 187th Infantry, reinforced later that day by the returning 1st Battalion of the 87th Infantry.

By March 6th, the ridge had been mostly cleared and the Afghan militia felt emboldened enough to get into the fight. This was the start of Operation GLOCK: a heavy pounding of the Whale by air power for three days followed by a sweep by various Afghan militia and their American advisers. It would run until March 12th during which time, Task Force RAKKASAN held in place on the eastern ridge on the far side of the valley. By the 10th, Major-General Hagenbeck considered the militia's sweep of the Whale to be insufficient and thus the stage was set for Operation HARPOON.[27]

Major Wolanski had first heard about Operation ANACONDA on March 4th. The rumour flying around Kandahar was that the Americans were getting a "shit kicking" in Paktia but were making progress. On the 6th rumours circulated about the commitment of American aviation and field artillery, as well as the Canadian battle group. Nothing came of this and in fact the Americans had no field artillery in the Afghanistan theatre to commit in any event. On the 7th, the winds were too high for the use of either attack helicopters or mortars, at which point several people remembered Wolanski's displeasure back in Canada about not taking guns. On the 8th Wolanski took half of the mortar group on what he euphemistically called a "training march" that involved man-packing the mortars and ammunition around the airfield along with individual personal gear, and conducting a quick action every 500 metres.

Wolanski repeated the march on the 9th, with the other half of the battery. As well, C Company finally arrived from Canada along with the battery's gun position officer, Lieutenant Mark Batten. It was an important day for more than that. That day the battle group finally received a warning order for ANACONDA which placed it on 30 minutes' notice to move.[28] The arrival of the 3rd Battalion of the

187th Infantry from the United States made it possible for the Canadians to leave Kandahar for operations. The newcomers would take up security of the airfield.[29]

The battalion's command group was loaded on a C-130 Hercules during the afternoon of the 10th and flown to Bagram Airfield, about forty kilometres northeast of Kabul. The facilities here were a welcome change from the austere environment at KAF: hot showers and "good chow" in the nearby dining facility. Here too, they met up with Company A ("Strike Company") of the Americans' 4th Battalion of the 31st Infantry Regiment, which would be with them for the duration of the operation.

The overall command fell to Colonel Kevin Wilkerson of the 2nd Brigade, 10th Mountain Division—Task Force COMMANDO. Lieutenant-Colonel Stogran, the senior ground force commander, would develop the tactical plan.

Initially, he had been told that they would deploy into the Naka Valley south of Takur Ghar to stop enemy exfiltration. By the end of the day on the 10th, however, after some initial confusion, it was clear the target would be the Whale itself.

The mortar line, in the meantime, was still at KAF and had loaded up their gear. Kevin Johnson recalls:

> Ordered to get ready to deploy up North. Tore our base plate [position] down and prepped our gear, and sat around in the sun. No orders, battle procedure or info being passed down.

> The average weight we were carrying with a mortar piece, a tri-pack of ammo, full battle rattle, water, rations and limited snivel gear[30] was about 160 [pounds] in 40 degrees. Wasn't pretty.[31]

They would follow the same routine for two more days in Kandahar while the command group, in Bagram, would spend the 11th and 12th planning for the attack on the Whale in what was now called Operation HARPOON.

Afghan militia too would be part of the operation. One group, acting prematurely, had made their way to the northern tip of the Whale on the evening of the 10th, where they had set up a large bonfire and waited for events. Their presence there interfered with the planned preliminary bombardment of the ridge. Another group, expected to sweep the valley floor from north to south, did not move in. Nonetheless, the Americans airlifted out their own Operation ANACONDA forces, which had been there for the last week. As this happened, the Afghan militia moved in again but abandoned the plan to instead stream through the valley to loot its villages.[32]

Two days later, on the 12th, the order finally came. Johnson: "Departed Kandahar via [Hercules] at 1320 and arrived at Bagram airbase at 1520. There were no seats in the [Hercules], so everyone had to sit on the floor squished in like sardines. We received orders at 1930 and got some shut eye. No time for battle procedure."[33]

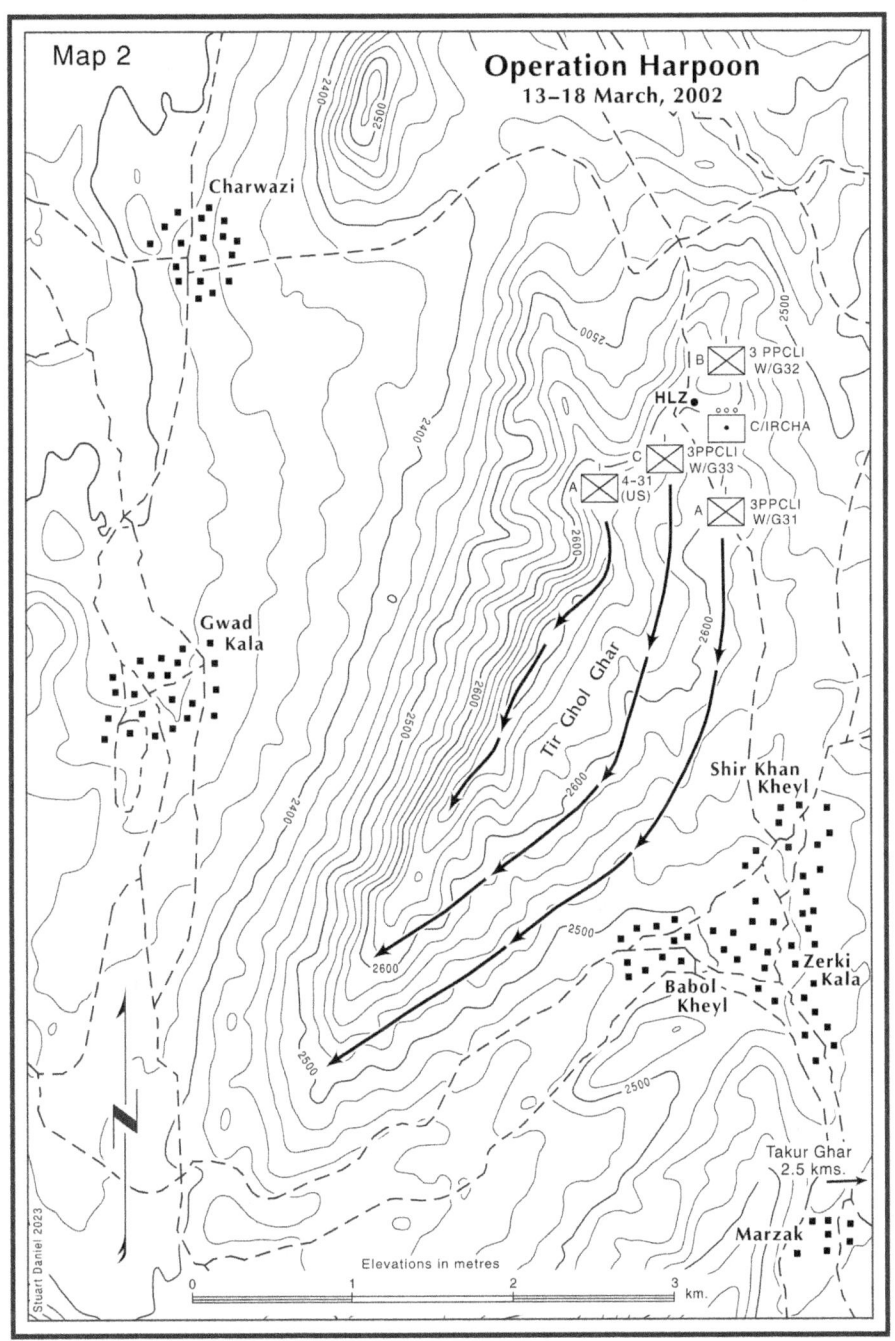

Map 2

Operation Harpoon
13–18 March, 2002

Charwazi

Gwad Kala

HLZ

B | 3 PPCLI W/G32

C/IRCHA

C | 3PPCLI W/G33

A | 4-31 (US)

A | 3PPCLI W/G31

Tir Ghol Ghar

Shir Khan Kheyl

Zerki Kala

Babol Kheyl

Takur Ghar
2.5 kms.

Marzak

Elevations in metres

0   1   2   3   km.

Stuart Daniel 2023

Lieutenant-Colonel Stogran's tactical plan was to sweep down the Whale from northeast to southwest with three companies up: A Company on the left, Strike Company on the right, C Company in immediate support and B Company in reserve.[34] The mortar group would move a few hundred metres downslope from Landing Zone SPEAR into a position where it could cover the entire length of the Whale and its slopes as well as the valley below, if required. It was time to get the force together.

On the 13th, they were off. Johnson:

> *Scheduled to be skids up at 0530. We didn't receive our mortars until 20 [minutes] before chalk assembly. [Machine gun] and 81mm ammo was issued on the tarmac. Every soldier in the [company] picked up a tri-pack of 81mm [ammunition] with the idea they would drop it off when they got off the chopper.*

> *We packed our rucks and went to the weigh scale. My ruck and kit weighed in at 171 lbs. I only weigh 180. Quick trip through to the padre, who said a prayer for us and then on to the Chinook. We packed 43 fully loaded soldiers into the chopper right up to the back of the ramp. I had to hook in. Skids up at 0535 and skids down at the landing zone at 0620.[35]*

Surprisingly, the mortars had not been cross loaded across multiple aircraft. If their helicopter had to return to base for a malfunction or crashed or was shot down, the entire platoon would have been out of action.[36] Johnson continues,

> *The flight was peaceful until the last half [hour] when they began contour flying through the mountains. "One minute" warning was given. The [landing zone] was a small bowl on the side of the mountain. The Chinook hovered, with only the ramp touching the ground. Everyone ran off the chopper and amongst the down draft and blowing dirt, tried to orient themselves. I almost wiped out coming off the chopper because my left leg was asleep. The infantry dropped all the tri-packs in a pile as soon as they got off the chopper.*

> *The mortar [group] eventually regrouped near the [ammunition] dump. A quick recce was conducted, and we moved to the base plate [position] about 400m down into a ravine. We set up the mortars, recorded, set security and then humped back up the steep hill to the [landing zone] to retrieve the rest of the tri-packs. Took us about ten trips. Pretty exhausted by then.[37]*

A Company was securing the landing zone while B Company looked for the enemy towards the north. Since there had not been enough airlift to bring the battalion in with one go, additional personnel and equipment flowed in by helicopter. Johnson recalls,

Throughout the night, Predator drones cruised above our [position] with B-52s dropping a lot of ordnance across the valley. Quite the light show. We established a two-hour, two-man [observation post] shift at the C6 [machine gun position] equipped with [night vision goggles] and an [infrared] strobe. No one slept that night. Some [personnel] didn't bring sleeping bags and at that altitude in the mountains, it dropped to below zero. Chinooks were arriving all night, dropping off supplies and sandblasting our [position] every time they hovered.[38]

On the 14th, with the north end of the Whale secure, the battalion moved out as previously planned. Captain Kennedy's G31 moved with A Company; Captain Grebstad's G32 with B; and Sergeant Carmichael's G33 with C. Major Wolanski's G39 moved with the battalion's command group. With them was an attached team of US Air Force enlisted terminal attack controllers[39] from the 10th Mountain Division.

While the mortar group sat and waited, the FOOs were having a hard slog as they hiked up and down the difficult terrain, weighed down by their kit, searching every cave or crevice for signs of the enemy. The sounds of gun fights came up to them from down in the valley. Stogran assumed the enemy was abandoning the Whale to exfiltrate eastward and were running into the Afghan militia down below.[40]

Stogran was concerned about the slow pace. He decided it was necessary to create company patrol bases (PB), drop rucksacks, and carry on with a lightened load to fan out and scour the hillsides, before returning to the PB, picking up rucksacks and moving on.[41] Wolanski's crew kept up the pace, but the US Air Force team with him experienced severe problems. While freezing cold at night, the day was blisteringly hot and the airmen, overdressed in Gore-Tex, were struggling in the heat to the point where they flat out sat down and refused to go on. They were extracted by helicopter and replaced by a US Air Force captain that night.[42]

Captain David Grebstad's role on the mountain had come about by circumstance. He had joined the army as a reservist with the 116th Independent Field Battery, RCA in Kenora, Ontario. Nine years later, he would transfer to the regular force, where in the fall of 2001, he was a gun line officer with C Battery. When the battery was finally required to provide a contingent to work with the Americans, it found itself with enough mortar line staff, but in need of a second FOO. Grebstad had not yet attended the regular force FOO course, but he had previously taken the reserve force one. So it was that they had given him command of G32.

At 0821 hours on March 15th, B Company was clearing the western slope of the Whale and Grebstad found himself looking down at a ravine facing the company. He had called in two fire missions the previous day on suspected positions, but each mission had been shut down by the FSCC. This time, he recalls,

We were clearing an area, and we had been given some [intelligence] on

where machine guns had been set up where the Americans had been fighting previous to us. So we thought we saw some movement in and around...this former machine gun nest. So I got eyes on and I just put a fire mission in and three or four rounds [of fire for effect] is all that I think I fired.[43]

Grebstad freely admits that the competition between his team and Kennedy's G31 was fairly strong as to who would fire the first high explosive rounds on Operation HARPOON. Kennedy's crew had fired the first illumination mission with Delta's 120mm mortars back at KAF. Grebstad's mission was on target; but they found nothing.

While the enemy had largely abandoned the Whale, not everyone had gotten the message. Late that day, not long before sundown, while clearing the spine, the recce platoon came upon an enemy bunker at what would be the topographical high point roughly half-way along the ridge. Strike Company was called forward and conducted a quick attack using AT-4s.[44] By dusk the Company had killed the three defenders there. It would be the battalion's only actual contact with a live enemy on the operation.[45]

Remnants of the enemy's presence could, literally, be found all over the mountain. The battle group found numerous caches of weapons and documents. They seized the documents for intelligence. Engineers blew up the weapons and ammunition in place.

One such discovery came from a patrol near the mortar base plate position. A cave under an overhang was located near where a bomb had been dropped prior to the air assault. In the midmorning, a team from the mortar group and some engineers with a C6 machine gun went over to investigate. Bombardier Ryan Herbert and Gunner Randy Blowes were dispatched with M72 rocket launchers. An engineer officer with Vector binoculars lazed the cave and measured that it was 425 metres away. That exceeded the range graduation on the M72's sight by 125 metres. Bombardier Hebert recalls:

Okay, so I'm aiming for the sky. I pop off my shot and I was five metres shy... And then Randy Blowes—it was probably the second M72 he ever fired in his life—and he dumped her down in the valley. And then here's the stupid thing. They had a C6 out there and the C6 was supposed to shoot at the cave while the assault element went around the ridgeline to assault the cave...The C6 opens up on the cave and he hits to the left of the target and his Number 2 yells to him, "Go right!" So he lets out another burst and again to the left of the target. [the number 2] yells "Go right!" And he now holds the trigger and again left of the cave and it goes on back and forth like that until he's letting out a half a belt burst and they're yelling at him, "Go right! Go right! Go right!" And then he's out of ammo. Here's the face palm moment. They say "Good shooting there, Corporal Wright."[46]

A search of the cave found it unoccupied but containing rocket-propelled grenades, 82mm mortar ammunition and 107mm rockets which the engineers blew up in place.

Further up the ridgeline they found the bodies of two enemy killed earlier during Operation ANACONDA. An American Defense Intelligence Agency team came to take DNA samples. More searches of the area found yet more caches, all of which the engineers blew up.

The night of the 16th/17th had brought a large amount of helicopter activity to the mountain. The mortar line woke up the next morning to find that the battalion was slowly pulling out.

That day was mostly quiet at the base plate position as they followed the progress of the battalion on the radio. As troops were pulling out, they would come and pick up tri-packs of mortar ammunition to take back to the base with them. With the reduction of allied troops on the mountain, the mortar group beefed up its defences with tripwire flares and Claymore mines.

The only stranger in their area, however, was a tame donkey, which had wandered up to the area where the enemy bodies had been found. From there it made its way to hang around the base plate position. While it would eagerly lap water from canteen cups, it was more discerning in its diet, and shunned the Canadians' individual meal pack rations. As the donkey tended to wander around, Bombardier Shawn Walker, one of the artillery technicians, decided it was at risk of being fired upon by nervous sentries at night, and needed some additional protection. He used the contents of an infrared glow stick to write "DONKEY" in large letters on both its sides.

At around 0400 hours, a trip flare suddenly ignited and everyone manned their posts, prepared for the worst to the extent that a call for the mortars to fire on the final protective fire target came down. The group held back with mortar rounds literally ready to drop and Claymores ready to be triggered. Things were tense, especially as nothing happened, and time dragged on, seemingly for an eternity of apprehension. Calls to the outposts for further information finally ended up with a response by the radio operator reporting that it was a donkey. "How" came the query from headquarters, "do you know it's a donkey?" The outpost replied, "It's got written on the side of it - 'donkey'!"[47]

Within the hour, the battery had packed up its gear, and with the aid of a Gator all terrain vehicle that had been left behind, moved 800 metres down the side of the mountain to their pickup zone. It was now March 18th. With the glimmer of the dawn's light touching the mountains, they would be the last of the battle group to leave the Whale for Bagram Airfield. They would stay there until the 22nd, when aircraft shuttled them back to KAF for further tours of airfield security and training.[48]

OPERATION MOUNTAIN LION

WITH THEIR RETURN TO KANDAHAR AIRFIELD, the battle group started a program of sending troops off for a short period of rest and relaxation. This was not the same program as the later home leave travel assistance program which would provide a financial allowance to deployed members to reconnect with family at home or a third location and which would leave contingents short-handed during combat operations. This was something shorter and simpler. Warrant Officer David Poss recalls,

> We had one three or four-day [rest and relaxation]...They flew us out by [Hercules] from [Kandahar] to Mirage [Dubai]...They [gave] us cash at the airfield; they line us up and gave us a couple of hundred dollars US; I think it was. Our hotel was paid for by [the Department of National Defence] and then they gave us money for transportation and entertainment they called it so basically you got whatever—$700 Canadian or whatever the amount came to.[1]

Sergeant Donnie Simpson remembers the trip as well,

> No one had civilian clothes. At best you had [physical training] gear that was just desert beaten. So picture this: Like 50 to 100 guys hitting this biggest mall in the world. They're wearing combat boots, cut-off shorts and most of them with a [Patricia] t-shirt or us with the regimental t-shirt and you're walking around in the most expensive mall in the world looking to buy clothes so that you can go swimming...[2]

Interestingly, rooms at the hotel, which was a resort on the Persian Gulf, were not allocated on a rank basis. Simpson recalls being given a standard type of hotel room and a few minutes after getting into it having a knock on the door where a private from A Company stood wanting to speak to him,

"Sarge! You've got to come and see this." So he takes me down [to his room] and his room is a double wide door and I open it up and come to find out he has a ground floor suite like something that would probably cost you $2,000 a night to stay at...And I just looked at him and said, "Kid. Don't say anything to anybody and just enjoy it." Of course, he was the hub now and all his buddies would come to that room to party.[3]

By April 2002, Tarnak Farms was operating steadily as an austere multi-purpose training facility for allied troops operating out of KAF.

A Company planned a live-fire exercise for the night of April 17th and invited Captain Tyler Kennedy's G31, as their dedicated forward observation officer, to participate. Equipment shortages that the battery faced caused the crew of G31 to decline the invitation. Kennedy, Sergeant Donnie Simpson and Bombardier Donnie Bishop recall that night:

Kennedy: For better or for worse, I just want to say that the fact that we only had one set of [night vision goggles] in the party, was one of the driving things that kept us off the ranges that night at Tarnak Farms.

Bishop: I say that all the time, Tyler. You're not alone on that one, buddy. I say that all the time.

Simpson: And I always say that when I came back from the [orders] group with the [company commander] and said "Hey. They want us to go to Tarnak Farms and give them help with the range that night," and Ranger Fred [Wolanski] said "No. You're going to do [martial arts training] with us tomorrow". And I always thank Fred for that cause you know we would have been standing right beside Marc [Leger].

Kennedy: I saw the [company commander] at lunch that day and he said "Coming out tonight?" and I said "Well, Sir, I mean you're doing a night shoot and it's not a lot to us because we don't have the mortars and only one set of [night vision goggles] between the four of us so if you're good, we'll stay back."[4]

That night a US Air Force pilot "exhibiting arrogance and lack of flight discipline"[5] dropped a bomb on A Company, killing four and wounding eight.

One of the four who died that night was Sergeant Marc Leger, who wasn't even supposed to have been in Afghanistan. Marc had been the second in command of A Company's stores. Being newly promoted, he was over-ranked for the deployment. He insisted on going, however, and was allowed to go.

Leger had been one of G31's favourite Patricias. A company quartermaster can make a soldier's life blissful or miserable. Leger worked hard to do the former and always treated the gunners fair and square. His professionalism stood in sharp contrast to the attitude that others displayed towards the gunners.

Prior to the incident, Leger had made a deal with Donnie Bishop to provide Bishop with a two-man tent if Bishop lent Leger his pair of Gore-Tex boots for an operation. Bishop had been sharing a four-man tent with someone else and wanted a tent of his own. Bishop lent him the boots and Leger issued the tent. Leger had returned the boots to Bishop prior to the 17th, but almost twenty years later Bishop had never worn the boots again nor been able to part with them.[6]

A Company was given a bit of time to mourn their loss, but there wouldn't be much time. Combined Joint Task Force MOUNTAIN had directed a series of battalion or lower level operations to be taken over the next three months under a campaign plan called Operation MOUNTAIN LION. It had begun on April 15th but had been in the planning stages from right after Operation ANACONDA.

MOUNTAIN LION's objective was to root out and defeat any remaining al-Qaeda forces in the Gardez and Khost regions and to secure the conditions for a loya jirga[7] to take place in Kabul in June. It would differ in that rather than relying on local Afghan forces such as ANACONDA had, these operations would rely primarily on airmobile insertions of coalition light infantry, including a newly arrived force of British Marines.[8] The Canadians would be taking part and threw themselves into training for their role.

One such exercise was a live-fire one which took place at the edge of the massive Registan Desert, some 15 kilometres south of KAF on April 19th, a few short days after the Tarnak Farms incident. The mortars were deployed in a line with a centre of arc facing almost due south into the desert. In the middle of a time-on-target fire plan, they found themselves laying on a target at almost right angles to the mortars' centre of arc, firing over each other's heads. It was obvious to the mortar line that something wasn't right and the command post requested a verification of the observer's call for fire data. The response was to fire on the coordinates they had been originally given. The rounds ended up impacting close to a village, fortunately, causing neither casualties nor damage. The error had been in a transposition of two digits in the northings of the target grid ordered by the observer.[9]

Major Wolanski had reported the incident immediately to Lieutenant-Colonel Stogran and suggested that the matter be dealt with as both a technical and disciplinary matter. He suggested that it ought to be dealt with in discussion with the commanding officer of the 1st Regiment, Royal Canadian Horse Artillery (1 RCHA). Stogran agreed. The battalion's mortar platoon commander disagreed, feeling it was inadequate. As a result Stogran ordered an investigation to be conducted by the officer commanding the administration company. That investigation over the next month also looked into the bad blood between the gunners' mortar line and its infantry leadership. In the result, nothing further was done regarding the error, but by June 21st the mortar group reverted to Wolanski's command.[10]

On April 22nd, 2002, Sergeant Kevin Johnson found himself to be the right man with the right skills in the right place. Back in 1995, prior to 1 RCHA's scheduled deployment to Croatia as an infantry battalion, the regiment had offered Johnson the infantry sniper and infantry reconnaissance (recce) patrolman courses. Lieutenant-Colonel Andrew Leslie, its commanding officer at the time, had wanted to ensure that he had his own sniper section. Johnson passed both courses, but the deployment was later cancelled. Johnson's training was not wasted, however, as he was picked up as a sniper by the 2nd Battalion, Princess Patricia's Canadian Light Infantry for a tour to Bosnia in 1997. This time, he did deploy. And again, in 2000, he deployed there, this time with the Lord Strathcona's Horse (Royal Canadians), as their sniper detachment commander.[11]

After Operation ANACONDA, the 3rd Battalion's sniper section was in trouble. One of the snipers had to be repatriated to Canada because of a family emergency. More problematic was that another—the section commander—had been accused of a war crime during the operation and was sent home for a disciplinary investigation. Much later, when the investigation was completed, a decision was made not to proceed with any disciplinary charges for lack of evidence. In fact, all five of the battalion's snipers would later be awarded a mention in dispatches[12] and the American Bronze Star with a (V) device[13] for their work with the 1st and 2nd Battalions, 187th Infantry.

In the meantime, however, the battalion needed two snipers. The first would be a soldier from A Company, and the second would be Johnson, who because of both his rank and prior experience was made the battalion recce platoon's sniper section commander.

Notwithstanding that the situation within the sniper section was strained, Johnson was happy. The change in job removed him from the mortar line where the friction with the two infantrymen assigned to lead the mortar group remained palpable and ongoing. He immediately conducted an equipment serviceability verification, ran an austere range to confirm zero on the two MacMillan tactical .50 calibre sniper rifles and other weapon systems, and then rapidly deployed the snipers on two sequential three-week operations.

A Company's tragedy on the 17th resulted in another change of plans. The company had been scheduled to fly into an old Soviet base at Khost on Operation WHITE FOX which was a part of Operation MOUNTAIN LION. A Company, however, had been given a short breather to mourn its dead. Their role on the operation went to B Company's 5 and 6 Platoons[14] and Captain David Grebstad's G32. Their task was to provide security for special forces operations out of the Khost base. No mortars, other than the rifle platoons' 60mm mortars, would accompany them. The plan was that all the fire support required would come through close air support. Lift restrictions meant that Grebstad and Gunner Patrick Coté were the only members of G32 to go. The two of them would split a 19-hour shift, seven days a week. Grebstad: "We spent a month there ... We spent a lot of time staring at the mountains and, once again, not much happened. There [were] a couple of times when your average rocket attack came in and it never actually landed too close."[15]

For Grebstad, Khost drove home some of the Canadian army's problems. They had sent him out without any dedicated fire support, having to rely solely on air support, but without any training as a forward air controller (FAC). Furthermore, they only had an older AN/PRC 113 radio to contact the airborne operations centre. On the few occasions they tried to contact them, no one answered. He recalls, "We deployed over there with—not just us but the whole coalition—threw all our eggs in one basket and when it came to fire support said, 'No, we're going to rely on the aircraft,' and then 3rd Battalion battle group deploys with no real way to access that."[16]

Grebstad wasn't without resources, however. Their headquarters was collocated with a Special Forces Operational Detachment Bravo[17] which had an abundance of resources at hand. Grebstad:

This one time, we had...several incoming rockets and we could see the point of origin because it was in this valley pretty far off. Even though I couldn't do anything about it, I could see it. This Special Forces dude comes up into my [observation post] and within minutes he had a B-52 on station and said "I have 24 JDAMs[18] to drop on them, if you want." In the end we didn't because the firing stops [and] we knew there were A-Teams and [friendly Afghan] elements out in the area.

We had some [Afghans] collocated with us...this rusty old T-55 drove out of nowhere...belching oil everywhere and it parked right below me and they just did indirect fire ... and they were impacting where the point of origin [of the rockets] was. And there was this battery of four Afghan artillery with us—an M1938, a D-30—shitty old guns, none of which had any sights, and everything was fired. I think they just eyeballed it through the barrel...These guys just were launching stuff downrange. I had the [Detachment Bravo commander] with me at my [observation post] and I said, "You know we don't know where anybody is out there. Maybe we should stop shooting."[19]

They did. After a month, in which Grebstad lost 30 pounds, he and Coté returned to KAF.

On April 22nd, while most of B Company watched over Khost, Task Force RAKKASAN issued a warning order to the battle group for Operation TORII,[20] a battalion-level sensitive site exploitation operation; effectively a recce-in-force to gather information and evidence on al-Qaeda.

The objective area for this task was Tora Bora, the area where Osama bin Laden had made his last stand against coalition forces in November 2001. As nothing had been heard from bin Laden since his ill-fated defence, it was thought that he may have actually died there. The intent was for elements of the battle group to search the area of the cave complexes, look for bodies and intelligence, and hopefully discover the fate of bin Laden. For this mission they would stage out of Bagram airfield.

Concurrently, and operating in the same area, Johnson and his snipers were tasked with Operation BLACK DEVIL, a covert operation looking for al-Qaeda mortar base plate and rocket positions.[21]

With the operations in Afghanistan not even a year old, critical recce, surveillance and intelligence resources were already being pulled away for future operations in Iraq.[22] The actual start of the operation had to be delayed because the initial landing zones, which had been chosen from air photos, were not practicable. US Special Forces were required to go into the extremely rugged country first to find landing zones. This gave the troops more time for mission rehearsals in Bagram.

Some took longer to get from Kandahar to Bagram than others. Bombardier Ryan Herbert recalls the trip for the mortars and recce platoon:

> *The Tora Bora trip. That was a bit of a Gong Show. We got on our C-130 to leave Kandahar and there's no seat in the airplane. There's just the bare floor and they said, "Sit on the floor." So it's like "whatever, it's a short flight." Over Bagram they turned us away because there is a storm...so we then turned back to Kandahar and they turned us away because there is a sandstorm. So we then flew to, I think Jacobabad, Pakistan, to get fuel but us, as Canadians, had no agreement to be in Pakistan so we had to get back on the plane.*

> *Then we flew all the way to Camp Snoopy in Oman. That was then a Gong Show because it was us and [the recce platoon] and they had a kitchen, a mess hall. The guys were in there—pounding back ice cream. They had a Burger King. I had a Whopper...*

Within the day they flew back to Bagram where they boarded Chinooks for Tora Bora.

> *At Tora Bora, we got dropped off on a mountain top, like we always do. We*

moved off the [landing zone] and set up...our mortar position and there are a fair [number] of pine trees so we dug our little shell scrapes and we built little pine shelters...It was awesome to get out of the sun during the days and they held the heat for us during the nights. We were so well camouflaged that numerous times we had to jump out and wave our hands to get the Chinooks to not land on us.[23]

The battle-group had been inserted on May 4th and had operated quickly and efficiently, with the recce platoon establishing a screen in the mountains. Meanwhile A and C Companies, assisted by Afghan guides, US Special Forces, and US forensic scientists, scrambled up and down the extremely rugged mountains combing for caves, trenches, bunkers, and graves for any information they might contain. Combat engineers moved tons of earth with explosives to uncover any caves that the air strikes had buried. The engineers destroyed any al-Qaeda defensive positions, once searched, to deny their future use to the enemy.

C Company proceeded into the valley to collect DNA samples from al-Qaeda bodies buried in a shrine near the village of Ali Khel. The locals were welcoming once they understood that they weren't there to burn poppy fields or desecrate graves. The locals actually helped while the troops followed proper Muslim traditions.[24]

Upon initial occupation of the position, Bombardier Herbert had found a small enemy bunker adjacent to their mortar base plate position. As they were pulling out, the engineers prepared to destroy it with approximately 75 pounds of explosives. Herbert threw a pair of socks that he had worn all week onto the explosives. After the blast, he found that it had blown the socks all the way back over to his mortar, relatively undamaged.[25]

With the mountainside thoroughly searched, DNA collected, and defences destroyed, helicopters extracted the battle group back to Bagram on May 7th.[26] Once again, the mortars were the last to be lifted out.[27] The next day, the battle group returned to KAF for further cycles of training and airfield defence.

The upcoming summer would register several hallmarks. On May 30th, Combined Joint Task Force MOUNTAIN would transfer authority for tactical operations in Afghanistan to Combined Joint Task Force-180, a small headquarters formed by XVIII Airborne Corps. The corps had more important things to think about than Afghanistan—namely Iraq. The Afghans' loya jirga would take place on June 11th. Finally, the International Security and Assistance Force would transfer authority in Kabul from the British to the Turks on June 22nd.

It was time to think about next steps and Canada announced that its 750 soldiers would be withdrawn by August, although naval, air, and special forces would remain.[28] The British followed suit and on June 20th announced that their Marines would come home starting July 4th.[29]

Change, and an end of the mission, might have been in the air, but operations and training continued.

On June 12th, an overloaded MC-130H Combat Talon[30] crashed on takeoff from an improved airstrip near Gardez with three fatalities amongst the ten occupants. Captain Tyler Kennedy and G31 were tasked to respond with the quick reaction platoon to supply security for the crash site investigation team. However, only Sergeant Simpson and Bombardier Bishop deployed as Captain Tyler Kennedy was left out of battle from an injury received during a wrestling match. The two of them would handle the communications with both the fast air and helicopters. They recollect,

> *Simpson: We had every air asset in southeast Afghanistan at our fingertips. We showed up at the airport with 3 Platoon and there were more air force guys getting on the helicopters than the security detail ... I had Tyler's [AN/ PRC-66 UHF] set and was talking to "Bossman" the [airborne warning and control system]. We had a brigadier-general on the ground walking around with us in his office shoes and a flight suit in the middle of Afghanistan. It was one of those wartime surreal experiences that you only expect to see in a movie.*
>
> *Bishop: The only one I can ever think of to compare it to was "We Were Soldiers". When they're coming off the plane to take pictures. That's what I compare it to because that's what it was.*
>
> *Simpson: And that's the kind of stuff we were doing there towards the end.[31]*

But it wasn't the only thing.

Within the week, the battle group received a warning order for another operation, which was to be a part of the ongoing Operation MOUNTAIN LION. It wasn't so much that Task Force RAKKASAN had directed the operation. Instead, the Canadians sought another operation before the battle group went home. Stogran: "I recognized by that point in time it had already been announced that we were coming out after six months. I wanted one last operation. We hadn't really been tested in terms of a firefight. I was referring to us at that time as 'have guns, will travel'..."[32]

American special operations forces had approached the Canadians to provide the conventional force for one of their operations, but eventually they scrubbed the mission. Stogran continues,

But we were given this other operation in Zabul Province. I guess, tit for tat, they wanted to get us employed. The coalition had a long-term plan to do Zabul Province in three phases, as I recall. And so I went to Colonel Lennington and I said, "Look if you can give me my Coyotes, and if I can use recce platoon, we will do all three phases very quickly."[33]

This task, Operation CHEROKEE SKY, would for the first time encompass the entire battle group. Included were the Coyotes of recce squadron of the Lord Strathcona's Horse (Royal Canadians). These light armoured surveillance and recce vehicles would set up blocking positions in the Shinkay Valley, near Qalat in Zabul Province, while all three rifle companies air assaulted in supported by a ground attack by local Afghan militia. The aim: to take out any al-Qaeda or Taliban present there.

There was a considerable lag between conceiving of the operation and mounting it, time that the battle group spent in training and rehearsing. The battery also tested out some new ways of dealing with the ammunition transport problem. Bombardier Herbert recalls:

That last [operation]...we were playing with some different ideas because we were going to be dropped off nowhere near the main [landing zone] so we loaded up a pair of John Deere Gators with mortar bombs. We had it right down to the frame. You couldn't put a single round more onto it. That kind of worked. Then we tried it with an Iltis. We loaded up the Iltis with mortar bombs. It could haul more, but it was a tight squeeze into the back of a Chinook. Finding someone to drive, more or less, thread the needle, was a bit of a challenge...We took [the Iltis] on the [operation] solely just to be an [ammunition] limber.[34]

While they considered the vehicle a wonderful idea to save the lugging of the ammunition by hand, on reflection, the time that the Chinook needed to stay on the ground, potentially very rugged ground and under fire while unloading, made the technique questionable.

Once again, the mortar line was separated from the rest of the battalion and it went into a defensive position while they awaited calls for fire. Calls that never came. The battalion spent the better part of a week sweeping through expected enemy locations, recovering weapons caches, and distributing blankets and food supplies to the locals, but engaging in no actual contacts.[35]

Once again, Sergeant Johnson's sniper section deployed, this time on a three-week strategic recce mission in the Qalat area of Zabul together with US Special Forces.

The intention had been to surprise the local governor who intelligence sources had suspected of being in collusion with the enemy. The deception plan included having the recce platoon, along with the snipers, who deployed in advance, being kitted out in American gear and driving civilian pattern vehicles so that there would be no suggestion that the green-clad,[36] Canadian battalion was coming. The deployment did not achieve total surprise. Stogran was sure that the governor had tried to dupe him by having coalition forces round up some locals to pawn off as captured Taliban, and by crediting the Canadians with having found some 30 Stinger anti-aircraft missiles which in fact they hadn't.[37]

When Operation CHEROKEE SKY ended on July 4th, it also signaled the end of Operation MOUNTAIN LION.[38] It was time to pack up for home and to reflect on all that they had learned and done. It was also a time when everyone would slap each other's backs, congratulate themselves on a successful campaign, and look towards a few years of rebuilding Afghanistan into a pseudo-western image.

Almost immediately upon the battle group's return to KAF after Operation CHEROKEE SKY, it had in short order held a briefing on redeployment, celebrated a belated Canada Day barbecue, received a redeployment start date, conducted a field exercise at Tarnak Farms for a "Mexican unload" of their surplus ammunition, and hosted visits by both Brigadier-General Gauthier, commander of Canada's Joint Task Force-Southwest Asia, and the new Minister of National Defence, John McCallum.

In between activities, they packed away and readied gear for shipping. Once again, the battalion didn't see things the same way as the gunners. Captain Grebstad, in addition to his duties with G32, also filled in as the acting battery captain, the battery's principal administrative officer, on occasions when Kennedy—who also doubled as the battery captain—wasn't there. When it came to the redeployment Grebstad observed,

> So the plan came out and said, "...you are to turn over all your equipment too, we're going to fold it all into the [battalion's administrative] company. They'll take everything back complete in one." Like we'll put our rifles in with theirs, we'll put our [binoculars] in with theirs. And I said, "This is a really bad idea. We should have C Battery's stuff segregated because it's all got to come back to Shilo..."[39]

Grebstad and Wolanski protested and argued their case but were overruled.

> Eventually they said, "No. Shut up. Put it all in the bin." So we put it all in the bin and don't you know it, everything got lost...It all ended up in Edmonton...it all went into 3rd Battalion's stores and then no one could find anything because tags were ripped off...and no one had the time or people to go start checking serial numbers...when we got back from leave...we all got a

stack of [miscellaneous loss reports] that at least someone had prepared for us, basically saying we've lost all of our kit that we had over there.[40]

Redeployment took place in the last week of July, starting with a C-5 Galaxy flight from KAF to Diego Garcia, an American Navy and Air Force base on a British island in the middle of the Indian Ocean roughly 2,000 kilometres south of India. Here they were put up for the night on cots in a gymnasium. Grebstad recalls that, "We were dry the whole time [in Afghanistan]. We didn't get eased back into alcohol. Everyone kind of went nuts as soon as they got to Diego Garcia. Everyone just started pounding booze."[41]

The next day they boarded chartered Air Malaysia flights for Guam. Grebstad considered Guam a particularly good choice as it routinely hosts large numbers of American sailors and is used to such visits and could easily handle 700 Canadians. National Defence Headquarters had reached out to Personnel Support Programs in Shilo to help out with the decompression, including greeting everyone as they landed.

Guam would be a five-day stay at a seaside resort hotel. While the battalion had a few briefings in the morning followed by the rest of the day left to their own devices, the battery would form up for morning physical training—often as the rest of the battalion was coming back from a night out drinking. This would be followed by 5-kilometre runs through town in the tropical humidity. This quickly became a morale issue. In fairness, the battery was following an activities table for decompression set out for them by Ottawa. As far as the troops were concerned, however, they were the only ones in the battle group following the timetable and the program was doing the exact opposite of decompression. Most would have preferred to simply lie around the beach rather than have a full schedule of sitting in a room watching PowerPoint presentations from 9 to 3. Some of these included discussions on the "Light Forces Working Group", a euphemism for "reinvigorate the Airborne, again." As one anonymous gunner put it, "It was decompression, and the guns didn't decompress."

With Guam behind them, the battery flew back to Edmonton and then Winnipeg for the bus trip home to Shilo. They had started and ended their journey on a bus but in between had circumnavigated the globe.

What lessons then came out of Operation APOLLO? The battalion would produce a PowerPoint presentation with 73 slides listing their observations and recommendations. Only three would relate to gunner issues. The lack of enemy contacts and the resulting few engagements by the mortars had brought very little of an artillery nature home to the infantry. What then were the key lessons learned by the gunners?

Major Wolanski had made several observations. Foremost among them was the issue of guns versus mortars. The choice to take mortars had been driven by the Americans' limited airlift and everyone's tunnel vision reliance on close air support. Afghanistan would probably become the most permissive environment for the use of air that anyone has ever seen or will ever see, but weather had denied air support at times while helicopters had been shot out of the sky by things as mundane as rocket-propelled grenades and machine guns.

The limited range of the mortars—Canadians did not even have the 120mm option the Americans had—and turbulent wind conditions in the mountains made mortars a poor choice for counter bombardment of enemy mortar and rocket firing positions. The Americans, too, recognized this and would quickly give a nod to a few guns. The month after the Canadians flew home, Battery C of the 1ˢᵗ Battalion of the 319ᵗʰ Airborne Field Artillery Regiment would deploy with a stripped-down battery of M119 105mm howitzers.[42]

The absence of artillery surveillance and target acquisition (STA) resources became clear quickly after the first rocket attacks struck Kandahar. The primitive crater analysis conducted by Wolanski, while interesting, provided no effective capability to strike back. Here too, the Americans quickly corrected their capability deficiencies by introducing AN/TPQ 36 Firefinder radars from the 3ʳᵈ Battalion of the 320ᵗʰ Field Artillery Regiment to KAF.[43] Canadians had no such capability in their inventory.

Tied to counter-battery work was the observation that command and control of fire support assets were too top-driven. Clearance to fire needed to go from the battle group, through the brigade headquarters, all the way to the fire support coordination centre in Bagram.

Problematic as well, especially in a theatre which relied heavily on air support, was the inadequacy of training and equipping of Canadian FACs. Canadian FACs were trained in NATO procedures, but most of the air resources were American and all of it was controlled by the Americans, so that Canadians had to retrain to American standards. The lack of LTM 91 Laser target designators and AN/PRC 117 radios in the Canadians' inventory also made it difficult to convince American authorities in theatre that Canadians could control American aircraft.[44]

What then was the bottom line of what the Canadian army learned about the employment of artillery in Canada's first war since Korea?

Unsurprisingly perhaps, very little.

The 3ʳᵈ Battalion's commanding officer had always been a vigorous proponent of light infantry battalions, which he felt were threatened within the army. He had strongly advocated on their behalf before Operation APOLLO. That position did not change afterward. Operation APOLLO's minimal use of indirect fire resources and overwhelming reliance on air resources, coupled with the rapid collapse of the

Taliban regime and al-Qaeda in Afghanistan, if anything, reinforced the status quo path to transforming the army into a lighter, more flexible organization.

The artillery very much remained, looking for a way to demonstrate its relevance. To many, its very existence was threatened. Afghanistan, meanwhile, was now a symbol of success. Rapid strikes by air power, special operations forces and light conventional forces had subjugated the country, making it ripe for nation-building. There were challenges, to be sure, but generally there was a feeling of optimism as various countries assumed a variety of roles required for that.[45]

Canada too would play its part. But first there would be an interlude.

THE FIRST INTERLUDE:
SUMMER 2002-SUMMER 2003

EVEN BEFORE THE END OF C BATTERY'S MISSION, changes were happening throughout the world. Changes which would affect Canada's future commitment to Afghanistan.

In Afghanistan, the enemy was changing. At the time of 9/11, the Taliban had been a conventional force hosting guest terrorists who used the country as a home base for their operations elsewhere. Now, they and their protégés were fleeing the country in droves through a web of ratlines. It appeared early in 2002 that Afghanistan was ready to rebuild.[1]

Neither the Taliban nor their affiliates, however, were dead and buried by any stretch of the imagination. Their leadership had fled the country to take up residence in Pakistan. There they established themselves in and around the west-central city of Quetta, a mere 200 kilometres southeast of Kandahar. Many of the Taliban's fighters had faded back into their local communities, waiting to see what the future held for them.

Al-Qaeda's leadership had also relocated to Pakistan, with bin Laden moving several times before finding a home in Abbottabad in northern Pakistan, within close proximity of the Pakistan Military Academy. Al-Qaeda's influence in Afghanistan was waning. Its attention would soon transition to other parts of the world. In its place, a third force was gaining prominence.

Gulbuddin Hekmatyar had twice been the prime minister of Afghanistan in the 1990s before the country's takeover by the Taliban. His Hezb-e-Islami Gulbuddin party had been a major force. Pakistan had initially provided them support in order to help form a friendly Pashtun government. That support had faded after the Taliban's successes.

By the summer of 2002, his rabid opposition to Hamid Karzai and reports that he was seeking to align himself with both al-Qaeda and the Taliban earned his organization the distinction as the primary threat to the nascent Afghan government in Kabul.[2] Less hostile, but also a serious threat, were Afghanistan's many warlords, drug lords, and their heavily armed militias scattered throughout the country.

Left behind in Afghanistan were the American Special Forces' operational detachments–who had united with and trained various anti-Taliban militias–a fledgling international contingent in Kabul, and a handful of conventional American army units. There also remained several Tier 1[3] elements such as those of the US Joint Special Operations Command, but their thinking was already elsewhere. It was already clear that President Bush was taking the show to Iraq and that the enemy now strategizing in Pakistan was of a lesser interest.[4]

The US Army's XVIII Airborne Corps was now the senior operational headquarters in the Afghan theatre. It was transforming itself into a combined joint headquarters capable of synchronizing the activities of land, sea and air resources as well as ground and allied organizations. It had adopted the designation Combined Joint Task Force-180. A significant constraint imposed upon the headquarters by the Pentagon was to withhold half of the headquarters from deploying, thereby permitting them the flexibility to prepare for potential airborne operations elsewhere.[5] The planning for what was soon to become Operation IRAQI FREEDOM, was already well underway. Notwithstanding this shift in focus and the initial successes in Afghanistan, President Bush, in a speech at the Virginia Military Institute in April, acknowledged that the war in Afghanistan was not over and that they were in it for the long haul.[6]

Combined Joint Task Force-180 assumed command of conventional coalition operations outside of Kabul's city limits in late May 2002. In doing so, it would pursue four lines of effort: security; civil-military; information; and training Afghan security forces. Of these, security would take priority for the rest of 2002, but thereafter, as Afghanistan stabilized, priority would transition to humanitarian assistance, support to the Afghan government through reconstruction, and Afghan security forces training.[7] As the year progressed, Combined Joint Task Force-180 took command of the Combined Joint Civil Military Operations Task Force. It also assumed operational control over Combined Joint Special Operations Task Force-Afghanistan, which had most recently been conducting training of Afghan security forces. Finally it took command of the newly arrived Combined Joint Task Force 82 made up of elements of the divisional headquarters, a brigade headquarters, and other units from the 82nd Airborne Division.[8]

It was during this time that initial, low-impact reconstruction efforts evolved into what would by early 2003 be the first three pilot provincial reconstruction teams; Gardez, Bamian, and Kunduz. President Karzai had preferred the term "provincial" rather than "regional" to emphasize that these teams did not work for local regional warlords or leaders.[9]

Progress was also made with the organizational development of a national army for Afghanistan. The initial blueprint agreed upon between the Afghan government and the international security forces, was given some structure, although not without difficulties. Initially, the US Office of Military Cooperation-Afghanistan worked with coalition partners such as the French to train officers, and the United Kingdom to train non-commissioned officers, while other allies took on the training of various other elements. As the training task grew, it was given a new name; Combined Joint Task Force PHOENIX.[10] It was at first staffed by the 2nd Brigade of the 10th Mountain Division, but thereafter the role was assigned to brigades provided by the US Army National Guard. This was another clear indicator that the main effort for US forces was shifting to Iraq.

While Canada had been fighting alongside the Americans in the south, another force had set up operations in the north within the confines of the capital city of Kabul. On December 20th, 2001, at the Bonn Conference,[11] United Nations (UN) Security Council Resolution 1386, created the International Security and Assistance Force (ISAF) to help Afghanistan's fledgling provisional government. ISAF's headquarters was a divisional one. As its operational field force, ISAF had a single brigade called the Kabul Multinational Brigade with three battle groups. The overall size of ISAF varied depending upon the contributing nations' commitments, but generally ran at just under five thousand troops.

For its first three rotations, ISAF I through III, several countries volunteered to form six-month rotations. The 3rd (UK) Division formed the first deployment as ISAF I. This was the same organization that had rebuffed Canada's participation leaving Canada free to take part in the Americans' Operation ENDURING FREEDOM.[12] ISAF I, operating from December 2001 to June 2002, was succeeded by Turkey's ISAF II. In February 2003 the Turks passed control to ISAF III, a joint German and Dutch force based on the headquarters of I German-Netherlands Corps.

Even before the start of ISAF III, however, it had become clear that finding one nation to organize and command the force was becoming difficult, and that the North Atlantic Treaty Organization (NATO), as an entity, would need to take over responsibility for ISAF IV and subsequent rotations. As a result, in 2002 there were two separate allied forces operating in Afghanistan: ISAF inside Kabul and the US, with select allied forces, everywhere else. But what of Canada?

With the homecoming of the 3rd Battalion, Princess Patricia's Canadian Light Infantry at the end of July of 2002, there was an operational pause. The battalion's deployment had been structured as a one-of and there was no plan for another Canadian rotation to Afghanistan. Around the world, there had been quiet anticipation that with al-Qaeda and the Taliban on the run, the mission would wind down. The spring and summer of 2002 had been seen as one of both optimism and anxiety, as plans moved to another loya jirga—a grand assembly—to be held in Kabul on October 1st, 2003. The loya jirga of 2002 had elected a transitional administration under Hamid Karzai; 2003 was planned to approve a constitution. What was becoming clear, however, was that even if the Taliban was for the moment out of the picture, there were still many diverse, and heavily armed, warlords to be concerned about.

Notwithstanding that the battle group had left Afghanistan, Canada had not entirely left the region. Under Operation APOLLO there had also been a naval and air contingent which continued to operate in the Persian Gulf region together with a support base. Camp Mirage, set up at the Al-Minhad Air Base in the United Arab Emirates, originally supported CP-140 Aurora maritime patrol aircraft. It had expanded its operations and now provided a vital logistics link back to Canada for all Canadian Forces operations in the region.[13]

Canada's government was still very much interested in demonstrating its commitment to the Americans in the War on Terror. Why then had Canada's army not remained inside Afghanistan in the first place? The answer was simple. Operations in the Balkans were consuming a significant portion of the army's resources. Chief of Defence Staff, General Ray Henault, had concluded that Canada's military, especially its army, could not continuously sustain two operations of that magnitude. He had convinced the government not to support any further operations in Afghanistan at that time.[14] What then changed the government's mind a mere half year later?

At the end of 2002, Jean Chrétien was just starting his 10th, and last, year as the prime minister of Canada. The Minister of National Defence, John McCallum, on the other hand, was a newcomer having taken over the role from Art Eggleton on June 26th, 2002. Much of Eggleton's tenure over the previous five years was consumed by the post-Somalia fallout. This had resulted in major changes in the *National Defence Act*, including changes to the military justice system and the governance of military police.

Eggleton had resigned under a cloud due, in part, to allegations of misleading Parliament regarding the capture of Taliban detainees by Canadian troops in Afghanistan. Canada's Joint Task Force 2, had taken such detainees, but Eggleton claimed he had not been told. In addition, there were allegations he had been in breach of ethics guidelines for having a research contract awarded to a former girlfriend. Chrétien was concurrently dealing with leadership challenges within the

Liberal Party, particularly the resignation of Paul Martin. Martin would subsequently become Prime Minister on December 12th, 2003.

McCallum's tenure as Minister of National Defence started off well for the Canadian Forces. The 2003 defence budget added US$1.5 billion from the previous year, raising it from US$8.5 billion to US$9.96 billion in 2003. This increase did not change the percentage of the gross domestic product spent on defence, as it remained at 1.2% for both years. It did, however, reverse the trend of a declining defence budget during a period known as the "Decade of Darkness". Under the Chrétien regime the budget had steadily dropped from a high in 1990 of US$11.41 billion (1.96%) to US$8.5 billion (1.2%) in 2002. McCallum wasn't without his own issues, as a series of incidents in late 2002 and early 2003 brought him criticism and censure in the press. McCallum, however, stayed on as Minister until December 11th, 2003.[15]

It was obvious to everyone that the Americans were heading into Iraq. Within the office of the Deputy Chief of Defence Staff, a small group was working on plans to see how Canada could, or would support that mission if asked to do so by the government.[16] The planners were convinced that the request would never come because Prime Minister Chrétien opposed such involvement. Options were discussed, however. In evaluating those options, two key questions needed answering: did Canada have the combat capability; and did Canada have the global command and control capability to support the various options? Afghanistan would probably require a battle group while Iraq would probably have been more challenging requiring more than that.

When Canada had originally declined to lead a follow-on rotation of ISAF due to its Bosnia commitments, there had been a second factor which had its roots in the 1997 "Great Lakes Fiasco" in the Congo. Not long after the Rwandan genocide General Maurice Baril with staff from the 1st Canadian Division headquarters went to the Congo to assess a United Nations (UN) humanitarian mission there under Operation ASSURANCE. The mission fell apart for a number of reasons including lack of major power support and also the fact that Canada did not have the requisite command, control and logistics capability to lead such a mission.[17] The after-action review of the operation had two viewpoints. Within the army it was that Canada had a capability gap which needed to be addressed. Conversely, within the office of the Deputy Chief of Defence Staff the view was that Canada can't do this type of leadership mission and shouldn't do it. Ultimately it would be a question of how much risk the government was willing to take.[18]

Chrétien's opposition to Iraq was deep and varied. While some have speculated that Chrétien was opposed to supporting this mission because there was no UN Security Council resolution supporting such a mission, the real reasons were likely more political. Many Canadians strongly opposed the venture and if nothing else, the Prime Minister was without equal in reading the public's mood. By January 2003, a mere 23% of Canadians supported such action, while in Québec only 7% approved. Québec was heading to an election in April 2003, which many saw as a vote of confidence in Chrétien's Québec policies.[19] As a result, the idea of committing the Canadian Forces to a mission in Iraq did not have the government's nor the Canadian public's support. Moreover, Canadian intelligence estimates concluded that Iraq no longer had any weapons of mass destruction of any consequence in its arsenal and that there was no convincing evidence that it was reconstituting its nuclear weapons program.[20] Individuals who heard the Prime Minister speak on the issue at the time confirmed that he accepted these Canadian assessments rather than the ones coming from the UK or the US.[21]

The Chretien government had a conundrum: How would President Bush react to a refusal by Canada to join the coalition he was forming? Was there a solution that could meet the mood of the country and the intelligence assessment, and still keep the US from thinking that Canada had forsworn the unconditional support that it had previously given?

By early 2003, many discussions were being held within the Prime Minister's Office concerning how to placate the Americans.[22] Luckily there was a solution on the horizon. Germany, like Canada, had resolved not to join the Iraq coalition and had already invested heavily in a presence in Afghanistan with ISAF. While Canada's senior military leaders remained in the dark, communications were happening from late November 2002 to February 2003 between the German government and McCallum as to how Canada, with admittedly limited resources, could fit in with Germany's efforts. In short, if both countries could make a credible commitment to ISAF, it would give them both solid grounds for not participating in the ongoing buildup for Iraq.[23] This plan included the provision that NATO, as a whole, rather than any one country, would take over the responsibility for ISAF.

McCallum had gone so far as to meet with the US Secretary of Defence, Donald Rumsfeld on January 9th without staff present.[24] A decision was not long in coming. Discussions in Canada quickly turned to the mission being not merely a military one, but a "Whole of Government" effort focused on stabilizing the Afghan government. Chrétien's view was that while he couldn't recommend to Canadians a mission in Iraq, he could recommend a humanitarian one in Afghanistan.[25]

Support for the German-Canadian effort soon grew as France and several other European Iraq holdouts declared their support for a NATO ISAF mission targeted on improving the security of Kabul. On February 4th, McCallum made the proposal of Canada's return to Afghanistan to cabinet where it gained acceptance as the best possible choice for the country, a position made even more palatable by the commitment and support of what was then termed the Department of Foreign Affairs and International Trade.[26] The talk now turned to the question of who would provide the leadership for the mission.

On February 12th, Prime Minister Chrétien publicly announced that Canada would deploy a battle group to Kabul. The same day, McCallum announced at a NATO meeting in Brussels that Canada would contribute 1,900 troops to the ISAF IV rotation in Kabul in the summer of 2003, and it would assume command of the Kabul Multinational Brigade.[27] Lieutenant-General Mike Jeffery had no advance warning of this commitment. He learned of the decision to go back into Afghanistan the same day that the rest of the country did on the 12th in a telephone call with the Minister. Further announcements stated that Canada would supply a deputy commander to ISAF IV and that Canada would take command of the ISAF V rotation in 2004.

With the commitments made, one needs to ask what was the state of Canada's army by this time? At the end of 2002, Jeffery's vision for change for the army was well defined. Called "Advancing With Purpose: The Army Strategy" it mapped out a multi-faceted 10-year plan to take the "Army of Today" to the "Army of Tomorrow". There was also a provision for a longer term view with an "Army of the Future" looking to a 10 to 30 year horizon. The plan was to transform the army from being optimized for Cold-War symmetrical warfare fought in open terrain and contiguous battlespace to one optimized for asymmetrical warfare in complex terrain in a non-contiguous battlespace. In the former, battalion-sized units are the building blocks to create brigade groups while in the latter company-sized subunits are the building blocks for a deployable battle group.[28]

A key element would be the basic composition of the army as a whole. The strategy called for one armoured regiment (with Leopard C2 tanks), two reconnaissance (recce) regiments (with Coyotes), six mechanized infantry battalions (with light armoured vehicles (LAV)), three light infantry battalions, and three artillery regiments. These would stand at tiered readiness with from 30 to 60 days for the light battalions to 90 to 180 days for the armoured regiment.[29]

What of the artillery?

While the broad concept was for companies as the building blocks, the overarching structure would still be the three brigades. Each of the brigades would have two mechanized and one light infantry battalion, however one brigade, the 1st Canadian Mechanized Brigade Group, would be weighted towards heavy with a tank regiment. Artillery would be tailored to match. One regiment, the one with the tank-equipped brigade, would be a medium regiment, initially equipped with three M109 batteries, a mortar battery and a yet to be created target acquisition battery. Two regiments would be light regiments each with an LG1 battery, a mortar battery and a yet to be formed target acquisition battery.[30] The medium guns would be at low readiness and the guns and mortars at tiered readiness.[31]

Air defence, too, would transform into a part of a direct fire structure and settle into one composite air defence battery and a regiment with three very short range air defence batteries.[32]

Running in parallel to these reforms was the Land Force Reserve Restructure project which had the aim of converging the reserve force and the regular force into a unified force within the Army of the Future for 2020.[33] What that meant for reserve artillery units was, as yet, undefined.

The transformation strategy matured as the year went on. By the time Mike Jeffery retired in 2003, there was an interim model for the army to be reached by 2007. This would structure the army for force generation using the then current equipment suite. For the regular force artillery, this would still be the LG1 and the M109 howitzers albeit 81mm mortars were now also starting to make their way into the regiments. For example, D Battery trained 24 gunners to operate mortars in preparation for its role as part of a rapid reaction unit.[34] With the interim model came the concept of the three-part readiness cycle where 1/3 of the army would be ready, 1/3 reconstituting after readiness and 1/3 training and building capabilities to be ready.[35]

At this time, as well, there was a look forward at what equipment could be part of the Army of the Future. Two systems were highlighted. The Leopard C2s to be replaced by something in the nature of an American Stryker 105mm Mobile Gun System and the M109 with something in the nature of the Swedish Bofors 155mm medium wheeled self-propelled howitzer. No actual project or funding for the medium artillery was in place.[36] Major Tim Young, at this time, left his job with the artillery school to work in Ottawa in a lieutenant-colonel's position at the Director Land Requirements 2 which had the mandate for artillery equipment. He recalls, "So DLR was really interesting because we had no projects that were … we had projects on the books, but no funded projects. And so that was the key that everybody else or most of the other sections in DLR had funded projects but us. So we were basically given sustainment funding for things that we were doing, [Indirect Fire Computer Control System], the software upgrades."[37] Young would soon switch jobs. The Director Land Requirements was required to give up a position to the Director Land Strategic Planning to work on the stand up of the Canadian Manoeuvre Training Centre which itself would require the transfer of approximately 300 positions from across the army.[38]

As Lieutenant-General Mike Jeffery was looking forward to retirement in May of 2003, the vision was held by many that large-scale, peer-to-peer conflict was over. 9/11 and Operation APOLLO had reinforced that view. Lieutenant-General Rick

Hillier, Jeffrey's successor as Chief of Land Staff, would be instrumental in taking the army forward into the next stage of transformation.[39]

Questions were being asked about what need there really was for some of the "esoteric" elements of the army. The artillery was slowly being pushed away from operating at the regimental level, and above, to becoming a force focusing on the battery and the troop. Its ability to instantly mass overwhelming firepower at a critical point in time and space was seen less and less as a necessity based on the former-Yugoslavia and Somalia and now Afghanistan experiences.

Capital expenditures—money earmarked for replacing aging military equipment and purchasing new capabilities—had dropped from a high of 30% of the defence budget in 1983 to between 13 and 17% by 2003.[40] The result was an ever increasing, perceived need to shed costly high-end capabilities that were deemed to be no longer affordable or necessary for an army focused on failed states and operations other than war.

A case in point was the hot debate within the armoured corps about the contemplated 105mm Mobile Gun System versus the existing Leopard tank. General Hillier, among others, was of the view that Leopard tanks, although recently upgraded to the tune of $145 million, had had their day. In their view future operations would be better served with the lighter, Mobile Gun Systems. Others, including members of the opposition party in Parliament believed that the loss of the tanks would leave Canadian soldiers at risk and denigrate Canada to a third-rate military.[41] Clearly, such a divestiture would lead to an "unbalancing" of the force whereby Canada's ability to fight in a peer conflict would quickly fade. Where the tanks were headed, the M109 self-propelled howitzers and M113 tracked armoured personnel carriers were sure to follow.

From the very beginning, the army's transformation strategy tried to balance the realities of funding shortfalls, rusting-out equipment, burned-out personnel, and vague political direction. That strategy, however, was receiving criticism that it was not "doctrine-based". One infantry officer, writing in the Canadian Army Doctrine and Training Bulletin, argued that the army was merely "capabilities-based"[42] without an overarching national strategy derived from war plans.[43]

A capability-based force without an overarching doctrine can lead to difficulties. The elimination of mortar and pioneer platoons from the infantry battalions, for personnel rather than doctrinal issues, in favour of artillery and engineer "modules" to be added to battle groups was one example.[44] Another was the replacements of the tanks with the creation of a "direct fire unit" combining the air defence artillery's Air Defence Anti Tank Systems, the infantry's Tube-launched, Optically-tracked, Wire-guided anti-tank weapons with the yet to be acquired armoured corps' Mobile Gun Systems.[45] Abandoning the tried-and-true echelon system of combat service support for *ad hoc* aggregated national support elements designed to operate out of base camps in the Balkans was a third.[46] The purchase of 203 LAV-based Coyote recce vehicles in 1993[47] to replace the Lynx recce vehicle was a fourth. It took seven years of trial and error to discover that it was poor at recce but probably the best surveillance equipment on the market. The lack of a supporting doctrine at the time of its introduction led to years of misuse[48] which continued through attempts to evolve the sound concept of integrating the coordination of intelligence, surveillance, target acquisition and recce (ISTAR) resources within the brigade into the less sound desire to actually regroup such resources into a single ISTAR unit.[49]

All of these initiatives have their genesis in the desire among some of the army's leadership and government to build a lighter, more responsive, more flexible force to meet what were considered to be the future challenges of the world: failed states such as Yugoslavia and Afghanistan which were consuming significant amounts of the army's resources.

A parallel, but doctrinally different concept was evolving in the United States. The American army's smallest Cold-War self-contained "unit of action" was the division, which was deemed too large for many future missions and as such, a reorganization was initiated to create brigade combat teams. By moving various divisional resources, such as artillery, engineer and logistics elements, to the division's brigades, US brigade combat teams came to resemble Canadian brigade groups which, because of the small size of Canada's army, had by necessity existed for over a half of a century.[50]

The initial brigade combat team concept had one major flaw: infantry brigade combat teams could be deployed rapidly but were too light to take on major combat or to manoeuvre quickly once deployed. Armoured brigade combat teams had the staying power once deployed but took far too long to deploy. Accordingly, an interim, middleweight, brigade combat team was created that was basically an infantry force equipped with air transportable LAVs which would form part of a rapid response force.[51]

The Interim Brigade Combat Team would subsequently be renamed the Stryker Brigade Combat Team because it would be based on the Stryker series of eight-wheeled armoured vehicles which, in turn, were based on the same general chassis as the Canadian LAV. The Stryker Brigade Combat Team development paralleled the new medium-weight Canadian Mechanized Brigade Groups with some significant differences and one major exception: the American version was never to be anything but a bridge to fill the capability gap between the Americans' light and heavy brigade combat teams, while for Canada, the medium weight mechanized brigade group was the sole capability with no fall back to a heavy force.[52]

Many in Canada questioned building a medium weight, modular, capability-based army which was planning on divesting itself of its heavy capabilities. These skeptics were quickly branded with being mired in Cold War concepts and unwilling to see the true nature of the future battlefield.

The winds of change were poised to sweep through and leave behind disastrous consequences for Canada's artillery, as it was less and less being seen as an essential combat arm. The interlude since C Battery had left Afghanistan had been filled with change—more was coming. With the Americans scaling down their effort there in favour of an action against Iraq, the Canadian government had committed itself to play a major role with ISAF in Kabul. With all of the political decisions in place, it was now up to the Canadian Forces and government planners to generate a plan and to build a force; a force within which gunners would once again play a role.

THE ROAD TO KABUL

WITH THE MINISTER OF NATIONAL DEFENCE having given a broad mandate and a general limitation on the numbers to be deployed, the task now fell to a host of people to determine the organization for this new upcoming deployment designated Operation ATHENA.[1] There had been a few limited warning orders about the upcoming mission but the immediate presumption was the task would go to Land Force Central Area which, at that time, had been tasked to provide the army's then high readiness brigade—2 Canadian Mechanized Brigade Group in Petawawa, Ontario. The brigade already had the task to provide Roto 13 for Operation PALLADIUM in Bosnia-Herzegovina that fall. This task would not change. As the brigade's close support artillery regiment, it was logical that the 2nd Regiment, Royal Canadian Horse Artillery (2 RCHA), augmented by other gunners, would provide the artillery component.

The artillery's chronicle of Operation ATHENA comes in two quite distinct but interrelated parts: the rapid rebirth of an artillery target acquisition capability—which had previously withered on the vine; and what would become the continuing struggle for relevance of the artillery's guns. The former's rise was to be dramatic at the beginning, while the latter would be highlighted by periods of frustration interspersed with moments of satisfaction. Both would intermittently progress over the course of the various deployments to Afghanistan.

The announcement of the Kabul mission, caused the staff within National Defence Headquarters to scramble.[2] As General Hillier would later put it, the sudden commitment to a brigade-level operation came as a surprise and reverberated throughout the army.[3]

Not everyone in the army was excited by the prospect of this deployment. "... in late May 2003, in a retirement address, [Lieutenant-General] Mike Jeffery, then Chief of the Land Staff, said he was worried about the army's future, pointing out that the commitment of two six month rotations of about 1,800 soldiers to Afghanistan meant about a third of the army's deployable forces were committed internationally."[4]

Two key appointments needed to be filled almost immediately. Since Canada was expected to lead the Kabul Multinational Brigade, it would need to provide a brigade commander. Second, since this was to be an International Security Assistance Force (ISAF) rotation dominated by both Germany and Canada, there was a requirement for a senior Canadian commander within ISAF, specifically a deputy commander.

The logical choice for command of the Kabul Multinational Brigade was the commander of 2 Canadian Mechanized Brigade Group, Colonel Peter Devlin, an infantryman with roots in The Royal Canadian Regiment. He would deploy that fall as an acting brigadier-general.[5] The commander of Land Force Central Area, Brigadier-General Andrew Leslie, a gunner, became the deputy commander of ISAF IV. Ottawa would promote him to major-general[6] before deployment. Both would subsequently rise to the rank of lieutenant-general and become commanders of the army.

Brigadier-General Leslie was in his office when the Prime Minister's announcement was made public. He was quickly called in to discuss the deployment and to lead a "Whole of Government" reconnaissance (recce) team to Kabul to meet with their counterparts of the current German/Dutch ISAF III rotation. While General Leslie had not received or reviewed Major Wolanski's Operation APOLLO lessons learned report, he became aware of the information it contained in a meeting with him.[7]

Among many other things, Leslie's trip confirmed that the Germans were flying a short range, all weather unmanned aerial vehicle (UAV), the EMT X-2000 Luna, as their tactical surveillance UAV, and that the Dutch had deployed AN/TPQ-36 Firefinder counter-mortar radars. Accordingly, he confirmed the need for both UAVs and radars as surveillance and target acquisition (STA) requirements for Canada's Kabul mission. Guns, rather than mortars, were identified as the doctrinally correct weapon system to strike back against any hostile mortars and rockets. Guns would also be employed in a "show of force" role for the Kabul Multinational Brigade. Coincidentally, American forces under Operation ENDURING FREEDOM, had come to a similar conclusion. In the latter part of 2002, they deployed field artillery battalions[8] equipped with their light 105mm M119A2s howitzers in addition to the 81mm and 120mm mortar systems that were already in theatre.[9]

Leslie brought these requirements back to Canada together with others including the decision to deploy an airspace coordination centre (ASCC), an electronic warfare capability, an all-source intelligence cell, and signals intelligence resources.[10] While neither guns, UAVs, nor radars were on the original draft Canadian table of organization and equipment, General Ray Henault, the Chief of Defence Staff, quickly approved them and forwarded the document to McCallum for approval. Neither he, nor the Prime Minister, made any amendments prior to granting it.[11] Leslie described both of them as very supportive in accepting his recommendations.

The list of required capabilities for procurement was handed over to the office of the Director Land Force Readiness who was double-hatted as the Director Army Operations.[12] Leslie described the subsequent actions by the procurement system in identifying, sourcing, and procuring the kit—a process which he considered usually terrible at best—as a magnificent job.[13]

Choosing a gun to deploy was a straightforward task. There were only three choices: the 155mm M109A4+; the 105mm C3; and the 105mm LG1. The M109 was deemed too heavy and the C3's role was becoming more of a training gun. The LG1 had already been used in a similar role in the Balkans. The LG1 was, therefore, considered the obvious choice, and F Battery, 2 RCHA had been equipped with six of them for several years.

On the other hand, UAVs and radars simply weren't in the army's inventory. Within days, the Director Land Force Readiness issued an unforecasted operational requirement to the Director Land Requirements. Under normal circumstances, equipment is acquired after a lengthy, deliberate staff process. This process considers key factors such as; the requirement for a given piece of equipment, how it is to be fielded, the number of pieces required, the personnel required to operate it, how it is to be maintained over its life-cycle, and the overall cost associated with it. An unforecasted operational requirement, on the other hand, merely requires the acquisition of a piece or several pieces of equipment to fulfill a specific need for a limited specific mission. Given that the UAVs and radars were going to be used immediately in Kabul, they would be obtained through that process.

While the army had made locating artillery a low priority for many years, gunners on operations quickly identified its importance at even as low as the battle group level. C Battery's Fred Wolanski on Operation APOLLO had seen the value of the Americans' AN/TPQ 36 Firefinder radar in determining highly accurate locations for enemy mortar and rocket launch sites, and he had stated that fact in his after action report. He'd similarly reported back the unsuitability of the 81mm mortar as a counter-battery weapons system because of its short range and often unstable projectile flight in the frequent high winds of the Afghan mountains.[14]

Wolanski's observations, however, had not translated into any concrete change in priorities for the artillery. The Canadian military's wheels of identifying and procuring new capabilities grind slowly. The "one-of" mentality of Operation APOLLO had left its lessons learned languishing. No one was about to change the priorities within the army from a single campaign in a desolate land on the other side of the Earth. Funding limitations, which necessitated the need to prioritize equipment acquisitions, were a real and immediate concern and, at times, overruled demonstrated needs.

All of that is not to say that there was a complete absence of activity on the target acquisition brief in Ottawa. Captains Nathaniel Ng[15] and Ray Dupuis, worked under the leadership of Major Bud Walsh in the Directorate of Land Requirements 8. Their section was for special projects and was tasked to look at an omnibus of smaller ones. They were evaluating the concepts of integrating both tactical UAVs and counter mortar radars as part of their directorate's intelligence, surveillance, target acquisition and reconnaissance (ISTAR) project. While ordinarily artillery projects were part and parcel to the staff at the Directorate of Land Requirements 2, these two capabilities had a prospective role to play within the ISTAR project. Ng and Dupuis' scope of work was to look at such things as high-bandwidth, high-speed data links, and automated data processing systems for the technical integration of various generic intelligence resources such as UAVs, radars, and the equipment that was part of the new Coyote armoured recce vehicle's suite.[16] It was a long-term project which was not specifically looking at immediate needs, but for the development of a future capability for the army. The selection of specific equipment was still a long way off, as was the development of how a given ISTAR unit[17] would function doctrinally.[18]

In April 2002, the Directorate of Land Requirements 8, in conjunction with the Directorate of Air Requirements and the Canadian Forces Experimentation Centre conducted Exercise ROBUST RAM in Suffield, Alberta. The aim of the exercise was to test some concepts partly in furtherance of the Canadian Forces' Joint Unmanned Surveillance and Target Acquisition System (JUSTAS) project. To do so, they had flown a forerunner of the MQ-1 Predator UAV from General Atomics called the Improved-GNAT.

Improved-GNAT was a medium level, long-endurance aircraft more envisioned for operation by the Royal Canadian Air Force (RCAF) rather than the army. Also tested at the time was a CL-327 Guardian UAV from Bombardier Aerospace, and the AeroVironment Pointer, a miniature UAV. The CL-327 was an improved version of the older CL-227 Sentinel (or "Peanut") developed by Canadair in the 1970s. The Improved-GNAT was designed for mid-level tactical recce, and thus more of an army resource than an RCAF one.[19] Interestingly, the lease for the Improved-GNAT was extended after the exercise to provide surveillance support to security operations for the 28th Group of Eight[20] Summit held at Kananaskis, Alberta, in late June 2002.[21]

The key outcome of Ex ROBUST RAM was a validation of the concept that

Canada required a family of UAVs that operated at the high, medium, and low levels, with the lower tactical-level category being an army asset. The separation of UAV categories and their respective "ownership" by the RCAF for the strategic high and medium levels, or the army for the low tactical levels was not a contentious issue at the time for the RCAF. That position would change.[22]

Canada was not a newcomer to the use of counter mortar radars, but their use had ended with the retirement of the 1950s era AN/MPQ-501s in 1988.[23] Canada's allies had also been slow and spotty in developing the capability beyond its 1950s roots with more modern, more capable technologies—peace tends to do that. By the late 1970s, however, the US had brought the AN/TPQ-36 Firefinder system to operational status, and by the mid-1980s, the longer range AN/TPQ-37. By the end of the century, both radars had found homes within target acquisition batteries with the American army's heavy divisions, at the corps level and with multiple-launch rocket system battalions. In addition, target acquisition platoons were incorporated into the establishments for separate brigades and the interim establishments for the newly developed brigade combat teams and for high-mobility artillery rocket systems battalions.

While several European countries were jointly developing the Euro-ART COBRA AESA, this system was still a few years away from initial operating capability. Norway and Sweden, however, had cooperated on developing Ericsson Microwave Systems' Artillery Hunting Radars also known as ARTHUR. It entered into service with both countries and several more, including the UK where it was being used by both their army and the Royal Marines.

Fortunately, with Ng and Dupuis already working on a long range project for integrating radars and UAVs for their project, much of the research and staff work for what was now a critical and immediate unforecasted operational requirement was already in process. They were able to produce a statement of operational requirements for both products in just a few short weeks. With funding allocated, they could hand off the projects to their counterparts in the office of the Director General Land Equipment Program Management 8 for procurement.[24] With the ongoing work on the main project, that directorate, working with Public Works and Government Services Canada, was able to rapidly staff a statement of work, which stipulated to civilian vendors the deliverables and services required to be met under the separate UAV and radar contracts. The turnaround time for bids was very brief; within approximately a week.

For the UAV contract two companies issued bids: the American AAI Corporation's Shadow 200,[25] which served with the American army and Marines; and the French SAGEM Sperwer,[26] which served with the French, Danes and Swedes. Unfortunately, the Shadow bid was deemed non-compliant with the requirements, as there was no guarantee that it could meet the minimum operating temperature required for training to be conducted in Canada year-round. There was really no alternative to Sperwer. Fortunately, its airframe, based on some of the best 1980s era technology, was in 2003 still one of the better systems around.

The system consisted of a ground control station and data terminal housed in a shelter on a vehicle, a truck mounted hydraulic launch catapult and several UAVs. The system supported simultaneous control of two UAVs and could transmit an image to a remote viewer connected to the control station by wire. The UAV itself carried a forward-looking infrared imagery radar (FLIR) payload, providing high resolution day and night imagery and target geo-location with an accuracy of 20 meters.[27]

The Canadian Forces gave SAGEM an initial contract of $33 million for two ground stations, four aircraft, one launcher, two ground data terminals, four remote video terminals, three simulators, three generator trailers, and associated training and support.[28] With time being short, Canada could not reconfigure a vehicle to accept the launcher assembly, and as a result, borrowed a French 10-tonne Renault Kerax from SAGEM for the initial deployment.

The decision concerning which radar to acquire was equally simple. There were only two options available; the US Hughes AN/TPQ-36 Firefinder, and the Ericsson ARTHUR.

The difficulty with the Firefinder, in a word, was "Iraq". With the Americans ramping up for a large-scale operation in Iraq, it had already earmarked all the existing radars for operational use. As a result, it would be out of the question to borrow any from them, and there was no time to order any from the manufacturer.

The ARTHUR had a similar problem, but since several of its contracts were on a lease-to-buy basis, such as with the UK, there was more room to negotiate. Both Sweden and Norway would agree to Canada's use of some of their radars, so long as the lease went through the manufacturer Ericsson, who would fully refurbish the radars before returning them. In the end, Sweden leased the Canadians four radars mounted on a tracked BV-206 chassis. Under the terms of the lease, Ericsson would receive the monetary benefits, while the Swedish armed forces would receive fully refurbished radars.[29]

The original lease discussed was a mirror image of the lease-to-buy held with the British army but the "buy" component was not acceptable for Canada as the radar was being acquired for a limited operation, and not as a long-term equipment purchase.

A contentious issue with the lease of the radars was the limited number of operating hours imposed by Ericsson. This was not a problem under the UK lease where the radars were primarily used for training and shut down for most of the time. However under operational conditions, the radars had to be operating for long periods of time, and any imposed restriction on their use would be problematic. The operational purpose of the radars was to protect one headquarters and the operational requirement was for a minimum of 12 hours radiating daily, cycling between four radars; two operating, and another two out of service for maintenance.[30]

Ericsson agreed to amend the contract to a straight 18-month lease, but with provisions similar to the British one limiting each radar's use to 1,500 emission hours and 3,000 kilometres of prime mover mileage. A further, as yet, unrecognized limitation of the contract would be a lack of a provision for an in-theatre field service representative. Maintenance support lines would prove to be tenuous.[31]

While people in Ottawa were working diligently to stand up the radar and UAV capabilities, others were turning their attention to training. The brigade training event in Wainwright in April of 2003 had been scheduled as the culminating point for 2 Canadian Mechanized Brigade Group's operational readiness training. Conceived to provide a check on the deteriorating collective training expertise of Canada's army, it was designed to work together with a new managed readiness system as the army's only properly structured, combined arms, level 8 collective training event for 2003.[32] Exercise RESOLUTE WARRIOR's stated aim was to assess the SABRE Brigade Group's capability under future operating conditions and to prepare specific units for high readiness missions.[33] The context of the collective training exercise was very much aimed more towards the traditional Eurocentric, Cold War theatre of operations, where an artillery regiment provided direct support to mechanized operations at the brigade and lower levels. There was very little training programmed that would prepare anyone for counter insurgency operations in an Asian theatre of operations. Exercise RESOLUTE WARRIOR had two hallmarks; it was the very first of a series of managed brigade-level training events conducted in over a decade, and it was to be the very last time that 2 RCHA fielded an 18-gun regiment.[34] As part of its annual September through to the end of April training cycle, 2 RCHA would fire some 6,000 rounds that year.

Rumours of a deployment to Afghanistan had floated around Petawawa from well before the brigade training event with various individuals aware that they had already been tentatively designated for deployment. Others were still in the dark, but everyone not already confirmed for Bosnia was lobbying hard for a position.

The 3rd Battalion, The Royal Canadian Regiment was rumoured to get the task. As the brigade's light infantry battalion, the 3rd Battalion was habitually paired with F Battery's six 105mm LG1s. The Battery, using the Grizzly armoured vehicle, general purpose as gun tractors, provided the battalion with direct support just as the 1st and 2nd Battalions, the brigade's two mechanized battalions, were supported by the twelve M109s of D and E Battery respectively.

Confirmation of the rumours that the 3rd Battalion would deploy came towards the end of Exercise RESOLUTE WARRIOR. F Battery's tasking would come shortly thereafter. What wasn't immediately certain was whether the battery would deploy with guns or with mortars.[35]

As the exercise was winding down confirmation finally came that F Battery would deploy with its guns, but with its gunline manpower limited to the size of a mortar platoon. This restriction reduced the number of guns to four, which in turn required reorganizing the entire gunline into four strong gun detachments.[36] Similarly, the battery would deploy without any of its usual echelon beyond the battery quartermaster sergeant. All medical and service support personnel would be provided by a centralized support element. In all, F Battery would leave some 20 of its members behind in Petawawa.

While the size of the gunline might have been limited, the forward observation officer (FOO) and forward air controller (FAC) detachments were not. F Battery's commander, Major Darryl Russell, his technician Warrant Officer Robert Beaudry and the battery's fire support coordination centre (FSCC) would be set up with the battalion's tactical operations centre. They would be supported by four FOO/FAC detachments. Captain Nick Williams from F Battery was slated as call sign G31. His detachment was augmented by Sergeant Wayne MacLean from E Battery as the detachment commander. Captain Jennifer Causey from E Battery received the word prior to Exercise RESOLUTE WARRIOR that her detachment was to be augmented by a FAC qualified detachment commander, and would be attached to F Battery as G32. Captains John O'Brian from D Battery and David Brassard from F Battery would round out the battery as G33 and G34 respectively. Williams' detachment would be the only one deploying using an Iltis.[37] The other three would be equipped with light armoured vehicle (LAV) command post variants, which provided each of them an extra radio installation.[38]

While the Battery's personnel were tentatively scheduled to deploy in the middle of the fast approaching summer, its equipment had to be shipped out almost immediately. Rather than returning it to Petawawa, it would be shipped from Wainwright to the 4th Canadian Movement Control Unit in Montreal for transshipment onward to Afghanistan by sea and truck convoys.

Supervising the preparation of the equipment fell on several personnel including Warrant Officer Dale Batton, the battery quartermaster sergeant of E Battery who would be deploying as F Battery's battery sergeant major and Warrant Officer Dennis Franken who was the battery's command post technical warrant officer. Franken would also double as a gun troop sergeant major. F Battery's current battery sergeant major was posted to Gagetown the upcoming summer.

Two command post vehicles were prepared. One was the battery's regular main command post light support vehicle, wheeled.[39] The battery's alternate command post vehicle was considered mechanically unsound, and the battery captain's office van was hastily reconfigured by the regiment's signals personnel with appropriate radio installations as an alternate command post and recce vehicle. This reconfiguration would cause no end of difficulty for the logistics personnel in Montreal who had to reconcile the vehicle's documented equipment configuration code number of a single radio installation with the dual installation that they were presented with.[40]

The battery's gun tractors—which at the time were Grizzly armoured vehicles, general purpose[41]—were left behind in exchange for four medium logistics vehicles, wheeled.[42] Two heavy logistics vehicles, wheeled[43] comprised the battery's ammunition section while four LAVs were being prepared for shipment as the battery commander's FSCC and for three of the four FOOs.[44] Two additional light support vehicles, wheeled—one for the battery sergeant major, the other for the battery quartermaster sergeant—and three Iltis—one for the battery commander, one for the battery captain, and one for the fourth FOO—rounded out the battery's equipment holdings.

All the vehicles and the four guns were left at a warehouse in Wainwright. The guns would be flat-bedded and the vehicles rail-shipped to Montreal. All the additional equipment whether for vehicles, guns or detachments was packed in tri-wall containers and left as well. It too would subsequently make its way to Montreal where everything would be repacked into sea containers. The equipment would not be seen again by the battery until its arrival in Kabul.

With the exercise over and the battery's equipment packed for shipment, F Battery's personnel returned to Petawawa with the rest of the brigade where not much additional training would take place.

F Battery wasn't the only element of 2 RCHA scheduled to deploy. The regiment also sourced three coordination centres for the brigade headquarters; an FSCC, an ASCC, and a brigade artillery intelligence officer. While the regimental headquarters would remain in Petawawa, the regiment's commanding officer, Lieutenant-Colonel Kevin Cotten, and its regimental sergeant major, Chief Warrant Officer Gino Moretti, would be deploying in other roles as the commanding officer of brigade troops and with the civil-military cooperation cell.

The regiment's FSCC, on the other hand, would accompany the brigade headquarters to Kabul in its more traditional role. For them, the word that they could be going had come down even before the departure for Wainwright. During a preparatory command post exercise set up on the Mattawa Plain, word started to circulate throughout the brigade headquarters' command post complex that it would be deploying. As would be the case later in Wainwright, almost immediately everyone started lobbying to find themselves a job in order to be a part of the upcoming operation.[45]

From 2 RCHA, Captain Mark Leach, the regiment's operations officer, Warrant Officer Ron Fillier, its operations warrant officer, Master Bombardier Keyvan Sajadi, and Bombardiers Bobby Hall, Darren Conway, John Terry, and Rob Fekete were all slated to go. Captain Todd Scharlach, the regimental command post officer, was subsequently brought in as the assistant operations officer.

Exercise RESOLUTE WARRIOR afforded an opportunity for the regiment's FSCC to bring together their own crew with the two other gunner coordination cells: the brigade artillery intelligence officer would come from the Royal Canadian Artillery School (RCAS), and the ASCC from the 4th Air Defence Regiment, RCA (4 AD Regt), both in Gagetown, New Brunswick.

While work was progressing quickly in Ottawa on the acquisition of UAVs and radars, the RCAS hadn't been idle either. Some work had been ongoing at the school within its limited locating capability for several years, but with the Operation ATHENA task, matters now moved into top gear.

Canadian artillery has extensive doctrine for the coordination of artillery intelligence and locating functions just as it does for field and air defence gunnery.[46] In short, while locating resources notionally exist at the division level, coordination functions are carried out both at division level by a division artillery intelligence officer and at the brigade level by a brigade artillery intelligence officer who is normally part of the brigade's close support artillery regiment.

To say that this doctrine has its foundation in the Cold War field army concept, which itself was in the process of being rejected by the army's leadership, is to state the obvious. Intrinsic with the overall function of artillery, however, is the need to coordinate and mass the resources of whatever indirect fire power is available within a theatre of operations. Even if Canada no longer had the operational wherewithal to form and deploy a division and had chosen, or been forced by circumstances, to focus on deploying a battle group with a pared-down brigade headquarters, Canadian gunners still needed the ability to coordinate their own and their allies' indirect fire resources.

While some of the challenges that 2 RCHA faced in providing artillery support to the Kabul multinational brigade under Operation ATHENA were like those faced in Bosnia-Herzegovina on Operation PALLADIUM—such as the need for FSCCs, FOOs, FACs, and, at times, guns—the sudden procurement of both UAVs and radar capabilities called for a level of expertise in the brigade headquarters and the field that was not readily available within the regiment.

The entire process of standing up 2 RCHA's target acquisition contingent became a machine with many moving parts. While acquisition was ongoing in Ottawa, personnel were being identified for specific roles shortly after the Minister of National Defence's announcement. The commanding officer of 2 RCHA asked for, and the RCAS agreed to provide technical assistance and training support to 2 RCHA, as well as a six-person detachment to work as the brigade artillery intelligence officer cell within 2 RCHA's brigade FSCC.

Two locating instructors in gunnery, Captains Dave Buchanan and Richard Little, designated for Rotos 0 and 1 respectively, formed the leadership of the school's target acquisition support. That, however, would change before deployment. Rounding out the cell for Roto 0 were Warrant Officer Art Snodgrass, Master Bombardier Pat Benard, and Bombardiers Scott French, Chris Coughlan and Brian Beach. Captain Little had the overall lead of the preparations for the deployment.

The cell came together quickly and almost immediately departed for Exercise RESOLUTE WARRIOR in Wainwright.[47] Here was the first opportunity to test out the command-and-control architecture of the fledgling cell and to even work with an ad hoc Vindicator UAV with a crude imagery system provided by Meggit. Meggit was the company that provided aerial targets for Canadian air defence artillery units. No simulated radars were put into play.

The brigade issued the basic equipment to the cell; a tent, a truck with a radio, and a table in the command post complex next to the brigade's ISTAR coordination cell. Other than that, all that the team had were the laptops that they had brought with them from Gagetown. To most of the members of the team, their participation at Wainwright was more an experiment of ad hoc, hastily designed procedures than a collective training confirmatory exercise of tried and true tactics, techniques, and procedures.[48]

ISTAR as a collective process was also a new concept to 2 Canadian Mechanized Brigade Group. For the armoured corps, like the artillery, the early years of the new millennium were a period of turmoil with planned divestitures of equipment. They had already lost the tracked Lynx recce vehicles, and their Leopard tanks would be next. Doctrine was up in the air as to how to convert from a heavy Cold War mechanized force with new ideas for an envisioned wheeled, more mobile, and agile structure. The concept was being developed concurrently with a new direct fire support unit designed to replace the soon to disappear tanks. The 1st Battalion, The Royal Canadian Regiment had even been conducting an experiment to create an ISTAR Company by taking their combat support company and its recce platoon and anti-armour platoon and 4 AD Regt's Air Defence Anti-Tank systems and using them in their anti-armour role. As the brigade training event in Wainwright progressed and the Kabul tasking developed, the Royal Canadian Dragoons' recce squadron, less their assault troop, was earmarked to provide a headquarters and two five-car recce troops to form the core of the brigade's ISTAR company, into which the brigade would integrate additional sensor elements, such as an electronic warfare troop, the contemplated radar and UAV troops, and any other elements that could be provided from other nations.[49]

There were three major outcomes for surveillance and target acquisition (STA) from Exercise RESOLUTE WARRIOR. First, the RCAS tasked Little to now lead the cell on Roto 0, while Buchanan would take over Roto 1. Next, the brigade headquarters had made the point several times that the cell was not there to only provide brigade artillery intelligence, but also to act in a more general intelligence and coordination manner, and as a result the name of the cell changed to the target acquisition coordination centre (TACC)[50] and Little became the TACC operations officer. Finally, rather than being nested in the FSCC, the TACC was to be a part of the newly established brigade ISTAR coordination centre.

Little objected to the latter on the basis of the ISTAR coordination centre not requiring another duty officer and that ISTAR was not doctrinally responsible for the counter-battery battle. The brigade accepted that rationale and thus the TACC would form its own cell within the Kabul Multinational Brigade headquarters where it would be responsible for the counter-rocket and missile defence battle. It would also coordinate all of the brigade's radars and UAVs, including the German Luna detachment which would remain in place for the upcoming German/Canadian ISAF IV.

The participation of 4 AD Regt on Exercise RESOLUTE WARRIOR appears to have been a last minute decision. 4 AD Regt had been tasked with providing an ASCC and a number of Air Defence Anti Tank Systems to the exercise only a month prior. Their attendance had less to do with air defence or operations in Kabul, than it had to do with the early concepts of employing the missiles' anti-armour capabilities in experimental ISTAR and direct fire unit organizations.[51] The commitment of an ASCC to Kabul would not be confirmed until early Spring of 2003.

Each of 4 AD Regt's three ASCCs were located near, and were designed to operate with, one of the army's three brigade groups for the purpose of coordinating the use of the brigade's airspace amongst all of its users—such as aircraft, aviation, artillery, and UAVs. From an organizational perspective, ASCCs are nested into the larger air coordination network that exists in a given theatre of operations.

Operation ATHENA was to be Canada's first ASCC deployment since 4 AD Regt had been part of 4 Canadian Mechanized Brigade Group in Europe, over 20 years prior. Moreover, this deployment would be its first operational one. Doctrinally, the ASCC would only be deployed with a brigade if there were air defence resources allocated to it. Prior ISAF rotations had not employed one and neither had one been deployed on Op PALLADIUM in Bosnia.

Canadian planners were concerned about two issues; the upcoming employment of the UAV, and the requirement for airspace coordination in the complex airspace around both Kabul, and the nearby Bagram air base. Just as important was the previous summer's release of the report of the board of inquiry into the Tarnak Farms incident.[52] While the death of four and the wounding of eight Canadian soldiers from the 3rd Battalion, Princess Patricia's Canadian Light Infantry at Tarnak during Operation APOLLO rested on the US Air Force pilot who dropped the bomb, systemic deficiencies in the Americans' coordination and control of the airspace were also identified. The deployment of an integral ASCC would allow the brigade to resolve both issues within the Kabul Multinational Brigade headquarters, setting the standard for its deployment and employment in a multinational operation.

Captain Mike Notaro, the commander of the ASCC assigned to 2 Canadian Mechanized Brigade Group had deployed with the brigade to Wainwright and there started the work of integrating Little's use of an improvised UAV into their processes. Notaro would be promoted to the rank of major and take command of the 1st Air Defence Regiment, RCA in Pembroke that summer. As the G3[53] Air Defence within 2 Canadian Mechanized Brigade Group, he would also lead a joint team from 1st Air Defence Regiment, RCA and 4 AD Regt consisting of Captain Nigel Grout, Sergeants Adrian Mirosnikov, Eric Harrington, and Frank Vidal and Larry Scott, and Master Bombardier Adam Weaver, Master Corporal Ian Thompson, and Gunner Jonny Goodman.[54]

A brief recce to Qatar to liaise with the American combined air operations centre quickly established that the Americans were less concerned about the Canadian UAV integration then the Canadians were. They already had experience operating their own UAVs in-theatre. The recce concluded that more coordination would be necessary with the agencies on the ground in Afghanistan.[55]

Unlike F Battery, the brigade's FSCC, TACC and the ASCC had no vehicles or equipment to pack and ship beyond their battle boxes.[56] All equipment, beyond personal gear and some specialized communications equipment for the ASCC, would be provided in-theatre.

The order to generate a UAV troop and a radar troop for Roto 0 was given to 2 RCHA during Exercise RESOLUTE WARRIOR. Since E Battery had already received the task to generate a FSCC and FOO detachments for Bosnia, and since F Battery was generating the close support battery for Kabul, the only question remaining was: which organization would provide the personnel for the locating elements?

Upon their return from Wainwright, Lieutenant Dan Matheson of E Battery and Warrant Officer Andy Skinner of D Battery were advised that there might very well be an opportunity for them to go to Afghanistan. The irony in their potential deployment was they would not be employed as field gunners, but as locating gunners leading the newly established radar troop as its troop commander and troop sergeant major, respectively. Similarly, it wasn't until he arrived back to Petawawa that E Battery's Warrant Officer Rob Bartlett was advised that rather than being sent over to Kabul in a defence and security platoon role, he and E Battery's Captain Ian Plummer would now be the troop sergeant major and troop commander of a newly created UAV troop.

D and E Batteries would provide the majority of the personnel for the two troops with the remainder coming from the rest of the regiment.[57] Once the establishment for the artillery component of Operation ATHENA was sourced, the 2 RCHA command team left behind in Petawawa–right down to the master bombardier level–was extremely thin on the ground.[58]

Pre-deployment training and administration for Radar Troop and UAV Troop would, on a few occasions, coincide with other elements of the contingent, but for the most part, it would turn out to be radically different.

Immediately following their return from Wainwright, the TACC detachment returned to Gagetown for pre-deployment leave for much of the month of May before traveling to Petawawa for the month of June to participate in 2 Canadian Mechanized Brigade Group's theatre mission specific training. Much of this training had little value for them. A simulated command post exercise was a failure because the simulator was not set up for counter-insurgency operations. Qualifying on the ranges on the C7 rifle was eventually scrapped after a week of constantly being bumped day after day for other, higher priority serials, or due to lack of ammunition. Notwithstanding this, Little used this time to great effect, providing considerable advice in preparing 2 RCHA's designated target acquisition personnel for their new roles.

The pre-deployment training that was afforded the rest of 2 RCHA, was generally considered adequate to most of those involved even though it was considerably less than what future Operation ATHENA rotations to Kandahar would receive. In large part this was due to the brigade's already high state of training and the short period of time remaining prior to deployment.

Mission specific training was hastily prepared. It consisted of: cultural awareness lectures, including, geography, language, and history of Afghanistan; some riot control training; some scenario based training; some range work; training on rules of engagement; mine awareness; and rotation through the administrative "sausage machine" of the brigade's departure assistance group.[59] A request from the 3rd

Battalion, The Royal Canadian Regiment for some battlefield inoculation fire was abandoned because only two guns remained with 2 RCHA's rear party.

Some of the members of F Battery thought the training was not much different from the training that was conducted on previous deployments to Bosnia. No one recalled any of the lessons learned from the prior year's Operation APOLLO deployment being filtered down to the battery.[60] Many felt that, while the battery was ready for Kabul, the administrative system was not well prepared for dealing with the families left behind in the event that casualties should occur. The general impression amongst the troops was that there wasn't much going on in Afghanistan,[61] and that F Battery was "good to go". That said, one member noted: "We didn't know what we didn't know."[62]

In the meantime, the training was taking a decidedly different direction for the members of the UAV and radar troops. While the remainder of F Battery completed their deployment training through a well established training system on equipment that had already been in service for many years, the opposite happened to these troops. The simultaneous development of the tactics, techniques and procedures to employ these two new capabilities, the requirement for personnel to train within the context of Operation ATHENA, and the administrative process to field the equipment all conflicted to create friction, continuous change, and fragmented training.

Warrant Officer Kerry Willcox from the RCAS had been working in the standards cell and, amongst other things, had been developing a strawman structure for notional radar and UAV troops. He also attended the RCAF's Basic Flight Safety Course in March of 2004. Willcox was no stranger to locating. He had been a surveyor since 1980, was a graduate of the year-long Gunnery Career Course, Depth Fire in the UK in 1994/5 following which, he was posted as a locating assistant instructor in gunnery to the RCAS.

By the end of March, Willcox and two members from the Directorate of Land Requirements were sent to The Netherlands to meet with the Dutch 101 Remotely Piloted Vehicle Battery to view their Sperwer system and to learn how they deployed and used it. Similarly, extensive research was underway in examining and developing tactics, techniques and procedures for the potential radar systems.

Back in Petawawa, 2 RCHA had also worked quickly. Matheson and Skinner were provided with a list of names of 2 RCHA personnel with some additions from 4 AD Regt, and were politely told that the list of names would not change. They were further advised that within the week they would all be heading to Norway for four weeks of training on the ARTHUR. 4 AD Regt personnel were added to the troop because the chain of command considered that their familiarity with air defence radar systems would be beneficial in learning how to operate the ARTHUR. In the end, once everyone was trained, there was little distinction between the operators because the two rader systems worked differently in practice.[63]

The organization of the troop was initially based on the doctrine set out in an older Cold War era publication. It used a structure of four radars, a recce detachment, and maintainers for a total of 24 to 27 personnel.[64] Prior to leaving for Norway, however, there had still not been any conclusive discussion about who the troop would work for or who it would report to as these aspects of the deployment were still under consideration.

The radar troop, accompanied by Willcox as their assistant instructor in gunnery, deployed to a hunting lodge at the Norwegian village of Hjerkinn—some 300 plus kilometres north of Oslo—to learn the intricacies of both the radars and their BV 206 prime movers at an adjacent Norwegian army training centre. Spanning the months of May and June, Swedish personnel instructed the troop on the use of the Norwegian equipment. The troop received only the barest of instructions on the theoretical aspects of radar systems, a shortcoming which would cause difficulty for them later in the complex terrain around Kabul.

The culminating event of the training was using the radars to track live fire rockets from a Norwegian multiple launch rocket system, which was deployed by Norwegian reservists.[65] Officials from Ericsson predicted that little would be gained from this exercise, as the range that the rockets were firing at was too short for the ARTHUR to track them effectively. As predicted, the troop failed to pick up any rockets fired but, nevertheless, Ericsson awarded tie clips to the troop which are only awarded to those who have experienced using the radars on live fire targets.

A separate problem was that the range at Hjerkinn was relatively clean of radar clutter, except for the odd bird. The lack of this clutter during training would be in sharp contrast to the high clutter environment they would soon experience in Kabul. Notwithstanding these technical issues, everyone deemed the course a success, and the troop returned to Petawawa. By this time, a decision had been made as to where to place the troop. They ended up as part of the Royal Canadian Dragoons' still experimental ISTAR Company.

The troop threw itself wholeheartedly into this new affiliation, moving into the Dragoons' lines, and attending their orders and training sessions. The Dragoons reciprocated and made the troop feel to be part of the team. While Ericsson had deployed a laptop based training simulator to Petawawa, other training interfered heavily, leaving the troop members virtually no time to use the equipment.[66]

One problem identified was that there were no replacements trained to either change out individuals who might prove unsuitable for deployment, nor to replace any operators during the rotation. It was fortunate that the initial pre-deployment training was fairly basic, and that no one was removed from training notwithstanding that there were some reservations about a few individuals.[67]

Returning from the training in Norway didn't stop things for Warrant Officer Willcox. Almost immediately after his return to Gagetown he was off again, this time to the British Royal School of Artillery in Larkhill to look at BAE Systems' Phoenix UAV. This trip was followed by another to 29 Commando Regiment, Royal Artillery in Plymouth together with Sergeant Moe Campbell of 2 RCHA's radar troop and a Directorate of Land Requirements representative. Here they learned about the Marines' experiences with the ARTHUR.

The four leased ARTHUR systems were scheduled to be flown from Norway by an Antonov 225 to arrive on the ground in Kabul just prior to the main party in August. This caused concern for the troop, as they believed that the theatre activation team made up of individuals from The Royal Canadian Regiment's 2nd Battalion would not have the wherewithal to handle their delicate equipment. They lobbied hard to get some members of the troop placed on the advance party to receive the equipment. In the end, while some of the troop's gunners deployed on the advance party, they arrived after the radars had already been unloaded. Fortunately there was no noticeable damage.[68]

While the radar troop was to deploy together with the rest of the task force, the UAV troop would have a completely different experience. Their significantly longer training requirements made it impossible for them to arrive in theatre until some time in October. Warrant Officer Bartlett, like Skinner, was given a non-negotiable list of personnel who would make up the troop. He was left to assign jobs to his people based on their individual qualifications. High on his list of prerequisites for ground control station staff were individuals who had observation post training and experience. Similar to the situation with the radar troop, the list of personnel did not include any spares. As the training would be so specialized, it too would be impossible to replace a member if it became necessary.

After a brief period of leave, the newly formed troop established a relationship with the Dragoons' ISTAR Company, and together with them, started pre-deployment training. This included everything from first aid to the proper way to stack up and clear a house.

Next, and while still in Petawawa, all members of the troop were required to undertake a three-month Transport Canada mandated advanced flight training course, which was conducted throughout that summer by the Brampton Flight School. The training was the initial flight training taken by all civilian pilots—less the practical flight phase. It consisted of a wide range of topics from refueling aircraft and flight planning, to all aspects of weather.[69]

Unbeknown to the troop, a new issue respecting UAVs had been percolating. The question of whether the UAVs would be an army or an RCAF asset had been slowly developing throughout the higher echelons of the Canadian Forces. With the identification of a tactical UAV requirement for Kabul, and a funded program for its acquisition, the staff at 1 Canadian Air Division began to pay closer attention to their employment. While the scope of responsibility between the RCAF and the army was theoretically made between the strategic and the tactical levels of UAVs, the army's Sperwer was now facing some very real practical issues.

Previously, during Exercise RESOLUTE WARRIOR in Wainwright, there had been a flight safety incident where range control had cleared a helicopter into the training area, but the helicopter had failed to contact and coordinate a safe transit route with the air cell at the brigade headquarters. The helicopter flew into a restricted operating zone immediately to the front of the Vindicator UAV's launch pad, just as it was being prepared for a day's operations. The target acquisition control centre filed a mandated Transport Canada flight safety incident report, and as a result the RCAF was required to investigate. In addition, the RCAS sent Art Snodgrass to attend a fourteen-day flight investigation course in Winnipeg. During this course, he presented the details of the incident where an RCAF brigadier-general in attendance commented that the "army had no right to fly anything."[70]

The speed of the army's initiative to acquire a UAV,[71] had caught the RCAF by surprise and it was now developing concerns with respect to the control of an aerial system by the army. They took a closer look at Little's team and 2 RCHA's UAV troop.[72] This scrutiny resulted in two initiatives being implemented by the RCAF: the insertion of an RCAF aircrew member into the UAV troop's ground control stations during missions, and a further RCAF staff officer to operate within the Kabul Multinational Brigade's headquarters.

At the operational level within the troop, a UAV is piloted out of one of the ground control station modules by an air vehicle operator who is assisted by a payload operator. Both are bombardiers or master bombardiers, and are supervised by a sergeant who is the mission commander. Additional crews operate the launcher and recovery sites, and provide maintenance and parachute repacking services for the aircraft. The RCAF, having become aware that there was funding available for the army to acquire and operate tactical level UAVs, initially insisted that the mission commander and air vehicle operators be RCAF personnel. Concurrently, the Canadian Forces' Intelligence Branch was pushing for the payload operators to be an intelligence technician. The army maintained that the positions would all be gunners, but the RCAF then insisted that they would not sign off on Sperwer's airworthiness unless a pilot was added to the team to oversee operations as air vehicle commanders. The RCAF based much of this argument on: the presence of an airport in Kabul with both civilian and military air traffic; the airframe's ability to fly at altitudes of up to 16,000 feet; and its significant size and weight.[73] To say that there were to be tensions between the RCAF and gunner personnel is an understatement.[74] The end result was that an RCAF air crew member was added into the ground control modules as a fourth person to oversee airworthiness, and from that point forward, two pilots and two navigators joined the troop for training.

While Ian Plummer remained with the troop for the rest of the flight school training, Bartlett, together with several personnel from the Directorate of Land Requirements and several other individuals from Ottawa, flew to SAGEM's facilities near Paris, France to organize training on the Sperwer. Upon arrival, they had to solve an immediate problem. SAGEM had prepared to train only one ground control crew while the troop was organized into two crews. SAGEM suggested that both crews receive the initial training, and they would then pick out the best operators and form them into one crew to finish the training. Those issues had to be discussed at a level above that of the troop. The result was that the entire troop would complete all phases of training. The troop now prepared for a lengthy stay in France. While they did, the rest of Roto 0s gunners boarded aircraft ready to depart for Kabul.

WELCOME TO THE
INTERNATIONAL SECURITY ASSISTANCE FORCE

ROTO 0 WAS ARRIVING AT A VERY INTERESTING TIME in Kabul's history. The Taliban had only been driven out a year previously and there were major power shifts underway with the Americans steering much of the agenda. While one could see where the general Afghan political situation was heading, local conditions were not so clear. The Americans had hammered out an agreement the previous October between the Coalition and the Afghan national government as to the Afghan army's size and structure. They had turned to their allies to assist with its training. The French established officer and general staff training, the British conducted non-commissioned officer training, while the American Special Forces trained many of the troops.

On May 27th, 2003. the Americans' 10th Mountain Division resumed the reins of Combined Joint Task Force-180[1] from XVIII Airborne Corps which was now focused fully on Iraq. Operation ENDURING FREEDOM in Afghanistan had become an economy of force operation for the Americans notwithstanding that the enormity of the training mission there had become clear. Task Force PHOENIX, which stood up to expand the training of the Afghan army, had at first used active duty army troops from the 10th Mountain Division but now used troops from various National Guard brigades.

The program was starting to pay modest dividends, but mostly the true Afghan military power was still being held by a loose grouping of warlords and drug lords. The latter employed militias which were more like mercenary forces for hire with very questionable loyalties. These operated under the catch-all label of the Afghan Militia Force[2], which was minimally controlled by the Afghan Ministry of Defence.

The Afghan militia was low on equipment and personnel, but high on graft.[3] It was a situation which was reminiscent of that after the fall of the Soviet-backed Afghan government which had precipitated the rise of the Taliban. The support or enmity of these factions depended very much upon how allied policies affected their

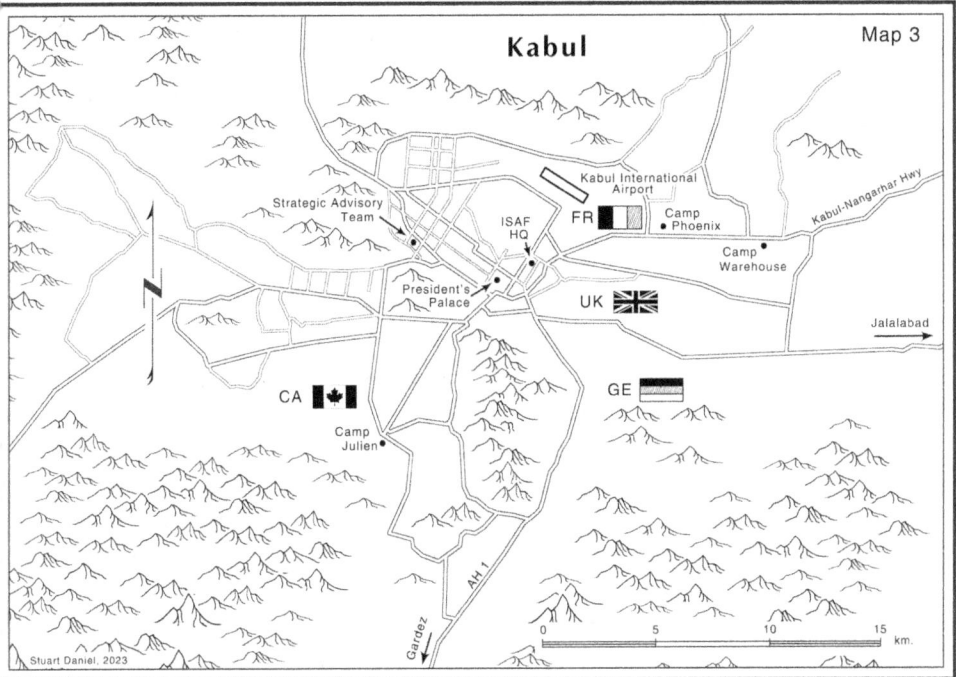

Kabul

Map 3

Strategic Advisory Team

Kabul International Airport

ISAF HQ

FR

Camp Phoenix

Kabul-Nangarhar Hwy

Camp Warehouse

President's Palace

UK

Jalalabad

CA

GE

Camp Julien

AH 1

Gardez

0   5   10   15 km.

Stuart Daniel, 2023

interests. Disarming them under the UN-backed Disarmament, Demobilization and Reintegration program, a pilot for which would start in Kunduz Province that fall,[4] was as much of a priority for the International Security Assistance Force (ISAF) as was building a true national army.

The populace itself was ambivalent to ISAF's presence. In general, ISAF was unwelcome, but less so than the Taliban. While the Afghan militia's leaders still carried powerful influence in the local communities where the bulk of them came from, they were fragmented and without a unified chain of command. The warlords and drug lords were problematic but predictable as one could determine which territory belonged to whom and one could cautiously work around them.

The wild card in the mix were the militias themselves. Some were pro-Pakistani, some pro-Iranian, and many were just simply anti-Western.[5] One of the key tasks for ISAF would be the bolstering of the new pro-western government which would be formed at the upcoming loya jirga—an Afghan grand assembly—scheduled for October. One of the ways that ISAF intended to assist the new government was through the planned disarming of the warlords to accompany the building of a new national military.[6]

To meet these challenges, the Canadians would deploy to three major locations. Those within the ISAF headquarters were located in a complex in the centre of downtown Kabul not far from the American and several other embassies. Those who formed the Kabul Multinational Brigade headquarters worked out of Camp WAREHOUSE, an international camp shared with a German airborne battalion—with an attached Bulgarian infantry company for camp security—Britons, Swedes and many other smaller contingents. It was located some 10 kilometres due east of Kabul's city centre. Finally, the bulk of the Canadian battle group operated out of Camp JULIEN which was located approximately nine kilometers south of downtown Kabul.

The deployment of the 2nd Regiment, Royal Canadian Horse Artillery (2 RCHA) to Kabul went seamlessly, starting with CC-150 Polaris flights from Canada into Camp Mirage in Dubai, United Arab Emirates. Camp Mirage was well set up to receive them and quickly moved them on to Afghanistan. Hercules CC-130 Hercules flew them into Kabul's international airport—guarded by ISAF's French contingent. Here they were met by the brigade's commander, Colonel Devlin, and his brigade regimental sergeant major. The new arrivals were issued ammunition and taken in light armoured vehicle (LAV) convoys to Camp JULIEN while their kit followed them in trucks.

Camp JULIEN derived its name from the 3rd Battalion, The Royal Canadian Regiment's advance party and the 2nd Battalion's theatre activation team. They had named it after one of their own; the 3rd Battalion's Lance Corporal George Julien, who had received the Military Medal for his actions in Korea in 1953. At the time the camp was still under construction.

One thing that the Canadians had not received, neither prior to leaving Canada nor in transit, was arid region camouflage uniforms. Once again, like their predecessors on Operation APOLLO Canadians would be deploying into a brown and tan desert region wearing "relish green" temperate woodland clothing. Notwithstanding that this shortcoming had been previously identified and was to have been rectified by the summer of 2002, such uniforms had not been issued to the battle group.

At JULIEN, after a brief stay in what was to become the fire hall, F Battery was generally broken down into tactical groupings with detachments being loosely grouped together. They were assigned Weatherhavens which can best be described as soft-sided World War Two Quonset huts which sleep eight comfortably.

To an extent, there were some differing viewpoints over the quartering. Enough Weatherhavens were assigned to the battery so that each was occupied by approximately six personnel notwithstanding their larger capacity. While some desired to have complete detachments tactically grouped together irrespective of rank and gender, the final decision was made to assign officers, senior Non-Commissioned members and female personnel to segregated quarters. This adoption of a garrison mentality in personnel management had the consequence that, on occasions, not all the appropriate officers or non commissioned officers were involved in discussions and decisions which affected them or their detachments simply because of where their assigned bed space was located. Others, who ordinarily had no problem with fully integrated detachment accommodation on exercises, appreciated the measure of separation afforded them on a six-month tour.

The arrival experience for brigade headquarters staff was slightly different. The previous rotation of the Kabul Multinational Brigade had not deployed a fire support coordination centre (FSCC), an airspace coordination centre (ASCC), a target acquisition coordination centre (TACC), nor any brigade-level fire support resources. As a result, besides settling into the camp, there was also the task of establishing a whole new aspect to the operation with only the most basic of handovers.

Captain Little's TACC team, for example, had arrived early in Kabul on July 12th. Their stay at JULIEN was brief. After collecting their kit, receiving a briefing on the hazards facing them, being issued Mefloquine antimalarial medicine, exchanging their "transportation rifles" for "tour rifles,"[7] and getting a quick meal, they were taken by LAV through the city to Camp WAREHOUSE which was also still undergoing construction.

Here, in the heat and dust, they grabbed cots in some scattered modular tents, and were placed on hard rations for a few days while they acclimatized to the altitude and their new jobs. Rations changed quickly to dining at the German kitchen which prepared meals in what the Canadians considered Gasthaus-style.[8] With the Germans also came about a dozen canteens, all of which sold beer.

Little set up shop within the operations cell on the secured third floor of the brigade's headquarters. This was located in an older Soviet-era, three-storey building whose marble floors and walls were pock-marked by bullet holes. Here, they reported administratively to the commanding officer of the brigade troops, 2 RCHA's Lieutenant-Colonel Kevin Cotten who doubled as the brigade's fire support coordinator. Operationally, however, they reported to the brigade's G3 and liaised directly with the brigade's FSCC, the ASCC and the intelligence, surveillance, target acquisition, and reconnaissance (ISTAR) coordination centre.

After two weeks, their accommodations also changed to Weatherhavens. Fairly quickly, conditions improved as CANEX[9] opened a small kit shop and a canteen which eventually provided up to two beers per person per day. A part-time local barber appeared, followed by field kitchens which, a few weeks later, were replaced by a full dining facility.

At WAREHOUSE, a gate separated the Canadians' compound from the other contingents. Behind it reigned a garrison mentality appreciated by very few. Having gunner officers and troops "jacked up" by some random regimental sergeant major for not wearing gloves with their combat jacket or for wearing tan boots rather than the mandated black boots with "winter dress" were but the silly end of the issue. Perhaps more serious was the fact that while the tent rows were neatly aligned, no significant protective measures had been taken beyond a low HESCO[10] revetment around each Weatherhaven in case of a rocket strike.

Accommodation at WAREHOUSE, like at JULIEN, was segregated with officers, non-commissioned members and other ranks and male and female personnel living separate from each other. No attempt was made to integrate housing into operational or functional teams.

Another indicator of the garrison mentality was that the team from the Canadian Mapping and Charting Establishment had been press-ganged into turning out parking signs on their large-scale printer as a priority,[11] rather than more operationally oriented tasks such as establishing registration points. Bit-by-bit, though, truck-load after truck-load of gravel replaced the powdery moon dust that covered every vertical surface while HESCO barriers rose around the perimeter.

Equipment was also at a premium. The TACC deployed with its own laptops and was provided with a Defence Wide Area Network[12] drop within the office. A radio, with which to communicate with the surveillance and target acquisition (STA) resources, did not show up until early September in time for the planned loya jirga. Until then, they had to borrow other people's radios. While the team had access to an air defence system integrator terminal—which ordinarily is used to push air control radar feeds to an ASCC—the secure data linkages it needed to function did not yet exist and the terminal therefore ended up being the resting place for the shared coffee maker for much of the tour. The maps were paper ones. The FalconView electronic mapping system did not become operational in the theatre until late in Roto 0's deployment when a work around for data updates was implemented through a secure email feed. Once it finally started operating, the system proved very useful.[13]

Once on the ground, the ASCCs Major Notaro went about coordinating airspace parameters with Kabul's air traffic controllers, the German contingent's aviation commander, and the J3 Air/Aviation staff at ISAF headquarters. The meeting with the airport's senior air traffic controller proved that while limitations had been placed on the German Luna unmanned aerial vehicle's (UAV) operation with respect to Kabul's airport, there were clear deficiencies with respect to any air control plan. There was a lack of consideration of live ranges around Kabul, and there was little interaction with the Americans' combined air operations centre in Qatar other than for the coordination of civilian traffic. In addition, Combined Joint Task Force-180, which was operating out of Bagram, had an air corridor that ran through a portion of Kabul's airspace, and through which they flew regularly without notifying or coordinating with Kabul.

ISAF headquarters essentially proved to have no resources to conduct airspace coordination, and they very quickly tasked Notaro to also assume the duties of the ISAF ASCC. Most problematic was Major Notaro's visit to Bagram when he visited Combined Joint Task Force-180's army aviation coordination center at their airspace operations center. They advised him that while they were responsible for all airspace coordination for the entire Afghan theatre, they were unaware of ISAF other than that they had some vague notion that there was some little peacekeeping force in Kabul. With respect to range facilities, the various records regarding their location did not match, and there were significant deficiencies in knowledge between the two forces. As a result, the potential for another Tarnak Farms incident had been high.[14]

Notaro dealt with these issues over the next several weeks and along the way discovered that some of the discrepancies in range location information was due to the fact that the German maps being used by ISAF were not accurate. Some of them had inaccuracies of up to five kilometers. The team from the Canadian Mapping and Charting Establishment was brought in to produce accurate locations and dimensions for all known ISAF ranges albeit that new and unknown ranges built by American special operations forces kept popping up.

Over the first few weeks, Notaro's liaison and coordination discussions with the US airspace management cell in Bagram were critical to the ASCC's operations. During a pivotal visit to Bagram, Notaro and Sergeant Mirosnikov raised concerns that his cell was printing, deciphering, and plotting airspace control measures on a map and talc overlay which was time consuming and prone to mistakes. It became apparent that Bagram used digital means to plot, submit and display approved airspace control measures. Fortunately, the program was called Tacview and Notaro's staff were very familiar with its parent software program FalconView. After a few hours of training, this vital program would save several hours of work each day, and time sensitive and accurate information of approvals and denials could be immediately coordinated.

Notwithstanding the efforts of the ASCC, coordination problems plagued the cell for the entire tour. While Combined Joint Task Force-180 had placed a restricted zone called a special usage area on the American embassy, it took considerable negotiation with them before the same courtesy was extended to the ISAF headquarters and the eight ISAF installations around Kabul. It was some time before the Americans accepted that the airspace over all of ISAF's areas of operation should become a jointly managed one.[15]

Other problem issues revolved around the fact that civilian air traffic, Afghan military helicopters, special operations forces, and some allied aircraft were notorious for not following coordination rules or Kabul air traffic control direction. This, in part, had led to very restrictive flight parameters for UAVs. One such constraint was to restrict night flights by UAVs, which was particularly strange, as there was virtually no air traffic at night over Kabul. ASCC coordination with the Kabul air traffic controller led to the development of a more flexible system. To complicate matters even more, within ISAF there were several agencies who felt they were the only airspace users within their particular area of operation, and they worked in isolation from all of the other agencies. The ASCC established biweekly coordination meetings, which were soon attended by up to 35 organizations' representatives. These meetings permitted ISAF to properly coordinate airspace requirements throughout its area of operations.

It became quite clear from the deficiencies of airspace control by prior ISAF rotations that very few countries outside of the US have the ability to set up a complex air management system. This meant that in order to conduct integrated airspace management, a Canadian ASCC required a secure US data feed in order to share the data needed to participate in their system. No such feed existed, although workarounds were put in place through the American J3 Air at ISAF headquarters. Nevertheless, the air control orders received were user-unfriendly with the Canadian systems until mapping software was acquired through the Americans.

The ASCC had been deployed, in part, to facilitate the coordination of the Canadian UAVs but it also found itself having to conduct airspace coordination for the two German UAVs; the light EMT ALADIN miniature UAV, and the heavier LUNA. Coordination for both the LUNA and the SPERWER required detailed parameters being set up with other users, primarily the Kabul air traffic controllers. Nevertheless, once they were established, the management and coordination of the required airspace became routine. Since missions for these heavier aircraft were almost always preplanned, sufficient time was available to set up the necessary restricted operating zone around the launch and recovery sites, the search area, and any transit corridor needed between the two. There was also enough time to disseminate the notices to all of the other airspace users.

Miniature UAVs, on the other hand, were more difficult to coordinate because of the often impromptu nature of their missions dictated by the lower level tactical organizations that were employing them. The primary conflict would be with ISAF and coalition helicopters, and in some circumstances, civilian air traffic near Kabul airport. With respect to usage within the ISAF area of operations, miniature UAV users were instructed to give the ASCC a fifteen minute warning of their impending usage, so that an advisory could be disseminated. For the terrain adjacent to the Kabul airport, special restrictions were imposed where the authority to employ the miniature UAVs was held at the highest level with the commander of ISAF. The ASCC was responsible for coordinating the overflight in these special restricted areas.

Things were much simpler for the FSCC. Captain Mark Leach, the regiment's operations officer and his technician, Warrant Officer Ron Fillier had quickly set up a 24/7 operation in a room shared with the ASCC. Their equipment needs were modest. Both artillery command and ring radio networks[16] were set up in addition to the Defence Wide Area Network and a brigade command computer network.

There were rudimentary attempts to install components of the army's nascent Athena tactical command and control system, but essentially the FSCC continued to use voice radio, and a map board and pins to track the location status of all elements of the regiment and their tactical situation.

A quick survey of the brigade's fire support resources found very little beyond the Canadian guns to coordinate. Some contingents had deployed with mortars, but had little expectation of using them, and even less inclination to having their fire coordinated. Essentially F Battery's guns were the main game in town. Important to the guns' employment was the lack of intelligence to drive the targeting process. With limited intelligence, the use of artillery became a reactive resource, rather than a proactive tool to take the fight to the enemy. Notwithstanding this, the physical presence of the guns did offer a show of force as was originally intended by General Leslie.

Equipment was also an issue for F Battery as it went to draw its gear from the national support element. While everything had been packed by the battle group in Wainwright, much repacking had gone on in Montreal, as it was loaded into sea containers. For whatever reason, some equipment, including radios and antennae were separated from their vehicles and trailers. Gun stores, including breech blocks, were separated from the guns. Everything was distributed amongst some three hundred sea containers that had arrived in Kabul. Many of these did not have load lists. Over a period of several days, the battery's quartermaster sergeant ended up searching numerous containers until everything could be accounted for.[17]

Other issues arose. The priority of work that the Mapping and Charting Establishment cell had been assigned by the camp's regimental sergeant major also reared its head for the battery. Having moved halfway around the world, it was necessary to calibrate electronic equipment for the region. Ordinarily the Mapping and Charting Establishment personnel would establish calibration points where all users of electronic positioning and navigation equipment, such as for the LAVs, could calibrate it. No such points had been provided. Accordingly, Warrant Officer

Franken, as the battery's technical warrant, made a call back to the Royal Canadian Artillery School in Gagetown to discuss and agree upon the best methodology to set up their own calibration points. That was eventually achieved by the use of two gun laying and positioning systems connected to defense advanced GPS receivers.[18] Two calibration points were set up for use by the entire battle group.

Meteorological data was also not generally available. Franken obtained ground meteorological data from the Germans and used it to determine the correction of the moment for the guns as best they could. This problem was manifest from an issue with the battery's meteorological detachment in Kabul. They were lacking gas for their weather balloons. When gas did finally arrive from Pakistan, the fittings for the gas cylinders didn't correspond, and it wasn't until approximately two months before the tour ended that Canadian meteorological data finally became available. Even then it was only available twice per day.[19]

In a matter of five days, with all of the equipment gathered, the battery's gun position was set up in the southwest corner of Camp JULIEN, about 800 metres away from where the battery was quartered. The position covered the battle group's main area of operation to the south and the west. Both the guns and their command post were situated in the open, protected solely by the camp's inadequate low perimeter HESCO wall. Within a short time, the decision was made to dig in.

Digging by hand in the super compacted and dry soil was entirely out of the question. Two days of such efforts produced a two-inch deep pit. Discussions with the multinational engineer group indicated that military engineer support was unavailable so the digging had to be done by local contractors. It was a laborious process that ended up breaking four backhoe buckets. The initial gun pit, dug to a two-foot depth complete with an ammo bunker and a crew bunker, took a month to complete.

The radar troop's deployment experience was similar to that of the others at JULIEN. Almost immediately after their boots were on the ground, the troop was split with two radars remaining at Camp JULIEN under Lieutenant Matheson and two deploying to Camp WAREHOUSE under Warrant Officer Skinner. There was time for a brief handover from the outgoing ISAF III Dutch AN/TPQ-36 radar detachment. While the two radars worked on different frequency bands and algorithms, the briefings provided valuable information about the challenges that the Canadian radars would face while working in Kabul.

Essentially, Kabul sits in a valley some 40 kilometers across, surrounded by mountains. The valley itself is bifurcated by one major ridge line that runs roughly north to south and several minor ones which divide Kabul into two parts. Everything—from the mountains, to unshielded civilian power transmission lines that had power surges, to aircraft with rotating propellers or rotors—would provide feedback to the radars that needed to be tuned and filtered out.[20] Of the two radars set up at Camp JULIEN, one quickly became unserviceable, albeit this issue was not formally identified until a subsequent routine maintenance check much later. It was beyond any local repair capability and wouldn't be fixed until a technical assistance visit team from Ericsson arrived late in the tour. The technicians fortunately had brought both the tools and parts necessary to complete the repair.

A much greater issue with the radars, however, was the lease. Under its terms the radars had a total of 750 hours of operation for the entirety of Roto 0. This worked out to an average of 3.5 hours per day. Much of the problem stemmed from the fact that contract negotiations were based on a single radar site, but the complex terrain around Kabul dictated that two sites were required.

The Dutch had run a 24/7 operation with their radars, but at the handover they had no information to offer as to when the Taliban were most likely to be active. Captain Little had to gather data from several disparate sources in order to determine when the best time was for the Canadian radars to be operating. An extensive hunt for information provided seemingly unrelated data until he noticed that most Afghans did not wear watches but timed their workdays on sunrise and sunsets. These timings shifted considerably throughout the year because of the heights of the surrounding mountains. Most of the attacks happened within four hours after the local sunset.[21]

The analysis of additional information provided by Chief Warrant Officer Moretti, 2 RCHA's regimental sergeant major, who had deployed in a civil-military cooperation role, revealed a correlation between the setting sun and moon phases as to when the Taliban were likely to attack. Another layer of intelligence as to tracking mercenary movements into theatre, related to an increased accuracy and range of rockets fired during this time frame. This allowed Little to eliminate some random outliers from the pattern. The net result of this artillery intelligence estimate was a fairly accurate picture of when the radars should be most active. The three subsequent rocket strikes hitting Kabul during Roto 0 all fell within the predicted time ranges thus validating the conclusions reached from the artillery intelligence estimate. It also substantiated the requirement for artillery intelligence resources in theatres of operations.

While the gun line was busy digging in at Camp JULIEN, the forward observation officer (FOO) detachments and battery reconnaissance (recce) detachment were sent out on their own to familiarize themselves with their areas of operation and to find viable observation posts and gun positions. With the French at Kabul Airport, the Germans, Italians and British at Camp WAREHOUSE,[22] and the Americans training the Afghan army close to WAREHOUSE, it necessitated that these detachments would spend much time traveling through the city. The teeming local population was heavily interested every time a pair of Iltis or a LAV—especially if commanded by a woman—passed through its midst.

None of the other nations were too enthused by the presence of the guns. Perhaps a year of unremarkable, inactivity by ISAF had jaded their viewpoint on the need for artillery. More likely it was that the presence of guns was inimical to their European attitude of how to run a stabilization mission. In the end, while the battery was a brigade resource, the majority of its activities were in support of the Canadian battle group's operations.[23]

While not generally involved in the "presence patrols" conducted by the 3rd Battalion, The Royal Canadian Regiment within the city, the FOOs did accompany the various elements of the battle group and the ISTAR company on specific tasks. Some of these tasks included: the provision of an additional force protection resource by virtue of their LAVs; deploying as part of the quick reaction force (QRF); conducting mounted and dismounted patrols outside of the built up areas; supporting cordon and search operations; providing overwatch at armament collection points when warlords were turning their various equipment over to the central government; and providing security overwatch at the loya jirga.

When not liaising or attending a specific battle group operation, the FOOs were sent out, either alone or in pairs, to set up surveillance posts under Operation BASEBALL. One in particular, a recurring one at the edge of the Canadian and German areas of operation received a lot of attention. Some felt there was a certain level of complacency in such taskings due to the low level of security that the crew of a single LAV could provide for itself.

The FOOs also quickly discovered the inadequacy of their equipment. While the artillery only had old night observation devices, long-range for dismounted night vision equipment—and in one case as the all-purpose replacement for a LAV's night vision equipment that had been broken down for an extensive period of time—the 3rd Battalion's recce platoon had been issued with night vision capable Vector binoculars. Fortunately, the platoon was prepared to share their "Gucci kit" with its gunners.

Once established, the battery organized a live fire shakeout exercise on August 21st at a spartan range facility set up by the American military for the training of the Afghan army. To get to the range, the battery needed to conduct a road move from Camp JULIEN north through Kabul, then east some 20 kilometres past Camp WAREHOUSE and then on for another 20 kilometres beyond that. The unarmoured gun tractors were modified with seats placed down the centerline of the cargo compartment facing outwards with a mesh installed hanging outboard to prevent any objects from being thrown in. The Iltis was slightly modified with blast blankets on the floor and piled up gear to allow troops in the rear to sit higher, face outward and have some blast protection.

Notwithstanding continued garrison-mentality criticism by the national support element's ammunition technicians, the battery refused to have its ammunition trucks display the mandated "Explosives" signs as it was felt that it was better not to advertise their contents to the world. Coincidentally, obtaining a resupply of ammunition would also require a drive through the city to the brigade's ammunition point, which was located a few kilometres east of Camp WAREHOUSE. While these provisions were felt to be adequate at the time, on reflection and with the hindsight brought on by later experiences in Kandahar, most now consider that they lived in a fantasy world and had been blessed with good luck in that they never had to test their preparations in action.

The range day itself went well with both small arms and LG1s firing. The latter sent approximately 30 rounds per gun down range.[24]

For the TACC things were a bit shaky at first.

About a month into the deployment, the office of the Deputy Chief of Defence Staff[25] noted the fact that there was now such a cell on the brigade headquarters' establishment and that its personnel came from Gagetown. The deployed force had expanded beyond that initially announced and planned for. Directions had limited participation to personnel from Land Force Central Area, and there was some concern that the organization was ballooning as individuals and agencies were grafting themselves onto the deployment. A heads-up came down to Captain Little that his detachment's tour would be cut short. A quick explanation upward through the chain of command pointed out the cell's connection to the doctrinal brigade artillery intelligence function which quelled the concerns in Ottawa.

Similarly, it took some time for the TACC's role within the headquarters to gel. Since it was no longer considered part of the FSCC, and 2 RCHA's commanding officer was employed as the commanding officer of brigade troops, there was no direct "ownership" of Little's detachment by 2 RCHA. The newly formed ISTAR company, a part of the battle group, had no connection to the brigade headquarters as far as personnel went, other than those of the ISTAR coordination centre who operated there. The brigade headquarters itself considered the TACC as a bolt-on component much like the G3 Air. Physically, the TACC shared an office with the ISTAR coordination centre which was linked to the office of the G3 Operations, while the brigade FSCC was in its own, disconnected office.

The radar troop had a similar problem regarding who owned who. The troop was initially under command of the ISTAR company, both in Petawawa and immediately upon deployment. That relationship would subsequently change. In the meantime, the troop conducted recces around Kabul to find additional locations during daytime using two unarmoured Iltis, a practice which with 20/20 hindsight might have been more suitable for Bosnia than it was for Kabul.[26] To this point in time, the threat had been benign, more theoretical than actual. That was about to change.

September 11th, 2003 brought the first change. That day, around 2150 hours, perhaps in celebration of the anniversary of the attacks in New York and the Pentagon, a rocket was fired into Camp WAREHOUSE impacting near a sea container. The strike was memorable for another gunner who had made his way to Kabul by a different route.

Captain John Stewart from the 7th Toronto Regiment, RCA had a varied career. With a degree in Latin American Studies he had also had training as an infantry officer and as an intelligence officer and spent time attached to the Special Service Force. More recently he had been asked to take a multi-year attachment as a civilian-military cooperation officer and had taken the course at the Pearson Peacekeeping Centre. His team had not participated in any of the brigade's pre-deployment training. Instead they had conducted their training in-house including Stewart attending the Partnership for Peace Training Centre in Türkiye. Much of the thinking in the field had been shaped by Canada's Bosnia experience which had gravitated towards construction work. For Afghanistan the aim was more in line with connecting with the community in such a way as to build an exit strategy to be able to leave the country capable of carrying on.

He had taken a year's leave of absence from his full-time job at a national bank to head up the small multinational civilian-military cooperation centre at the brigade's headquarters. It directed the activities of thirteen individual teams from seven different countries that provided vital interaction between ISAF and the local population. Much of the first part of the tour dealt with working on ways to create employment opportunities for individuals left without jobs as a result of the demilitarization programs. In one case a warlord's battalion-sized "army" gave up their weapons—everything from assault rifles to long-range rocket launchers—and were converted into a construction company. Throughout this he leaned heavily on local resources including a continuing relationship with a German nun who had been in Afghanistan for 30 years.

On the 11th, Stewart was walking past the seacan when he heard the rocket come in. He was just 27 metres away from the point of impact and was thrown against the metal support bar of a nearby tent but luckily unhurt.[27] The camp remained on alert until 0130 hours. Warrant Officer Snodgrass conducted a crater analysis[28] which established that the rocket had been fired from nearby.[29]

As an aside, the value of artillery intelligence training took some time to be recognized with respect to crater analysis. Little found resistance within the engineer support coordination centre to the artillery being involved in the process. The assistance he and his team provided in analyzing the point of origin of the rocket strike did result in acceptance of the value of the artillery intelligence process by the engineers.[30] The situation did, however, underline the fact that well over a half century of not actively practicing artillery intelligence functions and skills in the presence of the other arms had clearly lulled some of them into a belief that those skills simply did not exist or were no longer a gunner role.[31] The two skill sets did complement each other and were combined for later missions.[32]

The suspected firing position of the rocket exposed a problem. An analysis of the distances between Camp WAREHOUSE and Camp JULIEN established that while guns hypothetically located at Camp WAREHOUSE could fire south as far as Camp JULIEN, the same was not possible in reverse. This was due to the fact that the prevailing northerly winds would provide a tailwind boost in range to a southbound projectile while there would be a headwind resistance on a northbound one. Camp WAREHOUSE was thus effectively without close in artillery support. As well, consideration was given to the fact that should the battle group ever have to withdraw while in contact from Camp JULIEN to the Kabul airport or to Bagram airfield, guns located at Camp WAREHOUSE could provide continuous fire support for the move.

The decision was made to deploy Lieutenant Sarah Heer's[33] two-gun troop and a FOO detachment into Camp WAREHOUSE. Two days later it was decided to make this a permanent arrangement. Heer's troop was recalled to Camp JULIEN and the battery's command post officer, Lieutenant Kathy Haire,[34] Warrant Officer Dennis Franken, and their troop of two guns were sent north under the escort of two LAVs. The troop also took along one of the ammunition trucks and two Iltises which were used as runarounds and shared with the radar detachment already at WAREHOUSE. As for the observers, Captains Nick Williams, Jen Causey and John O'Brien's detachments stayed in JULIEN while Captain Dave Brassard's detachment moved to Camp WAREHOUSE.[35]

One consideration with the tactical configuration in the area of operations was the necessity for Haire and Franken, like Skinner from the radar troop, to frequently drive in their Iltises through Kabul to attend the battery commander's orders group at Camp JULIEN. This practice, again with 20/20 hindsight, exposed them all to unnecessary risk.

The deployment raised issues with both the signals squadron, who managed the Canadian extension of Camp WAREHOUSE, as well as the Germans who had overall management of the camp and its security. The signals squadron, while locating the gunners' quarters closer to their gun position than they had been at Camp JULIEN, again insisted that the troop be split up by rank and gender rather than tactically grouped. They did, however, provide an extra segment of modular tenting for use as a battery office. The German's concern was equally philosophical and centred on their objections to having "offensive" weapons systems set up within their camp at a time when they were focusing on establishing close relations to support the local population. For Haire, the larger concern was the gun position was initially exposed to the general Afghan public, as it was only separated from them by razor wire.

In the end, the troop set up a gun position on the edge of the helipad within the perimeter of the camp, but just outside of the Canadians' extension. That location occasionally played havoc with the command post vehicle's penthouse tent whenever a helicopter landed.

The newly established gun position allowed the troop to provide fire support over an area: beyond the Kabul airport to the west; south down to Camp JULIEN; east along the Kabul-Nangarhar Highway in the direction of Jalalabad and the Khyber Pass; and north along the Kabul-Bagram Highway in the direction of the Bagram airfield, albeit with the odd crest clearance problem created by high mountain peaks.

No attempt was made to dig in at WAREHOUSE although arrangements were made for additional protection through a low HESCO wall around the guns.[36] The Germans were particularly displeased with the presence of the ammunition vehicle at the edge of their helipad. It was to have been replaced by a sea-container. Despite attempts by the battery commander and battery quartermaster sergeant to arrange one through the national support element—which to most gunners' eyes continued to function as if it was still in garrison in Petawawa—nothing happened for several months until General Leslie, on an unrelated visit to the camp, was made aware of the problem and caused it to be quickly corrected.

The September 11th rocket incident also had consequences for the radars. Neither of the Camp WAREHOUSE's two radars had been oriented to the direction from which the rocket had been fired. As a result, one of the radars was moved to the other side of the Nangarhar Highway into the Multinational Engineer Group's camp. From here it could better provide surveillance over the point of origin of the rockets.

While the initial command and control relationship with the ISTAR company had proved eminently suitable for the troop, it changed after the September 11th rocket attack. Operational control of the troop passed from the ISTAR company to F Battery. This change was ostensibly undertaken to shorten and re-establish the doctrinal sensor-to-shooter link between the radars and the guns. The ISTAR company supported the change, as it had found that the counter mortar radars simply did not lend themselves well to the more general ground surveillance tasks performed by the company, particularly their own man-portable surveillance and target acquisition radars.[37]

The debate as to whether counter mortar radars were an artillery resource or a part of the fledgling ISTAR organization showed that while the Directorate of Land Requirements 8 may have been working on some technical concepts to integrate ISTAR components, the doctrine respecting their use had not yet been settled one way or the other. Considering the severe command and control limitations that the guns were under in returning any form of fire, and the time needed to receive the authority to fire from higher headquarters, the rationale of whether the sensor-to-shooter link was truly shortened was questionable. The debate would continue for several years to come under the unique circumstances of Kabul and the future, more volatile, yet still unique, Kandahar deployment where engaging targets solely on radar data would not be permitted.

The changeover proved difficult in more practical ways. No relationship between the radar troop and F Battery had formed prior to the deployment. Before the change in affiliation, the troop's practice had been that the troop commander, with his two radars, remained collocated with the ISTAR company commander at Camp JULIEN, while its troop sergeant major, with the two other radars, was collocated with the TACC and the ISTAR coordination centre at Camp WAREHOUSE.

With the new arrangement, the troop commander was now collocated with the battery commander at JULIEN. The troop sergeant major and his two radars remained isolated from the battery and the battle group notwithstanding that a troop of two guns had been moved to Camp WAREHOUSE. In effect, since the radars covered significantly different arcs, the JULIEN radar detachment connected to the battery's FSCC in Camp JULIEN and the Camp WAREHOUSE radar detachment continued to work with the TACC as it had done before.

The radars' clutter issues lessened over time as the crews became more experienced in their use and more skilled in techniques to filter it out. Nonetheless, there were still many false indications of rocket or mortar launches which in themselves created a problem with how to report them to the operational headquarters.

It became obvious from the sheer number of false indications that such reports could not be sent as they happened, and eventually a system of consolidated reports for the last half hour or hour were submitted to the TACC. It took some time to determine what other headquarters would want such reports. The ISTAR coordination centre had initially accepted them but later declined them. The brigade's FSCC was wary of such reports, and eventually only reports which the troop was convinced were of an actual attack were to be submitted. In such cases, a FOO or recce element could be sent out to examine the point of origin of the incident. No link between the radars and the battle group's tactical operations centre was ever established, although the troop commander attended the battle group's evening orders group where he would report any significant occurrences.[38]

While the bulk of the artillery's Kabul contingent had now settled in, one component was still missing as it continued to train in France.

7

ALL TOGETHER NOW: SPERWER ARRIVES

OCTOBER 2ND MARKED THE SECOND CHANGE and the first major tragedy for the battlegroup. G31—Captain Nick Williams; Sergeant Wayne MacLean, Master Bombardier Moe Mcgarrigle, and Bombardier Jay Killeen—had just returned from a patrol with elements of "Para" Company[1] when one of the company's Iltis light utility vehicles, still outside the wire, struck an explosive device in a wadi. It killed Sergeant Short of Para Company and Corporal Beerenfenger who had volunteered that day to accompany the patrol. Three other members of the patrol were wounded. G31 had crossed the same wadi in their Iltis only a few minutes before. The battle group was immediately put into lock down but the crew of G31, being a brigade asset, and at that point considering themselves not subject to the lock down, switched from their own unarmoured Iltis, in which they had patrolled, into a light armoured vehicle (LAV). They picked up several dismounts and snipers from the battalion's reconnaissance (recce) platoon and returned to the site of the strike. While the recce platoon members dealt with the incident site, G31 and the snipers provided security as an outer cordon.[2]

The incident was devastating for the battle group. Up until the strike, everyone understood that there were risks, but there was an air of general denial of the seriousness of the situation—some described it as flippancy. Forward observation officer (FOO) detachments, for example, would go out in a single LAV with a crew of as few as four which, after all the stations in the vehicle were manned, left only one dismount for security. October 2nd, changed everything.

The month of October also brought about somewhat of a crisis for the radar troop. The battery had arranged a day of shooting with the radars for the 11th, however, the radars didn't function and accordingly everyone went back to camp without a round being fired.

Logistics support for the radar troop, like everyone else, came through the national support element. Most aspects, such as rations and quarters, were no issue. One item, however, maintenance—specifically the lack of spare parts for the radars and the BV-206—was a problem.

The radars, being specialized and sophisticated electronic equipment, were susceptible to Afghanistan's heat and its fine powdery dust. Except for a technical assistance visit from Ericsson, maintenance was a matter of plug and play of components. There were only two technicians on the troop's establishment; a vehicle technician trained on the BV-206 and a signals technician trained to work on the various generators required to power the radars.

For the radars themselves, any component that went down was a priority issue for the troop, as the whole radar went down with the component. Unfortunately, a radar part had no higher priority for the national support element than a part for an Iltis for which temporary replacement vehicles were available within the theatre. When one radar went down for a long time, it became a cannibalization source of spare parts for the other three. It was not a good practice, but one which could be substantiated due to the hourly use limitations which rarely involved the use of over one radar at a time for each camp.

As the rotation neared its end and the lack of spare parts continued to plague the rader troop, Lieutenant Matheson took the bull by the horns, and much to the displeasure of the national support element, bypassed them and called Ericsson directly. This call eventually resulted in two outcomes: a technical assistance visit by Ericsson in February 2004 in time to recondition all four radars for the next contingent; and a more streamlined supply chain whereby parts could be ordered directly from the factory and sent to the troop via DHL or FedEx courier.[3]

While the range day on October 11th, had to be cancelled, another on the 27th went off very well. F Battery's observers—together with elements of an Italian mortar platoon—deployed to the Wais-e Qarni ranges, to the east of the city, for a special shoot. Lieutenant Heer's troop from Camp JULIEN moved up to Camp WAREHOUSE's helipad to set up next to Lieutenant Haire's troop. Over the next few hours, in the presence of a substantial brigade and international audience, the battery fired some 36 high explosive extended range (HEER) rounds.[4] Not only was this the first time that such rounds had been fired by Canadians in an operational setting, it was the first time that any Canadians other than some at the Royal Canadian Artillery School (RCAS) had fired them. While the exercise proved a success, both from the point of view of firing such rounds and firing them from within the Camp WAREHOUSE gun position, unbeknownst to the participants these rounds were already having a negative effect on the LG1's barrels which would become a major problem over the next few years.

The battery would be visited by a similar audience including, Generals Leslie and Devlin, on December 4th when it deployed to an American expedient range to conduct a live fire training exercise in celebration of Saint Barbara's Day. As November and December had come, the temperatures dropped and some snow covered the ground the day of the shoot. The exercise included direct fire engagements using high explosive squash head (HESH) ammunition against an old Soviet BMP armoured personnel carrier hulk. The target was effectively destroyed and, even considering that the targets may have been a little close, the LG1 proved to be a very accurate gun for direct fire. Every mission achieved a first-round hit. The day ended with all four guns returning to Camp JULIEN for a barbecue with the engineers.

Back in September 2003, everyone in the Canadian contingent and in Ottawa knew Sperwer was coming and there was an overwhelming excitement about it.[5] It wasn't until October 29th, 2003, however, that the unmanned aerial vehicle (UAV) troop actually arrived in theatre and established themselves in Camp JULIEN. Here they would remain for the rest of the tour.

The actual training for the troop had started in France in July and had run for three months. During that period of time, the Canadian-led multinational brigade in Kabul would rely solely on the German Luna for its UAV support.

In France, the troop—together with the ubiquitous Warrant Officer Wilcox—who had only been back to Gagetown for two days after his trip to the UK—was joined by five RCAF officers. The RCAF contingent consisted of: a major destined for the brigade headquarters; and two pilots and two navigators who would work directly in the UAV troop. In addition, a handful of RCAF maintainers were there to learn the servicing aspects of the aircraft. While most of the troop and RCAF personnel worked harmoniously, several interpersonal incidents were perceived to be an ongoing agenda on the part of some of the RCAF personnel to undermine any attempt by the army to manage these more complex tactical air surveillance systems.[6]

Training on the employment of the Sperwer simulator started at SAGEM's facilities in Éragny, France, which is located on the northern outskirts of Paris. The troop itself stayed in nearby Cergy, just north of Paris. The initial training ran for a few weeks before the troop moved to the French army's training area at Camp de Mourmelon, approximately 25 kilometers southeast of the city of Reims, where the troop was quartered. For over a month, the troop received more simulator training and conducted several practical flights.[7]

The training was generally considered adequate but disorganized, likely as a result of the rushed and heavily modified schedule.[8] The conditions for flying the aircraft in the gently rolling terrain of France, however, would prove quite a different experience from that of the much more rugged and higher altitudes that the troop would find surrounding the city of Kabul. While there was information passed on by SAGEM respecting the altitude limitations of their aircraft, the difference in the terrain would result in a series of challenges that the troop would only discover once they flew the UAVs under operational conditions.

The compressed timelines left virtually no opportunity to integrate the operation of the Sperwer with the other surveillance and target acquisition (STA) elements of the rotation. In short, while the radar troop and the UAV troop had been taught the fundamentals of how to operate their equipment and how to acquire targets, there had been no collective training to integrate them into the brigade or battle group. Neither had there been time to conduct an operational evaluation of the equipment prior to deployment. Finally, there had been no training provided on how to turn the "sense" function into an appropriate "act" response. Similarly, while the target acquisition coordination centre's (TACC) personnel had theoretical knowledge of the functioning of the radars and UAVs, none of them had acquired practical experience with the actual equipment. Finally, the Directorate of Land Requirements 8's project to integrate these varied intelligence, surveillance, target acquisition and reconnaissance (ISTAR) systems was still a developing concept. It had not been tested, evaluated and declared as a viable, functioning system. The tools to do so properly simply had not existed, and workaround methods had to be developed throughout the course of the deployment.[9]

The newly added RCAF major for the brigade headquarters had been boldly titled the G3 UAV. There was an immediate chain of command issue as to who worked for who vis-à-vis the G3 UAV and the commander of the TACC. The brigade's chief of staff directed that the G3 UAV worked for Captain Little who had already been successfully coordinating much of the German Luna UAV operations. While the UAV troop was getting Sperwer operationally ready, the newly arrived G3 UAV observed how the TACC, the German Luna detachment, and the newly arrived UAV troop operated. He became comfortable with the fact that the processes not only met but exceeded those of an aviation unit. Notwithstanding, he subsequently moved out of the TACC and co-located himself with the G3 Air and G3 Aviation.[10]

One particular challenge that illustrated the tension over UAV operations in theatre was the adoption of the Dutch army's training guidelines for the operation of Sperwer in Europe. 1 Canadian Air Division directed that these guidelines be adopted as direction for operations in Kabul without ever having had the opportunity to validate their value in a collective operational or training environment. This created problems. The key issue was that the Dutch guidelines did not allow Sperwer to be flown over any terrain in the Netherlands that had a population of over seven people per square kilometre. In contrast, Kabul is a city situated in a valley that is surrounded by mountains. Virtually the entire valley had a population density greater than the Dutch guideline, thus making UAV operations conforming to the direction extremely challenging. An RCAF major from 1 Canadian Air Division came on a technical assistance visit to brief Captain Little and, in part, to ensure that the Dutch guidelines were in fact followed. Captain Little quickly gave the major the opportunity to brief the brigade's chief of staff, Colonel Karl McQuillan, on the "seven people" issue. Colonel McQuillan quickly convinced the visitor that this direction was basically silly and the major agreed to bring the matter back to his headquarters for reconsideration. The brigade commander, in the interim, authorized the use of Sperwer and care was taken to avoid populated areas. Eventually, in February 2004, two days before Captain Little rotated back to Canada, 1 Canadian Air Division changed the direction to read that the Sperwer was not to purposely fly over heavily populated centres.[11]

In addition to the RCAF personnel deploying with the UAV troop, an eight-person testing team deployed to help bring Sperwer to its initial operating capability. Several technicians from SAGEM, a Dutch army officer, and a Dutch senior non-commissioned officer with Sperwer experience also arrived as technical advisers. From time-to-time the troop was also visited by personnel from Denmark's Sperwer UAV unit. The Danes were having challenges getting their own Sperwers airworthy, and as a result, they had deployed their personnel in a civil-military cooperation role.[12]

For the month of November and into December, the UAV troop's primary focus was to shake out the troop, test fly their four aircraft, and achieve initial operating capability status. That process was hindered largely by technical problems associated with the equipment.

On November 6th, 2003, a week after arrival in theatre, the newly designated CU-161 Sperwer had its first flight in Afghanistan. A successful mission was flown by aircraft number 161001. Not all missions would be.

One of the first issues that arose was as a result of the combination of the high altitude[13] and the temperature[14] of Kabul. In order to compensate for the thin air and to achieve take-off, the aircraft needed to be launched at a much greater pressure from the pneumatic launcher than it would have needed in France. This problem was compounded by the fact that in order to reduce the launch weight of the aircraft, it could not be fully fueled. The additional momentum imparted on the aircraft by the pneumatic launcher caused more launch stress to be placed on each lightened airframe, particularly on the wings. The resulting cracks to the wings necessitated two aircraft being taken out of service for repairs early on in the deployment.

The first major incident happened on November 12th to aircraft number 161004, which suffered Category "B" damage—very serious: damage to multiple major components—as a result of a hard landing on recovery. This was followed on November 21st, when aircraft number 161003 was undergoing a test flight. As the aircraft was returning for recovery, the parachute failed to deploy due to a spring failure, causing the aircraft to crash. It was subsequently written off. ISTAR company requested the battle group to have its quick reaction force (QRF) accompany the troop to recover the aircraft, but they refused as it was unpiloted. As a result, the ISTAR company had to collapse several observation posts to provide the needed security for the recovery team. To complicate matters further, the Canadian national command element's public affairs officer rushed out to direct that the ISTAR company ensure that none of the media have access to the crashed aircraft or its personnel. Nevertheless, as the flatbed carrying the aircraft arrived back at camp, the UAV project manager from Ottawa gave a press briefing with the crashed Sperwer as a backdrop.[15]

At this time, all four of the original aircraft were now out of service, albeit three were repairable and had been sent back to SAGEM. There were, however, two additional aircraft at Camp JULIEN, still in their packing crates. Captain Iain Clark, the administrative officer—later the battle captain—of the ISTAR company authorized their assembly and use.[16] Testing continued and initial operating capability for the aircraft was granted on November 29.[17] Operational missions could now begin.

The much anticipated and delayed loya jirga was finally held at the Kabul Polytechnic Institute on December 14. In all, some 504 delegates assembled in Kabul for the purpose of approving a new constitution for Afghanistan. The International Security Assistance Force (ISAF) had recognized for some time that such an assembly would offer a rare target of opportunity for those who were opposed to reform, but also that the security of the event should be seen to be in the hands of the Afghans themselves. As such, while the Afghan security forces handled security inside the perimeter, ISAF's personnel effectively created an outer cordon. Along with the bulk of ISAF, F Battery's FOOs were deployed to strategic observation posts to provide overwatch.

For the radar troop, the issue of the radars' lack of available operating hours came to a head in the weeks prior to the loya jirga, when the radars had once again been off during a rocket strike.[18] After that incident, General Leslie directed that the radars were to be operated full-time during the assembly. They were. Ericsson was persuaded to make adjustments to the lease compensating for the one radar that had been down. The radars would subsequently return to a reduced schedule for the rest of this and the next tour. To make matters worse for the troop, one of the leased BV-206 prime movers became unserviceable when it was necessary to reposition the radars for the loya jirga. Again, the uniqueness of the vehicle and the inability of the national support element to have it repaired led to the entire radar unit being flat-bedded across Kabul and back.

Mechanical problems for the UAV troop's aircraft did not end with their certification. When aircraft number 161006 suffered Category "C" damage—serious: damage to a major component—on December 17th, Sperwer operations were suspended until mid-January. The event highlighted the fact that the system was relatively immature and lacked reliability.[19] To add to the major issues, the national support element was not able to supply spare parts for the Renault truck launcher, which was becoming a familiar trend for all of the specialized equipment. Luckily, scrounging with the Germans found parts for German vehicles which could, with some ingenuity, be made to work.[20]

In Ottawa, the unease and disquiet over the technical issues with Sperwer in November had turned to furrowed eyebrows in December, and by January it would be just short of despondency.[21] While the troop and ISTAR company had been pragmatic and managed their expectations, the increased number of technical problems caused concern all the way up the chain of command. The total loss of yet another aircraft—number 161005—on January 19, 2004 caused a crisis. In that case the aircraft had been on a training mission practicing autopilot recovery procedures and, while it was on its fourth practice approach, the RCAF air vehicle commander ordered the air vehicle operator, against her objections, to descend the aircraft. On the previous three circuits the aircraft had descended ever closer to a ridge line and, on the last approach, impacted on the ridge.

This crash highlighted two issues. First, when ISTAR company advised Ottawa of the aircraft's tail number, it raised attention to the fact that the two boxed aircraft in Kabul, which had been unpacked, assembled and put into operation, had actually not yet been bought by Canada. Ottawa officially completed the sale the next month. Second, this loss now left the ISTAR company with only one serviceable aircraft, with two destroyed and three undergoing repair. Questions were being raised from above as to how to move forward. The answer from Clark was simply that he would continue to fly the aircraft until they had none left. They were not about to save the sole operational airframe in the back of the compound, waiting around for the perfect mission.[22]

Notwithstanding the technical issues and the concern they fostered in Ottawa, the impression the Sperwer made in theatre was favourable. The sensors were excellent and fulfilled the aircraft's role to provide surveillance, recce, security, escort over-watch, target acquisition and battle damage assessment. In particular, it proved very useful in identifying Afghan militia weapon caches which included not just armoured vehicles but even SCUD missile and FROG rocket launchers[23]. There was certainly potential for the Sperwer. Once repaired, previously damaged aircraft went back into service and, eventually in April of 2004 Canada would sign a contract amendment to get two replacement aircraft for the two that had been written-off. They would not be the last Sperwers that Canada was to lose or acquire.

December also saw the start of several operational illumination missions for the battery.

The first was fired from Camp JULIEN in support of G31 while at an Operation BASEBALL observation post. The observation post was situated close to the boundary between the Canadian and German areas of operation It became an area of concern due to frequent activities observed around a number of buried sea containers which were assessed as a potential rocket launch site into the nearby camp.

Shortly before Christmas, G31 observed activity around a house at night and ordered an illumination mission to better assess the activity. The mission itself was challenging and had to be fired at high angle because of the range and the crest of the mountain that G31 was located on. The key technical consideration for this mission was to ensure that the area where the round's carrier shell would land was clear of potential collateral damage.[24]

A total of ten rounds were fired on that mission. Three failed to function presumably as a result of the rounds being fired at a high angle,[25] at a high charge, and through the use of unreliable M577 fuzes. Warrant Officer Franken subsequently provided the probable impact locations to engineers to recover or destroy the blinds.[26] All 10 rounds, the three blinds and the seven empty carrier shells were all found within 30 meters of their predicted grid references.

The second and final illumination mission was also noteworthy.

A night in mid-January started off like any other until brigade headquarters received a call from a deployed element of the Norwegian Telemark task force. The element had spotted a suspicious party of individuals assembling a rail launcher in a field pointing roughly in the direction of Camp WAREHOUSE. The Norweigens were preparing to engage it with 30mm cannon fire from their CV9030N infantry fighting vehicles.[27]

The operations cell quickly scanned the location of their deployed forces and determined that, other than the Norwegians, there were no friendly forces in the area. Fortunately the brigade commander, Colonel Devlin was present in the headquarters as the brigade's G3 and the artillery's assistant operations officer, Captain Todd Scharlach, were discussing the situation. Scharlach recommended having Dave Brassard's G34 fire a few illuminating rounds to provide the Norwegians better visibility to confirm their target. The advice was taken by the G3 to the commander who quickly authorized the mission.

The call for fire was sent to Heer and Franken's troop at Camp WAREHOUSE.

The suspected launcher location was less than two kilometres away to the north of the troop and not far from the Kabul Afghan army training centre. It was approximately the same area where the prior September 11th rocket attack had originated. The troop scrambled to "take post" and, with the exception of the properly dressed command post duty staff, most arrived in shorts, t-shirts, and flip-flops.

The line gun-target ran directly over the camp's main gate and a guard tower, which combined with the short range, created a crest problem which once again necessitated a high angle engagement. It had taken a mere four minutes from the call for fire to the engagement of the target. Both guns at this point were manned and commanded by young gunners, as the detachment commanders and seconds-in-command, quartered further away, had not yet arrived. Franken, having computed the data, then left the command post to supervise the gun line while Heer ran the command post. Scharlach gave clearance to fire within a minute of when the CP had sent them the bearing, range and maximum ordinate of the mission.

The engagement caused great consternation for the German contingent in several respects. The Germans had never been too fond of the presence of the guns in their camp in the first place. The effect of the guns firing directly over the camp in the middle of the night, scattering the guards at the main gate, did nothing but reinforce their distaste for their presence. More important was the determination that the suspected target launcher was not, in fact, a Taliban crew setting up a rocket but the German UAV detachment preparing their LUNA for a launch. The Germans had failed to report to the brigade headquarters that they were about to conduct a UAV mission. Rather than being thankful that the illumination mission had prevented a blue-on-blue fratricide engagement by the Norwegians, the Germans' focused on the fact that the fire mission's high angle illumination carrier shells had impacted an estimated 15 or so metres away from their launch vehicle.[28]

One of the last tasks Roto 0 was involved in arose out of fighting that had broken out in Mazar-e Sharif in Northern Afghanistan in late 2003. As a result of this the United Nations (UN) Assistance Mission in Afghanistan under its Afghan New Beginnings Program set up four heavy weapons cantonments around Kabul. Here, under the supervision of ISAF, elements of the Afghan militia could turn in everything from light field artillery[29] to FROG rocket launchers for a reward. Once the equipment was turned-in, live ammunition was separated from it, and then the equipment was rendered inoperable by stripping key components away from it.

The program started operations in January 2004 and on January 23, Chief Warrant Officer Moretti received an old Russian BM 21 multi-barrel rocket launcher with ammunition at one of the sites. Moretti, a Master Gunner[30] got the system functional with a battery from a truck and disposed of the rockets by firing them into the side of a nearby mountain. Over the next two years the program removed as much as 98% of the Afghan militia's heavy weapons.

While there had been challenges for the brigade's fire support coordination centre (FSCC) and the gun battery in their deployment, the overall experience had been one of doing work they were familiar with but in unfamiliar circumstances and surroundings. Not so for the artillery STA components. As Roto 0 came to a close in February 2004, they still had teething problems to work out.

The full integration of systems was still lacking. For example, key staff in the brigade were unable to see any real-time, high-resolution imagery from the Sperwer. The UAV's sensor did produce an excellent image within the ground control station. It also had the capability to transmit a live image to a remote terminal which was connected to the ground control station by wire. In practice this permitted the battlegroup tactical operations centre in Camp JULIEN to see a live feed, but no such feed was available to the brigade headquarters which received a lower resolution copy of the flight well after the fact.

For both ISTAR company and the TACC, the handover to the incoming roto from 5ᵉ Groupe-brigade mécanisé du Canada from Valcartier, Quebec was a challenge. As the new contingent began to arrive, it was obvious that their brigade headquarters would follow a different setup than the one that the 2ⁿᵈ Canadian Mechanized Brigade Group had built. All of the coordination centres and cells were being turned into an operations support group under the FSCC's commander. While many of the tactics, techniques and procedures for the UAV troop and the radar troop were maintained—they were after all NATO standard ones—it was also clear in a number of ways that the new crew had their own way of working and they weren't about to spend much time reviewing the handover packages that had been prepared for them.[31]

Redeployment itself varied from group to group and involved long and tiring flights home through Camp Mirage without any time for decompression along the way. Back in Petawawa there was generally a three to four half-day cycle through an arrival assistance group and post operation debriefs, followed by leave. For the team from Gagetown, there were no organized procedures beyond a three-day arrival assistance group that was conducted in Trenton. Captain John Stewart's experience was even more surreal.

Forty-eight hours after having left his job with the civilian-military cooperation team buttoned up in a Bison driving through Kabul, he had gone through in-clearance in Trenton. Here he went through a medical debrief—with someone he felt wasn't really listening to him anyway—and had taken the bus from Trenton to Dennison Armouries in Toronto where, since it was Sunday, he was met by—no one.

A quick phone call told him to report to the armouries on Monday for a half day parading every day for the week. No one knew what to do with him. Reconnecting with friends that he had been away from for over half a year was strained and he ended up spending the next two months before returning to his civilian job reconnecting by telephone with Swedes and Germans he had served with in Kabul. For him, returning home was a horrible experience with feelings of loneliness and depression. Stewart would stay with the civilian-military cooperation detachment providing lectures on his experiences throughout various NATO countries until returning to the artillery in 2010.[32]

What then can we take away from the experiences of Operation ATHENA Roto 0?

What stands out is the stand up of the STA operations. Neither the UAVs nor the radars nor the TACC functions were new to the artillery. These capabilities had been there off and on—from operational use to experimentation—for well over a century. However, by letting the skills atrophy beyond the theoretical ones retained by a very small cadre of experts at the RCAS, the artillery had neither the necessary equipment in the inventory nor any trained operators in its use. While the Directorates of Land Force Readiness and of Land Force Requirements did yeoman service in identifying and procuring interim off-the-shelf systems, they were not necessarily the optimal ones and neither were they procured as sustainable capabilities. They were, at this point, nothing more nor less than yet another stop gap solution for yet another one-of mission. Much of it came with operational and logistical limitations—and, just as importantly, its operators were neither fully trained nor experienced in their operation when deployed.

While the gunners were inexperienced in the equipments' use and can be praised for their flexibility and enthusiasm to adapt, the supported arms were almost entirely unaware of what capabilities these systems, and even the guns, could bring to the fight. One can rightfully ask: if General Leslie, a gunner, had not been appointed contingent commander and deputy commander for ISAF, would Canada have even included UAVs and radars—or for that matter, even guns—with this operation?

The practice of cutting capabilities every time there is a perceived funding crisis is endemic within the army in general and the artillery in particular. It must be remembered that discussions respecting the unsuitability of the M109, like the tank, to what was predicted would be the future operational model for the army were already well underway. The M109s looming departure, and thus the 155mm round it fired, was predicted to create a ten-year capability gap in indirect fire support.[33] That capability gap would, however, not stop the upcoming divestiture.

Roto 0 had proven that the artillery did well in keeping its head in the game by sending a few select instructors in gunnery and assistant instructors in gunnery on foreign courses to retain some skills, but that does not translate into an easy path to re-establishing an operational capability once lost in the field.

This first Kabul rotation, while challenging, did not test the artillery's emergent STA troops with anything other than very modest enemy activity. This gave the rotation adequate time to get better at their craft. However, even a full year after the decision was made to go into Kabul, it was still a novel experiment undergoing teething issues. It would take several more years before the artillery's approach changed from a reactive to a proactive one. As we shall see, as STA grew in significance, it would do so at the expense of other artillery capabilities such as its ground-based air defence, its self-propelled guns, and its ability to provide massed firepower. But that was for a time yet to come. First, another regiment would take up the mission in Kabul.

8

NE FAIS PAS DE MAL[1]

ROTO 1 WOULD BE A DUPLICATE OF ROTO 0 but with one major difference; this time, Canada would also command the International Security Assistance Force (ISAF) mission. Canada had made the offer to do so in the spring of 2003. The North Atlantic Treaty Organization (NATO) had accepted. Who that commander would be was unknown. The position required a lieutenant-general. The army had two: the then Chief of the Land Staff, Lieutenant-General Mike Jeffery, a gunner; and his deputy, Lieutenant-General Rick Hillier, an armour officer promoted to that rank the previous December. Hillier expected that he would take over as Chief of the Land Staff the following summer, but Jeffery retired earlier in May. That left only Hillier in the running for the ISAF job and mostly settled the issue. The government, however, did not submit his name to NATO until later in the fall.

Things would be very different for Hillier than they had been for Leslie. While Leslie had been the deputy commander of ISAF, he'd also worn three additional hats: command authority for the Canadian contingent; commander of Canada's Task Force KABUL; and commander of Operation ATHENA, which included Camp Mirage in Dubai.

For Hillier's roto, Ottawa—possibly on the presumption that it had given Leslie too much leeway—narrowed the authority. Colonel Alain Tremblay, was appointed as commander of Task Force KABUL, and therefore would be the Canadian contingent's commander. Tremblay's chain of command reached back to Ottawa and not to Hillier.

Paradoxically, one of the primary lessons that came out of the 3rd Battalion, Princess Patricia's Canadian Light Infantry's deployment on Operation APOLLO concerned Canada's system of operational control. The link between the deployed battle group and Canada was cumbersome and unsustainable.[2]

Things had been manageable for Leslie—largely because he would not consult with the Deputy Chief of Defence Staff's people unless absolutely necessary.[3] It would be different for Hillier. If he wanted to task the Canadians, he would have to get the authority for that from Tremblay. Tremblay would often have to get permission from the Deputy Chief of Defence Staff group in Ottawa.[4] This could, and did, encompass significant delay. As a result, the Canadian contingent would not be the "go-to guys" for Hillier. He would end up using the more responsive Norwegians.[5]

Canada wasn't the only issue for Hillier. He would find the bureaucracy that permeated NATO's Joint Forces Command Headquarters in Brunssum equally challenging. He felt that it lacked a strategy and had an inability to provide direction or even communicate clear objectives.[6]

Hillier's experience on Operation ATHENA would become the driver for his 2006 transformation of the Canadian Forces' command and control structure when he later became Chief of the Defence Staff.

While Hillier dealt with the intricacies of forming a multinational headquarters for Kabul, the 5ᵉ Régiment d'artillerie légère du Canada (5 RALC) had already been looking at their upcoming deployment for some time. At the beginning of 2003, Batterie R had been preparing to support the 3ᵉ Battalion, Royal 22ᵉ Régiment at 2 Canadian Mechanized Brigade Group's brigade training event in Wainwright in April. The battalion was taking part in its capacity as the Force de réaction immédiate (terrestre).[7] The preparation for the exercise was nearing completion when the word for Canada's initial deployment to Kabul came. Briefly, the personnel in 5 RALC thought that they and the 3ᵉ Battalion would take Roto 0. The army dashed their hopes and even cancelled their participation in the exercise. It gave the assignment to the 2ⁿᵈ Regiment, Royal Canadian Horse Artillery (2 RCHA), and warned le 5ᵉ Groupe-brigade mécanisé du Canada to provide the follow up Roto 1.[8] Just like 2 Canadian Mechanized Brigade Group, le 5ᵉ Groupe-brigade mécanisé du Canada would provide the Kabul Multinational Brigade headquarters. It would also provide an infantry battle group composed of: the 3ᵉ Battalion of the Royal 22ᵉ Régiment; a reconnaissance (recce) squadron from 12ᵉ Régiment blindé du Canada, and 5 RALC's LG1 equipped Batterie R.

Roto 1 would become a full regimental effort for 5 RALC, just as it had for 2 RCHA. In addition to Batterie R, Batterie X would form the core of the surveillance and target acquisition (STA) contingent, while regimental headquarters and Batterie Q would fill in positions throughout the brigade.

Time blessed them. Their deployment would not take place until early 2004. The brigade would profit from the experiences of its predecessor, tailoring both its structure and its training. Training would not start until after the summer's annual posting season.

Batterie R's commander was Major Marc LaFortune. He had previously served as an instructor in gunnery at the Royal Canadian Artillery School (RCAS) and as a staff officer with the army's individual training section at the Combat Training Centre's headquarters. Lafortune felt the battery's forward observation officers (FOO) and forward air controllers (FAC) would benefit from integrating into the battle group. He moved the designated teams of Captains Francis Poitras, Martin Simard, Jessy Brunet, and Russ Eyestone into the 3ᵉ Battalion's lines. The rest of the battery and its augmentees reorganized themselves into a fire support coordination centre (FSCC), two two-gun LG-1 troops and a tiny echelon. Captains Francois Aziz-Beaulieu and Karl LaPrade would deploy as the battery captain and gun position officer respectively, while Lieutenants Marie Noel Blanchet and Marie-Eve Bégin would be the troop commanders. The battery quartermaster sergeant, Warrant Officer Luc Gravel, would deploy as the battery sergeant major. The incumbent in that position, Master Warrant Officer Yves Courtemanche, would instead deploy in a civil-military cooperation role. Warrant Officer Gabby Pinard would go as the battery tech warrant.

One by one, other personnel started being tasked with roles on the mission. Captain Dave Buchanan, an instructor in gunnery in Gagetown, had known since switching rotos with Captain Rich Little that he would deploy as the commander of the brigade's target acquisition coordination centre (TACC).

Anglophone personnel from Gagetown would form his team. Four of them, Warrant Officer Ken MacLeod, Master Bombardier Keith McLaren and Bombardiers Dominic Antle and Dan White, were surveyors working at the RCAS. Two more, Master Bombardier Anthony Tullett and Bombardier Peter Silva, were air defenders then assigned to W Battery's air defence troop in Gagetown. When asked if they'd be interested in going, they readily jumped at the chance.[9]

The Roto 1 TACC would function differently than Roto 0's had.

2 Canadian Mechanized Brigade Group had formed a new intelligence, surveillance, target acquisition, and reconnaissance (ISTAR) company based on its recce squadron with a small coordination centre at brigade headquarters. Le 5ᵉ Groupe-brigade mécanisé du Canada would look at ISTAR as a process, rather than as an organization. The ISTAR company therefore ceased to exist, and the recce squadron was reborn. The coordination centre became a collection of subject matter experts of various intelligence, surveillance and recce assets including the artillery's radars and unmanned aerial vehicles (UAV), all operating under the auspices of a G3. Buchanan's team and representatives from the UAV troop and the radar troop were all merged into the brigade's ISTAR coordination centre. Here, they effectively

assumed, amongst other roles, the doctrinal functions of an artillery surveillance and target acquisition battery headquarters.[10]

In some ways, some of Roto 0's structure survived. The Sperwer troop remained attached for administration to the recce squadron, while the radars remained attached for administration to the gun battery.[11]

While 58ᵉ Batterie d'Artillerie Antiaérienne was part of the reserve force's le 6ᵉ Régiment d'artillerie de campagne, ARC in Lévis, Quebec, the battery had been organized as a total force sub-unit. Its roughly 30 regular force and 100 reserve force members, operating out of Valcartier, were tasked to provide two Javelin missile troops and an airspace coordination centre (ASCC) to the 4th Air Defence Regiment, RCA (4 AD Regt), and to be under tactical control to le 5ᵉ Groupe-brigade mécanisé du Canada from time-to-time.[12] In the spring of 2003, the battery was on the road to high readiness and scheduled to attend the collective training exercise in Wainwright alongside the 3ᵉ Battalion and Batterie R. Ottawa cancelled the attendance of 58ᵉ Batterie along with the rest of the Valcartier contingent. Subsequently, in the late spring, 4 AD Regt was warned to deploy that battery's ASCC with the brigade headquarters on Roto 1.

At the time, the battery's ASCC was more a concept on paper than a functioning entity. Its personnel understood the principles of air control measures from the varying courses they had attended, but in Captain Jean-François Claveau's mind, "the main challenge that we had just before Afghanistan was that there was no ASCC training ... So we knew a bunch of definitions ... But how do we apply them?"[13]

The battery's training had primarily focused on its air defence role. Further, it had equipment challenges. For example, its members had never been able to make their air defence systems integrator work.

The tasking was for seven members. The selected personnel immediately started their training. Scheduled to accompany Captain Claveau were Warrant Officer François Vidal, Sergeant Daniel Gagnon, Master Bombardiers Bruno Plamondon and Guy Cloutier, and Gnr Réjean Raubichaud, a radar technician from 4 AD Regt. The battery was missing a major, and early in the fall, Ottawa added Major Mark Murphy to fill the slot of G3 ASCC in the brigade headquarters.

Individual gunners from the regiment were also finding their way into other jobs within the Kabul Multinational Brigade. 5 RALC's commanding officer, Lieutenant-Colonel Eric Tremblay, would deploy as the brigade's deputy chief of staff and commander brigade troops. Captains Stéphane Dumas and Marie-Christine Harvey would serve as military aide and executive aide, respectively, to the brigade's commander, Brigadier-General Jocelyn Lacroix.[14] The regimental sergeant major, Chief Warrant Officer Christian Desrosiers, would deploy with the brigade's civil-military cooperation detachment.[15]

Major Dany Fortin, newly posted to 5 RALC to take command of Batterie X, had recently been serving as le 5e Brigade's G3 Operations. With his battery being broken up for surveillance tasks, Fortin started looking for a deployment job and quickly found himself back at brigade headquarters where, once again, he would be G3 Operations. With him, in the brigade's FSCC, would be Captain Jean-François Duval, 5 RALC's operations officer.[16] Fortin described his portion of the headquarters as a joint operations centre using a standard "G" staff system. It incorporated the FSCC, the G3 UAV, the G3 ISTAR and the G3 ASCC, all reporting to the G3, a Canadian lieutenant-colonel.[17]

While commanded by a Canadian, the headquarters, and the Kabul Multinational Brigade itself, would truly be a multinational affair. The brigade headquarters would grow to 172 people from 16 different countries, albeit primarily Canadian, German, and French. Fortin's deputy G3 would come from France. The brigade's staff work and working language would, by necessity, be English. Regrettably, only Germany would send personnel to Canada to take part in pre-deployment training. Of those who attended training, only a few were the same individuals who would subsequently show up in Afghanistan. Those that did attend helped the brigade headquarters to become more familiar with the European way of doing staff duties.[18]

5 RALC had been gutted by the time it had filled all the deployment positions.[19]

The regiment continued its spring training while the task force organization fell into place. Regimental schools and confirmation exercises occupied the late winter and early spring of 2004, concurrent with which all batteries developed knowledge of Afghanistan.[20] With the oncoming summer, training ceased for the annual posting season and the regiment's dispersal on leave.

The brigade promptly started pre-deployment training in September with theatre mission specific training. This comprised briefings and activities held in Valcartier, whereby the headquarters and the battle group prepared for the cultural conditions that they would encounter.

Training also included aspects of asymmetrical threats and warfare. This culminated, during the first three weeks of October, with two brigade exercises in Valcartier. Here the brigade left the regiment mostly to its own devices to conduct battery and regimental live-fire exercises.

Exercise ATHÉNA AGUERIE I, running from October 6-10, and Exercise ATHÉNA AGUERIE II, from October 18-22 , validated Batterie R's readiness for deployment. In addition, the exercises taught everyone about dealing with attacks by belligerents and interacting with civilians.[21]

As the battery gelled, LaFortune changed its name to "Batterie Athéna" in recognition of its personnel coming not only from Batterie R, but from across the regiment. The newly renamed battery immediately took part in another series of exercises that stretched throughout the month of November and into early December.[22] Exercise ATHÉNA MOBILE, carried out in Valcartier from November 2–8, was noteworthy for two reasons. It would be the last time that 5 RALC's M109s deployed for a regimental exercise and it was the first time that the regiment attempted to do an airmobile lift of the LG1.

Airmobile training with the Italian 105mm L5 pack howitzers and CH-135 Twin Huey helicopters[23] had, in years past, been the bread and butter of Canada's light forces. The heavier weight of the LG1 and the lower lift capability of the CH-146 Griffon had ended this type of training. Word had filtered back that Roto 0 was using German CH-53 Sea Stallions to move the LG1s and LaFortune decided he would prepare the battery for that. Personnel remembering how to rig guns for helicopters set their minds to the problem. After some study, in which the RCAF cleared the Griffon for only administrative moves of the LG1, 430 Tactical Helicopter Squadron stripped a Griffon of much of its interior furnishings. A forward arming and refuelling point was set up close to the battery to lean out the aircraft's fuel to save weight. The weight was such a crucial factor that the crew even stripped the LG-1 of its breech block.[24] All that done, the Griffon was used to sling lift the gun—but only for a short distance. It taught the crews the process of rigging the gun. It was, however, not a viable procedure to use with Griffons.

There were neither the resources nor the time available to move everyone to Wainwright for a national brigade training event like 2 Brigade had gone through. Instead, 5ᵉ Brigade had to develop their own "BTE 3.5" with resources from within Secteur Québec des Forces terrestres.[25] This would be a two-part exercise. First would be Exercise LION RÉSOLU. Batterie Athéna would join the rest of the battle group at Fort Drum in upper New York state from November 15th to December 8th. Here, the battle group and the brigade headquarters would deploy respectively into separate and simulated Camps JULIEN and WAREHOUSE. They would recreate that scenario immediately thereafter in the city of Sherbrooke for Exercise LION ROYAL to more closely recreate the geographic situation in Kabul. In combination, the two exercises practiced the troops in patrolling in mountainous, urban and airfield environments supported by many dry fire missions.

Fortin recalled, "I thought those two together were filled with, pardon the expression, but, 'you can't make this shit up type of events', right? All kinds of things that you go; 'you know this is never going to happen this way' ... I had this list of things, events that occurred during the tour, and you know what? This is exactly ... exactly like some of the things that we discussed in training."[26]

While the rest of the regiment prepared for its deployment, Batterie X personnel were also preparing for their roles. Like their predecessors on Roto 0, the radar troop and the UAV troop would not take part in the battery's pre-deployment training. The radar troop, under its troop commander Lieutenant Patrick Gilbert and troop sergeant major Warrant Officer Jean Beaulieu, set off for Norway for several weeks in mid-November. Like Roto 0, they too would conduct their final exercise with live fire from a Norwegian M270 multiple launch rocket system battery[27].

The Sperwer troop, under Captain Pierre Gagnon and troop sergeant major Warrant Officer Patrice Nugent, undertook basic flight training in Canada and Sperwer training in France from early November to mid-December.[28] Neither troop's equipment would show up in Canada or at Fort Drum for integrated training with the battle group. The radar troop did make use of the radar simulator system after returning to Valcartier prior to deployment.[29] For Gagnon's UAV troop, the training was better than Roto 0's because of the additional lead time and language similarities with the trainers in France, but only marginally so. At the end of the training, the level of expertise was not what they had hoped for. The unforgiving terrain around Kabul would not be the place to enhance those skills.

Buchanan's TACC left Gagetown to join 5 RALC's pre-deployment training in September. They stayed with them, with the exceptions of weekend and pre-deployment leave, until deploying in January. Throughout, they took part in all the brigade headquarters' command post and field exercises. Here, they learned the intricacies of how the brigade's interpretation of ISTAR should function.[30] The crew of Roto 1's ASCC participated fully in all the garrison and the field training exercises, in each case trying as much as possible to replicate the situation they would face in Kabul. Claveau recalls that,

> Roto 0, before us, was instrumental to our success. We had good communications with them and they were exchanging a lot with us...we knew the map was on the left...we knew all the speed dials on the phone... each time we were replicating how they were working in Afghanistan...It was almost a seamless transition when we arrived because of them...as they were developing and knowing things they were always informing us and we would adapt that format.[31]

The predeployment training had prepared the regiment to face anything. As it turned out, it would have to face very little.[32] The push from Hillier had been clear and LaFortune paraphrased the intent: "don't mess this up ... don't be doing an indirect fire camp and blow up a couple of nomads...it's all about gaining the support of the

Kabul locals...do no harm."[33] Unlike the previous roto, Batterie Athéna would not even fire an illumination mission operationally.[34]

To say that the battery fired no operational missions, however, is not to say that the battery did not keep busy.

Its handover from Roto 0 went smoothly, and in no time the battery had established itself in Kabul. Of the over 200 gunners deployed, roughly forty percent manned the two guns, one half of the radar troop, and the brigade's various staff positions in Camp WAREHOUSE. Co-located with the battle group at Camp JULIEN, the rest of the battery manned the remaining two guns, the remaining radars, the UAV troop, the battery's FSCC, and the FOO detachments.[35]

Batterie Athéna had arrived with a slightly altered attitude from their predecessors. The casualties taken during Roto 0 had raised everyone's awareness of the dangers involved. Warrant Officer Gabby Pinard, the battery's tech warrant, noticed that Camp JULIEN's guns were in gun pits. No such protection existed for the guns or ammunition at WAREHOUSE. They took steps to build up the position's defences with HESCO barriers. The administrative distribution of the battery's personnel separated between officers and non-commissioned members and by gender around camp continued to be a problem which was never rectified.[36]

For the FOOs, there were still no observation post variants of the light armoured vehicle (LAV). They did, however, have the addition of AN/PRC-117 Multiband Manpack Radios,[37] which facilitated communications with the six newly arrived Dutch AH-64D Apache attack helicopters of the 1 (Netherlands) Helicopter Detachment. Not only did the helicopters' mobility and firepower provide for a dramatic show of force, their presence was a vital and immediate intelligence source through which the FOOs could brief their supported companies on details concerning their objectives.[38]

The battery's FOOs continued the patterns established by their predecessors, including the routine of manning observation posts. One early occupation of it on the night of February 17th and 18th caused a minor problem for the two detachments involved. Master Bombardier Éric Normand recalls:

> *Both crews were under the command of [Captain] Brunet for G33 and my crew, G34, under the command of [Captain] Sébastien Lemieux. After a few hours in place and while we had a bridge in our observation area we could see a vehicle stop to leave a man who disappeared under the bridge. We then reported the event and a few moments later the man left. A few times we saw this man come and go, always disappearing under the bridge.*
>
> *...we made a request for 105 mm fire in order to illuminate the observation area. I remember very well that we had estimated that the carrier shell would fall on the side of the mountain and that there was no danger for the*

population. The firing request refused, we continued to observe and report the comings and goings of this stranger.

At dawn when the time to leave arrived, discussions took place as to the possibility that explosives had been placed under the bridge and the decision to take an alternative route (after doing a recce of the map) was taken. It was then, with G34 in the lead, that after driving a few kilometers on this narrow road, it gave way under the weight of the VBL,[39] leaving us in a most precarious position. The VBL, leaning sharply to the right, was supported only by trees. We assessed the situation and tried to free ourselves from this unfortunate situation for several long minutes before the Afghans came towards us and who, with the help of rocks, managed to guide our driver so that he could move the VBL out of our way. [U]nfortunate situation. That's when the crew [of] G33 turned back as G34 continued on those narrow roads, repeatedly brushing past buildings as we passed through villages.[40]

The radar troop arrived with the main body of Batterie Athéna and immediately took over the equipment from Roto 0. Like its predecessor, it was split between Camp JULIEN and Camp WAREHOUSE with Lieutenant Gilbert set up at the former and Master Warrant Officer Beaulieu at the latter. Each detachment now had five operators instead of four, but still had to operate under the restrictive contract limitations, which only allowed sporadic *ad hoc* operations during quiet times. When required for specific tasks, the troop would implement operations on a 24/7 basis. Like their predecessors, operations were primarily static from positions inside the camp, which provided adequate coverage. The rare out-of-camp deployments necessitated adding a close protection detail for security, as the troop's manning was inadequate to provide both operators and security.

Aside from the continuing clutter generated by the environment around Kabul, the biggest headache for the troop was maintenance. The fine talcum powdery dust and the rising summer heat were a constant threat to the equipment. It required daily vacuuming as well as air conditioning to keep the equipment functional. Fortunately, the previous roto's deployment had to a large measure resolved the issue of technical assistance and spare parts for the contingent. The handover from Roto 0 had taken place during a technical assistance visit and as a result, the troop could address many technical and tactical issues on the spot. Two further visits, one in mid-tour—which passed on lessons learned from the British in Iraq—and one at the end, kept the equipment functioning and prepared for its return to the contractor.[41]

The TACC deployed to Kabul spread amongst several flights. Tullett and Silva's flight took them from Quebec to Scotland, Zagreb, Camp Mirage in the United

Arab Emirates, and then Kabul. In Zagreb they were let off the plane for a smoke while the aircraft refueled. Here the two air defenders had the chance to look over a lineup of Soviet-era jets and helicopters near the runway—aircraft, which until then, had been the primary object as targets for much of their training.

The weather in Kabul, in January, had also been a surprise. They'd left a snow-covered Quebec and spent a night at Mirage in conditions akin to a hot sauna. In Kabul, they were back in the snow, albeit it didn't stay long.

The first impression of Kabul for the ASCC's Claveau was that, "the only colour is sand. Everything is the same colour … But it was beautiful. I still remember it was beautiful. The mountains; all the mountains. That was spectacular. I can imagine why Kabul was one of the top five destinations in the sixties or seventies for tourism. It's majestic. Surrounded by very, very high mountains with snow."[42]

Physically, the team's accommodations and work conditions had changed very little from those for Roto 0. They remained in the same room as the engineer support coordination centre. They ran a three-man daytime ISTAR shift on one side of the room. A two-man engineer shift worked on the opposite side. A plotting table occupied the centre and a communications stack sat in one corner. The room faced the highway outside; for protection, they covered the windows with blast blankets. The cells all drew heavily from their interconnection with several surveillance asset subject matter experts throughout the brigade and headquarters. With time, the group grew to include representation from G3 Air and Aviation. Communications remained mostly by radio and a live video feed from the Sperwers. Operations were for the most part low-key but that didn't reduce the danger from improvised explosive devices or rockets. Both Camp WAREHOUSE and Camp JULIEN were targeted throughout the tour. Lieutenant-Colonel Eric Tremblay at brigade headquarters recalls one attack in particular. A group of Canadian engineers from the explosive ordnance disposal team had been in their tent and had decided to step out for a smoke break. While they were smoking, a rocket came in and destroyed the tent. No one was injured. In another incident, one Norwegian soldier was killed and another wounded in an attack with a rocket propelled grenade on the road just outside Camp WAREHOUSE.[43]

Captain Buchanan considered his brigade's coordination centre implementation superior to the previous roto's ISTAR company concept.[44] It was certainly robust enough for Kabul, and probably workable in a low-intensity conflict where the opponents limited indirect fire attacks to the odd rocket randomly flung into a grid square. The question for the future would be whether, doctrinally, counter-battery activities are so distinct from general surveillance activities that they merit an independent organization more directly tied in with a network of dedicated target acquisition and counterstrike capabilities? A second question to be answered would be; at what level should these resources be held and controlled?

With ISAF V, things had not changed materially for the ASCC from Operation ATHENA's Roto 0. There was still no airspace coordination cell at ISAF headquarters which was the equivalent of a divisional headquarters. Within the American system, airspace coordination is doctrinally a division-level resource. At brigade level, such elements are established out of organic resources and attached tactical air control parties. While prior to Kabul, Canada did have ASCCs through the three air defence batteries that would be under the tactical control of the three brigade groups; their tactics, techniques and procedures were more theoretical than practical. Those of other NATO nations were even less robust. Canada, having provided the Kabul Multinational Brigade headquarters, would indeed continue to carry the responsibility for all things airspace coordination for the entire Kabul area of operations. It even extended beyond to the new ISAF provincial reconstruction teams, and for ISAF troop movements beyond Kabul.

Notaro's Roto 0 team would firmly lay the groundwork for the operations of Sperwer and would go a long way to taming some of the residual chaos that had existed prior to Roto 0's arrival. One thing that Roto 1's team accomplished that Roto 0 hadn't been able to was to convince the Americans to add the ISAF training areas as restricted operating zones. With this they had gone a long way to minimizing the risk of another Tarnak Farms incident.

While the system was an effective command-and-control system, some of the issues from Roto 0 remained. Principal amongst those was the lack of an American SIPRNet[45] connection within the brigade. This was needed to transfer airspace control orders, air tasking orders, and special instructions between the brigade and Combined Joint Task Force 76 from the Combined Air Operations Centre in Qatar. A workaround system, via the American liaison team at ISAF headquarters, continued to be their primary connection.[46] Using the FalconView software to convert this text-based data into easily understood raster maps[47] for graphical displays enhanced the team's operations when deconflicting airspace requirements from users. While planned requests were required 72 hours in advance for processing and coordinating with the Americans, procedures were also in place for immediate requests to be handled by telephone. Another matter that was not resolved during either Roto 0, or Roto 1, was a satisfactory integration of the Americans' ground-based radar at Bagram with the team's air defence system integrator terminal. The best that they could do was to continue to go through the secure telephone workaround previously set up by Roto 0.

Many of the issues experienced by both rotos revolved around the fact that the number of multi-national airspace users had soared. As a result, the possibility of incidents would be more likely in the chaotic environment of an insurgency in a failed state situation. The problem would subsequently become clear for Roto 2, whose leadership at ISAF and the Kabul Multinational Brigade headquarters would come from a European nation. Hillier was so concerned about their replacements' capabilities that he asked Claveau to stay in Kabul for an additional month to help with the transition.[48]

Roto 0 and 1's experiences clarified that airspace coordination was here to stay but would need to improve technically and in training. Roto 1 created an extensive lessons learned report, including a website and a training package for the RCAS. They, in turn, would create an ASCC section that July and would start running some 40 courses over the next four years. Not every lesson learned found immediate acceptance. As an example, during discussions with the Data Link Advisory Panel for the ADATS 400 project, Major Murphy received pushback from the developers as to the operational usefulness of the FalconView software.[49] Fortunately, subsequent teams deploying to Kandahar accepted and learned from those lessons.

The brigade exercised command and control within the brigade through the Canadians' new Iris digital communications system, developed under the Tactical Command, Control and Communications System project. The communications squadron deployed Iris, and Canadian signalers, to all unit command posts reporting on the brigade net. This new equipment, including its situational awareness system, was not without problems. The brigade had only recently received the equipment. Their experience clearly highlighted the problems caused by rushing new equipment into a theatre of operations without the necessary time and training to make the users proficient in its operation.[50]

Intelligence sharing would also be a challenge as not everyone within the headquarters had the same level of Five Eyes[51] access to the various streams of information that were supplied.

Rules of engagement, which differed from country to country, turned out to be manageable. On the other hand, the fact that General Hillier was not the Canadian contingent commander, as Leslie had been, resulted in unnecessary difficulties. Neither Hillier nor LaCroix, the brigade commander, had control over the national command element or the national support element which rested with Colonel Tremblay, the commander of Task Force KABUL. Any operation that either of them wished to undertake using Canadian troops would require getting the authority to do so from Tremblay, often requiring a referral back to the Deputy Chief of Defence Staff in Ottawa. Their approval could take anywhere from 40 minutes to several days.

The centralization of the various units' combat service support into one agency created unnecessary problems. Each unit now had to deal with a separate agency in the planning of service support, adding one or more intermediate steps. When units had their own service support resources, a unit could plan its support based on its resources available, such as transport. With the national support element, the unit's requests had to be made with no knowledge of what resources would be available to fill such requests at any given time. As a result, the unit might need to alter its plans accordingly.[52] Centralized combat service support was a process contrary to standing doctrine within the Canadian Forces and while aspects of it might be workable in a scenario of limited tasks of limited durations such as Rotos 0 and 1, it would be challenging, particularly for maintenance.[53] The staff inside the national support element, and some staff officers in Ottawa, did not share that opinion and believed that their operation optimized combat service support.[54]

Early March brought two significant events to the Canadian contingent in Kabul. The first was the arrival of 60 brand new Mercedes-Benz G-Wagon light utility vehicles, wheeled to replace the aging, unarmoured Iltises.[55] The second, and much more relevant to the gunners, was the first live-fire exercise to be conducted by Batterie Athéna since its arrival in theatre.

On March 11th, the two guns, the command post, and several FOO parties from Camp WAREHOUSE conducted a road move a dozen kilometres to the southeast to the range in the Wais-e Qarni region. The exercise was brief—the guns only fired 19 rounds—but it verified that both the guns and their crews were operational.[56] Another exercise on May 6th showed the value in the battery having practiced the art of moving the LG1s by air. On that day, German Sea Stallion helicopters were brought in for an air mobile exercise and lifted the guns from both camps. The exercise was noteworthy for having issues with locals in the impact area and receiving fire missions from non-Canadian observers, a practice that required extra care in the command post to ensure that nothing was lost in translation.[57]

The UAV troop's arrival in theatre had not taken place until mid-March. Its handover from Roto 0 was particularly important because of the many lessons learned by their predecessors about operating the Sperwer in the harsh conditions prevailing around Kabul. The troop had to deal with a new mode of landing the Sperwers because of the terrain, which differed from that faced in France. This procedure, once tweaked, proved to be more accurate than the textbook method.[58]

In April, Canada ordered two more aircraft to replace the two destroyed ones.[59] This brought the overall aircraft holdings back up to six, albeit some of those were still under repair. The two replacements would not arrive in time to deploy to Kabul. Instead, Ottawa would order them sent directly to Canada.

There were concerns that aircraft were not performing up to the manufacturer's claims.[60] Spares were being used up at a very high rate and it was decided that both the recovery and launch systems were unsound.[61] Hillier opined that, for the mission in Kabul, Sperwer was an "atrocious" vehicle.[62] As Tullett would later recall,

> We had a lot of problems with Sperwer. Sperwer was really, really good. It had a really good surveillance package on it; it had a fantastic camera, but a crappy airframe and an even crappier motor. In January, you know, the air density wasn't too bad. We could fly in the afternoon and fly in the evening but as the tour went on and progressed and the hotter the weather got, we had to fly later and later in the day and for shorter periods because the airplane just couldn't stay in the air.

> I do remember on one occasion, Pete Silva and I were in the office and we're looking at the feed and he said to me "Is there something wrong with the Sperwer?"...and I looked at the feed and the next thing you know the phone rings and it's the Sperwer guys from JULIEN saying "Hey. We got an issue with the Sperwer. Gonna lose it." And it had everything to do with air density. They couldn't keep it in the sky and we basically lost it slowly coming out of the sky and do a nosedive into a building in downtown Kabul...Now we have this airframe that someone is going to have to pick up. They had the QRF [quick reaction force] go and get it.[63]

Notwithstanding these flaws, there was a sufficient promise of operational benefits in the concept. Plans were already being made for the system's redeployment to Valcartier at the end of the tour and for its future use. The fact that Sperwer was not sufficiently developed and that the training, while adequate, did not create the expertise for the hard conditions encountered simply meant that changes would have to be made.

As Roto 1 was coming to an end in August 2004, so too would the artillery's role in Kabul. Canada's commitment had only been for two brigade headquarters rotations. The next two rotations would be for significantly smaller battle groups. Each would be built around a recce squadron, an infantry company, and an engineer squadron from the 1st and 2nd Canadian Mechanized Brigade Groups in Edmonton and Petawawa, respectively. This reduction reached back to 2003, with the mission's original commitment. Hillier, on his first day as the new Chief of Land Staff, had convinced both the Minister of National Defence and the then Chief of Defence Staff, General Ray Henault, that with the Bosnia missions and with Kabul, the army would burn out by August 2004. As a result, the government planned Rotos 2 and 3 to be substantially smaller from the very beginning.[64] Rotos 0 and 1 had some 2,100 personnel with 643 major pieces of equipment. National Defence Headquarters pared this down for the subsequent rotos to 710 personnel with 511 major pieces of equipment.[65] Batterie Athéna packed up its guns and Sperwers together with their ancillary equipment to send back to Canada. The ARTHUR radars went back to their manufacturer for refurbishment and returned to their original Scandinavian owners.

Hillier's departure in early August 2004 constituted the end of the ISAF V rotation and the start of Eurocorps' ISAF VI under General Jean-Louis Py of France. The handover of the Kabul Multinational Brigade headquarters from le 5ᵉ Groupe-brigade mécanisé du Canada would not go smoothly. The determination that Eurocorps' Franco-German Brigade would take over the headquarters did not get made until very late in the rotation. Moreover, some of the outgoing brigade staff felt that their replacements were not ready, as the Eurocorps staff did not conduct a pre-deployment recce, and new staff were being added to their headquarters up to the very last minute. A French colonel replaced Major Fortin. Despite the rank inflation, several of the positions in the headquarters remained unfilled. Further, Brigadier-General Jocelyn Lacroix and Fortin were concerned about intelligence that a potential coup was fomenting, causing Fortin to sleep in his office during the last week of his tour. Both volunteered to stay on. In the end, Hillier ordered them to go home.[66]

With the excitement of an operational deployment on their minds, 5 RALC's Kabul contingent had spent little time concerning themselves about events back home. In fact, big changes were happening there. Batterie Q and the regimental headquarters had been busy conducting conversion training to the LG1s and preparing for the withdrawal of the M109s from service. Steps were underway to transform the regiment to a new establishment consisting of light guns, mortars, and locating devices. Batterie X was to be equipped with LG1s, Batterie Q with 81 mm mortars and the Sperwer UAVs slated to return from Kabul, and Batterie R with 81 mm mortars and 105 mm C3 howitzers borrowed from the reserve force. The transformation was completed on September 25th, as the regiment recognized the M109s long service in conjunction with a parade to exercise its right to the Freedom of the City of Quebec City.[67]

What did the mission in Kabul accomplish? Just as the United Nations Protection Force operations in the Balkans had been an important step in moving from Cyprus-centric United Nations operations to a theatre where war was still ongoing, so Kabul marked a new milestone. The year that Rotos 0 and 1 had spent there had been a critical step for the army and the artillery in learning how to operate in counterinsurgencies and in the violent environment that they would face in 2006.[68] In part this consisted of relearning old doctrinal lessons from World War Two but with newer guns, locating devices and staff procedures. As well, it was a precursor to a new epoch of war fighting in a non-contiguous battlespace. Aside from its NATO commitments, the army's operational deployments had slowly transitioned from peacekeeping to peace enforcement and were now poised to change further along the spectrum of conflict to war fighting. The Kabul experience would continue on a smaller scale and without the artillery for another year. For the guns, there would be another long interval and a major reset.

THE SECOND INTERLUDE:
SUMMER 2004 - FALL 2005

BATTERIE ATHÉNA'S GUNS HAD GONE HOME. Operation ATHENA continued.

Under General Jean-Louis Py's Eurocorps, the International Security Assistance Force (ISAF) VI had finished its initial expansion stage beyond Kabul in October. With Stage 1, Germany had taken responsibility for the nine provinces of Regional Command (North). Turkey's General Etham Erdagi, would follow Py and take up the reins of ISAF VII in February 2005. During this rotation, ISAF began its Stage 2 expansion into the four provinces comprising Regional Command (West) where Italy would take command.

The Americans would continue to operate separately from ISAF in the east and in the south under Operation ENDURING FREEDOM. There was, however, already a plan in the works for ISAF to relieve the Americans in the six southern provinces. ISAF planned its Stage 3 expansion to take place in the summer of 2006. The process would start under ISAF VIII, a longer, nine-month tour led by the Italians beginning in August 2005 and planned to finish under ISAF IX, also a nine-month tour led by the British, beginning in May 2006.

Canada's Roto 2 of Operation ATHENA began on August 9th, 2004. Its Task Force KABUL structure differed substantially from its predecessors. With the brigade headquarters, the artillery and the bulk of the battlegroup gone, what remained were the national command element and the national support element. To this, National Defence headquarters added a reconnaissance (recce) squadron from the Lord Strathcona's Horse (Royal Canadians) and B Company from the 1st Battalion, Princess Patricia's Light Infantry with two platoons—one each from A and B Companies—to provide camp security and a mounted quick reaction force (QRF). 11 Field Squadron from 1 Combat Engineer Regiment, an all-source intelligence centre, a civil-military co-operation detachment, a military police detachment, an embedded training team and medical resources rounded out the contingent. Without an intervening Canadian brigade group or battlegroup headquarters, the Canadian Task Force KABUL commander had operational command of the various tactical subunits.

Joining them was an 80 member mission drawdown team provided by the Canadian Forces Joint Support Group. They had already begun the complicated task of tearing down, cleaning, servicing, and packing all equipment, which would be surplus to the needs of the remaining Kabul rotations. The team would either return excess equipment to Canada or put it in storage for a future provincial reconstruction team (PRT) mission.[1]

Roto 2 experienced an almost immediate deterioration of the security situation in its area of operations, with a noticeable increase in improvised explosive devices (IED) and rocket attacks. Conversely, an expected increase in violence leading up to the presidential election on October 9th did not occur. Instead, it happened in the election's aftermath as Afghan security forces stood down and went on leave. The various coordinated attacks that followed clarified that the Taliban were very much working on their own timetable.[2]

In mid-February 2005, Roto 3 arrived. Structured similarly to Roto 2, it drew its infantry from A (Duke's) Company of the 1st Battalion, The Royal Canadian Regiment, its recce squadron from the Royal Canadian Dragoons and its engineers from 23 Field Squadron of 2 Combat Engineer Regiment.

This rotation would continue to provide a recce element and a quick reaction force while continuing with the tear down of Camp JULIEN to prepare for returning the land to the Afghan government.

While the artillery's role had ended with Roto 1, gunners did continue to serve in Kabul during Rotos 2 and 3 as well as for what would start off as Roto 4 and transition into Operation ARCHER.[3]

As early as Roto 0 of Operation ATHENA, there had been Canadian involvement in the training for the Afghan army. At first, 21 personnel formed an embedded training team with the 1st Kandak[4] of the 1st Brigade of the 201st Corps, which was based in the presidential palace in Kabul. Their activities included a program of instruction by Master Warrant Officer Nelson Lizotte. Lizotte operated out of the Americans' Camp PHOENIX, near Camp WAREHOUSE. He and several members of F Battery trained the Kandak's support company in the operation of old Soviet and Chinese 82mm mortars.[5] Lizotte had the mortars and the ammunition but no firing tables. To solve this problem, he went to the battery to see Warrant Officer Dennis Franken for a set of 81mm mortar firing tables which he used to develop ones for the 82mm mortars.[6]

Training efforts became more formalized under Operation ARCHER, which began on October 7th, 2004. With this operation, Canada integrated its *ad hoc* training efforts with those of the Americans. Under Operation ARCHER, four Canadian staff officers joined those of the headquarters of the American's Combined Forces Command-Afghanistan in Kabul. Another two went to the Combined Joint Task Force-76 headquarters in Bagram, and fourteen personnel joined Combined Joint Task Force PHOENIX III in Kabul. PHOENIX III was formed primarily from the Indiana Army National Guard's 76th Infantry Brigade Combat Team.

In the early spring of 2005, Major Mike Sullivan, the battery commander of F Battery, 2nd Regiment, Royal Canadian Horse Artillery (2 RCHA), received a warning order that some of his officers and several other members of the brigade and a few reservists, would join the Florida Army National Guard's 53rd Infantry Brigade Combat Team.[7] The 53rd would relieve the 76th for Combined Joint Task Force PHOENIX IV. Joining Sullivan would be Captains Jason Chetwynd and David Brassard, and Lieutenant Tom Hicks, all from F Battery, as well three other captains, a warrant officer, and five sergeants from other units.

The team proceeded through 2 Canadian Mechanized Brigade Group's Roto 4 pre-deployment training for a scheduled August 2005 deployment. The training included some excellent cross-cultural instruction from Professors Jim Murray of Optimal Solutions International and Sergei Plekhanov of York University. Sullivan also went on a recce to Kabul, where he encountered both a flood and rioting at the Kabul Military Training Center amongst a Kandak split on tribal lines. The team deployed a bit early, in July.

PHOENIX split the training for the Afghan army in Kabul into several lines of effort. The American National Guard taught basic training, the French presented officer training, the British did non-commissioned officer training, and the Germans provided armour training on ancient T-54s, T-55s and T-62s tanks. For a period, Mongolian artillerymen trained Afghans on old Soviet D-30 122mm howitzers. US Marines were also involved. They now provided the embedded training teams for Kabul's 201st Corps. Canada's role would be collective training.

By the time Sullivan's team deployed, the Canadian brigade headquarters was gone. Task Force KABUL had pulled all remaining Canadian troops into Camp JULIEN at the far southern end of the city. As a result, Sullivan's team moved into accommodations in the northeastern part of the city with the US Marines who proved to be excellent hosts.

Combined Forces Command-Afghanistan mandated a training system to rapidly grow the Afghan National Army. Essentially, once recruits entered the centre, they were split into soldier, officer and non-commissioned officer streams. Those in the soldier stream receive a seven-week basic training course followed by a six-week course of advanced individual training in their specialty. Upon completion of this individual training period the instructors combined all soldiers, officers and non-commissioned officers into a Kandak. This Kandak was then turned over to the Canadians for three weeks of collective light infantry training before being sent off to their new duty post. This last phase of collective training did not include any of the combined arms enablers such as tanks or artillery.

The brigade provided fifteen interpreters to Sullivan's team. For the collective training phase, each Kandak was now under its own leadership. Effectively, each of Sullivan's trainers was supervising a platoon of roughly 30 Afghans. Notwithstanding the availability of interpreters, language remained a problem. The American Central Intelligence Agency handlers who vetted recruits, had deliberately blended each Kandak at intake into mixed tribal groups.[8] Most training had to be doubly translated into both Pashto and Dari.

Upon his arrival, Sullivan changed two things immediately. First, he locally renamed his contingent from the Canadian Afghanistan National Training Centre to the National Training Centre (Canada-Afghanistan). The Americans had teasingly referred to its former acronym—CANTC—as "Can't See". Second, and much more important, Sullivan introduced live-fire exercises into the training regime. In order to conduct standardized preparatory training prior to any live-fire exercises, Sullivan requisitioned all the blank ammunition and blank firing attachments available for the various Kalashnikov rifle variants in use.

Sullivan's single most significant negative observation about the training system was that it did not cater to the norms of Afghan culture. While the Central Intelligence Agency's mixing of intakes into cross-cultural groups may have lessened the chance of creating Kandaks more loyal to a tribal region rather than the central government, it also created language and cohesion problems. Similarly, western concepts of delegation simply did not work well in an Afghan setting. He observed that,

> In a culture that if you are weak, you delegate things; to come up with a tactical system, a doctrine that is based on respect and successive delegation of command and control, it might be slightly out of line. General Karimi had said that [non-commissioned officer] in the Afghan language basically means "officer failure" and he suggested several times that we want to re-look at the concept...In their system, officers account for bullets, hand out individual rounds for a live fire range. This is not our system, but again, we try to impose our own system on them.

Sullivan's team soldiered on until January 2006 when they were replaced by a new rotation furnished from personnel in 1st Canadian Mechanized Brigade Group.

With the departure of Roto 1, airspace coordination underwent a major change. NATO's Eurocorps formed ISAF VI and placed its airspace coordination functions around a French air defence detachment in the Kabul Multinational Brigade headquarters. While this detachment had the framework of a system left to them by the Canadians, they had only a superficial knowledge of airspace management measures. Concurrently, within the ISAF headquarters, a newly formed Theatre Air Operations Centre, staffed primarily by aviators who had little understanding of ground-based tactical operations, increased its control over ISAF's operational airspace.

Canada's Roto 2 contribution to ISAF VI airspace management was Captain Linda Shrum, an air defence artillery officer, who arrived at the Kabul Multinational Brigade shortly after Roto 1's departure. Shrum, trained both as a field and air defence artillery officer, could bridge the training and doctrinal void which plagued most NATO countries regarding tactical level joint operations in complex terrain like Afghanistan.

Her solution to the problem was to create a joint operating centre called the Tactical Airspace Operations Cell within the Kabul Multinational Brigade headquarters. It merged the airspace coordination cell with the air and aviation cells, and integrated airspace operational control into the brigade's joint operations centre. Unfortunately, the structure did not survive long. A new senior European staff officer arrived to take charge of the airspace control and air and aviation cells, and things changed. A decreased capacity in the airspace control cell for ISAF VII resulted in the more complex tasks being shipped up from the Kabul Multinational Brigade directly to the ISAF Tactical Air Operations Cell.[9]

Canadian airspace coordination experiences spanning Rotos 0 to 2 in Kabul clarified that there was a capability gap within NATO regarding integrating joint airspace coordination into tactical level operations in complex theatres. For Canadian gunners, the experience that they had gained in Kabul would soon serve them well on other missions.

Roto 0 and 1's primary goals under Generals Leslie and Hillier, had been to provide security during the constitutional *Loya Jirga,* and the disarmament of the Afghan militias. There had also been a subtle, but growing shift to taking ISAF beyond Kabul, and to the creation of an effective and stable government. To further this aim, Hillier had tasked some twenty of his Canadian officers as strategic planning staff. Their purpose was to teach the Afghans the fundamentals of responsible government.[10] That team returned to Canada with General Hillier at the end of Roto 1. ISAF's leadership did not continue this concept on subsequent rotations.

Once Hillier became the Chief of the Defence Staff, however, and at the request of Hamid Karzai, he won the support of the Canadian government to continue the initiative. He also obtained grudging acceptance from the Department of Foreign Affairs and International Trade for such a mission.

In June 2005, Colonel Michael Capstick, a gunner officer working at the army's headquarters in Ottawa, was at his home when he received a call to meet with Hillier the next morning. The meeting was a short one. Hillier offered Mike the job of heading what would soon be called the Strategic Advisory Team-Afghanistan and promised him whatever resources he needed to get the job done.

Capstick's first call was to Lieutenant-Colonel Ivars Mezitis, the commanding officer of the 1st Regiment, Royal Canadian Horse Artillery (1 RCHA), to arrange for Sergeant John MacPherson—Mike's former driver—to be assigned to be the team's chief administrator and logistician. Major Tim Lannan would be the third and final gunner to get the call. His job would be to work as an advisor to the Afghan Rural Redevelopment Ministry.

True to Hillier's word, all obstacles within National Defence were quickly overcome. Things would not go so smoothly with Foreign Affairs' bureaucracy, whose resistance to the idea was subtle but palpable from the first planning meeting.[11] Notwithstanding only grudging cooperation from Foreign Affairs, Capstick brought together a team of twelve military officers—from all three elements and both the regular and reserve forces—two National Defence civilians and a member from the Canadian International Development Agency. They would report directly to the Chief of Defence Staff[12] and deploy under a new operation named Operation ARGUS.

The team deployed in August 2005 for what would be a fifteen month rotation. Capstick quickly secured the support of Canada's Head of Mission, Christopher Alexander and Head of Aid, Dr. Nipa Banerjee respectively. He also developed a relationship with Dr. Ishaq Naderi, the Senior Economic Advisor to President Karzai.[13]

The key to the team's success was that it did not offer advice to the Afghan ministries regarding specific fields, such as agriculture or health. Instead, they offered advice on the mechanics of operational and strategic organization and planning.

Two issues, however, would plague the team and, in fact, the overall effort in Afghanistan. For the team itself, the issue was inter-agency jealousy. Several non-governmental organizations opposed the idea of the military advising the Afghan government. This wasn't helped by critics within the Department of Foreign Affairs and International Trade and the Privy Council Office. Hillier was of the view that these agencies didn't want the military to take credit when those agencies themselves were failing to provide the staff that they had promised.[14]

For Afghanistan, the issue was the fact that, at the international level, there was no unity of the military stability and force generation efforts on the one hand,

and the humanitarian and reconstruction assistance efforts on the other. The brief tours of senior commanders, even once the Americans started commanding ISAF, mitigated against a continuing, coherent strategy. Capstick would subsequently say that it was long past due for the Secretaries General of the UN and NATO to agree to appoint a powerful, high-profile joint representative to coordinate all aspects of the international civil-military effort.[15]

Other rotations would follow, but Canada would stand the team down in 2008 when Colonel Serge Labbe was its commander. Historian David Bercuson concluded that once Alexander left the embassy in Kabul, the Strategic Advisory Team-Afghanistan's days were numbered. His successors reduced the cooperation he had fostered and worked to close the team down.[16]

While individual gunners toiled away in Afghanistan during 2004 and 2005, events were unfolding in Ottawa, which would have major consequences for Canada's artillery.

In August of 2004, Hillier returned to Canada and resumed his job as Chief of Land Staff but with plans to retire. He had known before returning to Ottawa that Canada would stay in Afghanistan after the Kabul mission ended. The Chief of Defence Staff, General Ray Henault, told Hillier that the NATO was strongly pressuring Canada to take on the Regional Command (West) PRT in Herat. Hillier advocated that there was more visibility for Canada to take over the operation and development of Kabul International Airport. The government, however, was resistant to both Herat and Kabul airport and favoured a mission in Kandahar.[17]

As summer turned to fall, it became apparent that Canada would need a new Chief of Defence Staff. Henault had been elected to the position of Chairman of NATO's Military Committee. Hillier delayed his retirement and threw his hat into the ring. After a meeting with the Prime Minister in December, Hillier felt he had the job. The Minister of National Defence, Bill Graham, announced the decision on January 14th, 2005. Hillier, at that time, was working on the government's upcoming defence policy paper. It was to be the first such paper that Canada had issued in ten years and was very much meant to orient Canada towards a new focus on international engagement.

On February 13th, 2005, Defence Minister Graham announced Canada was considering doubling the size of its force in Afghanistan from 600 to 1,200 and taking over the American PRT in Kandahar in August of that year. He even speculated that it could include a brigade in the spring of 2006, which could take part in combat operations under the Americans' Operation ENDURING FREEDOM.[18]

The final decision to send additional troops—a battle group and a brigade headquarters—occurred at a meeting between the Prime Minister, his inner circle, and Hillier on March 21st, 2005.[19] Hillier followed this with an announcement that Canada would deploy to, and put its focus on, Kandahar.[20] By the end of the month, Lieutenant-Colonel Ian Hope, the commanding officer of the 1st Battalion, Princess Patricia's Canadian Light Infantry, had been told his battalion would form the core of the battle group and they would deploy to Kandahar early in 2006.[21]

Wasting little time, Canada announced on May 17th its firm plans to deploy 1,250 troops to Kandahar, starting with a PRT.[22] The mission would also involve the Canadian International Development Agency, the Department of Foreign Affairs and International Trade, the Royal Canadian Mounted Police and the Department of Correctional Service Canada. Since ISAF would not be expanding into the south until the summer of 2006, the Canadian contingent would work with the Americans while taking over their responsibilities bit-by-bit. Canada added this new commitment to the existing Operation ARCHER. The public would soon realize that the size of the mission had grown.

While planning the move to Kandahar was underway, the government released its new defence policy paper in April, alongside one for foreign affairs. It promised that "the Canadian Forces will pursue their transformation efforts with renewed vigour and focus".[23] As expected, it shifted direction from a Cold War scenario to failed states, terrorism, the spread of weapons of mass destruction, and regional flashpoints.[24]

Hillier's theme in the defence policy paper was to completely transform the Canadian Forces. He planned to take them from a Cold War-oriented military which was both bureaucratic and process-focused into one which was combat-capable and modern.[25] Throughout the spring of 2005 he worked on his vision, and by the first of July, steps were being taken to reform the Canadian Forces' command-and-control structure. The Deputy Chief of Defence Staff's organization transformed into a more focused, agile and responsive Canadian Expeditionary Force Command. It assumed control over all such operations on February 1st, 2006.[26]

While National Defence Headquarters wrestled with the challenge of transforming to a new mission and organization,[27] Canada's army continued with its own transformation plans. These had hit full stride when Hillier was Chief of Land Staff. It did so now with the advertised "renewed vigour". What that renewed vigour would mean for the artillery was the question.

As early as 2004, Major Bruno Di Ilio, Director Land Requirements 2-3, gave a briefing to the instructor in gunnery course at Gagetown, which addressed the then current equipment situation within the artillery. A key component was that the army recommended disposal of the recently upgraded 155mm M109A4+, which equipped six of the nine regular force field batteries. These were considered as "not suitable to support the land force". The briefing also described that there was no expectation that the Future Indirect Fire Capability project would have a replacement gun in service until 2015. In short, there would be a ten-year capability gap where the artillery would only have the 105 mm C3 and LG1 light howitzers.[28] There were some thoughts on digitizing and modernizing these guns by mounting them on a vehicle under the Mobile Artillery Vehicle System project. While new equipment such as the light armoured vehicle (LAV) observation post vehicle and other projects to enhance digitization were seen as positive indicators of modernization, the outlook for a possible indirect fire delivery system looked bleak.

For air defence, the picture was equally dismal. The Oerlikon Twin 35mm GDF-005 and Skyguard FC Radar were nearing the end of their life cycle. The writing had been on the wall for them for some time considering that their original purpose had been airfield defence in Germany.[29] Their demise was sealed when the Chief of Land Staff signed the Air Defence Transformation Warning Order which would see the regiment amalgamated with the Lord Starthcona's Horse (Royal Canadians) as a direct fire unit. The Oerlikons fired their last rounds on April 26th, 2005.[30] Their crews converted to the Air Defence Anti-Tank System which had been in service since 1989. The Very Short Range Air Defence (VSHORAD) Javelin Man Portable Air Defence System (MANPADS) was being retired from service also, as it was being considered "unnecessary" within the army.[31] As the Javelin was being withdrawn from service, the reserve force air defence units became redundant, and would subsequently revert to field artillery units. Their three Airspace Coordination Centres (ASCC) would be absorbed directly into 4th Air Defence Regiment, RCA (4 AD Regt).

While the Air Defence Anti-Tank System was being kept—and in fact being considered for modernization onto a LAV chassis under the Multi-Mission Effects Vehicle project—it had less to do with air defence and more to do with the notion of marrying the system into a direct fire unit. This also involved the infantry's Tube-launched, Optically tracked, Wire guided Under Armour anti-armour missile system,, and the Mobile Gun System, all based on the LAV chassis. The latter was funded but had not yet been acquired. The concept was exercised several times but with Leopard C1 tanks playing the role of the as yet unacquired Mobile Gun System. In 2004, 4 AD Regt fired more missiles in the anti-tank role than in the air defence role. The direct fire unit was very much a part of the artillery and the armoured corps' fight to remain relevant in an infantry-centric army.[32]

At the end of the day, the air defence branch would lose 151 regulars and every single reservist from what had been a high of 475 regulars and 430 reservists. If there was a bright spot, it was that airspace coordination was here to stay. The path was clear, even if depressing. Events would soon muddy it.

If losing guns and air defence personnel wasn't enough, during 2004 to 2005, the RCAF had continued its push to take over Sperwer. By May 2005, there had been a decision to stand up two RCAF led rotations for Kandahar in 2006.[33] The agreement was that the RCAF would be the force generator and the army the force employer. 1 Wing, specifically 408 Tactical Helicopter Squadron from Edmonton, would have the lead. A new establishment for a tactical unmanned aerial vehicle (UAV) flight of 56 personnel drawn from both the RCAF and the army—including several gunners—came together in Valcartier in May 2005 to start their training. They would use the Sperwers that had returned with the 5e Régiment d'artillerie légère du Canada (5 RALC) from Kabul. SAGEM again led the training, and once again in French for a mixed French and English-speaking audience.[34]

The artillery, which had "gone through more than a decade of trying to remain relevant,"[35] did not give way entirely and pushed for a broader continued role in the UAV field. It wasn't about to give up a new capability easily and was staffing an unforecast operational requirement up to the Vice Chief of Defence Staff to deploy a miniature UAV to Kandahar. Options included the Elbit Skylark and the EADS Tracker.[36]

This initiative had an interesting genesis. Upon their return from Roto 1, Tony Tullett, promoted to Sergeant while in Kabul, and Bombardier Peter Sova had gone back to W Battery's air defence troop. Here they were asked if they were interested in joining a new surveillance and target acquisition (STA) troop being stood up in Gagetown under Captain Scott Lang, an air defence officer, and Warrant Officer Brian Williams. They were definitely interested. The troop soon grew to around twenty all ranks with Master Bombardier Keith McLean and Bombardier Dominic Antle joining them along with others from Roto 0. Their purpose was to explore the ins and outs of operating various types of commercial remote control aircraft, simulators, and sensor systems in order to develop tactics, techniques, and procedures to use this new equipment. Along the way, they experimented with yet another modified Vindicator target drone produced by Meggitt.

This experimentation progressed throughout the latter part of 2004 and into 2005 when they received word that Canada would deploy a yet to be chosen miniature UAV as part of Task Force 3-06 in the later part of 2006. The process would eventually end on an exceedingly rainy day on the Golan Heights where an evaluation team from Ottawa never left their bus while they observed Tullett's group operate a Skylark in the rain.[37] Skylark would get the nod for acquisition.

For the field artillery, nowhere was the Canadian Force's vigorous transformation clearer than in the implementation directive issued to it in July by the then Chief of Land Staff, Lieutenant-General Marc Caron.[38] This directive would shape the field artillery for decades to come and constituted its response to remaining relevant within the framework of the transforming army.[39] Effectively, it stated that the regular force field artillery would transform from being primarily gun centric in order to provide the personnel needed to increase the number of forward observation officers (FOO), to flesh out the fire support coordination centres (FSCC), and to create an surveillance and target acquisition function consisting of miniature UAVs and weapon locating sensors. The directive would:

- reduce gun detachments from 54 to 24 (concurrently reducing each regiment from three six-gun to two four-gun batteries);
- create 9 FSCC detachments;[40]
- increase the number of FOO detachments from 18 to 27; and
- convert three gun batteries to a total of 6 miniature UAV troops and 3 weapon locating sensor troops.

Just as important, the concept of operations provided that artillery regiments would cease being force employers but simply become force generation structures that would produce batteries and such personnel as necessary for a formation-level FSCC. The Director Land Strategic Plans had concluded that the army could only sustain one battlegroup and a brigade headquarters in one theatre rotating every six months while simultaneously sustaining a second battlegroup in another theatre. The artillery would support the former with a single gun battery, the necessary elements to coordinate fire at the formation level and an ASCC. Hence, there was no role for the deployment of an artillery regiment. Another contentious issue arising out of these discussions was that combat service support would operate out of a national support element structure, as it had been in Kabul.[41] This decision would later impact the artillery's greatest logistics requirement—the timely supply of ammunition. The army had created the operational model that it would follow throughout its commitment to Afghanistan.

The stated intent for the artillery was to "direct, coordinate and deliver precise lethal and non-lethal effects from integral, joint and coalition assets".[42] For the artillery, the mission element would become the troop grouped into composite batteries. The directive recognized that four gun detachments per battery were inadequate, and it directed that the reserves be prepared to augment each deployment with two formed detachments and individual augmentees.

Under the directive, the M109s, on which training had already been stopped, were to be withdrawn from service[43]. 1 RCHA fired its last rounds on February 25th and, after 37 years of service the guns were retired.[44]

It was also clear at this time that the artillery's only other "operational gun", the LG1, was showing dangerous signs of barrel cracking. Chief Warrant Officer Ken Whitnall, who would become the life cycle materiel manager for the army's howitzer fleet notes that when the guns returned from Kabul they,

> ...were placed in depot holding pending a service contract with GIAT for inspection and repair.

> As the repatriated LG1s were going through inspection and repair in 2004, cracks were discovered...at the muzzle brake keyway. As a result, the entire LG1 fleet had the barrels removed and sent to a contractor in Toronto for [non destructive testing] for cracks ... By 2005, after inspecting all the howitzers and spare barrels in stock there were only 9 serviceable LG1 barrels in the CF. At the time there was still the requirement to have a deployable [battery] so 6 serviceable barrels were mounted on LG1s at 5 RALC, one good barrel was on a gun at 1 RCHA Shilo...All LG1 howitzers aside from the 7 guns that had serviceable barrels mounted had cracked barrels mounted and were under firing restrictions.[45]

This was not the LG1's only problem. During 2003 and 2004, wear determination trials were held using the 105mm C132 High Explosive-Extended Range ammunition with both the LG1 and C3 howitzers. Whitnall:

> During the C132 development the driving band was changed from copper-bronze to sintered iron. Both the LG1 and the C3 have progressive rifling with the C3 being the more difficult to achieve stable results. The sintered iron driving band was needed for the zone 2 firings.

> The important data in my mind coming from those trials was [that] a brand new LG1 barrel was rendered non-operational after firing less than 600 rounds of C132 Zone 2 (high zone). [The Directorate of Ammunition] knew the C132 HEER [high explosive extended range] round was going to erode the barrels more than normal due to the propellant used; however, the extent of the wear was not fully known until the wear determination trials. Unfortunately 80,000 rounds of C132 were already in stock.[46]

The C3 howitzer had problems of its own. RDM, the Dutch company that had converted Canada's C1 howitzers to C3s and had a support contract for them, went bankrupt in 2004. Nedefco, the company that had bought RDM's tools, spares, and its service contract also went bankrupt later that year. Whitnall recalls that, "By 2006, [the Directorate Armament Sustainment Programme Management 3] had been trying to sustain the C3 fleet by using available spares from depot stock. By ...2006 1/3 of the C3 fleet was non-operational due to recoil mechanisms needing rebuild."[47] Moreover, "The results of the C132 wear determination trials were interesting...because it showed the accuracy of the C3 using the C132 was poor at the far terminal end even with a serviceable barrel."[48]

A new gun was needed for operational deployments ... and quickly.

The Chief of Land Staff's field artillery transformation directive, while not specifying any one gun in particular, resolved that "the Army will acquire a lightweight 155 mm howitzer and the requisite precision munitions as soon as practical". This was not of the class of guns being contemplated for the unfunded Future Indirect Fires procurement project, which was to provide an eventual in-service replacement for the LG1s and the divested M109s. The needs were more immediate and so the search was on for a suitable gun to support the upcoming commitment of a battle group to Operation ARCHER.

The original table of organization given to Brigadier General Fraser called for a 105mm howitzer which was the calibre which was used to good effect by the Americans in Afghanistan and would be used by the British as well. A recce visit to Afghanistan confirmed the view that the operational requirements would be better fulfilled by a 155mm calibre gun which would provide better effects, longer range and thereby less need to move the guns improving gun troops' safety. The visit also confirmed for Fraser the need to have an artillery advisor and expert in his headquarters.[49]

It would, once again, go the route of another unforecasted operational requirement.

Under consideration, if it was available, was the "Triple Seven"—the M777 Lightweight 155mm Towed Howitzer—which was just entering service in the US. Concurrently, staff checks were being conducted at the Royal Canadian Artillery School to determine if its predecessor, the old venerable M198 155mm towed howitzer, which the M777 was replacing in the US inventory, would serve if the new M777 was not available in time.

At that time, the M777 was not even in full scale production. What was coming off the assembly line, in the fall of 2005, was a "low rate initial production" run of 94 guns destined mainly for the US Marine Corps and later the US Army.[50] Accessing the M777 required that either one or the other of those organizations cede their guns and earmark them for Canada.

Major-General Leslie, the then Assistant Chief of the Land Staff, recalls:

First and foremost, there's a couple of unsung heroes which were literally game changers in the acquisition of the M777. Dan Ross, [the Assistant Deputy Minister (Material)]...Another was Colonel Chris Simonds...who at the time was in the Minister's office as the Military [Executive Assistant] to the Minister.

So based on the analysis, the requirement for the range and the precision and the air transportability and there's a whole host of other factors that indicated that [a self propelled] gun wouldn't cut it—we needed something that could be moved around relatively easily, certainly by heavy helicopter...There [were] very few choices - a quick analysis was done by [Director Land Requirements]—it looked more and more that the brand new Triple 7 now coming off the assembly line down in the States mainly for delivery to the Marine Corps and later the US Army, would be the weapon system of choice

...we had a good relationship with the Commandant of the Marine Corps... the Marines had availability and there was enthusiasm to support.

Dan Ross led; marshaled all the instruments of power that he had as [Assistant Deputy Minister (Materiel)]. I worked the town at my level, he did incredibly good work at his and Chris Simonds convinced, essentially convinced a variety of folk at the political level that this had to get done... Dozens, hundreds of people were all pulling in the same direction. It was a magnificent effort...[51]

Brigadier-General Fraser as well, made contact with the deputy commandant of the Marines and solicited and gained his support for the Canadians.[52] Leslie recalls that the original number of six guns was as a result of "horse trading".[53]

We wanted to equip a regiment based on the argument that you wanted to train with what you were going to send your soldiers overseas to fight on. That didn't receive a lot of support because there were many other things we had to get. And yes, we were leveraging the Afghan experience to reequip the army and that train of thought carried on for the next four or five years but we were also basing the asks for equipment on need and we had to prioritize.

And one of the big constraints, probably the one single largest, was [that] at the same time that we were asking the United States to give us six incredibly advanced, well actually state-of-the-art technology worldwide, they themselves had more troops than us by an order of magnitude in harm's way and they needed them as well and there's really only one source and we got the Commandant to agree to give us six of his guns. But asking for twelve or eighteen would have meant his soldiers would have been disadvantaged.[54]

With the decision on which gun and how many made, procurement took over.

The Lightweight 155mm Towed Howitzer project stood up in the Directorate of Land Requirements with Major Bruno Di Ilio as the project director. Under it, approval was sought for the purchase of up to twelve M777s with associated operator and maintenance stores and equipment, a howitzer digitization system, two years of logistics support, a number of XM982 Excalibur projectiles and modular charges and training all by way of a Foreign Military Sale for an all up price of $96,206,000.[55]

The project received Chief of Defence Staff approval for the purchase of six M777s and thirty Excalibur rounds on August 31, 2005.[56] Treasury Board approval came on October 17, 2005.[57]

With procurement underway, A Battery's commander, Major Steve Gallagher, deployed on a tactical recce to Kandahar to meet with Task Force GUN DEVIL,[58] and review how they employed their artillery. His report[59] was followed at the end of November by a training directive for the first six M777s issued by the Land Force Doctrine and Training System headquarters.[60]

A second group of six M777s would become available in 2006 when there was a pause after the Marines had equipped and sent their Marine Expeditionary Force into Iraq.[61] Ken Whitnall recalls that,

> *The first 6 guns were purchased from the USMC under [a Foreign Military Sale (FMS)] case for [an unforecasted operational requirement]. The first FMS case with the US included a standard spares pack for each gun, user training and tech training. The second 6 guns were also purchased from the USMC, another FMS case. The second FMS case included the standard spares pack for each gun, more tech training and a vast list of spares above and beyond the standard spares packs.*
>
> *There was also a third FMS case based on another [unforecasted operational requirement] that was outlined as a rental contract for us to receive 2 guns to replace guns that were damaged in theatre and had a long lead repair times in the UK and US. Every time we needed M777 spares we did not have, it was another FMS case with the US based on the [unforecasted operational requirement] as we did not have any support contract with the US or BAE as the whole M777 fleet at that time was a [unforecasted operational requirement] fleet. The US M777 JPMO (Joint Project Management Office) was very accommodating to us because we were in the fight in Afghanistan. More than once the US robbed M777 parts from their production line and redirected them to Canada for use in theatre. The M777 production in Hattiesburg was all scheduled for just-in-time parts delivery. The Canadian requirement for additional spares to sustain operations was all unscheduled.[62]*

Many saw the army's divestment of the M109 as a mistake. This included the then Assistant Deputy Minister (Materiel), Dan Ross, a former gunner, who had taken over the job in May 2005.[63] The army had already taken all the key decisions about transforming the artillery before Ross took on his job. The Chief of Land Staff directive only encapsulated the prior internal discussion within the army. Ross did not like the direction that the army had taken.

> We had this managed readiness concept. I called it managed unreadiness, because that's what it was. You're picking this very tiny piece of the army to be ready to go do something—maybe one rotation—and the rest of it was parked against the fence. The army could not afford its maintenance bills, could not afford its fuel bills...
>
> It was fundamentally resource allocation starvation that forced almost ad hoc responses and policies and strategies...
>
> From mid 1990s to around 2005, the army decided it needed to divest capabilities for two reasons. One, the infantry didn't think they needed it because no one had shot at them for fifteen years and, secondly, the maintenance and operational costs were too high. And that is a complicated question in itself. So we started to see the decisions that started with Mike Jeffery fighting the battle for M109s and lost. He won the battle briefly. Rick Hillier came in and the M109s were gone. Then the plan was to divest all Leopards; divest TOW Under Armour; divest Eryx missile systems...And then no new investments in things like electronic warfare or UAVs and so on. So combined with resource starvation...the army was in this long, long glide slope of divesting capabilities. Everything except stuff that's in an infantry company, effectively. So, they convinced themselves they are a LAV-based army and if the rifle company had their 60mm mortars and [general-purpose machine guns] and LAVs, life was good enough.[64]

These decisions had an effect in Afghanistan. Ross: "Of course, once when we went down from Kabul down to Kandahar and actually started to get shot at, Andy [Leslie] and I had to rebuild fundamental capabilities of the army. The LAV 3 armour is seven millimetres thick. On the belly it's three millimetres thick. Casualties resulted from the inadequacy of both the mobility and the protection of the LAV 3."[65]

While finances played a role, Ross was of the view that the decisions made were primarily the army's. "Some of this was political, but not very much ... I would say it was 75% internal to the army. The divestment of capability was 75% internal ... To be fair to both Hillier and Caron, there was a lot of pressure on army funding that was kind of unique and much, much more severe than it was on the air force or the navy."[66]

For the artillery, the equipment situation had reached a crisis point. In September 2005, Ross went to look at all the army's equipment in one place at the Combat Training Centre in Gagetown where, many years before, he had served as an instructor in gunnery. The visit included a tour of the artillery school's gun shed. He recalls,

> *The gun shed was almost empty. There [were] two M109s wrapped up in plastic—they were going to be shipped to Montreal to be chopped up—and there were a few LG1s on the floor and a few C3s...The bottom line of that visit was that the army had one operational gun; Canada had one operational gun because the C3s had the wheels falling off ... and [Director Land Requirements (DLR)] wasn't allocating any national procurement money for maintenance of artillery. The LG1s had shot out 27 barrels of the 28 by the defective ammunition that [Director General Land Equipment Program Management (DGLEPM)] had designed and bought. The driving bands were too hard, and they had ripped out the rifling halfway down the barrel...*
>
> *So I came back to Ottawa, and I was actually extremely upset and I talked to DGLEPM and I said "I need new barrels for the LG1s" and he said "Well there's no money." [I] said "Why's there no money?" and he said "Because [Director Land Requirements] does not allocate [national procurement funds] for artillery systems."[67] So it was a couple of million dollars and they did not have a couple of million dollars to re-barrel LG1s, nor was there interest in repairing the suspensions of the C3s and, as I said, the M109 conversation had already passed.[68]*

Ross reallocated funds from the broader program to buy 28 barrels and gave direction on remediating the C3 problem. Both were eventually actioned.

Ross was convinced that the army could have modernized and upgraded at least some of the 76 M109s to M109A6 Paladin status. He strongly believed in a balanced fleet. The army didn't or believed it couldn't.[69] Ross:

> *So what we ended up getting was nothing that had protection and mobility ... we bought twelve [M777s by Foreign Military Sales (FMS)] and we bought the final twenty-five FMS and then the army said "Okay. Well, that's good enough. We really only need eight operational guns times three regiments and that's good enough." But unless you have a Chinook, or a monster truck, and a great big road and a big, flat, dry field, [its] actually not very employable.[70]*

Throughout, no discussion took place as to putting any of the M109s into reserve. A number of them were cut up for scrap. Ross stopped their destruction in favour of having them converted into memorials and to have twenty-six put into storage along with six M578 tracked recovery vehicles for a few years. These last few M109s too eventually went the memorial route in 2008. Ross was adamant that, "From a business point of view, there were some really, really bad decisions made. I mean, the cost of what it would have taken to upgrade twenty-five A5s (sic) to A6 Paladins and buy half as many M777s would have been a good business case."[71]

The American army had learned a lesson about the role of the artillery in the recent war in Iraq. General (Retd) Barry R McCaffrey, the commanding general of the 24th Infantry Division (mechanized) considered the artillery to be the dominant tactical weapon during Operation DESERT STORM because of its ability to deliver numerous, rapid effects—from suppression to illumination to smoke—at all times, in all weather.[72]

It was a lesson that had clearly sailed over the heads of those transforming Canada's army.

Having directives on transformation is one thing, achieving them is an entirely different set of problems. By September of 2005 an outline for the artillery transformation plan was readied for an upcoming artillery working group meeting for early October.[73] It would point to 2008 as the year when all the moving parts would finally be in place.

While the artillery was wrestling with vital issues, the pace of the move to Kandahar did not lessen. Events unfurled rapidly in Afghanistan.

On June 29th 2005, a 220 person theatre activation team from the Canadian Forces Joint Operations Support Group departed Kingston for Kandahar. Operation ATHENA's Roto 3, after having moved some equipment south, completed its tour in Kabul. Duke's Company, 1st Battalion, The Royal Canadian Regiment, returned home in time for a unit change in command to Lieutenant-Colonel Omer Lavoie. His job was to prepare his battalion for its mission to Afghanistan as Task Force 3-06 in the summer of 2006.

ATHENA Roto 4, replaced Roto 3. This new roto was a small battlegroup composed principally of D Squadron Royal Canadian Dragoons, G Company 2nd Battalion, The Royal Canadian Regiment and 24 Field Squadron, 2 Combat Engineer Regiment, all under the command of the Dragoons' Lieutenant-Colonel Lowell Thomas. Their role would be to provide security for the Kabul mission as it closed down the Canadian presence in Camp JULIEN and moved south.

Lieutenant Justin Brunelle, the gun position officer of F Battery, 2 RCHA, put his scheduled FOO course for 2005 on hold. Instead, he answered the call for an extra duty officer to work in the Dragoons' headquarters. He arrived in Kabul in the early summer, surprised to find the area lush with greenery rather than the high desert he had been expecting. Brunelle would spend the next two months in Kabul while the tear-down of JULIEN reached its climax.

Meanwhile, in Kandahar, on August 16th, 2005, the Americans officially transferred their PRT to 250 personnel from 1 Canadian Mechanized Brigade Group. This new Canadian unit now started up its work under Operation ARCHER. On October 13th, they would rename their base to Camp NATHAN SMITH in honour of one of the 3rd Battalion, Princess Patricia's Canadian Light Infantry soldiers killed in the Tarnak Farms friendly fire incident.

In August as well, Brigadier-General David Fraser, the commander of 1 Canadian Mechanized Brigade Group, came for a recce to Kandahar. He was designated to become the commander of Regional Command (South) and to command the Canadian brigade headquarters in Kandahar, starting early in 2006. His subordinate Canadian battle group would pave the way for British troops destined for Helmand, a Dutch contingent that would operate in Uruzgan, and an eventual transition of Regional Command (South) from the Americans to ISAF.[74]

Operation ATHENA Roto 4 ended on October 18th. Lieutenant-Colonel Thomas' tiny battlegroup now also transitioned to the existing Operation ARCHER. and turned its attention to convoying the rest of the personnel and equipment from Kabul to Kandahar.[75] For some six weeks, Brunelle worked out of the Americans' tactical operations centre in Bagram as a liaison officer. His role: assist with synchronizing the air support coverage for the Canadian convoys.

The operation had G Company working out of two American forward operating bases—GHAZNI, at the south end of the city of Ghazni, and LAGMAN, at the north end of the city of Qalat. They were part of a "steel tunnel" along Highway 1 that the convoys would pass through at night, escorted by a route clearance element from 24 Field Squadron and the Dragoons. While intelligence had provided clear indications of what pockets of threats existed along the route, no attacks of any consequence occurred. Camp JULIEN officially closed on November 29th, 2005.[76]

With the move complete, the remnants of Thomas's battle group no longer had any tactical function and were quickly dispersed. One who wasn't dispersed was Master Bombardier Steve Merson from 2 RCHA who had initially deployed with the battle group's G3. Merson had temporarily filled in as a driver for Colonel Michael Capstick in Kabul and was asked to continue on with the job. Finding little to do after having been moved to Kandahar, he agreed to the driver job and flew back to Kabul. He recalls:

> I ended up...doing kind of a close protection...for [Capstick] because I was the driver, I also took care of his security. Everywhere he went, I went with him ...We lived next to the embassy, the Pakistan Embassy, in downtown Kabul. It was called [Operation] ARGUS and it was the infrastructure. So he would go in...the place where the government was, Karzai and all them.

So I had a C-8 [assault rifle]. I had a nine [millimetre pistol]. I had a different kind of webbing. I had a South African SUV—armoured—with police lights in the front and a siren because I remember four lanes of traffic in Kabul that the colonel would always hit the siren to move everybody. But I had to slap his hand because he's a colonel, he's a target.[77]

Beyond driving for Capstick, Merson would be assigned at times to drive and provide security for various visitors from non-government agencies or government departments. On one occasion a dispute about where a civilian bus could stop drew a large crowd in front of the compound and Merson needed to be called out to assist one of the interpreters and the Canadians' two civilian armed gate guards to disperse them. Subsequently it was decided that a working dog would be of assistance in any future such incident and Merson went to the Americans to see what was available. Merson recalls: "So there was one dog. He was a Dutch Shepherd and he was all ribs. There was no meat on him because the [Afghan army] had been using them and they don't feed them. So when he came back, there was nothing to him. So of course I said, 'I want that one.'"[78] The dog was revived and thrived on a diet of Nutter Butter cookies provided by Merson and hunks of hamburger from Capstick and would thereafter accompany Merson whenever he did his rounds.

Back in Kandahar, a small group of some 60 personnel from the battle group, including Brunelle, remained and filled in wherever needed. Brunelle himself returned to Canada just before Christmas, while Lieutenant-Colonel Thomas remained until Task Force ORION arrived.

With ORION, Canada's guns would return to Afghanistan. Over the coming year, Canadian soldiers who had rarely seen an artillery round impact, even from kilometres away, would quickly learn to truly appreciate the meaning of the words "Danger Close."

10

PREPARING FOR THE RETURN TO KANDAHAR

THE MEMBERS OF A BATTERY, 1st Regiment, Royal Canadian Horse Artillery (1 RCHA) did not envision having an active tour in Kandahar. Initially they weren't sure that they would be taking guns with them or even sure that they were going at all. Their road to Afghanistan had started innocently enough in October 2004 when General Hillier, then the Chief of Land Staff, gave Lieutenant-Colonel Ian Hope, commanding officer of the 1st Battalion, a heads-up for a mission that his battalion might be destined for in Afghanistan in early 2006.[1] At the time, the International Security Assistance Force (ISAF) was expanding its reach across Afghanistan. A Canadian brigade-led reconnaissance (recce) party had visited there on October 21, 2004.[2] That quickly developed into informal discussions with the British and the Dutch about jointly taking over Regional Command (South) from the Americans. Canada would assume the leadership role first and possibly take over the Americans' provincial reconstruction team (PRT) role in Kandahar.[3]

Hope had served in Kabul on ISAF's staff when Lieutenant-General Hillier had commanded there in 2004. He had only taken command of the 1st Battalion the summer of 2004. By the fall of that year, elements of the battalion's B Company with a platoon from A Company were in Kabul. The rest of the battalion was shifting gears back to mechanized operations using the light armoured vehicles (LAV).[4]

On February 25, 2005, 1 RCHA lined up their dozen M109s at "King" observation post in Shilo during Exercise LAST MISSION and fired a final "Regiment Right."[5] Not even a month later, on March 21, 2005 the government decided to send a battle group to augment the PRT destined for Kandahar. General Hillier, now newly appointed as the Chief of Defence Staff, now advised that the battle group was definitely going there and would do so as part of the American-led Operation ENDURING FREEDOM.[6] The battalion would not be employed in a limited area, as had been the case with the previous rotations to Kabul, but as a more mobile force spearheading the deployment of British and Dutch contingents.

Canada already had personnel working with the Americans under Canada's Operation ARCHER and this new force would join that mission.

Colonel David Fraser had been appointed the commander of 1 Canadian Mechanized Brigade Group in Edmonton in June 2005. Shortly after that he was promoted to Brigadier-General and designated as commander of both the Canadian contingent in Afghanistan and of the multinational brigade headquarters to be deployed to Kandahar. The brigade would eventually include nine separate nations, operating four battle groups, elements of the Royal Air Force Regiment and four provincial reconstruction teams. Planning could now start in earnest but problems were encountered early on. In the summer of 2005, Fraser had met with Major-General Ben Freakley, the commander of the Americans' 10th Mountain Division during a staff exercise at Fort Drum in New York. Freakley's divisional headquarters would take command of Combined Joint Task Force-76 in Afghanistan in February 2006. He would be Fraser's boss in theatre. It quickly became clear that Freakley assumed that his own 4th Brigade Combat Team from Fort Polk in Louisiana, and not the Canadians, would take over Regional Command (South). He was unaware that the multinational brigade would be part of his command. The Canadian team went home while matters were sorted out.[7]

Similarly, it was likely, but still not immediately certain, that the battle group would include a gun battery. An early draft establishment had only two rifle companies and the battery manning the PRT.[8] The battle group's operational concept was based on a counterinsurgency situation with some limited combat involving a section or perhaps a platoon at a time. This was in line with ISAF's thinking which tried to distance itself from the so-called War on Terror orientation of Operation ENDURING FREEDOM. Both the proposed British and Dutch contingents operated under similar premises. The North Atlantic Treaty Organization (NATO) aimed to pursue a classic heart-and-minds strategy, but while there was a general acceptance that the mission would be one of nation-building, both the British and Dutch would bring along their own howitzers.

In the spring of 2005, the Americans occupied Kandahar with a battle group of four manoeuvre companies, a gun battery, and several special operations forces units. In total, there were 1,500 to 2,000 allied troops; Canada was sending 800. Seeing indications that Kandahar might go hot, the idea of the battery as the PRT was quickly cancelled.[9]

While the contingent's initial organization had not included a battery of guns, it did have a brigade fire support coordination centre (FSCC) to be furnished by 1 RCHA. Lieutenant-Colonel Peter Williams, the regiment's newly appointed commanding officer, was designated to go. He'd already informally earmarked A

Battery to go when he joined a strategic recce to Kandahar in August with a select staff from the brigade and the battle group.

The recce confirmed that guns and a third infantry company were needed.[10] The proposed Canadian establishment was discussed between Brigadier-General Fraser and Lieutenant-General Carron, the then Chief of Land Staff following the recce. Fraser recalls: "The PRT needed a protection company and the Battle Group needed three [manoeuvre] companies. This adjustment was made based upon the operational needs on the ground ... we squeezed as much into the orbat as was sustainable over the duration of the mission."[11]

Both the brigade and the battle group commanders were adamant that guns were required. A major factor in this decision was the inclusion of a field battery in the order of battle of the American unit that the Canadians would be replacing. It would take a decision by the Chief of Defence Staff on August 31, 2005 to finally make it a certainty.[12] On the other hand, it was decided that radars were not a necessity as there had been no insurgent mortar activity at the airfield.[13] Besides, Canada had none. The leased ARTHURs had long ago been returned to their Scandinavian owners.

The team also concluded that the 105mm round was inadequate in terms of both range and terminal effects. There was also the knowledge that the army was considering a lightweight 155mm howitzer and precision ammunition by way of the Excalibur global positioning system-guided round. The intent of fielding these included reducing collateral damage to non-combatants through increased precision. After a discussion with Lieutenant-Colonel Hope, Brigadier-General Fraser also decided to include 81mm mortars in the order of battle, albeit on the golf bag principle.[14]

Even without the clarity of hindsight, it is difficult to see how any other solution could have been considered. There was the benefit of a potential range of 30 kilometres, two-thirds again more than that provided by 105mm high explosive extended range ammunition, and without the prospect of shooting out the barrels. Besides being able to reach out much farther, this also reduced the requirement to move the guns, thus increasing availability and reducing vulnerability on the move.

On the downside, no one in the logistics world really appreciated the challenges inherent in satisfying the voracious appetite for ammunition of even as few as four 155mm howitzers. Resupply would have to be by road, using the transport resources of the national support element. While the Americans had CH-47 Chinook medium-lift helicopters, and the British and Dutch would bring theirs, Canada had disposed of its limited fleet more than a decade earlier—ironically most of them to the Dutch. Any delivery of ammunition by air would depend on the generosity of allies.

With no definitive word on which gun would go, planning within 1 RCHA proceeded on the basis that the battle group would include a 105mm field battery. Even as the gun type to be deployed remained up in the air, the battery also had to cope with uncertainty over how many gunners would be sent. As is usual on operational deployments, there is an initial high-level staff estimate made which receives government approval. Generally there is reluctance to go back to the government for additional positions once the lower levels have worked out the details. This results in manning limitations that often appear arbitrary to those in the field. Compounding the problem was the concept of giving soldiers leave for up to three weeks during the tour. This would seriously reduce the number of assigned troops available during operations. The battle group had argued strenuously against such leave, but National Defence Headquarters had insisted on it.[15]

Planning proceeded on the basis that the battery would have a manpower ceiling of 100. This was based on the experience gained with Operation ATHENA deployments to Kabul where that battery had been equipped with 105mm LG1s but was largely restricted to two permanent camps. Furthermore, as it was anticipated that the battery would not do much firing, it did not have any ammunition lift capability other than the gun tractors. In fact, it did not have any echelon at all.[16] The first draft establishment, received on June 28, 2005 had six guns (four manned by regulars and two manned by reservists) and only two forward observation officer (FOO) parties. There was no guarantee that a meteorological section would deploy.[17]

Within a month, there were informal indications that the battery would be reduced to four guns. On August 3, 2005 the G3 of 1 Canadian Mechanized Brigade Group informed Lieutenant-Colonel Williams that the manning of A Battery was capped at eighty-eight all ranks. This was soon confirmed when the 1st Battalion's proposed table of organization and equipment was received that reflected four gun detachments and three FOO parties. The proposed manning was less than satisfactory. The figure of eighty-eight was based on the seven-person gun detachments of the LG1, while the FOO parties, for example, were made up of five personnel including someone cross-trained as a forward air controller (FAC); a more practical minimum was six all ranks.

All this led to a lack of stability in the manpower planning for the battery. There was a considerable difference in the ranks and trades between a subunit of six guns and two FOO parties compared to one with four guns and three FOO parties. The battery sergeant major, Master Warrant Officer Paul Parsons juggled and tracked the organization for several months on a whiteboard in his office. He had some frustrating moments.

Not least among the questions that Parsons had to contend with was that of who would be the battery's commander. The summer of 2005 would be marked as a change of command of A Battery from that of Major Anne Reiffenstein, the

Canadian artillery's first female battery commander, to Major Steve Gallagher. Reiffenstein lobbied hard to stay on the extra year and to take her battery overseas, but ultimately her posting to Kingston went ahead.

In the end, Parsons had 110 personnel to choose from, including several reservists. That gave him some flexibility and a pool of reinforcements.[18]

There was very little time to work out the details. 1 Canadian Mechanized Brigade Group had a brigade training event, Exercise PHOENIX RAM, scheduled in Wainwright, Alberta for September 6 to October 22, 2005. Here, the complete battle group, including A Battery, would be stood up for pre-deployment training in counter-insurgency operations. At the time this was also referred to as a "Three-Block War" describing a situation where a unit could be fighting on one block, conducting peace keeping on another and providing humanitarian aid on a third.[19] Besides the units from the brigade itself, a battalion of the Royal 22e Régiment and Batterie X of the 5e Régiment d'artillerie légère du Canada (5 RALC) would participate on the exercise.

To say that the battle group, now designated as Task Force 1-06, would train for a counter-insurgency mission in Afghanistan would turn out to be a tad optimistic. The exercise, which was directed by the Canadian Manoeuvre Training Centre and the Land Force Doctrine and Training System would turn much more to conventional war. In Brigadier-General Fraser's view, the operations in theatre turned out to be more than merely counter insurgency and, in hindsight, were the right thing to do in the circumstances.[20]

Steve Gallagher had made it clear to his troops that this would not be just a peacekeeping mission.[21] On the other hand, much of NATO believed, at least outwardly, that the expansion into Southern Afghanistan would not be actively opposed by major forces. What was missing was that the enemy would have a vote and was already well underway in building up its resources for an offensive. The allies certainly did not give enough credence to the traditional reaction of many Afghans to foreign intruders.

With the M109s being taken out of service and the LG1s suffering barrel issues Gallagher recalled,

> The [previous] commanding officer, Lieutenant Colonel Ivy Miezitis had requested two batteries of C3's to support the upcoming [brigade training event] to replace the LG1's with the cracked barrels. Of the six LG1's held by 1 RCHA, only one was cleared to fire without restriction. G4 Maintenance at 1 [Canadian Mechanized Brigade Group] headquarters advised on 17 June 2005 that the five cracked barrels would need to be modified and would be returned to the Regiment by end March 2006. [In other words, after the

battle group deployed.] At this time it was extremely unclear what guns I would be training the [battery] on.[22]

While the immediate question turned on what gun to take to Wainwright, the larger issues of what gun to take to Afghanistan still loomed. With deployment scheduled for early 2006, to suggest that it was still unclear which gun would equip A Battery for the mission was, to say the least, disturbing. Moreover, in the workup training, the battery commander and his FOOs could not advise their supported arm colleagues on how best to employ artillery based on the detailed characteristics of their guns. The battery held some LG1s, but these operated under the restrictions noted above, even during the work up training. Furthermore, no live firing, especially under danger close conditions, was planned.

The Chief of Land Staff's directive of July 20, 2005 had hinted at a possible solution: the acquisition of a lightweight 155mm howitzer. Staff work was already underway to find a solution and 1 RCHA was aware of that. Lieutenant-Colonel Jim Willis, Director Land Requirements 2, had indicated in a July 19, 2005 email that an attempt was being made to get M777s from the United States. This correspondence spoke about borrowing guns from the production run for the United States Marine Corps, while pursuing formal procurement through the Foreign Military Sales program. Delivery of the guns was expected in the October/November 2005 time frame. It was contingent on the Chief of the Land Staff being successful in persuading the Commandant of the Marine Corps to greenlight the action. In the meantime, the battle group manoeuvre companies would prepare for battle without employing the specific guns that would support them in action.

Going into Exercise PHOENIX RAM, the artillery's contribution to the deploying establishment was still shaking out.

Parsons and Gallagher had allocated key positions within A Battery. Joining Gallagher in the battery commander's tactical party would be his technician, Sergeant Jeffrey Dickson and the battery sergeant major, Master Warrant Officer Paul Parsons himself. The battery's FSCC would be commanded by the battery's second in command, Captain Howie Nelson with his technician Warrant Officer Darcy Cyr. Cyr had been a troop sergeant major and was also the regiment's supervisory FAC.

There were three FOO detachments: G11 would be Captain Bob Meade and his technician and FAC Master Bombardier John Furber; G12 was Captain Mike Smith with Sergeant Jason Ladouceur; and G13 would be Captain Nichola Goddard and Sergeant Dave Redford. Captain Howard Han would be the battery's administrative officer and Warrant Officer John Gero, the battery's quartermaster sergeant.

Last, but not least, would be the two gun troops led by Lieutenant Rob

O'Donnell with Warrant Officer Brian Jensen for A Troop and Lieutenant Andrew Nicholson and Warrant Officer Gord Brooks for B Troop. Warrant Officer Shawn Quinlan would fill the tech warrant position, Sergeants Christopher Damjanoff and Eldon Seaward would be the recce technicians, and Sergeants Paul Dolomont, Darrell Stubbington, Robert Pethick and Master Bombardier Douglas Quinn would be the four detachment commanders.[23]

Artillery reservists would man twenty-four positions in Afghanistan; roughly half of those would be in A Battery, mostly manning positions in the gun detachments but also including some command post personnel and one detachment commander.[24]

Gunners from 1 RCHA would also join Brigadier-General David Fraser's headquarters. There were, actually, two headquarters. The senior one for Canadians was Joint Task Force[25] AFGHANISTAN, which made up the national command element for all Canadian forces in theatre. In addition, he commanded the multinational brigade-sized headquarters, which would henceforth be called Coalition Task Force AEGIS.[26]

Coalition Task Force AEGIS was scheduled to assume the command of Regional Command (South) on March 1, 2006 from the Americans' Task Force BAYONET. BAYONET was based on the American 173rd Airborne Brigade Combat Team from Vicenza, Italy. Regional Command (South), at that time, was not yet a part of ISAF. It was scheduled to continue operating under the Americans' Combined Joint Task Force 76 until August 1, 2006 when ISAF would assume control over the region and over Coalition Task Force AEGIS.[27]

AEGIS would start operations as a multinational brigade with the Canadian battle group, the PRT and two American battalions—the 2nd Battalion of the 4th Infantry Regiment in Qalat and the 2nd Battalion of the 10th Aviation Regiment in Kandahar. It would quickly thereafter grow in size as new troops arrived from the British—the 3rd Battalion, the Parachute Regiment—for Helmand, the Dutch and Australians—the 13 Infanteriebataljon and the Special Operations Task Group respectively—for Uruzgan and the Romanians—the 141st Infantry battalion—for Zabul.

Williams' job had now settled into a dual role. Rather than simply "Fires", Williams would deploy as AEGIS's chief of fires and effects.[28] The concept of merging kinetic effects—artillery, close air support, attack aviation—with non-kinetic effects aimed at nation-building and development such as psychological operations, information operations, public affairs and civilian-military cooperation teams, had been used by Combined Joint Task Force 76 when they deployed in March 2005. They had required the same from their subordinate brigades. Each day, Combined Joint Task Force 76 would run a joint fires board intending to ensure unity of effort and to synchronize kinetic fires and non-kinetic effects within their area of operations.[29]

Williams would spend much of his time on the non-kinetic side of the house because that's where the major effort of Canada's deployment was aimed. The side more oriented to fire support coordination would fall to Williams' subordinate, Captain Tyler Kennedy, 1 RCHA's operations officer. He had deployed in the rank of major (while so employed) as the targeting officer and chief of fires at AEGIS.[30]

Another gunner, Major Tim Bishop, would join the brigade staff but not in a gunner role. Bishop had started as a reservist in the 3rd Field Artillery Regiment, RCA, but had transferred to the regular force in 1983 and by September 2005 was 1 Canadian Mechanized Brigade Group's G3 Operations. As such, he had been responsible for planning Exercise PHOENIX RAM under Fraser's direction. Halfway through the exercise he was appointed the G3/chief of operations for Coalition Task Force AEGIS to replace another officer. Bishop would deploy as a lieutenant-colonel (while so employed) and would, in 2007, be promoted to that rank substantively and assume command of 1 RCHA from Williams. Bishop, in his role at AEGIS, " ... was responsible for the contact fight, so ran the minute to minute operations 24/7 with my team in the joint operations centre."[31] Bishop would later receive the Meritorious Service Medal for his service in Afghanistan. The citation reads,

> *Acting Lieutenant-Colonel Bishop is recognized for the superb professionalism he displayed during Operation ARCHER Rotation 1, which took place in Afghanistan from February to August 2006. Responsible for the Canadian-led multinational brigade, he monitored and directed the combat operations of over 6,000 coalition combat soldiers, as well as fighter-jet and helicopter crews, directly contributing to the successes of the brigade. His selfless dedication and astute management ensured effective military operations in an area of some 200,000 square kilometres. Acting Lieutenant-Colonel Bishop's outstanding performance in this complex, multinational environment brings great credit to the Canadian Forces and to Canada.*[32]

The top non-commissioned member job in the brigade would go to a gunner as well. Chief Warrant Officer, and Master Gunner, Mike McDonald had been appointed as the 1 Canadian Mechanized Brigade Group's sergeant major and would deploy in that role for Task Force AEGIS. Throughout the tour he would keep a steady watch on morale and provide advice to the command team. He would receive a Meritorious Service Decoration for his steadfast leadership.

Other gunners would serve elsewhere: The regiment's Captain Lisa Haveman, amongst others, would join the PRT.[33] Colonel Michael Capstick would continue in his role with the Strategic Advisory Team for which service he too would receive a Meritorious Service Medal. His citation read,

> From August 2005 to August 2006, Colonel Capstick commanded the Strategic Advisory Team in Afghanistan. Epitomizing the Team Canada approach to international security challenges, his team achieved results in support of Afghanistan's government. Through leadership and resourcefulness, he earned the trust and confidence of Afghan authorities. His efforts and influence have been felt throughout Kabul and the international community. His team has been influential in the implementation of the Afghan National Development Strategy and the Afghan Compact, which, together, provide a blueprint for the future of Afghanistan.[34]

Other gunner agencies were mobilizing as well. In Gagetown, 4 Air Defence Regiment, RCA (4 AD Regt) would raise an airspace coordination centre (ASCC) manned by Captains Paul Hillier and Rory Moore, Sergeant Boyd Payne, Bombardiers Allison Babin and Fred MacLaren and four others. This would be a first for them as in previous rotations they had deployed the centre solely as a brigade asset. This time, it would also form part of the battle group's tactical operations centre.[35] Three of them would be deployed to the brigade headquarters, while six would work with the battle group. For the battle group ASCC, its mandate was to coordinate all of the battle group's resources that used or affected the area of operation's airspace. Artillery had to be deconflicted with fixed wing aircraft and helicopters especially when close air support was in use. This included the Sperwer tactical unmanned aerial vehicle (UAV) which was having its debut in support of ground combat operations.[36]

The brigade ASCC, meanwhile, concerned itself with the overall coordination of the whole of the brigade's area of operation. That wasn't to be their sole function, however. Part way through the tour, Captain Moore would find himself assigned to a new detachment in Coalition Task Force AEGIS responsible for coordinating activities with the Afghan National Security Forces.[37] In part, this was to help integrate the AEGIS's operations with that of the Afghans and, in part, to help bring the new Canadian operational mentoring and liaison teams on line.[38]

For both cells, the airspace coordination would be done through the establishment of restricted operating zones, monitoring mIRC[39] chat rooms and the use of the air defence systems integrator, a command and control system that connects to and integrates data from various airspace resources such as radars for real-time situational awareness.[40]

After the withdrawal of Sperwer from Kabul, the army and the air force had come to an agreement that thereafter, the air force would become the force generator of tactical UAV, while the army would be their force employer. The personnel manning the equipment, a flight of fifty-six in all, would come from both. Mission commanders, air vehicle operators and maintenance staff came from the air force; payload operators and much of the ground team came from the artillery; other personnel, such as intelligence operators, meteorological technicians, supply staff and so on, came from various other agencies.

In Valcartier, 5ᵉ Régiment d'artillerie légère du Canada (5 RALC) had already started reorganizing itself to turn Batterie Q into a surveillance and target acquisition (STA) battery. It would eventually have two troops of miniature UAVs[41] and one troop of weapon locating sensors. The Vice Chief of Defence Staff had signed off on the procurement of such systems under an unforecasted operational requirement, but as late as August, it wasn't clear whether such a system would be available in time for Gallagher's battery. In fact, the miniature UAVs wouldn't make their debut until the next roto. Similarly, radars and acoustic sensors were also identified for acquisition under another unforecasted operational requirement but would not make it into A Battery's inventory. Some forecasts at the time estimated that these systems would enter service in early 2007.[42]

While the miniature UAVs would not make it for Task Force 1-06, personnel from Batterie Q, however, would deploy. Twenty-five of them joined 408 Tactical Helicopter Squadron's Sperwer-equipped tactical UAV flight.

The flight had assembled for the first time in Valcartier in May 2005 for a six-week ground training session, once again in French, from SAGEM staff. 2005 would be the last time SAGEM would conduct the training, as thereafter Canadian military staff would do it in-house. Flight training for Roto 1—those destined to deploy concurrently with Task Force 1-06—would begin in August in Suffield, Alberta, and run for five weeks, following which they moved to Wainwright to join the brigade for Exercise PHOENIX RAM. Here they would also meet up with the personnel of Roto 2 who would do their flight training with them, followed by both rotos taking their formal validation for deployment.[43] The equipment would then be prepared for shipment to Kandahar.

Gallagher wasn't concerned that he would not have surveillance and target acquisition resources beyond the Sperwer and whatever assets the American would have available. The wide-ranging area of operations and the mobile operations they envisaged made the use of such assets difficult in any event.

While the regiments were busy dealing with the turmoil that artillery transformation would generate, the Royal Canadian Artillery School (RCAS) was facing an unrivaled pace of change. Not only was there transformation of the basic structure of the regiments, but the RCAS would have to deal with the arrival of a whole new inventory of equipment and ammunition and do so under wartime conditions. Each item would require capability evaluation, the determination and development of tactics, techniques, procedures and battle task standards for its employment, technical assistance visits, and the necessary and appropriate training and maintenance program to field and sustain the equipment on operations. To say that the RCAS faced a major challenge would have been the understatement of the year.

With the negotiations for the acquisition of six M777s well underway, two assistant instructors in gunnery from the RCAS, Warrant Officers J.R. Arsène "Bone" Veronneau and John Lannigan, had joined the United States Marine Corps detachment at the US Army Artillery School at Fort Sill, Oklahoma in August for a conversion course on the equipment. This visit proved very useful, and the team identified several issues to be resolved. They returned to Gagetown to draft the gun drill manual for subsequent training. The work which had been going forward at a frantic pace in several headquarters was about to be handed over to the troops. The M777 was coming.

11

ENTER THE TRIPLE SEVEN

WHILE OTHER MEMBERS OF THE ARTILLERY worked at the minutiae of acquiring and fielding a new gun, the 1st Regiment, Royal Canadian Horse Artillery (1 RCHA) went to Wainwright as a unit. A Battery, however, would spend its time mostly separated from the other guns. The battery bivouaced with the Task Force 1-06 battle group which had now been renamed to Task Force ORION.

Prior to deploying to Wainwright, 1 RCHA had conducted extensive live fire training so that its technical procedures were down pat. It was a good thing they had as they would see little firing during the brigade exercise. A Battery would have just four days at the end firing barely 100 rounds.

In Wainwright, the new Canadian Manoeuvre and Training Centre assisted with the brigade's training event. While the overall brigade exercise focused on conventional war, for the gunners of A Battery, the exercise ran a bit differently. The battery itself was broken up and the two gun troops were assigned to work with specific companies. Both the forward observation officer (FOO) and the gun troop's troop commander would attend the company commander's orders group. The battle group conducted individual exercises as mobile operations where each troop would follow a bound behind its assigned company. This training would pay dividends once the battery deployed to Afghanistan where it would range widely throughout the area of operations.

One thing that became immediately clear after the strategic reconnaissance (recce) was that with the gun troops dispersed, Parsons, the battery sergeant major would not be walking the gun line. In training, A Troop worked primarily with the 1st Battalion's mechanized A Company and B Troop primarily with the mechanized C Company. B Company, provided by the 2nd Battalion, Princess Patricia's Canadian Light Infantry from Shilo, was mounted in light utility vehicles, wheeled—the lightly armoured Mercedes G-Wagons. The intent was that B Company would provide close protection for the provincial reconstruction team (PRT) in and around the City of Kandahar. While B Company would, from time to time, have a FOO, it would have no gun troop assigned to it.

The battery's quartermaster sergeant, Warrant Officer John Gero, would remain back at Kandahar Airfield (KAF), but there would be no battery echelon. The national support element would handle logistics out of KAF. What they would do was have the battery sergeant major become part of the battery commander's tactical party, deploying with him in his light armoured vehicle (LAV) every time that the battle group commander deployed forward with his tactical command post—which would be almost continuously. Parsons concluded: "There was no playbook ... This wasn't the old school mentality of fighting a war ... This was like nothing I had ever trained for before."[1]

Several other gunners at Wainwright disagreed with this non-traditional way of operating. They did not approve of the decision to split the troops and have the battery sergeant major travelling with the battery commander. Parsons, on the other hand, was on board with it. He quickly decided, "I wasn't fighting getting into the car. I adopted that very quickly because if I wanted a fucking tour I better talk myself into (the battery commander's) car ... I could have talked myself out of that tour ... with two guns here and two guns forty [kilometres] away."[2] The two troops would be self-contained, each with its own recce party and command post. For security reasons, the recce party would move with the main gun group and never go forward on its own.

One concern for some in the battery was the stories brought back by C Battery about their relationship with their battalion on Operation APOLLO. Here A Battery would have a pleasant surprise. Their relationship with the 1st Battalion would be entirely different. "We built up a relationship with those guys second to none ... They opened their arms up ... we did the same thing ... It was a phenomenal working relationship."[3]

While the FOOs and gun troops were exercising for escorts, cordons and search, and deliberate attacks with their companies, they would also do a mortar conversion course and live fire exercise.[4] The fire support coordination centre (FSCC) was busy practicing their skills. Warrant Officer Darcy Cyr recalls, "The FSCC was fully integrated into the [battle group headquarters] and rehearsed clearance of fires, as well as artillery, air, and aviation coordination and deconfliction."[5]

Cyr's duties also extended to the battery's forward air controllers (FAC).

As the FAC training coordinator, I was responsible for ensuring that the FACs were appropriately trained and ready to go. As Canadian aircraft support was limited at the best of times, this involved a lot of extra time on [temporary duty] in between the regularly scheduled [task force] workup training as I took the FACs on a wide range of [close air support training] events all over the US to the various squadrons to leverage available aircraft support. The USAF was, and still is, eager to support coalition FAC training. It was beneficial to my FACs because it allowed them to experience different aircraft [tactics, techniques and procedures], different ranges, and a wide variety of voices on the radio nets. Additionally, these would be the types of platforms that would actually be supporting us in theatre—not Canadian CF-18s—so we needed to be intimately familiar with them...I don't think anyone expected [close air support], or really gunnery, to end up being what it was.[6]

Much of the training was catch-as-catch-can and Cyr ended up taking four of his controllers away from the Canadian training in Wainwright to go to Arizona to catch some runs with American A-10s. Working with the Americans had another advantage. It took them away from the heavily scripted exercises, with large safety distances, common at the time for Canadians, to the more realistic training the Americans had brought back from Iraq.[7]

The brigade training event, Exercise PHOENIX RAM, had two major aims. The first was to fulfill the army's requirements for the training of the brigade and in particular to look at the ongoing developments of the direct fire unit.

There was an agenda of transformation to prove the concept of the direct fire squadrons with the [Lord Strathcona's Horse (Royal Canadians)]...That was the focus of the exercise along with preparing the brigade headquarters to be a multinational headquarters.[8]

The direct fire unit included participation by 4th Air Defence Regiment's Air Defence Anti-Tank Systems working with the tanks of A Squadron of the Lord Strathcona's Horse (Royal Canadians) and the Tube-launched, Optically-tacked, Wire-guided missiles of E Company of the 1st Battalion, Princess Patricia's Canadian Light Infantry.

In addition to the brigade's collective training, was additional training for the battle group. This was mission focused and included an operational evaluation exercise. The battalion felt this training had shortcomings. Among these both the battery and the battalion considered the mandatory peacetime training safety distances as problematic for the howitzers as they were for the FACs.

The closest round of artillery that we had on one range...the closest round of 155 (sic) was probably almost two kilometres away from the manoeuvre subunits...which is why after the exercise we did a tactical reconnaissance in Kandahar and we came back and I argued and won the fight to get the battle group deployed four weeks early to Kandahar to train in theatre.[9]

The tactical recce also confirmed in Gallagher's mind that he did not have enough depth in FACs, so he arranged a course in Gagetown in emergency close air support.[10] Captains Nichola Goddard and Bob Meade and Sergeant Dave Redford attended the course in December and from the field could assist air support missions being conducted from the FSCC by the fully certified FACs.[11]

While the gunners slated for deployment had been busy in Wainwright, other actions were proceeding in Ottawa. September saw a Royal Canadian Artillery School (RCAS) commandant's planning session take place to map out an agenda for the artillery working group's meeting set for October 4 and 5, 2005.[12] This would outline the road forward to the multi-year implementation of the army commander's field artillery transformation directive. Key to the plan was the development of the mission element concept which effectively provided that a regiment generates composite batteries for deployment. A battery would comprise a requisite battle group FSCC and FOOs and various types and numbers of troops—gun troops and surveillance and target acquisition (STA) troops. The regiment might also be tasked to deploy a brigade-level FSCC but would not be expected to deploy as a full, multi-battery regiment.

On October 4, 2005 Lieutenant-Colonel Jim Willis and his staff gave the working group a briefing on the status of the M777 acquisition process and mapped out the many activities underway to ensure the gun's availability for Task Force ORION.[13] Treasury Board approval for what was now a purchase and not merely a loan, came on October 17th. Gallagher now knew that he'd have his guns. The question was when?[14]

People were busy making it happen. Warrant Officers Veronneau and Lannigan, having developed the Canadianized gun drills, returned to Fort Sill on October 24, 2005 accompanied by Major Paul Payne, the Chief Instructor in Gunnery at the RCAS, Master Gunner Kevin Smith, and Warrant Officer Andy Johnson. Also attending was Warrant Officer Dick Elson from 1 RCHA. Their purpose was to take a week and trial the Canadian conversion training course on the M777. There was originally some push-back from the Americans that the course was too short—five days dry and five days live-fire training—and that it didn't first do the full Marine Corps conversion course before teaching the Canadian add-ons. That was resolved by Major Bruno Di Ilio in favour of the Canadian method on the condition that the dry part of the course be run as a pilot course at Sill for evaluation.

The pilot ran from November 14 to 18, 2005. Two gun detachments, one each from B Battery 1 RCHA, led by Sergeant Jim Aucoin, and F Battery, 2nd Regiment, Royal Canadian Horse Artillery (2 RCHA), led by Master Bombardier Chesley Reid arrived to undergo the training.[15] The standard of these gunners was so high that the head of the Marine team accused the Canadians of stacking the detachments with picked personnel. This was not the case, but admittedly, it would have been unlikely that the batteries would have included any duds in the first place. However, it said volumes about the standard of Canadian gunners, and even more so when they were in the front window.[16]

During the fall, maintenance personnel trained at a variety of locations in the United States and the United Kingdom. In Canada, work was also underway to complete various equipment upgrades and trials involved with the howitzers and their ancillary equipment. A key one dealt with the introduction of a digital gun management system for late 2006.[17] One issue still not settled was what vehicle or vehicles would tow the gun and carry the detachments in theatre.

With the adoption of the M777 a certainty, Gallagher agitated for an increase in the size of each of his gun detachments to ten personnel, vice seven for an LG1. A similar push was on from the RCAS team that had been working on fielding the gun. To them, it was clear that a seven-member detachment would be inadequate for the M777 in an operational environment.[18] The increase in size took the battery back from eighty-eight to one hundred all ranks. This was finally approved on November 9, 2005 which was cutting it a bit fine.

In fact, in more normal times, the conversion to new equipment could have stretched over several months. Gallagher estimated that conversion of his experienced gun detachments would require from seven to ten days for gun drill followed by three days in the field, including live firing. He was allowed five days in garrison and three days for live firing. In retrospect it was by no means sufficient, but it had to do.

Also cutting it close was the proof firing of the M777s destined for 1 RCHA and Canadian acceptance trials of new classes of American ammunition and fuzes. These were conducted at the Yuma Proving Grounds in Arizona under the supervision of personnel from the Directorate of Armament Sustainment Programme Management. On November 21, 2005 the proof firing specifications having been reviewed and the objectives of the ammunition trial program achieved, four brand-new M777s were loaded onto two flatbed trailers for transport to Shilo.

Lieutenant-Colonel Peter Williams recalled the four M777s arriving in Shilo on the night of Thursday, November 24, 2005. The American training team, led by US Marine Major Pope had given up their Thanksgiving weekend to be with the Canadians. On Sunday, the battery's quartermaster sergeant, Warrant Officer John Gero received and signed for the guns. It was fortuitous that it was Gero who received them. The guns came minus cleaning staves, bore bushes, bell rammers, and primer vent bits and reamers, as these items were to come from the M198 howitzers the M777s would replace one-for-one in American battalions. Fortunately Gero had managed to keep these items in stock from the M109s that had been turned in the previous spring.[19] The quartermaster staff completed the paperwork and kitted out and immediately issued the guns to each of the Numbers 1. Detachment training began on Monday with the assistance of the American training team and a Canadian training team from the RCAS.

As training started in Shilo, Brigadier-General Stuart Beare's staff at the Land Force Doctrine and Training System headquarters in Kingston issued a training directive which set out in detail the processes to be followed across the army for all initial and steady state individual and collective training on the M777 in support of Operation ARCHER.[20] Many of the activities identified were already well under way.

A Battery was into its first week of training when a pause was called for a dedication ceremony. Williams recalled, "We dedicated the new colours with live fire (behind the RCA Officers Mess) that Friday, December 2, 2005, with the then Colonel Commandant [Major-General John Arch MacInnis] and [Brigadier-General] Fraser in attendance."[21] Gunner William Swanson, the battery's youngest gunner, fired the first round. The next week progressed to live fire on Ex TITANIUM GUNNER.[22]

The Marines' Major Pope and his team continued to be impressed with how rapidly the Canadian gunners, including reservists, were adapting to the M777. Marines were used to reservists manning guns but were surprised to learn that, unlike the Marine Corps, which did not have women in the combat arms, female Canadian gunners had started serving in the artillery over twenty years previously. It was clear to the team that the female gunners contributed equally to the high standard of performance they were witnessing in 1 RCHA.

This being Shilo in December, the weather played a part as well. Besides the obvious discomfort to the Americans attending, the cold caused problems with the hydraulics. It startled the BAE manufacturer's representative how fast it happened, worse than what he'd seen in Alaska for stressing the gun.[23]

While BAE advertised the trails on the gun as "self-embedding", the frozen ground of Shilo had a vote in that. Master Gunner Kevin Smith and Warrant Officer Veronneau had gone to a Home Depot to pick up some cut-off saws and jackhammers to cut divots in the frozen soil for the trails. Nevertheless, one night at last light, the trails on one gun popped out and slid backward, nearly taking out Sergeant Paul Dolomont, the Number 1.[24]

There was one final, very important matter that required immediate attention before the regiment sent the guns to Winnipeg for loading on an Antonov for the flight to Afghanistan. Each of the new guns soon had a plaque mounted on a conspicuous place on the top carriage. These had previously been presented to A Battery by the 1ˢᵗ Battalion, The Royal Canadian Regiment in recognition of their support in Korea.[25]

While the artillery was cutting it close, so too was the brigade. One final exercise prior to deployment involved only a few gunners. Since Coalition Task Force AEGIS headquarters was a multinational one, the brigade planned an exercise to have everyone work together. Tim Bishop recalls: "Bringing together the multinational team in [December and January] in Edmonton proved an exercise in logistics and travel given the troops were coming from all over the world to form our [headquarters] (the G5 was Australian for example). So getting them there and trained just prior to deployment was difficult and given the temperature in Edmonton—not ideal for deploying to Afghanistan."[26]

Preceding the battle group and deploying to Afghanistan in December was Captain Steve Hunter. Steve, like many other gunners, had started his career in the reserves which, in his case, was 30ᵗʰ Field Regiment, Royal Canadian Artillery in Ottawa. After a few years in 2 RCHA, he went on for special forces selection and training and becoming the second artillery officer to be qualified as an assaulter with Joint Task Force 2.[27] For the next six months he would deploy as the S3 (operations officer) for the Canadian special operations task force in Kandahar. It would operate separate from the Canadian conventional forces there but in the same battlespace. He credits his artillery background as being part of the foundation for his success in that role. "I was really privileged from my artillery background. So although I was going into the special operations community, largely associated with infantry, I think, especially the role I played in 05, 06, as the S3, my artillery background and the time I spent in command posts and really doing fire planning and all that type of stuff was instrumental to what I got to do as the S3 over there."[28]

With the equipment on its way to Afghanistan, with the family support cell in Shilo reinforced with additional personnel, and with Debbie Gallagher's able team ready to help the families with whatever assistance they needed—from transportation to snow removal to child care—there was nothing left to do but take some pre-deployment leave and prepare to board the planes.

Expectations as to what the upcoming seven months would bring were mixed, running the scale from peaceful humanitarian support to heavy fighting; mostly the former. Only time, and the Taliban, would tell. Just to make sure that the Canadians understood, the insurgents sent a clear message on January 15, 2006 when Glyn Berry, a diplomat attached to the PRT, and two others were killed and ten—including three Canadian soldiers—were wounded in a car bomb attack in Kandahar.

12

OPERATION ENDURING FREEDOM

THINGS WERE CHANGING IN CANADA. Canadian Expeditionary Force Command (CEFCOM) would stand up on February 1, 2006 and Stephen Harper would be sworn in as the new Prime Minister on February 6, 2006. Meanwhile, the members of A Battery were among the earliest of the Task Force ORION contingent to arrive in Kandahar. The first group landed in late January, the rest in early February. Of course, they weren't the first Canadians, or even the first members of the 1st Regiment, Royal Canadian Horse Artillery, to come to Kandahar. The regiment's own C Battery had that distinction having deployed a small mortar group a few years prior on Operation APOLLO. Kandahar was new to A Battery, however. They'd been briefed about the situation, but the experience of setting foot in the country was nothing like what they had expected.

At the time, Regional Command (South) comprised six provinces. Kandahar, Helmand, Uruzgan, Nimruz, Zabul, and Daykundi; names that would stand out repeatedly. Together they covered an area of slightly over 200,000 square kilometres, making it a little less than twice the size of Southern Ontario. To say that the region is defined by its geography is to trivialize the problem. The southern part of Nimruz, Helmand and Kandahar is dominated by vast, hard-packed desert while northern Daykundi is mostly mountainous. Uruzgan and Zabul have mixed flat and mountainous terrain.

Kandahar City is the region's largest population centre and the country's second largest city. It sits astride Afghanistan's ring road, National Highway 1, at a junction with another main route, National Highway 4. Highway 4 connects Kandahar to Pakistan at the border town of Spin Boldak. With a population of around 500,000, it is also the south's economic hub. The bulk of the remaining population of just short of 3 million is mostly rural, living along seasonally lush river valleys that are fed by the winter snows from the mountains. The principal ones are the Helmand River, running north to south through Daykundi, Uruzgan and Helmand, and the

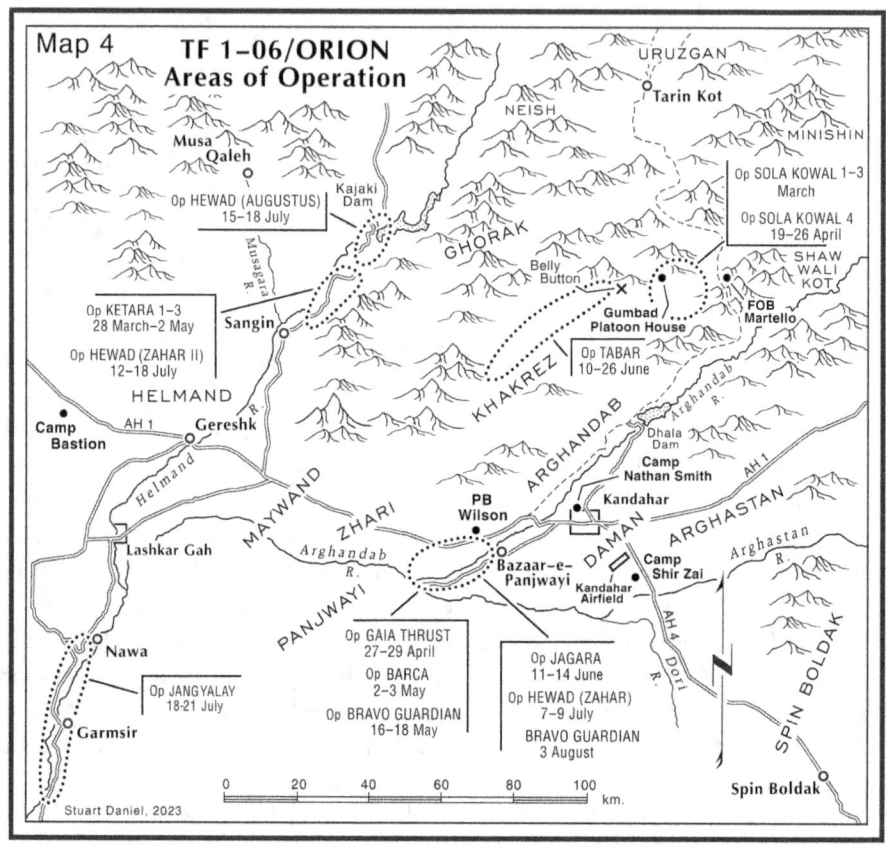

Map 4

TF 1–06/ORION Areas of Operation

Stuart Daniel, 2023

Arghandab River running northeast to southwest across Zabul and Kandahar to join up with the Helmand River.[1]

Weather varies from cool to cold, wet winters to blistering hot summers where temperatures of 40 to 50° Celsius are common. The wet winters also dictate the spring growing season for both market garden crops and the vast narcotics—primarily opium—fields. This employs much of the population during the springtime and then releases it for what is referred to as the summer "fighting season".

Afghanistan's people are predominantly tribal and within Regional Command (South) the main ethnic group is Pashtun. The Taliban are mostly Pashtun tribesmen who blend in relatively easily amongst the local population. There had been an ongoing strategic Taliban campaign since 2004 aimed at the south. One of its objectives was to isolate, infiltrate and, in the end, capture Kandahar City.[2]

Operating under the direction of the exiled Quetta Shura,[3] the Taliban's lines of communications in the south had been established from Pakistan into the border regions of Kandahar, Zabul and Uruzgan. Their campaign initially was to gain access to Kandahar City from the north. Checked in 2004, Mullah Dadullah Lang, the Taliban's operational commander in Afghanistan, took 2005 to move westward into the Baghran and Sangin districts on the Helmand River and from there started another front moving eastward into the Zhari and Panjwayi districts of Kandahar in early 2006.[4] By January 2006, it was estimated that some 200 core Taliban and foreign fighters were in Kandahar province with another 400-600 in Helmand and more yet to the north. The force would grow as more fighters infiltrated and the local population would swell their ranks once the opium harvest finished in the late spring. Those in Kandahar would triple by summer.[5] But even those estimates would be low. In fact, the situation was much worse than anyone expected. Eventually, after the events of August 2006, the Allies would start to understand that the Taliban had, in fact, been working on a complex and deliberate multi-year plan for a major offensive into Helmand and Kandahar for that year.[6] For the first half of the year, however, It was not only a plan that allied intelligence would miss but also a scenario that allied leadership would continue to dismiss even as evidence from the field showed a strengthening insurgency. For the time being, the incoming Canadian, British, Dutch and Australian troops had a completely different idea of what they would be facing.

Opposing the Taliban in the south were the Americans of Task Force BAYONET, a brigade-sized formation based on the 173rd Airborne Brigade Combat Team from Vicenza, Italy. It had deployed a composite battle group in Kandahar based on the 3rd Battalion of the 319th Airborne Field Artillery Regiment, known as Task Force GUN DEVILS. GUN DEVILS had reorganized itself to be primarily an infantry battalion but with one battery of 105mm M119 towed howitzers.[7]

In addition, Kandahar was the home base of what was now a Canadian provincial reconstruction team (PRT)—which had been there since the fall of 2005—and a variety of special operations forces and American aviation units. In addition, there was a growing element of Afghan security forces, both army and police, which had varying support from American special and conventional forces' embedded training teams. The plan was for the Americans to leave the south to concentrate in Regional Command (East) while the small but growing Afghan forces would remain in place.

With the collapse of the Soviet-backed Afghan government in 1992, an army of sorts had remained in Afghanistan through local militias loosely gathered into corps. Kandahar had been the home of the 2nd Corps. These forces, with their dubious loyalty, were a problem for the national government. Shortly after the collapse of the Taliban regime, in order to stabilize the country, the International Security Assistance Force (ISAF) and the fledgling Afghan Kharzai government instituted a plan to demobilize the existing Afghan army in favour of the building of a new national army. This was done and the 205th "Hero" Corps was formed and headquartered at Camp Shirzai on the southeastern edge of the Kandahar Airfield (KAF).

Training progressed slowly, and by the end of 2005 there were really only two battalion-sized Afghan kandaks in operation.[8] The US Army had overall responsibility for their training. Unfortunately, under Combined Joint Task Force PHOENIX—the formation tasked with training the Afghan army—the Americans were quite limited in manpower. Training had become primarily a US Army National Guard responsibility.[9] As of July 2005, the headquarters of the 53rd Infantry Brigade Combat Team from the Florida National Guard led PHOENIX IV. While PHOENIX trainers came from several nations, many of them, and especially the embedded training teams that accompanied the Afghans to the field, were guardsmen.[10] The plan for Kandahar was that a Canadian operational mentoring and liaison team would eventually replace the Americans.

Even worse was the situation for the Afghan police. The responsibility for creating an Afghan national police force fell to the Germans who were falling short.

> *The German approach focused on slowly building a modern police force, capable of engaging in highly technical aspects of law enforcement and of working with a functioning judicial system upholding the rule of law throughout the country. Regrettably, the high rate of Afghan illiteracy, limited resources for or understanding of technology, and a virtually nonexistent judicial system undermined this approach.[11]*

Afghan national police units varied in quality from brave fighters to highly corrupt thugs. The population universally hated them.[12] Problematic was that the success of any counterinsurgency depended on them. While military operations could clear an area of the enemy, only a dependable, local police presence would keep a cleared area stabilized enough to keep it secure against further incursions.

Canadian troops arriving in theatre came on passenger flights, stopping off at Camp Mirage, where they transferred to C-130 Hercules aircraft for the last leg to KAF.

For most, Kandahar was an eye-opener. Major Gallagher: "When the [battle group] arrived in [January] the weather was extremely wet. There were many rain storms that absolutely poured, making the powder-like sand extremely difficult to travel through."[13]

The first A Battery element arrived on January 21, 2006. Warrant Officer Darcy Cyr recalls:

> *When we arrived in Kandahar, the entire [battle group] was housed in massive tent warehouse-like structures that we simply called BATs (big ass tents). There [were] ample shower and bathroom facilities. We took the LAVs*

[light armoured vehicle] down to an area south of Kandahar City that we knew as the 'Red Desert' to test fire all the weapons as well as our personal weapons. We also conducted some [close air support] training with AH-64s at that location.[14]

Warrant Officer John Gero would recall that from the moment they landed they were immediately run through weapons zeroing, a combat first aid session, instructions on using the personal radios and the theatre rules of engagement. They were tired and not able to go to bed in their tents until late the next day.[15] They would be in those tents for the first six weeks without electricity and denied the use of Coleman lanterns. Individual meal packs supplied for the first month were all the same menu—a breakfast one. To relieve the tedium, one troop bought a goat from a farmer which he roasted for them on a grill taken from a Bison carrier.[16]

The guns were not immediately available upon arrival, but the battle group had insisted that the battery arrive with its mortars and so they had been part of the equipment the battery carried with them on their flights—an interesting exercise in security in its own right.[17] Over the next two weeks, the rest of the battery and battle group and its equipment were mostly on the ground and doing the shakeout training in the local area that they had insisted on. For the battery that included mortar firing exercises.[18]

Ammunition became an immediate problem. During November's tactical reconnaissance (recce), Major Gallagher had consulted with GUN DEVILS' battery commander and formed an understanding of the artillery fight and what he would need to support it. He'd prepared a detailed requisition of the amount and type of ammunition needed—including a 100 round basic load with multifunction fuzes for each gun—and submitted it up the chain of command. Upon arrival, Sergeant Major Parsons inspected the holdings in the ammunition compound and found what was there differed from what had been requested. The logisticians had substituted their own views on what was needed.[19]

Just as bad was the fact that the logistics system would not allow the battery to store ammunition near where the guns were deployed for the defence of the airfield. It was instead required to be held in KAF's ammunition compound, which entailed up to an hour round trip and thus made timely artillery return fire impossible.[20] That was perhaps unnecessary in any event. While the American multi-role radar at the airfield could determine a good point of origin for any rocket fired at the airfield—there being no mortar attacks at the time—the battery couldn't get authority to engage those with indirect fire without visual confirmation. Parsons recalls the battery doing maybe a half dozen deployments at the airfield but only firing one illumination mission.[21] This was fired by Smith's G12 at a possible rocket launch site using Nickerson's B Troop—G1B.[22] Gallagher requested and was given permission to take those missions from his task list.[23]

Captain Howie Nelson had the challenge of setting up the battery's fire support coordination centre (FSCC) in Task Force ORION's tactical operations centre. GUN DEVILS had not had an FSCC, nor did they have any joint terminal attack controllers (JTAC), so to a large extent he was working from scratch. Luckily Nelson was a forward air controller (FAC) and had Cyr with him as his FSCC Warrant Officer and supervisory FAC. The availability of two controllers would pay dividends when air strikes had to be run from the tactical operations centre when no FAC was in the area of contact with the enemy.[24]

By mid-February, the battle group was engaging in an excellent handover with GUN DEVILS, including several skirmishes with the Taliban. Early on, the Canadians were under pressure from the American brigade commander to show their willingness and ability to fight and assume tactical missions. Hope felt the battle group wasn't quite ready for that and continued training.[25] Exercising the battery continued into mid-February, as well. Task Force GUN DEVILS conducted a live fire exercise combining its own 105mm guns with A Battery's M777s, during which the latter fired some 150 rounds. The exercise—which would be both the first and last time that A Battery would deploy as a battery rather than as separate troops[26]—took place within range of the Gumbad platoon house, an outpost in the northern Shah Wali Kot region previously established by the GUN DEVILS.

The cold and rainy conditions were miserable and the battery ended up getting guns stuck several times, necessitating using the battery commander's LAV—G19—to tow them out with a cable to the muzzle. This highlighted the shortcoming of not having a battery echelon with a wrecker, as well as the inability to teach self-recovery of the heavy guns and their even heavier tow vehicles in the short time they had for training with them in Shilo.[27]

The first round of the first fire mission ran into a problem. The two gun numbers ramming the projectile weren't quite in sync and, as a result, it wasn't properly seated in the chamber. As the barrel was elevated the projectile fell back onto the propellant so that when the gun was fired, some of the expanding gas escaped. The result was that the round landed short of the target by approximately a kilometre—close to a farmer and a flock of sheep. Major Gallagher and the FOO, Mike Smith, ended the mission and went over to determine if anyone or anything had been injured. Fortunately, they hadn't been.

While the guns were training, the battle group's 2 Platoon, at the nearby Gumbad platoon house, was receiving a minor rocket-propelled grenade attack. A fortuitous 105mm illuminating round had revealed and spooked the Taliban. The battle group commander, who was also in the area with Lieutenant-Colonel Bert

Ges, commander of Task Force GUN DEVILS, turned part of the batteries' practice into a show of force mission with A Battery firing high explosive under Battery B of the 3-319th's coordinated illumination to support 2 Platoon.[28] The Taliban melted away. Hope recalls being criticized by Ottawa that the ammunition expenditure on the exercise had been excessive.[29]

Be that as it may, training would continue until February 19, 2006 when Task Force ORION assumed control over the area of operations from Task Force GUN DEVILS.[30] A Battery reported its first operational round fired from an M777 during a show of force mission on February 20, 2006. The credited detachment was Sergeant Paul Dolomont's 15A.[31]

For the next two weeks, the battle group carried out missions under the direction of Task Force BAYONET until Fraser's Coalition Task Force AEGIS would stand up and release BAYONET to move north.[32]

February and March were not yet the fighting season in Afghanistan. Task Force GUN DEVILS had not been involved in much patrolling before the handover, and, while the learning curve was steep, there was time for the battery to ease into a routine.[33] This started with a series of minor deployments and missions under Operation PHAROS which were essentially show of force missions using illuminating ammunition and high explosive for area denial.[34] The tasks would take some portion or another of the battery outside the wire of KAF every time an element of the battle group went out. B Company, the rifle company originally assigned to the PRT, had already been brought into the fight. With three companies deploying, often twenty or more kilometres apart, there was little time available for the guns to rest and refit.[35]

During this period, the weather would change from the early conditions, which had made it difficult for moving the gun troops. "On one occasion it took 6 hrs to move 10 [kilometres], with recovery after recovery. M777 had to be winched with LAVs. Around March the climate changed and there was almost no rain. There weren't even clouds in the sky making the daytime temperatures reach mid 50 degrees [Celsius]."[36]

The weather wasn't the only thing changing in March. AEGIS was taking over Regional Command (South).[37] Tim Bishop found out that some of the Americans' promises made to them during the two recces weren't being kept. He recalls,

We had an agreement for what the Americans were to leave behind in terms of communications gear but in the end improvisation and some very good work by our signals troops kept us in the fight as the Americans redeployed most of their gear. By far the biggest challenge was [to] try and duplicate the redundant communications architecture in time to assume command while completing the relief in place...For our arrival we had planned to take over the hard shelters that the Americans had built and occupied but they were not available (the Americans were supposed to vacate but elected not to) so we were initially in tents and then we moved in with other Canadians on site until the Americans departed and rooms were available. [Lieutenant-colonels] were 2 to a room and below that were 4 and above. Some were still in tents at the end of the tour given the magnitude of construction required to ensure everyone had adequate space...

Luckily the food and other amenities set up by the Americans [were] very useful in the transition as that part of the logistical challenges was relatively seamless.

Equipment was a challenge throughout the tour as our plan for communications architecture continued to evolve as we were working to 10 Mountain [Division headquarters] and they expected us to tap into the US systems that were just not available to us. We worked it out, but it wasn't easy. Something as simple as a video [teleconference] on secure means took a long time to solve given the unlike systems and the US's reluctance to use anything but US systems.[38]

The Americans had promised Bishop feeds in the tactical operations centre to their Predator unmanned combat aerial vehicles. All that he found there were wires on the wall. It wouldn't be until June that a system finally became operational in several restricted areas, as not every member nation represented in the AEGIS multinational brigade headquarters had clearance to see Predator data. Neither did they have Sperwer feeds. Those were left with the battle group headquarters.[39]

With Coalition Task Force AEGIS now taking up the role of a multinational brigade headquarters, it became clear to Gallagher that the brigade's fires and effects cell still saw itself in the role of a traditional doctrinal brigade artillery operations cell. Gallagher noted,

So the idea was—and this was [Regional Command (South)]—that guns are commanded at the highest level, controlled at the lowest; that they would assign me tasks and that could be a mortar task separate from the guns, drop the guns in KAF and take the mortars and support the Brits or support someone else...And if I take mortars out, if I take four mortars out, I've taken two Triple Sevens out of action. So we carried the mortar tubes with us.

I never asked Hope or a company or a platoon of LAVs for local [defence] support. I based all my [deployment] estimates off a hard drive that the US battery commander had left me with FalconView imagery—that I

could geo-rectify and import in—that was based on all sorts of aircraft and surveillance—dated, very dated, imagery—that I used to select gun positions ...We used those mortar tubes, four mortar tubes per troop, on two different bearings to cover for local defence.[40]

Gallagher's concern was leaving the battle group without indirect fire support while deployed away and how to employ the golf bag principle while providing fire support. In the end it did not become an issue as when the troops did deploy to support others they did so as part of a combat team. Moreover, troops often switched to the mortars for close targets.

These early operations made one thing clear to the battle group. The access to incredibly detailed intelligence that they had been promised during pre-deployment training simply wasn't there. "This lack of detailed intelligence, combined with the big blunt nature of our LAV-based capability, made it impossible to plan and execute rapid deliberate precision operations out of KAF ... Therefore, we began to deploy forward into company and platoon areas of operations and lived amidst the locals in the face of the enemy, out of the back of the LAVs."[41]

Where the companies went, the guns would follow.

While operations were still relatively quiet, the battle group started to suffer casualties. On March 3, two would die (one immediately, one later) in a traffic accident. On March 4, 2006 a suicide bomber hit the battle group commander's own vehicle gravely wounding one soldier. On March 5, 2006 Captain Trevor Greene, from the PRT, was seriously injured when attacked with an ax in the Shah Wali Kot region while meeting with villagers at a shura.[42]

The areas where the Taliban were making themselves felt were along Highway 4 between Kandahar and the airfield and in the Shah Wali Kot and Mienishin districts to the north. The latter were of significance to Regional Command (South) as they sat astride the main routes leading from the city of Kandahar to the city of Tarin Kot in Uruzgan, where the Dutch and Australians would deploy. There were unconfirmed reports of between 200-700 Taliban massing there.[43]

Highway 4 was left to B Company. A and C Companies, with G11 and G13, and several platoons of the Afghan army and police, deployed north on a series of smaller operations under the umbrella of Operation SOLA KOWEL (Peace Maker). The first two of these operations would run from March 8th to the 23rd and range across an area of some 20 by 20 kilometres, roughly centred on a geographic feature of mountain ridges near the Gumbad platoon house which would become known to Canadians thereafter as the "Belly Button."[44]

A and B Troops deployed into austere gun positions to the north of the various objective areas, providing support to the whole force. The road move in had shown a weakness: towing the M777. The battery had only had the guns for a few days in Shilo. There had been far too little time to teach the proper handling of the heavy tow vehicles and the very long gun. On the way out, a vehicle accident in the stop-and-go traffic of Kandahar City had sent the guns back to KAF for a day of maintenance and to regroup. Incidentally Gallagher needed to reclaim the gun tractor involved in the accident from the military police, who were insisting it be impounded until their investigation was complete.[45]

The subsequent six-hour road move, much of it over difficult terrain, showed another weakness: the guns' tires. Sharp rocks would lacerate them. The battery had come with only sixteen spares. Losing them on the move not only slowed down the road move, as stops were made for replacement, but quickly depleted the dwindling supply of spare tires.

In the end, the guns made it to their positions and provided a number of show of force missions. These missions supported the companies in their efforts to gather information on the Taliban and to connect with the locals in the area. While no fighting had taken place, intelligence reports confirmed that there were fewer Taliban in the area than estimated and that the battle group's aggressive operations had completely disrupted their intentions to take the Shah Wali Kot.[46]

The difficulties experienced in moving the guns by road pointed out two more problem areas. Canada had no helicopters deployed and any plan for an air mobile operation with them would require the assistance of kind strangers, principally the American aviation units in Kandahar. Compounding that was the fact that Canada had not, as yet, developed any drills for the lifting of the gun. In part, this was because of the short time since acquiring the M777s but also because Canada's Griffon helicopters couldn't even move an LG1 except for very short distances. The RCAF lifting a Triple Seven was out of the question.

B Troop's commander, Captain Andrew Nicholson, felt that the command side of the force didn't understand the gravity of the situation of road moves. The practice was already developing that rather than moving a bound behind the infantry as had been practiced in Wainwright, the guns would move a day ahead of them to occupy a gun position with a time to be ready before first light. The purpose of this was to provide cover for the main party's move. There would, however, be no security force for the gun troop; they would always provide their own and started referring to themselves as "infartillery." Gun positions were occupied using a box formation placing a Bison armoured personnel carrier at each corner to provide all-around local defence. Most of their tactics were being learned on-the-job in theatre rather than having been part of their training.[47]

Parsons decided they needed to experiment with the air lift process. He obtained slings, devised a lift method, and arranged for an American Chinook to do a small test lift for a few yards. Photos were taken which made their way back to the Royal Canadian Artillery School which prompted an email rocket from the school's Sergeant Major Instructor in Gunnery pointing out that the battery was not authorized to "fly" the gun as the drills had yet to be developed with the air force.[48] Other than this short test lift, the battery would never actually fly the guns in theatre. The two troops stayed bound to the rough roads, which would progressively be more subject to ambushes and seeded with improvised explosive devices. If nothing else, the gun troops' deployments to the north had taught them that they needed to be self-reliant, as help was a long, long way away. It was preferable to stay put in austere gun positions as opposed to having to drive back and forth to KAF. The troops simply hated driving through Kandahar City.[49]

Another issue arising in March was the differing conceptual views of operations held by the nationalities. Within ISAF, the operational plan specified that the PRT would be the leading edge of NATO's effort and that the military was there to enable that.[50] Canada, the Dutch and the British all saw it that way. For example, Lieutenant-Colonel Stuart Tootal, the battle group commander of the incoming British para battalion clearly saw the mission given to him as a peace support operation. The British started off their deployment with the view that any use of force was a last resort. They never expected that it would include hunting down the Taliban.[51] Tootal would later be amazed at how much 105mm ammunition was expended in support of one of his outposts.

Hope, too, saw things in this way. "As an operating concept, I intended [that] the 1 PPCLI [battle group] become an extension of the PRT so that I could coordinate and synchronize all [task force] tasks in a unified effort under one chain of command."[52]

By the end of March, everyone was seeing things in a more kinetic way. Artillery was already playing a role, and the battle group, with Gallagher's input, sent an initial theatre lessons learned report on fire support to the Land Force Doctrine and Training System headquarters. The salient points included:

Doctrine. The independent two-gun firing troop in support of a dispersed company should be a recognized method of providing fire support for counter-insurgency operations...

Doctrine. Gun batteries must be prepared to provide fire support in any direction, given the nature of the counter-insurgency battle;

Doctrine. The [FAC][53] task should be a primary duty and not a secondary task. A pool of [FACs] should be available at unit level of (sic) higher for assignment to support elements conducting operations; and

Training. FOO parties must train to fight their vehicle in ambushes. They must also possess strong dismounted FOO skills to include the ability to move dismounted with infantry elements in mountainous terrain.[54]

The Americans too were seeing the effort in more kinetic terms. Major-General Benjamin Freakley, the incoming commander of Combined Joint Task Force-76—which for the time being still had overall command of Regional Command (South) as well as Regional Command (East)—had asked the Afghan Minister of Defence for permission to conduct a major operation.[55] Planning for what would become Operation MOUNTAIN LION, reusing the name initially used in 2003, started in March and would kick off on April 11, 2006. It would concentrate American forces and resources in Regional Command (East) in a program of "clear-hold-build-engage" missions.[56] The plan also called for the Americans to come back in May and help ease the British, Dutch, and Australians into the south under a second major operation, Operation MOUNTAIN THRUST.[57]

As usual, the enemy would have a vote, and events would pull Canadians far away from the Belly Button and from Kandahar province into the neighbouring Helmand province. April would shape up far differently from March.

13

Operation MOUNTAIN LION Redux

BRITISH ADVANCE PARTIES were already operating in Afghanistan, but the main body from the 3rd Battalion of the Parachute Regiment was not scheduled to arrive until April. For the time being, operations in Helmand were still being conducted by American Special Forces Operational Detachments-Alpha and Afghan forces operating with American embedded training teams.

For well over 200 kilometres south of the Kajaki Dam, the Helmand River is a narrow band of lush green fields and villages just a few kilometres wide on either side. It is an area heavily invested in opium production, and heavily infested by the Taliban who had sworn to oppose the British arrival. The Sangin district centre was one such area of very high Taliban activity. Not far to the east lies the 1880 battlefield of Maiwand. Here a force of some 25,000 Afghan tribesmen defeated some 500 British troops and 2,000 of their Indian levies. It was still a point of pride for the Afghans. Much closer, just six kilometres to the south of Sangin, the Americans had built a small defended locality called Fire Base WOLF, but which would soon be renamed to Forward Operating Base (FOB) ROBINSON after US Special Forces Staff Sergeant Christopher Robinson who was killed in Sangin on March 25th.[1]

Early in March, Coalition Task Force AEGIS had been directed to create a platoon-sized quick reaction force (QRF) which, together with two American AH-64 attack helicopters, could be rapidly deployed by ground or by American helicopters to assist any force in the south in trouble.[2] One of the contingency plans developed for them early on was a plan to reinforce ROBINSON.[3]

In the early morning hours of March 28, 2006 an Afghan convoy en route to ROBINSON from Kajaki was subjected to significant and coordinated attacks. The convoy suffered casualties, but continued to slowly make its way to the base. AEGIS directed the QRF to deploy to ROBINSON to support the Americans there.

One member of that force was Warrant Officer Darcy Cyr, the technical warrant officer for Task Force ORION's fire support coordination centre (FSCC). His role was to be the QRF's forward air controller (FAC) whenever the battle group received a quick reaction assignment. He recalls,

> During my tour, I deployed on at least 5 separate QRF tasks that I can recall. Three were inserted by Chinook and two by ground ...

> [Intelligence] suggested the insurgents were going to attempt to overrun [ROBINSON], so the decision was made to launch the QRF that night. We deployed by Chinook shortly thereafter ... [4]

On arrival at ROBINSON, Cyr met the American combat controller on site and together the two men provided air support to the beleaguered outpost.

> There were enemy attacks the night we arrived. I called in airstrikes on several enemy positions using AH-64s, Harriers (UK), and A-10s from my location on a wooden tower in the centre of the FOB. It was chaotic. We had friendly forces outside the main perimeter as well as inside. [Afghan national security forces] were engaging from their adjacent compound. Coordination was confusing. Communications were sporadic between all personnel, and situational awareness was nearly impossible to gain. We suffered multiple wounded that night and 2 dead, a US medic, and [Private Robert Howard] Costall from 1 PPCLI. [5]

The American detachment at ROBINSON had been operating non-stop while under continuous Taliban attack for weeks. Cyr and the American controller worked with night vision goggles, bringing in medevacs, unmanned aerial vehicles (UAV), attack helicopters and jets, "racking and stacking" them in 2,000 foot blocks as aircraft checked in and out, some to refuel others to return to base to rearm. The two were stuck in the tower because the Taliban had a heavy machine gun set up 1,200–1,500 metres away that could rake the position. However, when it became necessary to make a call for casualty evacuation, and when communications were a problem, Cyr left the tower to gather the information required, an action for which he received a mention in dispatches.

> Warrant Officer Cyr was deployed with A-Battery, Princess Patricia's Canadian Light Infantry, 1st Battle Group (sic), during Operation ARCHER Rotation 1. On 28 March 2006, while serving as the forward air controller for the Quick Reaction Force at Forward Operating Base Robinson, he left the compound under enemy fire to assess the tactical situation. Having difficulty relaying the casualty evacuation request to headquarters, Warrant Officer Cyr ran back inside the compound at great personal risk. His success in transmitting the casualty removal request contributed to the safe evacuation

of three seriously wounded soldiers. His courage and dedication to duty were exemplary and brought honour to Canada.[6]

This would not be Cyr's sole contribution. Hope recalls, "The decisive point of the defensive fight came when the Canadian [FAC, Warrant Officer] Cyr, coordinated a [Joint Direct Attack Munition] strike upon a compound containing 30 Taliban—killing them all and causing the others to realize they could not win this fight. They withdrew by first light."[7]

As there was no artillery in the area, Cyr would stay at Robinson for the next week, bringing in air support. The artillery situation was about to change.

With Operation SOLA KOWEL 3 winding down in the Belly Button area, the battle group was about to undertake a bold move. On the night of March 31st the battle group withdrew 100 kilometres to Kandahar Airfield (KAF), where it replenished. The next morning, C Company (augmented by a platoon from A Company) and supported by their forward observation officer (FOO), Nichola Goddard's G13 left KAF. Moving with them were the battle group's tactical headquarters including Gallagher's G19, Nicholson's B Troop, a surveillance detachment, some engineers and the Sperwer tactical UAV Flight. Ahead of them was a 150 kilometre day and night cross-country move to Helmand.[8]

This was the start of a series of operations which would last for five weeks. The first—Operation KETARA 1—involved the C Company group pushing their way into ROBINSON. This enabled the troop's mortars to provide close-in support, if required. The Sperwer flight, meanwhile, deployed into another small base, FOB PRICE, just off the Number 1 Highway but on the west side of the river.

With the battle group, including B Troop, now secure within ROBINSON, C Company and Goddard started several aggressive cordon and search operations for Taliban leaders in the area. B Troop's commander, Andrew Nicholson, recalls the first major one,

> *We used to have these little huddles at night ... and Bill [Fletcher, the officer commanding C Company] said, "We're going outside the wire tomorrow. I'm going to take [Nichola Goddard] with me. We're going to do a clean sweep through Sangin. We anticipate that we're going to take some fire, but here's what I want you to do, Andrew. I don't want you to fire a single round in preparation. We're not going to soften the buildings up. Bayonets lead the way." And so I was "Okay. No problems, Sir. I've got lots of munitions on the truck. We'll be listening on the radio if anything changes. You let us know and we'll be ready to go."...*
>
> *They left at first light. They came up on the first objective and they got swacked*

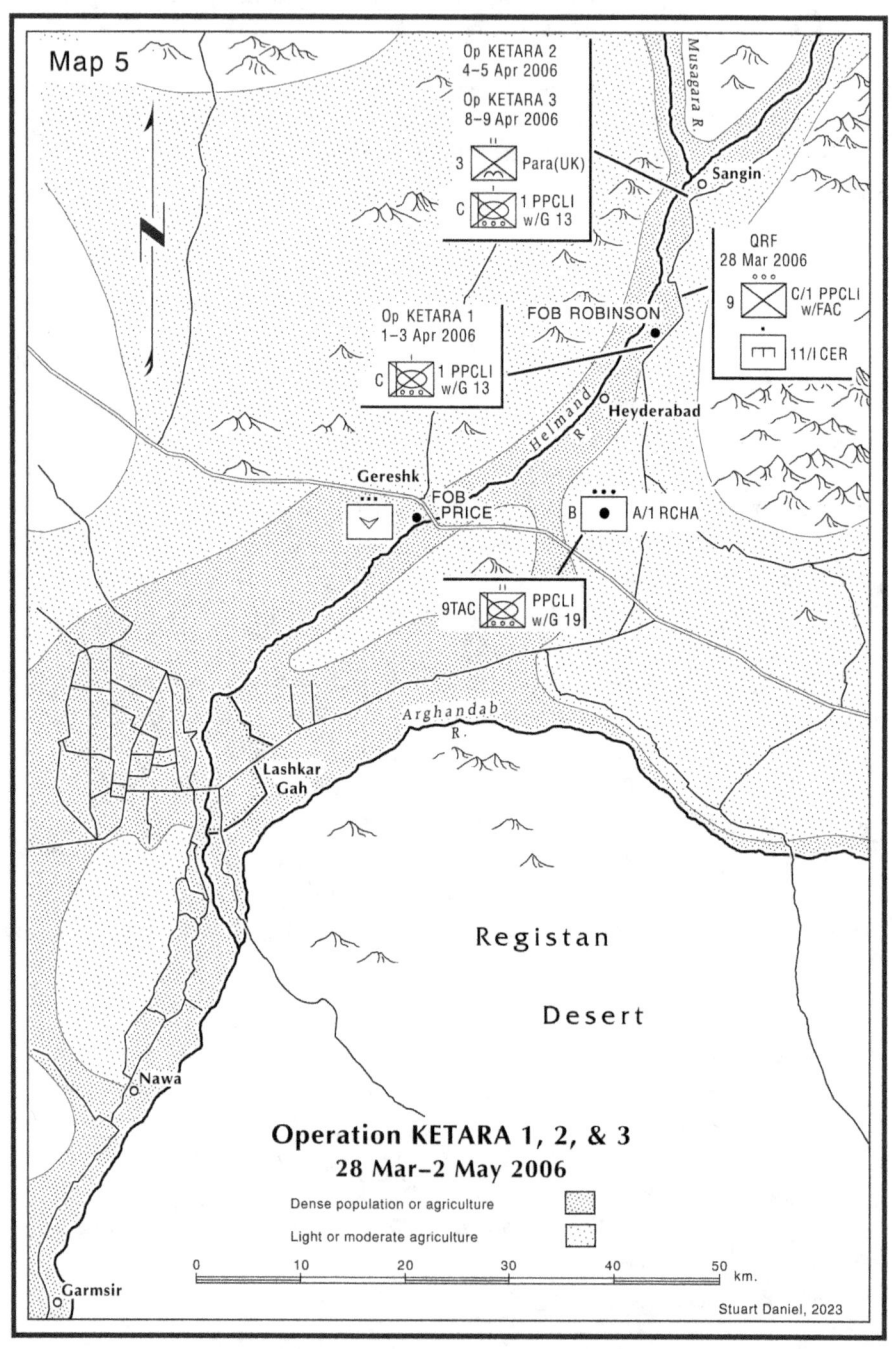

Map 5

Op KETARA 2
4–5 Apr 2006

Op KETARA 3
8–9 Apr 2006

3 | Para(UK)

C | 1 PPCLI
w/G 13

QRF
28 Mar 2006

9 | C/1 PPCLI
w/FAC

| 11/I CER

Op KETARA 1
1–3 Apr 2006

C | 1 PPCLI
w/G 13

FOB ROBINSON

Sangin

Heyderabad

Gereshk

FOB
PRICE

B | A/1 RCHA

9TAC | PPCLI
w/G 19

Musagara R.

Helmand R.

Arghandab R.

Lashkar
Gah

Nawa

Registan

Desert

Operation KETARA 1, 2, & 3
28 Mar–2 May 2006

Dense population or agriculture

Light or moderate agriculture

0   10   20   30   40   50 km.

Garmsir

Stuart Daniel, 2023

pretty hard ... They were pinned down so hard that they tried to fight their way out but had limited success to which Nichola had to come in and hastily come up with a fire plan to break this contact...And what she did then for this particular mission was she would call "target!" and then shift the fires to a new target and we just continuously fired [on this one mission] for seven hours...It was over a hundred rounds. [9]

The mission concluded just after lunch, at which point Nicholson received a satellite telephone call from AEGIS questioning who had authorized a 100-plus-rounds fire mission and asking him if it made sense to fire that many rounds in one mission. Nicholson explained he had the authority from the battery commander to fire up to half of his ammunition load without needing to ask for authorization, and then explained to them the details of how the mission had operated. While this seemed to satisfy AEGIS, it left Nicholson puzzled why the "delivery system" was being queried about a mission rather than the FOO or the battery commander.

Further operations for the rest of April followed suit.

C Company Group conducted more cordon and search operations trying to isolate high-value targets around Sangin district identified through several intelligence means, including Sperwer missions. These often included cooperation with American Special Forces and Afghan security forces. The aim of much of this was to define the intelligence picture for the British, who would soon be deploying. During one such operation, Operation KETARA 2 while C Company was deployed, the gun troop inside the wire at ROBINSON received several bursts of ineffective small arms fire. The source was never located; no fire was returned, and no casualties received.

As KETARA progressed, Gallagher swapped out the two troops. He returned B Troop to KAF to refit and then move up to Gumbad while A Troop went to ROBINSON. [10] A Troop's move proved eventful when 15A's Bison armoured personnel carrier hit an improvised explosive device (IED) some 400 metres short of the FOB blowing up the second left road wheel. Bombardier Corey Rein, the gun detachment's 3rd in command, was crew commanding and thrown up out of the hatch and back down into it again with the blast. On the way down, he broke the vehicle's master switch.

Almost immediately, an American Special Forces medic left the base, running out to be of assistance. Fortunately, the blast had remained outside the vehicle, but the detachment commander, Sergeant Paul Dolomont, received back injuries that would keep him out of the field for much of the rest of the tour. The others were just shaken up and bruised.

The broken master switch required that the vehicle be dragged the rest of the way to the FOB with the detachment's stores now piled into the overloaded

10-tonne gun tractor. The Bison would later be recovered by mechanics from the national support element, who lashed up the broken road wheel and drove it back to KAF for repair. As for Rein, he had been wearing an old pair of jungle boots and had been chewing cherry Trident gum at the time of the blast. Thereafter, every time they had to do a move, he would chew that gum and wear those boots, which, by the end of the tour, were being held together by gun tape.[11]

A few days later, Rein was commanding the detachment from between the trails of its gun during a show of force fire mission, when he received a personal satellite telephone call from the regiment's commanding officer, Lieutenant-Colonel Peter Williams. Williams had called to let him know that his promotion to master bombardier had just come through. Rein thanked him and carried on with the mission.[12]

A Troop would stay at ROBINSON until April 27, 2006 when it was ordered to "Cease Firing" and head back east to take part in Operation GAIA THRUST. Their deployment would be delayed. One of the 10-tonnes broke a control arm on the front wheels in the rough terrain. It immobilized the vehicle and required recovery. The vehicle replaced, the troop moved on, only to have it happen to another truck.[13] The rest of C Company, including Goddard's G13, would follow a few days later on May 1 and 2, 2006.[14]

March and April had defined the battle group leadership's method of operation for the battery's commander. While the tactical operations centre and the FSCC continued to operate out of the buildings at KAF, "9er TAC" stayed close to the action. This group included Gallagher's light armoured vehicle (LAV) G19, the engineer squadron commander's LAV, E19, and two lightly armoured G-Wagons in support. 9er TAC provided intimate leadership and frequently acted like another manoeuvre element which could, for example, occupy blocking positions. The group would grow in time with the addition of a Bison, a Nyala mine protected vehicle and a mobile electronic warfare team.[15]

During this period, Sperwer proved not as useful for reconnaissance (recce) as had been hoped. It was often supplanted by more capable American assets such as Predators, and attack helicopters, and other aircraft which could transmit imagery from their sensors to small, hand-held remotely operated video enhanced receivers—ROVERs—that were available to American joint terminal attack controllers (JTAC) in the field. Canadians did not yet have ROVERs. The loud noise from Sperwer's engine, however, made it a very useful deception device and the battle group would have it fly over areas to focus the Taliban's attention away from the real objectives and troop movements.

The absence of ROVERs and infrared laser designators to illuminate targets to aircraft were a noticeable shortcoming for the Canadian FACs. None of ORION's training had prepared them for the capabilities of the American enabling systems. The time at ROBINSON was well spent in being educated by the American Special Forces as to what assets were available, what their limitations were, and how best to use them.[16]

By this time in the deployment, Captain Howie Nelson and Warrant Officer Darcy Cyr's FSCC had settled into their jobs and were putting together lessons learned of their own as to fire support by both guns and air.

Initially, the training had been for a fully mobile battle group tactical operations centre to work in the field. That had changed quickly as it settled into buildings at KAF while the commanding officer circulated on the battlefield in his 9er TAC. As a result, communications worked well. Major Gallagher's LAV observation post vehicle even had one of the new Iris digital communication system's situational awareness sub-system screens. Unfortunately, it didn't have the necessary hard drives to make it work. The field-expedient fix was to put a big cork board and map over the screen and go back to using pins to mark troop locations.[17] Besides the standard military radios, both satellite radios and Iridium telephones were available for communications between the various command-and-control centres. An internet relay chat client, mIRC[18] allowed instant messaging to flow between users within discrete channels.

As an example, when the battle group's FSCC monitored a fire mission on the battery's fires net, users would immediately put data into the system where it would be monitored by all higher headquarters and relevant agencies. Where higher headquarters approval for the mission or airspace clearance or coordination with other force elements—such as special operations forces—would be required, the clearance would return by the same means. Similarly, in the event of contact with insurgents by troops in the field, the system would be used to initiate the push forward of air resources. A reply would assign aircraft and the battery would task one of its three FACs in the field to control it or, sometimes, Nelson and Cyr would themselves take over control of the strike from the FSCC.[19]

Many of Nelson and Cyr's observations related to the quality of the support offered at the front. The FOO's LAV observation post vehicles were showing themself to be excellent assets, but proper equipment for FACs, such as ROVERs and target designators, was lacking. Once again, the infantry had Vector binoculars while the artillery, years after the experiences and observations of Operation APOLLO and Kabul, still didn't.[20] Cyr noted,

> *The [FAC] and FOO must have their own mobility. The targeting suite in an [LAV] can't be 'shared' during a firefight. Most [troops in contact] situations require both [artillery] and [close air support], so both the FOO and [FAC]*

must have timely access to their targeting/[communications] equipment. In Afghanistan, usually the [FAC] rode in the back of the LAV (if mounted) and operated out of the personnel hatch, with no integrated targeting equipment. Having the [FAC] trying to look around or over the turret while the 25mm cannon is firing, to acquire a target without getting shot, is not the best way to conduct business, never mind trying to utilize handheld equipment such as a laser designator or Video Down Link receiver, and write down [close air support] fire orders.[21]

On top of that, combining them in a single LAV created the risk that one mine strike or IED would take out a company's entire fire support team.[22]

Training was also a noticeable issue. Cyr pointed out,

[FACs] need to be trained to an extremely high level of proficiency. Unlike a FOO, who has multiple independent doublechecks prior to a round leaving the tube, the [FAC] has no double check. Most of the time, the pilot has limited or no situational awareness as he is just arriving over the scene of an incredibly chaotic situation. He only knows what information the [FAC] passes him, and may not ever see the target. When the [FAC] does make an error, it can be strategic in scope.[23]

Both the air space coordination centre (ASCC) and the FSCC made good use of the FalconView software to track airspace data, but there were no laptops for the FACs in the field to use it.[24] American air enablers were proving themselves invaluable, especially in times of danger close operations. Both the Predator and most aircraft delivered precision missiles and bombs which could be quickly and accurately placed close to friendly troops. While the M777 was also very accurate, it required special procedures to creep rounds in close to friendly troops.[25] The much anticipated precision Excalibur rounds would not be available for quite some time.

While G13 had been busy with C Company in Helmand, Captain Bob Meade's G11 with Master Bombardier Furber—FAC call sign "Slayer 11"—and Captain O'Donnell's A Troop—and subsequently B Troop after the change-round—had continued their support of A Company and Recce Platoon in the north around the Shah Wali Kot and Mienishin Districts. Here they started building a new base to augment the Gumbad platoon house and conducted aggressive patrols. FOB MARTELLO, overlooking the Taliban-sympathetic village of Elbak, wouldn't be complete until the beginning of summer. Nonetheless it was already adding security for the soon-to-arrive Dutch along the vulnerable route to Tarin Kot. To call MARTELLO a completed base would be a kindness. Some described it as a temporary parking lot on the floor of a horseshoe-shaped valley. It was located there primarily to interfere with a Taliban ratline. Gumbad platoon house itself consisted of little more than a compound reinforced by some concertina barbed wire.

By the latter half of April, G11 and B Troop would support yet another Operation SOLA KOWEL; the fourth of that name. It aimed to engage with local leadership in the Mianishin District and to disrupt Taliban activities in the area.[26]

The road from KAF to Gumbad and MARTELLO was a difficult one, but needed to be used several times a week to transport personnel and supplies between Kandahar and the Shah Wali Kot due to the lack of helicopter support for the task force. By April 22, 2006 five vehicles had already been hit by IEDs, seriously injuring ten men. On that day, during Operation SOLA KOWEL 4, a report came in of another vehicle struck. At first there were cheers in the tactical operations centre as most of the vehicle's occupants were reported as "Priority Four", the medical term for "does not require medical attention." This rapidly turned to dismay when their situation was further described as "Vital Signs Absent", indicating probable fatalities.[27] Bombardier Myles Mansell, Lieutenant William Turner, and Corporals Matthew Dinning and Randy Payne were killed on the road near Gumbad when the G-Wagon they were riding in hit a quadruple-stack of anti-tank mines.[28]

Myles had been a reservist with the 5th (British Columbia) Field Artillery Regiment, RCA in Victoria. At 25, just months after becoming engaged, he had deployed to Afghanistan as a member of the provincial reconstruction team because he had wanted to help Afghans get the freedom which Canadians took for granted.[29] He had been working in the quartermaster stores in KAF and had volunteered to accompany the brigade commander's tactical headquarters as part of his close protection detail.

Turner too had a gunner background. He had started his military service with 11th Field Artillery Regiment, RCA in Guelph before moving to Edmonton, where he served with 20th Field Artillery Regiment, RCA and subsequently as a civil-military cooperation officer out of Land Force Western Area headquarters.

The four of them had been part of a convoy on the way back to Kandahar. General Fraser had been visiting the area and was flying back by helicopter. Members of his close protection detail were travelling back in the G-Wagon. Turner, who had been working out of Gumbad, had hopped aboard for a ride back to Kandahar for a break.

Back in Canada, Master Bombardier Steve Merson had only returned forty days earlier to the regiment in Petawawa after having completed his tour driving Colonel Mike Capstick in Kabul. Master Warrant Officer Mike Provencher asked him if he was prepared to escort Mansell home. Merson considered it his honour to do so. He found out subsequently that two of the other casualties, Dinning and Payne, were both individuals he had come to know while in Kabul. Unfortunately they received no briefing on what their job would all entail. They essentially took a car to Trenton to escort them first to the coroner in Toronto and then with Mansell on to Victoria. In Victoria for the funeral Merson was the one who carried Mansell's medal and beret on the pillow. Mansell's mom hugged him and thanked him for bringing their son home.[30]

While C Company was frequently engaged in Helmand during April, 9er TAC did not confine itself there. On April 14, 2006 it was present near Howz-e-Madad and Sangsar village in Zhari District where a poorly run Afghan national police attack had left them with many casualties. Too eager to get into the fight, the police had not waited for or coordinated their attack with the Canadians' B Company.[31]

B Company had started off patrolling Kandahar and the vital Highway 4 route unsupported by guns. They did, from time to time, have Captain Mike Smith's G12 as both a FOO and FAC—Slayer 12—but Smith also served occasionally with the battle group's QRF. He and his team would also do tours working out of the Gumbad platoon house and at MARTELLO.[32]

With the April 14, 2006 incident came a dawning recognition that the Taliban were gaining strength in the Panjwayi and Zhari districts. There was an initial misinterpretation that this massing had more to do with the poppy harvest than a looming attack.[33] Notwithstanding this interpretation, B Company was being targeted more in this region than it had been before. Lieutenant-Colonel Hope resolved that April would culminate with an operation in Zhari during the period from April 27 to 29, 2006 called Operation GAIA THRUST. Joining B Company would be three Afghan army platoons and two Afghan police platoons. The objective was to cordon off an area south of the Highway at Howz-e-Madad roughly five kilometres deep by eight kilometres wide and have the Afghan troops search a half dozen key objective areas.

G12 was brought down from Gumbad in support. Gallagher's G19 and A Troop, recently released from ROBINSON, would also participate. A Troop would set up in an austere gun position some two kilometres north of the Number 1 Highway and ten kilometres northwest of the centre of the search area.

For Gallagher's G19, the operation would be highlighted at noon on April 28, 2006 when the tactical headquarters that he was moving with came under intense small-arms and rocket-propelled grenade fire shortly after one vehicle had become stuck in the powdery sand. It took some twenty minutes to recover the stuck vehicle and another damaged vehicle while in continuous contact. The event brought home a clear and loud lesson; the Taliban were not running away. They were standing and fighting. It was a signal for all who would listen.

Early May saw A Troop back covering the Kandahar-Tarin Kot Highway at MARTELLO. With Captain Bob O'Donnell on leave, Captain Sean Tremblay was running the troop. One gunner mentioned to Tremblay that the interpreter was acting strangely. He had not only taken the unusual step of wearing his helmet and armoured vest, but had also built himself a little fort out of water bottles. The interpreter had heard Taliban radio chatter intercepts to the effect that an attack on the gun position was contemplated. Rather than reporting it immediately, he had first taken protective measures. The radio chatter clarified that they were under observation, but the observer hadn't developed a good head count of the troop and that the Taliban commander wanted to first have his supper before deciding whether to attack.

Tremblay ordered a stand-to and passed the information up to the FSCC. Anticipating an attack, he asked for permission to do a "Killer Junior" test-fire shoot. Effectively, a "Killer Junior" is a direct fire open action using an airburst round. This was granted, and after determining the area clear of noncombatants, was executed, providing the gun detachments with their first experience of that procedure on the M777. With the troop now trained, Tremblay asked for and was granted permission to fire some mortar rounds into the Taliban observer's area. These were followed by Taliban radio transmissions which made it clear the Taliban were no longer going to attack.[34]

While A Troop had gone back to the north, B Company did not remain idle in

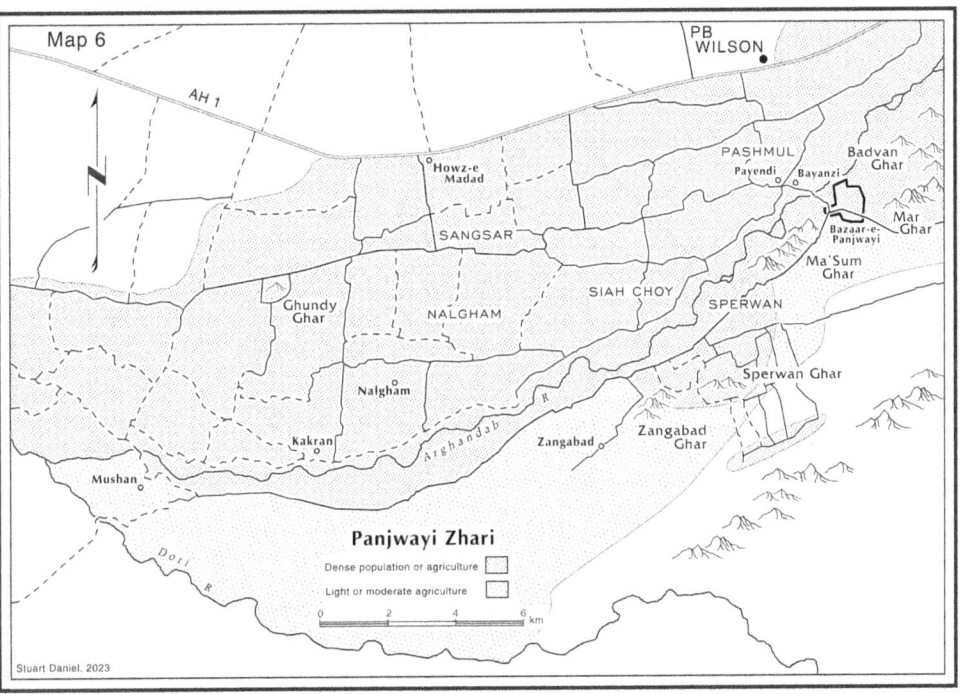

Zhari. During the period from May 2 to 13, 2006 it conducted sweeping operations in Panjwayi and Zhari called Operation BARCA. The purpose was to disrupt the Taliban and gather intelligence as to their activities. On May 14, 2006 Hope undertook a recce in the region with the chief of the Governor's immediate reaction police and resolved to take some action in the area.[35]

While the battle group turned its attention onto Zhari/Panjwayi, Operation MOUNTAIN LION would continue on, primarily in Regional Command (East), until the end of June. Task Force AEGIS's focus would stay on the south under Operation MOUNTAIN THRUST.

For Major-General Freakley, Commander of Combined Joint Task Force 76, the period May 15 to July 31, 2006 would be the lead-up to the transition of Regional Command (South) from his command to that of ISAF. To provide for that, he had initiated Operation MOUNTAIN THRUST. He realized the difficulties that the staggered introduction of the various NATO forces would bring and had asked to have his 4th Brigade Combat Team brought in from Louisiana to assist with the transition. His request was denied. That left him only his 3rd Brigade Combat Team and the 1st Battalion of the 3rd Marines from Hawai'i. They would remain primarily in Regional Command (East) focusing on Operation MOUNTAIN LION. The burden in the south would fall on the as-yet incomplete Coalition Task Force AEGIS. It had only two manoeuvre task forces on the ground: Task Force ORION, and in Zabul, US Lieutenant-Colonel Frank Sturek's 2nd Battalion of the 4th Infantry Regiment with elements of the Romanian 341st Infantry Battalion "Rechinii Albi".[36] The aim would be to set conditions to bring the British fully into Helmand and the Dutch into Uruzgan.

For Task Force ORION this was problematic, as the upcoming operations would frequently take them, and just as importantly their American combat enabling support elements, away from Panjwayi and Zhari, just as the Taliban were showing signs of massing there.[37]

Operation BARCA and a recce of Zhari had identified the necessity for future operations here. The battle group slated Operation BRAVO GUARDIAN in the Pashmul area of Zhari for May 16 to 18, 2006. BRAVO GUARDIAN would hurt.

Like so many operations in Afghanistan, Operation BRAVO GUARDIAN would start with preliminary movements into the area of operations in the darkness of the early morning hours.

The initial objective was to conduct a sweep from Bazaar-e-Panjwayi towards Nalgham township in the southwestern part of Zhari. To that end, 9er TAC, with an Afghan police platoon, had set up a blocking position to Nalgham's northwest at Ghundy Ghar.

C Company, with one of its platoons, one from B Company, and an Afghan platoon, strung itself out in blocking positions along Highway 1 to the north. Another C Company platoon, Call Sign 32, and Nichola Goddard's G13 were attached to B Company. C Company's third platoon formed the battalion's immediate reaction force. B Company's regular forward observer, Captain Mike Smith, had returned to Gumbad.

B Company, which was scheduled to conduct the sweep, with two of its own platoons, the attached one from C Company, one Afghan platoon, and Goddard's G13, moved into Bazaar-e-Panjwayi just south of the Arghandab River. Captain Rob O'Donnell's A Troop would provide fire support throughout from the north side of Highway 1. The troop was reduced to a single gun as the second had been damaged trying to negotiate a winding security barrier exiting KAF and was left behind for repairs. The remaining gun would be double-scaled on fire missions firing not only the rounds it would ordinarily fire but also those of the absent gun.[38]

The operation would not unfold as planned, however. As the companies launched on the morning of May 17, 2006 insurgents were spotted in Pashmul to the north of Bazaar-e-Panjwayi. Radio orders directed B Company to move into the village complexes there. They did so and were quickly engaged in a hard-fought defence by the Taliban in the complex terrain that made up the area. Goddard and her crew, who were manoeuvering with 5 Platoon, responded with both artillery and attack helicopter support.[39] B Company captured some 32 suspected insurgents and found signs of mass casualty evacuations.[40]

The fight ebbed and flowed until, near dusk, B Company's Number 5 Platoon and Goddard's FOO detachment were caught in a major ambush at a structure near the village of Bayanzi which would thereafter be called the "white school". While originally built as a school, the Taliban had taken it over. G13 was supporting 5 Platoon when their LAV was hit by a flurry of rocket-propelled grenades (RPG). Sergeant Michael Denine, a section commander in C Company's Number 8 Platoon, recalls,

Around this time we got a call over the net that I will never forget. Master Bombardier Jeff Fehr, [her] driver, said she got killed.[41] And then you just hear the net light up. I was like, "Get the fuck out of there." Her car got hit maybe four or five times on the one side. It was a mess trying to get them out of there, but they got them out. We ended up calling in a B-1 bomber to effect it.[42]

The bomber had been called by AEGIS to overfly in a "show-of-force" fly-by, but a show-of-force wouldn't do it. Howie Nelson, at ORION's FSCC, interrupted with a "Break! Break! Break!" and demanded a live drop. Nelson sensed that AEGIS was reluctant to act unless they had a 98% solution. They wanted to help but were falling short. Nelson screamed at AEGIS to force a live drop.[43] They did and 5 Platoon extracted itself in a process during which Master Bombardier Jeff Fehr, the senior-most non-commissioned team member—Sergeant Dave Redford was away on leave—excelled. Fehr received a mention in dispatches which read,

> On May 17, 2006 during Operation BRAVO GUARDIAN, [Master Bombardier Fehr's] platoon came under enemy fire in an ambush. When his commander was fatally wounded, he assumed command of the light armoured vehicle, successfully egressing out of the area under a barrage of rocket-propelled grenades and small arms fire. He continued to command the crew effectively, coordinating fire support and managing the engagement. [Master Bombardier] Fehr's decisive actions under enemy fire undoubtedly prevented more casualties and brought great credit to the Canadian Armed Forces and to Canada.[44]

At A Troop's gun line, they could hear the infantry's gunfire but had no actual idea of what was happening. The first hint of anything unusual was Fehr calling in for "Five Rounds Fire For Effect"—no adjustment—just straight into "Fire For Effect". It wouldn't be until forty-five minutes later that the news of Nichola's death reached the guns.[45]

Nichola had done much of her work under the close observation of Task Force ORION's commander, Lieutenant-Colonel Ian Hope. His words perhaps best sum up the type of gunner she was during those few, all too short, months in Afghanistan,

> She had served as the FOO with C and B Companies and in the performance of her duties [Captain] Goddard lived almost continuously in the field, in austere FOB, and in company leaguers situated routinely in open fields near remote villages; always in the vicinity of known enemy sanctuaries. In such circumstances, sleeping on the ground under the stars and working in conditions of extreme heat and dust, she led her FOO party with a superb mix of cheerfulness and competence...

> Working with only limited [Task Force] support, and remaining long hours in positions exposed to enemy observation and fire, she defined the objective areas, confirmed company group approaches and, for the first time since the Korean War, executed high explosive and illumination fire missions in support of Canadian troop manoeuvres against a known enemy. In addition, she coordinated a complex mix of artillery, aircraft, and electronic warfare assets, with technical perfection and with unwavering calmness that won for her [the] complete trust and respect of all ranks. Her willingness to volunteer

for dangerous tasks, her acceptance of risk in continual presence of the enemy, and her continuous demonstration of the highest leadership skills parallel the highest manifestations of leadership and courage in Canadian military history.[46]

Her battery commander, Steve Gallagher, would later say that as a gunner officer, "she got good, real good. Bill Fletcher [the company commander she worked for in Afghanistan] always wanted to hear what she had to say. She had a keen battle sense, just like those hockey players that can see the other side's play before they actually do it."[47]

She would posthumously be awarded the Meritorious Service Medal.[48]

1st Regiment, Royal Canadian Horse Artillery would also honour her memory by naming a new trigonometrical point in the Canadian Forces Base Shilo training area as "Trig GODDARD". The base was about to issue a new training area map, and the regiment was able to get Trig GODDARD included on it. The ceremony included A Battery deploying to the field and Nichola's FOO party calling in a fire mission. Nichola's husband Jason Beam, as well as her parents, Tim and Sally Goddard, attended. They had the opportunity to meet members of Nichola's crew and to ride in the type of LAV in which Nichola and her party operated.

But beyond her work ethic as a gunner, others remember her human side. Howie Nelson recalls when Nichola had first joined the regiment, she had asked him as to whether people dressed up in costumes at work for Halloween. He replied that they certainly did, and she dressed up that morning as a witch. Howie recalled how happy she had been to do that, but at the last second, he found that he simply couldn't go through with the prank and admitted the truth.

The battle group had only a short time to mourn their loss. Pashmul became a joint special operations area for the period of May 18 to 23, 2006, which required the battle group to move out to make way for special operations forces. ORION shifted its focus to the Shah Wali Kot on Operation NARINJI TABAR during this period. Meanwhile, in Canada, Captain Andrew Charchuk was pulled off the FAC course he was attending in Gagetown, and sent to be the replacement FOO for G13.

While awaiting his arrival, things became even worse for G13. No one else in the crew had been injured on May 17, 2006 but a few days later, after Captain Goddard's ramp ceremony, Major Gallagher decided the crew should go back into the field to support a lay-back patrol set out at night to ambush suspected Taliban. The patrol had not made contact and G13 went out in their LAV to pick them up off the highway. They did this by dropping their ramp while the infantry hopped on board. During this process, the Taliban sprung their own ambush and hammered G13 with small arms and RPG fire. While the vehicle took off at speed for Patrol Base WILSON with the ramp still down, Bombardier Chris Gauthier took a hit to his right hand that severed the index finger and thumb. He was medevaced to Kandahar. The rest of the crew followed by ground transport shortly after and were met by social workers.

While the Canadians had previously experienced losses, the gunners had been hit particularly hard in this period of a few weeks: first Myles Mansell and Bill Turner at the end of April and now Nichola Goddard and Gauthier. But the war wasn't about to pause. B Troop's commander, Captain Andrew Nicholson, noted that May 17, 2006 was a pinnacle. From that date forward, the operations and battles became much more aggressive.[49] Everyone in Task Force ORION realized now that they were experiencing a sea change. The Taliban were in Zhari/Panjwayi in strength and meaning to fight. That word, however, had not yet made an impact higher up.

14

OPERATION MOUNTAIN THRUST

MOUNTAIN THRUST would take the Canadians away from Zhari/Panjwayi and back to Helmand to assist the British. Before departing, however, there was time for one more battle group operation in Pashmul. With the special operations forces missions following Goddard's death now completed, B and C Companies deployed in the early morning hours of May 24, 2006 on Operation YADGAR. While two platoons screened the east and south, C Company and B Company pushed into Pashmul from the north and west, respectively. B Troop set up its guns a few kilometres to the north just across the Number 1 Highway near to Howz-e-Madad. G19, in the meantime, occupied the heights of Ma'Sum Ghar on overwatch with 9er TAC.[1]

The first contact came through an ambush in midmorning and was quickly responded to with artillery fire. Patrols continued and the battle group leaguered up on the battlefield before resuming its operation the next day. Enemy action was significantly heavier the next day and "deadly accurate" artillery support[2] and close air support was needed to overcome the insurgents who withdrew to the southwest. The next day, the battlegroup again followed and continued engaging. It was becoming clear that the necessary action was to fix the enemy with fire and then manoeuvre onto them for close-quarters fighting, a skill that would take time and several engagements to develop.[3]

The Combined Joint Task Force 76 command team met with the Canadians on May 29, 2006. Two matters were raised by ORION's command team. The first was that the enemy was massing in Zhari, something which the divisional staff had not yet picked up on. The second, was that there were only a few dozen Afghan army troops supporting the battle group. It was appreciated that the plans for Operation MOUNTAIN THRUST would take Canadian troops away from the area and they were directed do what they could before they left.[4]

Two of Task Force ORION's companies would remain in the area conducting platoon-level patrols and leadership engagements until June 10, 2006. They would shift to the north in two distinct phases. The first, Operation JAGRA, would run from June 11 to 14, 2006 and be a major effort by both B and C Companies at deception and in suppressing activity in Zhari/Panjwayi. B Company would then remain behind in Zhari while C Company moved north into Khakrez, Ghorak, Shah Wali Kot and Mianishin. Here, it and A Company, which was already in the north, would conduct a series of operations collectively called Operation TABAR.

During the period from June 8 to 10, 2006 the two gun troops conducted a switch round. B Troop, which had been in an austere position just to the north of Highway 1 in Zhari, moved further north to replace A Troop which had spent over three weeks at Gumbad. B Troop deployed to the nearby Forward Operating Base (FOB) MARTELLO where they were greeted by the Regiment's Colonel Commandant, Major-General (Retired) John Arch MacInnis, who had come to Afghanistan to visit the troops. As B Troop settled in, General MacInnis accompanied A Troop on their road trip back to Kandahar Airfield (KAF). The troop had been scheduled for 3 days of rest and refit. This, however, was cut to 36 hours in order for the troop to move to an austere position directly north of Ghundy Ghar on the far side of the Number 1 Highway in time to support Operation JAGRA.[5]

Operation JAGRA began with B and C Companies deploying by deception moves to their start positions. C Company, together with G13 and an Afghan army platoon and some Afghan police assembled near Ghundy Ghar. B Company with G12 and similar Afghan attachments assembled south of the Arghandab River near the town of Mushan. From there they swept east-southeast in a line so that both companies were south of the Arghandab River in Panjwayi before hooking back northward across the river into Zhari, heading towards Patrol Base (PB) WILSON. Throughout this operation, Gallagher's G19 remained at Ma'Sum Ghar with 9er TAC.

A massive information operations campaign and several clearance missions characterized the operation against pockets of insurgents. The Taliban would, on occasion, hold for 24 to 36 hours before breaking contact and withdrawing. The battle group's lack of air resources—who were busy supporting the Americans in Regional Command (East)—made it extremely difficult for Canadian troops to keep in contact with the enemy.[6] The result was that, notwithstanding the contacts, the companies were unsuccessful in pinpointing major Taliban strongholds.

The operation ended on June 14, 2006 with G13 and C Company ordered northward to join Operation TABAR. B Company and G12 stayed behind, keeping watch on Zhari.

Once C Company arrived in the north, there would be three major battle group operations as follows: Operation TABAR KUTEL from June 17 to 21, 2006 in the districts of Khakrez and Ghorak to the west; Operation TABAR POLAD on June 24 and 25, 2006 an airmobile insertion with a ground force link-up in the east in the Charnatu area; and Operation TABAR ROGH on June 26 and 27, 2006 in the northern area of Gumbad and Zamto Kalay.[7]

Operation TABAR KUTEL, characterized by bold sweeping moves across northern Kandahar, was designed to confuse the insurgents as much as come to grips with them. On its last day, the light armoured vehicle (LAV) of C Company's second-in-command struck an improvised explosive device (IED), seriously wounding two.

A and C Companies went east, while the 9er TAC group swung west in an attempted high-speed deception move through Ghorak district. Captain Howie Nelson, the battery's second-in-command, was forward with them as the acting battery commander. The battery's quartermaster sergeant, Warrant Officer John Gero, was also acting as the battery sergeant major while Major Gallagher and Master Warrant Officer Parsons were on leave. Nelson recalls,

> We were following the companies as they went and pushed for MOUNTAIN THRUST and...[the commanding officer] almost used his TAC as...the fourth manoeuvre unit of ORION. So it was us [G19] and he had himself, his car. The battalion sergeant major had his own vehicle, the [engineer support coordination centre] and [G19] were a kind of convoy of four vehicles and he used us as the fourth manoeuvre piece.[8]

Several blown tires had severely reduced progress, and the group leaguered up for repairs. The next morning, June 22, 2006 they set out west in the direction of Maywand, running off the maps that they had with them when Nelson's G19 struck an improvised explosive device (IED) just after first light.[9]

> All of a sudden we hear this "Boom" and everything goes black. I was following Colonel Hope and [was two cars behind] and he must have just missed the IED by an inch because I was driving in his wheel tracks and my car actually hit it and blew us up. Everyone was okay. My driver was a little bit scratched up. The blast went through the vehicle so much that it actually threw me up out of the turret and I smashed my hip as I landed on the turret and I landed back inside...The dust settles and Colonel Hope circles the wagons.[10]

They assessed the situation and hooked G19 up to drag it to a safe place. During this process, they received some small arms fire and returned fire at what was obviously the trigger man, who escaped on a motorbike to a nearby village.

It took some eight hours for recovery to come and take G19 away by flatbed and then to meet up with a platoon from B Company. The group now made its return to

KAF, linking up further with a resupply convoy.[11] Their LAV gone, Nelson and Gero hitched a ride in the commanding officer's LAV.

The attacks were far from over. On the western edge of the city, a suicide vehicle-borne IED attacked the now 50-vehicle convoy. The explosion peppered the battle group commander's LAV with shrapnel and flame, seriously injuring the air sentry, Master Corporal Gregory White, who was standing in the rear hatch next to where Nelson and Gero were sitting. White sustained a major wound to his arm. Nelson and Gero both worked on him, rendering first aid and applying a tourniquet. In fact, it would take three tourniquets to control the bleeding.[12]

Gero scouted for a helicopter landing zone for a medevac but there wasn't one nearby, so instead Hope rushed his LAV to Camp NATHAN SMITH to get White medical treatment.[13] It was clear that the command group was being targeted and that information about the group's movement was being given to the Taliban by members of the Afghan police.[14]

For Nelson and Gero, the situation was not quite over. As their ride raced off to Camp NATHAN SMITH, they were left by the side of the road to hitchhike back to KAF in one of the logistics vehicles. Gero was dropped off at the maintenance compound, where two American soldiers sitting on a pallet took one look at him and inquired if he was all right. It was the first time Gero realized he was covered in blood.[15]

On his arrival, Nelson discovered that news of their experiences had not only reached the KAF before them but also Canada and Major Gallagher, who was in Camp Mirage, on his way back to Afghanistan. Gallagher phoned Nelson to inquire how he was, and Nelson's immediate reply was, "Sorry, Dad. Wrecked your car."[16]

Two more TABAR operations would follow.

The first, Operation TABAR POLAD, would target the town of Chernatu in Mianishin district, a well known insurgent centre. Chernatu had first seen Canadian action on December 4 and 5, 2005 when a team from Joint Task Force 2 was sent in after a high value target. That operation had received very high resistance on insertion, resulting in the loss of an American CH-47 Chinook helicopter and the wounding of several Canadian and Afghan security forces personnel.[17]

TABAR POLAD would go on June 24 and 25, 2006 and would also be an airmobile assault supported by a ground forces link-up. This time, however, it would be at battle group strength and supported by the guns of B Troop. The airmobile assault force would include one platoon from each of A Company, C Company, and from the Afghan army landing in a Helicopter Landing Zone previously secured by the battalion's reconnaissance (recce) platoon. The rest of the force moved by ground into blocking positions. While there was significant electronic activity, little resistance was offered and the battle group's remaining time in the area was mostly spent in leadership engagements and reinforcing the legitimacy of the national government.[18] The conditions were now set for the Dutch to make their entry into Uruzgan.

With that accomplished, and notwithstanding that during the latter part of June, B Company and US Special Forces elements were experiencing attacks in Zhari, the battle group completed plans for G13 and C Company to move some 80 kilometres to the southeast of KAF. Their mission would be to move to Spin Boldak near the Pakistan border and take over the FOB there from the French and American Special Forces. C Company was scheduled to start its occupation on July 2, 2006 the day after Canada Day, when the new Tim Horton's—which had already had a soft opening—was to be officially opened at KAF. On June 30, 2006 however, two 107mm rockets had overflown the ammunition depot and would hit the airfield. One struck between two of the wings of the tented dining facility, injuring eight Canadians.[19]

The most seriously injured was Master Bombardier Bounyarat Makthepharak from 30th Field Artillery Regiment, RCA in Ottawa. Mak had arrived in Afghanistan a mere week before. It wasn't his first operational tour, having previously deployed as part of force protection to both Bosnia with the 2nd Battalion of the Princess Patricia's Canadian Light Infantry and to Kabul with Duke's Company of the 1st Battalion of The Royal Canadian Regiment. He had deployed once again in the force protection role.

Splinters had entered his back, with some damaging one lung, collapsing both, and also embedding close to his heart. Mak can only remember having gone to get some ice cream and then waking up in Germany at the US Army's Landstuhl Regional Medical Centre. While he'd been unconscious, the doctors at the Role 3 Multinational Medical Unit in Kandahar had opened his chest and performed skilful surgery to save his life. After a week in Germany, he was flown to Ottawa, where he was again hospitalized for a week before being allowed to recover at home. That recovery would take the better part of a year and a half.[20] In 2008, he was well enough to transfer as a master bombardier to the regular force, where he was posted to the 2nd Regiment, Royal Canadian Horse Artillery (2 RCHA) and deployed back to Afghanistan in 2010 for seven months as part of the national support element assisting with upgrading tracked LAVs.[21]

G13 and C Company would not have much time to settle in at Spin Boldak. General Freakley granted a deviation from Operation MOUNTAIN THRUST's plans, in order to allow the battle group to run a brief operation in Pashmul in Zhari to deal with the growing Taliban threat there, before moving west to help the hard-

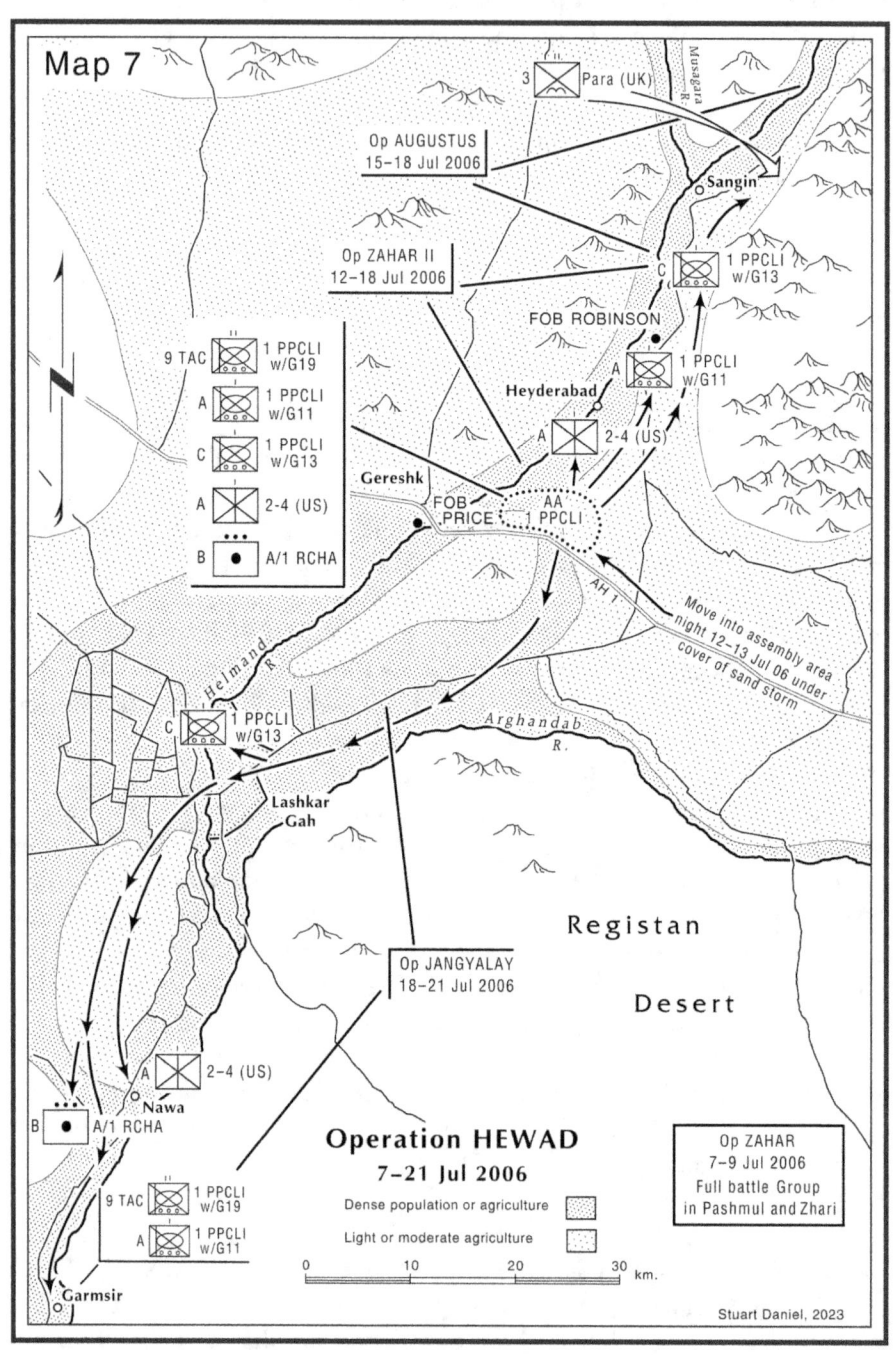

Map 7

3))))) Para (UK)

Op AUGUSTUS
15–18 Jul 2006

Op ZAHAR II
12–18 Jul 2006

Musagra R.

Sangin

C [XX] 1 PPCLI
w/G13

FOB ROBINSON

9 TAC [XX] 1 PPCLI
w/G19

A [XX] 1 PPCLI
w/G11

C [XX] 1 PPCLI
w/G13

A [XX] 2-4 (US)

B [•] A/1 RCHA

A [XX] 1 PPCLI
w/G11

Heyderabad

A [XX] 2-4 (US)

Gereshk

FOB
PRICE

AA
1 PPCLI

Helmand R.

AH 1

Move into assembly area
night 12–13 Jul 06 under
cover of sand storm

Arghandab R.

C [XX] 1 PPCLI
w/G13

Lashkar
Gah

Registan

Op JANGYALAY
18–21 Jul 2006

Desert

A [XX] 2-4 (US)

Nawa

B [•] A/1 RCHA

Operation HEWAD
7–21 Jul 2006

Dense population or agriculture

Light or moderate agriculture

9 TAC [XX] 1 PPCLI
w/G19

A [XX] 1 PPCLI
w/G11

Op ZAHAR
7–9 Jul 2006
Full battle Group
in Pashmul and Zhari

0   10   20   30 km.

Garmsir

Stuart Daniel, 2023

pressed British in Helmand. C Company would leave one platoon at the border, detach another as a quick reaction force (QRF), and with what was left, join the battle group.

The overall operation in Helmand would be called Operation HEWAD and was scheduled for the middle two weeks of July. For ORION, the first phase—the Zhari phase—would be Operation ZAHAR. The battle group would include parts of each of its three companies, two Afghan army companies, a recce squadron of the British Household Cavalry and both of A Battery's gun troops. It took place from July 7 to 9, 2006 in Zhari District, specifically Shakur Ghundy in Pashmul.

The original deployment plan had envisioned B Company working with the provincial reconstruction team and consequently they joined them at Camp NATHAN SMITH in Kandahar City. Increasingly, B Company, and Smith's G12, were tasked to serve as a manoeuvre company like A and C Companies and operate in Panjwayi and Zhari to deal with the growing Taliban threat there. As late as June 24, 2006 B Company had been operating in Panjwayi. Sergeant Jason Ladouceur, G12's fire effects detachment commander, recalls, "On 24 June during the battle of Mushan the Company and G12 got awarded an American combat patch from the US psychological operations crew that was with us. It is something nice to hang on the wall. Basically, from that point on we fought with B [Company] day in and day out during all operations during the numerous battles for [Panjwayi]."[22]

B Company and G12 had moved into the Panjwayi district centre for a while but had regrouped at NATHAN SMITH to prepare for ZAHAR.[23]

Operation ZAHAR commenced with a silent night insertion by the entire force. This included adding Afghan soldiers with each section and holding the rest in reserve so as not to be given away by the Afghans' typical use of headlights on their pickups. The three companies and the recce platoon moved to effectively surround the objective area. The first contact came rapidly as one A Company platoon made contact barely a half hour after midnight on the morning of the 8th. For A Company, having been up north, this would be the first time in the tour that they would come to grips with their enemy and be able to fight back.[24] The contacts quickly spread and soon the companies started taking prisoners and engaging in firefights. The battle group spent the next twelve hours slowly tightening the noose around the area.

Moving with C Company was G13, now joined by Captain Andrew Charchuk, taking part in his first action. On the way in before midnight, they met groups of women and children fleeing the area, a bad sign. The advance continued until, at around 0300 hours on July 8, 2006 flurries of small arms and rocket-propelled grenade (RPG) fire struck from both sides. They answered with the company's 25mm cannons and 7.62mm machine guns. The firefight lasted two hours before things quieted down. From radio contacts, it was clear that not only C Company, but the other two companies and the recce platoon had all been engaged at the same time.

Once again, rather than what would have typically been the end as the enemy scattered, the attacks would resume after dawn. To Charchuk's left, B Company was the first to receive a volley of some 20 RPGs. C Company's lead platoon also came under attack from a grape drying hut and the company commander issued orders for a quick dismounted attack. Charchuk climbed out of his turret and went to the back ramp to get the rest of his crew. As Master Bombardier Jeff Fehr exited the vehicle Charchuk saw his face go pale. They were dismounting only twenty metres away from where Nichola Goddard had been killed. Nonetheless, they carried on.[25]

The team took up a position—measured with a laser rangefinder at 89 metres away from the enemy—and started a danger close engagement. The first round was placed at 350 metres out but subsequent ones were quickly walked back in onto the target. Charchuk recalls being almost deafened by the sounds of the shells coming in and impacting near to them. He reflected on the fact that this wasn't something that his forward observation officer course had prepared him for. With a small correction, the next rounds, a mix of 50 percent ground burst and 50 percent air burst were brought in to 85 metres to awe inspiring and sheer frightening effect.[26]

G11 was engaged as well with A Company. In the early morning hours, the company was moving through the compounds and houses, clearing them as they pursued several machine gunners and rocket-propelled grenade operators. The company paused and Slayer 11 called in an A-10 for a 500-pound bomb run. The bomb came in and landed close—far too close—and off target. Many Canadian forward air controllers (FACs) still did not have laser designators with which to clearly identify a target for the aircraft. Even when they did, they were not able to set up the battery-powered, tripod-mounted designator while working out of the air-sentry hatch of a LAV. Instead, they talked the aircraft on to the target. This time mistakes were made[27] and the bomb landed within feet of A Company's 1 Platoon. Fortunately, it landed on very soft ground and caused no casualties. One soldier, Private Robert Adams, was a mere two metres from the car-sized crater. He would be evacuated with bleeding from the ear and the new nickname Danger Close Adams.[28]

The day continued with dismounted attacks, including G13 participating in the detailed work of clearing compounds and buildings.[29]

The dawn of the 9th brought no let-up. The companies continued their advance against heavy opposition. This was no longer the usual engagements where the Taliban would fire a few rounds and scatter. They were staying put. They were causing casualties. In attacking one compound in the morning, C Company's 8 Platoon lost Corporal Anthony Boneca, a reservist from the Lake Superior Scottish Regiment.

While Charchuk's team was preparing an artillery mission to take out the compound where Boneca had been hit, a Predator checked in with them. They engaged the compound with its Hellfire missile notwithstanding that they were closer than the safe distance of the blast. A direct hit did not stop the resistance. Charchuk followed up with 18 rounds of 155mm from the guns at a distance of 82 metres. Two rockets from an American Apache attack helicopter were next and caused secondary detonations as a hidden Taliban ammunition cache started exploding, ending the fight.[30]

The next day proved uneventful, with the Taliban finally dispersing. With that, the battery turned its eyes west to Helmand.

While the bulk of the battle group prepared for Operation HEWAD, B Company, G12 and A Troop remained behind in Zhari. Here they spent time crowded into the tiny PB WILSON with B Company and a contingent of police. They were frequently rocketed and mortared. The minimum range of the M777 made it necessary for the troop to respond with its 81mm mortars instead. One of the major suspected Taliban observation posts was a grape drying hut within a kilometre directly south of the base. A Troop would leave one of its 81mm mortars permanently laid on this target, while the other three shifted to other likely targets. The grape hut would have its role to play in August.

Enemy fire usually tried to bracket the base and would stop once counter fire went out at them. Occasionally enemy fire would fall inside the base; the gunners would take cover in their armoured vehicles until the target was identified, at which point they took post in the open to return fire. In one instance—just as they were about to go into fire for effect—an enemy round fell within 15 metres of the mortar line peppering them with rocks and dirt. The round had also landed about one metre away from a gun tractor loaded with ammunition and diesel fuel. Splinters ripped through the tires, wheel hubs and brake line, damaging six vehicles in all. Luckily, no one was hurt and 40 outgoing rounds on the grape hut stopped further incoming fire. Captain O'Donnell kept the mortar fins from the incoming round as a good luck talisman.[31]

Operations to support the British 3rd Battalion of the Parachute Regiment in Helmand would start with a road move by 150 vehicles from PB WILSON into an open leaguer in Maywand just off the Number 1 Highway.

For Operation HEWAD, General Freakley had assigned D ("Devil" or "Devil Dogs") Company of the 10th Mountain Division's 2nd Battalion, 4th Infantry Regiment from Fort Polk, Louisiana to the brigade which, in turn, placed it under ORION's operational control.[32] To heighten security, the battle group fed misinformation as to its intentions to various Afghan police officers. Intelligence intercepts confirmed the Taliban were concerned about this shift of forces. A massive sand storm on the evening of July 12, 2006 helped the battle group even more, and the force slipped unseen into a hidden patch of desert just south of Heyderabad.[33] While briefly grouped here, the contingent received an overnight visit from the new Chief of the Land Staff, Lieutenant-General Andrew Leslie. Leslie had been originally schedule to fly forward with Brigadier General Fraser—who had overall command of the operation—but blowing dust had cancelled the airlift so the two had come forward by road in Fraser's tactical headquarters "Niner Niner,"[34]

As a first mission, A Company and G11, under the cover of B Troop's guns, departed for Heyderabad to seize an enemy cell there. B Troop provided support from the position it had occupied near 9er TAC in the battle group's leaguer. A firefight ensued in which A Company killed 14 insurgents and found intelligence and IED material.[35]

Next, on July 13, 2006, there would be a push by C Company and G13 to Sangin to assist in the resupply of a British platoon running out of food and water. Captain Charchuk recalls,

> When we arrived in Sangin the locals began throwing rocks and anything they could at us—this was not a friendly place. We pushed into the District Centre, and during the last few hundred metres we began receiving mortar fire. They never taught me on my LAV Crew Commander course how to command a vehicle with all the hatches closed, using periscopes in an urban environment. I truly did it by sense of touch, meaning as we hit the wall to the left I would tell the driver to turn a little right!! We resupplied the Brits and, unfortunately, it turned dark and we couldn't get out of there, so we had to spend the night. We were attacked with small arms, RPG and mortars three times that night; I still can't believe that the Brits have spent over a month living there under those conditions.[36]

On July 14, 2006 the mission turned to Operation AUGUSTUS, which would launch the next morning. This would be a brigade operation spearheaded by an airmobile battle-group insertion of two companies of the British parachute battalion to seize several Taliban compounds near Sangin. Task Force ORION would set up several company-sized cut-off positions around the area while the Americans supplied air support with an AC-130 gunship, Apache attack helicopters and A-10 attack aircraft. Gallagher moved B Troop forward to an intermediate position within range of the entire area of operations.

C Company and G13 had pulled out of Sangin but had been turned around to go back for AUGUSTUS. Charchuk:

> This was turning out to be the longest three-day operation ever!!! Enroute we

were engaged by an 82mm mortar from across a valley. I engaged them with our artillery, it felt a lot more like shooting in Shilo as they were 2.8 km away as opposed to the 100m or less my previous engagements had been. We went round for round with them in what Rob [O'Donnell], the troop commander firing the guns for us, called an indirect fire duel. In the end, he said the score was Andrew 1 Taliban 0 and there is no worry of that mortar ever firing again.[37]

C Company was back in time to man their positions as the Paras' assault went in. It was while redeploying at the end of this operation that C Company ran into trouble while tasked to do a battle damage assessment. Charchuk noted,

The company quickly came under attack from what was later estimated as 100+ fighters. For about 15 minutes we lost communications with the company commander and a whole section of infantry as they were basically overrun. The section had last been seen going into a ditch that was subsequently hit with a volley of about 15 RPGs; I thought we had lost them all. I had Brit Apaches check in and they did an absolutely brilliant job at repelling the enemy...After about an hour-long fight, the company broke contact (but lived up to the nickname the soldiers had given us, ("Contact [Charlie]") and we levelled several compounds with artillery. Somehow we escaped without a scratch, truly amazing.[38]

During the operation, Chief Warrant Officer Mike McDonald, the brigade's sergeant major, who had deployed forward with the brigade's tactical headquarters, had the opportunity to visit with the British gunners from 7th Parachute Regiment, Royal Horse Artillery when they heard the sound of a mortar firing. He recalls:

Initially when the mortar fired our LAV Gunner asked "what was that noise" and I said "it sounds like a mortar so we must be adjusting some targets." Then a (I believe the British "Tech [warrant officer]") jumps out of a bunker, wearing only a pair of combat boots and a pair of desert shorts and yells "Incoming, take cover" in a very Monty Pythonish voice. We kind of chuckled and went about our business. Another round was fired and again we heard the "Incoming, take cover" followed by the impact, which was a little closer. The same happened a third time when we realized we were the target and all tried to dive in the back of the LAV. One of the British howitzers answered and neutralized the target.[39]

The battle group continued in some minor actions, working with the British around Sangin for a few more days, but it seemed the enemy had pulled back. On July 17, 2006 the battle group resupplied for its expected next-day move back to Kandahar.

3 Para's commanding officer, Stuart Tootal, was sorry to see C Company go. His battalion had become used to working with the Canadian troops and been impressed by their professionalism and courage.[40]

While the resupply was ongoing, 9er TAC took the opportunity to move south to link up with DEVIL Company, which had been operating near Heyderabad with only fleeting contacts during the previous few days. The Americans had, however, just become embroiled in a heavy firefight, and the command team went forward to a ridge to observe. They quickly took the measure of the fight and, as Gallagher identified targets, the two LAVs started engaging insurgents as close as 125 metres away with their 25mm cannons. G19's first round was a disappointment. Gallagher recalls, "I say [to Bombardier Golding, the gunner] 'Okay. Go" and all I hear is a click from the 25."[41]

The gun had misfired. In peacetime this would have required an armourer to come and clear the gun; as it was, there was nothing for it but for Golding to do it himself. He quickly removed the misfired round and threw it out of the turret hatch.

As the Taliban facing Devil Company attempted to withdraw into more complex terrain, the two LAV's crews supported the Americans' pursuit with fire from their 25mm cannons and the guns from B Troop. Towards the end of the day, an air strike hit a weapons cache so large that the secondary explosions lasted for an hour after the strike.[42]

In the evening, with DEVIL Company's action won, the command team returned to the battle group's Bison tactical command post vehicle for a brief rest before the return to Kandahar the next day. That was not to be. Just before midnight, radio orders—an unusual event—from the brigade commander gave the battle group a new mission. The district centres of Garmser and Nawa had fallen to the Taliban that day and thus exposed the town of Lashkar Gah, which was Helmand provincial capital. Fraser ordered the battle group to retake both Garmser and Nawa by 4:30 pm the next day. There was just one question: "Where are Nawa and Garmser?" Both were well off the edges of the battle group's maps for this operation. They lay on the Helmand River, well to the south. Lashkar Gah was the nearest, some 60 kilometres southwest as the crow flies. Garmser was the furthest, 110 kilometres southwest, with Nawa between the two. The route there would be anything but straightforward. Operation OR JANGYALAY had started.

A helicopter recce set out at first light on the 18th while the battle group prepared to move. Quick orders dispatched C Company with G13 to protect Lashkar Gah. A Company and DEVIL Company, which remained attached, initially also headed for Lashkar Gah. Here they crossed the Helmand River and then continued southward well to the west of the river. G19 with 9er TAC, meanwhile, took off on yet another off-road, cross-country "Sunday Drive" through the Afghan desert. By now Gallagher had learned to use his OziExplorer software tied to his global positioning system to keep an electronic trail of breadcrumbs of the journey to help him find the best routes back.

DEVIL Company was the first to strike. Its attack on Nawa was unopposed. A Company, with G11, continued on heading further south to retake Garmser. Unfortunately, B Troop ran into a problem.

To keep a foot on the ground and because of the long distances involved, Gallagher had decided to step up the troop to gun positions he had selected along the way by sending one gun forward with a dismounted command post and a couple of dismounted laptop computers.[43] He recalls, "Whoever led that gun in didn't do a proper drive-around the position and although what I thought was pretty flat and good terrain, ended up to be a big sinkhole and they sunk the gun and were stuck. Now I've got one gun that is stuck and out of action and one that's at [maximum] range."[44]

The situation prevented the troop from being in position in time to support A Company. That hadn't stopped Meade's G11, however. Like G19, Meade too had an issue with their 25mm gun. They had been engaging at Garmser with their 25mm when the gun jammed. Bombardier Clark Cummings, a driver/signaler for the vehicle, took action which resulted in his receiving the following Mention in Dispatches:

> On 18 July 2006, while engaged in a firefight at the Garmser District Centre, his light armoured vehicle's main gun jammed. Despite continuous direct and indirect fire from rocket-propelled grenades, small arms and mortar rounds, [Bombardier] Cummings left his vehicle to secure a hand crank from another vehicle to repair the main gun. His actions were instrumental in allowing his team to remedy the misfire and carry on with the firefight. [Bombardier] Cummings's dedication, resolve, and willingness to put himself in harm's way for the good of the mission reflect exceptionally well on him as well as on the Canadian Armed Forces.[45]

B Troop, by last light, had consolidated in a gun position on the west side of the Helmand River approximately halfway between the two towns. It could now support both companies and offer protection to the battle group's supply route. By 6:30 pm,[46] the troop started firing to support A Company. They engaged the Taliban throughout the night and started assaulting the town at first light.[47] Ammunition, or more properly, the lack of it, was now becoming a problem for B Troop.

May 17, 2006 had been a watershed and the operational tempo and ammunition expenditures had increased dramatically over those of the previous three months. AEGIS, directing operations, had pushed Task Force ORION with its single gun troop to the farthest ends of the supply chain—over a hundred and sixty kilometres—and had extended the scope of the operation in both time and intensity. As A Company sat in front of Garmser, Gallagher had a problem: "We were firing a ton of bullets and that's when I was trying to get emergency resupplied and they said there were no choppers ... I was pissed because Bob Meade was firing [rocket assisted projectile] rounds at maximum range with outrageous [probable errors range] and I was being told I couldn't get any bullets."[48]

From the very beginning, when Major Gallagher's suggested basic load was changed by the logistics chain, ammunition resupply had, from time to time for several reasons, been a problem.

Foremost, neither the battle group nor the battery had an ammunition section allocated in support. This issue hearkens back to the fact that the battle group had lost its administrative company and company echelons—much like the battery had lost its echelon—to be subsumed into the national support element. The battalion's highly experienced ammunition non-commissioned member ended up being employed as a postal clerk. On occasions, the companies would run short of 25mm.[49]

For the battery, each gun tractor carried 100 to 110 rounds of 155mm and 100 to 300 rounds of 81mm in addition to the detachment's equipment, food, water and a part of the troop's defensive stores.[50] A fully loaded B Troop would have started Operation AUGUSTUS with only around 200 rounds of 155mm.

Captain Howie Nelson, the battery's second-in-in command, thought that the "ammunition resupply sucked" and the situation—with the troops always deployed over long distances and the increased rate of fire—called for the battery to have its own echelon. In his view, the national support element did not understand artillery resupply.[51]

At Kandahar, Warrant Officer Gero found himself involved in ammunition management, a function that does not fall on a battery quartermaster sergeant. Each gun in the battery had an allocated basic load of all natures of ammunition. Gun troops at the end of each fire mission would report their ammunition expenditure to the fire support coordination centre (FSCC). Gero would liaise with them each morning to check against expenditures and arrange a replenishment when required. Only when a national support element combat logistics patrol became available, could it be brought out to the guns. The battery itself had no allocated vehicles for that task, but Gero frequently received requests to have one or more of his people drive a vehicle on a combat logistics patrol.[52]

The national support element's temporary depot munitions had given Gero a bit of latitude by allocating him two SeaCans for ammunition storage on site: one for projectiles and one for propellants and other items. At most, these held one hundred rounds. This was adequate until mid-May for the routine "topping-up" of the troops whenever they came into KAF.

With the two troops so widely dispersed, the battery sergeant major, now travelling with the battery commander, had little to do with ammunition. Paul Parsons put it this way, "For twenty odd years I was trained to do this [handle ammunition resupply] but my very first live [operation], it didn't mean [anything]"[53]

With B Troop running out of ammunition, Gallagher pushed his own FSCC to make something happen. Major Rob Rooney, the legal advisor to Task Force ORION who was at the FSCC at that time, tells what happened next.

So we looked around and we tried to figure out how to get some resupply to them real fast, basically just water and 155 projectiles, and we're looking around for the air liaison officer, who was an air traffic controller in Cold Lake, and he wasn't there. Afterwards we found out where he was. He'd grabbed the bicycle that he and I shared ... and he went tearing off to the flight line and grabbed some Americans who had just landed a Chinook and said, "Our trucks...can't get the resupply to our guns. Can you help?" and the American pilots said, "We're way beyond what we're allowed to fly per day."[54]

The air liaison officer pressed the issue, and the Americans agreed to fly the mission. Gallagher recalls, "And then that next morning—it was a gorgeous morning. The dew was coming up, sort of the fog in the low ground ... Black Hawks, no it was a Chinook that came in kicking pallets off the ramp and the guys were running with the bullets right from the pallet right to the guns."[55]

While the incident highlighted the problem with the basic logistics structure and the problem of keeping troops resupplied over long distances through hostile territory, it also brought out another, even worse, problem: the Canadians were running out of artillery ammunition. A major failure in planning for and stocking sufficient ammunition for upcoming operations was rearing its head.

Doctrinally, artillery ammunition resupply is an operational and not an administrative function. The planning of ammunition expenditure is the responsibility of the divisional artillery commander and his staff in conjunction with the division's logistics staff.[56] In the absence of a Canadian divisional headquarters, that responsibility ought to have fallen on Coalition Task Force AEGIS, who ought to understand the tempo of upcoming operations, and its associated national command element and national support element who understand the supply system.

The system, however, was not working under well-established doctrine. How command and control of ammunition supply was to function was being rewritten using procedures and manning structures used in the permissive environment of the Balkans and Kabul, as opposed to doctrinal ones developed by hard combat experience. For artillery munitions it would be a bone of contention between the brigade's staff, including the national support element's commander, Lieutenant-Colonel John Conrad, and the battle group.[57]

AEGIS considered the problem to arise from under-reporting of ammunition expenditures by Task Force ORION during July[58] compounded by heavy expenditures by the incoming Task Force 3-06.[59] However, the issue had been noticed within the national support element well before that. As Lieutenant-Colonel John Conrad himself put it,

> When we reached the cut-off date for ordering ammunition in mid-July for the next phase of operations, I had the mistaken impression that we had much more of all types of ammunition than we actually had. Our last order for ammunition from Canada had been dangerously small. We ordered too little to effect a full replenishment of our holdings. Major Bob Herold, my chief of ammunition, saw the pending problem and he begged me to order in more. I got angry at Bob believing that he had not fully understood the study of ammunition consumption and the relentless pursuit of a day of supply data.[60]

Conrad, in a footnote, alleges that the battery was responsible for forecasting reasonable operational 155mm long term requirements.[61] That, however, begs the question that Gallagher's initial pre-mission basic load forecast had been ignored and changed; that the battery was reporting its expenditures on an as-it-happens basis; that the uptick in tempo ought to have been obvious to everyone; and, most importantly, that the planning for future campaigns was AEGIS's responsibility, especially now that ORION was shortly to be replaced by Task Force 3-06 based on the 1st Battalion, of The Royal Canadian Regiment.

In fairness to both the Coalition Task Force AEGIS's headquarters and the national support element, they were both doing jobs which deviated from doctrine. Fraser:

> John Conrad inherited a system built on NATO war stocks. These tables did not reflect the reality on the ground. Conrad did outstanding work rebuilding ammo tables that reflected what we needed. It took time to rebalance the books and ammo was not an issue during [the Task Force] 1-06 period. It was during [Task Force] 3-06. For different reasons. Ammo management is always a critical factor. And quite frankly in counter insurgency operations, some units fired as much ammo as what the Ukrainians are (metaphorically) [firing] against the Russians.[62]

For AEGIS, especially the "fires" section, had been augmented by other non-kinetic capabilities to be the joint fires and effects cell. This added a very large amount of staff time to non-kinetic effects as well as kinetic ones. While Lieutenant-Colonel Williams had some additional multinational staff to handle non-kinetic effects, the kinetic "fires" side had a staff of only four for 24/7 operations, less than what would normally be a brigade level FSCC. The FSCC was situated in AEGIS's joint operations centre and acted in accordance with Lieutenant-Colonel Williams' instructions. Coordinating and employing the non-kinetic aspects was new for many of the members of the joint fires and effects cell. Thus, there was a steep learning curve throughout the tour, particularly as they dealt with several campaign plans all of which needed to be regularly assessed in terms of their progress towards achieving objectives.

The national support element was also short of manpower being tasked to not only provide the battle group's logistics, but those of the entire Canadian contingent. Logistics, like the artillery, had not been a priority matter for the army. Lieutenant-Colonel John Conrad has expressed both his pride in his organization and his frustrations with the system. He says,

> ...military logistics in the Canadian Forces is viewed as something less than merely non-elite. Military logistics in Canada is viewed with near disdain ...

> ...The Army has not been greatly interested in improving logistics support to the combat arms because it has not really been in the line of work where logistics was a life and death necessity. The focus of Army leadership was on protecting the combat arms in a long series of budget cuts.[63]

Conrad's national support element was designed on the Kabul experience, where the entire force was contained in two small camps and operated over a relatively small area of operations for a few days before coming back to base to resupply. Kandahar simply wasn't like that, and in July, the force was spread from Helmand to the Pakistan border to the northern Shah-Wali-Kot.[64] The physical aspect of getting ammunition delivered to the guns who spent most of their time far from KAF in ever more intense combat was daunting. With no organic Canadian helicopters, resupply depended to an extent on occasional cooperation of other nations' helicopters but mostly on the ground-based combat logistics patrols who were frequently the targets of IEDs. That vulnerability was about to be shown on several deadly occasions.

Last, but by no means least, was that the true picture of the Taliban's offensive plans had not yet been fully appreciated by higher headquarters.

ORION would spend four days in the Nawa/Garmser area involved in some 20 firefights before turning the area over to British troops on the 22nd. As late as the last day, A Company became involved in a major fight requiring G11 to call in an airstrike, dropping two bombs.[65] This time, however, the move back to Kandahar was a definite go. Orders were issued for the move and the companies would go in individual serials. A Battery was slated to be last in the order of march.

Major Gallagher had concerns about the move, much of which was essentially a cross-country trip. He handed B Troop's commander, Andrew Nicholson, a copy of the OziExplorer breadcrumb trail he had made for him to follow, knowing that the route had been proven. B Troop followed the route and in fact bypassed much of the column, Rather than being at the tail end, they ended up leading the battle group into the commodity point the national support element had set up to replenish the battle group's fuel and other supplies needed to reach KAF.[66] For the troop this may have been a fortunate turn of events. Near the Arghandab River crossing, a suicide bomber struck the support convoy—which was now at the tail end—killing two and injuring ten. A second bomber also struck, causing many Afghan casualties but no further Canadian ones.[67]

With its return to Kandahar province, the battlegroup could again focus on its own area of operations, as the countdown continued toward the transfer of authority for Regional Command (South) to ISAF. Before that could happen, however, one last incident of note occurred on July 27, 2006.

An American resupply convoy was making its way across the northern end of the province, within range of the guns at MARTELLO, when it took some casualties in an ambush by three or four Taliban snipers. The Americans vectored a Predator in to get some eyes on the target. The convoy broke contact, but the Predator stayed in pursuit of the enemy and at this point contacted ORION's FSCC as the Americans had no joint terminal attack controller (JTAC) of their own available. They read Captain Howie Nelson, who operated as a FAC as call sign Slayer 18, into the mission. Nelson recalls,

> We followed them along. We waited until they took up, basically, a hideout position in a grape hut...At that point I was able to engage them with a Hellfire and take out at least three of the individuals...[We] continued surveillance on the area and at that point it was noticed that two vehicles were moving into the area to recover the bodies and at that point there [had only been] one Hellfire left on the Predator; [it] had been used up so I did have guns in range. I called up one of the troops to engage...[I] gave the adjust fire and the first round actually impacted right beside the grape hut so I went right into fire for effect. After that point, the grape hut was destroyed as well as one of the vehicles was destroyed; the other was damaged and immediately pulled out of the area. It was noticed at that point that there was still some movement so I immediately did a "Repeat". I believe that the initial engagement had been two Rounds Fire For Effect from two guns in the troop. The Repeat came down and finished off the grape hut, destroyed the vehicle and all the remaining insurgents were killed. I recorded the target.[68]

It would be the first ever adjustment of Canadian artillery through a Predator.

Because of this and other missions, the battle group bestowed the nickname "Hellfire Howie" on Nelson.

15

Operation BRAVO CORRIDOR · August 3, 2006

THE END OF OPERATION OR JANGYALAY would be the last commitment for Task Force ORION in Helmand, but not in Panjwayi or Zhari. B Company in particular, working with their armoured Mercedes G-Wagons out of Patrol Base (PB) WILSON, had been involved in several contacts throughout July. Just around the corner was the July 31, 2006 transfer of authority for Regional Command (South) from the Americans' Combined Joint Task Force 76 of Operation ENDURING FREEDOM to the International Security Assistance Force (ISAF). Coincidentally, while some Canadians elsewhere remained under the ambit of Operation ARCHER, the vast majority of the troops in the south would now be deployed once again under Canada's Operation ATHENA.[1] Coalition Task Force AEGIS would continue as the headquarters for Regional Command (South) for a few more months. The transfer of authority of the battle space from Task Force ORION to the incoming Task Force 3-06, however, was to follow just a few weeks later in mid-August.

Up to this point, the relationship between the battle group and its guns had been excellent. Much of the fire and air strikes had, by necessity, been close in to the troops, well within the "danger close" distances, and while the risk of a blue-on-blue incident couldn't be dismissed, the battle groups' troops loved the guns.[2] On more than one occasion, the timely fire delivered by A Battery had made the difference for the infantry that was in contact with the enemy. A series of circumstances were about to fray that relationship.

Regardless of the general peacefulness of Regional Commands (Capital), (North) and (West), Regional Command (South) was at war. July 31, 2006 came as the Taliban's fighting season was about to hit full stride and all the signs were there that they were hell-bent on opposing the entry of the British in Helmand and on making a statement of strength in Kandahar.

ORION's commanding officer caused a warning order to be sent out on July 29, 2006 for Operation BRAVO CORRIDOR.[3] He explains that,

It started on the 1st of August and really kicked off on the 2nd. We were manoeuvering on the 1st. B Company on the 2nd did a lot of stuff. The purpose of B Company and BRAVO CORRIDOR was to try and keep open Highway 1 between Kandahar City and Lashkar Gah because there's a lot of ambushes popping up there. [We] wanted to start clearing ambush sites and keep that road open and the district centre—the Zhari District Centre—just north of Highway 1. [We] wanted to make sure that was not under threat because it seemed to be getting some fire; sporadic fire.

At the same time north of Panjwayi District Centre, across the Arghandab River, we had reports of mass evacuations of people; reports of white flags of the Taliban. We did not have any intelligence of their being there. Which didn't mean they were not there, just [that] we didn't have any hard evidence.

So we devised a concept of operations where B Company would push off of Highway 1 moving south and I would take an ad hoc group of one rifle platoon, [reconnaissance (recce)] platoon, an engineer field section, and push up from the white school in the south—Bayanzi it's called with a market, a bazaar there—push north and link up with Bravo Company and we would clear that road—it's a very intricate windy road. It's where Nichola Goddard got killed on May 17, 2006. By doing this we'll probably figure out if there is enemy presence in there and we could [also do] sensitive site exploitation. The locals had said that the Taliban had been in the bazaar and in the schools and we said, okay, we'll go in and see if we can find anything there.[4]

Leading up to this, there had been concerns within Coalition Task Force AEGIS about the upcoming transfer of authority. Lieutenant-Colonel Tim Bishop, the G3/Chief Operations at Coalition Task Force AEGIS, recalls:

ISAF were trying to track the battle but weren't as slick at it as the US headquarters. The US headquarters had been there forever and had been through several tours in Afghanistan and knew the business. The ISAF headquarters, not so much, and certainly not the level of contact we've had, we'd been under for months. So that is sort of the start difference between the headquarters we'd worked with all along and had built up from February to July, through February starting slow with the level of operations building up to full-on fighting season in July.

And then you have what I would say is a cold ISAF headquarters who is suddenly taking on all of [Regional Command (South)] in contact. I'm going

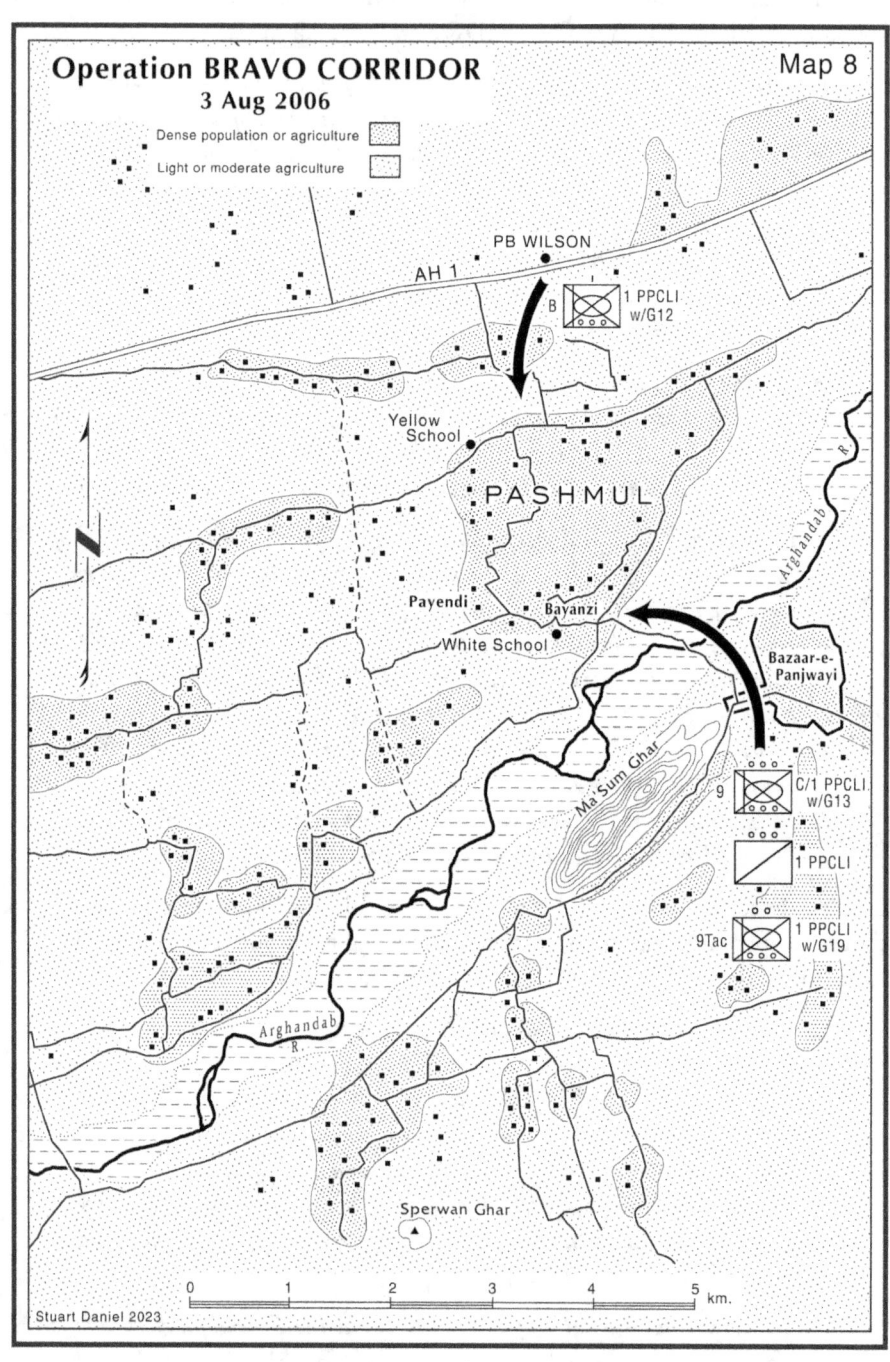

Operation BRAVO CORRIDOR
3 Aug 2006

Map 8

Dense population or agriculture
Light or moderate agriculture

PB WILSON

AH 1

B 1 PPCLI
w/G12

Yellow
School

PASHMUL

Payendi

Bayanzi

White School

Bazaar-e-
Panjwayi

Ma'Sum Ghar

Arghandab R.

9 C/1 PPCLI
w/G13

1 PPCLI

9Tac 1 PPCLI
w/G19

Arghandab
R.

Sperwan Ghar

0   1   2   3   4   5
km.

Stuart Daniel 2023

to say there's a bit of an overwhelming feeling of "Is ISAF headquarters going to be able to respond in a timely way and understand the fight in the intimate way that we do so that they can provide us with the value-added in a contact situation?"⁵

That trepidation was shared at ORION. Ian Hope would later say,

Under Operation Enduring Freedom there was a prevailing philosophy of "mission command", with echelons of headquarters pushing resources to the commander in the fight, and asking him what more he needed. There was never second-guessing or micro-management of the battalion's battles. Under ISAF the philosophy was reverting to one of tight control of everything by general officers many hundreds of kilometres away.⁶

Brigadier-General Fraser points out that: "The same approach to mission command continued from Aegis to Orion throughout their time in-theatre. The issue was one [of] risk and how [Americans under Operation Enduring Freedom] versus ISAF viewed it. We were in a transition and it took time to get into a rhythm with our new [headquarters]."⁷

With the transfer of authority to ISAF would come a new set of rules of engagement which were significantly less permissive than those that ORION had operated under with the Americans. Lieutenant-Colonel Peter Williams, at AEGIS, recalls that the new rules of engagement "... seemed a lot more restrictive in terms of authorities who could authorize certain kinds of engagements and parameters for collateral damage."⁸

For Williams, the change to ISAF focused on dealing with a different headquarters on the "non-kinetic effects" side of his job description. His battle rhythm contended with attending three morning meetings each day: an intelligence briefing with the J2 staff looking at the last twenty-four hours of activity with a look ahead for the near term; a teleconference with the fire support coordination centre (FSCC) in Kabul together with those of the other regional commands to confirm air requests and other fires for the next twenty-four to forty-eight hour time frame; and a meeting with the chief of staff and the other staff principles to discuss current issues. This was augmented with a chairing the regional command non-kinetic effects targeting meeting, and developing a back brief for the brigade commander about how the brigade was meeting ISAF's joint effects tasking order. In short, ISAF's focus on non-kinetic, reconstruction tasks was taking him away from the daily activities ongoing within the brigade's joint tactical operations centre.⁹

While Williams dealt mostly with the non-kinetic side of operations, which ISAF had been used to focusing on, others within the brigade were contending with the kinetic side which had been the bread and butter for them and the Americans up to now. There were multiple issues but the rules of engagement and the ISAF procedures were the most palpable.

Many saw these new rules of engagement as problematic, not only for what they did and didn't permit, but also because of the fact that they were being imposed on ORION at the tail end of what had developed into a very active campaign and when there were clear warning signs that the Taliban were massing for a major fight. Lieutenant-Colonel Tim Bishop:

> *...the evolution of the mission in July/[August 2006] where the [rules of engagement] changed proved challenging and at a very challenging time. [The battle group] had to work [through] a change that they [knew] about - but had to do so while in contact ...*

> *Obviously, there was a training piece that went along with the change over of the [rules of engagement] that we took very seriously because we knew that there was a potential impact on operations that we couldn't afford to muddle our way through; which of course is nearly exactly what happened on [August 3rd] but it was one of those things where we went from a battle group that was very slick at getting itself in trouble, understanding the [rules of engagement] and then get themselves out of trouble using the [rules of engagement] as, not a supporting document, but as "this is what we're allowed to do so let's get on and do it." That was how clear their understanding was until the 31st of July. Where the transition happened was, our higher headquarters, the ISAF headquarters, was clear that attacking infrastructure—specifically stuff that would be valuable in the rebuilding of the country—was always going to be a matter of discussion.*[10]

Lieutenant-Colonel Williams recalls a team coming down from ISAF in Kabul to meet at brigade level to discuss the changes and the manner in which ISAF operated, and that certain parameters were different and would require briefing up to ISAF's headquarters.[11] Difficult as things were at AEGIS, at ORION they were far worse. Ian Hope recalls, "Our [rules of engagement] hadn't changed from [Operation ENDURING FREEDOM] because we hadn't received any new [rules of engagement]. We hadn't been briefed. We'd been told cryptically 'It's gonna change, gonna change, gonna change.' But we hadn't been told how, certainly hadn't been told the safety distances."[12]

At the end, it all came in a rush. Major Rob Rooney, ORION's legal advisor, had been on leave and returned "a couple of weeks" before the changeover. He recalled that when he returned,

> *I hadn't received any [copies of the new rules of engagement]. I hadn't received*

any drafts...I was completely out of it. That caused a lot of concern. I couldn't believe that they were going to change the [rules of engagement] in the middle of a tour because at that point you got five months of combat in and we probably had 160 of those days were in active combat operations. And the guys were very—and we're talking right down to private level—they were very confident in their use of the [old rules of engagement]. They knew what [those] rules were and they knew what they were doing.[13]

Rooney recalls receiving the new rules of engagement "... maybe more than 12 and less than 24 hours" before they took effect. ORION had not received the soldier's cards that are normally issued concurrently. Master Corporal Michael Podolas confirms this. Podolas was a section second in command in A Company's 3 Platoon spending much of his tour in the north at Gumbad and MARTELLO. He'd asked to fill in a vacant position with 2 Platoon at the Kandahar Airfield (KAF) which was tasked as the reserve for the upcoming operation. He recalls,

Absolutely on the first set of [rules of engagement], we knew them cold and had reviewed them and had [worked] through them in great detail.

The new ones, as of 1 [August], other than some discussion that things were changing (and not for the good in our opinion at the time) we never went over them in great detail nor...did we receive soldier's cards.[14]

AEGIS's Tim Bishop confirms this. Technically, Canadian troops would not be using ISAF rules of engagement any more than they had actually used the American ones. All rules of engagement for Canadians are issued by Canada's Chief of Defence Staff. Ottawa would take whatever multinational rules of engagement might apply to them in theatre and factor their constraints in to develop a uniquely Canadian set, including soldier's cards, which would then be issued to Canadian troops. Bishop recalls, "There was a significant delay in getting the [rules of engagement] from Canada - For sure. Even the cards. I don't think we had new rules of engagement cards at the time that incident took place but we certainly had what was the rules of engagement. They were well known."[15]

Within the battery, too, things had come on very quickly. Captain Howie Nelson, the FSCC Officer, recalls,

We got the new [rules of engagement] but really the way it was going to work— this is something we didn't war game. "Here's the new [rules of engagement]. Let's do it." There wasn't a point where we were able to shop-talk how we were going to carry on with the higher headquarters; how this is going to work. I don't think they knew themselves how this is going to work.

So we would carry on with this [rules of engagement] and things are different, but it didn't seem like everybody was on the same page of how this is going to go forward. And we never had a chance to plan it out, talk it out, transition. It's like, "Oh! Here we go. We're ISAF now and this is the way forward. So do this..." But when a situation arose, or you needed higher [headquarters]; it was like they weren't ready to do the workaround to make it happen.[16]

The timing was truly inopportune. Additional factors would soon complicate matters even more. One of these was the standoff distances of impacting rounds from infrastructure. Major Gallagher recalls that one of the new rules of engagement addressed that issue. He recalls,

There was one figure as I walked out of the [tactical operations centre]—it was around 1 August for that mission on 3 August—and I turned to the [legal advisor], "What's this ISAF [rule of engagement, indicating a specific rule]? What's it mean?" And he said "you cannot use indirect fire 500 or 550 metres from a 2 metre by 2 metre structure with a roof or coalition forces or noncombatants—Afghans.[17]

The new rule about protecting infrastructure would soon create difficulties for the upcoming operation. If that wasn't bad enough, an obscure incident happened on the second day of ISAF's tenure, which would further complicate matters. Lieutenant-Colonel Ian Hope explains,

On the night of the 2nd of August, I was to give orders at Patrol Base WILSON, just north of Highway 1, north of the objective areas, to B Company, my ad hoc group, the [Afghan police], some [Afghan army] that were coming in there, guns and a number of others.

That whole patrol base received a lot of sniping fire that day. I remember at least four occasions where it was right over my head, bullet holes in the tent and I'm saying "you know this is not safe anymore, I could go live in the desert several [kilometres] north and be safer". And I didn't have snipers then, they were deployed with either A Company or C Company...so I didn't have that asset and we were scanning with [light armoured vehicles (LAV)] and all we could see was a grape drying hut. We couldn't make out much more than that and we were pretty convinced there was a sniper or group of snipers in that hut about six, seven hundred metres south of us and south of Highway 1 and I asked if G19 could do anything about it.[18]

As the target was too close to WILSON for an indirect fire mission by the guns, the agreed upon solution was to take one gun out and engage the grape drying hut with a few rounds of direct fire. Gallagher tasked Sergeant Paul Dolomont's

G15A, then being commanded by Master Bombardier Todd Engram, and Captain Mike Smith's G12 with the job. They deployed on open ground about 330 metres away from the target, while B Company deployed into several positions around the target in cut-off positions.

With the area secured and confirmed to be clear of non-combatants, G15A was given the order to engage. They sent a round down range that exploded against a wall immediately in front of the target. A video taken at the gun recorded the sound of a splinter coming backwards from the burst and within seconds, it's clear that Master Bombardier Corey Rein had been hit low down on his right calf, just above the top of his boot. He takes up the story from there:

I wasn't hurt very bad at all … We fired two more rounds and I record the gun and I'm still bleeding a little bit … I walked around and talked to a few people and go see the medic…He can't decide if the shrapnel is still in my leg so he's like "You gotta go back to KAF." So I'm laying on a stretcher waiting and of course it's just my luck that a big convoy that we weren't expecting full of chief warrant officers and generals and politicians roll in…and they hear there's a wounded soldier so they have to come over and they could tell it's not bad so they start making fun of me; all good natured, but it's embarrassing.[19]

A medevac helicopter arrived to pick him up.

So they grab two dudes from my troop, and they happen to be the two smallest dudes in the troop, to be stretcher bearers…The two little dudes pick me up and start running towards this helicopter…and they end up dropping me half way through and the American medics in the chopper lose their minds and jump out…and get me in the chopper finally.

And I'm excited about being in a Black Hawk, finally, with Apache's flying around me, so I'm trying to look out the window and I think that they thought I was struggling and they're trying to attach monitors and IVs to me …

And we land in KAF and I look out the window and I'm like "Oh God". There's got to be 30 different medical people waiting on the side of the airstrip. So I'm lying on the stretcher and they opened the sliding door of the Black Hawk and I just waved like an idiot, kind of like Forrest Gump did, and you could just see 29 of the people just throw their hands up in the air and go back in.[20]

Rein was left in the care of a Dutch doctor who initially had some problems discerning if the splinter was still embedded, because Rein had a small metal plate and screws in the leg from a previous surgery. Eventually, it was clear that the splinter had not stayed in the leg and the wound was closed with three stitches. Because it had been an open wound, he would be released immediately from the Role 3 Multinational Medical Unit but was required to remain in KAF helping to build ammunition pallets for the next ten days while ensuring no infection set in.

While Rein's wound was minor, it would have unfortunate and serious consequences.

Notwithstanding everything that was about to follow, G15A's direct shoot had done the job. Hope states, "It was very effective because there was nothing after that. I got on with orders."[21]

Later, around 2200 hours, Gallagher received a message to call Major Tyler Kennedy, AEGIS's chief of fires. Gallagher recalls that Kennedy told him,

> *Operational safe distances 725 [metres]! When I got that phone call that our safe distances had moved out to 725 [metres]—which is peacetime safe distance—and his reference was 381-001.[22] I was [regimental command post officer] for three years and I knew that book inside out and I said "there's nothing operational in it. That's not even the title. It's called 'Training Safety', so fuck off."...That's a staff officer. That's not command.[23]*

Nonetheless, Gallagher went to see the battle group's commander just before they rolled on August 3, 2006. Hope recalls,

> *He came to me and said "I just got a message from AEGIS that there's new restrictions on the use of fires." And he went through the restriction of—first of all, collateral damage estimates, CDEs—we've been doing all along. But he said there's now going to be a new distance for your 155s of 725 metres and 500 for the 81s. And I went "there's no place in Afghanistan where we can fire because everything is that close unless you're in the middle of the desert." And he goes "Yeah, I know, this is a problem." And I said "yeah, but this is not coming down the [operations] channel, it's not coming down the command net. I don't know what this is and did you get anything hard copy?" and he said, "No I just got this info."[24]*

Williams too recalled the incident of Master Bombardier Rein being injured by a splinter and restrictions being imposed, "And I think there were some temporary restrictions put in place just to make sure that—I can't recall the distances involved—there may have been some temporary restrictions put in place just to make sure that the soldiers were safe."[25]

The issue concerned the stand-off distance that should be kept from the impact of a round of a certain type and the location of our own troops and protected infrastructure. To determine this distance in combat situations, A Battery had been using the American JFIRE manual.[26] The combat risk-estimate distance it produces is a small fraction of the peace-time safety distance of 725 metres set out in the Canadian manual, "Operational Training, Training Safety."[27]

Captain Howie Nelson saw the change as problematic. With the concept of artillery fires being controlled at the lowest levels, forward observation officers (FOO) did not request permission to start a mission, they just engaged the targets on their own and their supported arms commander's initiative. Most of their engagements were in response to enemy contact and an immediate fire support response was required in accordance with the risk assessments made in the field. Where aircraft were involved, deconflicting airspace might be a necessity, but as for higher headquarters, while they had monitored missions, they had not interfered.[28]

The sudden imposition of such a mixture of wartime risk-estimate distances and range safety distances in the middle of a kinetic operation was, at the least, confusing at the battle group level. The problem was about to go from being merely theoretically to problematic.

August 3, 2006.

"A mess; confusion; multiple issues all piled on top of one another."[29]

"The real story of August the Third has not been written about."[30]

The events of that day are controversial and the full truth of why they happened may never be fully known even once the official records are made available. One can point to several contributing factors, but without all of the records, the final word will be elusive. One thing stood out; on that day, the artillery, for whatever reason, did not provide the fire support that the infantry so desperately needed and which A Battery would undoubtedly and unhesitatingly have delivered at any time prior to August 1, 2006.

The operation started quietly enough just after midnight with one Sperwer flight after another overflying the objective areas in the Pashmul district. The complicating factor for the operation was already obvious as the word "school" figured prominently in discussions on various communication channels; one school in the north in B Company's area and a second one in the south where a composite group was advancing.

At 0200 hours on August 3, 2006, 9er Tac, accompanied by a composite group made up of the battalion's recce platoon (call sign ORION 6), C Company's 9 Platoon (call sign ORION 33), an engineer detachment (E11F), Gallagher's G19 and Charchuck's G13, left PB WILSON. They moved east on Highway 1 to skirt the whole region and hook around to come up from the town of Bazaar-e-Panjwayi, before crossing the Arghandab River and pushing into Pashmul.

Two hours later, just before 0400 hours, B Company left PB WILSON heading directly south across Highway 1. With them moved Smith's G12. The aim was that the two pincers, formed by the composite group and B Company, would eventually meet up.

Afghan police accompanied both groups. Back at WILSON, A Troop stood ready with two M777 howitzers and four 81mm mortars to provide fire support. Besides the Sperwer flight, other multinational air and aviation assets stood by to lend support as needed.

At 0430 hours, having crossed the Arghandab River from south to north and about 500 metres east of the southern white school, 9 Platoon, leading the southern group with Captain Charchuk's G13, ran into eight to ten armed Taliban moving around. The platoon engaged them briefly. While attempting to manoeuvre, the acting platoon commander's LAV struck an improvised explosive device (IED), disabling it, killing one soldier and rendering the acting platoon commander unconscious. During the skirmish, a rocket-propelled grenade (RPG) hit G13's vehicle but its crew suffered no wounds. The group secured the area in order to recover the damaged vehicle and to have their two casualties medevaced. While paused to do this, they would receive sporadic small arms fire from various places in the Bayanzi area, including the white school.

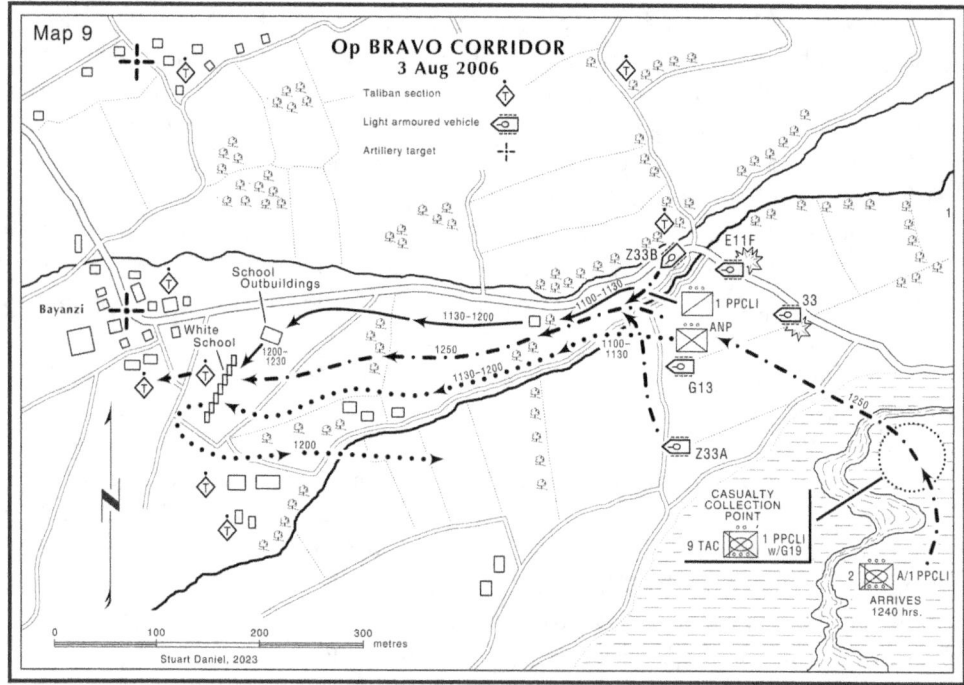

Concurrently, B Company pressed its advance in the north, but to this point without any enemy contacts.

In the south, troops found several additional IEDs strung around the area of the damaged LAV and the engineer detachment started rendering them ineffective. It had been the battle group's policy to recover all damaged equipment off the battlefield so as not to leave a propaganda opportunity for the Taliban. Hope called for a "show of force" fire mission into the area north of the white school in order to cover the vehicle recovery operation. Gallagher initiated the mission and shortly after 0600 hours, A Troop engaged with one M777. It fired one adjusting round, which fortuitously hit a nearby building of interest, notwithstanding that it had not been specifically targeted. Intercepted communications chatter from the building established that it now contained both wounded and dead Taliban.[31]

Almost concurrently, B Company came into contact with several enemy positions, including two mortars in a culvert. Smith's G12 started a fire mission engaging several "enemy in ditch" with two of A Troop's 81mm mortars.

While A Troop had gotten off an adjusting round on Gallagher's show of force mission in the south, no further rounds would be fired on that target. Within a few minutes of the shot, a message came down from AEGIS's chief of operations disapproving the mission. A few minutes later, at around 0620 hours, Gallagher's G19 started a new fire mission, this one on effective small arms fire coming from approximately 200 metres southwest of the white school. The troop fired seven rounds of high explosive on this new mission.

At 0624 hours, B Company reported that they had another enemy contact, this one at what they also called a "white school". B Company's white school was a structure very similar in shape to the one facing 9er TAC near Bayanzi, but located approximately 2,000 metres to the north by northwest. B Company's contact quickly escalated into four contacts.

By 0700 hours, the action in the south had died down, but 9er TAC had received cellphone intercept intelligence that a wounded medium value target was in the southern white school, and that this individual was calling for support to help him exfiltrate and to leave IEDs behind.[32] Hope reported this to AEGIS and requested authority to "block the enemy from getting out of [the] school" with 155mm.

At first, AEGIS approved this plan and allowed another show of force artillery mission. A minute later, AEGIS came back up requesting further information on what was in place to reduce collateral damage. The reply was that there was a medium value target trapped in the school, that the nearest platoon and the nearest buildings were 300 metres away, and that the only way to stop exfiltration was with 155mm.

AEGIS's chief of operations acknowledged the message and again approved this show of force mission. However, a few minutes later, and before any rounds had been fired, an order came down from the brigade commander to "Stand Down on Show of Force, Check Firing."[33] A discussion between Hope and Fraser ensued. Requests for clarification of the rules of engagement were requested and guidance provided including advice from the brigade's legal advisor.[34] AEGIS wanted to push on to the southern white school and suggested that a LAV should be pushed forward first. Hope replied he wouldn't do that because of the IED threat. AEGIS further stated that if the troops were engaged by fire, then they could engage. Hope instead advised that he was pulling out of the operation.[35]

Back in Kandahar, when the first contact came down, Captain Howie Nelson and Warrant Officer Darcy Cyr at the battery's FSCC started gathering in and pushing forward air resources, including an American B-1B bomber and two Dutch attack helicopters. Two British Harriers, an American Predator and other aircraft would soon also join in.

While things were about to get worse for the southern group, B Company was pressing into their objective area using air power brought in by their FOO and forward air controller. A complicating factor was that they too were engaging Taliban at a school, and throughout the fight, this school would also be frequently referred to as a "white school" but occasionally as a "yellow school." Neither of the two buildings were actually functioning as schools at the time. The involvement of the term "school" in their target description had not become an issue for B Company.

In the south, however, shortly after the "Check Firing" order and the decision to pull out, the engineer detachment's LAV, E11F, was moving to where it could provide better cover and demolition support for the recovery of the damaged LAV. While doing so, at around 0715 hours and near the first damaged vehicle, it also hit an IED, disabling the engineer LAV and injuring three Canadian soldiers and an Afghan interpreter. A call went out for a second recovery team from the national support element and a second medevac mission for the wounded. This new incident would clearly prolong the composite group's stay in the area while this recovery and medevac would take place.[36]

There were now two damaged LAVs located 500 metres directly east of the southern white school. A casualty collection point was set up between 200 and 300 metres further southeast in the dried-up floodplain of the Arghandab River. 9 Platoon's two remaining LAVs, Charchuk's G13, and dismounted troops provided security to the damaged vehicles. They faced principally westward towards the school and north towards where the initial show of force fire mission had occurred. The recovery teams coming from Kandahar would be approaching the casualty collection point from the east through the town of Bazaar-e-Panjwayi.

While AEGIS had imposed "Check Firing" shortly after 0700, no one there had followed up on the situation. For the artillery, "Check Firing" has a very specific meaning, which is that all firing from the affected guns stops until "Cancel Check Firing" is issued by the originator. A Troop asked Captain Howie Nelson to verify if "Cancel Check Firing" had been given. AEGIS had not done that, so at 0824 hours Nelson, seeing that the offending show of force mission was clearly over with, took it on his own initiative to give the order.[37]

During the interval between the second IED strike and 0900 hours, the battle group commander had further discussions with AEGIS, who advised him they were pushing Dutch attack helicopters and some Afghan police to him. The helicopters established contact with Charchuk but proved to be of limited value as their national caveats restricted them from operating at an altitude below 1,000 feet.

AEGIS still wanted a push on to the southern white school. Hope surveyed the area with his two platoon commanders, Captain Jon Hamilton for Recce Platoon and Sergeant Vaughan Ingram, now the acting platoon commander for Number 9 Platoon. He decided that they could push an Afghan police platoon forward to the school supported by a composite platoon formed from Recce Platoon and 9 Platoon. Concurrently, A Company's 2 Platoon was called forward from KAF to assist with the recovery and extraction. Calls were also sent out for additional Afghan police and air support.[38]

While all this was going on, B Company and Smith's G12 continued their fight to the north, using guns, mortars, a Predator, attack helicopters and strike aircraft. There was now intelligence that a medium value target, Haji Lala, might be laying up at the northern school. B Company moved to isolate it.

In the south, it took some time to organize the composite platoon and to await the arrival of the Afghan police. Eventually, only 26 police showed up to be supported by the 20 dismounts of the composite platoon and the fire from the remaining 9 Platoon LAVs. Just after 1000 hours, the police and the composite platoon moved towards the southern white school. They received small arms fire, which again came from the area in the north where the initial show of force mission had been fired. The platoon returned fire and the enemy's fire died down shortly thereafter.

At 1034 hours, the battery's FSCC received an email from AEGIS chief of fires, Major Tyler Kennedy, restating the 725 metre safety distance previously communicated verbally to Gallagher the night before. A caveat enabled the battle group commander to authorize fire to within half of that distance if troops were under some form of protected cover. On the other hand, the 500 metre restriction on two metre by two metre structures laid down by ISAF for 155mm fire remained unchanged.[39] AEGIS, however, did not forward this instruction to 9er TAC through the operations channel.[40]

Shortly after 1100 hours, the Afghan police started moving forward into the southern white school with the composite platoon providing overwatch. To their east, attempts were being made to pull the two damaged LAVs out of the ambush site to a place where the national support element's wrecker could load it on a flatbed. Major Gallagher recalls,

> At the end of the day, on the 3rd of August, we had two LAVs sitting on their bellies and if it wasn't for [Battery Sergeant Major Paul Parsons] putting [himself] at risk while bullets were coming down the side of our LAV while [he's] outside underneath that LAV hooking chains up...it was the engineer LAV that got blown up and [he] was underneath...We were doing a double LAV pull with chains dragging that LAV up out of the Arghandab.[41]

Throughout this period, intelligence reports from various airborne surveillance sources were reporting Taliban scattered around Pashmul and even south of the Arghandab River in Panjwayi in anywhere from section to platoon to even company strength. On several occasions, Afghan police reported mortars firing on their elements approximately one and one half to two and one half kilometres southwest of the southern white school. While AEGIS had dispatched two Dutch attack helicopters to the area they continued to be of little value due to the Dutch 1,000 foot altitude restriction making it difficult for them to distinguish the Taliban from the friendly forces. They never fired at all.

At the southern white school, the Afghan police started to receive small arms fire from the southwest at around 1135 hours. 9 Platoon's LAVs responded with 25mm fire. At around noon, the police moved beyond the school and received heavy fire from the bazaar at Bayanzi which caused them to retreat to the southeast, leaving the Canadians behind in two outbuildings on the northern flank of the school. The Talibans' fire now shifted onto the Canadian composite platoon, hitting it from three sides. Seeking better cover, the platoon moved into the school but continued to be hit by RPGs, small arms and machine gun fire.

With fire still coming from three sides, the troops were also plagued by heat exhaustion and radio problems. The platoon had been calling for artillery support. Both the battle group commander and Gallagher called for artillery support. For a half an hour, none was authorized. Their desperation was obvious to all the individuals who were listening in on the radio nets. The eventual denial of M777 fire came to them from brigade headquarters and was on the basis of collateral damage to infrastructure.[42]

Gallagher's initial requests had gone straight to AEGIS's chief of operations, Lieutenant-Colonel Tim Bishop, using his AN/PRC 117 radio. Once denied, Gallagher's subsequent communications went by satellite phone to his FSCC officer Captain Howie Nelson who relayed communications to the chief of fires, Major Tyler Kennedy. Everyone within Gallagher's vehicle and on up would have been aware of his anger and desperation to obtain authorization to engage with the guns.[43] For Captain Andrew Nicholson and his team, listening in on the radio nets in B Troop's command post far to the north at MARTELLO, the confusion and miscommunication was "painful to watch."[44]

Considerable activity had been ongoing at AEGIS's headquarters. Tim Bishop, who was in the brigade's tactical operations centre throughout that day, explains,

> There was a significant interaction between the ISAF headquarters and us trying to make sure they understood what was going on on the ground, what the level of contact looked like, what the objectives were and so on. There shouldn't have been because they were tracking the same battle that we were ...I do know that their concern appeared to be the use of "school" and then became the authority of what level of weapons and assets we were able to use to stop the firefight or at least win the firefight. Using close air support, attack helicopters, artillery...

> What resulted was a bit of a discussion between [Brigadier-General] Dave Fraser and [General David] Richards[45] and myself and my counterpart to try to get them to understand where we were at and what was happening on the ground.

> We had taken casualties already. We had already hit an IED. There was medical evacuation taking place and all this is transpiring while we're trying, and Ian Hope and his troops are manoeuvering to win the firefight and trying to get authority to use other assets.

> Dutch A-64s were brought into the fight because they were actually airplanes that were available nearby. We gave them off to the [tactical air control party]. The TACP tried to use them but the Dutch decided that their rules of engagement at the time, because the helicopters were not being engaged by the target, the helicopters could not therefore engage the target not understanding that troops on the ground were being engaged by the target therefore they were part of our force package and therefore they could engage and therefore it became a discussion between us and the Dutch and the commander of the Dutch saying "what the...why aren't these attack helicopters supporting the troops on the ground that are in contact because that's what we sent them to do."

> There's a bit of a left and right discussion, even intimate to our own force that is part of the education that we never envisioned is really going to be a problem. Later on, and not much later on, the Dutch were very good at understanding that they are part of the fight and part of the force and that protecting the force is part of their job ...

All this confusion unfortunately resulted in a couple of hours of time where Ian wasn't getting the support that he desperately needed to manoeuvre his force, and protect his force and do the medical evacuation and keep engaged in the fight in a meaningful way.

...There was definitely confusion that didn't need to happen and some of that confusion was multinational where before that with the US forces, there would have been no discussion at all. Had those AH-64s been US assets from Task Force NIGHTHAWK - no discussion.

...Added to the overall confusion of what the hell we were talking about— even though we were providing grid references where the actual contact came from—the fact that we were calling them "schools" and not maybe "school A" and "school B" and so on needed to be clearer. It became pretty clear to us early on that we were no longer talking about schools but we were talking about contacts at grid whatever and an ancillary building that was nearby that happened to be a school. But that, I think, also added to a level of confusion because you're still using the word school and you're still engaging something that ISAF valued as something post fight. That they didn't feel could be destroyed because it was part of the rebuilding of the country.[46]

There was the added confusion of where all the moving parts of the force were at that time. Again, Bishop recalls,

I do know that after they started manoeuvering forces we briefly lost a handle on where all of our friendly forces were and we were pretty concerned if we engaged we risked collateral damage to our own forces. We were relying pretty heavily on Ian at the time—Gallagher and Charchuk specifically—knew where all the Afghan forces were, all of the other ancillary forces including his own so if he did engage there was low risk to our force and when they asked for danger close I'm guessing because of the manoeuvering happening we did not have a clear enough picture where our own forces were to carry on with the use of kinetic force.[47]

Just before 1230 hours, a major firefight had occurred at the southern school. It had included a direct hit on the building from an 82mm anti-tank gun which the Taliban had used for the first time during ORION's rotation. Three Canadians were dead; seven wounded. Captain Hamilton's radio call from the school said it all. He made it abundantly clear that if support didn't come up immediately, if they didn't bring the LAVs up, his team would all die.[48]

With that call, events moved into high gear. Hope made a transmission over the brigade's "troops in contact" radio net for air support including a show of force flight. Captain Nelson, at the FSCC, called for the most immediate air support available. That call would be answered by a B-1B bomber, Call Sign Dark 20, which agreed to fly a mission directly over the southern school at the "lowest altitude". Within minutes, Dark 20 complied and set itself up for its run in.

But even before that could happen, the crews of 9 Platoon's two ZULU[49] LAVs, all too well aware of their comrades' dire circumstances, had volunteered to brave any potential IEDs to rescue them. Permission was given for them to go. Other LAVs had also been pushed forward to assist. A Company's Number 2 Platoon had arrived at the casualty collection point and were ordered to move forward and to follow 9 Platoon's ZULU LAVs and support them in their dash to the schools.[50]

9 Platoon's two ZULU LAVs thundered to the school, firing their whole load of ammunition in the process. Master Corporal Mike Podolas, with 2 Platoon, recalls: "[The 9 Platoon vehicles] went and saved [the troops at the school] ... They knew that there were probably other IEDs, and they led the charge ... [We, 2 Platoon,] got up to the white school and absolutely [9 Platoon] vehicles were there ... and they were loading wounded in."[51] 2 Platoon's LAVs took up positions in a line covering them. Podolas: "... from there the LAVs kept coming and going evacuating everybody back to the [casualty collection point] and the [command post]"[52]

At 1248 hours, with the extraction complete, the LAVs pulled back to the casualty extraction point. They were still receiving inaccurate Taliban fire, which threatened them and the incoming medevac helicopters, when the B-1B thundered overhead at what the troops estimated was 500 feet above the target, one half the altitude that the Dutch helicopters were restricted to. Smith's G12 requested a second flyby. Dark 20 complied.

At this time, with troops taking fire but under the cover of the buildings and their LAVs, Gallagher ran his LAV back to a position of observation and called in a fire mission onto the target that he had engaged early that morning. He quickly adjusted the rounds onto Taliban positions near the white school and, because the rounds were close to friendly troops, double scaled the adjusting gun so as to ensure that there would not be a gun with a cold barrel firing. Podolas remembers that, "We were happy to see that place get hit."[53]

Things were serious at the casualty collection point. Everyone from the commanding officer on down was lending a hand. Battery Sergeant Major Parsons counted twenty-two casualties, many with heat injuries, but all-in-all the tiny composite group in the south had lost four dead and thirteen wounded. Gallagher and Parsons used their own LAV to ferry wounded to the medevac's helicopter landing zone. At one point, the ramp of the LAV was awash in blood after carrying an Afghan interpreter with tourniquets on both legs. Emotions were high. Gallagher recalls, "I just remember one young soldier, and he was so distraught, and crying... and the only thing that I could do was hug him ... and say, 'It's gonna be okay.'"[54]

Podolas's platoon took on the burden of handling the three recent deceased so that 9 Platoon wouldn't have to face that trauma. At the same time, for him, this was one of the most positive moments. He recalls, "One of the greatest moments of why we train the way we train was watching [9 Platoon] reorganize themselves."[55]

With the acting platoon commander unconscious and medevaced after the initial IED strike and his replacement, Sergeant Ingram, killed at the school, Sergeant Patrick Tower, who had distinguished himself throughout the battle, took over 9 Platoon. Despite their losses, Tower quickly reorganized the platoon and their three remaining LAVs, then reported that the platoon was ready to carry on.[56] Tower and Sergeant William MacDonald would both be awarded Stars of Military Valour for their actions.

Things weren't over yet. B Company remained in the field to the north, engaging in sporadic contacts to draw attention away from their comrades to the south who were still engaged in recovering the two damaged LAVs.

At around 1400 hours, in Bazaar-e-Panwayi, to the east, a suicide bomber in a vehicle-borne IED attempted to hit one of the approaching recovery teams. An alert crew member on a Bison saw suspicious behaviour and engaged the vehicle with his C6 machine gun. The IED detonated and killed some 21 Afghan civilians and wounded another 13. For a few hours the quick reaction force (QRF), including Warrant Officer Darcy Cyr, deployed by road before being pulled back.[57]

A Troop was running short of ammunition as they continued to support B Company. At 1500 hours they called for an emergency resupply to be dropped inside the compound by a helicopter sling load, as close to the guns as possible. This was because they were short manned and wouldn't be able to recover a pallet load dropped outside. When additional manpower was found, this request was amended to allow a resupply by standard kicker pallets. By 1628 hours, two pallets of 48 rounds of high explosive with propellant and fuzes were on the way for delivery by 1800 hours.

Just after 1900 hours that night, G12 and B Company were off the field and back in WILSON. G13 and G19 would be back at KAF a little over an hour later.

16

REFLECTIONS AND ROTATIONS

AMONGST OTHER ISSUES, August the 3rd had been a failure of both strategic and tactical intelligence and a failure of the overarching policy to build a new national security force for Afghanistan.

The build up of the Taliban in Zhari had its roots in the summer of 2003 when the Taliban's leader, Mullah Omar, announced the formation of a new ten-member leadership council and called for an offensive strategy to be built for years down the road. The one-legged Mullah Dadullah Lang was given a key role in this process as the Taliban's leader of the southern provinces. He tracked down and reformed the scattered Taliban cadres, set up training camps, brought in allies from Iraq and elsewhere to help train his force, instituted the concept of improvised explosive devices (IED)—including suicide bombings which were novel for the Taliban—built up a foundation of moral grounds to fight the foreign invaders, set up a program of recruitment for new fighters built on linkages within the Pakistani security forces, and moved to southern Afghanistan to plan and gather support there.

Throughout 2004 and 2005 that support grew through campaigns of intimidation, murder of the opposition, manipulation of tribal grievances, and persuasion. It solidified as new recruits channeled their way in from the training camps.[1]

Concurrently, the US, the International Security Assistance Force (ISAF) and the new Afghan government were on a program to disassemble the pre-existing police and militias, which were organized on tribal lines, in favour of a national security force. By the end of 2005, they'd had great success in disarming the old security forces but had achieved only a very minor level of success in building the new force.[2]

By the end of 2005, the Taliban's building blocks were in place. Dadullah headed to northern Helmand to organize that front. The locals had flocked to his colours. After a brief return to Pakistan, he moved his headquarters to Maywand from where he would supervise the offensive which would now operate on three fronts: the northern Helmand districts of Musa Qala, Sangin, Nowzad, and Kajaki;

the southern Helmand districts of Garmser and Nawa; and the western Kandahar districts of Maywand, Zhari and Panjwayi. The ultimate goals for his estimated 4,000 fighters were to capture Kandahar City and Lashkar Gah.[3]

Everyone knew the Taliban were active in these areas. Their mass, their influence, the complexity of their organization, the sophistication of their strategy and state of their training, not so much. When Dadullah unleashed his first hostilities on the night of February 3, 2006 in Musa Qala, Sangin and Nowzad, the area of operations still belonged to the American Task Force BAYONET. The Americans too had missed the signs.

Helmand, of course, was not ORION's area of operations. The intelligence picture of what was happening there would be better understood by AEGIS, the Americans and later the British. ORION's area of operations was Kandahar province, and their evaluation was that while the battle group was conducting cross border operations in Helmand as part of Combined Joint Task Force 76's Operation MOUNTAIN THRUST, the Taliban had moved in and strongly reinforced and fortified Pashmul with insurgents of significantly higher quality. These were not merely small groups of less than a dozen local fighters, but platoon-sized groups acting in concert in well-organized defensive positions. ORION had sensed that things were different in May and again in July. There was, however, no concrete intelligence at higher command levels which confirmed those observations. But even within ORION, the available intelligence did not come close to defining the true nature of the enemy's strength in Pashmul. At AEGIS, they took note. Reflecting on August 3rd, Lieutenant-Colonel Tim Bishop stated,

> That was sort of the first time; a sustained level of contact, manoeuvre, significant manoeuvre, the enemy stood its ground, I mean there was a whole bunch of things that changed on that date that we had not seen before anywhere else. Generally they had come into contact, you'd fight for 30 minutes or so until the window of close air support happened and then they'd just disappear. The 3rd of August was different ... That's where it became clear to us that there was a significant build up in that pocket, although we had suspected, that was our first sort of confirmation. That's where we started building up [Operation] MEDUSA from.

> Understanding that; how much seemed to be concentrated there, how sophisticated their levels of operations seemed to be. Ian later found that they had positions to fall back into, they had medical supplies in protected areas, they had stuff there it was clear, after the fact of course, that they had anticipated using that as a strong point and as fighting positions in depth. Just a completely different dynamic than we faced before.[4]

In the fight's immediate aftermath, the overriding concern was that the combat-experienced Task Force ORION was going home just as the trained but untried Task Force 3-06 was arriving to face a new and dangerous enemy. Intelligence surfaced that the Taliban were planning something "big" for August 19, 2006. That day was not only the date of the transfer of authority from Task Force ORION to Task Force 3-06, but also Afghan Independence Day. ORION volunteered to stay in theatre. That proposal was rejected.[5] Both AEGIS and ORION worked rapidly to after-action the incident with the incoming battle group. On August 4, 2006 Major Mason Stalker, ORION's operations officer, sent out a final summary of Operation BRAVO CORRIDOR.[6]

Lieutenant-Colonel Ian Hope followed Stalker's report on August 5, 2006 with a letter to the brigade commander, raising concerns about the denial of the show of force fire missions, the friendly troop safety distance, and the collateral damage assessment procedures.[7]

Brigadier-General Fraser replied by letter on August 13, 2006[8] in which he stood by the decision to terminate the show of force mission because it fell within the 500-metre prohibition issued by ISAF and because there was no overriding self-defence exception available at the time it was being fired. He reiterated that he would review the situation respecting safe distances with Canadian Expeditionary Force Command but that in the interim, safe distances as set out in the Canadian Forces Publication *Operational Training-Training Safety* would apply. Among other considerations, for pre-planned fires of 155mm rounds no troops could be closer than 725 metres, but the commanding officer could authorize fire up to one half that distance if the troops were under cover. Any circumstance of fire closer than that reduced distance could only be authorized by the brigade commander himself. The commanding officer, however, could authorize closer fire in cases of self-defence. He closed by stating his opinion that neither issue contributed to the casualties on August 3, 2006.[9]

In short, AEGIS contended that whenever ORION asked for clarification on ISAF's more restrictive rules of engagement during this transition period, advice was given; that at no time was self defence ever a question; that AEGIS never lost sight of what was necessary; and that mission command was always provided.[10]

In ORION's fire support coordination centre, they saw things differently. In Captain Howie Nelson's view, there was a concerted effort by higher headquarters to manage things at a higher level and that they had lost sight of what they didn't need to do. He felt it was a trust issue. He saw it as them not recognizing that they had a qualified, highly skilled and highly trained battery commander on site.[11]

Over and above the exchange of correspondence, meetings were held including the commanders, principal operations officers and legal advisors, to clarify and resolve these issues to reduce the possibilities of any future misunderstandings or confusion.[12]

Time was running short for A Battery as members of the 2nd Regiment, Royal Canadian Horse Artillery's E Battery began to flow into theatre. While reliefs in place were starting, Howie Nelson had yet one more opportunity to go outside the wire. In Helmand, the district centre of Musa Qala had been under siege since May 18th when the Taliban killed some twenty Afghan National Police. The 3rd Battalion of the Parachute Regiment responded initially by putting in its Pathfinder Platoon. An initial attempt to relieve the Pathfinders had failed on July 6, 2006 but later that month the Danish 1st Light Reconnaissance Squadron was able to link up and reinforce the platoon. Another attempt to replace the Pathfinders on August 1, 2006 was again unsuccessful, leading to a major operation involving some 500 troops being mounted for August 6, 2006.

Operation MAR CHICHEL (Snakebite) would involve two parachute companies who would air assault supported by a ground-based advance of engineers, D Squadron of the Household Cavalry and a platoon-sized Canadian quick reaction force (QRF) mounted in light armoured vehicles (LAV). The operational plan was to establish a ground corridor, allowing the Pathfinders to drive out, to be replaced by an incoming platoon from the Royal Irish Regiment and a supply convoy coming in to replenish the Danes. Fire support would come from a troop of British 105mm L118 light guns, close air support and a mortar section. Nelson deployed as the forward observation officer (FOO)/forward air controller (FAC) for the Canadians. For Nelson, the operation stands out:

> There were parts of the tour where you were like 'this experience is dangerous' but at this point, at the very end of the tour, I honestly thought this is going to be where I meet my maker. I had a bad feeling about it ... The British didn't have any armoured vehicles and were getting their butts kicked so they asked for Canadian armour ... I didn't think I would make it out of that one.

> ...The problem was [the British] had to cross this dry river bed to get to this town... the Taliban had excellent fields of fire and what happens is that every time the British tried to cross this riverbed when they get there they'd get gunned down, so they couldn't. We had to use these LAVs of the [quick reaction force] to basically roll across and put down some suppressing fire ... so that the British could land and get their mobile infantry in ... In the end it was very successful. Basically, once we rolled up with four LAVs shooting some 25 mm they scattered pretty fast.[13]

The handover from Task Force ORION to the 1st Battalion, The Royal Canadian Regiment's Task Force 3-06 battle group would start in the initial week of August and end on August 19, 2006 with the official transfer of authority. For the Taliban, August the 19th was still a go although the recent battle on the 3rd had reduced that in scope from attacking Kandahar City to attacking just Bazaar-e-Panjwayi. Some 400 insurgents started to encircle the town.[14]

With the uptick in activity the two batteries would not have the type of relief in place that had been the norm for the batteries in Bosnia or Kabul; a return to camp, a 100% stock taking, a handover of equipment and a battery smoker. Instead it would take place in the field team-by-team, group-by-group. Personnel from E Battery would come out to relieve A Battery's gunners under combat conditions.

This was especially true for those in Zhari and Panjwayi. Here the Taliban, emboldened by their success earlier that month, set up gauntlets of ambushes with everything from small arms to rocket-propelled grenades (RPG). B Company's departure from Patrol Base (PB) WILSON, with their associated gunners of G12 and A Troop, was a case in point. They, now under the protection of their relief, ran through a five kilometre-long gauntlet involving an estimated 100 Taliban positioned anywhere from the ditches next to the road to some 200 metres off the road. RPGs were launched in some instances from so close that the fuzes did not have time to arm and they bounced harmlessly off the vehicles' armour.[15]

For Major Gallagher there would be a week of "left seat-right seat" with his replacement, E Battery's Major Greg Ivey, as they followed 9er TAC throughout the area of operations with the incoming battle group commander, Lieutenant-Colonel Omer Lavoie. On August 8, 2006 they had arrived at PB WILSON and were outside their vehicle chatting with Captain Ryan Stimpson, an officer from the 1st Regiment, Royal Canadian Horse Artillery (1 RCHA) attached to E Battery with his crew as a FOO. There was a "crump" that rocked and dusted a nearby light utility vehicle wheeled. Another vehicle was hit by a mortar bomb which failed to function. As mortar bombs continued to fall, they took cover in a LAV. A platoon was deployed to firing positions, and both battery commanders' crews assisted with controlling Dutch attack helicopters and firing illuminating rounds into the area of the "yellow school" which had been attacked by B Company on August 3. A subsequent crater analysis of the impact points confirmed that the mortar bombs had indeed come from within 500 metres of that location.

By August 16, 2006 the handover was complete and E Battery was in place awaiting the official transfer of authority on August 19. Within a few hours of that, their war would begin in earnest.[16]

Afghanistan was the place where events described as "the first time since Korea" became commonplace. It was no different for AEGIS and ORION. Predominant amongst those was the first operational use of the M777 howitzer by anyone, anywhere.

Notwithstanding that Canada's aim had been to deploy a security force in order to enable a robust whole-of-government campaign to build an effective and stable Afghan government, the enemy's vote had quickly morphed the mission into one where robust and kinetic military action played a much greater role than anticipated. ORION itself had been in over 100 contacts with the enemy and 50 of those had involved intense firefights, complex manoeuvres and artillery and air support.[17] On the reconstruction side, more than 80 projects had been initiated with 37 of those funded with CA$4.3 million. The human cost had been eighteen killed—including three gunners—seventy-three other soldiers physically wounded in action and many more bearing hidden scars deep inside.

Along the way, Canadian troops had been under command of the Americans and then a North Atlantic Treaty Organization multinational headquarters. Conversely, Canadians had been in command of Americans as well as multinational forces in combat.

For the artillery, which had initially been considered for the provincial reconstruction team, the statistics had been sobering. The gunners of A Battery had carried out over 114 operational fire missions, 41 of which had been in support of troops in contact. Their guns had fired 501 high explosive and 92 illumination 155 mm rounds and 308 high explosive and 52 illumination 81mm rounds in support of operations. They had conducted the first fire missions observed and adjusted by a Sperwer tactical unmanned aerial vehicle (UAV) as well as one with an American Predator UAV. They fired the first operational 155mm rocket assisted projectiles. Their "Slayer" FACs had conducted 135 operational close air support missions including dropping precision guided munitions in 11 troops in contact situations. The gunners working with the tactical UAVs flew 136 missions in 147 days and those with the airspace coordination centre spent every day of the tour deconflicting a complex airspace involving multiple international users at both the brigade and battlegroup level.[18]

Along the way a number of lessons had been learned and reported back for future rotations.

For the observers, the training for danger close missions had been inadequate and there was seldom the time available to follow the laid down procedures. A practice of offsetting the first round with as little as 120-200 metres and creeping back in 20-metre increments as well as double scaling a single gun was recommended. They had found that their proximity fuzed high explosive projectiles were unbelievably lethal.

Their man-portable surveillance and target acquisition (STA) radar, issued to each FOO party, proved to be an effective early warning system but was never used to engage indirect fire. The AN/PRC 117F multiband multimission manpack radio proved an invaluable tool to the FOOs with its ability to handle both ground-to-ground and ground-to-air communications. They found that the concept of an individual performing the combined role of FOO or FOO technician and FAC in the LAV did not work well. FAC needs to be a separate individual's primary role.

When choosing between guns as opposed to close air support, the high, first round accuracy of the M777 and its high availability made it preferable. Attack helicopters proved very useful but skill levels varied by nationality.[19] The preference for precision munitions to minimize collateral damage set out in the army's artillery transformation program and as handled in ISAF's rules of engagement were not yet mature without the availability of the Excalibur round in the field. However, the M777 with non-precision rounds proved highly accurate in its own right.[20] AEGIS's brigade sergeant major, Chief Warrant Officer Mike McDonald, witnessed that accuracy at work. He recalls:

> I was out visiting a unit of the Patricia's and ran across G12. Having been the [regimental sergeant major of 1 RCHA], I knew most of the soldiers, so was having a good chat with [Sergeant] Ladouceur when the infantry called for him to spool up a mission. The guns fired their first round and I heard the correction as "Right one three, Drop one two" (or something very similar). I had spent many years as a FOO Tech and a [battery commander's] Tech where it was drilled into us to correct for line then "be bold" on the bracket. Sgt Ladouceur saw the look on my face at the correction and said "RSM, I know what you're thinking, but with the lasers, accuracy of the guns etc. there is no need for the bold corrections, and unlike your days we are concerned about collateral damage." The target was inside a walled compound and the correction put two rounds in the compound. Needless to say I felt like a dinosaur, but was very proud of the professionalism and skills of the gunners during that mission.[21]

1 RCHA's gunners would be among the last to fly home. The battalion itself would need to leave for a change of command parade where the battalion would be turned over to Lieutenant-Colonel Dave Anderson. Gallagher and Parsons found themselves assigned to the last chalk out. They'd arrived on the first chalk and now vied for who would be the last to step onto the aircraft's ramp. Gallagher won.[22]

The trip home would be interrupted by a four-day stop in Cyprus for lectures and decompression. While several years of rotating troops from a combat zone had made this part of the operation's routine, it nonetheless stayed problematic in that teams that had fought together for six months were rotating home in fragmented groups due to the fact that reliefs in place would occur over several days and elements of a given team would rotate out ahead of others. The battery was, and even troops were, never fully together in Cyprus at any one given time.[23] Captain Howie Nelson recalls,

> It was nice to go to Cyprus but the problem is that we were spread out. We didn't have a chance to decompress as a group...We were put in many different hotels spread over several areas of the city we were in and it didn't let us decompress as a group. I felt very isolated. I wasn't anywhere near Steve Gallagher at the time yet I worked close to several—well for years before. We'd gone through something major and yet we were kind of spread over hell's half acre. I think it would have done everyone better if we'd been able to decompress as a group...The real decompression comes when you can have a beer with your buddy at the end of the day which we just weren't able to do.[24]

Likewise, the homecoming to Shilo was bittersweet.

At the top of that list was the fact that they weren't all coming home. While that hit all members of the regiment hard, it was particularly so for the officers. Captain Andrew Nicholson recalls,

> I knew it would be tough for me to come off the bus in Shilo because we had one less person; and that was Nic. And I knew Jay wasn't going to be there; her husband, widower, because he had nobody to receive. So we took that pretty hard...It was a different experience because we were down one ... It didn't feel right...Got home ... (My wife Lianne) gave me a huge hug and realized at that point, she's like "Jay can't do this". She goes "It's never going to be the same."...We lost a family member from the regiment... At the end of the day it proves the tightness of the Royal Regiment...We all have six degrees of separation. If you talk to someone long enough, you'll find a connection through some way.[25]

Nicholson too points out the rapid dispersion of the reservists upon redeployment as a fault.

> We did really well on the front end of bringing them in early but we didn't do it as well on the back end at letting them go too quickly. And I understand that everybody just wants to go home and see their families and so forth, but when you go back to 26th Field or 5 [Field] or 15 [Field], and you're the only person who deployed, there's no one else inside that unit that understands what he's gone through and you've just left your immediate family that you shared blood, sweat and tears with.[26]

It wasn't just the reservists that dispersed quickly. With the battery returning in the active posting season, people were rapidly dispersing—including the battery's commander, Steve Gallagher, who was off to Gagetown to become the Chief Instructor In Gunnery at the Royal Canadian Artillery School. His replacement, Major James Allen, wouldn't be around much either as within a short time he was tasked to be part of a board of inquiry into a "friendly fire" incident in Afghanistan.

Battery Sergeant Major, Paul Parsons was singularly unimpressed with the whole homecoming experience. Decompression lectures in Cyprus seemed more designed to convince him that his experiences should have given him post-traumatic stress disorder. He and his people were immediately thrown into a garrison mentality for the upcoming change of command parade and forced into the relish-green uniform rather than being allowed to bask for a few days in their tan arid ones. Then he found himself alone with his battery commander gone and his troops now under a new leadership team. His next job was up in the air and he was eventually made battery sergeant major of Headquarters Battery. He says, "All I'm getting at is I went back with no troops. I went back alone...I didn't have Gallagher to talk to no more...It was a weird, weird feeling."[27]

Equally concerning to him was the lack of interest anyone showed in sitting down to discuss lessons learned or asking him to provide a guest lecture on the deployment: "It's not a big deal, I guess, but I thought it was a big deal what we just went through."[28]

It had in fact been a big deal. A Battery had gone to war for the first time in over half a century, had fought in a way that no one had tried to before, and for the most part, had to figure it out while it was happening.[29]

The final words on A Battery's performance in Afghanistan should go to the battle group's commanding officer, Lieutenant-Colonel Ian Hope,

The responsibility we gave not only Steve [Gallagher] and his battery headquarters but the FOOs; the responsibility we gave to them—not just for indirect fire but for air control, airspace control, fast air—it would have crippled FOOs from other armies...They never failed. Not once, the whole time. It was amazing...

The battery was the most forward element of the battle group. Every sub-unit and sub-sub-unit of the battle group had a ratio of about 2/3 out of the wire, out of Kandahar Airfield, and 1/3 in the wire, sometimes 3 weeks out of [and] 1 week in Kandahar. The battery would be flat out and do three to four weeks [out] and 3 to four days at Kandahar airfield and back out 3 to 4 weeks...there were only four guns and they were spread out always at two locations because we were manoeuvering constantly all over the area and we wanted Canadian artillery to support Canadian manoeuvre. The battery didn't get a break.[30]

In recognition of this service, on October 31, 2006

> *A Battery had the distinguished honor of being presented with the PPCLI cipher for display on their guns. An honour for A Battery, this dedication symbolized the special bond developed in battle between the PPCLI and A Battery, 1 RCHA. Only once before has this honor been bestowed upon the Artillery, this was from [The Royal Canadian Regiment] following the Korean conflict, and it was also presented to A Battery.*[31]

A Battery had come home. In Afghanistan the Taliban's fighting season was in full swing with their troops marshaling in Pashmul. The next chapters belong to E Battery.

17

Task Force 3-06: The Road to High Readiness

From the very start we found ourselves in "no shit war fighting."[1]
- *Major Greg Ivey*

BATTERY SERGEANT MAJOR BOB MONTAGUE was blunt when he addressed the assembled members of E Battery. The 2nd Regiment, Royal Canadian Horse Artillery (2 RCHA) had just learned of their upcoming deployment to Afghanistan. "I would be surprised if we ever fired a shot over there ... if I ever fired a shot I would pull the plug and retire ..."[2]

As Montague later explained, without a hint of embarrassment, he indeed had vowed that he would retire if the battery fired a single round during its deployment. He noted:

> *I had been deployed to Egypt, Cyprus, Kosovo, [and] Afghanistan [in 2003] and assumed that we would be in a much similar situation. Throughout the workup training and preparations prior to deploying, I harped to my [non commissioned officers] that we needed to keep vigilant and keep our guard up. That we needed to ensure our troops remained alert and focused. One of the larger concerns was that we might fall into the Cyprus/Bosnia syndrome, where we sit for extended periods doing very little; further, that discipline and morale might degrade due to that.*
>
> *Early on in the [preparations], I stated time and time again that our biggest problem might very well be boredom and the problems associated with idleness.[3]*

Montague admits that he was soon proven wrong. The reports from A Battery, 1st Regiment, Royal Canadian Horse Artillery (1 RCHA) with Task Force ORION arrived during late Spring of 2006. They spoke of serious combat. Boredom would be the least of their problems. E Battery would deploy as part of Task Force 3-06, a battle group based on the 1st Battalion, The Royal Canadian Regiment from Petawawa, Ontario. It would find itself in a tough situation when it assumed responsibility for Kandahar province from Task Force ORION on August 19th, 2006. The signs of a Taliban resurgence were abundantly clear to those who were paying attention. The battle group had voiced its concerns over the last few months. The North Atlantic Treaty Organization's (NATO) senior leadership in Afghanistan was now finally paying attention.

It would fall to the newly arrived, but still untried, battle group to confront and fight the Taliban. Their enemy had swollen to perhaps 1,000 fighters hidden in the complex terrain that bordered the Arghandab River to the southwest of Kandahar City. Task Force 3-06, with the support of various international contingents, would fight NATO's first major battle ever. It would require some considerable negotiation and a lot of tact by Brigadier-General David Fraser and his Coalition Task Force AEGIS staff to create that support. It would also take some hard fighting from the battle group. If the truth be known, the battle was fought almost exclusively by Canadians and Americans. There would be assistance from the British, Danes, and Dutch, but the rest of the International Security Assistance Force (ISAF) watched from the sidelines.

By the time it began its end of tour handover, E Battery would have fired close to 8,000 rounds from its four M777 howitzers and eight 81mm mortars. That would be over 13 times as many as A Battery had fired before them in support of ORION. Indeed, on the very first day that Task Force 3-06 took over from Task Force ORION, the battle group's A Company found itself in a major battle. E Battery guns had to pound Taliban fighters while the battery's fire support coordination centre (FSCC) would direct aerial attacks against enemy positions in depth.

No. It would not be a boring tour.

National Defence Headquarters warned E Battery that they would deploy to Afghanistan in the fall of 2005, not long after A Battery knew that they'd be going first. Lavoie himself knew his battalion would deploy even before he took command of it in June 2005. The rotation would be challenging for 2 RCHA. Not only would they be deploying a battery in August 2006 but a second one, back-to-back, in February 2007. The regiment would have to field a small brigade "fires advisor" cell, two augmented battery FSCC detachments, six forward observation officer (FOO) detachments, two full gun batteries, and several surveillance and target acquisition (STA) troops for deployment out of their limited pool of gunners. Additional personnel would fill other positions, such as in Kandahar's provincial reconstruction team (PRT). The regiment also faced the challenges of the recently announced army's artillery transformation. This directive would turn one of its three gun batteries into a surveillance and target acquisition (STA) battery. It was a heavy commitment.

To an extent, the deploying batteries' austere establishment, similar to A Battery's, eased this problem. Like with A Battery, there was initial uncertainty as to the gun that they would take. That, fortunately, had settled on the M777 before any serious pre-deployment training would take place early in 2006.

There would be one significant change in E Battery's manning from that of A Battery. Its organization would include 16 additional personnel to generate a miniature unmanned aerial vehicle (UAV) troop equipped with Israeli Skylarks. These small aircraft—really radio-controlled model airplanes—would provide a capability for the infantry to peek over the next hill. While the addition of this troop was a step forward, the personnel deficiencies in, for example, the number of FOO parties, and the problems created by the centralization of administrative support in a national support element had not been addressed.

The battle group would also lack additional artillery STA systems to accurately find and fix enemy mortars and rockets. While the acquisition process remained ongoing, no radars or acoustic sensors would deploy with Task Force 3-06. Coupled with the permanent personnel shortages resulting from the home leave program, as well as normal attrition and possible casualties, this meant that E Battery would face challenges in providing continuous effective fire support.

While Brigadier-General Tim Grant and his chief of staff Lieutenant-Colonel Tom Bradley would come from the 1st Canadian Mechanized Brigade Group in Edmonton, many of his staff would be supplied by Land Force Central Area for the nine months starting on November 1, 2006.[4] That headquarters would have a significantly reduced role from that of its predecessor. Coalition Task Force AEGIS was a multinational brigade headquarters responsible for all of Regional Command (South). This included the British, Dutch, Australian and other contingents in the provinces of Kandahar, Helmand, Uruzgan, and Zabul.[5] AEGIS reported directly to ISAF Headquarters in Kabul. As of November 1, 2006, ISAF would form a new multinational headquarters to command Regional Command (South) under a Dutch major-general. Grant's headquarters, as Joint Task Force AFGHANISTAN, would be reduced to the command of all Canadian Forces operating under Operation ATHENA—Canada's operational deployment to the Afghanistan theatre of operations. In its dual role as Task Force KANDAHAR, it would have command or operational control over most of the forces in the Province of Kandahar.

Like E Battery, the battle group also faced manning difficulties. The army tasked Land Force Central Area as the force generation agency for Task Force 3-06 and much of the subsequent Task Force 1-07. To help with manpower, Ottawa added a rifle company from the Princess Patricia's Canadian Light Infantry to each of Task

Force 3-06 and 1-07. For Task Force 3-06, it would be A Company from the 2nd Battalion, Princess Patricia's Canadian Light Infantry in Shilo. With them would come a FOO detachment from 1 RCHA led by Captain Ryan Stimpson and Sergeant Robin Everett. Their call sign would be G21.

2 RCHA would fill out the rest of the positions.

Major Greg Ivey would deploy as the battery commander. Master Warrant Officer Bob Montague would go as the battery sergeant major and Sergeant Donald Barton as the battery commander's technician. Montague, like his A Battery predecessor, would now typically travel in the battery commander's light armoured vehicle's (LAV). Here he would man an air sentry hatch and be the rear gunner.

Ivey, an army brat who had graduated from the Royal Military College in 1995, had previously deployed operationally to Bosnia and Kosovo. He had qualified as an instructor in gunnery in 2001 and had served a tour in the Royal Canadian Artillery School (RCAS) in Gagetown. In 2005, he was posted to 2 RCHA as its operations officer. In February 2006, after his promotion to major, and just six months before the deployment, he was unexpectedly given command of E Battery when the incumbent had become unavailable.

Captain James Spears, Warrant Officer George MacDonald and Sergeant Shawn Attrux would deploy as the FSCC officer, FSCC warrant officer and second in command and FSCC third in command, respectively. The regiment's two FOO parties would be G22 led by Captain Ian Plummer and Sergeant Maurice McGarrigle and G23, led by Captain Dan Matheson and Sergeant James Myler. Captain Roger Pierce and Warrant Officer Rick Cameron would be the battery captain and battery quartermaster sergeant.

On the gun line, Captain Cory Gillis would deploy as the gun position officer, while Captain Ian Haney—from Guelph's 11th Field Artillery Regiment, RCA— and Lieutenants Caleb Walker and Francis Gould would be the command post officers—Haney and Gould with C Troop, Gillis and Walker with D Troop. Walker was a late comer to the battery. Originally with F Battery he had been on avalanche control in Rogers Pass and was a replacement for another officer after E Battery was already well into its training.[6] Warrant Officer Rodney Gallant and Sergeant Dennis Larade would deploy as the command post detachment commanders for C and D Troop respectively.

The two troop sergeants major would be Warrant Officers Paul Penny for C Troop and Maurice Campbell for D Troop. Gun detachment commanders would be Sergeants Timothy Hale and Kenneth Leet for C Troop, and Frank Hendrickson and Alexander Prentice for D Troop.

Finally, Sergeant David McGuinness would command the four-man meteorological detachment, elements of which came from Canadian Forces Base

Shearwater. Captain Andrew Lockridge, an STA instructor in gunnery from the RCAS and Warrant Officer Stephen Konynenberg, from the 1st Battalion, The Royal Canadian Regiment, would command the miniature UAV troop.

Warrant Officer Rod Gallant recalls that at the time the battery was tasked to deploy, its personnel strength stood at 90%. That would drop to approximately 70% when they subtracted individuals who could not deploy for various reasons. Being the first battery of the regiment to deploy, he was able to round out the command post staff with his pick from the regiment.[7]

2 RCHA would also rely heavily on the reserve force gunners of Land Force Central Area to fill out the establishment. In total 18 reserve gunners would answer the call from the 7th Toronto Regiment, and Guelph's 11th, Ottawa's 30th, Sault Ste Marie's 49th, and Brantford's 56th Field Artillery Regiments, RCA. Filling out the rest of the battery positions was no problem. Everyone was eager to go. Pierce, the battery captain would later recall:

> ...Ivey and I were both parachuted into the [battery] just as the level 4 live fire pre-deployment training started. We were not too familiar with who was [regular force] and who was [reserve force] and had a difficult time distinguishing the difference. At the end of the tour, Greg and I had a long discussion about this and agreed that everyone was "E [Battery]" ... not [regular force] plus Augmentees. For me it really reinforced the adage of the "[Royal Canadian Artillery] Family" and proved that a gunner is a gunner regardless of where they come from.
>
> I'm still convinced this was the right way to go, as it reinforced that we were one tightly congealed unit, regardless of our backgrounds. As far as I know that practice continued with follow-on [batteries].[8]

E Battery was an eclectic combination of field and air defence artillerymen. There were even a few airmen. This integration of personnel from a variety of units would succeed for many reasons, not least of which was that for the gunners, they all wore the same cap badge. This was a constant reminder that above all else they were members of the Royal Regiment of Canadian Artillery, and provided a head start on cohesion that was not necessarily available to the others arms.

Another factor was the RCHA flash proudly worn by all artillery members of the battery—regular and reserve. The latter almost did not happen. In an effort to highlight the contribution of the various units supporting the battle group, decrees had come down from above that all reservists would wear their own unit flashes. While this may have made sense for members of infantry and armoured regiments, it was seen as a retrograde move for gunners. Indeed, by not allowing reservists to wear the RCHA flash, it could be said that the regulars were not prepared to accept them as full members of the battery.

Pierce, as the battery administrative officer and second in command, appealed to the Task Force adjutant, who was initially reluctant to raise the issue. Pierce made the point that while this may seem unimportant to others, it was an important issue to the gunners, who truly considered themselves all members of one regiment. This was important for not only the morale of the battery, but for all members of the artillery. The chain of command bought into his argument, and while the rest of the reservists in Task Force 3-06 wore their parent unit flashes, all the field gunners proudly served on "the right of the line" as part of the RCHA.

E Battery's structure, like A Battery's before it, was still modeled on the original 2003-2004 deployments to Kabul. The Kabul batteries, equipped with the LG1, had been camp bound and had fired very few operational rounds. As had been the case with A Battery before it, E Battery's various elements were neither manned nor equipped to conduct prolonged 24/7 combat operations outside the wire, under the constant threat of enemy contact. This, of course, is exactly what they would end up doing.

Tactically, the battery had quickly adopted the practices of its predecessors. While the vehicles the gun line used in training were a mixture of unarmoured wheeled vehicles, and did not involve the armoured Bisons in use in Kandahar, the battery started to use the independent troop and local defence, force protection layout being used by A Battery.[9]

Major Ivey and Battery Sergeant Major Montague would travel together in their LAV, G29, as part of the battle group commander's tactical group. The three FOOs, in their respective LAV observation post vehicles, would be with their respective infantry companies; Stimpson's G21 with A Company, Plummer's G22 with B Company and Matheson's G23 with Charles Company.[10]

The FSCC, like its predecessor, would remain with Task Force 3-06's tactical operations centre at Kandahar Airfield (KAF). So too would the battery's small administrative element.

E Battery was slated to take over A Battery's equipment and so formed itself with each gun troop having a maximum of eight vehicles once deployed. There would be five Bison armoured personnel carriers—one for reconnaissance (recce), one as the command post, one for the troop sergeant major, and one each for the two gun detachments as troop carriers. Two heavy logistics vehicles, wheeled, would serve as gun tractors doubling as ammunition carriers. In addition there was a Bison designated for the meteorological detachment. In Canada, this detachment operated out of a specialized variant of the medium logistics vehicle, wheeled.

One key lesson coming back from Afghanistan was that the recce party did not move separately from the gun group for reasons of security. Recce would always move as part of the complete gun group.

The original plan, like A Battery's, envisioned the battery deploying as a single four-gun entity. That would change during training, as word came back from Afghanistan that most deployments were as independent troops. E Battery's gun line trained extensively to deploy as troops providing for their own security in austere gun positions. The deployment layout was in the form of a box with an armoured Bison at each corner. The guns deployed close together with the command post, gun tractors and the meteorological vehicle behind them, all within the box.

With Coalition Task Force AEGIS and its fires and effects cell remaining in place until November 1, 2006 there was no call on 2 RCHA to provide any artillery officers to AEGIS's headquarters. On that date, AEGIS was scheduled to hand off its functions respecting Kandahar province to Brigadier-General Tim Grant's incoming Task Force KANDAHAR headquarters. With AEGIS's role as the headquarters for ISAF's Regional Command (South) going to a new Dutch-led multinational headquarters, Grant's headquarters was built light right from the very start and did not have an artillery cell. Circumstances would see it grow with time.[11]

Similarly the 3-person airspace coordination centre (ASCC) at AEGIS would not require replacement in August as their tour would coincide with that of AEGIS. Then they too would go home without replacement as their function would be part of the new NATO-provided Regional Command (South) headquarters. On the other hand, the six-person ASCC team that was with Task Force ORION would require replacement by a new detachment from 4th Air Defence Regiment, RCA (4 AD Regt).

4 AD Regt assigned six air defenders under Captain Bill Warren, an air defence instructor in gunnery and Lieutenant Stephen Chledowski, to Task Force 3-06 in February 2006. They too would be involved in the Task Force's predeployment training alongside E Battery's FSCC.

There would , however, be no tactical air control party with the battle group, nor for that matter the incoming Task Force KANDAHAR headquarters. That function would remain solely at AEGIS's headquarters in the form of air force Major Pat Howell and two other non-Canadian officers. They too were scheduled to depart with AEGIS in November and their role assumed by the incoming Dutch Regional Command (South) headquarters.[12]

2 RCHA would also play a large role in manning the Task Force 3-06's PRT. In the fall of 2005, the regiment's commanding officer, Lieutenant-Colonel Simon Hetherington was called in to see his brigade commander, Colonel Al Howard,

a gunner as well. Howard told him that he had been selected as the commanding officer of the PRT for Operation ATHENA Roto 1 and asked if he was interested. Heatherington's response was, "What's a PRT?" Notwithstanding this, he was interested in the job. While originally scheduled to deploy in August, the situation in Kandahar was making it clear that the team needed an officer proficient in combat operations and therefore his deployment was moved up by six weeks. In June 2006, he transferred command of 2 RCHA to Lieutenant-Colonel Scott Johnson and deployed.[13] With him would go an 8-person team from F Battery to form his tactical headquarters and security detail.[14] Also deploying would be the regiment's deputy commanding officer Major Steve Murray, Master Warrant Officer Mike Louvelle as the PRT sergeant major, Bombardier Kelly Wood with the quartermaster, and another two dozen personnel filling various support roles.

The PRT would be structured much like its predecessor. There would be a handful of people from Foreign Affairs Canada, the Canadian International Development Agency and the Royal Canadian Mounted Police. The majority of the over 130 personnel came from the military including civil-military cooperation teams and a military police platoon. In addition they would be supported by an infantry company in the role of force protection. The PRT would grow over time as elements and personnel were added to it.

5e Régiment d'artillerie légère du Canada (5 RALC) would also be supplying some personnel to this roto albeit they would not participate in the pre-deployment training. The second roto of the tactical UAV flight had trained with the Task Force 1-06 roto in the fall of 2005. Subsequent to that all of the Sperwer systems had been deployed to Afghanistan. By the time they would arrive in Afghanistan early in August, they would have had no hands-on experience with their equipment for almost ten months.[15]

E Battery started its pre-deployment training immediately in the new year of 2006. The first four M777s, which had been used in training by A Battery, had, by now, been shipped to Afghanistan. This left two new guns to be shipped to Petawawa where they were immediately rotated between the two troops; one using M777s, the other using 105mm C3s.

The first challenge would be sharing the two M777s with others outside of E Battery. Not only was there a need to train E Battery's gunners on their use, but there was also a complex plan in play for the myriad of tasks needed to properly implement all the components associated with them. Colonel Bob Gunn, the Director Land Requirements, would issue a fielding plan for the system in March.[16] Implementation of that plan, however, had started even before its issue.

While E Battery would have the guns for training in February there were periods built into the plan where various individuals, primarily from the RCAS would travel to Petawawa to conduct trials. February also started off with thirteen weapons technicians and eleven fire control systems technicians from across the country making their way to Aberdeen, Maryland for several weeks training on their responsibilities for maintaining the guns.

Other activities during this period included trials to calibrate the newly acquired modular ammunition charge system with the gun and with the existing Indirect Fire Control Computer System; receiving, trialling and fielding a digitized gun management system; and developing, trialling and fielding a digital radio link to connect the gun management system with the command post computers. Further work would also need to be done to field the 30 Excalibur rounds that had been bought.

The digital gun management system was a concurrent project that stood up at the time of the original purchase of the M777. The contract went to SELEX Sensors and Airborne Systems, an Anglo/Italian company that had developed the Laser Inertial Artillery Pointing System (LINAPS) for the British artillery.[17] The complete system has the following components for each gun:

- An inertial navigation unit that contains a ring-laser gyro and quartz accelerometer-based inertial sensor assembly that provides inertial measurement of gun elevation and bearing angles, and a global positioning system receiver module, providing the gun's primary location data;
- A gun laying unit which is a touch-screen display, providing operators access to the control and display capabilities of the gun management system;
- A muzzle velocity indicator which provides muzzle velocity data and accuracy figures;
- A vehicle distance sensor which is an odometer providing wheel rotation information;
- A battery power management system to provide power to the system; and
- A detachment commander's display unit which is a handheld or tripod mounted, full-screen, portable, stylus terminal that provides an in-cab display of position and steering information to the driver, links the battery command post to the gun laying unit and reads the muzzle velocity and sends it to the command post.[18]

It would revolutionize operations at the gun line. To this point in time, fixing the actual geographic location of a gun and the direction it was pointing to was a complex, multistep process conducted by an artillery recce team. Now guns had the ability to fix and orient themselves making it possible to deploy individual guns scattered across a wide area but still be able to concentrate their fire. Similarly, passing fire orders from the command post to the guns had been done by someone in the command post reading the data off a computer screen, passing it to the gun by way of either radio, a wired speaker called a tannoy, or, in the worst case scenario, by shouting them out the back door of the command post, and finally setting the data on the gun's sight. Now the data would flow from the command post's computer directly into the gun laying unit and the detachment commander's display unit. Not only did the system save time in processes where every second counts, but it also reduced the possibility of an error creeping into the data during the transmission process.

At the RCAS, Captain Lorne Doucet, with Warrant Officers Alexander Sangster and Gabriel "Gabby" Pinard were appointed office of primary interest in conducting fielding and training of the system once delivered and integrated onto the M777. Steering of the acquisition and integration of the system's various components remained with Major Bruno D'Ilio at the Directorate of Land Requirements until he was replaced by Major Kevin Duff at the end of the summer 2006 trials.

Since the LINAPS had never been installed on an M777 before, the initial trials would not only be to test out the functionality of the system, but to develop a method of how to integrate it with the howitzer. Time blocks were set aside in Petawawa throughout February to July where the work being done at the RCAS and at the Land Software Engineering Centre would merge with and into the equipment and training in Petawawa. The challenge was not only to mount the system on the M777, but also to make its operating software bilingual, and to integrate and connect the system to the Indirect Fire Control Computer System in the command posts.[19]

To leave E Battery free to concentrate on their role for the upcoming deployment, much of the trials work was left to D Battery whose own pre-deployment training would not start until after the summer. As a side benefit, the trials would help D Battery with the digital transformation process when they started their own road to high readiness training.

By March, the positioning of the equipment on the gun had been resolved. In addition a small radio, the Raytheon Microlight Ultra High Frequency, Software Defined Radio, had come to the attention of the project team. It was considered an orphan system by the communications branch without other applications but with sufficient spare sets available within the army for the gunners' needs. It would become the temporary wireless connective link between the gun and the command post for several years to come.[20]

Collective training for E Battery started on March 18, 2006 with the battle group's Exercise THUNDERING BEAR II in Petawawa. A Company of the 2nd Battalion of the Princess Patricia's Canadian Light Infantry flew in from Shilo to round out the battle group. A Company would be issued the Mercedes G-Wagon Light Utility Vehicles Wheeled, both in Petawawa and early on in Afghanistan where they would start receiving LAVs. The other two companies operated out of LAVs. Major Mike Wright, the company's officer commanding, felt very welcome and part of the battle group right from the first moment of their arrival and found the training excellent. In his view, "Third Battalion [The Royal Canadian Regiment] set up a fantastic set of ranges for us there."[21]

The battery, naturally, found the training very infantry-centric and very much following the style of operations that had been the routine for Kabul. Major Greg Ivey recalls, "Our workup training was focused on these surgical infantry operations at night. These "hard-knock" versus "soft knock" operations, I think, still trickled out of our Kabul days. Even at the artillery school you could see the type of three-block war; using the artillery only as a precision weapon."[22] Each exercise evolution would be a company level deliberate operation. It would start with 100% intelligence and then the company would deploy.

It would be a challenging exercise for A Company and for some others as they were ravaged by an attack of the Norwalk virus, a highly contagious, intestinal viral infection which causes serious bouts of vomiting, diarrhea and stomach pains. Despite everything, the gunners were happy with their new gun and the tour. Sergeant Stan MacDonald of Army News filed a story in the late winter expressing how pleased the gunners were with their new gun and how "stoked" they were with the mission.

While the infantry's training was not challenging for the FOOs, the training for the forward air controllers (FAC) would be better. RCAF F-18 fighter jets out of Bagotville had a large supply of ordinance that they wanted to drop. They were prepared to provide a considerable number of hours of aircraft time. Through personal contact with the squadron through Captain Tim Spears, arrangements were made to incorporate the fighters into the battery's exercises. Both inert 1,000-pound bombs and live Mk 82 bombs were available, as was a tanker for air-to-air refueling allowing aircraft to stay on station longer. Spears was of the view that, "For us, the culmination of THUNDERING BEAR had trained us ... the scope of that exercise was way larger and way more than what [the Canadian Manoeuvre Training Centre] could put out at that time."[23]

Preparatory training at the Canadian Manoeuvre Training Centre in Wainwright for Task Force 3-06 ran from the last week of April and throughout May. It would follow generally the same outline as used for Task Force ORION. The Centre had been established in 2004 and helped develop and run the Canadian army's brigade training event in 2005. 2006, however, would be the first of the MAPLE

GUARDIAN series of exercises. Previous exercises focused on general training for combat readiness, while the new exercise focused on training a task force for deployment to Afghanistan.

The counter insurgency model that was exercised anticipated that there would be contacts with small groups of insurgents. Full scale combat operations were considered unlikely. The emphasis in training had been on limited kinetic operations, reinforcement of the authority of the central government, and support for the creation of democratic institutions. It was, more or less, the "Three Block War" model that was in vogue at the time. The focus was on a combination of counter-insurgency and nation building. Lavoie recalls:

> We were served fairly well on two sides. On the one side I had, at the time, Colonel Al Howard, [a gunner who] was the brigade commander...He set a pretty rigorous training plan in Petawawa which had included a lot of live fire and included a lot of close, all-arms cooperation and specifically with E Battery in support...[he] ran us through those paces of the conventional side, I would say, for probably three or four months.

> And then we had the benefit of being the first battle group to go through the Canadian Manoeuvre Training Centre [CMTC]. It was just getting on its feet when Ian Hope's battalion was training but he never went through a CMTC serial so we were the first ones to go through a CMTC serial which I characterize more as a mission rehearsal.

> So what 2 Brigade put us through would have prepared us for any type of conventional, high-intensity operation. CMTC probably, in a way, scaled it back a little bit. Not only was there live-fire manoeuvre and live-fire ranges; it was a mission rehearsal in the terms of full-spectrum of exercising the PRT under another gunner [Lieutenant-Colonel and, at the time, commanding officer of 2 RCHA] Simon Hetherington; exercising the battalion but more in the sense of counter-insurgency operations ...

> At the time, and in hindsight...I thought it was a pretty intense serial ... [At] the time it was, amongst the staff and the troops, "This is bullshit! You know, we're never going to experience these many incidents in a 24-hour period." And I came to be proven pretty wrong about that in the first week of September when we kicked off with MEDUSA. And I remind young soldiers now as a division commander and higher that "Your worst day in training is still better than your best day in combat." So you want to train for it on the one-way range before you get to figure it out on the two-way range.[24]

For the gunners, the training was repetitive and probably dragged on too long.

The concept of operations for the training still envisaged separate company areas of operation. The scenarios called for an infantry company securing the Tarin Kot Highway in the north at Forward Operating Base MARTELLO, a second company based in Kandahar City with the PRT, and a third securing Highway 1 west of the city. Elements of the Royal Canadian Dragoons' Intelligence, Surveillance, Target Acquisition and Reconnaissance (ISTAR) Squadron[25] would be in Spin Boldak screening the border and securing the commercial lifeline of Highway 4 that connected Kandahar with Pakistan.

The cutbacks in all arms operational training over the previous decade along with the experience in the Balkans and around Kabul had resulted in the infantry of the battle group having had little to no experience in working with the artillery. Only a few had taken some all-arms calls for fire training. The focus was on the selective use of artillery with individual rounds on a discrete target as opposed to area neutralization missions where large volumes of fire are used to neutralize a larger target's effectiveness. While the battery had become very proficient in applying fire under a variety of conditions and scenarios, the standard of all arms cooperation had fallen short. Indeed, all arms training may have been only a buzzword, with each arm training separately, with little to no coordination. As an example, Captain Piers Pappin, the commander of 4 Platoon, would later comment,

> *Prior to deployment, I had never seen an M777 for real let alone understanding [its] capability (it was fired during our work-up in [Wainwright] but the crazy '[training] safety' distance (several [kilometres], and us under cover I think) from our [position] didn't allow us to truly appreciate it.*
>
> *The best we were able to do insofar as training with the All-Arms Call for Fire was using our own 60mm mortars and the Arty simulator (we used this quite a bit).*
>
> *On conducting my [Relief in Place] in-country, the outgoing [platoon] ensured we spent some time calling-in live fire (myself and the [Section Commanders]).*[26]

Pappin would note that in theatre, "We would walk the 155 in towards us as close as 40 [metres] as we hunkered down tight to a dirt wall (concrete hard) or in a wadi."[27]

In hindsight, Lieutenant-Colonel Omer Lavoie agrees,

> *At the time I was pretty happy with the integration of both the guns and, of course, the mortars as well during the training events, particularly in Petawawa, because I remember a lot of nights being out practicing company or battle group attacks in the middle of the night with Colonel Howard right behind me and him on the fire control nets, the gunner one, when he saw*

things he wasn't happy with and have the guns either redo it or adjust or whatever. So I was pretty happy going into it.

But, to your point, when we got into the fight, I wished then that—and of course in training there's a whole bunch of limitations that preclude you from doing "danger close"—so, yeah, in hindsight, and I think other battle groups who followed me were able to adjust that. There were a lot more "danger close" missions than we ever anticipated or had trained for. But, I'd say to their credit; well whether it was the FOOs or the [mortar fire controllers] or even often an all-arms call for fire, it got mastered pretty quickly.[28]

At Wainwright, the battery's FACs would only see dry runs with Alpha Jets, and barely four hours of additional F-18 time. Spears: "From a training perspective [the Canadian Manoeuvre Training Centre] wasn't a crescendo; we'd already peaked at THUNDERING BEAR."[29]

While the FACs might have had good training during THUNDERING BEAR, the training and essential equipment still did not come together. The FACs did not have infrared pointers nor remotely operated video enhanced receivers—ROVERS—which could provide them with imagery from an aircraft's targeting pods. There were vague expectations that the equipment would be available for them in theatre, but no one actually knew what that would be. Greg Ivey indicated: "The FAC parties were extremely limited in terms of what they had at their disposal."[30]

Further, no one in Canada had yet fully appreciated the problems of a FAC working out of the back hatch of a LAV while in contact and which A Battery was experiencing in Afghanistan. Moreover, they had not completed any night runs, something required for certification for controlling American aircraft. That would have to wait for Afghanistan as well.

Problems would appear for others as well. One of those was Sergeant Anthony Tullet. Tullet was part of the STA troop in Gagetown. He had been intimately involved in the development of the artillery's miniature UAV program and the selection of the Israeli Elbit Skylark. He and several other gunners from Gagetown were joining E Battery's miniature UAV troop. The newly acquired Skylarks arrived just before deploying on Exercise MAPLE GUARDIAN. Tullet found that the aircraft had been "Canadianized" with slightly different antennae than those found on the manufacturer's Israeli ones. The test aircraft had worked perfectly in Israel. It could fly out to the advertised 10 kilometre range. In Petawawa it barely made it out 3 kilometres before losing contact and then automatically returning to its launch location. The problem was so bad that the Troop had to get a field representative from Israel to run diagnostics on the system. He identified the antenna as the culprit and suggested a fix which was implemented. The fix worked, however, there would be another, more complex issue, which wouldn't arise until the system was deployed in theatre.

Training of the Task Force 3-06 PRT improved over that of its predecessors.[31] When first stood up, the Task Force followed the existing model, namely that the PRT was subordinate to the battle group which designed and directed its training. That continued until just before deploying to the Canadian Manoeuvre Training Centre. At that time, it was decided that the PRT would become an independent unit reporting to Joint Task Force-Afghanistan.

Lieutenant-Colonel Heatherington, an instructor in gunnery, took two recce trips to Kandahar where he met with the existing team and was able to bring the information learned back to the Canadian Manoeuvre Training Centre staff who were quite receptive to incorporating scenarios into the exercise.

> *Training scenarios were injected to include high-level meetings with [Afghan] officials, the design and delivery of projects, working with [Non Government Organizations] and other [Canadian] government departments, etc... Specific training was done in negotiations. The remainder of the PRT training followed the requisite individual and collective battle task standards for deployment. In the case of the PRT, we participated in convoy [operations], including responding to [an] ambush.[32]*

It was clear that training for the PRT would be an evolutionary process going forward as the teams in theatre developed techniques to deal with novel situations that they faced. Task Force 3-06's training had adapted to the Task Force 1-06 experience. Future serials at the Canadian Manoeuvre Training Centre would similarly learn and adapt future training.

As the training reached its end in May, with reports of heavy fighting coming back from the front, it was clear that many of the assumptions behind the concept of operations and force structure were no longer valid. Tim Spears recalls:

> *MAPLE GUARDIAN is something that we had to do, and we took it [seriously] but there was a lot of animosity between the battle group and the [Canadian Manoeuvre Training Centre] staff on that exercise. It was not jovial by any stretch...When we were doing the company level attacks they were pretty canned...Now MAPLE GUARDIAN started to develop better from lessons learned in theatre after our tour, I think. And they got better quickly.[33]*

Lavoie concedes that there were issues, but that the outcome was good,

> *I think we were well served. There were some friction points between us and*

[the Canadian Manoeuvre Training Centre], them being a brand-new organization and us being a battle group getting prepped to what by that point in time we thought was going to be a combat operation and they, sort of, had to stick to their script. So if anything, for me it was I don't want to focus on the low-intensity stuff, I want to focus on the high-intensity because if I can do that then I can probably do anything.[34]

Notwithstanding that the training had ended and the battery was in the final stages of preparing for deployment, the actual threat facing them wasn't yet clear. Ivey acknowledges that the word coming back from Kandahar hadn't been alarming before Wainwright. He says,

I don't think anyone in the battery was expecting an Operation MEDUSA two or three months earlier. Even our exercise in Wainwright, despite the discussion about having to go into combat...Nichola Goddard was killed while we were in Wainwright and almost immediately after [Task Force] 3-06 had completed its [tactical recce] ... even then I don't think anyone was expecting the type of build-up that took place and the severity of a potential Taliban takeover of Kandahar City and Kandahar Province...

We didn't know what we didn't know...Even on MAPLE GUARDIAN, the last workup exercise, the confirmation exercise...it was disjointed, better than anything I had ever done, I had ever experienced as a gunner officer, but again, still very disjointed...

The E [Battery] FSCC and artillery elements of that exercise always seemed to have been an afterthought. They didn't necessarily connect with the manoeuvre activities that were taking place and in many cases I would argue we were almost, not left out of battle per se, but we weren't necessarily inculcated quite well into the battle group planning process with the leadership of that battle group. The focus was on the engineers and their tasks during that exercise.

The agenda did not allow us to integrate as well as we should have before we deployed over.[35]

It is questionable just how much word of the reality of the situation on the ground in Afghanistan came back to Canada to influence the training. As an example, during Wainwright Captain Corey Gillis was still of the view that, as the gun position officer, he would be running a four-gun fire unit rather than the individual troop deployments that A Battery had fallen into.[36] In Afghanistan, meanwhile, the nature of the fight was clearly evolving and was about to do so in a radical way. Task Force 3-06's training was complete by the time that ORION experienced the events of

August 3, 2006 in Pashmul. Even then, the full impact of that day's activities, as well as those in Helmand in July, hadn't fully sunk in. Even the most pessimistic intelligence report fell far short of the reality of the situation in Afghanistan that the next roto of gunners would be facing.

18

The New Kids on the Block

MULLAH DADULLAH LANG HAD PLAYED A LONG GAME in the south. Over several years, he had quietly built up a force of 4,000 well-led, well-trained Taliban fighters. This force, organized into three fronts—northern Helmand, southern Helmand and western Kandahar—had two objectives; the two provincial capitals of Lashkar Gah and Kandahar City. Task Force ORION had seen the start of the northern Helmand front early in the tour in April. In July, supporting the British Parachute Regiment's battle group, they had seen both of the Helmand fronts in full swing around Sangin, Garmser and Nawa. The British would be tied down there for a long time to come.

The Taliban had started their reoccupation of Kandahar province in early 2006 by moving into western Panjwayi. In April, at the request of the local population, they moved their strength across the Arghandab into Zhari.[1] While Task Force ORION had conducted several operations there, other International Security Assistance Force (ISAF) and American priorities prevented them from leaving any permanent force behind. The Taliban strength grew. ORION's Operation BRAVO GUARDIAN in Zhari in May, when Captain Goddard was killed, was hailed as a great success by local Kandaharis but did not stop the Taliban's buildup.

ORION had poked the Taliban third front's sleeping bear on August 3, 2006 in Pashmul. Notwithstanding that fight, the Kandahar front remained relatively quiet for a few weeks. The insurgents' offensive there was not scheduled to start until August 19, 2006, Afghan Independence Day. Concurrently, the relief in place of the combat hardened ORION with the novice Task Force 3-06 would be in full swing.

Dadullah, in anticipation of the overall campaign, now sat firmly ensconced in Maywand, from where he could keep an eye on all three fronts. His goal was clear: capture the south as an entryway to the rest of the country.[2]

While the Taliban's organization was by no means trouble free, by all appearances its leadership was generally unified and focused on a specific aim. The same could not be said for the North Atlantic Treaty Organization (NATO) allies.

The United States continued to be distracted by and focused on Iraq. Secretary of Defence, Donald Rumsfeld had been looking at reducing America's troop commitment in Afghanistan to between 10,000 and 12,000. The reduction was to follow the October, 2005 Afghan elections. The Americans would stay focused only on the eastern border. NATO was expected to step up in the rest of the country.[3]

When Rumsfeld visited Kabul in December, he realized that the situation was deteriorating. This hadn't changed his mind. He blamed the problem on poor governance and did nothing to strengthen the development of the Afghan army. Instead, he was reassessing its size downward from 70,000 to 45,000-52,000. He also withdrew one American brigade of 3,000 troops.

President Hamid Karzai, in the meantime, was in a snit. The British had insisted that he remove his governor in Helmand, Sher Mohammed. It was an intrusion into Afghan politics and Karzai, rightly or wrongly, blamed the return of the Taliban there on Mohammed's removal. Coupled with this was the demobilization of the pre-existing Afghan militias. These local forces had been seen as a threat to Karzai's national government. The slow growth of the Afghan National Army and the total disaster that was the Afghan National Police, meant that the southern security situation was poor at best.

While the Taliban had roughly 4,000 fighters in Helmand and Kandahar provinces, the allies had approximately 5,700 soldiers and police. Many of these were either fixed in the cities or otherwise non deployable. In total, 1,850 soldiers and police were in the field in the south. Another 1,200 were in Kandahar City and Lashkar Gah. They could be called on occasionally as a reserve.[4] Missing too was unity of command. While an ISAF command structure existed, it was divided and responsive to national factions. Even within the Afghan security forces, Karzai had chosen not to appoint any single commander. Instead numerous Afghan governors and agencies reported directly to him.

> Together, they should have been strong enough to defeat the Taliban...Yet the government and their tribal allies were divided, riven by feuds and competition. Staunch opponents of the Taliban had their armed men stripped away by other opponents of the Taliban. So when the Taliban attacked, a few tribes fought, but others either switched sides or sat things out.[5]

Task Force 3-06's rotation had commenced midway through the summer of 2006. The battle group, including E Battery, flowed into the theatre in several waves a few days apart. Typically, a "chalk" made up of troops from a variety of units would leave Petawawa during the day, undergo a brief processing in Trenton, and then depart by CC-150 Polaris for Camp Mirage. As an example, the G22 forward observation officer (FOO) party, less Bombardier Johnson, left Petawawa at 1100 hours on July 31, 2006, arrived in Trenton at 1430 and were "wheels up" at 1600 hours. They arrived in Dubai at 2000 hours on August 1, 2006, a day which their observation post log simply described as "Really Hot". Here they drew their weapons, ammunition and ballistic plates and departed by multi-engine CC-130 Hercules for Kandahar Airfield (KAF) at 2230 hours.

Major Ivey described his arrival in KAF as,

> *A quick walk off the tarmac and into a bombed out reception hanger was enough to have everyone dripping with sweat. The camp sergeant major's representative gathered everyone into a semi-circle and started talking. I assume he was briefing on the dos and don'ts of the camp, [but] we couldn't actually hear anything over the drone of the aircraft engines. [We] grabbed our kit and moved to temporary quarters. Two hours later we were on the rifle range zeroing our personal weapons and pistols at first light. Gloves had to be worn when picking up anything metallic due to the heat.[6]*

There was little time to reset the body clocks. Captain Plummer's G22 FOO party, the first into theatre, spent the remainder of August 2, 2006 and all the next day acclimatizing and exploring the camp. This wasn't his first time in Afghanistan. He had started his career as a reservist with the 49th Field Artillery Regiment, RCA in Sault Ste Marie but transferred to the regular force in 1999. In the summer of 2003 he had deployed with F Battery to Kabul as the troop commander of Canada's first ever Sperwer tactical unmanned aerial vehicle (UAV) troop.

Now, he and his detachment followed up their arrival with a short period of training and signing over of kit. On two of their first evenings, they experienced "Welcome to Afghanistan" rocket attacks. Most teams had three to four days in KAF. Partially this was to receive some of their equipment but mostly it was to acclimatize them to the blistering fifty degrees Celsius summer heat.

Warrant Officer Rod Gallant was also a veteran of the previous F Battery Kabul deployment. Kandahar was a totally different environment from what he had experienced before; the cool mountains replaced by the sweltering heat of what was mostly an open desert.[7]

For some of the incoming rotation the reality of the situation was brought home by their attendance at the ramp ceremonies for those killed on August the 3rd. It was a sobering moment.[8]

As their respective companies shook out and were given tasks, the FOO parties did the same. Captain Ryan Stimpson's G21 was deployed with A Company. Equipped with a mixture of the lightly armoured G-Wagons and LAVs, the company was earmarked to work with the provincial reconstruction team (PRT) out of Kandahar. They would also cover the outpost at Patrol Base (PB) WILSON previously handled by ORION's B Company and their outgoing FOO, G12's Captain Mike Smith.

The PRT now had the task of working on the Afghan development zone concept that ISAF's British commander, General Richards, had articulated the month before. The implementation of this ISAF designed program would come through Task Force AEGIS in the south by way of joint effects tasking orders which were normally issued monthly and gave the Regional Commands a list of low, medium and high priority tasks to be achieved over the short, medium and long term. Lieutenant-Colonel Peter Williams, the chief fires and effects in AEGIS:

> As I recall the short term was the next 2 months, medium was the 3rd month out and long term was beyond the three month point. I recall the establishment of the [Afghan development zones] was one of the key high priority tasks for the short term. Other tasks included delivering Reconstruction and Development, countering Taliban messaging and helping build ANA capacity. On the latter, this would largely fall to the [operational mentoring and liaison team] once it was established.[9]

The intent of these zones, a variation of the long-standing counter-insurgency ink-blot concept, would drive a common military and non-military effort across all of ISAF.[10]

For the Canadian team, however, resources would prove to be an impediment for the first part of the tour and limited the effects that it could deliver. Lieutenant-Colonel Hetherington recalls,

> This was due largely to our inability to move across the [area of operations]. While there had been a [company] from the battle group initially tasked with supporting the PRT with transportation and protection, [operations] in PANJWAII and [ZHARI] districts necessitated the [company] rejoin the [battle group]. This left the PRT with limited resources with which to conduct activities. In 2006, we were still driving in armoured G-Wagons. In fact, I was actually ambushed while travelling in one of these—and they don't really feel too armoured when that happens.[11]

Things wouldn't change until late in the year when a fourth rifle company was deployed for force protection for the PRT.

By the end of Task Force ORION's tour, PB WILSON had become the battle group's centre of mass. It constituted both the Zahri district centre and an Afghan police station.

During their 6 month tour, ORION had ranged far and wide. They had been in the Shah Wali Kot in the north, to help ease the Dutch/Australian forces into

Uruzgan. They had gone west, to help first the Americans and then the British in Helmand. By August, ORION was concentrating on Zhari district and keeping the vital Highway 1 ring road to Lashkar Gah open. PB WILSON was key to the success of that. Task Force ORION's B Company had worked on the Zhari problem while much of the rest of the battle group was deployed to Helmand.

The enormity of the Taliban's infestation of Zhari, however, didn't strike home at AEGIS until the events of August 3rd. At that point it became clear to Brigadier-General Fraser that something needed to be done there and planning began for what would become Operation MEDUSA.[12] That plan would develop into a four-phase operation: shape; strike; exploit; and stabilize. Supporting the kinetic operations, particularly in the last phase, would be a number of non-kinetic activities including information operations to counter Taliban messaging. This included having a media quick response force to deal with local media and the distribution of portable hand-cranked radios to the local population to assist in getting the ISAF and Afghan government's message out.[13]

There would be no fixed timeline for any phase. The operation would move from one phase to the next phase once conditions were deemed right. Key to the length of time that the shaping operations would run was when sufficient enablers would be available, particularly from the Americans, to start the strike phase. The estimates were that this would not be until mid to late September.[14]

The plan went to General Richards—as well as to Generals Freakley, Gauthier and Hillier[15]—in the second week of August. "Shaping" would entail exploiting intelligence, surveillance, and reconnaissance (recce) assets to find and fix Taliban leadership, improvised explosive device (IED) factories, ambush sites, supply caches, indirect fire assets such as mortars, supply and movement routes and the like, and degrade them. Simultaneously, the brigade staff would designate objectives to be taken during the "strike" phase.

Shaping operations started even while Task Force ORION and Task Force 3-06 were still in mid rotation.[16] PB WILSON's proximity to the highly active ambush sites on Highway 1 made it critical to the upcoming operation.

The briefing to Richards went well, and Richards confirmed to Fraser that Operation MEDUSA would be NATO's main effort.[17] That, however, did not translate into "boots-on-the-ground." Once the canvas of other national ISAF forces started it quickly became clear that participation would be limited. The Germans, the French, and the Italians, all declined to participate. The caveats put on their forces by the various NATO countries were the primary impediment.[18]

Others would eventually commit but for the time being Fraser and his staff were left scrounging for resources. While the brigade staff planned, the new battle group was settling into their jobs.

PB WILSON would subsequently be expanded, but at the time of E Battery's arrival in 2006 it was still just a small compound. It had three buildings and a courtyard enclosed by seven-foot tall concrete walls. In all, WILSON was an adequate base to house a company-sized element, albeit under somewhat unappealing conditions. It also made a convenient target for Taliban snipers and mortars.

Mortar attacks on WILSON were a daily occurrence during the relief in place. The mortars were sited no more than two to four kilometres to the south of the PB. They were almost invisible amongst the thick vegetation and walled compounds. The accuracy and rate of fire indicated that the crews were well trained, coordinated and had an adequate supply of ammunition.

WILSON would become the home for Captain Ryan Stimpson's G21 and A Company. Besides the mortaring, they had already been involved in firefights along Highway 1 on an almost daily basis.. A stretch of road to WILSON's east had earned the nickname "Ambush Alley". Snipers and machine guns and rocket propelled grenades were routinely fired at traffic.

Captain Ian Plummer's G22 had been assigned to B Company which was tasked into the Shah Wali Kot, to the north of Kandahar City. Amongst other things, they patrolled the Tarin Kot-Kandahar highway through the Arghandab district. The Dutch had moved into Uruzgan and this highway was their main line of communication with KAF.

Captain Dan Matheson and most of G23 were amongst the last to leave Canada. They arrived at KAF early in the morning of August 10, 2006. Notwithstanding the time they arrived and how tired they were, by 0800 hours that morning they were on the rifle range zeroing their weapons. While August 11, 2006 was given to them as a day off, it also ended up being their first ramp ceremony.

The handover between Captain Dan Matheson's G23 crew and that of the outgoing G13 happened at KAF on August 12th and 13th during a rocket attack. Their light armoured vehicle (LAV), the former home of both Captains Nicola Goddard and Andrew Charchuck and their crew, was a mess and showed every sign of having been ridden hard during six months of combat. The next day they and Charles Company departed for a short hop to Spin Boldak on the Pakistan border. It was a worrisome drive. Just a few days earlier, on August 11, 2006 Corporal Andrew Eykelenboom, a medic from 1 Field Ambulance in Edmonton on his last mission before returning home, was killed on the highway coming back from Spin Boldak to KAF. The G-Wagon he was in was hit by a suicide bomber.

For a few days, G23 accompanied Major Matthew Sprague's Charles Company conducting patrols from the border town into the "Red Desert." That wouldn't last. Trouble was brewing in Panjwayi.

These first few days with the outgoing A Battery had quickly driven home to the

FOO parties the difference between how they had trained in Canada and the reality of Afghanistan. Major Ivey recalls,

> By the first week of the [relief in place] each FOO party had already experienced combat, normally deliberate ambushes along the 40 [kilometre] stretch of road from KAF through Kandahar City to the Zhari-Panjwai districts...

> The parties quickly realized the importance of crew drills, LAV gunnery skill sets, and a thorough knowledge of company [standard operating procedures]. Although our previous training tended to push our FOOs to the flanks or good positions of observation in open ground, the reality of counter-insurgency in complex terrain quickly altered our mind set. During a firefight, the enemy isn't choosy about who he engages and the FOO is as susceptible to enemy fire as the lead infantry section. Second, the lack of reaction time and space in complex terrain forces the FOO party to be another 25mm platform concurrent to fire support.[19]

While the battery's four miniature UAV detachments were to supplement the observation capability of the FOOs with the battle group's rifle companies, that did not happen on deployment. Major Ivey: "[FOO] parties and [miniature UAV] detachments were to provide a robust surveillance and target acquisition (STA) capability that would focus on interdicting and preventing the enemy from operating within the [area of operations] ... [miniature UAVs] were also to be pushed to the sub-units based on surge operations."[20]

Despite promises that the equipment would be on the ground in Kandahar when the troop arrived, it did not arrive until September. Even then, serious technical issues would dog the aircraft.

The two gun troops had completed their reliefs in place at austere gun positions. Both troops remained "trails down" and ready for action as A Battery continued to support Task Force ORION's operations.

As the relief progressed, A Battery's more junior ranks were transported back to KAF by road or air while the more senior remained in place to guide the newcomers. C Troop took over B Troop's gun position located a few kilometres west of PB WILSON. From here, they could cover south into lower Zhari and into Panjwayi all along the Arghandab River. D Troop would be at Forward Operating Base (FOB) MARTELLO in the northern part of the battle group area. The move to MARTELLO was a stressful one which gave the troop's personnel their first experience driving through the chaos of Kandahar City. It was dark by the time they got there, causing the packet to miss the turnoff to the FOB and having to turn around in the dark in the rugged terrain.[21]

Like the FOOs, the gun lines were able to quickly capitalize on the experience gained by A Battery during its tour. They adapted to the various changes which were made to the training program and to the equipment they took over.

The battery had a number of female members, who functioned well in these austere conditions. Unlike the previous base-camp experiences of Kabul a few years earlier, they all shared the same accommodations where everyone slept fully dressed, ready to fire the guns at a moment's notice. If a female had to remove or adjust her clothing, the males would turn and face away until she was dressed again. The battery quartermaster sergeant at KAF grew accustomed to sending feminine hygiene products out periodically. Battery Sergeant Major Montague opined that if the female soldiers had been treated differently and given, for example, segregated quarters, cohesion and morale would have suffered.

Deployment drills concentrated on the independent troop box format and on the Bisons which formed the armoured component of the troop. Additional night observation devices and man portable surveillance radars were obtained for the gun position. The concept of operations, however, still reflected a relatively low intensity mission. Perhaps most serious, besides the few number of guns for such a huge area of operations, was the lack of proficiency in the conduct of tactical air support missions, including the employment of Predator armed UAVs and attack helicopters.

Back in KAF, the battle group's fire support coordination centre (FSCC) officer, Captain Tim Spears couldn't help but notice the stressful situation all around him in the ORION tactical operations centre. Spears had none of the issues in setting up an FSCC from scratch that Captain Howie Nelson had to deal with six months previously. He inherited a fully functioning operation and was given an excellent handover from A Battery's crew. The absence of a tactical air control party at TF 3-06 tactical operations centre would, however, create difficulties. Captain Spears recalls,

> *Yes, we were handed off a good functioning FSCC set up from TF 1-06, they just never had to deal with the volume and complexity of task and asset our circumstances dictated. However, we had no Tactical Air Control Party (TACP), so all Requests, [Special Instructions], [Close Air Support] Control and Terminal Attack Control were [my] responsibility. With No TACP, we cobbled together a makeshift [organization] and the [airspace coordination centre (ASCC)] rolled into very close [coordination] with the FSCC and we tried to make it work. [Captain Bill Warren] and his crew were very familiar with all the air space control requirements and all the rules, [regulations] etc.*

THE NEW KIDS ON THE BLOCK | 269

so his cell was instrumental to helping us try to get our arms around Operation MEDUSA and the integration of all the [Flight Safety, Air, Aviation] that would be jammed in a very small area. The [High-Density Airspace Control Zone] started as 25 [nautical miles square] and was eventually reduced to 10 [nautical miles square]. We had literally bitten off more than we could chew and had to reduce the amount of control we were dealing with as it was completely exhausting and overwhelming. Bill and his crew played a vital role in planning, monitoring, and providing feedback to [the battle group headquarters] and more importantly the FSCC/TACP on the airspace in real time.[22]

Unfortunately, the relationship between the existing Task Force ORION and Coalition Task Force AEGIS was anything but comfortable. Spears remembers,

We were the first chalks in. When we left Canada, on August 2nd, we were heading to a theatre of operations that had Stage 2 Insurgency issues happening. There'd been a car bombing. There had been a little bit of rattling the sabres here and there… there was nothing earth shattering. And then when we arrived in Mirage, there were people on blow-horns yelling at us, "Line up here to get your gear!…Welcome to the war!"…August 3rd had just kind of went and unhinged everything, and changed the dynamic dramatically.[23]

Once on the ground and doing a left seat/right seat transition with Nelson it became very clear to Spears that there were issues between Task Forces AEGIS and ORION. That was a concern as AEGIS would remain until November. The newcomers were rapidly having to assimilate the fact that the tactical reality had changed in theatre from what they had believed a mere week before. Spears recalls,

The situation changed dramatically in a very short period of time. When Task Force 1-06 went into Panjwayi on [August 3], the dysfunction of the relationship between [AEGIS/Regional Command (South)] and [Task Force 1-06/ORION] refused to let anybody believe that there could be any significant [Taliban] build up in Panjwayi because [AEGIS] had kind of a mode …with regards to reconstruction happening. [Panjwayi] was a model district in terms of rehabilitating Afghanistan in those time frames. What they didn't realize was that was part of the Taliban, part of al-Qaeda, and the Taliban's game plan…with Task Force ORION trying to get the UK into Helmand, and get the Dutch into Uruzgan, they were spread out all over the place, it gave [the Taliban] the ability to build up right in [the brigade's] backyard right under the guise of all of this other reconstruction that was going on.

When we landed we were in a full Stage 3 insurgency situation with the insurgents moving toward conventional forces and transitioning to conventional operations against Kandahar City.

Everybody was just gob-smacked. We all just kind of went, "What happened?"

If I go back to that dynamic between [AEGIS/Regional Command (South)] and Task Force ORION it seemed to me like there was a lot of information that was being collected that would lead, or that might have led to intelligence being analyzed that would have [given] them an idea of what was going on. Nobody wanted to, kind of, believe it. There was a little bit of a disbelief; a little bit of a looking through rose-coloured glasses...[24]

Brigadier-General Fraser acknowledges that "even the Americans were surprised by the change in [Taliban] tactics and their congregating their top [ten] commanders and 500 fighters in [Panjwayi] for the fight that became MEDUSA."[25]

Captain Steve Hunter had also experienced the lack of concrete intelligence during his six month tour in the first half of 2006 with the Canadian special operations task force.

I would tell you that there was a false sense of security, I think, at least in the late months of 2005 and early 2006. There was a sense that something bigger was going on, but we didn't have the technology and the enablers that we had in the later years...We really lacked that in those early years...From a special operations perspective, we are an intelligence led organization. Everything comes down to intelligence...And again, we just didn't have the technology to really understand what was going on at the time.[26]

Spears saw that much of the problem was with the all source intelligence centre that functioned as part of AEGIS. He believed that,

Intelligence officers and the intelligence community were very much used to templating the Soviet military and the Cold War...they could follow those templates...but the insurgency required more thinking on your feet and more analyzing and really digging in and the all-source cell was this place where information went in but not a lot ever came out.[27]

Brigadier-General David Fraser supports that conclusion, in part. While Dadullah had been building up his offensive over several years, even before the Canadians' arrival, the Americans had not seen it coming either. Fraser had taken several visits to his predecessor formation, Task Force BAYONET, and his headquarters had been tracking their progress over six months and, at the time of the transfer of authority in March of 2006, there had been no surprises except for the inexperience of his own people—"we had been peacekeepers"—and the failure in intelligence from his all-source intelligence cell. He recalls,

> *And remember we took over from the best, the US, and the US didn't know either. So MEDUSA was a strategic surprise to all of us. Now, in hindsight, it shouldn't have been, but it was. And when I say [the all-source intelligence cell] failed, it was again, they were inexperienced. They were working at strategic [intelligence]; we were doing tactical [intelligence]. They were producing like a product a week; I needed a product an hour.*

> *The hundred and some odd of them that they had...the limiting factor in any organization is how many analysts you have and we didn't have enough analysts. So, I walked away from them, literally, for about a month and I went back to the Americans and I had a little room in my headquarters where I had three people talking to three computers. They gave me all the [intelligence] I needed. And then after a month, when the all-source intelligence cell got up to speed with what the [operational] tempo was, they were fine.*[28]

That would have been in April or May. Fraser disagreed with there being an increased level of Taliban activity and states that one needs to distinguish between what activities were initiated by ORION and what was actually happening. His view is that things actually changed during the battle group's transfer of authority.

> *It was strategically when NATO came in that's when the Taliban took and accelerated their operations. Up until that point they were building up for the NATO transition. And that was in August.*

> *It was Amrullah Saleh the head of the [National Directorate of Security], that I had relationships with, coupled with the Americans who actually confirmed the intelligence picture for us; what was going on. And that was all in, I would say in July, the July period. So May, July, [Saleh] sent his deputy down [for] two weeks and then we knew [the Taliban] were getting ready for the NATO transition.*[29]

It is correct that the Taliban hadn't initiated any major activity in the period May to July in the Zhari/Panjwayi theatre. They were lying low. What Task Force ORION had seen and reported, however, were increasing numbers of organized Taliban who were fighting in a much more determined way than they had done previously whenever they were bumped. When ORION brought their concerns to the attention of Combined Joint Task Force-76, on the eve of the battle group's involvement in Operation MOUNTAIN THRUST, it became clear that that headquarters' intelligence had not fully appreciated the extent to which the enemy's forces appeared to be massing in Zhari and Panjwayi.[30]

The incoming Captain Spears' view on the then existing intelligence assessments was that, "There were certain [human intelligence] sources that Brigadier-General Fraser would absolutely not refute anything that they said and they were probably only right about 20% of the time ... He was convinced that they were the only ones that could give him the information that he needed."[31]

Intelligence issues aside, the turmoil that the new ISAF-originated rules of engagement had caused for Task Force ORION were also a concern for the incoming gunners. Spears recalls, "We were deeply concerned about [the rules of engagement issue] upon our arrival."[32]

Spears reported that there had been discussion about delaying the transition to ISAF because ISAF was not ready to take over Regional Command (South). The political will pushed it forward. Notwithstanding their concern, the adoption of the ISAF rules of engagement, ended up not being a problem for E Battery. Spears:

> For us, I don't want to say a little more normal. It was harder for Task Force 1-06, it was hard for Hope and his crew, because they had been under [Operation ENDURING FREEDOM rules of engagement] up until that point. August 1st things were changing and they had to adapt to the changes that weren't well briefed and well understood. You could see the looks on their faces after we arrived there after 3 [August]. They were whipped. They were beat up.[33]

E Battery and Task Force 3-06, on the other hand, simply stepped into the new rules of engagement from square one.

The relief in place for the battle groups' command teams had started on August 9, 2006. E Battery had completed its handover with A Battery on August 16, 2006. From that day forward, they had taken over responsibility for direct support of the battle group. The actual transfer of command authority from Task Force ORION to Task Force 3-06 was scheduled to take place at 1600 hours on August 19, 2006. Aggressive actions by ORION throughout early August had resulted in daily contacts with the insurgents. Available intelligence pointed at a major operation for the Taliban for August 19, 2006.

Steve Gallagher, the outgoing battery commander, and Greg Ivey had spent the 16th doing a last minute tour of Zhari with the two battle group commanders' tactical groups. Insurgent mortars struck shortly after their arrival at PB WILSON.[34] Stimpson's crew was there when the two battery commanders and their battery sergeants major—Bob Montague and Paul Parsons—had arrived. They were standing and talking just as the first round went through the roof of a truck, not twenty paces from them. It failed to detonate. A second mortar bomb detonated beside an ammunition vehicle, shredding its tires. The gunners had had a very close call. Others had been less lucky. The attack slightly wounded six A Company soldiers.

After the third round fell, Gallagher recalls, "... we ran back to my LAV and mounted up. We drove to the front gate where a round fell in front of us and one behind."[35]

In the LAV were both battery commanders' parties. Accompanying them out was a platoon from A Company. Having left PB WILSON, together they set up an overwatch position trying to find the mortar and its observers. They had Dutch attack helicopters available and later fired 81mm illumination but to no avail.

Upon their return to WILSON, the two battery commanders and two battery sergeants major, proceeded to do a mortar crater analysis. Gallagher recalls, "Greg [Ivey] and I used Montague's dental floss tied to a rock and a protractor. I asked the gun [command post] to calculate range—81 and 82 mm were close—and used my Timex compass to find direction. If memory serves me correct we were about 500 [metres] off."[36]

The rounds had come from the vicinity of the abandoned "yellow school" southwest of WILSON across Highway 1. It was the same northern one which had been Task Force ORION's B Company objective on August 3rd. Sentries at WILSON maintained observation of the position and, during a subsequent engagement, spotted the smoke of a mortar firing. The guns responded. While the results are not known, the mortaring abruptly ceased and was not resumed.

During the night of August 16/17, 2006, the battle group commander's tactical group moved to Panjwayi district centre, arriving at first light the next morning. Here they were surprised to find that the Afghan police and army had forces occupying the hill feature of Ma'Sum Ghar.

This 100 to 150 metre-high ridge, on the south shore of the Arghandab River dominated the terrain of Pashmul to the north and the district centre town of Bazaar-e-Panjwayi just to the east. A mere one and one half kilometers to the north sat the now infamous August 3rd "white school". Simply put, possession of Ma'sum Ghar was key to denying the Taliban control of the town as well as the terrain around it on both sides of the river.

The two battle group commanders learned that the Afghan police were there without any allied embedded training teams. They had deployed to defend the district centre and had been experiencing brazen probes by the Taliban.

Before returning to KAF, the two commanders resolved to have A Company deploy its company headquarters and a platoon to assist the police.[37] Lavoie called the incoming A Company's officer commanding, Major Mike Wright, and directed him to occupy Ma'Sum Ghar by last light on the 19th.[38] Stimpson's G21 FOO party would accompany them.

At Task Force AEGIS, meanwhile, staff were working on the detailed plan for Operation MEDUSA. The shaping operations were progressing and as targets were identified they'd be pounded down by artillery fire. In Brigadier-General Fraser's mind the launch of the strike phase was still contemplated as not happening until some time in mid to late September.[39] In fact, Fraser was scheduled to leave immediately after the upcoming transfer of authority ceremony for Kabul and Canada. Here he would brief his superiors on the plan and to enjoy a few days leave.

AEGIS staff weren't the only ones who had been planning for MEDUSA. The frequent mortar attacks and ambushes along Highway 1 had galvanized Lieutenant-Colonel Lavoie. He recalls,

> *The way it unfolded was that it goes back to...my vehicle being hit by a mortar round. And not yet being in command but not happy that the Taliban had that freedom of action, and combined with that, I think on the same day or the day before, been ambushed on Highway 1. Likewise that was a recurring event. And, I wasn't going to put up with that.[40]*

So, even before taking command, he had started his staff on planning for what was to be the "Strike" phase of MEDUSA. He recalls that prior to Brigadier-General Fraser going back to Canada on the August 19, 2006,

> *Very early into the planning for MEDUSA...When we were doing the staff tables for it, we figured that we needed to have at least 5,000 rounds [of 155mm] to start and then have a resupply of 500 per day to continue the fight ...And then I asked the obvious question "What do we have in theatre right now?" And the answer came back, "Something like 300." And I go, "You've got to be shitting me."*

> *I went right over to General Fraser's headquarters, knocked on his door, and said, "You know, we need a significant resupply operation going on here. And I'm going to have to conduct shaping operations until we get what we need in the way of artillery ammunition."*

> *At that point in time his poor chief of staff, Shane Schreiber, happened to walk by and Fraser just dismissed me, "No. We have plenty of artillery ammunition." And I said, "No, Sir. We have 300 rounds—that might not even be one day of fight."*

> *And poor Shane happened to walk by at the wrong time and [Fraser said] "Shane, tell Lavoie how much artillery ammunition we have in theatre."*

THE NEW KIDS ON THE BLOCK | 275

And Shane goes, "He's right, we only have 300." And of course General Fraser wasn't too happy...That kicked off this massive initiative to bring artillery into theatre ...[41]

The 300 rounds represented what was in the compound in KAF. There were more yet on the four gun tractors in the field. Nonetheless, he was correct in that a massive resupply initiative needed to start.

Weapons are a matter of particular interest to all soldiers. They spend untold hours researching, debating and criticizing the weapons they have been given or which they would like to have. This is logical since weapons are literally a matter of life and death for them. Gunners may debate the merit of this gun versus that one, but the gun isn't their weapon. Every young gunner has it drilled into his head from day one of training that the weapon of the artillery is the projectile. Everything else is just a system used to get the projectile to the right place at the right time. It is therefore equally logical that the failure to have adequate stocks of artillery ammunition on hand is not just a matter of serious concern to gunners; it's a crisis.

Major Bob Herold was the chief of ammunition, at the national support element. He had expressed his concern that the ammunition being ordered in July was "dangerously small". This had earned him a rebuke from his boss that "he had not fully understood the study of ammunition consumption and the relentless pursuit of a day of supply data".[42] That was coupled with the practice that artillery ammunition forecasts and stockpiling were treated primarily as a logistics function. It should have been an operations function as called for under existing doctrine.[43]

The problem, however, ran much deeper than that. It started, once again, with the logistics model which was based on operations in Bosnia and Kabul where artillery had played a minor role. Major Todd Scharlach, an instructor in gunnery, was the G3 Operations for 2 Canadian Mechanized Brigade Group. In early August 2006, he deployed to Afghanistan as the J3 for the headquarters of Task Force KANDAHAR/national command element. He recalls,

> *As part of my hand-over with the outgoing J3, we discussed [ammunition] (small arms, 25mm and [artillery]) usage rates, which for the outgoing roto were all quite low, and compared them to [ammunition] that was in the [ammunition] compound at KAF. The [Deputy Chief of Defence Staff] allocation for artillery [ammunition] was roughly 2,000 [rounds] and between what was on the guns and what was held in the [ammunition] compound, we were in good shape for <u>expected</u> usage rates based on previous expenditures.*[44] *(original emphasis)*

Scharlach notes further,

At this time, there were concerns being expressed by [Canadian Operational Support Command] about the Net Explosive Quotient (NEQ) of the ammunition being stored in the compound. My understanding was that we were over our NEQ and that as such, [Canadian Operational Support Command] did not want to increase our [ammunition] holdings. In fact, they wanted to reduce the holdings [in order to] get us below our NEQ.[45]

The Canadian concept for logistics in Kandahar was aimed to achieve maximum efficiency and economy of effort based on centralized control under a national support element. Like its predecessor, E Battery had only been authorized to have a small administrative element based at KAF. It did not have any integral lift for ammunition other than the basic load on each gun tractor, which approximated 100 rounds of 155mm per gun.

This was an unfortunate decision. Neither the force planners nor the logisticians had any proper appreciation of the challenges involved in satisfying the voracious appetite for ammunition of hungry guns in a real war. The experiences gained in Bosnia and Kabul had been misleading. The logistics problem was compounded in a theatre of rough terrain, great distances, a constant threat of IEDs and competition for scarce aviation resources.

The guns, of course, weren't supposed to be doing a lot of shooting. Notwithstanding the highly kinetic nature of Task Force ORION's 27 named operations, A Battery, had fired just 114 operational fire missions—with only 41 in support of troops in contact. In total they had expended 501 high explosive and 92 illuminating rounds of 155mm and 308 high explosive and 52 illuminating rounds of 81mm. This was well within the ammunition allotment held at KAF.[46] Notwithstanding this, even A Battery had experienced periods where ammunition resupply had become an issue.

The Canadian Forces logistics policy, based on modern civilian "just in time" management practices, was to not stockpile ammunition. Careful tracking of the daily consumption of all natures of ammunition, had convinced the logisticians that the situation was manageable. As Lieutenant-Colonel John Conrad, the commanding officer of the national support element noted, "The era of brute logistics had passed and today the replenishment of Canadian ammunition is expensive and clinically handled. In the same way a motorist might study fuel consumption to work out his gas mileage, we sought to understand our usage of ammunition so we would know when we had hit the trigger to fill up once again."[47]

In their naiveté, they had not accounted for the fact that consumption rates based on a long period of inactivity will only work if the enemy does not pick up the tempo. Very little ammunition was consumed in the first half of A Battery's tour. The heavier fighting in the later stages had run down the stocks. This somehow had been missed by the tracking system. This paralleled the intelligence underestimation of the Taliban build-up in Kandahar.

The logisticians—and the operators at Task Force AEGIS—incorrectly assumed that the holdings in the KAF ammunition point were sufficient to meet the needs of MEDUSA's kinetic operations; at least until Task Force 3-06's headquarters started running staff checks. The window of opportunity to correct this problem was about to narrow.

Transfer of Command Authority

AUGUST 19, 2006 was about to turn into a very strange day indeed.

At 1600 hours the official transfer of command authority to Task Force 3-06 took place at Kandahar Airfield (KAF). The incoming and outgoing battle group tactical headquarters had traveled back to Kandahar to complete the handover and then conduct the ceremony. Steve Gallagher and Greg Ivey were both present.

Immediately after the completion of the ceremony Brigadier-General David Fraser flew to Kabul via Bagram. He left Task Force AEGIS in the care of his deputy commander, Colonel Steve Williams. Williams, from the Alaska Army National Guard, commanded Task Force GRIZZLY, the American's Kandahar-based national command element in Regional Command (South).

With the brigade commander winging off to Kabul and Canada, Colonel Williams, Task Force AEGIS's British chief of staff, Colonel Chris Vernon, and his assistant chief of staff, Canadian Lieutenant-Colonel Shane Schreiber, received an urgent invitation to attend at the compound of the Province of Kandahar's Governor Asadullah Khalid at 1700 hours. They, and Lieutenant-Colonel Lavoie, attended as requested, surprisingly finding a number of known and suspected Taliban present.

In short order they were told several points. First, that several of the local Panjwayi and Zhari tribal leaders present were making deals with, or contemplating making deals with, the Taliban. Second, this was due to the general belief that the Americans were leaving and that the International Security Assistance Force (ISAF) wouldn't fight but was only there for development. Third, that this impression had resulted from a well-intentioned, but horribly misleading, announcement from General Richards at ISAF headquarters that henceforth ISAF would conduct a development program, rather than engage in hostilities.

The Taliban information campaign had jumped at the opportunity to gain an advantage.

Notwithstanding the presence of several known and suspected Taliban, the team gave a brief and general outline of the MEDUSA plan to persuade those wavering that the allies would definitely fight while trying to preserve Kandahari lives and property.[1]

Complicating matters further, Governor Khalid had called in Abdul Razik, the commander of the predominantly Achakzai Afghan Border Police, to police what is traditional Noorzai territory in Panjwayi. This had infuriated the locals and support for the Taliban in that area had skyrocketed.[2]

Fraser was unaware of these events. He would first hear of the Khalid meeting some days later by way of a phone call to him while he was meeting with General Hillier at a change of command ceremony in Edmonton.

The events occurring at the governor's palace were also unknown to A Company's Major Mike Wright who, together with the light armoured vehicle (LAV) and G Wagon-equipped Number 3 Platoon,[3] and Captain Ryan Stimpson's forward observation officer (FOO) party, arrived at Ma'Sum Ghar sometime between 1700 and 1800 hours. Major Wright had prepared his estimate and issued orders back at Patrol Base (PB) WILSON, so his troops proceeded to their assigned areas on the long hilly ridge without further direction. To Wright's dismay, he realized that the terrain was "dramatically different" from what he had understood from his map study.

Wright directed his LAV Captain, Captain Mike Reekie, to site his vehicle on the south side of Ma'Sum Ghar facing the town of Bazaar-e-Panjwayi to guard the company's rear. Stimpson, meanwhile, moved his G21 vehicle to a site on the ridge from where he could observe north across the river into Zhari District, the primary area of interest.

At around 1845 hours, while Wright was still preparing his confirmatory orders based on his revised estimate after observing the ground, a rocket-propelled grenade whizzed over his vehicle. It was the first of many, many rounds that would be fired at A Company over the next several hours.[4]

By the time that the battle group commander and Ivey were summoned to the battle group's tactical operations centre, at 1930 hours, it was evident that a major attack was underway. In fact, it was already shaping up as the heaviest, deliberately planned, coordinated Taliban operation in Kandahar Province. "The [fire support coordination centre (FSCC) officer], Captain Spears, informed [Major Ivey] that C Troop was already engaged in a fire mission in support of G21 ... although the severity of the contact was not fully understood at this time."[5]

Eventually it was estimated that 300-500 insurgents were involved.[6]

Major Gallagher, who was still at KAF before flying home, was in the battle group's tactical operations centre at the time and recalls, "It was a massive attack, like we faced on the 3rd of August. It wasn't anticipated. They ran into a lot of forces that they didn't know were in the [area] at the time."[7]

The battle would rage on for several hours with the small group of A Company elements—the company headquarters, 3 Platoon and G21—and their Afghan allies fending off attacks on three sides. To complicate matters a vehicle had become stuck in the rugged terrain while manoeuvering and ammunition was becoming a concern. Gallagher recalls:

> *I happened to be sitting there in my PT shorts—where else was I going to go?—looking over the shoulder of Tim Spears in the FSCC and there was a vehicle that had become disabled at some point. And just to show you that you can do a [relief in place] in and out but little things … [Lieutenant-Colonel] Omer Lavoie looked right over at me, the only ORION person in that [tactical command post] that day, as most of the Patricias had left already, and said, "Who's the authority to [blow in place] the vehicle?" My answer was "Well, that would be you if you feel you can't recover it and you've got to blow it, then blow it"…"But" I said, "first of all get all the [communications equipment] out of it…but here's another alternative … set out an outer cordon around that vehicle and anything that comes in with a weapon, with a hostile intent, take it out."[8]*

They eventually managed to drag that vehicle out. After the initial hour of combat, however, A Company had been forced to pull back off the ridge to regroup. Afghan security forces, on the other hand, continued to hold on to the ridge. Gallagher recalls, "And at that time, Ian Hope came into the tactical operations centre and said, "Whoa. We've worked our entire tour to develop this trust and this relationship. Get back in there and save their ass. You can't leave them alone."[9]

To help the ground commander, Captain Spears' FSCC identified target areas to G21 and pushed a Predator unmanned aerial vehicle (UAV) into the area. Spears did not have a Remotely Operated Video Enhanced Receiver III[10] feed from the aircraft's targeting pod. He was able, however, to conduct a Type II[11] forward air control attack using the telephone link to the Predator's pilot at their control centre at the airfield. The pilot would describe to Spears what he could see and Spears would clear the aircraft for two Hellfire missile strikes on two groupings of Taliban. The strikes killed some twenty to thirty of them.[12] The artillery and Hellfire strikes shaped the conditions for A Company to re-enter the fight.

At the gun line, the ferocity of the fight had come as a bit of a shock. Warrant Officer Gallant recalled being engaged most of the night with him in the command post in his underwear. The complexity of the terrain caused a challenge. Engaging the south side of the steep Ma'Sum Ghar feature required firing at the targets at high angle so as not to impact on the north slope or crest.[13] The relief in place was over. This was E Battery's first fight.

Captain Stimpson's G21 contributed heavily to the engagement firing several fire missions including two with 10 rounds fire for effect each. In total Lieutenant Frank Gould's C Troop had fired 92 rounds that night. The next morning they needed a combat logistics patrol to resupply them with ammunition as the troop had fired off half of its basic load.

The guns weren't G21's only available weapons. Ivey:

By this time G21 had Dutch AH-64 Apaches on station and they were used quite effectively to destroy small groups of three to five fighters caught under culverts or in the ditches as they tried to maneuver. The fighting was so intense and chaotic at times that, as [Captain] Stimpson described, everyone in the party was engaging the enemy with every weapon they had.[14]

Captain Stimpson was manning the pintle-mounted C6 7.62mm, Sergeant Robin Everett was engaging the enemy with the 25mm cannon while the signaller, Bombardier Daniel Walsh was engaging with his [personal] weapon from the sentry hatch from the rear of the LAV.[15]

At first there had been chaos. E Battery's commander, Greg Ivey reflected on that night,

Admittedly, it was ugly in the battle group [tactical operations centre] as we all tried to make sense of the [situation reports] coming in and as we tried to go through the drills and procedures. Unfortunately we never went through a scenario like that in [training]. The FOO had targets and the FSCC was relaying on [the satellite] phone to the gun troop west of PB [WILSON]. We (with the commanding officer's tactical headquarters) had wrapped up the [transfer of command authority] ceremony protocols earlier in the day and were caught up in KAF. I clearly remember Steve Gallagher in the FSCC with me and he was trying to help. I remember sensing his frustration while we "the new guys" stumbled through what would have been [standard operating procedures] for their [tactical operations centre]. For us it was everything but [standard operating procedures]—it was much more trial by ritual. I (including Lieutenant-Colonel Lavoie) owe a lot to [Steve Gallagher] for his mentorship that night.

As the evening progressed, A Company's situation improved, the [tactical operation centre] regained its composure and the "warrior spirit". I had never seen that before in a command post. The next day we went out to PB

[WILSON] and [Lavoie] made it a point to go out and see the gun troop and recognize their accomplishments.[16]

Ivey learned two valuable lessons in those first few hours of combat on the 19th. He recalls,

As the [battle group commander] and staff studied the array of maps and listened attentively to the radio traffic, they quickly learned that patience was the key to fully understanding the situation on the ground ... The other lesson learned was that the ground commander must be trusted to provide the information and to make the right tactical decisions. There was an overwhelming sense of helplessness and frustration among the [battle group command post] staff as they listened to the radio and studied the maps.[17]

The fighting, for the most part, was over by midnight. A Company and its Afghan allies held the ridge. Estimates provided subsequently by ISAF would indicate that of the hundreds of insurgents involved in the attack 60 to 72 of them were killed that night.[18] Allied casualties were not certain but probably up to 7 members of the Afghan police.

Ivey recalls,

[The Taliban] were not expecting such a heavy response with UAV, [artillery] and indirect fire that night from A [Company]. We know from the [human intelligence] reports that followed in the next few days they were completely not expecting such a response and I think a lot of the [Taliban] fighters/ commanders did not understand the capabilities of Thermal/[infrared] sensors and UAV. To lose a hundred fighters in one night at one ambush is a good indicator that they were not prepared. I think the large number of [Taliban] fighters that took part in the ambush that night [was] a good indicator of their confidence in their [command and control] capability, their high morale and their understanding of [Canadian rules of engagement].[19]

There had already been an outline of Operation MEDUSA in the works, but August 19th spurred activities within Task Force 3-06. Lieutenant-Colonel Lavoie recalls,

It was a significant counterattack, somewhere with numbers as high as 300 Taliban going after what is essentially a mechanized infantry company supported by artillery, supported by close air. And that fight went through the night. It wasn't until 3 or 4 o'clock in the morning by the time I was actually able to get forward. And, long story short, when the sun rose, it was like a bit of a "holy shit" moment for us but for NATO because, okay, the intelligence is saying there's 50 or 60 insurgents in the area and I was attacked by 300 or so in a coordinated attack and fairly brazen going against mechanized forces, conventional forces. There's obviously an issue here with the intelligence picture. So that really illuminated it...

Probably, from August 20, 2006, within 5 or 6 days we had a plan. As I mentioned, General Fraser wasn't in theatre, so General Freakley and commander ISAF, British General Richards came down to Kandahar and I briefed them on the plan. We had a huge sand model room set up and I walked them through the entire plan and [Richards] approved it and his parting words was, he took me aside and he said "If you fail, NATO fails." Okay, no pressure there. He said, "I'll see you on the Arghandab in a few weeks."[20]

The plan was relatively simple in outline.

Effectively, the Taliban had already fixed themselves into a general location in the Pashmul area. All that was necessary was to hold them in place and bring the appropriate pressure to bear through artillery and air strikes to degrade and break the enemy into pockets and to allow both intelligence and recce to clearly identify and define the individual pockets of resistance for elimination.

Captain Chris Purdy, the battalion's intelligence officer explains that the battalion wanted, "A very clear picture of what was in there ... We then wanted to conduct a feint in order to get the Taliban to light up their [command and control nodes], to get the Taliban to reinforce so that we could see them moving into their forward positions."[21]

The feint would come from two directions, the north and the south. Lieutenant-Colonel Lavoie recalls,

The plan originally was fairly simple—attack from the north, attack from the south—hem them in. We had blocking forces east and west. And once they were hemmed in, I would decide. We still didn't have a very clear picture where their positions were. Then I would decide—Okay, I'll fix on one axis and I'll attack on the other and I'll pick and choose when and how I'll do that.[22]

The plan called for up to three days of artillery and close air support to strike the positions while the feints were operating. Lavoie:

We had planned for up to three, is what I would say. But clearly, the second that I would have had an opportunity to exploit a situation, based on intelligence and based on reconnaissance (recce), I wouldn't have cared if it was one day. But I would have cared that I would have the reliable intelligence to guide that change. So I was prepared to go in as fast as I could.[23]

Task Force 3-06 weren't the only ones working on the plan. There was one further thing that August 19th did. Ivey: "This event also woke up the entire task force. For all of [Gallagher's] efforts, the critical ammunition shortage finally became an issue that the chain of command could no longer avoid."[24]

With the situation at Ma'Sum Ghar stable after August 19, 2006, AEGIS and TF 3-06 now turned their attention back to shaping the battlefield in preparation for MEDUSA's "Strike Phase" and to solving the ammunition issue.

Complicating matters was the fact that resupplying low stocks of ammunition was not simple. Flights carrying explosives in quantities from Canada to Kandahar would need some two weeks' notice in order to obtain the necessary diplomatic clearances to transit other nations. At the time, Canada did not have any pre-approved international flight routes like the US had.[25]

Task Force ORION's expenditures had picked up at the end of their tour. Task Force 3-06 had begun to conduct operations with a rate of intensity higher than that of its predecessor. The furious fight at Ma'Sum Ghar on August 19 attested to that.

While waiting for ammunition stocks to build up, Task Force 3-06 continued doing shaping operations for MEDUSA. Lieutenant-Colonel Lavoie recalls,

> Because of that delay, for about, I don't know what it was, 9 or 10 days, I had to conduct shaping operations and deception operations to, on the one hand, not scare the Taliban away, but not give up what we were doing at the same time. It sort of worked in our favour in the end because there were things I had to clean up especially in the way of resupply—ambushes on Highway 1— [we] conducted a lot of company-level anti-ambush operations so that I could secure my line of communications from Kandahar forward for resupply...
>
> We were able to kill quite a few insurgents and stop, almost completely, the ambushes happening on Highway 1. So, while that was happening, the ammo was starting to build up in theatre and then I was satisfied by the time we got to D Day that we had enough to kick it off...[26]

The issue of who knew what or when about the ammunition situation is not a clear one by any means.

Lieutenant-Colonel John Conrad states that he had been aware of the issue in early August and had been trying to correct it. He describes being called in to see Brigadier-General Fraser and Lieutenant-Colonel Lavoie at 1900 hours August 19, 2006 and confronted with the fact that the Task Force was, "... running dangerously low on a number of types of ammunition ..."[27]

Conrad felt certain the stocks would be alright for MEDUSA. However, he too was scheduled to go home.

It was a few days later, on August 22, 2006 that Task Force 3-06 started its run of shaping operations which brought the ammunition issue which had been percolating since mid-July to a crisis point.

The events of August 19, 2006 - the meeting with Khalid and the attack on Ma'Sum Ghar—galvanized ISAF and Regional Command (East). Brigadier-General Fraser noted that things had immediately changed. Not only did General Richards agree that MEDUSA would be NATO's main effort but Major-General Freakley committed significant numbers of American resources. One complicating factor; they would only be available for the first few weeks of September.[28] It should be remembered that the "Strike" phase of Operation MEDUSA had been contemplated for the latter half of September. That phase was now going to be moved forward although no actual date had yet been set.

Even before August 22, 2006, the battle group and the battery had started repositioning elements to focus on Panjwayi and Zhari and to reinforce A Company and G21 who were already operating out of PB WILSON. Ian Plummer's G22 had patrolled to KAF from Forward Operating Base (FOB) MARTELLO on August 18, but then headed back again on August 19. Now B Company, G22 and Captain Cory Gillis's D Troop received orders to move from MARTELLO to the south for the shaping operations. Arrangements were made with the Dutch and Afghan police to take over MARTELLO and to secure the Kandahar-Tarin Kot highway for the foreseeable future.[29]

Charles Company and Captain Dan Matheson's G23 were brought back from the Pakistani border. Matheson's team had completed their relief in place on August 18 at which time A Battery's Captain Charchuk returned to KAF for his flight home. On August 19, Matheson received a warning order for future operations in Panjwayi. After a brief night in KAF on August 20, G23 made its way to PB WILSON where, for a day, the team started sharing the reception of very accurate Taliban mortar fire with G21.

One gunner who was not making his way back to Kandahar was Lieutenant-Colonel David "Buck" Buchanan. Buchanan hailed from the 1st Regiment, Royal Canadian Horse Artillery and was Brigadier-General Fraser's executive assistant. Buchanan, as well as several others of the staff, went on leave when their boss did. When Fraser hurriedly left Canada to return to Kandahar, he decided to let his team remain on leave rather than recalling them early. In Buchanan's case, he was sitting at home at the kitchen table with his wife when he found out from a newscast, much to his surprise and displeasure, that MEDUSA was starting.[30]

On August 22, Lavoie's companies started a series of deterrence patrols, supported with artillery and close air support. These would continue until August

29. Their aim was to secure the lines of communication and to prevent any further attacks on the Panjwayi district centre.[31]

With Charles Company gathering at PB WILSON, things were getting crowded at A Company's small base. On August 23, 2006 Charles Company's last platoon arrived. Now they, and Captain Dan Matheson's G23, set off for a leaguer on the southern banks of the Arghandab River near the town of Panjwayi.

They wouldn't go unmolested, however. Almost immediately after they left WILSON and turned east on their way towards Kandahar City they experienced the full effects of Highway 1's "Ambush Alley". The ambush ran for a full five kilometres with small arms and rocket-propelled grenade fire coming from both sides. The convoy responded vigorously with their own small arms as well as the LAV's 25mm and 7.62mm pintle mounted machine guns and even the M777s with 10 rounds of high explosive. G23's log entry for that day included the following,

Couldn't get heads wrapped around artillery as primary weapon when [rocket-propelled grenades] and [rifle] fire all around us. We killed some for sure...2 injured in the convoy and some minor vehicle damage. Stopped at an [Afghan army] base in Kandahar City to [reorganize] and deal with the casualties...Seems [an] interpreter was sending information about our convoy on his cell phone.[32]

The battle group's command element could see that merely doing a fighting run through "Ambush Alley" wasn't enough of a deterrent for the Taliban. Surprisingly, the insurgents continued to mount these attacks from the same area time after time. They showed little inclination to modify or scale back their efforts notwithstanding that while they inflicted only minor casualties to the coalition forces, they were suffering heavy casualties in return. Lieutenant-Colonel Lavoie resolved to aggressively search them out and destroy them with artillery and air power.

He and Major Ivey arranged to use the Sperwer tactical UAV to hunt Taliban at last light every night for a week. The Sperwer had both a respectable on-board camera— capable of night vision operation—and an equally effective target acquisition package that could provide accurate grid locations. This data could be displayed on a large screen television monitor in the battle group's tactical operation centre at KAF. Any insurgents located would be attacked using artillery or close air support, controlled by the FSCC Officer, Captain Tim Spears. It was a simple solution and an excellent example of modern artillery tactics which foreshadowed what would be employed on an industrial scale by both sides a decade and a half later in Ukraine.

Sperwer had some significant limitations caused by the high air temperature and low air density in the Kandahar area. This effectively ruled out daytime operations during the summer "fighting season." It also had relatively "short legs" compared to larger UAVs like the Predator. It could only remain on station for no more than five or six hours. Given its low operating ceiling—because of the air temperature/density factor—and its loud engine noise, it was unable to loiter undetected. The Taliban had already learned that.

Of the original eight aircraft bought for Kabul, two had been written off. Of the additional ten bought for delivery throughout 2006, two more had already been written off during Task Force ORION's tour. This would be the first tactical mission flown by the Sperwer since E Battery had assumed responsibility.

C Troop's gun detachments were ready in their austere position on the west edge of PB WILSON. As last light approached, they laid their two M777s to face east along Highway 1. Meanwhile the tactical UAV flight in KAF launched a Sperwer and began to search the area of interest. Almost immediately after it was on station, its sensor package registered activity. A group of about twenty people were sitting approximately 400 metres north of the highway in a lightly built-up area. While that was suspicious, it did not provide a clear demonstration of hostile intent. Male Afghans just hanging out in and of itself was not enough to justify an engagement under ISAF's rules of engagement.

Soon, however, they stood up and began to move in groups of two or three through the maze of grape fields towards the highway. Observers in the FSCC could see on the screen the rocket-propelled grenades and other weapons they were carrying. Their hostile intent was now clear.

Excitement mounted both there and on the gun position. The Taliban took an erratic course as they threaded their way through the rows of grape vines. It appeared as if some were having problems navigating the dense foliage. Finally, a group of about 15 stopped near a compound. It was long enough to allow C Troop to fire a round of fire for effect using the target location transmitted from the Sperwer.

The two high explosive rounds impacted close enough to the insurgents to spur them into a sprint to the compound. By this time a British Harrier fighter-bomber had arrived on station. Unfortunately, there was neither a forward air controller nor any other friendly troops in the area to actually provide eyes on the ground to confirm the target location. Tim Spears and his staff at the FSCC, however, could control the Harrier while watching the feed from the Sperwer.

Fire orders and situation reports were passed to C Troop via satellite phone. These were procedures that had never been practiced in the battle group's pre-deployment training. This novel way to engage the enemy was also new to the battle group and its legal advisor.

At this point the wheels almost came off the wagon. An urgent phone call from the liaison officer at the governor of Kandahar's palace caused a sudden shift in attention away from the insurgents in the compound. The local Afghan police had reported that artillery rounds had hit a compound west of the city, killing a family. Greg Ivey assured the battle group commander that the rounds had impacted in the target area, and they definitely had not landed in a compound. The Sperwer circled back over the target area and confirmed that the thermal signatures of the two, still warm, craters were well away from any buildings.

With that distraction out of the way, Captain Spears set about destroying the enemy-occupied compound. On the gun positions the two detachments waited for the orders to pound it with high explosive. Instead, as Bombardier Lucas Cunningham, an M777 gun number, recalled, "Much to our surprise my gun detachment was given fire orders for a MARK mission with a single illumination round. Not questioning why, we applied our data and fired the round. The illuminating [round] hit the compound dead centre, a direct hit."[33]

This mission had been fired to confirm that both the aircraft and the FSCC were looking at the same target. With the target identified, the FSCC cleared the Harrier hot and the pilot centred his sight on the compound and launched a 500-pound laser guided bomb.

Back on the gun position, in Bombardier Cunningham's words, "Just then in the distant night the sound of a fighter jet could be heard, followed by a huge flash of light and an echoing thunder. Over the radio we heard a British Harrier had been on standby to hit the compound. Well, our illumination round had provided the signal he needed and he unloaded a 500 [pound] bomb on the compound, leveling it."[34]

In the FSCC the Canadians watching the Sperwer's imagery on the screen, observed the bomb score a direct hit, destroying the compound. It was later determined, 12 of the 15 enemy who had taken refuge in it were killed. This was a significant achievement that came as an eye-opening revelation to the non-gunners in the tactical operations centre that evening. The entire engagement had taken about four hours, and indeed the relatively short-legged Sperwer was running low on fuel by the time that the Harrier delivered its bomb. Major Ivey remarked, "However, to the infantry and other combat arms present in the [battle group command post] that evening, it was a significant accomplishment that again strengthened the newfound respect for the artillery. An avid hunter, [Lavoie] referred to this type of operation as "jacking Taliban."[35]

Three enemy fighters miraculously escaped out of that compound that evening. They obviously spread the news to their friends because the battle group was never ambushed again along that stretch of Highway 1 for the remainder of the tour.[36]

D Troop had an uneventful deployment from FOB MARTELLO to PB WILSON, arriving there on August 25, 2006. The two troops, now deployed together as a battery, were visited that day by the battle group commander and Major Ivey.

Lieutenant-Colonel Lavoie took the opportunity to thank the guns for their service to date and to tell them that "the [battery] was punching above its weight and ... was responsible for the majority of the kills to date." He then took the opportunity to promote Francis Gould to the rank of captain and Marcy Maddison and Brenda Stansfield to master bombardiers.

With the next day came a move for both troops as a battery. The new position was one of two moves which were part of a deception plan to pull the Taliban's focus to the north. The first position was one just to the east of PB WILSON. The area turned out to be more built up than expected from the map recce. Warrant Officer Rod Gallant, C Troop's command post detachment commander was unhappy with the position. He recalls, "But we didn't like it ... There was a high speed route in between our gun line—again we were there with the four guns, the battery was there. A couple of hundred metres away we had compounds. It wasn't a good spot. I didn't like it. My Spidey-Senses were up. And that's where we had an engagement with the [Afghan police]."[37]

The gun line had deployed with all around protection with its Bison detachment carriers and troop sergeants major vehicles on the perimeter. Each was manned by a sentry in the commander's hatch armed with a pintle mounted 7.62mm machine gun.

It wasn't long before a white, unmarked Toyota pickup truck approached the battery's right flank at a high rate of speed. It had two personnel in the cab and several more in the back. Another vehicle followed behind. The closest sentry, Gunner Maureen Black, fired several warning shots but the vehicle didn't stop so she again engaged, this time firing shots into the vehicle. It came to a stop some 300 metres from the position. Several individuals jumped out of the vehicle with rocket-propelled grenades and small arms. They pointed some toward the right flank of the guns. Ivey notes, "One detachment commander clearly heard small arms fire over his head."[38]

An immediate concern was the ammo truck which had been parked near the right flank and whether this was an attempt to strike it with a vehicle-borne improvised explosive device.

C Troop's gunners hastily occupied their fighting positions and engaged with up to and including a .50 calibre machine gun. At one point Gallant's driver came to the back of the command post and asked to be given an M72 light anti-armour weapon kept there. Gallant gave it to him.

Reports were now coming in on the radio that the Afghan police were engaged in a firefight. Gallant relayed that to the officers who were outside controlling the defence. Firing was stopped and the situation assessed. The vehicle had, in fact, been an unmarked Afghan National Police vehicle. One policeman had been killed and several wounded. The Battery's personnel immediately provided medical treatment and arranged to have them medevaced.

While the injured were being treated, a motorcycle similarly approached at high speed, ignored warning shots and was engaged again wounding one individual on the motorcycle. Gallant: "Things were piling up."[39]

The incident was subsequently investigated by the Canadian Forces National Investigation Service which determined that the gun line had followed proper procedures.[40]

Soon after, the battery received move orders for a new gun position approximately 6 kilometres to the northwest of PB WILSON. This new position was in very open terrain away from both compounds and roads. In short, it was easy to secure and defend.

Here they would subsequently be joined by two 155mm tracked and armoured, Dutch Panzerhaubitzen 2000s, from the 14e Afdeling Veldartillerie, put under operational command of the Canadians. Ordinarily they operated out of Uruzgan province. There would also be a Danish ARTHUR counter mortar radar.[41] The six guns would remain collocated throughout the upcoming operation.[42] The spirit of international cooperation was high except on the sports field. Between missions the Canadians would play both soccer and football with the Dutch and Danes, augmented by British troops there to help with ammunition. The Anglo-Dutch-Danish team would thoroughly trounce the Canadians at soccer and the Canadians would return the favour during football.[43]

Ammunition stocks had shrunk to a dangerously low level. Major Todd Scharlach at Task Force KANDAHAR recalls,

> *As MEDUSA shaping operations started on or about 22 [August], E [Battery] started a five day run of expending roughly 150 [rounds] per day. On or about 27 [August], [Montague, the battery sergeant major of E Battery] was able to conduct an ammunition replenishment of 750 [rounds] from the [ammunition] compound. This effectively emptied the KAF [ammunition] compound of 155mm [ammunition], but still left roughly 1,200 [rounds] with the [battery]. It also caused the [Net Explosive Quotient] to drop below the red-line which made [Canadian Operational Support Command] happy. The situation was not reported to the [national command element] J4 or I at this time.[44]*

Orders for the "Strike" phase of Operation MEDUSA were issued on August 27, the same day that the battery obtained its 750 rounds replenishment. The replenishment triggered Battery Sergeant Major Bob Montague to talk his way into the ammunition compound to do a physical count of the artillery ammunition. Despite prior assurances that it held more than 2,000 rounds, Montague could find only 311. He wasted no time in bringing the bad news to Greg Ivey.

Accounts vary as to who knew what and when or what feelers and tentacles for sorting out the situation might have been sent out since the ammunition issue was first raised. Regardless, the national command element was vigorously addressing the problem on August 31. Scharlach:

> It was not until 31 [August] when E [Battery] sought another [ammunition replenishment] from the now empty compound that matters escalated to the J4 and I.

> I reached out to [Canadian Expeditionary Force Command] on the J3 [network] while J4 reached out to [Canadian Operational Support Command] on the J4 [network] to notify Ottawa of the situation.[45]

The diplomatic issues respecting the transport of ammunition now reared its head indicating that Canadian ammunition would not reach Afghanistan for at least two weeks. The solution would be two-fold:

> The J4, working through contacts in Theatre, was able to negotiate a deal with [the US Central Command], using a [Standard NATO Agreement] for replacement in kind, [and] was able to get 300 [rounds] the next day and a further 1,200 [rounds] over the next week. This extra 1,500 [rounds], plus a Commander directive to limit E [Battery] to 100 [rounds per day] allowed the [battle group] to get through its [operations] until 21 [September], when the Canadian [ammunition] arrived.[46]

With rounds on the gun platforms and more on their way, E Battery was now ready.

20

OPERATION MEDUSA: SEPTEMBER 2-5, 2006

WHILE OPERATION MEDUSA would have many moving parts, the plan that Task Force 3-06 had briefed and which had been approved was quite simple in concept.

The enemy was believed to be concentrated in Pashmul. The area of the infamous white school and stretching a kilometre west and north to Bayanzi and Payandi became Objective RUGBY. The words "white school" were dropped from the lexicon as the International Security Assistance Force (ISAF) was still protective of infrastructure.[1]

There would be a second major objective. Approximately a kilometre and a half to the south of Patrol Base (PB) WILSON was Objective CRICKET. Three other objectives—BASEBALL, LACROSSE and TENNIS—were identified in Zhari and one more—BILLIARDS—around Sperwan Ghar in Panjwayi district.

Task Force 3-06 intended to hit all objectives with artillery and close air support for up to roughly three days. During this time he would feint with a company in the north against BILLIARDS and with another in the south against RUGBY. Throughout, his intelligence, surveillance, target acquisition and reconnaissance (ISTAR) Squadron and other surveillance resources would gather information about the Taliban as they moved to occupy battle positions. As it stood, there was still inadequate intelligence defining the enemy's positions.

Not until the enemy was sufficiently located would Lieutenant-Colonel Lavoie decide whether the north or the south would become the main effort.[2] Lavoie: "But that all went to shit once the first day happened."[3]

Lavoie roughly divided his forces between north and south. He assigned two companies to the southern effort; the light armoured vehicle (LAV) equipped Charles Company with its forward observation officer (FOO), Matheson's G23, and A Company with Stimpson's G21.

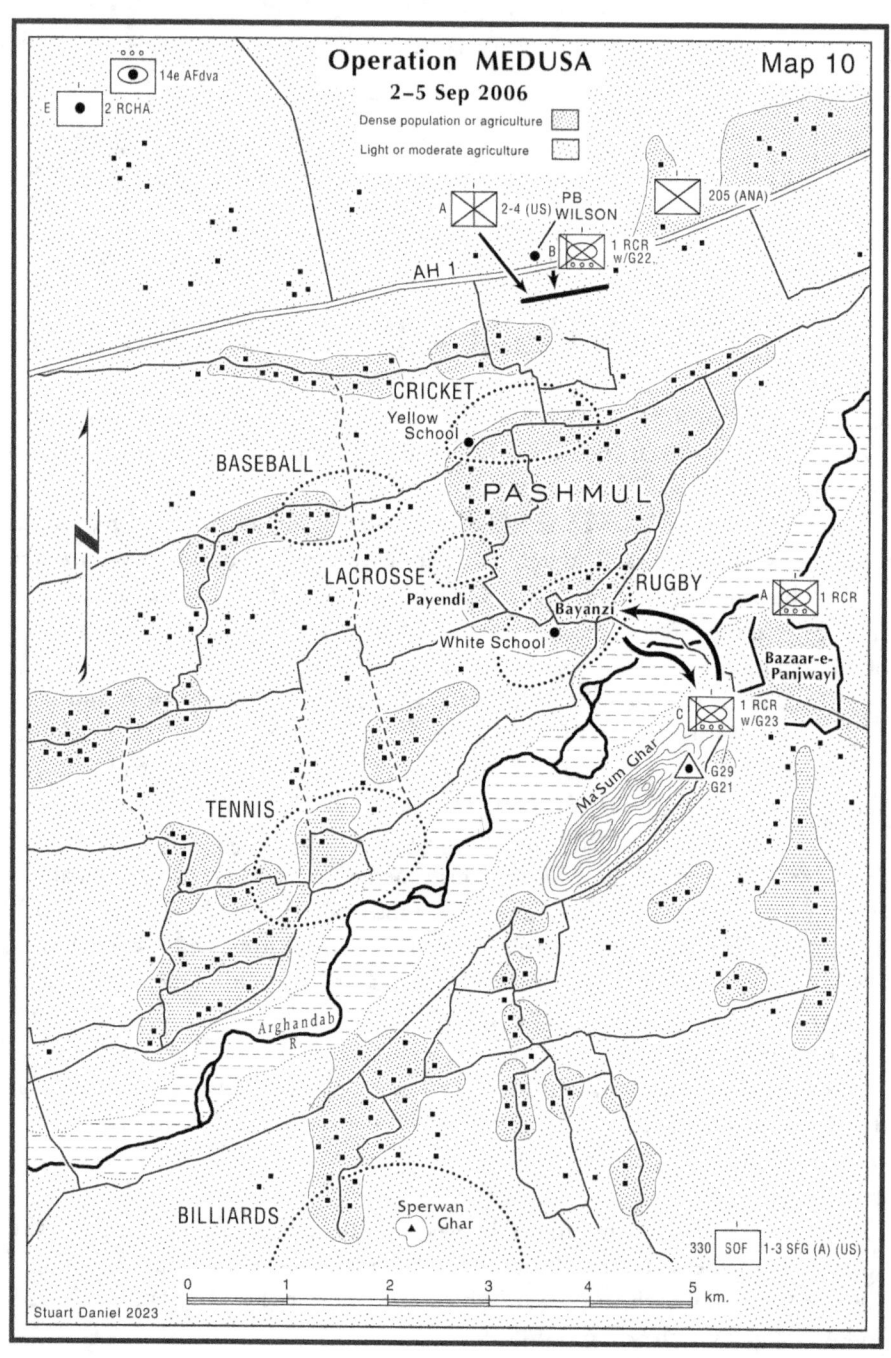

Operation MEDUSA
2–5 Sep 2006

Dense population or agriculture
Light or moderate agriculture

Map 10

14e AFdva

E   2 RCHA

A   2-4 (US)
PB WILSON
B   1 RCR w/G22

205 (ANA)

AH 1

CRICKET
Yellow School

BASEBALL

PASHMUL

LACROSSE
Payendi

RUGBY
Bayanzi

A   1 RCR

White School

Bazaar-e-Panjwayi

C   1 RCR w/G23

Ma Sum Ghar   G29
G21

TENNIS

Arghandab R

BILLIARDS   Sperwan Ghar

330   SOF   1-3 SFG (A) (US)

0   1   2   3   4   5 km.

Stuart Daniel 2023

The battle group's ISTAR Squadron would operate in the south and east providing surveillance in the vicinity of Panjwayi.

In the north, B Company and Plummer's G22 would advance south from PB WILSON across Highway 1 and a short distance into the fields beyond. In order to do this, B Company and G22 would move out of Forward Operating Base MARTELLO and briefly set up a leaguer at PB WILSON. They would then advance across the highway five hundred metres and string out on a broad front along a tree-lined wadi that meanders roughly parallel to the highway.

B Company would be joined in the north by the Americans' motorized Company A, 2nd Battalion, 4th Infantry Regiment, which went by the nickname Task Force MOHAWK. There would also be an Afghan army company from the 205th Afghan Corps. Both companies had been placed under Task Force 3-06's control for the operation.

TF 3-06 would not be alone. To the west, elements from Task Force 31^4 of the US Special Forces would deploy several days early to traverse the Registan Desert. These were led by Operational Detachment-Bravo 330—which was a company-level headquarters—and comprised three twelve-man Operational Detachments-Alpha, a special operations signal's intercept team, some Afghan army personnel and a Canadian liaison officer. Their task was to establish a blocking position to cut resupply and escape routes in the region running from Sperwan Ghar—Objective BILLIARDS—to Ma'Sum Ghar.^{5}

Major-General Freakley had also earmarked Company C (Comanche Company), 2nd Battalion 87th Infantry Regiment supported by two M119 105mm howitzers from Battery A, 5th Battalion, 25th Field Artillery Regiment as a possible reinforcement. In addition he designated the 1st Kandak of the 3rd Brigade of the 201st Afghan Corps as a reserve and allocated one high-mobility artillery rocket system (HIMARS) to add to the fire support.^{6}

Essentially, the mission for MEDUSA was to rapidly encircle the Taliban force, degrade it heavily with artillery and air strikes, probe it both electronically and by other surveillance and reconnaissance (recce) means until such time that Task Force 3-06 could determine whether the north or the south was the better option, and designate it as the main effort.

While the building blocks were falling into place, the guns had to do something about the mortaring that PB WILSON had been experiencing. Intelligence indicated that the Taliban had an indirect fire specialist who coordinated the activities of approximately ten 82mm mortars. In the final stages of the shaping operations for MEDUSA the fire support coordination centre (FSCC) officer, Captain Tim Spears, dealt with them. He set up a counter-mortar program whereby the Danish radars were coupled with the Canadian and Dutch guns. Every time an enemy mortar was located by the radars, the automatic response was five rounds of fire for effect from the guns. Spears remarks,

> At one point we had either killed their [subject matter expert] or we had destroyed enough mortars that they couldn't do that any more. So in August, leading up to MEDUSA, that was a big problem that we were able to get rid of prior to the start of Operation MEDUSA...Later on, that allowed the guys to go down through the north without any fear of getting mortared in the open or in any of those staging areas.[7]

In accordance with Task Force 3-06 plan the rifle companies moved out in the early morning hours of September 2, 2006 and took up their respective battle positions.

To the north, B Company, with G22, Task Force MOHAWK and an Afghan army company took up positions along a line approximately 500 metres south of Highway 1.

To the south, Charles company, with G23, moved in and seized Ma'Sum Ghar, while A Company, with G21, did the same on the east side of the town of Bazaar-e-Panjwayi. Lieutenant-Colonel Lavoie's tactical headquarters and G29 went to Ma'Sum Ghar. From here, they had a dominating view of the entire area of operations.

> "B" and "C" [company groups] were responsible for conducting feints north and south of Pashmul respectively. Concurrently A [Company Group] was to isolate Bazaar-e-Panjwayi in order to provide flank protection to "C" [Company Group]...If successful in their actions, the enemy would be pummeled and annihilated by precision guided munitions and indirect fire.[8]

Overall fire support was in the hands of Major Greg Ivey whose four guns of E Battery and the two Dutch guns, under his operational control, were in direct support of the battle group. He recalls, "The indirect fire mission for the Pashmul area was essentially to neutralize and destroy as much of the command and control and suspected strong points of the Taliban as possible."[9]

Ivey now called on his six guns and the general support of the American HIMARS rocket launcher and the close air and attack aviation support provided by the ISAF and the Americans. Ivey:

> We had approximately 10 hours of attack helicopters by day and five hours by night. We deployed three FOO parties in and around Pashmul area to essentially conduct preparatory fires to basically set the conditions for the battle group to move onto the objective on foot or in LAVs...At 0600 hours on 2 September, we had two FOO parties south along the Ma'Sum Ghar

mountain ridge, one FOO party in the north—each affiliated with their respective rifle company in the area. And it was a shock and awe start.[10]

The listed targets for the bombardment were Taliban commanders, improvised explosive device (IED) factories, mortars and rockets, service support nodes, intelligence, surveillance and recce resources, and propaganda operations which had become identified during the shaping operations of the previous week.[11]

Targets had been carefully selected and vetted for appropriate treatment. These were then added to a target list which was passed up through Regional Command (South) to ISAF headquarters and reviewed and approved by a targeting board. Air resources would come from far and wide including from a US aircraft carrier operating out of the Indian Ocean. Intensive preparations had been undertaken through an information operation to get the local population to leave the area. Many had moved into the city of Kandahar, often into the slums there, where they would stay for the foreseeable future.[12]

B Company's role in the north, as one of the two feinting forces, was to sit and look prepared to attack. They were not to get decisively engaged once they took up their positions along the wadi. However, no one had told two Taliban fighters about the master plan. While the Company sat quietly and held their positions, two individuals popped up on a wall and started opening up on 5 Platoon's LAVs with nothing but their AK assault rifles.

Plummer spun up his first combat fire mission to support 5 Platoon's plan to take out the snipers' position. He recalls,

> *I lazed the target...I opened up with proximity, 1 round fire for effect and the rounds landed. I lazed the centre of mass of those two rounds and then brought them on target so that the next one caved in the building and killed the Taliban on the roof. But afterwards, when the infantry platoon commanders came by, the one platoon commander who was closest said, "Yeah, Ian. There's a lot of shrapnel coming around. Is that normal? I just told my guys to dig in." ... When I turned back to my crew I said to the master bombardier, I said, "From now on we are going to open up with one round. We're going to open up with adjustment. We're going to push it 400 metres and we'll walk it back on the target. We're going to use [delay fuzes] until we're sure where that round's going to go."*[13]

Plummer now settled down for a quiet few days. Ivey and the remaining two FOOs located on Ma'Sum Ghar were to control the next three days of bombardment.

Ivey described the start of the operation, "We fired a quick stab ... from the battery[14] We had over 150 [close air support] sorties just to support the opening phase. And an equal number of attack aviation sorties ... And the whole intent of it was, reminiscent of World War I/World War II tactics, simply pound the crap out of the enemy on the north side of the river."[15]

A major objective of the massive fire plan was to get the Taliban to unmask their communications network to the allied electronic warfare intercept systems and thus become visible to other surveillance resources. As the fires came down, various systems started receiving information.

Tragically, at 0930 hours, one of those resources which had been providing real-time video feeds, was lost. A British Nimrod multi-engine surveillance aircraft with 14 souls on board, had caught fire due to a fuel leak while mid-air refueling. It crashed, killing everyone as it tried to make its way to Kandahar Airfield (KAF). The ISTAR Squadron was tasked to find and secure the crash site. This removed several additional surveillance assets on the first day of MEDUSA.[16] They had been assets which would have helped define the enemy locations and have allowed Lavoie to properly decide which direction to push from; the north or the south. As the day progressed, there was still not enough information to make that decision.

In the early afternoon of that day, Brigadier-General Fraser came forward to Charles Company's location. He directed that the battle group would immediately cross the Arghandab River.[17] Charles Company had already done some recce and preparatory work. Their conclusion was that the site where ORION's southern force had crossed on August 3, 2006 was the only suitable crossing site. Fraser ordered Charles Company's security platoon to be pushed across the river. This was done without incident, but Lavoie believed there was no benefit to be gained by leaving the platoon there overnight. He managed to convince Brigadier-General Fraser to allow them to be withdrawn at last light.[18]

As September 2, 2006 drew to a close, not much intelligence had yet been gathered about the enemy's fighting positions. In part this was due to the reduced intelligence gathering resources but also because the Taliban had the discipline to stay quiet throughout the initial bombardment.[19] It is at this point that the plan started to unravel. Lieutenant-Colonel Lavoie recalls,

> The plan was executed exactly on September 2, 2006 as how we'd planned it. Where it went off the rails was September 3, 2006 or the night of September 2, 2006, when after successfully taking all the battle positions that I wanted to take, and then allowing for two or three days of detailed reconnaissance supported by aerial and artillery bombardment, then I was going to decide where I was going to strike and not show my cards...[20]

Brigadier-General Fraser now pressed Lavoie to cut the additional two days of artillery and close air preparation and to have Charles Company cross over the Arghandab River into Zhari that night. Lavoie:

I received radio orders from Brigadier-General Fraser to resume the attack at zero one hundred ... Initially I said, "No. We can't do that, I don't have the reconnaissance"...So he and I had a private conversation. This is going on the battle group or the brigade net for all to hear. So we had a private conversation on a secure satellite phone and I was subsequently ordered to cross the river at first light which I was unhappy about...[21]

Brigadier-General Fraser was clear in his mind that it was the right time to move.

It was the actual assault onto the position—RUGBY—that we moved forward based on two things.

There was a two or three days further bombardment planned but from the intelligence point of view, I asked, "Is the enemy any..."—the bottom line was—the enemy had degraded to the point where they had done two reliefs in place; they were not able to fire their support weapons; we killed the top seven of their ten commanders; they were about as attrited as we'd ever seen. The intelligence picture...Didn't think it was ever going to get any better than that. [22]

At least some of that intelligence came from Governor Khalid. According to Fraser, the Afghan National Directorate of Security had received and confirmed several reports stating that the Taliban were fatigued. Fraser decided that his force was as ready to launch as it would ever be.[23]

While this information preceded the September 2, 2006 bombardment, it did come after a full week of shaping operations. Fraser explained further, "Number two and the most important reason—the Governor of Kandahar had told us that he and the Afghan tribal leadership would side with the Taliban leadership if we did not attack now. So we were about to lose the trust and confidence of the people and that trumps everything."[24]

The Taliban may very well have been fatigued. They may even have been attrited. They may even have been attrited to levels that intelligence hadn't seen before. Events of the following days, however, would prove, without any doubt, that the Taliban were still in Pashmul in strength. They remained organized, determined and capable of fighting.

Governor Khalid and a number of tribal elders had met with the Canadian leadership on August 19, 2006 and that meeting, and the assault on Ma'Sum Ghar, had brought the "strike" phase of MEDUSA forward from approximately mid-September or later to its beginning. It's hard to see how that, or another telephone call from the Governor on September 1, 2006 could precipitate the tactical decision to cut out two days of preparatory fires and recce to define the enemy's locations in Pashmul.

Fraser acknowledges that the ammunition crisis had been mitigated by September 2, 2006.[25]

There are other viewpoints.

Task Force AEGIS's assistant chief of staff, Lieutenant-Colonel Shane Schreiber agreed that there was pressure on the brigade at this time. This pressure did not come from Khalid. It came internally from Task Force AEGIS's higher headquarters. Schreiber recalls,

> We had reports that the Taliban were actually leaving ... that they were actually running away.

> When Major-General Benjamin Freakley [ISAF's Deputy-Commander for Security](sic)[26] heard that the enemy may be escaping he said "They're leaving, you're letting them out of the bag." That was his big fear, that the Taliban would get out of the bag and we'd have to fight them again later. So, he said, "The Taliban are leaving so you have to get in there and get after them." Lieutenant-General Richards [the ISAF commander] agreed with him, so we started to get a significant amount of pressure to get in there and to actually find out what was going on in Objective Rugby.[27]

Lieutenant-Colonel Bishop, the AEGIS chief of operations, agrees with Schreiber. He states,

> It became pretty clear early on that Fraser was being pushed really hard to cross the Arghandab and to get into the objectives way earlier than [Omer Lavoie] was planning to do it. He had planned a three day or so fire plan with every asset available in order to prepare the objectives and to make sure that there was some deception built into the plan, and so on. And as soon as the first day's significant contact happened, [ISAF commander General] Richards was pushing very hard for Fraser to get across the Arghandab in an immediate way.

> Fraser was also very keen to get across the Arghandab and was pushing [Lavoie] hard to do it which of course changes the fire plan from three days of preparation to essentially whatever you had available on the first day and then get on with it ...

> [Fraser] thought, at the time that if they got under significant attack, if the Taliban got under significant attack, he still believed that they were gonna try to withdraw or reposition somewhere and he wanted to be more

agile and get after them in the opening hours, so there's always a discussion between the battle group commander who is obviously dealing with it and the brigade commander who is, who has all kinds of other pressures on him to immediately get on with it so, I remember a whole lot of high level discussions going on at the time...

Certainly, from a Canadian perspective, we were in no hurry to take any more casualties at that point and clearly, Omer having been baptized by fire early on, was in no hurry to press us into a fight which he still hadn't a clear definition of. There's a reluctance on the battle group's part, rightly so, and there's this reticence on our part as a headquarters to move in a more deliberate way but then the pressure from elsewhere was to get on with it, so how do you square that circle?[28]

At the battle group level, there was no intelligence saying the Taliban were leaving. Captain Chris Purdy, Task Force 3-06's intelligence officer, took the view that,

The intelligence community was basically saying that we still know the enemy are there, the assessment is that they're going to stay and fight, especially within the particular vicinity of Bayenzi. They may fold in the surrounding areas, but [Bayenzi/Objective RUGBY] was going to be the Taliban's last stand right in that area. And due to the ground, they really were able to shape us into where we had to cross. The whole area was very canalizing.[29]

Major Greg Ivey, the battery commander, heard the discussion between Brigadier-General Fraser and the battle group commander, and later stated that the battle group had determined that, based on intelligence, surveillance and recce assessments, the enemy had not withdrawn.[30] He believed it was a classic case of intelligence developed by troops in contact being ignored in favour of analysis of sophisticated means conducted in the rear.[31]

The battery FSCC Officer, Captain Tim Spears said,

We had a plan in place, and Brigadier-General Fraser was not there, he was on leave, and he came back just as MEDUSA was kind of going and he completely changed the plan...[32]

For the battle group, and its gunners in particular, September 2, 2006 had been a good day. Over the next 36 hours that would change dramatically. Whether there had actually been sightings of Taliban fleeing or whether it was another elaborate Taliban ruse to pull Canadians into a kill zone, may never be known. The fact was they were still in Pashmul and Charles Company would find that out the hard way the next morning.

At first light on September 3, Captain Dan Matheson and his forward air controller (FAC), Sergeant James Myler had been preparing for Charles Company's advance. The company's operation couldn't really be called an attack, yet. It was more in the nature of an obstacle crossing followed by an advance to contact into an area where the enemy was expected to be.

One of the lessons learned from August 3, 2006 was that the Taliban had seeded the only road into Bayanzai with IEDs, and as such, the company should be prepared to go off-road. Off-road, however, was easier said than done considering the rugged nature of the terrain. The area was a hodge-podge of plowed fields, ditches, walls, hedges, berms, canals, and vineyards with 3 foot-tall, concrete-hard, mud rows.

Mobility support came by way of the battle group's field engineers of 23 Field Squadron. By mid-August they could not provide much. Major Gasparotto, the squadron commander would say, "Unfortunately, the Squadron was still incapable of offering any meaningful mobility support to the Battle Group as large quantities of our heavy equipment remained unserviceable."[33]

The solution was to weld armour plating to a just-repaired Zettelmeyer front end loader, and to scrounge up a British D6 Caterpillar armoured bulldozer, a D7 bulldozer borrowed from the Afghan army and a rented D8. These too were "Mad Maxed" with welded on steel plating.[34] At the last minute an American route clearance package was added to the squadron. The Zettelmeyer and the D6 were assigned to accompany Charles Company with the task of cutting breaches that the LAVs and other vehicles could navigate through.

While Matheson would accompany Charles Company on its advance, Major Ivey would be on Ma'Sum Ghar with the battle group's tactical headquarters. Captain Ryan Stimpson G21 would be nearby as an anchor observation post throughout the operation.

The company's start had been planned for 0400 hours but it was more like 0600 hours before they actually kicked off. The fire plan had been developed and sent out based on the lanes that the engineers were expected to breach.

Two things complicated matters. First, the fire plan had been sent down and involved both troops but while C Troop had completed a registration mission D Troop had not been able to. Matheson did not feel that as problematic as the two troops were roughly shooting the same targets anyway so he simply double scaled the rounds to be fired by C Troop.[35]

Greg Ivey recalls,

We pounded the enemy position and then we pushed the fires back into the enemy depth, into what we expected was their supporting positions ... at H-Hour, Captain Matheson used suppressant fires on that bank just to get the guys shaken out from their battle position on Ma'Sum Ghar onto the

Arghandab River ... Once they gained lodgment on the far side, or on the north side, of the river, Captain Matheson pushed the fires back into the Taliban depth. He also had close air support at the same time to strike even deeper, probably about 1,000 metres or so.[36]

The second issue proved more troublesome. Captain Matheson's G23's observation post log: "When we left the [line of departure] the breaches did not happen where we initially thought. We got [bottle-necked] near the only road [into] the objective."[37]

The company pushed on and eventually established two sequential breaches to let them get to the near side of the white school. 7 Platoon was pushed through the final breach and shook out into a line in a tall Marijuana field facing the school. While the Taliban maintained disciplined control of their fire, the movement of small groups of them was identified by surveillance devices and they were subsequently engaged. It was becoming quickly clear that the intelligence about a fleeing enemy had been dead wrong. With 7 Platoon deployed, G23's log recorded, "... all hell broke loose. Ambushed is a light term for what happened ... [as] we started sending LAVs through we got hit with [rocket-propelled grenades], AK [assault rifles], PKM [general purpose machine guns], RPK [squad machine guns] and [anti-armour 82mm] Recoilless rifle. The latter causing the most damage."[38]

The fire fight was furious with the Afghan army element accompanying the platoon fearlessly charging into the fray. The fight would last many hours. One of the lightly armoured G-Wagons was hit killing Warrant Officer Rick Nolan, the platoon's second in command; then the engineer section LAV was hit in the turret killing Sergeant Shane Stachnick; the Zettelmeyer was hit and disabled, and another LAV became bogged down in a ditch while trying to withdraw. Two others would die, Warrant Officer Frank Mellish and Private William Cushley. Eight others were wounded.

While the fight progressed and recovery of the dead, the wounded and the vehicles proceeded, Matheson's crew continued to provide fire support,

We did our best to bring fire in to support the push, extraction and strafed the target area. We used [attack helicopters] and Guns to support the extraction. We were the third last vehicle out. We emptied our primary and secondary [ammunition] bins and fired a box of 7.62. One bomb did not detonate and bounced close to friendlies. We picked up a section whose vehicle was made into a casualty vehicle. About 8 guys crammed into the back with Bowen and [Sergeant] Myler...It was a very hard fight. The boys did really well. Sad day for Charles Company...

We regrouped in the [wadi] and then pushed back to [Ma'Sum Ghar]. [Myler fired all the ammunition of two A-10s] No grape hut was left untouched and

no [wadi] left not strafed. [Myler] worked aircraft continuously that day destroying everything in sight.[39]

The bomb that did not detonate was a global positioning system-guided 1,000 pound one that went off-course after being dropped from a French Mirage. It had ended up landing within 20 feet of the company commander, Major Matthew Sprague and a number of his men. Ivey would say this about G23's performance,

> *When the company commander was prepared to withdraw, Captain Matheson brought air-burst rounds onto the marijuana fields and the corn fields, probably about 200 to 250 metres out in front of the company's dismounted troops to assist the extraction. At the same time there were buildings in depth that we suspected the Taliban were using to fire RPG [rocket propelled grenades] and 82 mm recoilless rifles so as best as we could we used [Hellfire] missiles from attack helicopters, as well as 500 and 1,000 pound laser guided munitions to neutralize those areas.*

> *[It] was a tough slog because it was probably the first time that the FOO had been put in a situation like that where he was with the company commander conducting the fire plan, using the 25mm cannon, controlling artillery at danger close distances under contact and his FAC in the back [of his LAV] was controlling aircraft all at the same time.*[40]

It wasn't just Matheson's crew that was affected. To the north Plummer's G22, as part of B Company's feint, were in shock listening in on the action to the south.[41] Spears, back at the FSCC, was of the view that it was the complete change in plans that had been forced on the battle group, "that led to Charles Company basically driving into the kill-zone on Objective [RUGBY] on 3 September and getting lit up extensively by a well-disciplined, well-prepared and very, very determined enemy force."[42]

G23 had fired 93 rounds of high explosive, dropped five bombs and eight Hellfire missiles in support of their company that day.

It wouldn't end there. The vehicles which couldn't be recovered were deliberately destroyed in place using close air support. The Taliban, now unmasked, were hit throughout the night by the FOOs on Ma'Sum Ghar. Nonplussed by this, the Taliban were announcing to the world that their morale was high and that they were winning the war. Rather than facing an insurgency that the coalition had feared was running, the Taliban were in fact reinforcing Pashmul. This newest battle at the white school was becoming a rallying cry for them.[43]

While the guns and aircraft pounded away, Charles Company rested, reorganized and refitted.

It would again be Charles Company that would give it another go in the south on September 4. B Company would still be threatening in the north to tie the Taliban down. A further feint in the north would be run by the Royal Canadian Dragoons' ISTAR Squadron, who were back and repositioned from their task at the Royal Air Force Nimrod's crash site. The plan this time would be to not only feign strength along the line of the wadi but to actually penetrate past it further into the south. The intent was to give the Taliban the impression of a larger attack in the north. H-Hour was set for first light; 0530 hours. The advance, however, would be called off before it even started.

In the south, two FACs, Slayer 13 and Slayer 15, had been conducting air attacks against suspected Taliban positions. A few hours before first light, a flight of two and subsequently a second flight of two A-10A Thunderbolt IIs had been dispatched to Charles Company's area of operations. They were properly cleared into Task Force 3-06's airspace. Both were advised of the target area and advised that friendly forces were positioned south of the Arghandab River. They checked in to their assigned FACs and commenced a series of bomb and 30mm gun runs into the area of the white school.

While these runs were occurring, Charles Company was waking up and going through their morning routine prior to their own advance which was scheduled for 0700 hours that morning.

As daylight was starting to increase, Slayer 13 cleared the aircraft in for another guided bomb unit drop to be followed by a strafing run on the white school. The strafing run would follow on after the bomb drop using the smoke generated by the prior bomb as the pilot's aim point. In the case of the last run, the pilot about to execute the strafing run had just removed his night vision goggles due to the increasing light level. As he began his attack, he mistook a garbage fire in the midst of Charles Company's position for the prior bomb burst and commenced firing with his 30mm cannon.

The instance that Slayer 13 saw the burst start, he called "Abort! Abort! Abort!". The pilot immediately broke off and his wingman terminated his approach. The burst had been limited to approximately 1/4 of what would be a full gun run. The FAC's quick action had clearly saved lives.

On the ground, the burst had hit the company's headquarters and a platoon as they were packing up after breakfast. Private Mark Anthony Graham was killed, and approximately thirty-five others were wounded, 5 of them seriously. Medevacs were immediately called for and everyone in the area, including the crew of Matheson's G23 rushed over to provide first aid to the injured. Included amongst the wounded was the company commander, Major Matthew Sprague.

To stop the Taliban from seeing what was going on Ivey called for smoke to be laid down along the river valley. That would lead to confusion for a large, twin-rotor Chinook helicopter medevac flight coming in. As the grey smoke screened off the ridge, the lead aircraft ignored the ground controller, overflew the position, missing the purple smoke marker, and headed to the north side of the Arghandab River where the screening smoke was spreading.[44]

The Chinook actually touched down in enemy territory for a second before lifting off, unmolested, and made its way to the proper landing zone. Major Ivey would later email a report to Lieutenant-Colonel Scott Johnson, commanding officer of the 2nd Regiment, Royal Canadian Horse Artillery which included the following entry,

> *You are by now well aware of the A-10 incident on the following day—G23 (the FAC in particular) was obviously shaken up. The bond between the FOO parties and companies is unbelievable—soldiers that were wounded in the strafing run literally hobbled and limped over to G23's LAV and hugged the guys saying "it wasn't your fault, we love you guys, it wasn't your fault". Very emotional times.[45]*

For Charles Company there would be no assault that day. The company returned to KAF. Lavoie and Ivey also headed back to KAF to hammer out a new approach. Matheson and G23, on the other hand, stayed on at Ma'Sum Ghar. Their log book would show the following entries for the next few days:

> *September 4...Charles [Company] headed into KAF for [reorganization] and refit. [Sergeant] Myler to go with. The troops don't blame us but we feel responsible...Close call all around for us. The boys again did really well helping treat the wounded and organizing litters. [Master Bombardier Kevin] Bannister conducted over watch for several hours. HIMARS mission tonight. Rockets sent from KAF and hitting targets on [Objective] RUGBY. Impressive to watch but not very effective. Perhaps psychologically, but they impacted like a Regimental fire mission with 1 [round Fire For Effect]*
>
> *September 5 - Bombing continues on Objective RUGBY. They give us the go ahead to rearrange the landscape and we are making short work of it.*
>
> *September 6 - More bombing.*
>
> *September 7 - Still more bombing.*
>
> *September 8 - Yet again more bombing.[46]*

Both the US Air Force and the Canadian Armed Forces convened boards of inquiries to examine the incident. The new battery commander for Shilo's A Battery, Major James Allen, was designated as a member to the Canadian board. The board's findings found the pilot as the sole cause of the incident. The board also made several additional findings which, while not causal to the incident, pointed to several deficiencies in how Canada trained, deployed, and equipped their FACs.[47] Almost all of these had previously been identified by the various artillery units. These included the following as listed in the report's executive summary:

> 5. *Although not causal to the incident, the Board finds that there were deficiencies with the FAC predeployment training and equipment. The FACs were not qualified Combat Ready Night High (CR-NH) before deploying to theatre, thus not meeting the requirements of the ISAF Standard Operating Procedure (SOP) 311. Furthermore, the pre-deployment training, while providing FACs with the minimum knowledge to conduct Close Air Support (CAS), was insufficient to prepare them for the conditions they faced during Op MEDUSA. In regards to equipment, the FACs were provided with the minimum required to control aircraft. Many of the controls involved CAS during the night where more sophisticated equipment such as infrared (IR) pointers and other such devices would have greatly facilitated identification of targets and friendly positions.*

> 6. *The air coordinating agencies such as the Brigade and Battle Group level Tactical Air Control Party (TACP) were not properly manned. Prior to deploying, the Brigade Headquarters (HQ) exercised in Canada with a complete TACP but did not deploy it. Significant effort was made in theatre to overcome these shortfalls and to qualify FACs CR-NH and the efforts made by some individuals is commendable. But the fact still remains that the FACs arrived in theatre without the requisite qualification and the TACP was not properly manned.*[48]

The lack of training also included that given to the manoeuvre forces,

> 223. *Furthermore, pre-deployment training did not adequately prepared (sic) FACs to assume their [Close Air Support] functions and never inoculated manoeuvre commanders or soldiers to the effects and employment of [Close Air Support].*[49]

The Report then lists eight examples of training inadequacies which include: lack of aircraft, lack of Danger Close training scenarios, lack of training including the supported manoeuvre commanders, assigning FAC duties as secondary duties within the FOO party, and no training on employing attack helicopters amongst others.

While there were a few individuals manning the tactical air control party at brigade, no such group existed at the battle group, and the job there had been taken on by the FSCC Officer, Captain Spears. He recalls,

> *In the planning of Medusa, [Regional Command (South)] made it clear they wanted to download all the requirements for control of air, [aviation] and fires to us at the [battle group headquarters]. [Regional Command (South)/Task Force AEGIS] only had 3 pilots in their TACP, and were supposed to provide [a] qualified Air Controller to assist with the high demand of Air assets for the [operation], however, they did not show up for the fight until much later in Medusa. We had the Air Defence Systems Integrator (ADSI) at the [battle group air space coordination centre (ASCC)], which allowed us to see the air picture from 2000' up. This meant we used procedural control from 2000' to the ground and positive control from 2500' up. Early in the task, [Captain Bill Warren, the ASCC officer,] and I realized we were going to need to work hand in glove in a combined effort to function as a [battle group] TACP of sorts. The ASCC was instrumental in [air support coordination] planning and the creation of the [High-Density Air Control Zone] for Medusa and [air support coordination] for all follow-on [operations]. By that time I had run 24/7 for several days and was completely exhausted. There were 3 FOO/ FAC parties to distribute the air/[aviation] push to and they had difficulty with the volume. With only me to control any shaping and close strike when they were in contact and couldn't control because of contact or close terrain [line-of-sight] issues. We did not have ROVER at this time so my feeds and contact with the Predator [squadron] and [tactical unmanned aerial vehicle] Sperwer [troop] were pivotal. A [Royal Canadian Navy liaison officer] and [Royal Air Force liaison officer] arrived in late [September] to help and it was greatly needed and appreciated but we really could have used it in late August.[50]*

Corrective action would come before the report was even published. In October another gunner, Major-General Stuart Beare, the commander of the Land Force Doctrine and Training System visited Afghanistan. He spent a night at the FSCC with Spears after having spent the previous night at Ma'Sum Ghar with Lavoie and Ivey while troops were in contact. He "observed the power of a disciplined, professional combined arms team in action."[51] Spears advised him about the TACP situation. Beare:

> *"Spears was the man who lit a fire in me on that. On return to Canada my first call was to Charlie Bouchard—Commander [1 Canadian Air Division]. Charlie was incredulous too. He is an old [tactical helicopter]*

guy—and got it right away. The decade of darkness allowed military leaders to effectively kill air/land skills—no [Air Ground Operations Section] and no command level attention to that vital role. We agreed immediately to fix that—and we did."[52]

While Task Force 3-06 reorganized and planned, artillery and close air support continued for the remainder of September 4 and 5. A and B Companies were still at effective strength. Charles Company's losses had dramatically reduced its combat power. More troops would be needed. A new plan was needed.

To the southwest Operational Detachment-Bravo 330 had been in contact with the enemy for several days around Objective BILLIARDS. The intelligence suggested the area of Objectives BILLIARDS (Sperwan Ghar) and TENNIS (Siah Choy) was a hornets' nest of Taliban, including a training centre. Some estimates concluded that there were up to 1,000 Taliban occupying the area.[53] The detachment had on September 4, 2006 drawn the conclusion that in holding Sperwan Ghar they had occupied the "key terrain" in the area. While only twenty metres high, this artificial hill, built by the Russians decades earlier, nonetheless had a commanding view of the surrounding area.

Task Force 31 approved a plan for two of their Detachments-Alpha to seize it. Their fire support would come from attack helicopters, A-10s, the odd B1 bomber, Predators, and AC-130 gunships. The latter would circle and engage targets with their 105mm, 40mm and 25mm cannons.

The detachments moved from their observation posts to Sperwan Ghar. The next day, in a furious battle, they seized and held it against a determined Taliban counter attack. On September 6, 2006 Fraser declared that Sperwan Ghar was now MEDUSA's major effort.[54]

Lavoie, meanwhile, realized that in the face of determined conventional resistance he would need tanks to enhance his force's mobility and in clearing the heavily fortified Taliban strong points. Discussions about the utility of tanks had started even while Task Force ORION was still in theatre. The issue at that time was the terrain and the tanks ability to resist IEDs.[55] Lieutenant-General Leslie, Chief of the Land Staff, in a telephone conversation with Lavoie now asks him if he could use some tanks. He agreed that he could. Again, the issue was the terrain.[56]

In a message to General Hillier on September 6, 2006 Fraser asked for six tanks. Hillier suggested a half squadron. That eventually grew to a 15-tank squadron. All that was immediately available were the venerable Leopard C2s from the Lord Strathcona's Horse (Royal Canadians) and an armoured engineer troop from 1 Combat Engineer Regiment from Edmonton, Alberta. The government, in an announcement on September 16, 2006 said the tanks were needed to "better facilitate 'the reconstruction and stabilization efforts in Afghanistan.'"[57]

It wouldn't end with just the Leopard C2s.

Previously, on June 6, 2006 the outgoing Chief of the Land Staff, Lieutenant-General Marc Caron had recommended to the Vice Chief of Defence Staff that the mobile gun system acquisition be cancelled. In part this was due to problems that the Americans were having with the system. That month, the Vice Chief halted funding on that project and, coincidentally, on the air defenders' multi-mission effects vehicle which was the proposed replacement for the Air Defence Anti-Tank systems in service with 4 Air Defence Regiment, Royal Canadian Artillery. Thus ended the direct fire unit initiative.[58]

Lieutenant-General Leslie and Dan Ross, the Assistant Deputy Minister (Material) now initiated a major new acquisition program. They would take the money previously allocated to buy the Stryker-based, eight-wheeled mobile gun systems and use it to purchase and upgrade Leopard 2 tanks from Germany and the Netherlands.[59]

The pressure on Brigadier-General Fraser from higher headquarters to get back into Pashmul and to clean it up was on again. So was the pressure from Ottawa to hold the line on casualties.[60] With ISAF's pressure, however, came some additional resources.

A fourth Special Operations Detachment-Alpha was moved onto Ma'Sum Ghar to relieve Canadian special operations forces there.[61] Company C (Comanche Company), 2nd Battalion 87th Infantry Regiment supported by two M119 105mm howitzers from Battery A, 5th Battalion, 25th Field Artillery Regiment would be brought in on the 8th and put under operational control of Operational Detachment-Bravo 330. They would stay for the remainder of Operation MEDUSA. In addition, Task Force 42, a British special forces group, operated in the Registan Desert to interdict Taliban supply lines.

Charles Company, its leadership now down a company commander, a company sergeant major, a platoon commander, three platoon warrant officers, and five of nine section commanders, had stepped up. A newly promoted sergeant became the company sergeant major while master corporals took the roles of a platoon commander and the platoon warrant officers. Privates became section commanders. On the 6th, Charles Company was back at Ma'Sum Ghar where it was reunited with Matheson's G23 and where it would become a part of Task Force GRIZZLY.

GRIZZLY had been formed by AEGIS. The Alaskan National Guard's Colonel Stephen Williams was appointed its commander. GRIZZLY would also include Task Force 3-06's ISTAR Squadron as well as an *ad hoc* group of Americans formed from their national support element in Kandahar. Its task would be to hold the

Ma'Sum Ghar/Bazaar-e-Panjwayi region and conduct enough deception activities to lead the Taliban to believe that the whole battle group was still in the south.

That left TF 3-06's tactical headquarters, with Ivey's G29, and A Company to move around from Ma'Sum Ghar to the north near PB WILSON where it joined B Company and Task Force MOHAWK.

While the companies reorganized and positioned themselves, 155mm ammunition had been arriving at KAF. As soon as it landed it was pushed forward to the gun line by both road and helicopter until there were 2,500 rounds stockpiled on the gun position. The lack of a battery echelon and an ammunition section meant that ammunition delivered by helicopter pallets would frequently have to be broken down into individual rounds and transported within Bisons from the helicopter landing zone to the gun platforms.[62] That raised a whole new question of what to do with it if the battery, or one of the gun troops, were given orders to move. Without its own echelon, the battery only had the ability to lift only some 400 rounds on its gun tractors.[63]

The question was a purely academic one; first it was payback time.

21

OPERATION MEDUSA: SEPTEMBER 6 - 17, 2006

AS OF SEPTEMBER 6, 2006, Operation MEDUSA now had two major areas of operation.

In the south, at Sperwan Ghar, was Operational Detachment-Bravo 330's with two special forces detachments and approximately a company of the Afghan army. Brigadier-General Fraser allocated a significant portion of his air power to them. Their task was to fix the Taliban in place and attrit them. On September 8, 2006 with the addition of another American rifle company with two 105mm howitzers attached under operational control, they were readying to push north across the Arghandab River toward Siah Choy. Captain Dan Matheson's G23 would stay in the south at Ma'sum Ghar with Charles Company and Task Force GRIZZLY for the time being, providing the appearance that the whole battle group was still there.

In the north, Task Force 3-06—minus Charles Company—would start its slow and deliberate southward grind to eradicate the Taliban defenses in Objective CRICKET. The scheme of manoeuvre was to advance the three companies—A, B and A Company 2-4 Infantry (US)—southwards with generally one company up, destroying all Taliban remaining in place. At the end of each day, they would consolidate and hold the ground gained. The following morning the battle group would conduct a passage of lines with a follow-on company moving through to take up the advance. The engineers used bulldozers and explosives to create run-up positions and lanes for the light armoured vehicles (LAV) and leveled a wide road with a cleared security zone 300 metres on either side. The width was based on the approximate effective range of a rocket propelled grenade.[1] The partial clearing of what would later become Route SUMMIT had begun.

B Company would take the lead first, and for the next six days, Stimpson's G21 and Plummer's G22 would exchange positions as lead and anchor forward observation officers (FOO), as their respective companies advanced.

The terrain in the north was highly complex. It was filled with fields,

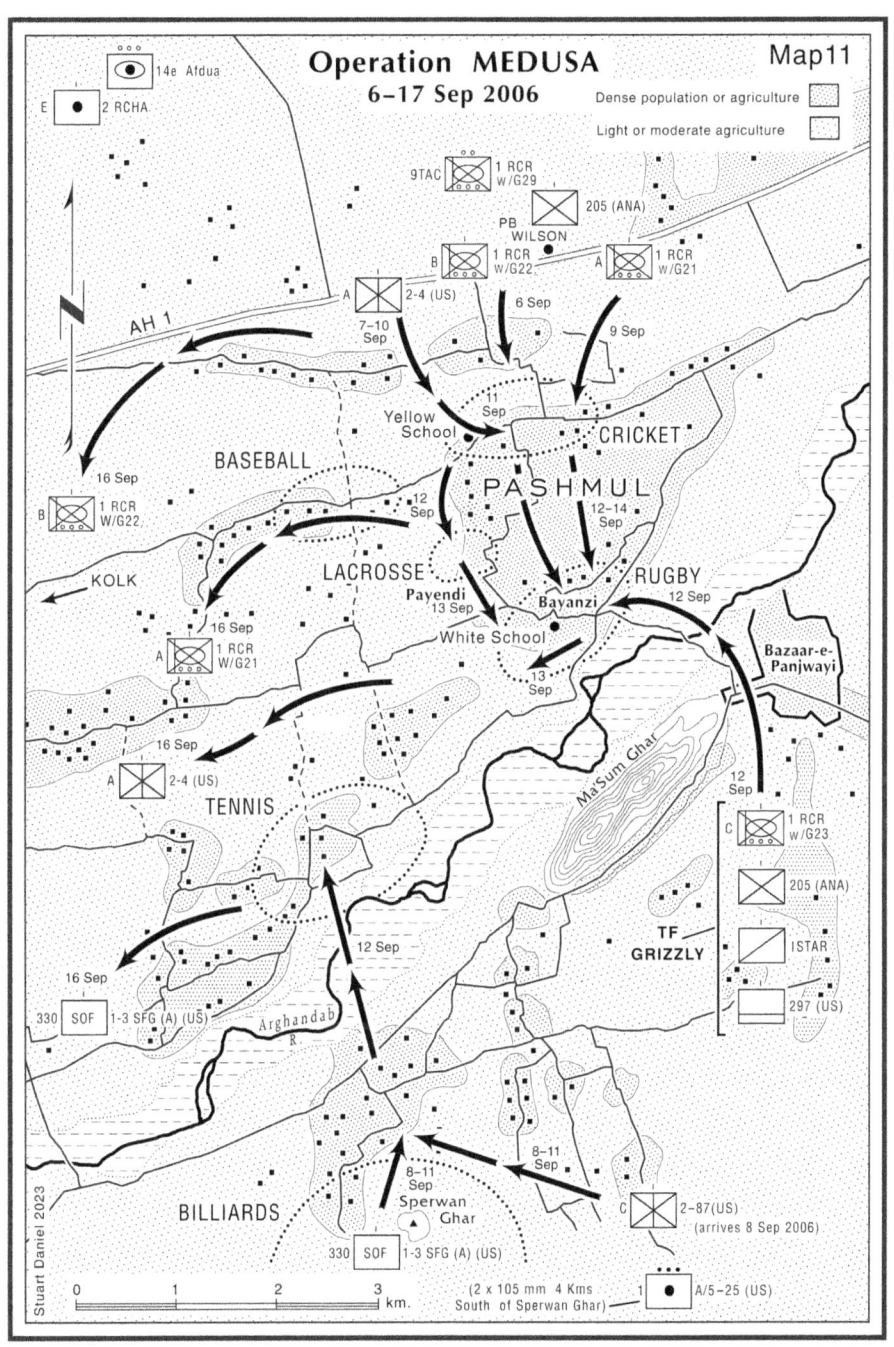

OPERATION MEDUSA: SEPTEMBER 6-17, 2006 | 313

compounds, hedgerows, walls, wadis, and canals which generally limited visibility to a few hundred metres at best. Mostly it was a fight where troops in contact required the fire support of danger close engagements. G22's Ian Plummer recalls one such bound,

> ...*A Company was forward now. I went forward to where they were, which was essentially going to be B Company's line of departure. The plan was for me to do the fire plan and at H-Hour [B Company] would just drive right through the centre of A Company's position with their LAVs, spread out, dismount and occupy buildings for the next bound...I had two targets, a smoke screen, and one or two [defensive fire targets]. All of these targets are danger close except the [defensive fire targets].*

> ...*When we did that bound...I did the screen first to our right flank...and then I engaged the objective ... then there was a bit of a problem. The [company's] LAVs had to stop because they couldn't see. There was so much dust and debris ...they went maybe a hundred metres past the line of departure. They stopped, waited for all the dust to come down and then continued their advance. For me, I grabbed my signaler. I hopped out and just ran behind [the dismounts] because there was only a few hundred metres—caught up [went to the lead section and set up observation]*[2]

At this point Task Force MOHAWK company was deployed just to their left and engaging their own targets using the guns from the Canadian/Dutch firebase north of the highway. Splinters from those rounds were impacting on the roof where Plummer, his signaller and a member of the B Company had set up.[3]

It was not an intelligence-driven fight. Major Ivey:

> *All the talk about leading with sensors and precision strike briefs very well but it definitely didn't happen that way here. We did not receive from [brigade] a single 6-figure grid reference of an enemy location. We were provided big goose eggs on the map and [PowerPoint] map symbols. We literally rolled up at [H-Hour], occupied [observation posts] and started engaging 'suspected' positions based on our best guess as to where they were hiding or occupying. At the tactical level, we pulled our own [intelligence] from what the FOOs observed and what recce could pull—completely bottom up.*[4]

To say that the fight wasn't intelligence driven is not the same as saying that there wasn't some intelligence respecting possible targets. Plummer recalls,

> *[Air] was actually really challenging. We ended up getting 24/7 [close air support]. And it was exhausting because...there [were] only a few of the ... [forward air controllers (FAC)] that were qualified combat ready. So you*

needed to get your night runs, your Day High and your Day Low runs and so
we were missing night runs. So when we got into theatre all the officers did the
handover and the sergeants went over and finished their night runs with the
Americans. So during [Operation] MEDUSA...those three sergeants...every
three hours were rotating [close air support]...when you threw in patrolling,
it was super exhausting.

...We were allowed to engage suspected positions, so we had intelligence
reports of... probably twenty or thirty of these. There were pictures and target
locations and because we were running short of artillery and the [battery
commander] said, whenever an aircraft comes on station you're to drop every
bomb and weapon system on any of those positions. My sergeant came to me
and said "Sir, I've dropped bombs on every one of those positions", and I'm
like "Keep dropping."...We really religiously stuck to those intelligence reported
positions.[5]

While the FACs directed aircraft, the battalion's reconnaissance (recce) platoon
would move forward at night and define the next day's objective. Day-by-day the
resistance increased...and then it suddenly slackened.

While the battle group continued to press in the north, Matheson's G23 on
Ma'Sum Ghar with C Company and the various elements of Task Force GRIZZLY
continued to make their presence felt. On September 9, 2006 a recoilless rifle, fired
out of Objective RUGBY, impacted close to G23's LAV. They responded with
more bombing. By September 10, 2006 pressure was being put on Matheson to fire
more artillery. Their part of the operation, however, had the lowest priority. With
the ammunition issue becoming better but still limited, the best that could be done
was making use of the new American white phosphorus rounds recently arrived in
theatre to lay in a smoke screen.

G23's observation post log for September 11, 2006 stated, "ICOM chatter tells
us we are doing well. The Taliban hate us and don't want to fight anymore. Yet we are
still getting shot at from across the waddie. Again very close to my vehicle and the
boys." Coincidentally, there was a visit at their observation post by a Major Harjit
Sajjan who provided them with some useful information on the Taliban.[6]

The systematic pounding from the north had broken the Taliban. Ivey described the
tactics as being simple and straightforward.

Once the assaulting troops gained lodgment onto their objective, the process
would start over. "The FOO would get up onto a compound with a dismounted
laser range finder, a map and a pair of binoculars and begin preparing the

next bound...Yeah. World War I tactics. We would just neutralize anything in front of us and then once fire had been lifted, we would push the infantry through and begin preparing the next bound.[7]

The northern portion of Objective CRICKET was seized on September 10, 2006. Task Force MOHAWK passed through and captured the southern end the next day. September 11, 2006 marked the battery's 1,000[th] round fired in combat. Barely into their first month of the tour they had already doubled the number of rounds fired by A Battery during their entire deployment.

While the battle group's relentless, grinding advance continued from the north, to the battle group's southwest at Sperwan Ghar, the American Special Forces' Operational Detachment Bravo 330 and its attached forces had defeated all attempts by the Taliban to drive them off. Having dealt with this sporadic resistance they now pushed northward to the Arghandab River on September 11, 2006 and crossed it on September 12. Resistance here would also be light as they secured Objective TENNIS at Siah Choy.[8]

Back in the north, with Objective CRICKET taken and the Taliban trying to pull back to the west, A Company pushed on. By September 12, Task Force MOHAWK had taken Objective LACROSSE.

On September 12 as well, Charles Company with Task Force GRIZZLY was given the green light to push across the Arghandab River and into the eastern end of RUGBY. Matheson prepared a fire plan but no one had advised him that the Afghan army unit hadn't been ready to step off at the allotted time. Consequently the majority of the smoke had already been fired before they were ready to cross. That proved to be irrelevant. When GRIZZLY eventually crossed the river it was unopposed. The next day, G23's log reflected, "[Charles Company] in better spirits on the net and the confidence has returned. They want to push as fast and as far as Grizzly 6 wants to. They push to the white school. No resistance yet."[9]

A threat warning forced them back, but on September 15, 2006 Charles Company had secured the white school and the southeastern end of Objective RUGBY.

Task Force MOHAWK, advancing from the north, moved into the west end of RUGBY on September 14, without resistance. By September 16, B Company had swung west and pushed some 5 to 6 kilometres west into a line running from Kolk north to Highway 1.

The next few days would see a consolidation of forces but essentially, the Taliban's offensive in Kandahar had crumbled and the survivors had fled. Ivey: "We found everything you would expect to find after a battle but we also found massive weapons caches, car batteries and remote garage door starters and 50 [kilograms] of nitrogen, Iranian and Pakistani money, communications gear among other things; so it was obvious that those who left, left in a hurry and not deliberately."[10]

Manoeuvre and intimate fire support had proven a game winning combination. On September 17, 2006 the strike phase of Operation MEDUSA was officially declared over.

Throughout the operation, while the FOOs had been manoeuvring with their respective companies, the gunline had stayed in one location. Its isolated position and good fields of view provided excellent security. It had also removed them from the threat of ambush and the mortars and rockets that they had experienced close to Patrol Base WILSON. As such, the guns could dedicate maximum effort to providing fire support to the infantry.

Ammunition resupply remained an issue. While the in-theatre quantities of 155mm ammunition had required daily firing limits, the actual delivery of that ammunition from Kandahar Airfield (KAF) to the gun position, through the by-now infamous "Ambush Alley" was of greater concern. Ground based combat logistics patrols were constantly high-risk targets. The creation of such a patrol with its requisite force protection packet had routinely proven difficult.

To help alleviate this issue, Battery Sergeant Major Montague was redeployed into his traditional role on the gunline. Not only did this help with the management of the delivery of over a thousand rounds of 155mm to the gun position, it also helped with the leadership and mentorship that a battery sergeant major brings to the troops.[11] Throughout, the battery quartermaster sergeant, Warrant Officer Rick Cameron, Master Bombardier Daniel Musgrave[12] from the 7th Toronto Regiment, Royal Canadian Artillery, and Bombardiers Andre Gravelle and Robert Frank did yeoman service in preparing and rigging trucks and kicker pallets for resupply of the gun line.[13] Cameron recalls,

> We used a lot of kicker pallets [which] we built and shipped. We did sling loads from KAF. And we did send some by road, which was not the smartest thing to do, I don't think. So we did all three. Once Medusa kicked off, the bullets were just flying out of the [ammunition] compound. I can remember working long nights there getting stuff [prepared] ready to go out the next morning. Pretty hectic. We had to build the kicker pallets right at the [battery quartermaster stores] using power tools.[14]

The process was anything but normal. Ordinarily a battery has an ammunition detachment to handle incoming ammunition brought forward by the regiment or the logistics system. No such detachment was permitted to the battery in order to meet the personnel cap that was put on the mission. Neither was there a regimental ammunition detachment. Instead the battery was limited in carrying only the ammunition that would fit on its gun tractors. Resupply was to come directly from KAF by combat logistics patrols operated by the national support element.

Ordinarily the battery quartermaster sergeant and his staff do not handle artillery ammunition. The situation with the national support element, however, was that the battery had no choice but to lean in and take on roles to fill the gaps in the system.

The commitment of American CH-47 Chinook helicopters made aerial resupply possible but also complicated the preparation and reception of ammunition resupply pallets. Ammunition arrived in KAF on separate pallets of projectiles, propelling charges and fuzes but, if sent to the guns by air, needed to be repacked onto pallets where each pallet contained a complete set of projectiles and their requisite charges and fuzes. Battery Sergeant Major Bob Montague describes how the process worked,

> Ammunition was often delivered in mixed pallets of projectiles, propelling charges and fuzes by Chinook helicopters...[At the gun position, the] helicopter would move slowly forward just off the ground with its ramp lowered and in a slight nose up attitude. The pallets would slide out, one after the other and end up in a compact line. If the troop was fortunate, there would be a vehicle with handling equipment available to deliver the pallets to the guns; otherwise, the pallets had to be dismantled and the ammunition loaded on a truck by hand.[15]

> [Cameron] led his small team who miraculously managed to organize, prepare, and ship thousands of rounds of 155 mm projectiles, fuses, and propellant to the battery...Preparing and organizing this ammunition into loads in KAF was a gargantuan task...[Cameron relied on Bombardier] Robert Frank, who was the face-to-face contact with staff at the [national support element] and [temporary depot munitions]...Frank did a fantastic job juggling the logistics, cutting through the minutia, and maintaining communication...[16]

The guns found themselves frequently firing directly over the heads of, or directly at, their supported companies. This required some discretion as to which guns were used where. The M777 was prized for its accuracy and speed of response. Daily registration missions[17] made it possible to open a fire mission in fire for effect without adjustment. Danger close missions were fired at a safe distance and then incrementally walked-in to their intended target.

There were some issues with respect to the Dutch Panzerhaubitzen. Their auto-loading system was quite complex, computerized and prone to heat failures. On occasion when there was a computer glitch, the entire system had to be rebooted. In general, these guns were slow. Ivey noted, "First off, I would take a Canadian [detachment] on a manual M777 over a fully automated [Panzerhaubitze 2000] any day. Our guys were reporting shot/rounds complete well before the first [Panzerhaubitze] fired its first round."[18]

Even though concentrated in one location, the guns were generally employed in two-gun troops. "There were times when all three [companies] were engaged in contact; during these times each FOO party had a troop at priority of fire."[19]

Notwithstanding that the Chief of the Land Staff's field artillery transformation directive of 2005 contemplated a future where precision fires would be the order of the day, Ivey found that,

> ...with little intelligence and lack of definition of where the enemy positions started or stopped ... we resorted to good ol' area neutralization ... We pounded the shit out of grape fields and compounds that the Taliban were using as likely forming up points, rally points and [command and communication] nodes ... Once on target, we would "massage" the area by moving the [mean point of impact] left or right 200 [metres] and then in depth 200 [metres] just to make sure that we spread the good news to all the bad guys.[20]

Here too, the speed of the M777 proved advantageous. While not able to call down a regimental mission, Ivey found that, "Two M777s that can fire off a total of [eighteen] 155mm projectiles onto the target area in under a minute is devastating."[21]

Fire discipline occasionally proved a problem. On one occasion the order "Smoke two rounds followed by five rounds fire for effect, six-zero seconds"—which orders all rounds to be smoke—resulted in the two Dutch guns firing two rounds of smoke followed by five rounds of high explosive which, fortunately, injured no one.

As the emergency resupply of American ammunition flowed into the theatre, the battery had to adjust to various differences on the fly.

Canada, at the time, used two types of smoke projectiles. The first was the M60 White Phosphorus smoke round that initiates in a single burst on the ground by way of a point detonating fuze. The other was the DM45A1 Hexachlorethane smoke round that expels several smoke canisters from the projectile's base in the air by way of the M577 mechanically timed fuze. The DM45A1 round proved problematic in the Afghanistan environment. The hard ground would frequently cause the canisters to bounce and spread too far thus lessening the screening effect.[22]

Amongst the ammunition received from the Americans was a new type of White Phosphorus round, the M825A1 round which no one in the battery had ever used before. That round functioned by way of expelling chemically infused White Phosphorous wedges into the air by way of an M762 electronically timed fuze. The fuze too, was new to the Canadians. It was, however, similar to the C32A1 multipurpose fuze in use with their high explosive projectiles and so the troops were able to rapidly work out procedures for its use in the field.

In addition was a question of whether or not the M825A1 round was legally permissible to be used. That was resolved favourably by referring the matter for an opinion through the battle group's legal advisor. An unexpected bonus was that the new round was more effective than either of the previous ones providing an excellent rapid screen. It did not "pillar" like the old White Phosphorus round and lasted longer on the ground than the old Hexachlorethane one.

While they were able to solve that problem another, while obvious, proved more difficult. At one point, having run short of C32A1 fuzes, someone in the troop decided to use the American M762 fuzes instead. This resulted in a number of dud rounds landing. A call to Captain Lorne Doucet at the Royal Canadian Artillery School, ammunition and equipment cell, eventually established that the M762 fuze, while similar, lacked the booster charge present on the C32A1 fuze which was needed to set off the high explosive filler in the round.[23] The Electronic Time Fuze M762 is used with projectiles carrying payloads that are expelled during projectile flight such as illumination and smoke projectiles.

Another complication arising from the newly arrived American ammunition were the propelling charges. Newly introduced to the Canadian artillery was the modular artillery charge system, which had a short-range type called the M232, and a longer-range type called the M232A1. Amongst the newly arrived ammunition was M232 propellant which, although appearing very similar to M232A1, was intended for the cancelled Americans' Crusader self-propelled artillery program. The M232 had a slower velocity than the M232A1. In addition, the Crusader had a very different chrome lined barrel while the M777's barrel was unchromed. As a result, the propellant's chemical properties caused much greater wear on the M777.[24]

The battery's fire control computer systems had data for both types of charges, and the shortage of propellant was such that the M232 was used. But with so little to distinguish between the two types of propellant, an accident was almost inevitable. The result was a round fired using the shorter range propellant but with the data for the other, longer range one. It impacted approximately 900 metres short of the target and just to the left and rear of a FOO party and several metres from a vehicle. Luckily it ricocheted and detonated further away.[25]

Once the difference in the two types of propellants was recognized, the proper data could be calculated quite readily. However, the barrel wear issue would remain and for several years into the future, M232 propellant would find its way onto the gun platforms even when other, less damaging, types of charges were available.[26]

Some individuals have minimized the effectiveness of artillery and air strikes in Pashmul on September 2, 2006 based on minimal damage observed on the bunker systems. This was based on their walkthroughs of the area after the battle.[27] This, however, begs the question as to whether the planned additional two days of shaping operations would have made a difference.

On the other hand, the effects of artillery and close air support as part of combined arms operations were clearly substantiated in all other phases of the battle. The battle group's commander clearly understood that.

> *"The Taliban didn't think we'd attack from the north," surmised Lavoie, "because the ground was impassable and no one had done that before." He explained that a clever deception in the south and the use of bulldozers to plough lanes through the grape vineyards and marijuana fields to make lanes for the LAV IIIs, as well as and B Company's utilization of the ground in conjunction with overwhelming fire from artillery and [close air support] at "danger close" range, overcame any and all opposition.[28]*

As did Brigadier-General Fraser who recognized the conventional nature of the fight that developed and who credited the Taliban's destruction in the battle to the integration of artillery and air support with the infantry's fire and movement.[29]

E Battery's commander, Major Ivey, expands on that,

> *The physical effect from all the artillery and [close air support] I think was quite obvious. We destroyed bunkers, fighting positions and other physical structures, and in the end denied them the use of those structures. However, use of [close air support] and artillery synchronized with direct fire weapons during counter-attacks on the strong points definitely disrupted enemy operations and created a psychological effect that is probably hard to measure but cannot be underestimated. Never knowing when or where artillery will strike has a significant impact on the enemy moral plane. As for interdicting and denying freedom of movement, this will only work when the enemy progresses from classic small-party, counter-insurgency to the point where they require larger [command, control] and coordination to conduct more complex operations. Massing of large enemy groups, the establishment of identifiable enemy nodes, and the establishment of "a front line" all lend well to "shaping" operations with artillery and [close air support]. The use of more accurate ammunition (not necessarily precision munitions but accurately placed dumb munitions) can also create the same effect.[30]*

For the International Security Assistance Force (ISAF), Operation MEDUSA had been a tactical success. Estimates as to what it had cost the Taliban varied from initial claims of around 500 killed to later estimates of 1,000. The fight had been a disaster for the Taliban.[31]

Following on after MEDUSA, ISAF launched Operation MOUNTAIN FURY starting on September 16th. Its focus would be on a series of major combat operations over the next four months by the Americans in the east and the British in the southwest. Canadians would turn to consolidating their gains from MEDUSA.

While Operation MEDUSA had come to a successful conclusion, it would not be the operation that saved Afghanistan. It might have bought the City of Kandahar and the Afghan national government some breathing space, but that wouldn't be enough. As Ivey clearly noted on September 20th, 2006,

> The challenge now is to keep a strong presence in that area so the Taliban can't filter back in. The day the guns fell silent, the population started to move back in (the entire area had been abandoned for almost a month since the Taliban and the foreign fighters moved in). For the first time in that area, kids were out on the roads and families came up and shook our hands. It made it all worthwhile. Ian Plummer had kids hanging around his [LAV observation post vehicle] all day.
>
> For the past few days, it has been quiet at the gun position. [Lieutenant-Colonel Lavoie] has made every effort to get out to see the guns and talk to the troops. We were able to get the [tactical] recce out there today as well. Tomorrow, the gun troops finally start the [relief in place] back to KAF for a well-deserved break.[32]

What was missing, however, was a strong Afghan security force presence to move in and hold the region. MEDUSA itself had been conceived in four phases: shape; strike; exploit; and stabilize. Afghan security forces had been important for the first three phases but they were critical to the fourth.

There had only been some 3,700 police for all of Helmand and Kandahar provinces and they had suffered 500 casualties and another 500 desertions. As for the Afghan army, most of those were employed with the American Special Forces. There was clearly a competition for the scarce Afghan manpower. Only a small handful would be available to help the Canadians in Pashmul.

Taliban improvised explosive device (IED) attacks resumed almost immediately. Captain Ian Plummer, with B Company, recalls,

> Driving back to KAF after MEDUSA [two] LAVs up from me (platoon commander Captain Piers Pappin) got hit by a [suicide vehicle borne] IED. (I was told the largest to hit Canadians at the time) knocked his driver unconscious and blew out all eight tires. The explosion was so big that I thought it hit the [company commander's] LAV between us. Something dented in the [company commander's] helmet. It also blew a handset off a dismounted radio in my bin and left [the insurgent's] body parts all over my LAV.[33]

No Canadian died in that incident. Harder hit was A Company on the 18th when a suicide bomber rode his bicycle into a group civilians and a group of soldiers on patrol. The bomb killed 4 Canadians and wounded 10 Canadians and 27 Afghan civilians including children.[34]

By October 2006, some 800 Taliban had seeped back into the area. In Helmand, the attacks had continued unabated and would even force the British into a peace agreement with the Taliban for Musa Qala. It wouldn't last long. Dadullah Lang's offensive may have suffered setbacks, even major setbacks, but overall, it would continue to be a rousing success. As historian Carter Malkasian would observe, "By the end of the year, Taliban had taken most of Zabul, Farah, Uruzgan and Ghazni. They controlled so much territory that, with Kandahar City almost surrounded, they could foreseeably threaten the survival of the Afghan government...The era of hope and opportunity relapsed into civil war, the new definition of Afghanistan."[35]

That was yet to come. In the immediate aftermath of MEDUSA, however, Canadian gunners would continue to support the battle group's efforts to stabilize Kandahar province.

22

CONSOLIDATION

BY THE END OF SEPTEMBER, A Company and Captain Ryan Stimpson's G21 moved to Ma'Sum Ghar. Captain Ian Plummer's G22, elements of B Company and D Troop deployed back to Forward Operating Base (FOB) MARTELLO relieving the Dutch who had occupied it during MEDUSA. Captain Dan Matheson's G23 and Charles Company made the move to Sperwan Ghar on September 23, 2006. For the next three weeks their log would record predominantly illumination missions, improvised explosive device (IED) events, games of poker and one air strike on two Taliban occupied compounds. Signal intelligence intercepts reported that 10 insurgents were killed in the strike.

C Troop also moved to Sperwan Ghar, but not without difficulties. Sergeant Ken Leet's gun dropped a wheel into a wadi and damaged the gun. It was towed to Sperwan Ghar, but further examination showed that the gun needed to go back to Kandahar Airfield (KAF) for maintenance.

It was picked up by an American Chinook which resulted in a further problem. Airlifting the M777 was a new art for everyone and unfortunately on setting the gun down in KAF, it was "pickled" before being safely placed onto the ground. The fall caused extensive damage to its carriage which would need specialized welding.[1]

The situation raised issues with respect to the serviceability of the guns. Ken Whitnall, a life cycle materiel manager for guns recalls,

> *The situation was constantly critical, the US was very accommodating as much as possible but in many cases parts were just not available as the pace of parts manufacturing was set to feed the assembly plant at BAE Hattiesburg which was still in the early stages of production. In hindsight, it was almost fortunate that CFR 016 in 2006 and CFR 017 in 2007 sustained damage to their cradles and had to be back loaded to Canada. Those 2 guns were extensively robbed for parts and assemblies in order to sustain other guns for [operations] and training. The fact they were damaged beyond repair and fit*

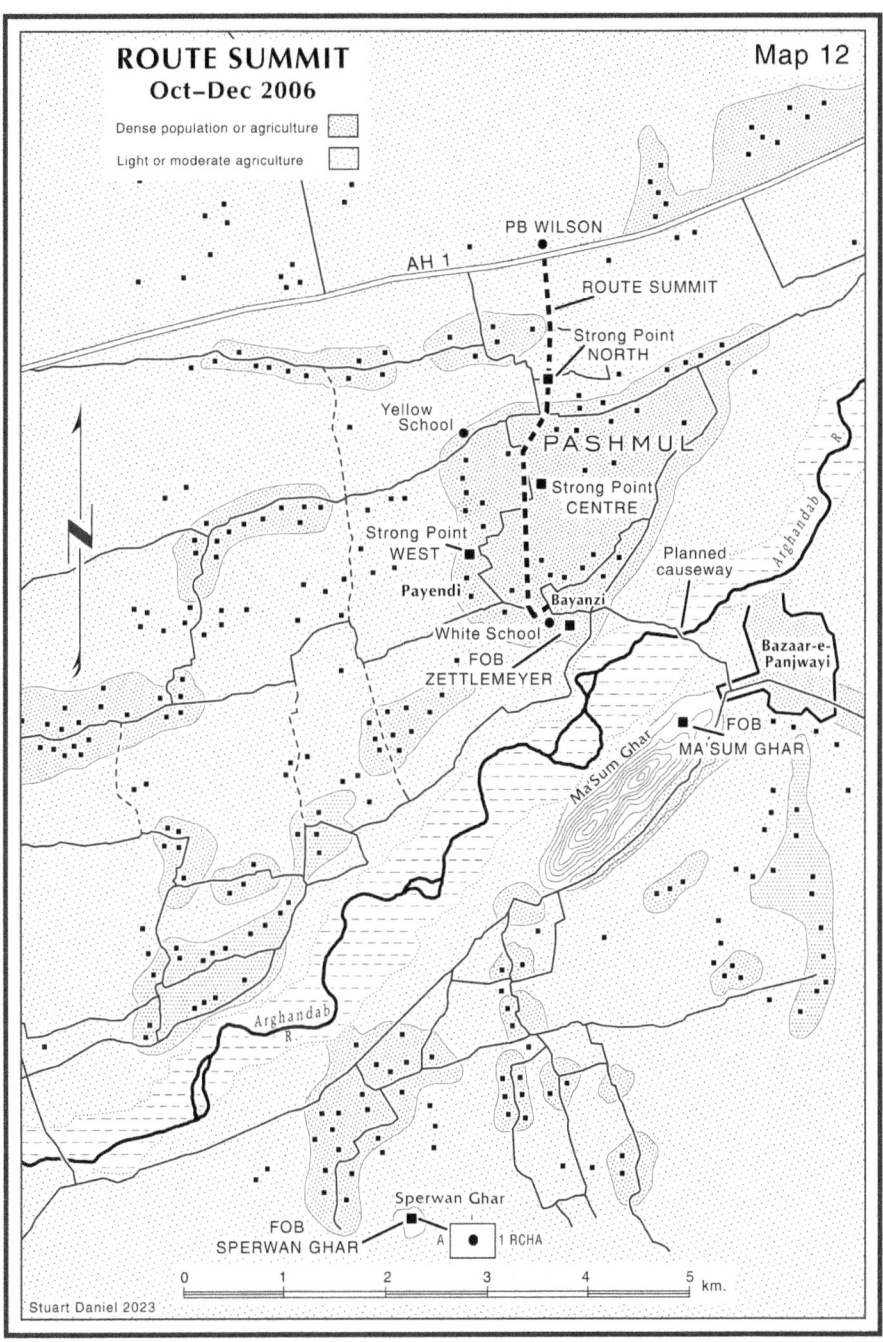

ROUTE SUMMIT
Oct–Dec 2006

Map 12

Dense population or agriculture

Light or moderate agriculture

PB WILSON

AH 1

ROUTE SUMMIT

Strong Point
NORTH

Yellow
School

PASHMUL

Strong Point
CENTRE

Strong Point
WEST

Planned
causeway

Arghandab R.

Payendi

Bayanzi

White School

Bazaar-e-
Panjwayi

FOB
ZETTLEMEYER

Ma'Sum Ghar

FOB
MA'SUM GHAR

Arghandab
R.

FOB
SPERWAN GHAR

Sperwan Ghar

A ● 1 RCHA

0   1   2   3   4   5 km.

Stuart Daniel 2023

for cannibalization did buy us some time. Two separate repair contracts were let to BAE for their repair but the list of removed assemblies for each gun was amended a couple times before the guns were finally shipped to Hattiesburg.[2]

The return of the Canadians to FOB MARTELLO came as a relief to the Dutch who were more than pleased to give the dust bowl back. MARTELLO had never been much more than an austere outpost walled with HESCO bastions and a few buildings set in a valley surrounded by hills. G22's position was on a ridge overlooking the valley. Here their light armoured vehicle (LAV) sat next to a small sandbagged bunker.

On October 2, 2006 shortly after their return, 122mm rockets flew at the observation post impacting within 30 to 50 metres of their LAV. The rockets had left a visible exhaust trail which pointed back at a Joshua tree across the way. The crew quickly spun up an 81mm mortar mission in response.

The next day was quiet but on October 4, 2006 another attack came in. This time everyone was more prepared for it. A patrol from B Company spotted the launch site within a few seconds. Unfortunately, they only had a map of Panjwayi with them rather than one for the Shah Wali Kot. D Troop fired a spotting round for the patrol. G22's Master Bombardier Justin Clarke recalls that the initial correction of "Add 4,000" pointed out that there were issues. D Troop's Captain Corey Gillis and the patrol would have to work out a different way to come up with a target grid reference. Eventually the troop responded with their rounds falling on the launch site.

The previous attack had also resulted in close air support being available for a response. In short order a British Harrier GR7 was brought in and attacked the launch site with rockets and an air burst bomb.

A patrol to the launch site subsequently did identify that it had been in use by the Taliban. A stone launch ramp covered in oil pointed towards G22's observation post. The Joshua tree in the distance had clearly been an aiming point that the insurgents used to help to accurately direct their fire. Curiously, shrapnel from the air strike had been tucked away and hidden under rocks around the site.

Engineers destroyed the Joshua tree with explosives. For the remainder of their time at MARTELLO, G22 was never again attacked by rockets.[3]

Lieutenant Walker remembers a similar situation at MARTELLO shortly after they had returned there from MEDUSA. The Dutch had experienced numerous attacks from the Taliban while the troop had been deployed south. Some of these had been so near that grenades had been thrown over the walls and into the compound. Now, upon their return, the troop and the rifle company that they supported were being mortared. Lieutenant Caleb Walker recalls, "We got mortared there a few times ... some of the mortars landed really close ... one of them landed 20 metres off the gun position."[4]

The company would send out daily clearing patrols around MARTELLO frequently augmented by one or another of the gunners from the troop's recce detachment. On this particular day, "Bombardier Jimmy Akeroyd was out with one of the clearing patrols ... they could see the puff of smoke where the mortar was firing and could work out where the mortars were coming from."[5] The patrol calculated the mortar's grid reference and relayed an all-arms call for fire on the company's radio net to Plummer's observation post which spun up a mission with the troop. The troop took post on the guns while the mortar rounds were landing around them and responded with counter mortar fire. Walker: "For that action, in helping to manage the team Warrant Officer [Maurice] Campbell [the troop sergeant major] got a [Commander Canadian Expeditionary Force Command] commendation for that. He was on the gun line, the tube line, the mortar rounds were coming in ... he was like standing out, standing up working with the team, motivating them."[6]

Between the patrol and the FOO, they "were able to adjust onto the mortar ... and they were able to destroy the mortar ... so we didn't get mortared for the rest of the time that we were up there."[7]

With Canadians in Kandahar wrestling with how to stabilize the post-MEDUSA situation, Gunners in Canada were working on putting meat on the bones of the army's 2005 field artillery transformation directive.

On October 3 and 4, 2006 senior gunners would be meeting for the artillery working group. The primary aim of the meeting was to revise and realign artillery transformation to the future army capabilities and force structure vision.[8] Lieutenant-General Mike Jeffery had set the initial transformation in motion. Lieutenant-General Marc Caron had issued the field artillery transformation directive. Since June, there had been a new chief in town. The army was once again in the hands of a gunner, Lieutenant-General Andrew Leslie. He would be the Chief of the Land Staff for the next four years.

In the summer of 2006, the incoming Commandant of the Royal Canadian Artillery School (RCAS), Lieutenant-Colonel Brian McPherson, had recognized the challenges that artillery transformation would bring. He had realigned staffing within the school to create a Chief Instructor in Gunnery cell within the Field Artillery School. Major Renald Dufour was appointed the Chief Instructor in Gunnery and Master Warrant Officer Kevin Smith, as its Master Gunner. Their task was to focus on current and future artillery transformation initiatives. They provided a presentation to guide the working group's discussions.[9]

First and foremost, the M777 had now become the prime operational gun for the army. The foreign military sale for an additional six howitzers and associated equipment and services for an estimated price of US$17,727,189.00 had been signed on September 26, 2006.[10] With twelve guns in hand, the artillery could deploy a battery of six guns and have another six guns for training and as spares. The remaining howitzer fleets were now relegated to the status of training fleets.[11]

The army commander's vision and direction had been set. The focus was clearly on the formation of battle groups tasked for Afghanistan for the foreseeable future. This meant modular artillery batteries. The objective for the workshop was how to implement the vision over the upcoming few years.

For the first year the emphasis was on converting the personnel gained from eliminating two gun detachments per battery into a more robust battery fire support coordination centre (FSCC) and a third forward observation officer (FOO) party. This group—the FSCC and FOOs—now known as tactical groups—would form the core of any deployed artillery battery. Mission-tasked batteries would be assembled by troop building blocks starting with a tactical group. To this would be added a varying number of gun troops and surveillance and target acquisition (STA) troops.[12]

The plan for the second year was to convert one gun battery in each of the three regiments—less their tactical group—into STA batteries. Each STA battery would be formed of two miniature unmanned aerial vehicle (UAV) troops and one radar and acoustic sensor troop.

The meeting also received an update as to the state of equipment acquisition. In addition to the six new M777s being fielded, it was confirmed that the artillery would maintain its commitment to the Sperwer flight until at least the end of Task Force 3-07. The Royal Canadian Air Force would continue to generate the capability until 2009. In addition, the ten Skylark miniature UAVs were being converted from analogue to digital systems. The end state would have four systems deployed in theatre and six at the RCAS in Gagetown.[13]

For acoustic sensors, the plan was to acquire three of the Leonardo Hostile Artillery Locating System II, or HALO II. One would be for deployment to theatre, one for the RCAS and one for whichever unit was on the road to high readiness. These would be in hand by November and deployable with Task Force 1-07 In January.[14]

For radars, the ongoing plan was to acquire between 10 and 12 AN/TPQ-50 lightweight counter-mortar radars. Actual numbers and distribution was not yet certain but they were expected by the end of 2007. Five would be deployed in theatre, three stay with the units, and the remainder at the RCAS.

At the further end of the horizon were considerations for a small UAV—something that fell in between the Skylark miniature UAV and the Sperwer tactical UAV—and an artillery locating radar system.[15]

Much of the discussion was how to affect the manning of these various systems and the training on them. There was no increase in manpower associated with their acquisition. The requirement for a ten person M777 detachment compounded this problem.

The training issue, naturally, addressed the limited availability of staff to grow training within the RCAS. Appropriate maintenance and support personnel for the equipment was also an issue, seeing that it was all coming under unforecast operational requirements. Dufour pointed out that, "The fielding of new capabilities ... mostly acquired through the [unforecast operational requirement], has generated many second and third order impacts translating directly into increased workload for the Centre of Excellence and the field force not fully accounted for."[16]

Being touched on as well were issues being faced by air defenders. They were looking at realigning to a mixed air defence and a counter rocket, artillery, and mortar—CRAM—capability. The final decision on canceling the upgrade of the tracked, missile-equipped air defence anti-tank systems into a LAV-based multi-mission effect vehicles for the 4th Air Defence Regiment, RCA (4 AD Regt) was only a month away, but contingency plans were already being considered.[17] Dan Ross, the Assistant Deputy Minister (Material) at the time recalls, "No one believed that you needed air defence at all. We were out of Europe, NATO had total air superiority in every mission they had been in, weaponized drones weren't on the radar screen by opponents at that point ... If you don't have a sponsor that believes in you, your capabilities disappear pretty quick."[18]

A few months later, Lieutenant-General Leslie would inform the House of Commons' Standing Committee on National Defence that the air defence anti-tank systems would probably remain in service until 2010.[19] The air defence community had been given a warning.

Underlying much of the discussion was the army's formative thinking which would lead toward the 2007 publication "Land Operations 2021: Adaptive Dispersed Operations—The Force Employment Concept for Canada's Army of Tomorrow."[20] At the heart of this concept were two entities: the joint, interagency, multinational and public (JIMP) enabled brigade or task force,[21] and the optimized battle group. Essentially these modular organizations would form the base structure of the army. What form these entities would take was to be the subject of further study and experimentation.[22]

One thing that was clear was that manpower was an issue. Reservists had been playing a significant role in augmenting deployed batteries and in Task Force Afghanistan as a whole. One of the conclusions of Dufour's report was that "the reserve part of Artillery transformation should be re-examined and formalized into [Land Force Reserve Restructure] key documents."[23]

While the future of the artillery looked more promising than it had when the M109s were withdrawn, there was much to do and many challenges to come to grips with.

In Afghanistan, October 5, 2006 marked a change for the Americans. On that day, Combined Joint Task Force-76 formally became the International Security Assistance Force's (ISAF) Regional Command (East) headquarters. Major-General Ben Freakley retained command of the American forces in the region but also became the deputy commander for security operations to ISAF under General Richards.[24]

While gunner leadership in Ottawa had been wrestling with a change agenda, Coalition Task Force AEGIS, had basked in a brief post-MEDUSA euphoria. It now turned its attention to stabilization through Richards' Afghan Development Zone initiative. Task Force 3-06 redeployed and re-tasked its forces accordingly.

The order of the day was "construction". Both the Sperwan Ghar and Ma'Sum Ghar land features needed extensive development to become proper FOBs. In order to connect these two new locations with the existing Patrol Base (PB) WILSON, and to allow a company to dominate the Pashmul area, a secure road was needed. Money was pledged by Canada, the US, and Germany. Route SUMMIT was a go. Getting the pledged funds paid out would be a chore and would force the construction to be dragged out.

Several platoon-sized outposts would be set out along the approximately 6 kilometres of the road. Strong Point NORTH, was located approximately a kilometres and a half south of PB WILSON. Strong Point CENTRE a further kilometre and a bit further down. The south would be anchored by a small FOB in the area of the white school. It was destined for the Afghan army and called FOB ZETTLEMYER. Eventually, circumstances dictated that a fourth—Strong Point WEST—needed to be added a little less than a half of a kilometre southwest of Strong Point CENTRE.

Having already suffered 15 killed and 85 wounded, and with the mandatory home leave program now in full swing, the battle group was stretched thin indeed.

Punctuating the construction were never-ending IED strikes. Even more unexploded IEDs were being turned up in the freshly dug road by the engineers' clearance teams. Clearly, the Taliban had their eye on the project and were taking advantage of knowing exactly where the Canadians were operating.

While construction was happening to the east, Matheson's G23 at Sperwan Ghar was asked to provide a show of force mission on October 12, 2006. It was for an Afghan army patrol accompanied by an American embedded training team member. The patrol's objective was a compound nicknamed "the Alamo". With the requested preparatory fire mission complete, Matheson decided to keep an eye on the patrol. Sure enough it ran into a major fire fight at the objective. C Troop, at the base of the Sperwan Ghar hill provided fire support to help them disengage. G23's log for that day stated,

> When [the patrol was] able to [withdraw] back, we opened up the floodgate
> of indirect [fire] and engaged the Alamo with 1 Gun and 3 Tubes. The time

of flight on the Gun was 7 seconds. We were punching holes in the walls. Slayer 13 dropped 3 X 500 [pound] and 2 X 1000 [pound bombs] and brought A10 in with a couple of strafe runs. We hit one grape hut, and it was destroyed completely. Definitely a secondary explosion as we know from MEDUSA that Grape Huts take more than one 500 [pound] bomb. Good day to be a gunner.[25]

The entry for the next day stated, "[intercepted communications] stated killed 30 [anti-coalition militia] and one Arab [commander] in yesterday's [troops in contact]."[26]

A further update on October 15, 2006 set the number of insurgents killed at 40. From this point forward the daily engagements started picking up.

In eastern Zhari, the first phase of building Route SUMMIT was the clearance of a swath several hundreds of meters wide through the heavily congested terrain. The work was engineer intensive involving the bulldozing of grape and marijuana fields, bulldozing walls and compounds, the explosive demolition of grape drying huts and the building of culverts for the numerous streams and canals.

It was midway during this phase, on October 14, that Major Greg Ivey's G29, found itself at Strong Point CENTRE. The strong point had recently become manned by Charles Company's 9 Platoon. It had previously been manned by elements from the intelligence, surveillance, target acquisition and reconnaissance (ISTAR) squadron. They had just traded places with Charles Company at Sperwan Ghar.

That morning, one of 9 Platoon's LAVs, Call Sign 33A, had been damaged by an IED in the road. It was recovered to PB WILSON where the section was medically checked out. The remaining two sections and the platoon headquarters were all at Strong Point CENTRE. Major Ivey picks up the story,

On 14 October 2006, the Commanding Officer's Tactical Group was conducting a line tour from the Forward Operating Base at Ma'Sum Ghar mountain back north to Patrol Base Wilson. The Commanding Officer's Tactical Group consisted of four armoured vehicles that travel in the following order of march: the Commanding Officer's LAV III, the Assistant Operations Officer's LAV III, the Regimental Sergeant Major in a RG-31 Nyala and the Battery Commander's LAV III. My vehicle was last in the order of march. This tactical group travels together and serves as the Commanding Officer's forward command post, or eyes and ears forward, as well as integral protection. In the Battery Commander's vehicle, the Battery Sergeant Major normally travels in the rear and provides rear area security for the vehicle. On this day, we also had two other passengers from the [miniature]

UAV Troop that we were taking back to Patrol Base Wilson: [Bombardier Theodore] Zaremba and [Master Bombardier William] Tiernay.

The line tour was to include a brief stop at one of Charles Company's platoon defensive positions and [Charles Company headquarters], known as Strong Point CENTRE since on this day … a local VIP visit was taking place.[27]

Their objective was to pick up a party of Afghan dignitaries and members of a civil-military cooperation element from the provincial reconstruction team (PRT). These individuals had been visiting the post, and were to be transported to PB WILSON. Considering the events later that day, it may be that the presence of these visitors prompted the Taliban to attack, but that is by no means certain. What was certain was that it was a well-coordinated attack hitting the battle group in five different locations simultaneously.[28] Ivey continues,

As we were transiting in a northerly direction along [Route SUMMIT] towards the Strong Point CENTRE, a threat warning was broadcast across battle group net indicating an attack on Canadian Forces in that area was imminent. As we slowed and dispersed the vehicles in front of the strong point, the Commanding Officer dismounted to discuss some issues with the Company Commander and to retrieve a few more passengers making their way back to Patrol Base Wilson. At this time, a second threat warning was broadcast indicating an imminent attack on Strong Point CENTRE. This threat warning was credible due to the nature of the source but it did not indicate whether it was a threat of mortars or a direct fire attack. At this stage the [tactical groups] vehicles were sitting still in front of the strong point; I ordered [my] driver to advance off of what I considered was a bit of a hill as I did not want be a stationary target. [Lieutenant-Colonel Lavoie] made his way back [to] his vehicle and mounted up as quickly as possible to move back to Patrol Base Wilson. Just as my vehicle started to roll forward with the remainder of the tactical group, rocket propelled grenades [(RPG)] and machine gun fire landed immediately behind my vehicle. The [tactical group] sped forward approximately 300 meters north, turned the LAVs back towards the enemy and returned fire as we took up new positions at [Strong Point CENTRE]. As we advanced back and took up firing positions, my gunner was firing the main gun while I was firing the pintle mounted C6 (until it jammed), and the crew did its best locate the enemy. It was during this time that two soldiers were killed and a number were injured from rocket-propelled grenades.

I initiated a fire mission immediately by giving our location, a direction of 4800 mils knowing the route ran directly north-south and added 600m to begin

a quick adjustment to cut off any exfiltration or support to the enemy firing positions; the enemy positions, although not confirmed immediately, would have had to have been within 150-400m based on the terrain to the south and west of Strong Point Centre. The enemy position was well concealed in a thick treed area near a canal or wadi system. We could see where the enemy was firing from but we could not see their exact locations. Furthermore, we believed that the attack was coordinated from a number of different locations, which meant that our flanks and rear were also at risk of attack. I personally saw at least ten rocket propelled grenades or anti-tank rounds impact around the strong point area. I also heard and saw the impact from machine gun fire onto the strong-point. The attack took place at approximately 1530 hours local. The sky was clear and the sun was off to the west. I distinctly remember the chaos on the battery [radio] net as we were trying to bark fire orders and [situation reports] to the command post over the noise and concussion of the main gun and C6s of our vehicle, coupled with the noise of the other LAVs to our left flank as we engaged what we could in a south west direction.

All [tactical group] vehicles were trying to jockey and stay mobile in what was a de facto fire base as best we could, but the ground was very limiting and we were still literally out in the open on [Route SUMMIT]. By this time the adjustment was underway and we brought the effects close in to the point where a lot of fragmentation was seen in and around our vehicles and I did not want to risk casualties to our left flank at Strong Point CENTRE because we knew there would be troops exposed outside vehicles and what not. We figured there was enough direct fire effects coming from the [company] position so I kept the artillery on top of the enemy and to their rear to suppress any reinforcement or withdrawal. As the Commanding Officer was jockeying for a new position of fire, his LAV became caught up in a grape ditch and it could not [manoeuvre] out on its own. We could also see it unfold off to our left. The vehicle and crew were trapped and exposed to enemy fire. [Lavoie] called for assistance over the radio so I manoeuvered the vehicle in front of the Commanding Officer's LAV and briefed the crew in the back over the intercom. [Battery Sergeant Major Bob Montague] could see what was going on through the back hatch so he knew what was happening and what needed to be done. As I positioned my vehicle in front of the Commanding Officer's vehicle, Monty dropped the ramp and dismounted with [Master Bombardier William] Tiernay without hesitation. [Corporal Joshua] Brophy and [Corporal Mark] Todorovic, both [The Royal Canadian Regiment] soldiers, dismounted from the Commanding Officer's LAV. These four soldiers conducted the recovery operation and local protection on the ground. My

[LAV] gunner maintained suppressing fire with the 25mm cannon while I focused on the artillery effects, which was now at a distance of 300 metres to our front, and the overall safety of our own vehicle. You could see fragmentation and small arms fire pinging off vehicles and kicking up dirt during this whole ordeal. The [commanding officer] laid down suppressing fire with the C6 pintle-mounted gun and his crew fired the multi-barrel smoke grenades over and in front of my vehicle to assist in screening our recovery procedure from enemy eyes. I won't lie, it scared the shit out of me at first because he didn't warn anyone that he would do that and my first though was that the front of my vehicle was going to catch fire with that shit going off everywhere in the bone dry heat...It should be noted that both Monty and Tiernay, despite not being LAV III qualified or even familiar with the recovery procedures for a LAV, dismounted to assist the soldiers under enemy fire.

Once the vehicle was towed forward and out of the grape ditch, both Monty and Tiernay proceeded to help put away the tow cables and equipment. He returned to the back of my LAV and raised the ramp and put his headset back on. We then moved back to a new firing position and both Monty and Tiernay continued to provide rear area security as if the event did not even happen.

However the event didn't end there...those remaining hours were more stressful than the actual combat earlier in the day. The [tactical group] spent the next 6 hours out in the open in a partial all-round defence assisting where we could with observation with Strong Point CENTRE. It was harrowing sitting there despite being in a relatively protected vehicle but we knew the enemy recoilless rifles and anti-armour weapons could cut through LAVs by this time. Daylight turned into darkness. We watched our arcs, we provided reports and returns, we didn't leave the vehicle; we cut the tops off of plastic water bottles to urinate and [simply threw] them out of the LAV. Batteries in our night vision gear would die and would require immediate replacement. A good lesson and reminder of the importance of basic soldier skills, vehicle drills and the need for all crew members to be completely familiar with the vehicle and where everything is kept.

Once the vehicle recovery operation and resupply activities at Strong Point CENTRE were complete, the [tactical group] moved back to Patrol Base Wilson. Most of the team met outside the [headquarters] building located inside the patrol base once we completed our own post op drills; we sat there for quite a while if I remember correctly, decompressed, and chatted about the day.[29]

Each of Montague, Tiernay, Brophy and Todorovic received a Mention in Dispatches for their actions that day.

The fight had been an intense one and had involved many. The LAV of Captain Dan Clark, the troop commander of 2 Troop, 23 Field Squadron, engaged and destroyed an enemy 82-mm recoilless rifle crew during the battle.[30]

It was 9 Platoon that had been hit the hardest, however. Their 33C LAV was parked close to an observation post manned by Private Jess Larochelle, which had come under heavy fire. A rocket-propelled grenade detonated after hitting the LAV's laser warning tower, spraying splinters down into the turret and killing Sergeant Darcy Tedford and Private Blake Williamson and wounding several others.

Master Corporal Jeremy LeBlanc, although wounded, rallied the section's survivors to return fire and tended to the wounded. He would be awarded the Medal of Military Valour.

Private Larochelle "although he was alone, severely injured and under sustained enemy fire in his exposed position at a ruined observation post, he aggressively provided covering fire [with a machine gun and light anti-armour weapons] over the otherwise undefended flank of his company's position." For this he would be awarded Canada's second highest award for valour, the Star of Military Valour.[31]

While the incident was one of tragedy and heroism there was also a touch of humour. G23's log would reflect the following for that day, "[G29's] first [troops in contact] and everything that they harp on us for came back to haunt them. No [situation reports] and stated they were in no position to conduct [forward air controller (FAC)] or Fire Missions. We've all been there so we understand the difficulty in coordination."[32]

While much of Charles Company had taken over the line at Route SUMMIT, Matheson's G23 had remained at what was now called FOB SPERWAN GHAR with C Troop. While things had quieted down again after the 12th, the gun troops were engaged in a mission virtually every day. On quiet days it might be just a few rounds of illumination and a registration mission. On heavier days, thirty or more high explosive rounds would be sent down range.

For G23, the tedium was interrupted on October 16, by a visit from the Canadian September 4, 2006 A-10 Incident Board of Inquiry. Concurrently new equipment, including infrared pointers, arrived for the FACs.

From time-to-time, E Battery would support local special forces missions. In particular, at SPERWAN GHAR, support would be provided to Task Force 31 elements who continued to operate from there. On October 18, Matheson accompanied a patrol, made up of members of Task Force 31 and the Afghan army, clearing the villages around the FOB.

The Americans had their own indirect fire support by way of a 120mm mortar and 100 rounds of high explosive, illuminating and white phosphorus. This came in a standard FOB kit that the US Special Forces utilized. They loaned it to the Canadians to use. Unfortunately, it did not come with any tabular firing tables. A late afternoon phone call on Friday, October 20 to the RCAS, caught Master Warrant Officer Kevin Smith just before going home. In very short order, and with the assistance of several others, Major Allan Finney, who was the Canadian Forces liaison officer at the US Army's Armament, Research, Development and Engineering Center at Picatinny Arsenal was able to obtain a set, digitize it and transmit it back to the battery.[33]

The mortar was also missing its sights. Warrant Officers Rod Gallant and Paul Penny found that the sights from one of the battery's 81mm mortars fit the bill and managed to get the whole system up and running. Firing data for bearing and range was produced by way of the Indirect Fire Control Computer Software and the elevation then determined using the tabular firing tables.[34]

On October 25, Matheson's G23 crew packed up and moved east to establish an observation post at the newly constructed Strong Point WEST. They occupied it the next day. The outpost was an Afghan compound which had been previously occupied by the Taliban. Small quantities of money, drugs and 7.62mm casings littered the area. Also found was an aiming post for a Soviet 82mm mortar. To aid in the position's defendability, the engineers had knocked out a section of the compound's wall so that the detachment's LAV could be backed into the yard.

To make the new crew feel welcome the Taliban mortared the compound the next day walking the rounds to within 15 metres of the compound perimeter. The detachment's FAC, Sergeant James Myler—Slayer 13—responded with a 1,000 pound bomb targeted on a suspected insurgent observation post. The following day the mortar started up again. This time the response was a heavy burst of high explosive and all the 30mm ammunition that two A-10s had brought with them. That quieted the Taliban down for the next day, giving G23 the opportunity to hand the position over to Stimpson's G21. Stimpson's crew would hold the position until November 2 to give G23 a few days at what was now FOB MA'SUM GHAR for some rest and change round on members coming and going on leave.[35]

Coping with 120mm mortars weren't the only new things that the gun line had to deal with. As October was coming to an end, digitization for the Triple Sevens had come to Afghanistan.

In Canada, by the end of July, firing trials had been done to determine the suitability of the new modular propelling charge systems with the range of Canadian fuzes. By the start of autumn, all the pieces for the system were complete. Mister Peter MacLean and his team at the Land Software Engineering Centre had done Yeoman service to have all the systems' software connected and working with each other. The system had been deployed with D Battery and was now ready for prime time in Afghanistan. It would be the closing of the first chapter of an extensive and complex program to rapidly deploy both a new howitzer and an incredibly sophisticated digital gun management system to the field under combat conditions.

In October a six-man technical assistance team was assembled to deploy to Afghanistan to install the equipment and to train the operators in its use. The first to go would be Mister David Ryan, the M777's life cycle materiel manager and Sergeant Peter Hoy, a radio operator working with the Microlight radio as well as two electrical and mechanical engineer technicians—Corporal Christian Gauvin and Corporal Justin Simms—to install the system on D Troop's two guns which were brought down from MARTELLO to KAF. In mid November Captain Lorne Doucet and Warrant Officer Alexander Sangster from the RCAS arrived to join the team.

With the first two howitzers digitized and tested out, they and the team moved out to FOB SPERWAN GHAR. Here the two digitized guns were set up in the middle of the position with the other guns flanking them. The team found itself having to conduct installation on the C Troop guns and the training for both of the troops' gun crews and command post staff in between operational fire missions. A few days of scheduled training ended up taking the better part of the week. Sangster at one point volunteered to fill in on a mortar detachment on a mission.[36]

Nonetheless, by the end of the month, all four of E Battery's guns were operating with the new system. The rapidity with which the system was deployed is particularly noteworthy. The Americans, who had been working on the M777 for several years, did not field their own Towed Artillery Digitization/Digital Fire-Control System for the gun until the following year.[37]

As October neared its end, the engineers' work on Phase 1 of Route SUMMIT—the work on demolishing and clearing a wide path from Highway 1 to the Arghandab River—was coming to an end. On October 21, 2006 the first signs of the incoming armour capability showed up. A Badger armoured engineer vehicle arrived and was assigned to 23 Field Squadron.

For Phase 2 the engineer effort of work was changing from the centrally controlled carving out of the route. Engineer resources were now decentralized and aimed at improving the strong points, the FOBs, and the two remaining sectors of Route SUMMIT itself. The companies were located with A Company at FOB MA'SUM GHAR, B Company at FOB MARTELLO, C Company at PB WILSON and the strong points, and the ISTAR squadron with both of E Battery's gun troops at FOB SPERWAN GHAR.[38]

Coalition Task Force AEGIS headquarters was going home. On November 1, 2006 it gave up its dual role by firstly transferring authority for Regional Command (South) to the command of Dutch Major-General Ton van Loon and his new multinational headquarters at KAF. Concurrently, command for the Canadian headquarters responsible for the Province of Kandahar went to Task Force KANDAHAR. Command changed to Brigadier-General Tim Grant, a former commander of 1 Canadian Mechanized Brigade Group in Edmonton. His staff, however, came from Petawawa's 2 Canadian Mechanized Brigade Group. Grant would also command Joint Task Force AFGHANISTAN which comprised all Canadian Forces not just in Afghanistan but in all of Southwest Asia.[39]

Going home with AEGIS were its principle artillery officers: its G3/chief of operations, Tim Bishop; its chief of fires and effects, Peter Williams; and its chief of fires, Tyler Kennedy. Replacing them at Regional Command (South) would be NATO officers; replacing them at Task Force KANDAHAR ... no one. With the reduced span of control, Task Force KANDAHAR was not provided with any artillery advisors, a situation that would continue until early into the new year.

Leaving with AEGIS as well was the brigade-level airspace coordination centre (ASCC) under 4 AD Regt's Major Blair Baker. Their function too would be taken over by van Loon's multinational Regional Command (South) headquarters. The 6-person ASCC at Task Force 3-06 under Captain Bill Warren would, however, carry on.

With the absence of an ASCC at Task Force KANDAHAR, the airspace coordination function was going through a doctrinal adjustment perhaps unique to Afghanistan. It was now a resource located only at Regional Command (South), which was growing into a divisional level headquarters, and at the Task Force 3-06 battle group headquarters. The unique structures of the national contingents and the geographic area each covered had a role to play in that. Unsurprisingly, more thought on how best to deploy ASCC resources would take place in the future. Further, the equipment holdings of the ASCCs (both at Task Force AEGIS and Task Force 3-06) were such as to keep it tied to buildings in KAF and dependent on the FSCC. The operational deployment of ASCCs in Afghanistan remained an evolutionary process. So too did the initiative back in Canada to develop a mobile ASCC mounted in a Bison armoured vehicle.

The lessons learned during this rotation highlighted the fact that Canada did not have its own radar in place to support the ASCC. It depended on an American radar nicknamed "TRUMPCARD" whose feed was filtered by the Americans and generally did not provide data below 5-7,000 feet. This meant that the ASCC did not always have full situational awareness of activities within its area of responsibility.[40]

It was clear that regardless of the future of air defence, the ASCC would have a role to play on future operations.

As Brigadier-General Tim Grant's headquarters got their feet on the ground, three new or augmented capabilities were entering the theatre of operations; capabilities that would add significant depth to the operations the Canadians could undertake.

Besides the Badger armoured engineer vehicles, Canada had sent over a squadron of 15 Leopard C2 tanks. They had been arriving since early October and were still being prepared for operations while their crews were training. The purpose of the tanks was to provide direct fire support to the infantry companies; support strong enough to punch through the concrete-like walls, grape huts and other buildings. It would give the battle group an option over and above precision artillery and air strikes.

In addition to the heavy armour, Canada was providing a hard but more subtle touch in the way of an expanded special operations forces capability.

Canadian special operations forces had been deployed to Afghanistan right from the beginning by way of the Tier 1 operators from Joint Task Force 2. On February 1, 2006 Canadian Special Operations Forces Command was formed and all special operations forces in Canada were placed under its command. More recently, on August 13, Canada had officially stood up the Canadian Special Operations Regiment, which was expected to grow to over 700 all ranks, but was still in its formative stages with less than half of that number.

In Afghanistan, Canadian special operations forces had taken a tactical pause starting in July while these organizations stood up. By October they had shaken themselves out and had prepared the necessary infrastructure in Afghanistan for their deployment. Starting that month, a Canadian Special Operations Task Force of some 250 operators and supporters from a squadron of Joint Task Force 2 and a company from the Canadian Special Operations Regiment, together with other enablers, deployed to Kandahar. They would be under the command of Lieutenant-Colonel Michael Rouleau.

Rouleau had started his military career as a gunner with the 5e Régiment d'artillerie légère du Canada. After nine years, he transferred to Joint Task Force 2 as an assaulter. In 1999 he took a brief break to be a civilian emergency response police officer, but returned to special operations after the September 11, 2001 attacks on the United States.[41]

Once deployed, the Task Force operated out of FOB GRACELAND on the western outskirts of Kandahar City. GRACELAND was also known by its US names of Camp GECKO and subsequently Firebase MAHOLIC. With this new deployment, the members of the Canadian Special Operations Regiment would take over the job of Tier 2 specialist support for Joint Task Force 2 that had previously been done by members of the American army's 75th Ranger Regiment.

This would be the only rotation with 250 personnel. Further rotations at that number were considered unsustainable.[42]

Last but not least, Canada was sending an additional LAV equipped company of 120 infantrymen from the Royal 22ᵉ Régiment under Major Louis Lapointe to form the force protection company for Lieutenant-Colonel Hetherington's PRT in Kandahar City. The task was to have originally fallen to A Company, but it had been continuously needed as a line company with the battle group. This brought Lieutenant-Colonel Hetherington's command up to roughly 330 military and a few individuals from the Department of Foreign Affairs, the Royal Canadian Mounted Police and the Canadian International Development Agency.[43]

This was a welcome situation for Grant's headquarters. With Operation MEDUSA behind them and some form of stability in the region, Task Force KANDAHAR could at last focus on a number of reconstruction projects. There were several issues which rose to the fore. Maintaining and growing the road network so that commerce could flourish was one of them. This included a stable border crossing at Spin Boldak. So was maintaining and rehabilitating the Dhala Dam located in the Shah Wali Kot, and providing irrigation to much of the Arghandab district.[44]

While construction on Route SUMMIT and the various FOBs continued, the battle group's rifle companies provided security and also undertook extensive patrolling throughout Panjwayi, Zhari, and around the Shah Wali Kot. Effectively throughout the month of November there wasn't a single day when the guns were not involved in at least one fire mission.

From time-to-time the guns themselves became the targets of attack. Bombardier Lucas Cunningham, a member of Sergeant Tim Hale's M777 gun detachment in C Troop at FOB SPERWAN GHAR remembers,

> We were in the FOB itself. [The] Taliban were using the black smoke from the FOB garbage pit to adjust their rocket and mortar rounds. They also used the slots in the grape huts to point their [assault rifles] out at us to shoot while staying hidden, however they were well out of effective range of the [rifles], probably about 400 [metres-plus] distance between us and them. We used our mortars in C [Troop] to chase away their mortar and rocket crews, while the Dragoons and Engineers used their LAV's and [Coyote surveillance vehicles] to dismantle the grape huts from the safety of the FOB. The Taliban only attacked us a few times like this, as they inflicted no casualties of any kind, and probably realized they were out gunned, like bringing a knife to a gunfight, except they brought rifles to an artillery troop and armoured and engineer troop.[45]

While the fighting season had died down with the weather—including a torrential rainstorm in the middle of the month that flooded out large swaths of Route

SUMMIT—IED's strikes were unending. The next Canadian fatalities would occur on November 27, 2006. That strike hit Task Force 3-06's tactical group as it was traveling west on Highway 1. The location was at the western edge of Kandahar City where an old Russian minefield lay opposite a small group of scattered buildings.

G29 was, once again, at the rear of the packet with Battery Sergeant Major Bob Montague keeping watch to the rear. To their front was the battle group's regimental sergeant major's Bison armoured personnel carrier.[46] Chief Warrant Officer Bobby Girouard had traded in his RG-31 for a Bison in order to be able to carry extra water, ammunition and medical supplies out to the troops as the tactical group made their rounds.[47] This was his first trip out since returning from leave.

Montague recalls the explosion happening to the front with a shower of debris raining down on their car. G29 proceeded past the blast site, which led to an initial impression that all vehicles had escaped unscathed. Unfortunately, Corporal Albert Storm, the Bison's driver, had been killed instantly. His foot had stayed pressed on the accelerator, so that the vehicle continued forward until it ran off the road about 200 metres further on.

Montague, and Master Warrant Officer Brad Montgomery, the engineer squadron's sergeant major, both ran to the stricken vehicle and were the first there. While Montague checked on Storm who had been killed by a head wound, Montgomery tried to help Girouard. Despite attempts at resuscitation, he too had died in the blast.

The attack had come by way of a suicide vehicle-borne IED in a van. What was left of the van could be stuffed into two barrack boxes. The rest of it, as well as the bomber himself, was scattered in small pieces around the blast site. In Montague's view the Taliban had missed a golden opportunity. If there had been an effective ground ambush coupled to the suicide bomber's attack, the tactical group would have been vulnerable and hard pressed to provide an effective defence.[48]

It wasn't just the Taliban, however, that were missing opportunities.

23

OPERATION BAAZ TSUKA: OUTREACH

WHEN GENERAL VAN LOON TOOK COMMAND of Regional Command (South) he faced multiple challenges, not least among which was the autonomy of the four major actors in the south: the Americans, British, Canadians, and the Dutch. Each had their own issues and approaches to the situations that confronted them. For the latter three, the mission had been sold by their governments to their people as helping the Afghans to reconstruct their devastated country through "whole of government" efforts. The Dutch government, in particular, distinguished their approach from that of the Americans. In the Netherlands the government distinguished between the American operations — an anti-terrorist campaign—with that of International Security Assistance Force's (ISAF)—one of reconstruction.[1]

For the Dutch, in Uruzgan, this approach would work in 2006. They would not be seriously challenged there until mid-summer of the following year. For the Americans, post-MEDUSA, this approach was problematic. Lieutenant-Colonel Don Bolduc, the commanding officer of Task Force 31 recalled,

> *One of the biggest obstacles was to convince [Major-General] van Loon that there could be no development without security. An active insurgency will not allow support to the locals. We needed to balance kinetic and non-kinetic operations in an intelligence-driven, full-spectrum campaign. It took about thirty days for him to realize this.[2]*

In fairness, the Dutch understood the basic concepts of counterinsurgency, albeit their emphasis remained on reconstruction. In an interview in late November, General Ton van Loon clearly stated that his priority was reconstruction. He planned to build on the Canadians' success during MEDUSA to spread into the rural areas to assist the population and the Afghan government.[3] Resources available to van Loon were an issue. His forces were short on helicopters, aircraft and psychological operations personnel. He also did not have a reserve which he could deploy in the event that the Taliban again threatened one of the regions as they had done in Pashmul.[4]

The Taliban, however, were not going to sit back.

> *The formation intelligence officers noted that the insurgents continued to conduct reinforcing and resupply operations with relative ease into the Zhari/ Panjwayi Districts as a result of ratlines coming out of the nearby Registan Desert and other lines of communication to the west...They further noted that the Taliban had established a very effective early warning network in the area and were capable of conducting coordinated ambushes on extremely short notice.[5]*

In response to this threat, ISAF ordered Regional Command (South) to conduct an operation to separate the hard-core Taliban from the local population and local augmentees. The operation would be conducted in several phases with manoeuvre elements. Taliban command and control centres and individual insurgents were to be targeted, isolated, neutralized and destroyed.[6] ISAF's emphasis, however, was on the immediate follow up. "As each village was cleared, the teams would gather the elders for a shura (village council meeting) to explain the plan for providing security and support. This helped to gain the support of the local populace."[7]

These would be accompanied, or immediately followed, by the development and manning of security outposts and quick impact projects.

Operation BAAZ TSUKA—Dari for FALCON SUMMIT—would include a multinational force. In addition to the Canadian Task Force 3-06, the American Special Forces' Task Force 31 would once again be involved with members from the Afghan army and police. There was also to be a company from the Dutch 12 Infanterie Bataljon for one phase of the operation. British special forces would again screen the far western end of the Panjwayi/Zhari valley throughout.

For this operation, the battle group would be deploying out of Patrol Base (PB) WILSON, advancing west along Highway 1 to the town of Howz-e-Madad and from there south.

A Company and Stimpson's forward observation officer (FOO) detachment, G21, occupied what had now become a proper forward operating base (FOB) at MA'SUM GHAR. With them were the Leopard C2 tanks of B Squadron of the Lord Strathcona's Horse (Royal Canadians) which had arrived earlier that month.

Captain Matheson's G23, had been encamped at Strong Point WEST since November 2, 2006 with elements of Charles Company. They were finally relieved on December 10, 2006 by Captain Plummer's G22, who, together with B Company, had been whiling away the hours at FOB MARTELLO. B Company had stripped MARTELLO and turned it over to the Afghan Security Forces. That done, they moved down to PB WILSON and took up security of that base and the strong points along Route SUMMIT. This freed up Charles Company—reinforced to four platoons and with the tanks of B Squadron and an engineer troop—to form Canada's first war-time square combat team since Korea.

G23 would first move back to Kandahar Airfield (KAF) for three days of maintenance to their light armoured vehicle (LAV). That done, they headed out on December 17, 2006 to FOB MA'SUM GHAR. Here they married up with B Squadron's tanks. Over the next few days, Matheson would make several trips to PB WILSON to work out the details of the upcoming operation.

The deployment of the tanks had initially been a contentious issue with the regional command's Dutch leadership. It felt that tanks had no role in a counterinsurgency operation. When the tanks had arrived Lavoie had gone on leave fully expecting them to be used during his absence in combat team operations. Upon his return he found they were still in KAF and that Regional Command (South) had refused authority for them to deploy outside the wire.

He went to see Brigadier-General Tim Grant, the commander of Task Force KANDAHAR about the situation. When he said to Grant that he wanted to speak to General van Loon about it, Grant told him, "Good luck. Because I can't convince the guy to do it." Lavoie did speak with van Loon. He argued that a tank firing one round of 105mm high explosive squash head at a building occupied by insurgents was less destructive than a 155mm from an M777 . The general conceded and the tanks were released.[8] Strangely enough, the Afghan government had no issue with the tanks. Lieutenant-Colonel Tom Bradley, a Strathcona and the chief of staff for Task Force KANDAHAR notes, "...President Karzai [in discussions with General Grant] said the tanks were an accurate way ... to do accurate, pin-point fire and there was absolutely no issue from the Afghan perspective with the way that the tanks were applying lethal force on target because it was directly on the target".[9]

When Captain Ian Plummer's FOO party had left MARTELLO, so too did Captain Cory Gillis's D Troop. While G22 went to occupy Strong Point WEST, the gun troop had carried on to what now had also become a proper FOB at SPERWAN GHAR. Here they had fallen in next to C Troop to form a single gun position. Both troops would remain here for the duration of the battery's rotation. With the two troop command posts colocated and winter coming in, activities slowed down. Lieutenant Caleb Walker, as the junior one of the officers on the gunline found himself responsible for early morning "check bearings"[10] for the guns and mortars and, when not engaged in long games of Euchre or Poker, the construction of a "Mega Bunker" to hold the troop's personnel. Walker had some doubts about the bunker's robustness and was surprised that it was still standing when he returned with Task Force 3-08 a few years later. Notwithstanding that the gunline was now together, the austere conditions remained. Food continued to be boil-in-a bag individual meal packs rather than fresh cooked meals. Water was such a precious commodity that even field expedient showers were not in use. Laundry exchanges were infrequent and troops lived in the same clothes for a week or two at a time.[11]

G22, meanwhile, wrestled with the austere conditions at Strong Point WEST, which, despite everyone's best efforts, was still an unpleasant place. Upon being relieved by G22, G23's log reflected the following entry, "December 13 - [relief in place] with G22. Good to see them for many reasons primarily because we are finally out of this hole called West."[12]

The main complaint about Strong Point WEST was the limited arcs of visibility. At best, they had 800 metres of grape fields to the west which were made up of row upon row of four to six foot high berms. These allowed insurgents to move in both unseen and protected from direct fire. To the south the visibility was approximately 200 metres. Ensuring friendly troop safety required a careful watch over the detachment's arcs of observation, and a constant monitoring of the nets to keep track of where all elements were manoeuvring. Accessing fire support was not a problem with the guns at FOB SPERWAN GHAR, and air support was on station roughly three times per day.

Task Force 31 had once again deployed their company level headquarters, Operational Detachment-Bravo 330, to FOB SPERWAN GHAR. With them were four Operational Detachments-Alpha, and three platoon-sized Afghan army companies. They would also have an American route clearance package and a Canadian engineer troop attached, and would be able to call on support from the Canadian guns.[13]

Prior to Operation BAAZ TSUKA there had been an extensive information operations campaign to warn the local population of what was about to happen. Phase 1 kicked off on December 17, 2006 when Task Force 31 pushed westward in Panjwayi district from FOB SPERWAN GHAR along the southern bank of the Arghandab River. The fields were no longer lush or green and hot like they had been for MEDUSA. Everything was dry, the fields empty, and the weather decidedly cooler. Notwithstanding, the push was slow and deliberate, as the teams and their Afghan allies cleared buildings one by one, covered by both guns and air support. Over the next three days the battery averaged firing fifty rounds of high explosive per day, with some smoke and illumination thrown in for good measure.

On December 19, American and British forces marked a particular success. They had been tracking Mullah Akhtar Osmani by cell phone signals. He was one of the three principal leaders of the Taliban and head of operations in the south. His vehicle was struck with a precision bomb killing him.[14]

In the face of Task Force 31's pressure, the Taliban's Tier 1 fighters did not stand.

They quickly fled. Instead of firefights, each day, *shuras* were held in the villages, humanitarian aid delivered, and arrangements for setting up security were worked out. While the Taliban did not fight they did leave behind weapons caches, booby traps, and dug in defensive positions which slowed the progress of the advance.[15]

Task Force 3-06 commenced Phase 2 of Operation BAAZ TSUKA, on the morning of December 20, 2006. Matheson's G23 FOO party and two troops of tanks left FOB MA'SUM GHAR and met up with the rest of the elements of their combat team, including a troop of engineers, two companies of the Afghan army and police, and last but by no means least, elements from Lieutenant-Colonel Hetherington's provincial reconstruction team (PRT). Overhead, a pair of Apache attack helicopters flew top cover.[16] G23's logs recorded, "The enemy ran away when they saw us coming ... On the objective [Howz-e-Madad] at 0900 [hours] and set [the] outer cordon quickly ...[PRT] conducted a Shura with local elders and started handing out [humanitarian aid] and [medical aid]."[17]

That aid came in the way of Chief Warrant Officer Frank Grattan and his team from the PRT who brought two cargo containers filled with items that would be of value in a rural village. They contained everything from diesel generators and fuel to shovels and wheelbarrows and even construction material and dried fruit. The force stayed in place for two nights while the PRT arranged for another cargo container.[18]

Hetherington was of the view that, "the [civil-military cooperation] platoon ... was the most flexible element of the [PRT] and I employed them similar to FOOs: [civil-military cooperation detachments] would be attached to the [companies of the battle group] to provide liaison, advice and a conduit back to the [team]."[19]

The concept of the cargo containers had come from a member of the PRT's staff.

> *During BAAZ TSUKA, the incredibly bright and resourceful [civil-military cooperation platoon commander, Captain] Harry Chadwick, came up with the idea of CIMIC "Bombs". These were sea containers that contained a variety of items that could be delivered anywhere to assist villages that were unlikely to receive support from elsewhere. The sea containers could be repurposed to become a checkpoint for the local police. Unfortunately, Harry wasn't a Gunner, but damn, that was a great idea. And they worked.*[20]

Within Task Force KANDAHAR these cargo containers were dubbed, "Village in a Box".

A police checkpoint was constructed overnight but surveillance reports disclosed that the Taliban were not completely gone and were busy planting improvised explosive devices (IED) on the routes heading south from Howz-e-Madad. Eleven illuminating rounds were fired that night but no high explosive.[21]

The next day became slightly more active with Predator sightings of Taliban mixed in with women and children. They were not engaged. Further signs showed women and children moving south as Afghan army units probed in that direction. That night G23's position was overflown by two rockets that impacted 500 metres away. E Battery's engagements had decreased notably. For the period December 21 and 22, only ten high explosive, three smoke, and twenty-three illuminating rounds had been fired.[22]

Reports were coming in that the Taliban had decamped for Maywand and Helmand. While a push to the south with PRT engagements would continue, the bulk of the B Company combat team was to withdraw to MA'SUM GHAR. Instead, they only went as far as PB WILSON and then waited for further orders.

South of the Arghandab River, Task Force 31 had the same experience as they pushed further west. Villages were cleared, *shuras* held, fortified police checkpoints built and humanitarian aid distributed. One noticeable problem was that as checkpoints were built and manned by the Afghan army or police, their already low numbers available for further offensive operations dwindled.[23]

On December 21, 2006, Operational Detachment Alpha 331 escorted a force of the Starthconas' Leopard tanks forward from MA'SUM GHAR to the edge of the village of Mushan. Here they provided a fire base for a Chinook helicopter insertion of a company of Dutch infantry on the 22nd. The Dutch seized the village, held a *shura* distributed a bit of humanitarian aid, and departed the next day.[24]

Phase 3 started on December 27. For this phase, Task Force 31, again supported by the Dutch infantry company, would cross the Arghandab River and move onto the villages of Nalgham and Siah Choy, and ultimately Sangasar.[25]

Task Force 3-06 would also regroup for this phase.

Stimpson's G21 stayed with A Company. B Squadron left MA'SUM GHAR and redeployed to the far western end of the area of operations. B Company with Plummer's G22 stayed at PB WILSON and the Route SUMMIT strong points, while C Company split itself between MA'SUM GHAR and SPERWAN GHAR. Matheson's G23 remained primarily at MA'SUM GHAR but would occasionally travel over to SPERWAN GHAR.

The battle group's intelligence, surveillance, target acquisition and reconnaissance (ISTAR) squadron would at first operate throughout the area of operations but then concentrate on seizing and holding the artificial hill feature in the western end of Zhari called Gundy Ghar. Stimpson and G21 would be ordered west to join them there. These deployments would continue until January 22, 2007 when preparations for the relief in place with Task Force 1-07 would begin.[26]

With the exception of December 29, 2006 and the period January 5 to 8, 2007 as the move to Ghundy Ghar occurred, ammunition expenditures ran very low and mostly to smoke and illumination. During this brief January interval of four days, high explosive expenditures averaged fifty rounds per day, and on January 7, 2007, 102 smoke rounds were fired.

On December 29, 2006 what became a fairly desperate engagement, had started innocently enough. Captain Ian Plummer's G22 in Strong Point WEST had been caught up in the home leave program of musical chairs. This shuffle attempted to balance the level of experience across all of the FOO parties when key personnel were away. On December 17, 2006 Master Bombardier Justin Clarke, G22's fire effects technician, departed on leave, while G23's forward air controller (FAC), Sergeant Maurice McGarrigle moved over to G21 to fill in for Sergeant Robin Everett. In return G21's Master Bombardier David Munro[27] reported-in to fill the vacancy in G22.[28]

The next several days saw a somewhat unusual combination of routine and eclectic activities that included celebrating The Royal Canadian Regiment's birthday on December 21, 2006 with the Ortona Toast, an early Christmas Dinner with General Rick Hillier and comedian Rick Mercer on December 24, 2006, and a fire mission on Christmas Day. On December 28, 2006 Captain Plummer received a warning order to move to PB WILSON on the next day to join the ISTAR squadron. Accordingly, G22 drove the four kilometres from Strong Point WEST to PB WILSON at approximately 1200 hours on December 29, 2006 and settled in with the squadron.[29]

The squadron planned to send troops out on various tasks, but this would not start until a few days later. G22 found itself unemployed, so all the radios except one were switched off and it joined the squadron net. One member of the crew in turn would stand radio watch while the others caught up on their personal maintenance and looked after the vehicle and its equipment.

Captain Plummer walked over to the miniature unmanned aerial vehicle (UAV) troop tents to visit with Sergeant Jeffery Hinch (they had been reserve force non commissioned members and had done Qualification Level 3 training together in 1995.) He and Hinch were playing a board game of "Axis and Allies" when a runner arrived to fetch him to the command post and to have his crew rejoin the B Company net.[30]

By the confused traffic it was obvious something was going on, and it soon became clear it involved an attack on Strong Point WEST. The outpost was manned by Captain Piers Pappin's 4 Platoon along with an American embedded training team, and some Afghan army troops. It was, in Pappin's words, "a fairly conventional defensive position. We had built an obstacle belt out front and patrolled the terrain to our front (up to 2 kilometres out) very aggressively—all very doctrinal, clearing patrols in the morning, ambushes at night, etc."[31]

Captain Plummer recalled that,

> 21A [commanded by Sergeant Byron Sheppard] was in the southwest and the American [training] team was at the southeast corner viewing Route Summit. The former was facing...grape fields....Approximately 210 metres to the south of 21A was a grouping of buildings which ran East-West...and up to Route Summit.[32]

The Taliban had previously mounted attacks on the outpost using the grape fields for cover and concealment. Most only lasted for an hour or so, but this night would be different. Back in PB WILSON Captain Plummer assessed the situation as best he could and began to initiate fire missions. In his words it was,

> [v]ery confusing. I listened to find out what was going on, picked grids ... approximately 500 [metres] away to ensure safety ... Well next thing I did was send the [fire mission] and put [at my command] in effect. I then spoke with 21A or the [company commander] to see what they wanted me to do. I believe [a quick reaction force (QRF)], with Dan Matheson, was moving in around this time. The infantry told me to shoot ... I checked for patrols etc out there, spoke to Dan on the radio and started shooting. I then asked 21A for corrections. Basically he said to keep shooting ... I kept asking for corrections and they said either the enemy was still shooting or keep shooting guns. I used direction 6400 and moved the rounds generally [North] and [South] 500 [metres] from the strong point. I remember [Warrant Officer] Gallant ... asking constantly for [situation reports] and the Infantry net being super busy and unavailable for providing them to me. I just kept telling him repeat or Drop 50 repeat etc. I ended up having some air on station and (I think it was [G23's Captain Dan Matheson] or Sgt Myler) controlling an [attack helicopter] and no one could see anything. I was a bit concerned about dropping as I wasn't really sure where the [enemy] was so I didn't drop anything and kept firing arty to the [southwest].[33]

While G22 was engaging targets, Captain Dan Matheson and G23 came up from FOB SPERWAN GHAR with the company commander of Charles Company and 7 Platoon as the QRF. Since G22 had the artillery in hand, and the helicopters couldn't locate targets, Matheson's LAV joined in with the platoon in fighting with their LAVs' armament.[34]

Plummer continues,

> *I remember this lasting hours...Eventually Sergeant Sheppard said the enemy was south in the building and to shoot there. I picked a grid off the Falcon View, I was there earlier so knew which buildings. I think the Infantry had marked the buildings as aiming marks for their mortars as well even. Anyway I picked the grid, gave a direction of 6400 and Drop 200 to move the rounds 400 meters south for safety ... [G]enerally the rounds were on or up to 200 meters away. I did this for safety. The guns fire Proximity and Sergeant Sheppard says move the rounds north. I moved the rounds north 50 meters I believe then repeat. As I recall, this happened a couple of times. He says to move the rounds north 200 meters and made a point that it was definitely 200 meters. The enemy was in the field. I think he wanted me to go faster as well. I was doing the math of 200 meters south of the initial grid [followed by] the corrections and thought it was close but okay. I thought he was confident and sent "Add 200 Repeat". Well the rounds came in just to the south of the wall in Strong Point WEST, basically 20 [metres] from their LAV. I spoke to them the next day and they showed me. The next thing I hear is "Check firing, check firing you just blew up 21A" from the American [call sign]. I sent Check firing on the [artillery] net and waited to find out what happened. The [company commander and 2nd in command] were both trying to get a hold of 21A and I sat for the worst 3 minutes of my life. I was sure that I had killed them. Anyway after about 3 minutes Sergeant Sheppard got on the radio and told me to shoot south 200 meters. I have the correction and repeat.*[35]

The version of events of Sergeant Byron Sheppard, the section commander of call sign 21A, who clearly knew his business, closely matches that of their FOO. He says,

> *I will add that the enemy seemed to be everywhere, and I was sure they were trying to get inside our strong point. My LAV had taken several direct hits from RPG [rocket propelled grenade] fire, and my Crew Commander with the use of his thermal sight was sending me grids every time he spotted the enemy. We opened up with every weapons system we had, but the most effective weapon of all was then, [Captain] Plummer's M777. The enemy was firing at us from ditches, grape huts, and built up areas with thick mud roofs and walls. They made several attempts to cross the open stretch of ground from the village to our south to the gate of our strong point at which they were stopped several times with the call of a new fire mission. I have completed*

three tours in Afghanistan, and this was by far the longest and most intense firefight I have ever been involved in.

I do recall the one round of 155 that impacted close to our LAV and it was my mistake, and a bad correction on my part. It was simply a mistake of drop instead of add on my part. The number of rounds fired that night was very high, 112 [rounds] of 155[mm] and I can't even remember the number of 60mm we fired. But we did not take any friendly casualties that night and never saw any more enemy activity in that area for another 22 days and when they did attack later in Jan it was mostly hit and run.[36]

During this contact Captain Plummer had tried to control some aircraft, but they were unable to spot the enemy despite several attempts to do so. A B1B bomber did drop a GBU38 bomb south of the strong point, but Sergeant Sheppard did not see it detonate and declared it a dud. They called for a reattack and radioed their intent to the company commander. At this point the battle group commander advised that he had seen the detonation and cancelled the further run. After a long night of fighting the Taliban had had enough and broke contact. It had been a near run thing.[37]

The next morning Captain Plummer returned to the strong point with the company commander. He later recalled,

I felt pretty bad about everything and expected the troops to hate me to be honest. Anyway pretty much the first thing [Sergeant] Sheppard did was apologize for saying north 200 meters. I said it was my fault and that I hoped everyone was okay. I walked around to see the troops and they looked kind of like zombies. Tired and kind of spaced out. One of the [warrant officers] said they brought up a ton of 60 mm mortar ammo which was fired and the position had, I think 1 LAV manned, 3 [observation post] positions with a 60 mm position inside the walls. [Sergeant] Sheppard, after the round landed too close, had to run around and check on his guys which is why there was a 3 minute pause on the radio and no one could get a hold of him. He said the LAV would point to the south and get hit from the west. It would traverse west and then get hit from the south. We had fired some illuminating rounds the night before and I guess they told me not to do that as they figured the illuminating was working for the enemy to hit the LAV. I was pretty angry because if I was there, which I was the day before, I could have dropped bombs/arty all day long on the exact positions and stopped the [troops in contact] almost immediately. I was relieved that the section was okay and then I then went back to [PB WILSON] and carried on with ISTAR Squadron.[38]

The next morning patrols found blood trails and debris that indicated the Taliban had suffered some casualties. A few days later a member of the PRT had a *shura* with some local leaders who indicated something like 15-25 wounded Taliban. The defenders of Strong Point WEST suffered no casualties.[39]

Having joined up with the ISTAR Squadron, Plummer and G22 would now carry on to the west end of the area of operations for the better part of a month to seize, hold, and set up a police checkpoint at the artificial hill feature of Ghundy Ghar. As January turned to February and the imminent battle group relief in place, G22 would return to B Company and FOB MARTELLO to close out their tour.[40]

If there is one thing to say about the miniature UAV, it's that they failed to live up to their potential despite the best efforts of everyone involved.

One must take into consideration, however, where the Skylarks fit into the grand scheme of things. The top of the food chain belonged to the Predator. These large aircraft not only came armed with precision missiles that could immediately strike a target once found, but they also had an excellent surveillance package. Their sensors, like most American aircraft, could be linked to a small computer ground station like the remotely operated video enhanced receiver—ROVER—which was on wide distribution amongst American joint terminal attack controllers (JTAC), but only slowly making it into the hands of allied, including Canadian, FACs.[41] Predator feeds, and radio linkage to the Predator's pilots, quickly became the surveillance and precision attack tool of choice for the ground troops.

The second tool was the Canadian tactical UAV, the Sperwer, operated by the RCAF in a mixed RCAF and army flight of some 56 people. It was neither armed nor could it provide a ROVER feed. Instead it would provide its excellent video feed to a limited number of proprietary ground receivers. The previous roto had employed one of those with the commanding officer's tactical headquarters but Task Force 3-06 had opted to have these located at their tactical operations centre in KAF.

Sperwer had been useful but the noise of the aircraft limited its ability to "sneak and peek". In addition, spare parts and daytime heat continued to be a troubling issue. Nevertheless, the flight continued to experiment with techniques including the use of the vehicle to control indirect fire.[42] Notwithstanding that the "Flying Ski-Doo" was the butt of some jokes, it proved useful not only for reconnaissance, but as a diversion tactic the way it had for Task Force ORION. In short, in Lavoie's view, Sperwer was punching above its weight.[43]

Skylark had problems. Some were technical, others were conceptual.

On the technical side was the issue of frequency management. A Skylark was flown by way of a radio link between the operator and the aircraft. If the link was broken then the aircraft would automatically return to its point of launch. The problem encountered was that all too often that link would go down making the aircraft unreliable to the supported companies. The reason that the link went down took a long time to uncover but it was eventually determined after this tour that often it was as a result of friendly forces' frequency jamming provided by nearby Bison-mounted mobile electronic warfare teams. The jamming was mainly aimed to defeat enemy IED control systems. Attempts to get at the root cause of this was stymied by communications security concerns by people in the forward areas.[44]

Also problematic was that the Skylark's imagery went back solely to the operator who would need to be close to the local commander in order to provide him with the information revealed by the aircraft's imagery. The teams were never properly integrated into the companies to be able to do so. Everyone on the rotation understood the principles of miniature UAV operations but could never work out the practical aspects.[45]

Greg Ivey, the battery commander summed up his views on Skylark, like this,

> *The mini-UAV project and [operational] deployment has been nothing less than a disappointment. Bits of night kit have only just arrived despite having emails from [the Directorate of Land Requirements] stating that the kit would be in theatre before our arrival. I'm convinced that the [troop commander, troop sergeant major and liaison officer positions] are no value added—maybe the [troop sergeant major] but that's it. I think all these positions were based on some sort of centralized approach where mini-UAVs would be held at KAF and then missions tasked from a central location. I'm no UAV expert but I do know that the intent of the mini-UAV is for immediate tactical information—time and space do not permit a centralized approach. The [tactical] UAV yes, not for a mini. Each [detachment] of three guys gets farmed out [under operational control] to a [company]. It's such a simple concept but we've overcomplicated everything—I have an email from an air force [Lieutenant-Colonel in Ottawa] giving me "authorization" to fly, flight permits and a whole bunch of other crap that clouds the purpose of the mini-UAV...it is a model airplane that flies over the next bound for the [company commander]. Nothing more, nothing less. Others in Ottawa may argue but out here I don't care about flight permits and risk assessments—just fly the thing. It will be invaluable to the [companies] once it's up and running.[46]*

The upshot of the technical and employment issues was that the number of usable aircraft dwindled to zero due to various problems. The miniature UAV troop would spend much of its time providing security at PB WILSON rather than flying aircraft in support of patrols. In the words of Lieutenant-Colonel Lavoie, "Welcome to the infantry."[47] Captain Andrew Lockridge had started his job as troop commander of the miniature UAV troop very excited, but as the tour wore on and the problems became insurmountable everyone became very frustrated. The capability was stuck with an undeserved bad reputation.[48] It would be up to future troops to wrestle with the issues.

On January 15, 2007 Operation MOUNTAIN FURY would come to an end. Operation BAAZ TSUKA would be scaled back on January 22, and ended on February 7.[49] It was not so much because the job was done but because new rotations were happening. In many ways, BAAZ TSUKA set the conditions for the relief in place that followed being a quiet, uneventful handover.[50]

The British commander of ISAF, General Richards would soon be replaced by American General Dan McNeill. Major-General Freakley and his 10th Mountain Division team was on their way home as well, to be replaced in Regional Command (East) by Major-General Dan Rodriguez and Fort Bragg's 82nd Airborne Division under the designation Combined Joint Task Force-82. Their main troop contingent would be Task Force FURY formed by the Airborne's 4th Brigade Combat Team. In acknowledgment of 2006's uptick in Taliban activity, the outgoing Task Force SPARTAN—3rd Brigade Combat Team, 10th Mountain Division—would be extended in Afghanistan for an extra three months effectively doubling the American's combat power in Regional Command (East) for the early part of 2007.

No such luck for the Canadians. Task Force 3-06 was about to be replaced by Lieutenant-Colonel Rob Walker's Task Force 1-07 formed around the 2nd Battalion, The Royal Canadian Regiment from Gagetown. The gunners of E Battery would be turning over their guns to their sister battery, Major Dan Bobbitt's D Battery. They would arrive with a fourth FOO party, a third M777 troop, and additional surveillance and target acquisition (STA) equipment.

E Battery had arrived in the middle of a massive Taliban build up at the height of the fighting season. They would be leaving when enemy contacts were limited and fire missions few and far between. IED strikes, on the other hand, were becoming frustratingly commonplace. Rather than a sweltering summer with 50° Celsius temperatures, it was a cold and wet winter.

Battery Sergeant Major Montague recalls,

> When the battery deployed back to Canada, the handover was done in the field. The incoming troops were given issue cards for their particular items or vehicles, they carried out a kit check and signed the cards once satisfied. They arrived by helicopter and the aircraft returned carrying E Battery personnel. In contrast, when the battery deployed, the changeover with A Battery was done at KAF.[51]

G23's Master Bombardier Kevin Bannister diary from his last day in theatre read as follow,

[January] 29th 2007. (Last day in Panjuai)!! Woke up at 0200hrs for my shift. 0240hrs [chaos] comes over the radio, 4 [Afghan police] check points were in a [troops in contact].The QRF [quick reaction force] was called out. By the time they got there it was over. Taliban harassment force I guess, what a joke! The [contact] was at the far west of our position so after the quick [orders] Group we did a 20 [kilometre] patrol and found nothing, like I always said - farmers during the day, Taliban at night. No injuries this day, thank you, god. Got back at 0630hrs and slept until 1000hrs. Back to KAF tonight-can't wait. Called my boys on the [satellite] phone-talk about uplifting!! Donny, Steve and I did a Registration Mission before we left, (The Last Fire Mission G23 ever did as a team) Made up my [target] list for the next crew and left Panjuai for the last time. Thank god. Arrived at [FOB MA'SUM GHAR] at 1700hrs, met up with 129, his crew and [the commanding officer's tactical headquarters] and left [MA'SUM GHAR], still have to drive to KAF, not over yet (they like to hit us when the tours over- Taliban morale booster) MADE IT!! Yeah!! Arrived at KAF at 2330hrs. Took a long deserved shower and went to bed, finally a real bed. Well G23 we did it and went through a lot of heartbreaking and scary moments but got through it.[52]

The maintenance of their equipment and handover to D Battery's G13, whose personnel were provided from the 1st Regiment, Royal Canadian Horse Artillery (1 RCHA), would extend over several days. G13's FOO, Captain Jeff Francis would arrive later so most of the handover was handled by the incoming G13 Detachment Commander, Sergeant Clay Cochrane. They knew they were getting Captain Goddard's LAV but since its current crew had made it through unscathed, the new crew would dub itself "Lucky 13". Regrettably, that was not to be.[53]

Captain Matheson would deploy several times with the new D Battery detachment and their supported company. This company too were augmentees to TF 1-07 coming, in this case, from the Para Company of the 3rd Battalion of the Princes Patricia's Canadian Light Infantry.

For G22's Captain Ian Plummer, the relief was timely. The six month tour had worn him down and the physical activity with the heavy loads they had to carry and the living off individual meal packs had caused his weight to drop, including muscle loss, from 190 to 165 pounds. He recalls that, "it was a bit of shock to see a new motivated team and compare with my run down status."[54]

For the entire gun line, the relief in place went smoothly at FOB SPERWAN GHAR. Handovers were done within the FOB and the junior ranks sent back to KAF while the leadership stayed for anywhere from two to three days of "left seat/ right seat".[55]

G22's Master Bombardier Justin Clarke recalls leaving Afghanistan early because his wife was about to deliver their first son. They had been deployed at Strong Point WEST and he caught a ride to FOB SPERWAN GHAR and from there a Chinook to KAF.

For his chalk, decompression took place over four days at a hotel in Cyprus. Lectures on mental health and post traumatic stress started early each morning to the displeasure of the many who had made a late night of it the previous day. Afternoons and evenings were free time. While there was no one else from G22 with him, a few gunners from G21 and others from the battery were on the same flight giving them an opportunity to unwind together. There were a variety of choices of recreational activities available to choose from, and they were provided with some cash to pay for them.[56]

Clarke would also experience what would become a standard situation for many gunners. Almost immediately after coming off paternity leave, he was slotted into the next round of predeployment training for his role as an observation post detachment commander/JTAC with Captain Cory Gillis's G11 for Task Force 3-08.[57]

Redeployment for the remainder of the battery was a similar experience. Gunners were distributed amongst various returning flights with no troop complete on any one flight. Anywhere from 20 to 30 gunners would be in a given hotel in Cyprus at the same time. The relationship between the battery and the battalion was at a high point. In the words of Rod Gallant, the battalion "loved the gunners."[58]

Plummer too noted the fact that at the end of the tour, the battalion and its gunners came home as a single family. "The positive feeling, and even a sense of family, between E [Battery, the 1st Battalion, The Royal Canadian Regiment], and the battle group generally ... through the individuals who were on the tour continued, even now. As people left the units, the unit training seemed to revert to normal peacetime training practices little by little."[59]

The returning battle group also experienced a great reception as the serials arrived back in Petawawa. Unlike their predecessors from A Battery, E Battery reaped the benefits of coming home in February, well before the active posting season started. In consequence they would, for the most part, stay together as a group and decompress slowly. Reservists, unfortunately, would almost immediately be separated from the battery and quickly returned to their home units to mostly fend for themselves.

A point of friction, like it had been with Task Force ORION, was honours and awards.[60] The process raised two issues; the frequency with which submissions were downgraded and the pace at which they were awarded.

Leading the issue for Major Ivey was the, "draconian trend of playing down honours and awards..."[61] He opined that, in part, such awards are, "dependent on the chain of command and their creative writing skills ..."[62] In the particular case of Task Force 3-06,

> ...the problem our roto ran into was that a lot of the paperwork from the battlegroup was literally on field message pad because we were deployed outside the wire and we [surmised] that it lacked the detail or "staff look" that other rotos could produce. I've seen some of the write-ups from rotos after me that included [PowerPoint] diagrams of the actions and all kinds of other products that our roto and TF ORION's roto had no access to.[63]

All the awards put forward for the various FOOs were knocked down to commanders' commendations. There was a perception that perhaps Task Force KANDAHAR and Canadian Expeditionary Force Command were inundated with the sheer volume of "good deeds" done during the operation and thereby became acclimatized. The result was that performances meriting recognition were put down to people just doing their jobs.

As examples of the pace of such honours being granted Ivey pointed out a Chief of Defence Staff Commendation that took two years and a Meritorious Service Medal that had taken four years to be awarded. This slow pace of dealing with such recognition is not only detrimental to morale, but also complicates the ability of the chain of command to track the process due to the fact that many personnel are posted while the award is still being processed.[64]

What then had E Battery, and gunners in general, accomplished?

The battery had started its first day in theatre—August 19, 2006—involved in a major Taliban attack on Ma'Sum Ghar. Its engaging the enemy by way of guns and close air support had helped beat back a superior force and secure a piece of vital terrain.

Many Canadians have heard of Operation MEDUSA and associated it with North Atlantic Treaty Organization's (NATO) first battle.[65] In fact one can argue quite easily that Task Force ORION's engagement on August 3, 2006 was NATO's first fight and Task Force 3-06's on August 19, 2006 was NATO's first ever major combat victory.

With the September 6, 2006 reset of Operation MEDUSA in the north, E Battery had clearly proven its worth.

> Captain Purdy [Task Force 3-06's intelligence officer] reinforced the tactics used. "In the north it was overwhelming air power and artillery... We started getting reports that the enemy cannot move when they are being bombarded and this was a real sense of frustration for the Taliban." He described how the enemy indicated in their communications between themselves that

"we cannot complete our objective while we are being bombarded." Purdy assessed, "Artillery in this first stage of the battle was instrumental. We could not have pushed the Taliban out of that area without artillery."[66]

The pace never slowed. With the conventional threat defeated, Task Force 3-06 set about consolidating its gains and preparing the security environment for reconstruction. E Battery would never again engage in a set piece battle like MEDUSA. Notwithstanding this, time and time again, probes by the enemy, especially along SUMMIT, necessitated artillery and air support intervention.

Operation BAAZ TSUKA was more in the nature of engagement with the population that ISAF wanted to run. One that emphasized small but significant gains that facilitated reconstruction work.

Besides starting to get "Villages in a Box" into the communities and starting several major programs, the PRT had several other successes. There were now four Afghan-led provincial development committees to coordinate reconstruction and development work in the four provinces. In conjunction with this were additional funds flowing in from the US Agency for International Development and other foreign agencies for reconstruction work. In addition, each province now had Afghan-led provincial coordination centres which coordinated elements of the National Security Directorate, the Afghan National Police, and the Afghan National Army under the provincial governor's leadership to address security issues in the province.[67]

For Lieutenant-Colonel Hetherington, the PRT's greatest success was that it had set the conditions for the success of subsequent teams.[68] He would turn over the job to Lieutenant-Colonel Bob Chamberlain, a former commanding officer of 1 RCHA, who would be given a full year in the job to provide for continuity.

In Kabul, ISAF was pleased with Operation BAAZ TSUKA and was touting its success. A spokesman for ISAF in Kabul stated that the force had moved forward from September with the destruction of the Taliban's conventional force. In their minds, all that was left was an insurgency targeting weak points.[69]

But it was those weak points that would need artillery the most. If one had learned anything from the attacks on Strong Points CENTRE and WEST, it's that the Taliban will try to whittle down those weak points. If they were prepared to take on mechanized infantry sections and platoon-sized strong points, how much would they be deterred from attacking an Afghan police checkpoint? And how do Canadians rapidly support those if not by artillery and close air support?

In the end, Lieutenant-Colonel Omer Lavoie evaluated the artillery and close air support provided to his battle group as follows:

I think it exceeded my expectations in probably a couple of different ways. One was just how accurate it was with those 155s...there's the piece at how proficient the guns were even when it was an all-arms call for fire ... On close air support, in hindsight, I never would have dreamed in a million years that I would have that much air support. Greg [Ivey] would brief in the morning - I was always pretty impressed that between the [fire support coordination centre] and the [airspace coordination centre] they could actually deconflict all that and still put rounds effectively or bombs effectively on target. That was something that we never trained for at that level at all. In the beginning I was a little bit overwhelmed by it until I got used to it and I was really assured that the coordination that was going on was pretty seamless and pretty efficient.[70]

Statistically, E Battery had hit a home run right out of the ballpark. The gun line had fired approximately 6,500 rounds of 155mm, 100 rounds of 120mm mortar and 1,500 rounds of 81mm mortar in support of Task Force 3-06. Its FACs had handled 2,075 hours of close air support and 600 hours of attack aviation support, dropping 326 bombs and 50 Hellfire missiles.[71] They had fired 13 times the number of 155mm high explosive rounds and five times as many 81mm high explosive rounds under ISAF as A Battery had before them under Operation ENDURING FREEDOM. Like the 1st Battalion, Princess Patricia Canadian Light Infantry battle group, the 1st Battalion, The Royal Canadian Regiment battle group and the American's 1st Battalion, 3rd Special Forces Group (Airborne) would be awarded the Canadian Commander-in-Chief Unit Commendation for their actions that year.

E Battery had done its bit. It had come trained but had still learned or refined many of its tactics, techniques, and procedures while on the job in theatre. It had sent those lessons learned back to Canada to its successor. Because of that, D Battery was coming better prepared for whatever faced them.

D Battery was also coming with a few more guns.

EPILOGUE

IF THERE IS ONE THING that Canada's experience in Afghanistan has reinforced it's that Canada's gunners—like many of the nation's soldiers—are experts at making a silk purse out of a sow's ear. Their expertise, however, has been sorely tested over the last few decades through no fault of their own.

This book was started before Russia's criminal invasion of Ukraine and finished while that war had been raging for a year and a half. It's easy, from a gunners' viewpoint these days, to say over and over again "I told you so". It's easy for a military professional these days to see the utility of sufficient field guns, air defence, and vast stocks of munitions—not to mention missiles, unmanned aerial vehicles and a host of other weapon systems.

It wasn't that easy to see early on in this century as the army wrestled with the lack of resources coming out of the Decade of Darkness and wondered how to create and sustain a modern army. Clearly artillery was an easy target. Artillery, in quantity, is rarely required in peacetime except as a symbol of deterrence. True deterrence requires a credible and capable force that will lead an opponent to believe that aggression on their part will be met by failure. If not contained in the active army, the capabilities that make the force credible must at least be available as a mobilizable reserve.[1] The absence of artillery in all its forms sends a strong signal to an opponent—and allies—that the country does not have a credible force.

Over the years, austerity programs had either eliminated or significantly reduced critical artillery capabilities: surveillance and target acquisition (STA), air defence, even tube artillery. Hard to learn skill sets had atrophied. Even worse, as capabilities were cut, no funded projects existed to implement the requisite replacements contemplated in Lieutenant-General Mike Jeffery's vision for the future.

It was serendipity that the Director Land Requirements 8, working on an intelligence, surveillance, target acquisition, and reconnaissance (ISTAR) integration project, had amassed enough information to facilitate the rapid acquisitions of both unmanned aerial vehicles (UAV) and counter mortar radars as unforecasted operational requirements, and thus reactivate those capabilities in time for Kabul.

By the summer of 2005, the Chief of the Land Staff's transformation plan for the field artillery even relegated the artillery regiment to a mere force generator and not a force employer. No programmed funds to implement transformation were provided. It was once again the use of unforecasted operational requirement funding that provided for the acquisition of a limited number of M777 lightweight howitzers in time for Task Force ORION, and of a handful of UAVs, radars, and acoustic sensors subsequently. The fact that Canada was able to get six M777s from the Marines' low rate initial production run had more to do with personal relationships amongst senior leaders and the Americans' desire to see Canada succeed in Afghanistan than with sound force development planning.

Once again, it was the acquisition teams, the training teams, and the gunners themselves who made it possible to field these complex systems in a bare six months. It was the gunners who made it possible to make it routine to bring in danger close fire to within 80 metres of friendly forces.

The same can be said for the systems of close air support and airspace coordination. Each of these functions matured dramatically in the interval between the turn of the century and the end of Task Force 3-06's roto. Most often it was as a result of extraordinary efforts by individual gunners to leverage their own skills and personal contacts.

Many times these gunners were ones who had previous tours as either instructors in gunnery or assistant instructors in gunnery who had served or were serving at the Royal Canadian Artillery School. They were the gatekeepers of the artillery's corporate knowledge even as critical capabilities existed only in theory.

Gunners were stepping up everywhere. Batteries were deployed to war with 10 to 15 percent of their complement made up of reservists. Female gunners claimed their rightful place and proved their worth in combat. Many other gunners, both regular and reserve, were stepping up for other positions outside of the gun batteries; the tactical UAV flight, the provincial reconstruction team (PRT), the various headquarters, and on the operational mentoring and liaison teams. Up to this point, many, but not all who had deployed to Kandahar, had come from units in Ontario and the west but in the coming year units from the Maritimes and Quebec would be doing their part in large numbers as well.

The families of gunners too had stood up through the numerous support organizations. As news of the randomness of improvised explosive devices (IED) and rocket and mortar strikes came home, everyone realized that no one was totally safe. To underscore that point, three gunners had made the ultimate sacrifice. Others bore visible wounds and far too many would be returning home with invisible ones which too would impact their families. Everyone, gunners and families, knew that with the small size of Canada's artillery, they would in all probability go back for another tour.

There was optimism at the end of Task Force 3-06's tour that the chaos that had met the battle group in Zhari and Panjwayi in August had been controlled. Operation BAAZ TSUKA had followed the concept laid down by the International Security Assistance Force (ISAF) in its Afghan development zone process. If enough Afghan security forces, both military and police, could be trained and deployed prior to the next fighting season, then perhaps the region would be stable enough to keep down any Taliban resurgence.

Operations hereafter would, more often than not, be cynically referred to as rounds of "Whack-a-Mole", as successive combat teams and battle groups dealt with an elusive insurgency that, rather than massing, would sooner employ IEDs to wear down coalition resolve while working in small groups in the villages to win over or cow the population.

The next roto of artillery was certainly prepared to do its part. In Petawawa, D Battery was preparing for a six-gun, three-troop, four-forward observation officers deployment—a significant increase in the incoming battle group's combat support. Surveillance and target acquisition (STA) capabilities would expand with radars and acoustic systems, and there would be sightings of the promised Excalibur guided precision projectile. Not only would the tanks be staying but a program had started to replace them with significantly newer and more capable ones.

The trouble was that there were storm clouds on the horizon. "[The Afghan] government and their tribal allies were divided, riven by feuds and competition. Staunch opponents of the Taliban had armed men stripped away by other opponents of the Taliban. So when the Taliban attacked, few tribes fought, but others either switched sides or sat things out."[2]

While everything depended on a strong Afghan security force none was forthcoming.

> *The drift back to war might have been overcome if not for a series of regrettable mistakes. Most obvious among them is that the United States invaded Iraq, redirecting scarce resources and limiting its own options to help Afghanistan...Before this crisis [in 2006] and of greater importance from December 2001 onward, the United States rejected out of hand the idea of talking to the Taliban or allowing them into the political process ... Having given its adversary cause to fight, the United States then decided to build a small [Afghan] Army slowly. Not only did the United States fail to build a*

large Army, it failed to build a small capable one...These mistakes bore fruit in 2006.[3]

Afghanistan was not a country prone to accepting outsiders, "Rejection of foreign occupation runs deep in Afghan history ... A religious based call to fight infidel occupation spread."[4]

In the south, that applied equally to foreign occupiers or Afghan central government agencies branded as puppets of the occupiers. "After 2006, opportunities to end the conflict would narrow. The Taliban became larger and ensconced across the south and east. With vast ground under their control, the Taliban could mobilize fighters and raise revenue at an impressive rate."[5]

The incoming Task Force 1-07's D Battery, 2nd Regiment, Royal Canadian Horse Artillery was under no illusions as they landed. Their battery sergeant major, Master Warrant Officer Chad Wagar, had made no promise like E Battery's Master Warrant Officer Bob Montague had, that "if I ever fire a shot, I would pull the plug and retire". Fortunately for the regiment, it was a promise which Montague didn't keep.

At the beginning of this volume we had asked the question: can Canada's artillery, structured for small-scale, asymmetric operations, be restructured back to high-intensity peer conflict? A structure where it can offer a credible threat to a modern adversary such as the one now attacking Ukraine. The same adversary Canada is currently facing in Latvia. At the end of 2006 there was still a regiment's worth of M109s and the 30mm Oerlikon air defence guns in storage. What was left was twelve new M777s, a handful of 81mm mortars, some Air Defence Anti-Tank systems, two small fleets of mechanically challenged 105mm howitzers and the promise of some STA capabilities. Would they be enough? As 2007 dawned, however, that was not even a question being asked. Artillery transformation from a force structured to support tracked mechanized units in a European theatre to a lighter, more mobile force designed for failed-state scenarios had barely started. The focus was squarely on D Battery and Afghanistan.

D Battery had worked hard to be there. They'd started with very little, drawing the last resources they could from a regiment already heavily committed to Task Force 3-06. They would dig deep from the reserve units of Land Forces Central Area and Land Forces Atlantic Area. Their story would not just be the next chapter. It would be the first of many more chapters, each differing from the one before it as Canadian gunners, with just a few guns, adjusted to the changing threats in Afghanistan and the circumstances at home.

ENDNOTES

INTRODUCTION

1 Debbie Gallagher, interview by Brian Reid, Wolf Riedel, Kevin Smith May 19, 2021

2 Gunner is a generic term that applies to all members of the Canadian Forces who serve in the artillery. It is also a rank equivalent to the rank of private.

3 "E-mail newsletter a lifeline for military families," CBC News, February 28, 2006 https://www.cbc.ca/news/canada/e-mail-newsletter-a-lifeline-for-military-families-1.581619

4 Debbie Gallagher, interview by Brian Reid, Wolf Riedel, Kevin Smith May 19, 2021

5 Ibid.

6 A call sign is a unique designation on a radio net for a specific individual or group and their vehicle. The letter "G" or "Golf" indicates that it is artillery. G13 would indicate the third forward observation officer detachment in the first battery of a given artillery regiment.

7 The reserve force also has three independent field batteries.

PROLOGUE – ARTILLERY FOR THE NEW MILLENIUM

1 Rounds fired to produce a desired effect in the target area as opposed to rounds fired to adjust the guns onto the target.

2 A battery is a grouping of approximately 4 to 8 guns manned by roughly 80 to 150 gunners. It equates to an infantry company or a tank squadron all of which are also referred to as sub-units. Several sub-units grouped together form a unit. For Canadian artillery that unit is called a regiment and can comprise anywhere from 2 to 5 or more batteries.

3   In broad terms, field artillery consists of mobile guns capable of accompanying the army into the field while garrison artillery looks after heavier pieces more suitable for defending fortifications, coastal installations or sieges.

4   The Royal Regiment of Canadian Artillery, *Standing Orders Volume I History, Organization and Heritage* (Shilo: Royal Canadian Artillery Association, May 12, 2021), B-4/14. https://rca-arc.org/wp-content/uploads/2021/06/rca-standing-orders-2021-vol1.pdf. Hereafter referred to as RCA Standing Orders.

5   Ibid., B-9/14 - 10/14.

6   Subsequently designated the 105mm C1 and later converted to the C3 with a lengthened barrel.

7   *RCA Standing Orders*, B-11/14 - 12/14.

8   Lieutenant-Commander Paul Blumenstock, "Canada's Strategic Dilemma: Changing World Conditions and the Need for Organizational Reform of Defence." (MDS Research Project, Canadian Forces College, 2012)., 55. See also Captain Matthew McInnes, "First Principles and the Generation of Armoured Fighting Power," *Canadian Army Journal* 17, no. 3 (2017): 96

9   A battle group is a tailor-made military organization which, in Canada, is usually based on an infantry battalion augmented by other elements such as artillery, reconnaissance, armour and engineers. They vary in size from around 8-900 personnel or more.

10 Ian Hope, "Misunderstanding Mars and Minerva: The Canadian Army's Failure to Define an Operational Doctrine," *The Army Doctrine and Training Bulletin* 4, no. 4 (Winter 2001-2002): 18.

11 J.L. Granatstein, "Fighting the Bean Counters," *Legion Magazine* (November 1, 2002). - Note that "Mobile Command" was the name in use at the time for what was basically Canada's army.

12 Sean Maloney, "Purple Haze: Joint Planning in the Canadian Forces from Mobile Command to J-Staff, 1975-1991 (Part 1)," *The Army Doctrine and Training Bulletin* 5, no. 4 (Winter 2002-2003): 62-63.

13 Hope, "Misunderstanding Mars and Minerva," 20.

14 Sean Maloney, "RCAC History: Ch 19" A Brave New World 1990-2000 (draft)," in *The Royal Canadian Armoured Corps: An Illustrated History*, ed. John Marteinson and Michael R. McNorgan, Accessed June 12, 2021, http://www.seanmmaloney.com/old/pdfs/Ch19RCAC.pdf

15 Department of National Defence. "United Nations Protection Force (UNPROFOR)" (Ottawa: DND, last modified December 11, 2018), Accessed May 7, 2021. https://www.canada.ca/en/department-national-defence/services/military-history/history-heritage/past-operations/europe/canengbat-mandarin-harmony-cavalier-medusa-panorama.html.

16 John Boileau, "Canadian Peacekeepers in the Balkans," *The Canadian Encyclopedia 2019*. Accessed May 14, 2021. https://www.thecanadianencyclopedia.ca/en/article/canadian-peacekeepers-in-the-balkans. Note that Canada is still committed to Kosovo under Operation KOBALT in 2021.

17 10/90 means 10% regular force and 90% reserve force manning.

18 Philippe Lagasse, "Specialization and the Canadian Forces," *Occasional paper No. 40* (Ottawa: Norman Paterson School of International Affairs, Carleton University, 2003), 5-6. Accessed June 6, 2021. https://www3.carleton.ca/csds/docs/occasional_papers/npsia-40.pdf.

19 General Rick Hillier, *A Soldier First: Bullets, Bureaucrats and the Politics of War* (Toronto: HarperCollins, 2015), 43.

20 Mike Voith, "Military Readiness," *The Army Training and Doctrine Bulletin* 4, no. 2 (Summer 2001): 41.

21 Major Andrew B. Godefroy, "Transformation and the Army of Tomorrow," in B-GL-310-001/AF-001 *Towards Land Operations 2001: Studies in Support of the Army of Tomorrow Force Employment Concept*, ed. Major Andrew B. Godefroy and Mr. Peter Gizewski (Kingston: Department of National Defence, Directorate of Land Concepts and Design, 2009), 3-1.

22 Lieutenant-General Mike Jeffery, "Doctrine Development in Canada's Army in the 1990s," *The Canadian Army Journal* 17, no. 1 (2016): 17., and Lieutenant-General (Retd) Mike Jeffery, interview by Wolf Riedel, November 8 and 16, 2022, and January 4 and 27, 2023; and Mike Jeffery, Email to Wolf Riedel 4 January 2023.

23 Department of National Defence, *Advancing with Purpose: The Canadian Army Modernization Strategy*, 4th ed. (Ottawa: DND, December 2020).

24 Colonel (Retd) Bob Gunn, Director Artillery 2002-2006, interview by Wolf Riedel and Kevin Smith, March 31, 2022.

25 Lieutenant-Colonel André Harvey, "Directorate of the Army Training Update: The Brigade Training Event: Managed Versus Operational Readiness" *The Canadian Army Journal* 7, no. 1 (Spring 2004): 7.

26 During a House of Commons Standing Committee on National Defence and Veterans' Affairs meeting on December 4, 2002, Lieutenant-General Jeffery, then Chief of Land Staff, indicated he might be able to turn out a mechanized battle group on six months' notice and possibly even a brigade but would be challenged in sustaining such a force. See House of Commons, Standing Committee on National Defence and Veterans' Affairs, *Minutes of Proceedings and Evidence*, Wednesday, 4 December 2002, 1540-1545.

27 Lieutenant-General (Retd), Mike Jeffery, email to Wolf Riedel January 4, 2023. In 1989 the regular force had an authorized strength of 88,000. By 2000

it would drop to 68,500 and by 2002 would slip to 61,600. https://www. macrotrends.net/countries/CAN/canada/military-Army-size The artillery non commissioned member strength would slip from 2,538 in 1986 to 1,449 in 1996, The Royal Regiment of Canadian Artillery Strategic Capabilities Assessment, Accessed August 22, 2021 http://rca-arc.org/wp-content/ uploads/2018/10/RCA-Strategic-Capabilities-Assessment-26-Apr-16-EN.pdf

28 Lieutenant-General (Retd) Andrew Leslie, interview by Wolf Riedel and Kevin Smith, January 26, 2021.

29 Scott Taylor and Brian Nolan, *Tested Mettle: Canada's Peacekeepers at War* (Toronto: Esprit de Corps Books, 1998), 124.

30 Colonel (Retd) Bob Gunn, interview by Wolf Riedel and Kevin Smith, March 31, 2022, As an example at one point in 1996, Gunn as commandant of the Royal Canadian Artillery School was unable to source a mortar platoon from any of the nine regular force battalions to participate in an exercise but did find one from a reserve battalion.

31 Ibid.

32 The C3 being a C1 having been upgraded with a longer barrel for additional range.

33 Total force is a term used for a Canadian army unit composed of both regular force and reserve force personnel.

34 *RCA Standing Orders* 2-23/31 - 24/31.

35 Their future did not look bright. By 2006 their establishment would be reduced by 151 regular force positions and all the reserve ones.

36 Major Richard Little, "A Short History of Target Acquisition Artillery," *Canadian Army Journal* 11, no. 3 (Fall 2008): 43.

37 Sharon Hobson, "Plain Talk - Who Decides?" *Canadian Naval Review* 2, no. 2 (Summer 2006): 37.

38 Captain Kevin Johnson, email to Wolf Riedel December 14, 2022. Trials conducted in Wainwright in Sept/Oct 1998 established that an LG1 stripped of everything possible could only be lifted some 20 kilometres by a Griffon which had a restricted crew of two and a minimal fuel load. The same results were reported in a similar trial conducted in Valcartier in 2003 in preparation for operations to Kabul.

39 Little, "A Short History", 50.

40 Lieutenant-General (Retd) Mike Jeffery, email to Wolf Riedel January 4, 2023.

41 David Ochmanek et al., *U.S. Military Capabilities and Forces for a Dangerous World* (Santa Monica: RAND Corp, 2017), 45.

42 JL Granatstein, and Lieutenant-General (Retd) Charles Belzile, *The Special Commission on the Restructuring of the Reserves: Ten Years Later* (Calgary:

Canadian Defence & Foreign Affairs Institute, September 2005), 12.

43 Lieutenant-General (Retd) Mike Jeffery, email to Wolf Riedel, January 4, 2023

CHAPTER 1 – PREPARING FOR WAR

1   Bombardier is a rank in the artillery equivalent to the rank of corporal. There are also master bombardiers. Strangely enough master bombardier, like master corporal, has never become a rank since it was created at the time of unification of the Canadian Armed Forces in the mid 1960s. It is an appointment between the ranks of bombardier and sergeant and constitutes the first level of leadership.

2   On any artillery system the gunners are numbered. For the 81mm mortar the detachment commander is the #1, the gunner who lays the mortar for bearing and elevation is the #2 and the ammunition loader is the #3.

3   SEAL stands for Sea, Air, and Land and is the name of the US Navy's primary special operations force members and units.

4   The Chief of the Land Staff commands Canada's army

5   Lieutenant-General (Retd) Mike Jeffery, interview by Wolf Riedel, November 8 and 16, 2022, and January 4 and 27, 2023.

6   Lieutenant-Colonel Fred Wolanski, interview by Brian Reid and Kevin Smith, December 29, 2020.

7   "Third Battalion," *The Patrician* 53 (2001): 48-51.

8   Major Wayne Lundrigan, and Warrant Officer Ryan Hebert, interview by Brian Reid and Kevin Smith, January 24, 2021.

9   At that time the Deputy Chief of Defence Staff would have been the Canadian Forces' chief of staff for operations and would oversee the planning, coordination and conduct of all operations.

10 Lieutenant-General (Retd) Mike Jeffery, interview by Wolf Riedel, November 8 and 16, 2022, and January 4 and 27, 2023.

11 Dr. Donald P. Wright et al, *A Different Kind of War: The United States Army in Operation ENDURING FREEDOM (OEF): October 2001–September 2005* (Fort Leavenworth: Combat Studies Institute Press, 2010), 27-35.

12 Armed Forces Council is composed of the Chief of Defence Staff and all his most senior generals while the Defence Management Committee is the Deputy Minister of National Defence and the Chief of Defence Staff co-chairing all the three-star commanders of commands and civil service equivalent assisstant deputy ministers.

13 Lieutenant-General (Retd) Mike Jeffery, interview by Wolf Riedel, November 8 and 16, 2022, and January 4 and 27, 2023

14 Some batteries from the United Kingdom have the honour titles "Kabul" and "Maiwand" dating from the Afghan Wars in the 19th Century.

15 Wright, *A Different Kind of War*, 5-26.

16 United Nations, *United Nations Security Council Resolution 1368 S/Res/1368 (2001)* (New York: United Nations Security Council, 12 September 2001). http://unscr.com/en/resolutions/doc/1368. See also United Nations *Security Council Resolution 1373 S/Res/1373* (New York: United Nations Security Council, 28 September 2001). http://unscr.com/en/resolutions/doc/1373.

17 Wright, *A Different Kind of War*, 32.

18 US Army special operations forces are broken into two classes, Tier 1 which are classified organizations and Tier 2 which are not. The US Army's Tier 2 forces are the Special Forces Groups (also known as the "Green Berets"). Their basic unit is the Operational Detachment Alpha (or ODA) which consists of 12 men led by a captain and warrant officer and with two each specialists of operations, weapons, engineer, medical and signals. Six ODAs operate under an Operational Detachment Bravo which is a company headquarters run by a major. Three ODBs come under an Operational Detachment Charlie which is a battalion headquarters led by a Lieutenant-colonel. Three ODCs (later 4) form a Special Forces Group. Finally, The Operational Detachment Delta (or Delta Force) is the army's completely separate and classified Tier 1 special operations force which belongs to the US Joint Special Operations Command. Almost all of the war in Afghanistan prior to 2002 was fought and won by these and other special operations forces elements.

19 Wright, *A Different Kind of War*, 65.

20 United Nations, *United Nations Security Council Resolution 1386 S/Res/1386 (2001)* (New York: United Nations Security Council, 20 December 2001). http://unscr.com/en/resolutions/doc/1386.

21 General Rick Hillier, *A Soldier First: Bullets, Bureaucrats and the Politics of War* (New York: HarperCollins, 2010), 81.

22 Ibid., 242-243.

23 Ibid.

24 Lieutenant-General (Retd) Mike Jeffery, interview by Wolf Riedel, November 8 and 16, 2022, and January 4 and 27, 2023.

25 Colonel Patrick Stogran, interview by Angus Brown, August 1, 2006.

26 Captain Kevin Johnson, interview by Brian Reid and Kevin Smith, March 14, 2021.

27 Lieutenant-General (Retd) Mike Jeffery, interview by Wolf Riedel, November 8 and 16, 2022, and January 4 and 27, 2023.

28 Aaron Ettinger and Jeffery Rice, "Hell is other people's schedules: Canada's limited-term military commitments, 2001-2015," *International Journal* 71, no. 3 (September 2016): 378.

29 Edmund Degen, and Mark Reardon, *Modern War in an Ancient Land: The United States Army in Afghanistan 2001-2014 Vol I*, (Washington: Center of Military History, United States Army, 2021), 75-77.

30 Robert McElroy, "Afghanistan Fire Support for Operation Anaconda." *Field Artillery* (September-October 2002): 6.

31 Captain Joshua Mitchell, "A Case for Howitzers in Afghanistan," *Field Artillery* (November-December 2003): 6 and 9.

32 Lieutenant-Colonel Fred Wolanski, interview by Brian Reid and Kevin Smith, December 29, 2020; Lieutenant-General (Retd) Mike Jeffery, interview by Wolf Riedel, November 8 and 16, 2022, and January 4 and 27, 2023

33 Lieutenant-General (Retd), Mike Jeffery, Email to Wolf Riedel 4 January 2023.

34 Jack Watling, *The Future of Fires, Maximizing the UK's Tactical and Operational Firepower* Occasional Paper(London: Royal United Services Institute,, 2019), 2. The effectiveness of precision air delivered weapons, the end of the Cold War and switch to counterinsurgency operations combined to have many North Atlantic Treaty Organization countries reduce their artillery holdings.

35 Colonel (Retd) Tim Young, interview by Wolf Riedel and Kevin Smith, August 4, 2023.

36 Department of National Defence. Lieutenant-General Mike Jeffery, PowerPoint presentation "Advancing With Purpose: A Strategy for Canada's Army 2002", Slides 66 and 67; Lieutenant-General (Retd) Mike Jeffery, interview by Wolf Riedel, November 8 and 16, 2022, and January 4 and 27, 2023; Lieutenant-General (Retd) Mike Jeffery, email to Wolf Riedel, December 2, 2002.

37 Captain Kevin Johnson, interview by Brian Reid and Kevin Smith, March 14, 2021; Technically speaking an infantry mortar platoon has eight mortars divided into two four-tube groups similar to how a six-gun battery can be divided into two- or three-gun troops. The four-tube entity sent by C Battery is referred to as a platoon or group or even troop by various individuals.

38 Lieutenant-Colonel Fred Wolanski, interview by Brian Reid and Kevin Smith, December 29, 2020.

39 "First Battalion," *The Patrician* 53 (2001): 26

40 Lieutenant-Colonel Fred Wolanski, interview by Brian Reid and Kevin Smith, December 29, 2020.

41 Lieutenant-Colonel Fred Wolanski, email to Wolf Riedel, December 12, 2022.

42 Lieutenant-Colonel Fred Wolanski, interview by Brian Reid and Kevin Smith, December 29, 2020.

43 These were subsequently found in the battalion headquarters being used for sending emails home.

44 The Directorate of Land Requirements is responsible for formulating army

equipment acquisition programs. DLR2's responsibilities include artillery equipment.

45 Colonel (Retd) Tim Young, message to Wolf Riedel, March 16, 2023.

46 In the army individuals and groups are identified by their radio call signs. "G" or "Golf" is an indicator for artillery. The first number indicates the company or battery "3" identifying the third battery i.e. C Battery in the 1st Regiment, Royal Canadian Horse Artillery. The battery commander is G39. The FOOs are G31, G32 and G33 while the battery command post is G1, albeit the two mortar sections on APOLLO adopted the infantry mortar platoon call signs 52 and 53

CHAPTER 2 – INTO THE FIGHT

1 Master Warrant Officer (Retd) Donny Simpson, and Captain Dave Poss, interview by Brian Reid and Kevin Smith, December 30, 2020.

2 Ibid.

3 Ibid.

4 Ibid.

5 Ibid.

6 After Lisa retired from the regular force she became the commanding officer of 31 Signals Regiment in Hamilton. Ryan would similarly become the commanding officer of the 7th Toronto Regiment, RCA.

7 Major Wayne Lundrigan, and Warrant Officer Ryan Herbert, interview by Brian Reid and Kevin Smith, January 24, 2021

8 Senate of Canada, Lieutenant-Colonel Pat Stogran Testimony, *Debates of the Senate (Hansard)* no. 18, Tuesday, 19 November 2002, 1430.

9 Lieutenant-Colonel Tyler Kennedy, Master Warrant Officer (Retd) Donnie Simpson and Sergeant (Retd) Donnie Bishop, interview by Brian Reid and Kevin Smith, January 17, 2021

10 Lieutenant-Colonel Fred Wolanski, interview by Brian Reid and Kevin Smith, December 29, 2020.

11 Captain Kevin Johnson, interview by Brian Reid and Kevin Smith, March 14, 2021.

12 Lieutenant-Colonel Tyler Kennedy, Master Warrant Officer (Retd) Donnie Simpson and Sergeant (Retd) Donnie Bishop, interview by Brian Reid and Kevin Smith, January 17, 2021. The Canadian Mapping and Charting Establishment (MCE) was caught off guard by the speed of the deployment. Some initial products included Russian maps with a Military Grid Reference System (MGRS) overlaid. The issue led to the development within MCE of a more time efficient way of generating maps which has been adopted by several North Atlantic Treaty Organization countries. Captain (Retd) (Master

Gunner) Kevin Smith, email to Wolf Riedel, May 23, 2023.

13 Master Warrant Officer (Retd) Donny Simpson, and Captain Dave Poss, interview by Brian Reid and Kevin Smith, December 30, 2020

14 A gun laying and positioning system (GLPS) is a tripod mounted and integrated system that incorporates a north-seeking gyroscope, an eye safe laser range finder and a digital electronic theodolite.

15 Master Warrant Officer (Retd) Dennis Goodland, interview by Brian Reid and Kevin Smith, March 13, 2021.

16 Task Force K-BAR had originally started as Combined Special Operations Task Force-South and was a US Navy SEAL commanded grouping of special operations forces personnel from seven nations including Canada. All units participating were granted a Presidential Unit Citation by President George W. Bush in 2004.

17 Lieutenant-Colonel Fred Wolanski, interview by Brian Reid and Kevin Smith, December 29, 2020.

18 Lieutenant-Colonel Fred Wolanski, email to Wolf Riedel, December 12, 2022.

19 Lieutenant-Colonel Fred Wolanski, email to Wolf Riedel, December 12, 2022; Major Wayne Lundrigan, and Warrant Officer Ryan Herbert, interview by Brian Reid and Kevin Smith, 24 January, 2021

20 John McNabb, "Chemical and Biological Threats against Public Water Systems," in *Weapons of Mass Destruction and Terrorism*, ed. James J.F. Forest and Russel D. Howard (New York: McGraw Hill 2012), 340.

21 Lieutenant-Colonel P. Stogran, "Fledgling Swans Take Flight: The Third Battalion, Princess Patricia's Canadian Light Infantry in Afghanistan" *Canadian Army Journal* 7, no. 3-4 (Fall/Winter 2004): 16-17.

22 Lieutenant-Colonel Fred Wolanski, interview by Brian Reid and Kevin Smith, December 29, 2020.

23 Warrant Officer One Scott E. Prochniak, and Major Dennis Yates, "Counterfire in Afghanistan" *Field Artillery* (September-October 2002): 15

24 Lieutenant-Colonel Fred Wolanski, interview by Brian Reid and Kevin Smith, December 29, 2020

25 Wright et al, *A Different Kind of War,* 127, 135.

26 Ibid., 134-5; see also Sean Naylor, *Relentless Strike: The Secret History of Joint Special Operations Command* (New York: St Martin's Press, 2015),185-7; and Sean Naylor, *Not A Good Day to Die: The Untold Story of Operation Anaconda* (New York: Berkley Publishing Group, 2005).

27 The section dealing with Operation ANACONDA is a summary of Wright, "Chapter 6. Operation ANACONDA," A Different Kind of War, 127-180; Edmund Degen, and Mark Reardon, *Modern War in an Ancient Land: The*

United States Army in Afghanistan 2001-2014 Vol I, (Washington: Center of Military History, United States Army, 2021), 143 - 167; Naylor, *Not a Good Day*; and Naylor, "Chapter 14. Patton's Three Principles of War," *Relentless Strike,* 187-198.

28 Lieutenant-Colonel Fred Wolanski, interview by Brian Reid and Kevin Smith, December 29, 2020.

29 Degen and Reardon, *Modern War in an Ancient Land Vol I,* 165.

30 Snivel gear is an American army slang term for anything that is not operationally necessary but can make a soldier's life more comfortable; it can include anything from candy bars to Gore-Tex parkas.

31 Captain Kevin Johnson, interview by Brian Reid and Kevin Smith, March 14, 2021

32 Degen and Reardon, *Modern War in an Ancient Land Vol I,* 168.

33 Captain Kevin Johnson, interview by Brian Reid and Kevin Smith, March 14, 2021

34 Degen and Reardon, *Modern War in an Ancient Land Vol I,* 168.

35 Captain Kevin Johnson, interview by Brian Reid and Kevin Smith, March 14, 2021.

36 Major Wayne Lundrigan, and Warrant Officer Ryan Herbert, interview by Brian Reid and Kevin Smith, 24 January, 2021.

37 Captain Kevin Johnson, interview by Brian Reid and Kevin Smith, March 14, 2021.

38 Ibid.

39 Forward air controlling has a long history going back to the Second World War and coming into its own in Vietnam. Both officers and enlisted personnel did this duty with officers, more often than not, being pilots working from aircraft as airborne forward air controllers. By the 1990s, the USAF had concluded that the enlisted personnel who had assisted officer forward air controllers on the ground should be fully trained and employed as independent air controllers termed ETACs. This field later evolved into the common title of joint terminal attack controller which applies to all personnel from all services regardless of rank or nationality. See Charlie Pocock, et al., *A Brief History of Forward Air Controlling* (Polson: FAC Association, 2008)

40 Colonel Patrick Stogran, interview by Angus Brown, August 1, 2006

41 Wright et al, *A Different Kind of War,* 168.

42 Lieutenant-Colonel Fred Wolanski, interview by Brian Reid and Kevin Smith, December 29, 2020.

43 Lieutenant-Colonel David Grebstad, interview by Kevin Smith, January 31, 2021.

44 The AT-4 is the equivalent of the Canadian 84mm Carl Gustav anti-armour weapon. It fires a variety of ammunition.

45 Wright et al, *A Different Kind of War*, 169; See also Colonel Patrick Stogran, interview by Angus Brown, August 1, 2006. Stogran was quite displeased with the haphazard manner in which the American company was operated during this event. He asked the brigade commander to remove them from the operation and they were flown out on the 16th.

46 Major Wayne Lundrigan, and Warrant Officer Ryan Herbert, interview by Brian Reid and Kevin Smith, 24 January, 2021.

47 Master Warrant Officer (Retd) Donny Simpson, and Captain Dave Poss, interview by Brian Reid and Kevin Smith, December 30, 2020; Major Wayne Lundrigan, and Warrant Officer Ryan Herbert, interview by Brian Reid and Kevin Smith, 24 January, 2021.

48 Captain Kevin Johnson, interview by Brian Reid and Kevin Smith, March 14, 2021.

CHAPTER 3 – OPERATION MOUNTAIN LION

1   Master Warrant Officer (Retd) Donny Simpson, and Captain Dave Poss, interview by Brian Reid and Kevin Smith, December 30, 2020.

2   Ibid.

3   Ibid.

4   Lieutenant-Colonel Tyler Kennedy, Master Warrant Officer (Retd) Donnie Simpson and Sergeant (Retd) Donnie Bishop, interview by Brian Reid and Kevin Smith, January 17, 2021.

5   Lieutenant-General Bruce Carlson, "U.S. Air Force Verdict: Text of Decision, Approved Punishment—Schmidt Art 15" Accessed December 7, 2022 CBC News Online July 6, 2004, https://web.archive.org/web/20040804021748/http://www.cbc.ca/news/background/friendlyfire/verdict.html

6   Lieutenant-Colonel Tyler Kennedy, Master Warrant Officer (Retd) Donnie Simpson and Sergeant (Retd) Donnie Bishop, interview by Brian Reid and Kevin Smith, January 17, 2021.

7   In Afghanistan, a loya jirga is a grand council convened to elect a new head of state.

8   Edmund Degen, and Mark Reardon, *Modern War in an Ancient Land: The United States Army in Afghanistan 2001-2014 Vol 1* (Washington: Center of Military History, United States Army, 2021), 180-181.

9   Major Wayne Lundrigan, and Warrant Officer Ryan Herbert, interview by Brian Reid and Kevin Smith, 24 January, 2021.

10 Lieutenant-Colonel Fred Wolanski, email to Wolf Riedel, December 12, 2022.

11 Captain Kevin Johnson, interview by Brian Reid and Kevin Smith, March 14, 2021.

12 A mention in dispatches is an official report in which a member's name appears for their gallant or meritorious action in the face of the enemy.

13 The Bronze Star would also be awarded to the four members killed at Tarnak Farms as well as to several Canadian officers including C Battery's Major Fred Wolanski and Captain Jeff Wilson.

14 "Third Battalion, B Company," *The Patrician* 54, (2002): 38.

15 Lieutenant-Colonel David Grebstad, interview by Kevin Smith, January 31, 2021.

16 Ibid.

17 In the US Special Forces, Detachment Bravo is a company strength sub-unit commanding six Operational Detachments Alpha, more famously known as "A-Teams".

18 Joint Direct Attack Munition. A JDAM is a guidance kit that can be attached to a 500 to 2,000 lb "dumb" bomb to allow it to become a precision guided weapon.

19 Lieutenant-Colonel David Grebstad, interview by Kevin Smith, January 31, 2021.

20 A torii is a traditional Japanese gate at a Shinto shrine. The RAKKASANs adopted it as their unofficial patch in honour of the unit's parachuting into Okinawa just as the Second World War was ending. In some publications this operation is also called TOR II or TORI.

21 This raises an interesting question. Has any other gunner ever served as an infantry sniper in combat?

22 Degen and Reardon, *Modern War in an Ancient Land I*, 182.

23 Major Wayne Lundrigan, and Warrant Officer Ryan Herbert, interview by Brian Reid and Kevin Smith, 24 January, 2021.

24 Colonel Patrick Stogran, interview by Angus Brown, August 1, 2006.

25 Major Wayne Lundrigan, and Warrant Officer Ryan Herbert, interview by Brian Reid and Kevin Smith, 24 January, 2021.

26 Lieutenant-Colonel Fred Wolanski, interview by Brian Reid and Kevin Smith, December 29, 2020.

27 Major Wayne Lundrigan, and Warrant Officer Ryan Herbert, interview by Brian Reid and Kevin Smith, 24 January, 2021.

28 Nancy Teeple, *Canada in Afghanistan: 2001-2010 A Military Chronology* (Kingston: Defence R&D Canada, 2010), 13. One American historian, Degen and Reardon, *Modern War in an Ancient Land Vol I*, 182 erroneously states that the Tarnak "incident played a major role" in the decision to not send more

ground troops. In fact Canada had specifically stated when it initiated Operation APOLLO that its ground force contribution would be a single deployment for a maximum of six months.

29 Wright et al, *A Different Kind of War: The United States Army in Operation ENDURING FREEDOM, October 2001–September 2005* (Fort Leavenworth: Combat Studies Institute Press, 2010), 187.

30 The Combat Talon is a version of the C-130 cargo plane modified for combat use by special forces. It is designed to penetrate hostile airspace at low altitudes to pick up and drop off troops and supplies. It is equipped with special night-flying capability, can be refueled midair, and can land on short runways.

31 Lieutenant-Colonel Tyler Kennedy, Master Warrant Officer (Retd) Donnie Simpson and Sergeant (Retd) Donnie Bishop, interview by Brian Reid and Kevin Smith, January 17, 2021; Simpson, Master Warrant Officer (Retd) Donnie and Captain Dave Poss, interview by Brian Reid and Kevin Smith, December 30, 2020.

32 Colonel Patrick Stogran, interview by Angus Brown, August 1, 2006.

33 Ibid.

34 Major Wayne Lundrigan, and Warrant Officer Ryan Herbert, interview by Brian Reid and Kevin Smith, 24 January, 2021.

35 Wright et al, *A Different Kind of War*, 187.

36 Lieutenant-General (Retd) Mike Jeffery, interview by Wolf Riedel, November 8 and 16, 2022, and January 4 and 27, 2023. Canadian soldiers were switching from the one-tone combat uniform to the camouflage CADPAT at this time. While the new green woodland uniform was available, the planned arid desert pattern was not able to be produced in sufficient quantities for the operation.

37 Colonel Patrick Stogran, interview by Angus Brown, August 1, 2006; see also Lieutenant-Colonel P. Stogran, "Fledgling Swans Take Flight: The Third Battalion, Princess Patricia's Canadian Light Infantry in Afghanistan" *Canadian Army Journal* 7, no. 3-4 (Fall/Winter 2004): 17-18.

38 Wright et al, *A Different Kind of War*, 188.

39 Lieutenant-Colonel David Grebstad, interview by Kevin Smith, January 31, 2021.

40 Ibid.

41 Ibid.

42 Captain Joshua Mitchell, "A Case for Howitzers in Afghanistan," *Field Artillery* (November-December 2003): 6.

43 Warrant Officer One Scott E. Prochniak, and Major Dennis Yates, "Counterfire in Afghanistan," *Field Artillery* (September-October 2002): 15.

44 Lieutenant-Colonel Fred Wolanski, interview by Brian Reid and Kevin Smith,

December 29, 2020.

45 Wright et al, *A Different Kind of War*, 181, 191-199.

Chapter 4 – The First Interlude: Summer 2002 – Summer 2003

1 Donald Wright et al, *A Different Kind of War: The United States Army in Operation ENDURING FREEDOM October 2001 to September 2005* (Fort Leavenworth: Combat Studies Institute Press, 2010), 181.

2 Anssi Kulberg "Warlords and Governors in Today's Afghanistan" The Eurasian Politician (November 2002). http://users.jyu.fi/~aphamala/pe/2002/afgawhoswho.htm.

3 Tier 1 Special Missions Units are highly trained and specialized forces such as the US Army's 1st Special Forces Operational Detachment - Delta or Canada's Joint Task Force 2 (JTF2).

4 Sean Naylor, "Part III: Building the Machine," in *Relentless Strike: The Secret History of Joint Operations Command* (New York: St. Martin's Press, 2016), 198 - 290.

5 Wright, *A Different Kind of War*, 191-2.

6 Ibid., 183.

7 Ibid, 209-210.

8 Ibid, 211.

9 Ibid., 226-7.

10 Ibid., 231.

11 United Nations Security Council Resolution 1386, December 20, 2001, https://digitallibrary.un.org/record/454998?ln=en.

12 General Rick Hillier, *A Soldier First: Bullets, Bureaucrats and the Politics of War* (Toronto: Harper Collins, 2009), 242.

13 Lieutenant-Colonel Chris Marvin, interview by Wolf Riedel and Kevin Smith, April 16, 2021.

14 Dan Fitzsimmons, "Canada, the North Atlantic Treaty Organization (NATO) and the International Security Assistance Force (ISAF) in Afghanistan," *International Journal* 68, no. 2 (June 2013): 306; Lieutenant-General Mike Jeffery, Chief of the Land Staff, was also very much of this view. Lieutenant-General (Retd) Mike Jeffery, interview by Wolf Riedel, November 8 and 16, 2022, and January 4 and 27, 2023.

15 See for example Wikipedia https://en.wikipedia.org/wiki/John_McCallum.

16 Positions were deeply divided between the various services as to what could and should be done. See Fitzsimmons, "Canada, NATO and ISAF in Afghanistan," 307.

17 Dr Michael A. Hennessy, "Operation 'Assurance': Planning a Multi-National Force for Rwanda/Zaire," *Canadian Military Journal* 2, no. 2 (Spring 2001): 18-20.

18 Lieutenant-General (Retd) Mike Jeffery, interview by Wolf Riedel, November 8 and 16, 2022, and January 4 and 27, 2023.

19 Joseph Fiorino, "Why Canada Really Didn't Go Into Iraq in 2003" NATO Association of Canada, June 7, 2015. Why Canada Really Didn't Go To Iraq In 2003 – NAOC (natoassociation.ca) accessed February 7, 2021. See also Fitzsimmons, "Canada, NATO and ISAF in Afghanistan," 308.

20 Jim Bronskill, "Canadian intelligence assessment of Saddam's Iraq got it right, new paper says," The Canadian Press, CBC August 23, 2020. Canadian intelligence assessments of Saddam's Iraq got it right, new paper says | CBC News

21 Lieutenant-General (Retd) Mike Jeffery, interview by Wolf Riedel, November 8 and 16, 2022, and January 4 and 27, 2023.

22 Fitzsimmons, "Canada, NATO and ISAF in Afghanistan," 308.

23 Ibid., 310.

24 Lieutenant-General (Retd) Mike Jeffery, interview by Wolf Riedel, November 8 and 16, 2022, and January 4 and 27, 2023.

25 Lieutenant-General (Retd) Andrew Leslie, interview by Wolf Riedel, Brian Reid and Kevin Smith, May 6, 7 and 11, 2021.

26 Fitzsimmons, "Canada, NATO and ISAF in Afghanistan," 313.

27 Nancy Teeple, *Canada in Afghanistan: 2001-2010 A Military Chronology* (Ottawa: Defence R & D Canada,December 2010), 16.

28 Department of National Defence. *Canadian Army, Advancing With Purpose: The Army Strategy* (Kingston: Department of National Defence, May 2002).

29 Lieutenant-General Mike Jeffery, PowerPoint presentation "Advancing With Purpose: A Strategy for Canada's Army 2002," Slide 54.

30 Ibid., Slides 57-59.

31 Ibid., Slide 67.

32 Ibid., Slide 67.

33 Ibid., Slide 61.

34 *The Canadian Gunner 2002* 38 (June 2004): 9.

35 Department of National Defence. Lieutenant-General Mike Jeffery, PowerPoint presentation "Advancing With Purpose: A Strategy for Canada's Army 2 CMBG Professional Development 2003," Slide 15.

36 In 2003 the Swedish Bofors was in the test system stage. It would later mature into the Archer Artillery System.

37 Colonel (Retd) Tim Young, interview by Wolf Riedel and Kevin Smith, August

4, 2023.

38 Ibid.

39 Colonel (Retd) Bob Gunn, interview by Wolf Riedel and Kevin Smith, March 31, 2022

40 Philippe Lagasse, "Specialization and the Canadian Forces," Occasional Paper No. 40 (Ottawa: Norman Paterson School of International Affairs, Carleton University, 2003), 4-5. Accessed June, 6 2021. https://www3.carleton.ca/csds/docs/occasional_papers/npsia-40.pdf.

41 David Pugliese, "The Myth Surrounding Canadian Leopard Tanks in Afghanistan," Ottawa Citizen, May 27, 2018.

42 For a good overview of the Canadian army's capability development process over the years, see Major Andrew B. Godefroy, "Chasing the Silver Bullet: The Evolution of Capability Development in the Canadian Army," *Canadian Military Journal* 8, no. 2 (Spring 2007): 52-66.

43 Lieutenant-Colonel Ian Hope, "Misunderstanding Mars and Minerva: The Canadian Army's Failure to Define an Operational Doctrine," T*he Army Doctrine and Training Bulletin* 4, no. 4 (Winter 2001-2002): 27-28.

44 David Lambert "Adapting the Canadian Army Organisation: 'Transformation' and the Enduring Nature of Warfare," *Security Challenges* 6, no. 1, (Autumn 2010): 43.

45 Ibid., 50-56; see also Lieutenant-General Rick Hillier, "Army Transformation: Punching Above Our Weight," *The Army Doctrine and Training Bulletin* 6, no.3 (Fall/Winter 2003): 3-4.

46 Lambert, "Adapting the Canadian Army Organisation," 56-57.

47 While the army had been seeking to replace its aging mechanized carrier fleet with modern tracked infantry fighting vehicles, a political nudge to the light armoured vehicle chassis for the Coyote and subsequent Light Armoured Vehicle III for two thirds of the army's infantry battalions was pushed due to the ability to manufacture them in Canada. For details on the light armoured vehicle purchase see Major J. Craig Stone, "An Examination of the Armoured Personnel Carrier Replacement Project," *Canadian Military Journal* 2, no. 2 (Summer 2001): 59-66.

48   Major D.J.Senft, "The Medium Gun System is Coming! ... Now What?" *The Army Doctrine and Training Bulletin* 6, no.3 (Fall/Winter 2003): 26.

49 Captain Martin Rivard, "ISTAR Sensor Integration: A Non-melting Pot Option," *The Army Doctrine and Training Bulletin* 3, no. 3, (Fall 2000): 16.

50 Unsurprisingly, at the time of writing, faced by new challenges from Russia and China, the US Army is rebuilding the division structure and aggregating its brigade combat teams' artillery battalions into a divisional artillery brigade.

51 Studies determined early on and still do today that the US Army's goal of deploying a Stryker Brigade Combat Team anywhere in the world in 4 days is not achievable. See US General Accounting Office, *Military Transformation: Realistic Deployment Timelines Needed For Army Stryker Brigades* (Washington: GAO, June 30, 2003); and Alan VIck et al, *The Stryker Brigade Combat Team: Rethinking Strategic Responsiveness and Assessing Deployment Options* (Santa Monica, CA: RAND Project Air Force, 2002). Note that the name of the US General Accounting Office changed to US Government Accounting Office in June of 2004.

52 Among the further differences are that a Canadian brigade group has only two light armoured vehicle equipped battalions rather than three and has very limited anti-armour and artillery resources.

CHAPTER 5 - THE ROAD TO KABUL

1 The initial deployment on an operation is designated Rotation, or Roto, 0, so the first deployment to Kabul is described as ATHENA Roto 0; a second phase of Operation ATHENA started in Kandahar in 2005 which also started as a Roto 0. Accordingly the four rotations in Kabul are retroactively described as Op ATHENA Phase 1 and the Kandahar ones as Phase 2.

2 National Defence Headquarters integrates the primarily civilian staff of the Department of National Defence with the primarily military staff of the Canadian Armed Forces.

3 General Rick Hillier, *A Soldier First: Bullets, Bureaucrats and the Politics of War* (Toronto: HarperCollins, 2009), 193.

4 Senate of Canada, Standing Senate Committee on National Security and Defence, *Canadian Security Guide Book 2005: An Update of Security Problems in Search of Solutions* (Ottawa: Senate, December 2004), 14.

5 Albeit the formal announcement from the North Atlantic Treaty Organization wasn't made until July 16, 2003.

6 At the time the International Security Assistance Force (ISAF) was essentially a one-brigade divisional headquarters and the commander of ISAF I was a British major-general, a rank commensurate with a divisional headquarters. While the size of ISAF did not increase over the next three rotations, starting with the Turks on ISAF II the command position was upranked to lieutenant-general a rank ordinarily commensurate with command of a corps. In consequence the deputy commander position was also upranked to one of major-general.

7 Lieutenant-General (Retd) Andrew Leslie, interview by Wolf Riedel, Brian Reid and Kevin Smith, May 6, 7 and 11, 2021.

8 A US Army artillery battalion is generally a three-battery, 18-gun unit, the

rough equivalent of a Canadian artillery regiment at the time.

9 Captain Joshua Mitchell, "A Case for Howitzers in Afghanistan," *Field Artillery* (November-December 2003): 6.

10 The requirements for electronic warfare and signals intelligence were also key capabilities which were brought into consideration because of Brigadier-General Leslie's prior experience as the Canadian Forces J6 with responsibility for the communications field force, signals/electronic intelligence, and computer network operations.

11 Lieutenant-General (Retd) Andrew Leslie, interview by Wolf Riedel, Brian Reid and Kevin Smith, May 6, 7 and 11, 2021 and Colonel (Retd) Peter Williams, interview by Wolf Riedel and Kevin Smith, January 19 and 29, 2021.

12 Colonel (Retd) Peter Williams, interview by Wolf Riedel and Kevin Smith, January 19 and 29, 2021.

13 Lieutenant-General (Retd) Andrew Leslie, interview by Wolf Riedel, Brian Reid and Kevin Smith, May 6, 7 and 11, 2021.

14 Lieutenant-Colonel Fred Wolanski, interview by Brian Reid and Kevin Smith, December 29, 2020.

15 Captain Ng had also been an instructor in gunnery at the Royal Canadian Artillery School and in fact had, just prior to his posting to the Directorate of land requirements, held the same job in the locating field occupied by Captain Little in 2002-3.

16 Major P.A. Romano, "The Land Force Intelligence, Surveillance, Target Acquisition, and Reconnaissance Project: A Primer for Our Readers," *The Army Doctrine and Training Bulletin* 6, no. 1 (Spring 2003): 7-9.

17 Captain Martin Rivard, "ISTAR Sensor Integration: A Non-melting Pot Option," *The Army Doctrine and Training Bulletin* 3, no. 3 (Fall 2000): 16-19.

18 Captain Richard Little, "Target Acquisition Coordinating Centre-Lessons Learned For Both TUAV and CBTA Radar Introduction on Operations", *Canadian Army Journal* 7, 3-4 (Fall/Winter 2004): 67-73.

19 T.F.J , Leveridge *Sagem CU-161 Sperwer Canadian Armed Forces Serial 16101* (Ottawa: Canadian Aviation and Space Museum, 2013), 5-6.

20 The Group of Eight was an inter-governmental political forum of eight countries from 1997 until 2014.

21 Sandy Babcock, "Canadian Network Enabled Operations Initiative," Ottawa: Department of National Defence, June 2004, 11-12

22 Captain (Retd) Nat Ng, interview by Wolf Riedel and Kevin Smith, February 10, 2021.

23 There were six in total. One was saved at the Royal Canadian Artillery Museum in Shilo, Manitoba. The remainder had the radars removed

and their M113 chassis returned to standard APC configuration. Darren Baker, "M113A1 with AN/MPQ-501 Radar" Armorama January 8, 2012. https://armorama.kitmaker.net/modules.php?op=modload&name=SquawkBox&file=index&req=viewtopic&topic_id=187086&page=1.

24 Captain (Retd) Nat Ng, interview by Wolf Riedel and Kevin Smith, February 10, 2021. DGLEPM 8 is a section within the offices of the Assistant Deputy Minister Materiel which stood up concurrently with DLR 8 to look after the equipment acquisition functions for equipment requirements identified by DLR 8 and funded by the army.

25 Which evolved into the RQ-7 Shadow variants.

26 SAGEM's name has changed and at the time of writing is known as SAFRAN Electronics & Defense. The name "Sperwer" itself comes from the Dutch word for "Sparrow Hawk" - Leveridge, *Sagem CU-161 Sperwer*, 1.

27 Ibid., 1.

28 Ibid., 7.

29 Major (Retd) Ray Dupuis, interview by Wolf Riedel and Kevin Smith, April 15, 2021.

30 Ibid.

31 Little, "Target Acquisition Coordinating Centre, 71-72.

32 In the army, training progresses through levels of increasing complexity which at the relevant time went from Level 1 - Individual Battle Tasks to Level 8 - Formation (i.e. brigade group) Level Training.

33 Lieutenant-Colonel André Harvey, "Directorate of the Army Training Update: The Brigade Training Event: Managed Versus Operational Readiness," *Canadian Army Journal* 7, no.1 (Spring 2004): 7. (Note: A Sabre Brigade was a mechanized brigade group designated to be at high readiness in order to deploy on 90 days notice as an expeditionary force pursuant to the 1994 White Paper on Defence) The exercise would eventually evolve into the MAPLE RESOLVE series of exercises.

34 Chief Warrant Officer (Retd) Dennis Franken, interview by Wolf Riedel and Kevin Smith, March 21, 2021.

35 Ibid.

36 Ibid.

37 The Iltis was a two-axle light utility vehicle, wheeled (LUVW) with a ¼ ton capacity built by Bombardier in Canada under licence from Volkswagen.

38 Warrant Officer Wayne MacLean, interview by Wolf Riedel and Kevin Smith, March 11, 2021.

39 Light support vehicle, wheeled (LSVW) are two axle trucks with a 1.5 ton

capacity built by Western Star under license and based on the Italian Iveco VM 90.

40 Chief Warrant Officer (Retd) Dennis Franken, interview by Wolf Riedel and Kevin Smith, March 21, 2021.

41 Grizzly armoured vehicle, general purpose also known as AVGP - the infantry version of the six-wheeled forerunner to the light armoured vehicle built by GDLS and based on the Swiss MOWAG Piranha 1.

42 Medium logistics vehicle, wheeled (MLVW) - Artillery specially equipped vehicle - a three axle truck with a 2.5 ton capacity specially equipped for artillery usage built by Bombardier under license and based on the American M35.

43 Heavy logistics vehicle, wheeled (HLVW) - a three axle truck with a 10 ton capacity built by UTDC under license and based on the Austrian Steyr 1491.

44 These light armoured vehicles were not yet the specialized light armoured vehicle observation post variant which were only just entering service at the time.

45 Captain (Retd) Ron Fillier, interview by Wolf Riedel and Kevin Smith, March 12, 2021.

46 B-GL-371-003/FP-001 Field Artillery Operational Procedures. (Ottawa: Department of National Defence, August 27, 2000).

47 Major Richard Little, interview by Wolf Riedel and Kevin Smith, February 6 and 9, and October 26, 2021.

48 Bombardier (Retd) Scott French, interview by Wolf Riedel and Kevin Smith, February 17, 2021. "It was very much throwing stuff against the wall to see what would stick and then going with it."

49 Lieutenant-Colonel Iain Clark, interview by Wolf Riedel and Kevin Smith, March 16, 2021.

50 The term target acquisition coordination centre would be in vogue for some time but eventually transition into surveillance and target acquisition coordination centre in due course.

51 "4th Air Defence Regiment," *The Canadian Gunner 2003-4* 39, (February 2005): 15. Note that much of 4th Air Defence Regiment, RCA's activities in 2004 turned around the direct fire role to the extent that at the order of the Chief of Land Staff most of their missiles fired that year were in the anti-armour role. The regiment conducted its first level 4 training exercise since the 1990s.

52 Department of National Defence, "Board of Inquiry Minutes of Proceedings, A10-A Friendly Fire Incident 4 September 2006, Panjwayi District, Afghanistan," (Declassified and redacted) (Ottawa: Department of National Defence, 15 December 2006).

53 Within an army continental staff system, like the Canadians, the staff functions

are identified by the letter G and a number. The key ones are G1 for personnel, G2 for intelligence, G3 for operations, G4 for logistics. G3 Air Defence would indicate a staff function for operations in the field of air defence.

54 "4ᵗʰ Air Defence Regiment," 15.

55 Major Mike Notaro, "Airspace Coordination in Afghanistan," *The Bulletin* 10, no. 6 (November 2004): 2; Lieutenant-Colonel Mike Notaro, email to Wolf Riedel, May 31, 2021.

56 The regiment's fire support coordination centre's alternate headquarters HLVW van was in fact shipped to Kabul but was designated, from the very beginning, to be allocated to another unit.

57 Lieutenant-Colonel Dan Matheson, interview by Wolf Riedel and Kevin Smith, March 4, 2021.

58 Colonel (Retd) Peter Williams, interview by Wolf Riedel and Kevin Smith, January 19 and 29, 2021; interview by Wolf Riedel, Brian Reid and Kevin Smith, June 16, and December 17, 2021; and interview by Wolf Riedel, March 4, 2023.

59 A departure assistance group, or DAG, is a temporary organization set up by a unit or base to review and assist members with various administrative matters just prior to deploying on a mission.

60 Chief Warrant Officer (Retd) Dennis Franken, interview by Wolf Riedel and Kevin Smith, March 21, 2021.

61 Lieutenant-Colonel Jennifer Causey, interview by Wolf Riedel and Kevin Smith, March 8, 2021; and Chief Warrant Officer (Retd) Dennis Franken, interview by Wolf Riedel and Kevin Smith, March 21, 2021.

62 Lieutenant-Colonel Jennifer Causey, interview by Wolf Riedel and Kevin Smith, March 8, 2021.

63 Master Warrant Officer (retd) Andy Skinner, interview by Wolf Riedel and Kevin Smith, February 2, 2021.

64 Lieutenant-Colonel Dan Matheson, interview by Wolf Riedel and Kevin Smith, March 4, 2021.

65 Warrant Officer (retd) Kerry Willcox, interview by Wolf Riedel and Kevin Smith, February 19, 2021; and Lieutenant-Colonel Dan Matheson, interview by Wolf Riedel and Kevin Smith, March 4, 2021. Note that Norway subsequently mothballed their 12 M270 MLRSs in 2005.

66 Lieutenant-Colonel Dan Matheson, interview by Wolf Riedel and Kevin Smith, March 4, 2021; and Master Warrant Officer (retd) Andy Skinner, interview by Wolf Riedel and Kevin Smith, February 2, 2021.

67 Master Warrant Officer (retd) Andy Skinner, interview by Wolf Riedel and Kevin Smith, February 2, 2021.

68 Lieutenant-Colonel Dan Matheson, interview by Wolf Riedel and Kevin Smith, March 4, 2021.

69 Chief Warrant Officer (Retd) Rob Bartlett, interview by Wolf Riedel February 28, 2021; and Major Richard Little, interview by Wolf Riedel and Kevin Smith, February 6 and 9, and October 26, 2021.

70 Master Warrant Officer (Retd) Art Snodgrass, interview by Wolf Riedel and Kevin Smith, February 24, 2021.

71 Gary Schaub Jr. and Kristian Kristensen, "But who's flying the plane? Integrating UAVs into the Canadian and Danish armed forces," *International Journal* 70, no. 2 (June 2015): 257.

72 Master Warrant Officer (Retd) Art Snodgrass, interview by Wolf Riedel and Kevin Smith, February 24, 2021.

73 Major Richard Little, interview by Wolf Riedel and Kevin Smith, February 6 and 9, and October 26, 2021.

74 Chief Warrant Officer (Retd) Rob Bartlett, interview by Wolf Riedel February 28, 2021.

CHAPTER 6 - WELCOME TO THE INTERNATIONAL SECURITY ASSISTANCE FORCE

1 With a significantly leaner headquarters.

2 In some reference material also called the "Afghan Military Forces"

3 Special Inspector General for Afghanistan Reconstruction, *Reconstructing the Afghan National Defense and Security Forces: Lessons from the US Experience in Afghanistan* (Arlington, VA: SIGAR, September 2017), 16.

4 Peter Thruelsen, *From Soldier to Civilian: Disarmament, Demobilization, Reintegration in Afghanistan*, DIIS Report 2006:7 (Copenhagen: Danish Institute for International Studies, 2006), 24.

5 Major Richard Little, interview by Wolf Riedel and Kevin Smith, February 6 and 9, and October 26, 2021.

6 Lieutenant-General (Retd) Andrew Leslie, interview by Wolf Riedel and Kevin Smith, January 26, 2021.

7 In certain circumstances, "transportation" weapons would be issued temporarily for self defence to personnel moving into or out of a theatre of operations. These would subsequently be exchanged for weapons which would be issued to a person for use during the duration of the tour.

8 Cuisine more typical of a German restaurant or home rather than North American.

9 CANEX is the abbreviation for the Canadian Forces Exchange System and is a commercial service of the Canadian Forces Morale and Welfare Services

which provides a variety of retail and other products throughout Canada and on operations.

10 HESCO bastions are collapsible wire mesh containers with a heavy duty fabric liner filled with sand or gravel and used as a temporary to semi-permanent blast wall.

11 Major Richard Little, interview by Wolf Riedel and Kevin Smith, February 6 and 9, and October 26, 2021; and Captain (Retd) Ron Fillier, interview by Wolf Riedel and Kevin Smith, March 12, 2021.

12 The Defence Wide Area Network (DWAN) is one of the computer networks serving the Department of National Defence throughout the world.

13 Major Richard Little, interview by Wolf Riedel and Kevin Smith, February 6 and 9, and October 26, 2021.

14 Major Mike Notaro, "Airspace Coordination in Afghanistan," *The Bulletin* 10, no. 6 (November 2004): 1; Lieutenant-Colonel Mike Notaro,email to Wolf Riedel, May 31, 2021.

15 Notaro, "Airspace Coordination in Afghanistan," 4.

16 A regimental command net is used for all operational communications within an artillery regiment including calls for fire. A regimental ring net is a more restricted, technical communication channel between the regimental command post and the fire units. The regimental command post officer exchanges technical information with the firing gun lines on the regimental ring net minimizing the communication traffic on the regimental command net.

17 Chief Warrant Officer (Retd) Dennis Franken, email to Wolf Riedel, September 24, 2021.

18 Defence advanced GPS receivers (DAGRs) are dual frequency global positioning receivers.

19 Chief Warrant Officer (Retd) Dennis Franken, email to Wolf Riedel, September 24, 2021.

20 Major Richard Little, interview by Wolf Riedel and Kevin Smith, February 6 and 9, and October 26, 2021.

21 Ibid.

22 The French generally covered the northern AO, the Germans the east, the Italians International Security Assistance Force headquarters and the British the centre while Canada covered the south and west.

23 Lieutenant-Colonel Jennifer Causey, interview by Wolf Riedel and Kevin Smith, March 8, 2021.

24 Chief Warrant Officer (Retd) Dennis Franken, interview by Wolf Riedel and Kevin Smith, March 21, 2021.

25 The Deputy Chief of Defence Staff is a three-star general or flag officer who, at

the time, was the senior operations officer for the Canadian Armed Forces.

26 Lieutenant-Colonel Dan Matheson, interview by Wolf Riedel and Kevin Smith, March 4, 2021.

27 Major (Retd) John Stewart, interview by Wolf Riedel, September 5 and 6, 2023.

28 Crater analysis is a process by which the physical characteristics and debris found in and around a crater created by an explosive device is analyzed in order to determine what created it, and in the case of a projectile, the direction that it was launched from.

29 Master Warrant Officer (Retd) Art Snodgrass, interview by Wolf Riedel and Kevin Smith, February 24, 2021.

30 Major Richard Little, email to Wolf Riedel, December 14, 2021.

31 Ibid.; and Major Richard Little, interview by Wolf Riedel and Kevin Smith, February 6 and 9, and October 26, 2021.

32 Colonel (Retd) Tim Young, email to Wolf Riedel, March 1, 2022. Engineers focused on the forensics of the munitions that created the crater while artillery focused on the geometry that would indicate the point of origin. The engineers subsequently went to different levels of examination to do both.

33 Heer had conducted the recce of the gun position there and as such was more familiar with it.

34 Then Kathy Hanna.

35 Lieutenant-Colonel Jennifer Causey, interview by Wolf Riedel and Kevin Smith, March 8, 2021.

36 Only one other pit would be developed for the remaining gun at JULIEN.

37 Major Richard Little, interview by Wolf Riedel and Kevin Smith, February 6 and 9, and October 26, 2021; Lieutenant-Colonel Iain Clark, interview by Wolf Riedel and Kevin Smith, March 16, 2021; Brigadier-General Peter Devlin, "Canadian Soldiers Deploy to the Kabul Multi-National Brigade-July 2003," *The Bulletin* 10, no. 2 (January 2004): 3; and Brigadier-General Peter Devilin, "A Mid-Tour Update from the Commander KMNB - Op ATHENA Ro 0," *The Bulletin* 10, no. 2 (January 2004): 7.

38 Lieutenant-Colonel Dan Matheson, interview by Wolf Riedel and Kevin Smith, March 4, 2021.

CHAPTER 7 - ALL TOGETHER NOW: SPERWER ARRIVES

1 M Company 3rd Battalion, The Royal Canadian Regiment.

2 Warrant Officer Wayne MacLean, interview by Wolf Riedel and Kevin Smith, March 11, 2021.

3 Lieutenant-Colonel Dan Matheson, interview by Wolf Riedel and Kevin Smith, March 4, 2021.

4   Chief Warrant Officer (Retd) Dennis Franken, email to Wolf Riedel, September
     24, 2021. With an HE M1 cartridge an LG1 Mk II howitzer achieves a
     maximum range of 11.2 kilometres while with an HE Extended Range C
     132 cartridge the maximum range would be 18.5 kilometres. Department of
     National Defence, C-74-315-H00/TA-000 *Ammunition for 105 mm Howitzer*
     (Ottawa: Department of National Defence, September 24, 2004), 1-1-1.

5   Lieutenant-Colonel Iain Clark, interview by Wolf Riedel and Kevin Smith,
     March 16, 2021.

6   Chief Warrant Officer (Retd) Rob Bartlett, interview by Wolf Riedel February
     28, 2021; and Major Richard Little, interview by Wolf Riedel and Kevin Smith,
     February 6 and 9, and October 26, 2021.

7   Chief Warrant Officer (Retd) Rob Bartlett, interview by Wolf Riedel February
     28, 2021; and Warrant Officer (retd) Kerry Willcox, interview by Wolf Riedel
     and Kevin Smith, February 19, 2021.

8   Chief Warrant Officer (Retd) Rob Bartlett, interview by Wolf Riedel February
     28, 2021; and Captain I. Plummer, "Lessons Learned by the Op Athena Roto
     0 TUAV Troop-Units Undergoing Training With Civilian Companies," *The
     Bulletin* 11, no. 4 (June 2005).

9   Captain R.N.W. Little, "Target Acquisition Coordination Centre-Lessons
     Learned For Both TUAV and CBTA Radar Introduction on Operations,"
     Canadian Army Journal 7, no.3-4 (2004): 68-69, 70-71.

10   Major Richard Little, interview by Wolf Riedel and Kevin Smith, February 6
     and 9, and October 26, 2021.

11   Major Richard Little, interview by Wolf Riedel and Kevin Smith, February 6
     and 9, and October 26, 2021.

12   Denmark bought Sperwer in 2002 and after considerable difficulty with them
     divested themselves of their remaining 10 aircraft by selling them to Canada
     for $7.7 million in 2006. Justin Wastnage, "Denmark sells unwanted second-
     hand Sagem Sperwer Unmanned Aerial Vehicles to Canada at 10% of price"
     FlightGlobal, September 1, 2006.

13   Kabul itself sits at an elevation of approximately 1,800 metres above sea level
     and is surrounded and bisected by ridges and mountains that rise to several
     hundred to a thousand and more metres higher.

14   The average high temperature in June and July is 32° C while in January it drops
     to 5° C.

15   T.F.J., Leveridge, *Sagem CU-161 Sperwer Canadian Armed Forces Serial
     16101* (Ottawa: Canadian Aviation and Space Museum, 2013)., 26-27; Major
     Richard Little, interview by Wolf Riedel and Kevin Smith, February 6 and 9,
     and October 26, 2021; and Lieutenant-Colonel Iain Clark, interview by Wolf

Riedel and Kevin Smith, March 16, 2021.

16 Lieutenant-Colonel Iain Clark, interview by Wolf Riedel and Kevin Smith, March 16, 2021.

17 Leveridge, *Sagem CU-161 Sperwer*, 9.

18 The first had been on September 11th when a rocket impacted in Camp WAREHOUSE particularly close to Warrant Officer Snodgrass. Master Warrant Officer (Retd) Art Snodgrass, interview by Wolf Riedel and Kevin Smith, February 24, 2021.

19 Leveridge, *Sagem CU-161 Sperwer*, 10.

20 Major Richard Little, interview by Wolf Riedel and Kevin Smith, February 6 and 9, and October 26, 2021.

21 Lieutenant-Colonel Iain Clark, interview by Wolf Riedel and Kevin Smith, March 16, 2021.

22 Lieutenant-Colonel Iain Clark, interview by Wolf Riedel and Kevin Smith, March 16, 2021.

23 SCUD is the North Atlantic Treaty Organization nickname for a mobile Soviet ballistic missile with a range of some 180 km. FROG is a North Atlantic Treaty Organization nickname meaning Free Rocket Over Ground for a Soviet unguided rocket with a range of approximately 65 km.

24 Ordinarily, during training, the potential point of impact of an illumination round's carrier shell only matters in the case of a round malfunctioning and needing to be located so that it can be destroyed. On operations in which civilian collateral damage was viewed as a strategically important factor there is a need to determine the expected point of impact of the carrier shell—which is usually offset from the target being illuminated—as its mass can cause collateral damage, especially in a built up area, even though it no longer contains any explosive or illuminating filler material.

25 Very generally, a round fired from a gun will go further the higher the tube is elevated until approximately 45° at which point it will start to drop closer. When the barrel of a gun is elevated beyond that point the fire is termed high angle. High angle fire is used to go over high terrain or obstacles either close to the gun or the target or to achieve certain effects.

26 A blind is a projectile that has failed to function as intended and remains relatively intact.

27 A CV9030N is a Swedish tracked infantry fighting vehicle used by Norway.

28 Chief Warrant Officer (Retd) Dennis Franken, interview by Wolf Riedel and Kevin Smith, March 21, 2021.

29 The definition of what constitutes light artillery varies between countries and over time and is based more on the calibre and effect of the projectile rather than

the actual weight of the gun. By US and Canadian standards any gun up to and including 105mm is light. A 155mm would be designated medium. For Soviet equipment, which formed most of the Afghans' inventory, the venerable D-30 at 122mm would be classified as light while 152mm guns would be medium.

30   Master Gunners are Senior Non-Commissioned Members who have received extensive training and are subject matter experts in all technical aspects of gunnery.

31   Major Richard Little, interview by Wolf Riedel and Kevin Smith, February 6 and 9, and October 26, 2021; Lieutenant-Colonel Dan Matheson, interview by Wolf Riedel and Kevin Smith, March 4, 2021; and Master Warrant Officer (retd) Andy Skinner, interview by Wolf Riedel and Kevin Smith, February 2, 2021.

32   Major (Retd) John Stewart, interview with Wolf Riedel September 5 and 6, 2023.

33   Major Bruno Di Ilio, "Directorate of Land Requirements DLR 2" briefing to instructor in gunnery course slide deck (2004), Slide 13

CHAPTER 8 - NE FAIS PAS DE MAL

1   "Do no harm" - part of the advice given to the battery by General Hillier on deployment.

2   General Rick Hillier, "Chapter 13 Friendly Fire," in *A Soldier First: Bullets, Bureaucrats and the Politics of War* (Toronto: HarperCollins, 2009); and Colonel Patrick Stogran, interview by Angus Brown, August 1, 2006, 19-22.

3   David Bercuson, et al, *Lessons Learned? What Canada Should Learn from Afghanistan* (Calgary: Canadian Defence & Foreign Affairs Institute, 2011), 10.

4   Lieutenant-General (Retd) Andrew Leslie, interview by Wolf Riedel and Kevin Smith, January 26, 2021.

5   Hillier, "Chapter 13 Friendly Fire," in *A Soldier First.*

6   Hillier, "Chapter 15 Kabul," in *A Soldier First.*

7   FRI(T): Immediate Reaction Force (Land).

8   Colonel Marc LaFortune, interview by Wolf Riedel and Kevin Smith, April 8 and 9, 2021.

9   Master Warrant Officer (Master Gunner) Tony Tullet, interview by Wolf Riedel and Kevin Smith, October 20, 2021.

10 Captain D.C. Buchanan, "Intelligence Surveillance Target Acquisition and Reconnaissance Coordination Centre IISTAR CC - Providing the Commander's Situational Awareness," *The Bulletin* 11, no. 1 (February 2005): 13-14.

11 Ibid., Figure 1.

12 Lieutenant-Colonel Jean-François Claveau, interview by Wolf Riedel and Kevin Smith, March 18, 2022.

13 Ibid.

14 Colonel Marc LaFortune, interview by Wolf Riedel and Kevin Smith, April 8 and 9, 2021.

15 Ibid.

16 Major-General Danny Fortin, interview by Wolf Riedel and Kevin Smith, February 18, 2022.

17 Dany Fortin et al. "The Challenges of a Multinational Headquarters - Kabul Multinational Brigade," *The Bulletin* 11, no. 3 (April 2005): 10.

18 Ibid.

19 Colonel Marc LaFortune, interview by Wolf Riedel and Kevin Smith, April 8 and 9, 2021.

20 "5 RALC," *The Canadian Gunner 2003-2004* 39 (February 2005): 13-14.

21 Ibid.

22 Colonel Marc LaFortune, interview by Wolf Riedel and Kevin Smith, April 8 and 9, 2021.

23 The CH-135 Twin Huey was the Canadian version of the US Bell UH-1N Iroquois helicopter.

24 Colonel Marc LaFortune, interview by Wolf Riedel and Kevin Smith, April 8 and 9, 2021.

25 Major-General Danny Fortin, interview by Wolf Riedel and Kevin Smith, February 18, 2022. Land Force Quebec Area.

26 Ibid.

27 Major-General Danny Fortin, interview by Wolf Riedel and Kevin Smith, February 18, 2022.

28 "5 RALC," *The Canadian Gunner 2003-2004*, 14.

29 Colonel Marc LaFortune, interview by Wolf Riedel and Kevin Smith, April 8 and 9, 2021.

30 Master Warrant Officer (Master Gunner) Tony Tullet, interview by Wolf Riedel and Kevin Smith, October 20, 2021. Tullett praised 5 GMBC for how welcoming they were to the team and how well they looked after all of the team's needs. The only exception perhaps was the lack of a good cultural brief on Afghanistan.

31 Lieutenant-Colonel Jean-François Claveau, interview by Wolf Riedel and Kevin Smith, March 18, 2022.

32 Colonel Marc LaFortune, interview by Wolf Riedel and Kevin Smith, April 8 and 9, 2021.

33 Ibid.

34 Ibid.

35 "5 RALC," *The Canadian Gunner 2003-2004,* 13-14.

36 Warrant Officer (Retd) G."Gabby" Pinard, interview by Wolf Riedel and Kevin Smith, April 18, 2021.

37 The An/PRC 117 provides a capability to talk to ground forces via VHF and air and aviation via UHF and has a TAC SAT capability.

38 Captain GR Eyestone and Lieutenant PDD Gilbert, "Athena Battery ISTAR Assets Deployed" *The Bulletin* 11, no. 5 (August 2005): 4-5.

39 Véhicule blindé léger, the French term for light armoured vehicle.

40 Chief Warrant Officer Éric Normand, email to Wolf Riedel January 17, 2022.

41 Eyestone and Gilbert," Athena Battery," 4-5.

42 Lieutenant-Colonel Jean-François Claveau, interview by Wolf Riedel and Kevin Smith, March 18, 2022.

43 Major-General (Retd) Eric Tremblay, interview by Wolf Riedel, September 15, 2023.

44 Buchanan, "Intelligence Surveillance," 14.

45 Secret Internet Protocol Router Network.

46 Major M.F. Murphy, "Airspace Coordination in Operations," *The Bulletin* 11, no. 3 (April 2005): 8.

47 A raster map tile graphic is a dot matrix data structure that represents a generally rectangular grid of pixels viewable by a computer. By contrast, vector map tiles are made of mathematical interpretations of geometric features such as points, lines and polygons.

48 Lieutenant-Colonel Jean-François Claveau, interview by Wolf Riedel and Kevin Smith, March 18, 2022.

49 Lieutenant-Colonel Jean-François Claveau, interview by Wolf Riedel and Kevin Smith, March 18, 2022. Amongst other things ADATS 400 delivered was a digital command and control system to complement the ADATS Rectification of Command, Control and Communications Repair and Overhaul Project which, among other things, would deliver, by 2008, five Bison airspace coordination centre vehicles for 4th Air Defence Regiment, RCA.

50 Major D.W. Whittier, "The Weight Behind Our Punch - SAS and the Cost of A Knowledge-Based Army," *The Bulletin* 12, no. 1 (March 2006): 2.

51 The Five Eyes intelligence community only includes Australia, New Zealand, Canada, the UK and the US.

52 Captain P .Lévesque, "Combat Service Support (CSS)," *The Bulletin* 11, no. 7 (November 2005): 3-4.

53 Master Warrant Officer D. Cossette, "To Centralize or Not to Centralize:

Comments on the Reconnaissance Squadron Echelon Doctrine," *The Bulletin* 11, no. 7 (November 2005): 7.

54 Captain C. Munger, "Combat Service Support - Centralized or Decentralized - As Seen In The Context Of Op Athena Roto 1," *The Bulletin* 11, no. 7 (November 2005): 5-6.

55 A total of 802 LUVWs, 160 of them armoured and 1,061 GM Silverado MILCOTS replaced the Iltis fleet. ISAF Mirror 5, Apr 2004, P10.

56 Colonel Marc LaFortune, interview by Wolf Riedel and Kevin Smith, April 8 and 9, 2021; "KMNB in action," *ISAF Mirror 5*, (April 2004): 7.

57 Warrant Officer(Retd) Gabriel "Gabby" Pinard, emessage to Kevin Smith, 20 September, 2023, Colonel (Retd) Jean-François Duval email to Wolf Riedel, 20 September 2023.

58 Captain P. Gagnon, "UAVs in the Theatre of Operations," *The Bulletin* 11, no. 3 (April 2005): 17.

59 T.F.J. Leveridge, *Sagem CU-161 Sperwer Canadian Armed Forces Serial 16101* (Ottawa: Canadian Aviation and Space Museum, 2013), 26-28. Aircraft 161003 and 161005 replaced by 161007 and 161008.

60 Ibid., 10.

61 Ibid., 10.

62 Hillier, *A Soldier First*, 271.

63 Master Warrant Officer (Master Gunner) Tony Tullet, interview by Wolf Riedel and Kevin Smith, October 20, 2021.

64 Hillier, "Chapter 14 Four Stars," in *A Soldier First*. On reflection Hillier thought this a strategic mistake in that with the downsized mission, the pressure on the government for funding was removed.

65 Captain John C. Scott, "Sequencing for Future Success—Observations on the Task Force Kabul Mission Draw-Down," *The Bulletin* 12, no. 1 (March 2006): 7-9.

66 Major-General Danny Fortin, interview by Wolf Riedel and Kevin Smith, February 18, 2022.

67 Colonel Marc LaFortune, interview by Wolf Riedel and Kevin Smith, April 8 and 9, 2021; and "5 RALC," *The Canadian Gunner 2003-2004* 39 (February 2005): 13-14.

68 Major-General Danny Fortin, interview by Wolf Riedel and Kevin Smith, February 18, 2022.

CHAPTER 9 - THE SECOND INTERLUDE: SUMMER 2004 - FALL 2005

1 Colonel W.J. Ellis, "Comd TFK End Tour Report - Operation Athena Roto 2:

9 Aug 04 - 10 Feb 05," *The Bulletin* 11, no. 2 (March 2005): 4. See also Captain John C. Scott, "Sequencing For Future Success - Observation of Task Force Kabul Mission Draw-Down," *The Bulletin* 12, no. 1 (March 2006): 6.

2   Ibid., 8.

3   There is some ambiguity in the open source material on when Phase 1 of Operation Athena actually ended. The National Defence archived website states that Phase 1 ended in July 2005 when Roto 3 ended and that Phase 2 of Operation ATHENA started with Roto 0 in August 2005. See Government of Canada, "Operation ATHENA," Accessed July 17, 2023. https://www.canada.ca/en/department-national-defence/services/operations/military-operations/recently-completed/operation-athena.html. Conversely, "G Coy Deploys on Op Athena," *Pro Patria 87* (April 2007): 16 states that G Company deployed on Operation Athena Roto 4 in July 2005, that Athena ended on October 18th at which time G Company transitioned to Operation Archer Roto 0. Peter Pigott, *Canada in Afghanistan: The War So Far* (Toronto: Dundurn Press, 2007), 106 also states that Athena ended October 18th.

4   A Kandak is the Afghan term for a battalion of approximately 600 men.

5   Captain Michael Chagon, "Canadian Embedded Training Team," *The Bulletin* 10, no. 8 (December 2004): 6.

6   Chief Warrant Officer (Retd) Dennis Franken, email to Wolf Riedel, September 24, 2021.

7   Made up of soldiers from the Florida National Guard's 211th Infantry Regiment augmented by the Nebraska National Guard's 209th Infantry Regiment.

8   Colonel Mike Sullivan, interview by Wolf Riedel and Kevin Smith, September 22, 2021. Intakes were supervised by the Central Intelligence Agency and roughly blended into 44% Pashtuns, 25% Tajiks 10% Hazaras and 21% other.

9   Captain L.A. Shrum, "Lessons Not Yet Learned - Tactical Airspace Operations in Afghanistan" *The Bulletin* 11, no. 8 (December 2005): 2 and Captain L.A. Shrum, "Transformation and Airspace Operations in Afghanistan," *Canadian Military Journal* 7, no. 3 (Autumn 2006): 15.

10 David J. Bercuson et al, *Lessons learned? What Canada Should learn From Afghanistan* (Calgary: Canadian Defence & Foreign Affairs Institute, 2011), 6-7.

11 Colonel (Retd) Mike Capstick, telephone interview by Wolf Riedel, November 17, 2021. Foreign Affairs had even been resistant to opening an embassy in Afghanistan and essentially ran the operation on a shoestring.

12 Bercuson et al, *Lessons Learned*, 6.

13 Michel-Henri St. Louis, "The Strategic Advisory Team-Afghanistan - Part of The Comprehensive Approach to Stability Operations" *Canadian Military*

Journal 9, no. 3 (Winter 2009): 60.

14 Bercuson et al, *Lessons Learned*, 8.

15 Colonel Mike Capstick, "The Civil-Military Effort in Afghanistan: A Strategic Perspective," Journal of Military and Strategic Studies 10, no. 1 (Fall 2007): 25.

16 Bercuson et al, *Lessons Learned*, 8.

17 General Rick Hillier, *A Soldier First: Bullets, Bureaucrats and the Politics of War* (Toronto: HarperCollins, 2009), 314. Hillier states the government had already commenced planning to go to Kandahar before he returned from Kabul. Recollections and opinions vary as to the underlying reasons for the Martin government choosing Kandahar.

18 Associated Press "Canada to nearly double troops in Afghanistan: AP" Accessed June 10, 2021, 2021, CTV News February 14, 2005, https://web.archive.org/web/20061004011130/http://www.ctv.ca/servlet/ArticleNews/story/CTVNews/1108317447589_3/?hub=Canada.

19 Bill Shiller, "The Road to Kandahar: How Did We Get There?" Toronto Star, September 9, 2006.

20 Peter Pigott, *Canada in Afghanistan: The War So Far* (Toronto: Dundurn Press 2007), 104.

21 Lieutenant-Colonel Ian Hope, *Dancing With the Dushman: Command Imperatives For The Counter-Insurgency Fight in Afghanistan,* (Kingston: Canadian Defence Academy Press, 2008), 23.

22 "Canada sending more troops to Afghanistan" Accessed February 21, 2022, CBC News, May 17, 2005 https://www.cbc.ca/news/canada/canada-sending-more-troops-to-afghanistan-1.559176

23 Department of National Defence, *Canada's International Policy Statement: A Role of Pride and Influence in the World - Defence* (Ottawa: DND, 2005), 3.

24 Ibid., 3-6.

25 Hillier, *A Soldier First*, 250.

26 Lieutenant-General (Retired) Michael Jeffery, *Inside Canadian Forces Transformation: Institutional Leadership as a Catalyst for Change* (Kingston, Canadian Forces Defence Academy, 2009), 21-32. See also Hillier, *A Soldier First*, 266-268. Concurrently, three additional commands were formed: Canada Command; Canadian Operational Support Command; and Canadian Special Operations Forces Command.

27 For detailed studies of the Hillier initiated Transformation see: Jeffery, *Inside Canadian Forces Transformation*, and the shorter Lieutenant-General (Ret'd) Michael K. Jeffery, "Inside Canadian Forces Transformation," *Canadian Military Journal* 10, no. 2 (Spring 2009): 9-18.

28 Department of National Defence. Major Bruno, Di Ilio, "Directorate of Land

Requirements DLR 2" PowerPoint briefing to instructor in gunnery course 2004, Slide 13. In fairness, under Jeffery there had been no plan to divest the M109s nor had mechanical problems with the LG1 raised their heads. The direction to remove the former and the problems with the latter arose quickly under Hillier's watch.

29 Colonel (Retd) Bob Gunn, interview by Wolf Riedel and Kevin Smith, March 31, 2022.

30 "4th Air Defence Regiment," *The Canadian Gunner 40 2005* (February 2006): 12.

31 Ibid.

32 Ibid., and Colonel (Retd) Bob Gunn, interview by Wolf Riedel and Kevin Smith, March 31, 2022.

33 The artillery had fought strongly for Sperwer and had held onto it during Kabul but its weight and the altitude that it could operate at had put it into the category of a Tactical Unmanned Aerial Vehicle which was now an RCAF field. The RCAF's continuing argument for airworthiness certification requiring aircrew trained operators/supervisors finally won out albeit the army did keep a presence in the new organization. See Colonel (Retd) Bob Gunn, interview by Wolf Riedel and Kevin Smith, March 31, 2022.

34 T.F.J .Leveridge, *Sagem CU-161 Sperwer Canadian Armed Forces Serial 16101* (Ottawa: Canadian Aviation and Space Museum, 2013), 12.

35 Colonel Marc LaFortune, interview by Wolf Riedel and Kevin Smith, April 8 and 9, 2021. See also Colonel (Retd) Bob Gunn, interview by Wolf Riedel and Kevin Smith, March 31, 2022.

36 Major Jacques Gobin, email to Major Steve Gallagher, August, 5 2005.

37 Master Warrant Officer (Master Gunner) Tony Tullet, interview by Wolf Riedel and Kevin Smith, October 20, 2021.

38 Department of National Defence. Lieutenant-General Marc Caron, "3185-1(LFDI 2) Implementation Directive Transformation of Field Artillery" July 20, 2005. The artillery's restructure was a person-years neutral trade off in order to create what is necessary to maintain what the artillery is and does and to position the resources that the artillery has to be able to provide the things in the future that the army requires, per Colonel (Retd) Bob Gunn, interview by Wolf Riedel and Kevin Smith, March 31, 2022. Colonel Rocky LeCroix, Gunn's successor as the Director of Artillery in 2006 credits Gunn with having kept the core capabilities alive and having crafted much of the campaign plan to address the "hollow artillery" and position the Regiment for a seamless transition into the future. See *The Canadian Gunner 2006* 41a (February 2007): 5-6.

39 Concurrently, the air defence artillery was heading towards merging into

the armoured corps in its own attempt to remain relevant with continued experimentation in the concept of the direct fire unit.

40 In large part through the use of the existing 9 battery commanders and their teams

41 Colonel Peter Williams, email to Brian Reid, September 3, 2021.

42 Caron, "Implementation Directive," at paragraph 3.a.

43 Captain (Retd) Ken Whitnall, interview by Wolf Riedel, Brian Reid and Kevin Smith, September 23 and 27, 2021. Research was conducted to determine if the M109A4+ could be upgraded to an M109A6 Paladin but it was considered impractical for numerous reasons including that the production lines for A6 conversions had been closed for several years .

44 "Message from the Director of Artillery," *The Canadian Gunner 2005* 40 (February 2006): 5 & 7

45 Ibid. and Captain (Retd) Ken Whitnall, email to Wolf Riedel, March 9, 2022. GIAT subsequently admitted the cracks were the result of a design flaw. The barrels were redesigned and replaced at a prorated cost.

46 Ibid.

47 Ibid.

48 Captain (Retd) Ken Whitnall, email to Wolf Riedel, March 10, 2022.

49 Major-General (Retd) David Fraser, message to Wolf Riedel,October 6, 2023.

50 Low Rate Initial Production is a system to manufacture a number of guns to allow fielding and testing of both manufacturing processes as well as in service reliability and maintenance requirements.

51 Lieutenant-General (Retd) Andrew Leslie, interview by Wolf Riedel, Brian Reid and Kevin Smith, May 6, 7 and 11, 2021.

52 Major-General (Retd) David Fraser, message to Wolf Riedel,October 6, 2023.

53 Lieutenant-General (Retd) Andrew Leslie, interview by Wolf Riedel, Brian Reid and Kevin Smith, May 6, 7 and 11, 2021.

54 Ibid.

55 Department of National Defence. Synopsis Sheet (Effective Project Approval) Lightweight 155mm Towed Howitzer Project 00001017 Aug 05

56 Lieutenant-Colonel Jim Willis, email to Colonel Bob Gunn, September 1, 2005; Discussions with Raytheon, the manufacturer of Excalibur, indicated that all produced rounds were already earmarked to US troops but that they had the parts available for 27 rounds which could be assembled for Canada if approved for acquisition. A backup plan was agreed that if they could not be sold to Canada then three rounds would be provided in Yuma, AZ for test purposes and 24 would be delivered to 10 Mountain Division in Afghanistan and provided for Canada's use. The direct sale to Canada was cleared and the

backup plan was not needed. Colonel (Retd) Bob Gunn, interview by Wolf Riedel and Kevin Smith, March 31, 2022.

57 Lieutenant-Colonel Jim Willis, email to Major Bruno Di Ilio, October 17, 2005. Delivery of the first six guns was delayed by one week due to the plant having to close during Hurricane Katrina in late August 2005. Colonel (Retd) Bob Gunn, interview by Wolf Riedel and Kevin Smith, March 31, 2022.

58 3rd Battalion, 319th Airborne Field Artillery Regiment.

59 Department of National Defence. Gallagher, Major Steve, 3350-1(BC A) Artillery Tactical Recce Report, November 5, 2005.

60 Department of National Defence. Brigadier-General Stuart Beare, "Land Force Doctrine and Training System Headquarters, 4500-1 (ATA) Training Directive – M777 Lightweight Towed Howitzer", November 29, 2005.

61 Ibid.; See also Department of Public Works and Government Services. Sandi Branker, Public Works and Government Services Canada, Canadian Embassy Washington (Letter of Request (Restate) LOR-CN-P-P-082306-01", August 23. 2006.

62 Captain (Retd) Ken Whitnall, email to Wolf Riedel, March 10, 2022.

63 Brigadier-General Dan Ross had commanded 2nd Regiment, Royal Canadian Horse Artillery from 1990 to 1992, and Land Force Western Area from 1997 to 1999 after which he became Deputy to the Foreign Policy Advisor to the Prime Minister and Director of Operations for the Foreign and Defence Secretariat at the Privy Council Office. After retiring from the Canadian Forces in 2002 he held several senior civil service jobs before his tenure as the Assistant Deputy Minister (Material) from 2005 to 2012.

64 Brigadier-General (Retd) and Assistant Deputy Minister (Material) (Retd) Dan Ross, interview by Wolf Riedel, Brian Reid and Kevin Smith May 5, 2021.

65 Ibid.

66 Ibid.

67 Brigadier-General (Retd) and Assistant Deputy Minister (Material) (Retd) Dan Ross, interview by Wolf Riedel, Brian Reid and Kevin Smith May 5, 2021. National Procurement monies are expended by ADM(Mat) to support the army based upon the advice of the army G4 (Logistics) staff who manage in service equipment. Army staff had not, at this time, been recommending the expenditure of such funds to address the barrel issue: Colonel (Retd) Bob Gunn, emails to Wolf Riedel , April 4 and 12, 2022.

68 Brigadier-General (Retd) and Assistant Deputy Minister (Material) (Retd) Dan Ross, interview by Wolf Riedel, Brian Reid and Kevin Smith May 5, 2021.

69 Captain (Retd) Ken Whitnall, emails to Wolf Riedel, March 10, 2022. The conversion of an M109A4+ to an A6 would have first required a major

conversion to A5 and then another major conversion to A6. The production line for A5 had stopped in the US by that time and had already changed to A6 to A7 conversions. Accordingly, while feasible, the complication and cost were a factor and the willingness within the army to go this route, as it would do later for the Leopard tanks, simply wasn't there.

70 Brigadier-General (Retd) and Assistant Deputy Minister (Material) (Retd) Dan Ross, interview by Wolf Riedel, Brian Reid and Kevin Smith May 5, 2021.

71 Ibid.

72 Major-General Michael D. Maples, "Relevant and Ready: The FA Now and in the Future," *Field Artillery* (November-December 2003): 1.

73 Department of National Defence. PowerPoint brief for "Artillery Transformation: Commandant's Planning Session" September 2005.

74 Major-General (Ret'd) David Fraser and Brian Hanington, *Operation Medusa: The Furious Battle that Saved Afghanistan* (Toronto: McClelland and Stewart, 2018), 35-39.

75 "2 RCR" *Pro Patria 2005* 87 (April 2006): 16-20.

76 Major (Retd) Justin Brunelle, interview by Wolf Riedel and Kevin Smith, June 20, 2021.

77 Warrant Officer Steve Merson, interview by Mark Zuehlke and Kevin Smith, April 25, 2023.

78 Ibid.

CHAPTER 10 - PREPARING FOR THE RETURN TO KANDAHAR

1 Lieutenant-Colonel Ian Hope, *Dancing With the Dushman: Command Imperatives For The Counter-Insurgency Fight in Afghanistan* (Kingston: Canadian Defence Academy Press, 2008), 23.

2 Nancy Teeple, *Canada in Afghanistan: 2001-2010 A Military Chronology* (Kingston: Defence R&D Canada, 2010), 25.

3 Major-General (Ret'd) David Fraser, and Brian Hanington, *Operation Medusa: The Furious Battle that Saved Afghanistan* (Toronto: McClelland and Stewart, 2018), 35.

4 *The Patrician* 56, (2004): 17-19.

5 A "Regiment Right" has all the guns in the regiment fire sequentially at a given interval between each gun firing.

6 Hope, *Dancing With the Dushman*, 22-23.

7 Fraser and Hanington, *Operation Medusa*, 35-46.

8 Colonel (Retd) Ian Hope, interview by Brian Reid, Wolf Riedel and Kevin Smith, May 28 and June 10, 2021. In fact six gunners from 1st Regiment, Royal Canadian Horse Artillery did deploy with the PRT. *The Canadian Gunner*

2005 40 (February 2006): 6.

9 Colonel (Retd) Ian Hope, interview by Brian Reid, Wolf Riedel and Kevin Smith, May 28 and June 10, 2021.

10 Ibid.

11 Major-General (Retd) David Fraser, message to Wolf Riedel, October 6, 2023.

12 Even before the recce, Hope had spoken with Hillier and they had no illusions but that they were potentially going into a very serious environment that was going to grow worse as they transitioned into it.

13 Colonel (Retd) Tim Bishop, interview by Wolf Riedel, Brian Reid and Kevin Smith, July 26 and August 2, 2021 and Colonel (retd) Ian Hope, interview by Brian Reid, Wolf Riedel and Kevin Smith, May 28 and June 10, 2021.

14 Colonel (Retd) Ian Hope, interview by Brian Reid, Wolf Riedel and Kevin Smith, May 28 and June 10, 2021. The "Golf Bag" principle means that there would be one detachment employing both weapons. In practice an artillery detachment could man one gun or two mortars at any given time, but not both.

15 Ibid. Canadian Forces members on duty specified distances away from home for specified extended periods of time are entitled to periods of leave, subject to limitations that can be placed on such leave, to return home or to meet their family at a third location. Financial assistance for travel for such leave is provided under the home leave travel assistance (HLTA). Almost all tours were long enough to trigger such leave which, because of the financial assistance, was often referred to as HLTA or HLTA leave. Personnel going on HTLA leave were very rarely replaced by someone from outside the theatre of operations and accordingly left the deployed units short-handed during all but roughly the first and last months of the tour.

16 Typically a gun battery's echelon would have a quartermaster, a half dozen ammunition vehicles, a kitchen, an ambulance, a fuel truck, and vehicle, weapons and electronics technicians.

17 Lieutenant-Colonel Steve Gallagher, interview by Brian Reid, Wolf Riedel and Kevin Smith, May 17 and 18, 2021. A four person team would eventually deploy and obtain its gas from Pakistan. In addition to calculated met from balloon flights, the team would also develop meteorological data using the IGRADS - Integrated Grid Analysis and Display System from the internet.

18 Master Warrant Officer (Retd) Paul Parsons and Lieutenant-Colonel Steve Gallagher interview by Kevin Smith, May 25 and June 1, 2021.

19 Hope, *Dancing with the Dushman*, 22-23.

20 Major-General (Retd) David Fraser, message to Wolf Riedel, October 6, 2023.

21 Lieutenant-Colonel Howie Nelson, interview by Wolf Riedel, Brian Reid and Kevin Smith, January 21 and 28, 2022.

22 Lieutenant-Colonel Steve Gallagher, email to Brian Reid, January 13, 2021.

23 A Battery Task Force 1-06 88.xls spreadsheet, undated.

24 Lieutenant-Colonel Steve Gallagher, interview by Brian Reid, Wolf Riedel and Kevin Smith, May 17 and 18, 2021 and *The Canadian Gunner 2006* 41a, (February 2007): 6.

25 A "Joint" task force consists of elements from two or more services such as army, navy, air force, or marines.

26 Technically under US naming convention a task force made up from various countries would be called a Combined Task Force. AEGIS chose to call itself a Coalition Task Force but is occasionally also referred to as Combined Task Force AEGIS such as in American publications.

27 Subsequent to August 1, 2006 Combined Joint Task Force-76 would stay in theatre commanding Regional Command (East) until relieved by Combined Joint Task Force-82 (US 82nd Airborne Division) in mid-2007.

28 Lieutenant-Colonel P.J. Williams, "Effects Based Operations In Afghanistan," *The Quadrant* 22, no.3 (Winter 2006): 10. See also Peter J. Williams, "Being Effective in Snake Fighting - Lessons For The Canadian Forces in the Effects-Based Operations Era," *Canadian Military Journal* 10, no. 4 (Autumn 2010): 19.

29 Captain Daniel C. DiNicola et al, "Afghanistan: CJTF-76 Joint Fires Board in OEF 04-06," *Field Artillery* (March -April 2006): 35.

30 Colonel (Retd) Peter Williams, interview by Wolf Riedel, Brian Reid and Kevin Smith, June 16, 2021.

31 Colonel (Retd) Tim Bishop, interview by Wolf Riedel, Brian Reid and Kevin Smith, July 26 and August 2, 2021.

32 Governor General of Canada, Honours Recipients, https://www.gg.ca/en/honours/recipients

33 *The Canadian Gunner 2006* 41a, (February 2007): 6.

34 Governor General of Canada, Honours Recipients, https://www.gg.ca/en/honours/recipients

35 *The Canadian Gunner 2006* 41a, (February 2007): 13.

36 Captain Rory Moore, "Experiences of a Junior Officer" *The Quadrant* 23, no. 1 (Summer 2007): 5.

37 Ibid.

38 Ibid.

39 mIRC is a commercial Windows based Internet Relay Chat client.

40 4th Air Defence Regiment, RCA PowerPoint presentation "2006-7 TFK ASCC Ops", Undated.

41 Sperwer was the Forces' tactical unmanned aerial vehicle. The smaller Israeli

Elbit Skylark would be deployed as the miniature unmanned aerial vehicle.

42 See for example PowerPoint brief for "Artillery Transformation: Commandant's Planning Session" September 2005, slide 14.

43 T.F.J .Leveridge, *Sagem CU-161 Sperwer Canadian Armed Forces Serial 16101* (Ottawa: Canadian Aviation and Space Museum, 2013), 12.

CHAPTER 11 - ENTER THE TRIPLE SEVEN

1 Master Warrant Officer (Retd) Paul Parsons and Lieutenant-Colonel Steve Gallagher, interview by Kevin Smith, May 25 and June 1, 2021.

2 Ibid.

3 Ibid.

4 Lieutenant Lewis, "A Bty prepared for Task Force Orion," *The Quadrant* 21, no. 3 (Winter 2006): 9.

5 Captain (Retd) Darcy Cyr, interview by Wolf Riedel, Brian Reid and Kevin Smith, August 9, 2021.

6 Ibid.

7 Ibid.

8 Colonel (Retd) Ian Hope, interview by Brian Reid, Wolf Riedel and Kevin Smith, May 28, and June 10, 2021.

9 Ibid., Brigadier-General Fraser disagrees with the directed training having shortcomings and holds that the battle group "worked at the direction of the brigade and army requirements for the [operational evaluation] exercise ... the direction of the Army Commander and the [Chief of Defence Staff] was clear. We were all working to achieve a collective capability." Major-General (Retd) David Fraser, message to Wolf Riedel, October 6, 2023. The battle-group, including A Battery, were provided time in theatre for additional training.

10 Major Steve Gallagher, "3350-1, Artillery Tactical Recce Report," November 4, 2005.

11 Lieutenant-Colonel Steve Gallagher, interview by Brian Reid, Wolf Riedel and Kevin Smith, May 17 and 18, 2021.

12 PowerPoint brief for "Artillery Transformation: Commandant's Planning Session" September 2005.

13 Lieutenant-Colonel Jim Willis, Major Bruno Di Ilio and Major André Pageau, PowerPoint Brief "Lightweight 155mm Howitzer M777E1: Presentation to Artillery Working Group Meeting," October 4, 2005.

14 Lieutenant-Colonel Steve Gallagher, interview by Brian Reid, Wolf Riedel and Kevin Smith, May 17 and 18, 2021.

15 Captain (Retd) (Master Gunner) Kevin Smith, email to Brian Reid, August 9, 2018.

16 Captain (Retd) (Master Gunner) Kevin Smith, email to Wolf Riedel, April 19, 2022.

17 Draft Introduction Plan M777 Lightweight 155MM Towed Howitzer (LWTH) System, November 2005. See the 1st Regiment, Royal Canadian Horse Artillery, 2nd Regiment, Royal Canadian Horse Artillery and RCAS articles in *The Canadian Gunner 2005* 40 (February 2006) for additional details.

18 Captain (Retd) (Master Gunner) Kevin Smith, email to Wolf Riedel, December 26, 2022.

19 Master Warrant Officer (Retd) John Gero, interview by Wolf Riedel, February 22, 2023.

20 Brigadier-General Stuart Beare, "Land Force Doctrine and Training System Headquarters, 4500-1 (ATA) Training Directive – M777 Lightweight Towed Howitzer," (Kingston: DND, November 29, 2005).

21 Colonel (Retd) Peter Williams, message to Wolf Riedel, June 12, 2023.

22 Lewis, "A Bty prepared for Task Force Orion", 9.

23 Captain (Retd) (Master Gunner) Kevin Smith, email to Brian Reid, December 2, 2020.

24 Lieutenant-Colonel Andrew Nicholson, interview by Kevin Smith, May 3, 2022. The tools were placed in a Seacan and shipped to Afghanistan but never seen again.

25 Lieutenant-Colonel Steve Gallagher, interview by Brian Reid, Wolf Riedel and Kevin Smith, May 17 and 18, 2021; Originally The RCR crest was painted on the shields of the battery's 25-pounders, but these were later replaced by plaques. See G.D. Mitchell, (With B.A. Reid & W. Simcock) *RCHA – Right of the Line; An Anecdotal History of the Royal Canadian Horse Artillery From 1871* (Ottawa, RCHA History Committee, 1971), 178.

26 Colonel (Retd) Tim Bishop, interview by Wolf Riedel, Brian Reid and Kevin Smith, July 26 and August 2, 2021.

27 The first would have been then Captain, now Major-General, Mike Rouleau. Concurrently several artillery non-commissioned members were qualifying as assaulters.

28 Brigadier-General Steve Hunter, interviewed by Mark Zuehlke, Wolf Riedel and Kevin Smith, September 12, 2023.

CHAPTER 12 - OPERATION ENDURING FREEDOM

1 Institute for the Study of War, "Regional Command South" (Washington: Institute for the Study of War). Accessed February 4, 2023, Regional Command South | Institute for the Study of War (understandingwar.org).

2 Carl Forsberg, *Afghanistan Report 3: The Taliban Campaign for Kandahar*

(Washington: Institute for the Study of War, 2009), 21.

3   Named after their home base in the city of Quetta, Pakistan.

4   Forsberg, *Afghanistan Report 3*, 23.

5   Lieutenant-Colonel Ian Hope, *Dancing With the Dushman: Command Imperatives For The Counter-Insurgency Fight in Afghanistan* (Kingston: Canadian Defence Academy Press, 2008), 33-40.

6   Carter Malkasian, T*he American War in Afghanistan: A History* (New York: Oxford University Press, 2021), 115-129.

7   Lieutenant-Colonel Bertrand A. Ges, "3-319 AFAR TF Gun Devils: Providing FA Fires for Afghanistan and Maneuvering on the Enemy," *Field Artillery* (September-October 2006): 20. Task Force GUN DEVILS was a composite organization with two of its organic batteries and an attached infantry anti-armour company, an infantry company, an MP platoon, a Romanian rifle company, and two Afghan National Army Kandaks.

8   Forsberg, *Afghanistan Report 3,* 18-19.

9   Brian Neumann and Colin J. Williams, *The U.S. Army in Afghanistan Operation Enduring Freedom May 2005 - January 2009* (Washington: Center of Military History, 2020), 22. See also Edmund Degen and Mark Reardon, *Modern War in an Ancient Land: The United States Army in Afghanistan 2001-2014 Vol II* (Washington: Center of Military History, United States Army, 2021), 142-143.

10 Neumann and Williams, *The U.S. Army in Afghanistan*, 10-11, 23.

11 Ibid., 23.

12 Lieutenant-Colonel Ian Hope, *Dancing With the Dushman: Command Imperatives For The Counter-Insurgency Fight in Afghanistan* (Kingston: Canadian Defence Academy Press, 2008), 41-46.

13 Major Steve Gallagher, "Op Archer Task Force Orion January - August 2006" PowerPoint presentation, undated (approximately 2006-7), Notes to Slide 7.

14 Captain (Retd) Darcy Cyr, interview by Wolf Riedel, Brian Reid and Kevin Smith, August 9, 2021.

15 Master Warrant Officer (Retd) John Gero, interview by Wolf Riedel, February 22, 2023.

16 Master Warrant Officer (Retd) Paul Parsons and Lieutenant-Colonel Steve Gallagher, interview by Kevin Smith, May 25 and June 1, 2021.; Lieutenant-Colonel Steve Gallagher, interview by Brian Reid, Wolf Riedel and Kevin Smith, May 17 and 18, 2021.

17 Lieutenant-Colonel Steve Gallagher, interview by Brian Reid, Wolf Riedel and Kevin Smith, May 17 and 18, 2021.

18 *The Canadian Gunner 2006* 41a (February 2007): 7.

19 Major Steve Gallagher, email to Brian Reid, August 7, 2009.

20 Lieutenant-Colonel Steve Gallagher, interview by Brian Reid, Wolf Riedel and Kevin Smith, May 17 and 18, 2021.

21 Master Warrant Officer (Retd) Paul Parsons and Lieutenant-Colonel Steve Gallagher, interview by Kevin Smith, May 25 and June 1, 2021.

22 Lieutenant-Colonel Andrew Nicholson, interview by Kevin Smith, May 3, 2022.

23 Ibid.

24 Lieutenant-Colonel Howie Nelson, interview by Wolf Riedel, Brian Reid and Kevin Smith, January 21 and 28, 2022. See also Captain (Retd) Darcy Cyr, interview by Wolf Riedel, Brian Reid and Kevin Smith, August 9, 2021.

25 Hope, *Dancing With the Dushman*, 46.

26 Gallagher, "Op Archer" presentation, Slide 28.

27 Master Warrant Officer (Retd) Paul Parsons and Lieutenant-Colonel Steve Gallagher, interview by Kevin Smith, May 25 and June 1, 2021.

28 Hope, *Dancing With the Dushman*, 61. See also Lieutenant-Colonel Steve Gallagher, interview by Brian Reid, Wolf Riedel and Kevin Smith, May 17 and 18, 2021.

29 Colonel (Retd) Ian Hope, interview by Brian Reid, Wolf Riedel and Kevin Smith, May 28, and June 10, 2021.

30 Hope, *Dancing With the Dushman*, 45.

31 Lieutenant-Colonel Peter Williams, email to Major LP McGarry et al cc Major-General Andrew Leslie et al, February 20, 2006.

32 Hope, *Dancing With the Dushman*, 46.

33 Colonel (Retd) Tim Bishop, interview by Wolf Riedel, Brian Reid and Kevin Smith, July 26 and August 2, 2021.

34 Op PHAROS was an ongoing series of missions in the area local to Kandahar and ran from 27 February until 17 Apr 2006.

35 Colonel (Retd) Ian Hope, interview by Brian Reid, Wolf Riedel and Kevin Smith, May 28 and June 10, 2021. See also *The Canadian Gunner 2006* 41a (February 2007): 7.

36 *The Canadian Gunner 2006* 41a (February 2007): 7.

37 From this point forward, Coalition Task Force AEGIS assumed the role of Regional Command (South) which it retained until November 1, 2006.

38 Colonel (Retd) Tim Bishop, interview by Wolf Riedel, Brian Reid and Kevin Smith, July 26 and August 2, 2021.

39 Ibid.

40 Lieutenant-Colonel Steve Gallagher, interview by Brian Reid, Wolf Riedel and Kevin Smith, May 17 and 18, 2021.

41 Hope, *Dancing With the Dushman*, 55.

42 Ibid., 56-57.

43 Ibid., 64-65.

44 Lieutenant-Colonel Steve Gallagher, "TF ORION Op Archer Roto 1 Tour Summary," PowerPoint presentation as at August 12, 2006. Slide 4.

45 Lieutenant-Colonel Steve Gallagher, interview by Wolf Riedel, February 10, 2023.

46 Hope, *Dancing With the Dushman*, 66.

47 Lieutenant-Colonel Andrew Nicholson, interview by Kevin Smith, May 3, 2022.

48 The RCAF did not deliver that reference until 2009. The method Parsons created became the basis for all Canadian M777 batteries as an interim measure, although it too required modification for a double hookup method for some Chinook variants. The RCAF reference did not address the double hookup method, and again it was the gunners themselves, in collaboration with respective allies flying the Chinooks, that came up with a practical methods. Kevin Smith, message to Wolf Riedel, March 22, 2023.

49 Master Warrant Officer (Retd) Paul Parsons and Lieutenant-Colonel Steve Gallagher interview by Kevin Smith, May 25 and June 1, 2021.

50 Degen and Reardon, *Modern War in an Ancient Land Vol II*, 75.

51 Colonel Stuart Tootal, *Danger Close: The True Story of Helmand from the Leader of 3 Para* (London: John Murray Publishers, 2009). Kindle edition location 404.

52 Hope, *Dancing With the Dushman*, 50.

53 The term used by US forces for forward air controller (FAC) had changed to Joint Terminal Attack Controller and was finding itself into Canadian usage and was used here rather than FAC. The term FAC was subsequently replaced by JTAC in Canada as time and training changed.

54 Lieutenant-Colonel Ian Hope, "TF ORION 3350-3 (ALLO), Task Force Orion - Fire Support, Initial Theatre Lesson Report," March 26, 2006.

55 It was the first time the Americans had ever asked for permission.

56 Colonel Michael Cross, "Operation Mountain Lion: CJTF-76 in Afghanistan, Spring 2006," *Military Review* (January-February 2008): 23.

57 Neumann and Williams , *The U.S. Army in Afghanistan*, 28-29.

CHAPTER 13 - OPERATION MOUNTAIN LION REDUX

1 Since it is best known as Forward Operating Base Robinson that name will be used hereafter.

2 Major-General (Retd) David Fraser, message to Wolf Riedel, October 6, 2023.

The platoon was subsequently dispensed with as it could be better used on the ground and the reserve consisted solely of the two attack helicopters which Fraser considered more effective and efficient.

3   Lieutenant-General J.C.M. Gauthier, "CEFCOM 1080-1 (DComd), CEFCOM Review of BOI Report on the Action at FOB ROBINSON, Afghanistan, 28/29 Mar 2006 (redacted)", March 8, 2007.

4   Captain (Retd) Darcy Cyr, interview by Wolf Riedel, Brian Reid and Kevin Smith, August 9, 2021.

5   Ibid.

6   Department of National Defence. The Mention in Dispatches 1991-2016. Ottawa: Department of National Defence, 2016, 118. https://www.canada.ca/content/dam/themes/defence/caf/militaryhistory/dhh/honours/mention-in-dispatches.pdf

7   Lieutenant-Colonel Ian Hope, *Dancing With the Dushman: Command Imperatives For The Counter-Insurgency Fight in Afghanistan* (Kingston: Canadian Defence Academy Press, 2008), 72.

8   Ibid., 76-78.

9   Lieutenant-Colonel Andrew Nicholson, interview by Kevin Smith, May 3, 2022.

10   Lieutenant-Colonel Steve Gallagher, interview by Wolf Riedel, Feb 10, 2023.

11   Captain Robert O'Donnell, email to Brain Reid February 11, 2011.

12   Sergeant Corey Rein, interview by Wolf Riedel, February 16, 2023.

13   Ibid.

14   Lieutenant-Colonel Steve Gallagher, "TF ORION Op Archer Roto 1 Tour Summary," PowerPoint presentation as at August 12, 2006, Slide 6.

15   Hope, *Dancing With the Dushman*, 80-81.

16   Ibid., 82.

17   Lieutenant-Colonel Steve Gallagher, interview by Brian Reid, Wolf Riedel and Kevin Smith, May 17 and 18, 2021.

18   Cyr can't recall mIRC being used during training.

19   Captain (Retd) Darcy Cyr, interview by Wolf Riedel, Brian Reid and Kevin Smith, August 9, 2021.

20   Lieutenant-Colonel Steve Gallagher, interview by Brian Reid, Wolf Riedel and Kevin Smith, May 17 and 18, 2021.

21   Captain (Retd) Darcy Cyr, interview by Wolf Riedel, Brian Reid and Kevin Smith, August 9, 2021.

22   Ibid.

23   Ibid.

24   Ibid.

25 Ibid.

26 Hope, *Dancing With the Dushman*, 61; Lieutenant-Colonel Steve Gallagher, "TF ORION Op Archer Roto 1 Tour Summary," PowerPoint presentation as at August 12, 2006, Slide 5.

27 Lieutenant-Colonel Steve Gallagher, interview by Wolf Riedel, Feb 10, 2023.

28 Hope, *Dancing With the Dushman*, 63.

29 Tom Hawthorn, "Myles Mansell, stand easy," Globe and Mail May 4, 2006, accessed January 22, 2023. https://www.theglobeandmail.com/news/national/myles-mansell-stand-easy/article708273/

30 Warrant Officer Steve Merson, interview by Mark Zuehlke and Kevin Smith, April 25, 2023. Some of the circumstances experienced by Merson and the other escorts were, to say the least, difficult and disturbing and more so because they had not been briefed. Upon his return Merson advised his chain of command of what had transpired and action was taken to ensure that in future all escorts would be thoroughly briefed and prepared for their roles.

31 Hope, *Dancing With the Dushman*, 44-45.

32 Captain Mike Smith, "Aide Memoire for Discussion, With A Few Guns," submitted to Brian Reid, undated.

33 Hope, *Dancing With the Dushman*, 83.

34 Captain Robert O'Donnell, email to Brain Reid October 29, 2010.

35 Hope, *Dancing With the Dushman*, 85-86.

36 Edmund Degen and Mark Reardon, *Modern War in an Ancient Land: The United States Army in Afghanistan 2001-2014 Vol II* (Washington: Center of Military History, United States Army, 2021), 81-83; Brian Neumann and Colin J. Williams, *The U.S. Army in Afghanistan Operation Enduring Freedom May 2005 - January 2009* (Washington: Center of Military History, 2020), 27-28.

37 Hope, *Dancing With the Dushman*, 83-84.

38 Lieutenant-Colonel Steve Gallagher, interview by Wolf Riedel, February 10, 2023.

39 Christie Blatchford, *Fifteen Days* (Toronto: Doubleday Canada, 2007), 168.

40 Hope, *Dancing With the Dushman*, 86-87.

41 Some recall Fehr's message as being "This is G13. My Sunray's down." "Sunray" is the Canadian military radio term used to identify the call sign's commander.

42 Michael Thomas Victor Denine, "Dwindling Options," in *In Their Own Words: Canadian Stories of Valour and Bravery in Afghanistan 2001-2007*, ed. Craig Leslie Mantle et al (Kingston: Canadian Defence Academy Press, 2013), 91.

43 Lieutenant-Colonel Howie Nelson, interview by Wolf Riedel, Brian Reid and Kevin Smith, January 21 and 28, 2022.

44 *The Mention in Dispatches*, 128.

45 Sergeant Cory Rein, interview by Wolf Riedel, February 16, 2023.

46 Hope, *Dancing With the Dushman*, 89.

47 Major Steve Gallagher, email to Kevin Smith, May 17, 2007.

48 Governor General of Canada, Honours Recipients, https://www.gg.ca/en/honours/recipients

49 Lieutenant-Colonel Andrew Nicholson, interview by Kevin Smith, May 3, 2022.

CHAPTER 14 - OPERATION MOUNTAIN THRUST

1 Lieutenant-Colonel Ian Hope, *Dancing With the Dushman: Command Imperatives For the Counter-Insurgency Fight in Afghanistan* (Kingston: Canadian Defence Academy Press), 90-99.

2 Ibid., 96.

3 Ibid., 97-98.

4 Ibid., 98-99.

5 Captain RC Moon, "Colonel Commandant Visits A Battery," *The Quadrant* 22, no. 3 (Fall 2006): 10.

6 Hope, *Dancing With the Dushman*, 93 to 103; Lieutenant-Colonel Steve Gallagher, "TF ORION Op Archer Roto 1 Tour Summary," PowerPoint presentation as at August 12, 2006, Slide 12.

7 Lieutenant-Colonel Steve Gallagher, "TF ORION Op Archer Roto 1 Tour Summary," PowerPoint presentation as at August 12, 2006, Slide 13-14.

8 Lieutenant-Colonel Howie Nelson, interview by Wolf Riedel, Brian Reid and Kevin Smith, January 21 and 28, 2022.

9 Hope, *Dancing With the Dushman*, 105.

10 Lieutenant-Colonel Howie Nelson, interview by Wolf Riedel, Brian Reid and Kevin Smith, January 21 and 28, 2022.

11 Mobility kill recovery was a perpetual problem resulting from a combination of those resources being concentrated in the National Support Element in KAF and because the army had not purchased any light armoured vehicle-based recovery vehicles. Recovery was done by way of a wrecker and flatbed. See in part Colonel John Conrad, *What the Thunder Said: Reflections of a Canadian Officer in Kandahar* (Toronto: Dundurn Press, 2009), 150-151.

12 Lieutenant-Colonel Howie Nelson, interview by Wolf Riedel, Brian Reid and Kevin Smith, January 21 and 28, 2022; Master Warrant Officer (Retd) John Gero, interview by Wolf Riedel, February 22, 2023.

13 Lieutenant-Colonel Howie Nelson, interview by Wolf Riedel, Brian Reid and Kevin Smith, January 21 and 28, 2022; and Hope, Dushman, 107.

14 Hope, *Dancing With the Dushman*, 106-108.

15 Master Warrant Officer (Retd) John Gero, interview by Wolf Riedel, February 22, 2023.

16 Lieutenant-Colonel Howie Nelson, interview by Wolf Riedel, Brian Reid and Kevin Smith, January 21 and 28, 2022.

17 Colonel Bernd Horn, *No Ordinary Men: Special Operations Forces Missions in Afghanistan* (Toronto: Dundurn Press, 2016), 106-130.

18 Hope, *Dancing With the Dushman*, 109.

19 Conrad, *What the Thunder Said*, 177.

20 During which time he remained on Class C Reserve Service.

21 Sergeant Makthepharak Bounyarattanaphon, interview by Wolf Riedel and Kevin Smith, February 16, 2022.

22 Warrant Officer Jason Ladouceur, "Aide Memoire for Discussion, With A Few Guns" submitted to Brian Reid, undated.

23 Christopher Lorne Harding, "Helping a Buddy ... Under Fire," in *In Their Own Words: Canadian Stories of Valour and Bravery From Afghanistan, 2001-2007*, ed. Craig Leslie Mantle et al (Kingston: Canadian Defence Academy Press, 2013), 108-110.

24 Christie Blatchford, *Fifteen Days* (Toronto: Doubleday Canada,2007), 80.

25 Captain Andrew Charchuk, "Contact Charlie" A Forward Observation Officer with Task Force Orion," *Canadian Army Journal* 10, no. 2 (Summer 2007): 28.

26 Ibid., 29-30.

27 The forward air controller was decertified, retested successfully a week later and stayed in theatre.

28 Blatchford, *Fifteen Days*, 82-86.

29 Charchuk, "Contact Charlie," 30.

30 Ibid., 30-32.

31 Captain Robert O'Donnell, email to Brain Reid February 11, 2011.

32 Hope, *Dancing With the Dushman*, 118 and Major-General (Retd) David Fraser, message to Wolf Riedel, October 6, 2023.

33 Ibid., 118-119.

34 Sean M. Maloney, *Fighting for Afghanistan: A Rogue Historian at War.* (Annapolis: Naval Institute Press, 2011), 295.

35 Ibid., 119 - 120.

36 Charchuk, "Contact Charlie," 33.

37 Ibid.

38 Ibid.

39 Chief Warrant Officer and Master Gunner (Retd) Mike McDonald, email to Wolf Riedel, September 8, 2023.

40 Colonel Stuart Tootal, *Danger Close: The True Story of Helmand from the Leader of 3 Para* (London: John Murray Publishers, 2009), Kindle Location 2261.

41 Lieutenant-Colonel Steve Gallagher, email to Wolf Riedel, May 18, 2023.

42 Hope, *Dancing With the Dushman*, 128.

43 Loaded with the Indirect Fire Control Software Suite (IFCSS).

44 Lieutenant-Colonel Steve Gallagher, interview by Wolf Riedel, February 10, 2023.

45 *Mention in Dispatches*, 117.

46 Blatchford, *Fifteen Days*, 323.

47 Hope, *Dancing With the Dushman*, 124 - 138.

48 Master Warrant Officer (Retd) Paul Parsons, and Lieutenant-Colonel Steve Gallagher interview by Kevin Smith, May 25 and June 1, 2021.

49 Colonel (retd) Ian Hope, interview by Brian Reid, Wolf Riedel and Kevin Smith, May 28, and June 10, 2021.

50 Master Warrant Officer (Retd) John Gero, interview by Wolf Riedel, February 22, 2023.

51 Nelson, Lieutenant-Colonel Howie, interview by Wolf Riedel, Brian Reid and Kevin Smith, January 21 and 28, 2022.

52 Master Warrant Officer (Retd) John Gero, interview by Wolf Riedel, February 22, 2023.

53 Master Warrant Officer (Retd) Paul Parsons and Lieutenant-Colonel Steve Gallagher interview by Kevin Smith, May 25 and June 1, 2021.

54 Major (Retd) Rob Rooney, interview by Wolf Riedel, Brian Reid and Kevin Smith, May 31 and June 4, 2021.

55 Master Warrant Officer (Retd) Paul Parsons and Lieutenant-Colonel Steve Gallagher interview by Kevin Smith, May 25 and June 1, 2021. Chinook helicopters could deliver ammunition in two ways: as a sling load suspended under the helicopter or internally on pallets. If loaded internally the pallets were unloaded by sliding them out of the helicopter's rear ramp while the helicopter slowly moved forward to make room for each pallet. The action was referred to as "kicking" and the pallets as "kicker pallets".

56 Department of National Defence, B-GL-371-003/FP-001, *Field Artillery Operational Procedures* (Ottawa: DND Canada, 2000), 143-144.

57 Colonel (retd) Ian Hope, interview by Brian Reid, Wolf Riedel and Kevin Smith, May 28, and June 10, 2021.

58 Major-General (Ret'd) David Fraser and Brian Hanington, *Operation Medusa: The Furious Battle that Saved Afghanistan* (Toronto: McClelland and Stewart, 2018), 163-4.

59 Major-General (Retd) David Fraser, message to Wolf Riedel, October 6, 2023.

60 Conrad, *What the Thunder Said*, 137 - 138.

61 Ibid., 74.

62 Major-General (Retd) David Fraser, message to Wolf Riedel, October 6, 2023.

63 Conrad, *What The Thunder Said*, 40 and 68. Much of the same comment can be made with respect to the army's attitude for the combat support function of field and air defence artillery.

64 Ibid., 96 - 99.

65 Lieutenant-Colonel Steve Gallagher, "TF ORION Op Archer Roto 1 Tour Summary," PowerPoint presentation, as at August 12, 2006, Slide 18.

66 Lieutenant-Colonel Steve Gallagher, interview by Brian Reid, Wolf Riedel and Kevin Smith, May 17 and 18, 2021; See also Conrad, What The Thunder Said, 185.

67 Conrad, What The Thunder Said, 185 - 193.

68 Lieutenant-Colonel Howie Nelson, interview by Wolf Riedel, Brian Reid and Kevin Smith, January 21 and 28, 2022.

CHAPTER 15 - OPERATION BRAVO CORRIDOR - AUGUST 3, 2006

1 Operation ATHENA has been split into two Phases divided between rotations that operated in Kabul and those that were related to Kandahar.

2 Christie Blatchford, *Fifteen Days* (Toronto: Doubleday Canada, 2007), 72-73.

3 Major Mason Stalker, "TF ORION – Warning Order for Op BRAVO CORRIDOR (Frag O 93)," July 29, 2006.

4 Colonel (Retd) Ian Hope, interview by Brian Reid, Wolf Riedel and Kevin Smith, May 28, and June 10, 2021.

5 Colonel (Retd) Tim Bishop, interview by Wolf Riedel, Brian Reid and Kevin Smith, July 26 and August 2, 2021.

6 Lieutenant-Colonel Ian Hope, *Dancing With the Dushman: Command Imperatives For The Counter-Insurgency Fight in Afghanistan* (Kingston: Canadian Defence Academy Press, 2008), 15.

7 Major-General (Retd) David Fraser, message to Wolf Riedel, October 6, 2023.

8 Colonel (Retd) Peter Williams, interview by Wolf Riedel and Kevin Smith, January 19 and 29, 2021; by Wolf Riedel, Brian Reid and Kevin Smith, June 16, and December 17, 2021; by Wolf Riedel, March 4, 2023.

9 Ibid., and Colonel (Retd) Peter Williams, email to Wolf Riedel, July 13, 2023.

10 Colonel (Retd) Tim Bishop, interview by Wolf Riedel, Brian Reid and Kevin Smith, July 26 and August 2, 2021.

11 Colonel (Retd) Peter Williams, interview by Wolf Riedel, Brian Reid and Kevin Smith, December 17, 2021.

12 Colonel (Retd) Ian Hope, interview by Brian Reid, Wolf Riedel and Kevin

Smith, May 28, and June 10, 2021.

13   Major (Retd) Rob Rooney, interview by Wolf Riedel, Brian Reid and Kevin Smith, May 31 and June 4, 2021.

14   Major (Retd) Michael Podolas, message to Wolf Riedel, March 9, 2023.

15   Colonel (Retd) Tim Bishop, interview by Wolf Riedel, Brian Reid and Kevin Smith, July 26 and August 2, 2021.

16   Colonel (Retd) Tim Bishop, interview by Wolf Riedel, Brian Reid and Kevin Smith, July 26 and August 2, 2021.

17   Lieutenant-Colonel Steve Gallagher, interview by Brian Reid, Wolf Riedel and Kevin Smith, May 17 and 18, 2021.

18   Colonel (Retd) Ian Hope, interview by Brian Reid, Wolf Riedel and Kevin Smith, May 28, and June 10, 2021.

19   Sergeant Corey Rein, interview by Wolf Riedel, February 16, 2023.

20   Sergeant Corey Rein, interview by Wolf Riedel, February 16, 2023.

21   Colonel (Retd) Ian Hope, interview by Brian Reid, Wolf Riedel and Kevin Smith, May 28, and June 10, 2021.

22   Department of National Defence. B-GL-381-001/TS-000 *Operational Training, Training Safety.* Ottawa: DND, September 24, 2004.

23   Master Warrant Officer (Retd) Paul Parsons and Lieutenant-Colonel Steve Gallagher, interview by Kevin Smith, May 25 and June 1, 2021.

24   Colonel (Retd) Ian Hope, interview by Brian Reid, Wolf Riedel and Kevin Smith, May 28 and June 10, 2021.

25   Colonel (Retd) Peter Williams, interview by Wolf Riedel, Brian Reid and Kevin Smith, December 17, 2021.

26   Department of Defense, United States Army, FM 3-09.32 *JFIRE Multi-service Procedures for the Joint Application of Firepower* (Fort Monroe: US Army Training and Doctrine Command, October, 2004). At Appendix E, the manual sets out the "Risk-Estimate Distances" to assist a commander in determining the level of risk to his own troops from the effects of various natures of munitions including American bombs and rockets. In a combat situation, the key risk-estimate distance is the one at which there is a risk of 0.1% probability of incapacitation. For the 155mm High Explosive round, that distance at 1/3 of the range of the gun is 200 metres Splinters can very well fly beyond that distance, as did the one that struck Rein at approximately 330 metres, but at a lower than 0.1% probability that a splinter will incapacitate anyone.

27   Department of National Defence. B-GL-381-001/TS-000 *Operational Training, Training Safety.* Ottawa: DND, September 24, 2004, 4A2-12 and 4A5-1.

28   Lieutenant-Colonel Howie Nelson, interview by Wolf Riedel, Brian Reid and

Kevin Smith, January 21 and 28, 2022.

29 Captain (Retd) Darcy Cyr, interview by Wolf Riedel, Brian Reid and Kevin Smith, August 9, 2021.

30 Colonel (Retd) Ian Hope, interview by Brian Reid, Wolf Riedel and Kevin Smith, May 28, and June 10, 2021.

31 Lieutenant-Colonel Steve Gallagher, interview by Brian Reid, Wolf Riedel and Kevin Smith, May 17 and 18, 2021.

32 Hope in his interview of May 28, 2021 contemplates that this may have been either a mistaken intercept referring to the northern school or a ruse to lure his troops into a kill zone, a scenario also explored by Adnan Khan, "The View From Ambush Alley," *MacLeans.ca*, September 11, 2006, accessed May 20, 2021. https://archive.macleans.ca/article/2006/9/11/the-view-from-ambush-alley

33 Colonel (Retd) Ian Hope, interview by Brian Reid, Wolf Riedel and Kevin Smith, May 28, and June 10, 2021.

34 Major-General (Retd) David Fraser, message to Wolf Riedel, October 6, 2023.

35 Ibid. Hope took the suggestion that he push some of his troops forward as using them as bait and adamantly refused to do so.

36 It is at a time like this that the absence of a light armoured vehicle recovery variant from the army's inventory and the absence of an organic close support echelon able to deploy them rapidly, becomes very apparent. Interestingly, numerous M578 tracked and armoured light recovery vehicles from the decommissioned M109 batteries were still available in storage but never deployed.

37 Lieutenant-Colonel Howie Nelson, interview by Wolf Riedel, Brian Reid and Kevin Smith, January 21 and 28, 2022.

38 Colonel (Retd) Ian Hope, interview by Brian Reid, Wolf Riedel and Kevin Smith, May 28, and June 10, 2021.

39 Major Tyler Kennedy, email to Warrant Darcy Cyr "TF ORION FIRES" 1034 hours local, August 3, 2006.

40 Colonel (Retd) Ian Hope, interview by Brian Reid, Wolf Riedel and Kevin Smith, May 28, and June 10, 2021.

41 Master Warrant Officer (Retd) Paul Parsons and Lieutenant-Colonel Steve Gallagher, interview by Kevin Smith, May 25 and June 1, 2021.

42 Blatchford, *Fifteen Days*, 25.

43 While several individuals had listened in on this and other transmissions that morning, Lieutenant-Colonel Williams was not one of them. He had not been present when Fraser ordered the "Check Firing" or any of the subsequent discussions and surmises that he was away from the joint tactical operations centre for one or more of the meetings that were part of his daily routine.

Colonel (Retd) Peter Williams, interview by Wolf Riedel and Kevin Smith, January 19 and 29, 2021; by Wolf Riedel, Brian Reid and Kevin Smith, June 16, and December 17, 2021; by Wolf Riedel, March 4, 2023 and Colonel (Retd) Peter Williams, email to Wolf Riedel, July 13, 2023.

44 Lieutenant-Colonel Andrew Nicholson, interview by Kevin Smith, May 3, 2022.

45 Richards held the substantive rank of Lieutenant-General and was promoted to the acting rank of General for his tour of command of ISAF. General David Richards, *Taking Command* (London: Headline Publishing Group 2014), 286

46 Colonel (Retd) Tim Bishop, interview by Wolf Riedel, Brian Reid and Kevin Smith, July 26 and August 2, 2021.

47 Ibid.

48 Blachford, *Fifteen Days*, 27.

49 The prefix ZULU before a call sign indicates the vehicle is empty except for its driver and, in the case of a light armoured vehicle, its gunner and commander. The rest of the section would be dismounted.

50 Major (Retd) Michael Podolas, interview by Wolf Riedel, March 8, 2023.

51 Ibid.

52 Ibid.

53 Ibid.

54 Master Warrant Officer (Retd) Paul Parsons, and Lieutenant-Colonel Steve Gallagher interview by Kevin Smith, May 25 and June 1, 2021.

55 Major (Retd) Michael Podolas, interview by Wolf Riedel, March 8, 2023.

56 Tower and Reconnaissance Platoon's Sergeant William MacDonald were awarded Stars of Military Valour, Canada's second highest award for valour presented for "distinguished and valiant service in the presence of the enemy". Much more comprehensive accounts of that day's actions can be found at Blachford, *Fifteen Days*, 1.; Hope, *Dancing With Dushman*, 1.; and Sergeant William Kenneth Macdonald, "Pinned Down, Not Defeated," in *In Their Own Words: Canadian Stories of Valour and Bravery in Afghanistan 2001-2007*, ed. Craig Leslie Mantle et al (Kingston: Canadian Defence Academy Press, 2013), 125-126.

57 Captain (Retd) Darcy Cyr, interview by Wolf Riedel, Brian Reid and Kevin Smith, August 9, 2021.

CHAPTER 16 - REFLECTIONS AND ROTATIONS

1 Carter Malkasian, *The American War in Afghanistan: A History* (New York: Oxford University Press, 2021), 115-125.

2 Ibid., 125.

3   Ibid., 133.

4   Colonel (Retd) Tim Bishop, interview by Wolf Riedel, Brian Reid and Kevin Smith, July 26 and August 2, 2021.

5   Colonel (Retd) Ian Hope, interview by Brian Reid, Wolf Riedel and Kevin Smith, May 28, and June 10, 2021.

6   Major Mason Stalker, "TF ORION - Frag O 93 - Op BRAVO CORRIDOR - FINAL SUMMARY," August 5, 2006.

7   Lieutenant-Colonel Ian Hope, 1 PPCLI 3350-1 (CO), August 5, 2009.

8   Brigadier-General Dave Fraser, CFT AEGIS 3350-1 (Comd) "Authority to Fire and Indirect Safe Distances, August 13, 2006.

9   Ibid.

10 Major-General (Retd) David Fraser, message to Wolf Riedel, October 6, 2023.

11 Lieutenant-Colonel Howie Nelson, interview by Wolf Riedel, Brian Reid and Kevin Smith, January 21 and 28, 2022.

12 Colonel (Retd) Tim Bishop, interview by Wolf Riedel, Brian Reid and Kevin Smith, July 26 and August 2, 2021.

13 Lieutenant-Colonel Howie Nelson, interview by Wolf Riedel, Brian Reid and Kevin Smith, January 21 and 28, 2022.

14 Lieutenant-Colonel Ian Hope, *Dancing With the Dushman: Command Imperatives For The Counter-Insurgency Fight in Afghanistan* (Kingston: Canadian Defence Academy Press, 2008), 138 - 140.

15 Major Greg Ivey, interview by Brian Reid, August 7, 2008.

16 Master Warrant Officer (Retd) Paul Parsons and Lieutenant-Colonel Steve Gallagher, interview by Kevin Smith, May 25 and June 1, 2021. Major Greg Ivey, interview by Brian Reid, August 7, 2008.

17 Hope, *Dancing With the Dushman*, 17.

18 Lieutenant-Colonel Steve Gallagher, "TF ORION Op Archer Roto 1 Tour Summary," PowerPoint presentation, as at August 12, 2006, Slide 23-25.

19 Major Steve Gallagher, "Op Archer Task Force Orion January - August 2006," PowerPoint presentation, undated (approximately 2006-7), Slides 18-25.

20 Major David Grebstad, "The Role of Artillery in Afghanistan," *Canadian Army Journal* 10, no. 3 (Fall 2007): 16-17.

21 Chief Warrant Officer and Master Gunner (Retd) Mike McDonald, email to Wolf Riedel, September 8, 2023.

22 Master Warrant Officer (Retd) Paul Parsons and Lieutenant-Colonel Steve Gallagher, interview by Kevin Smith, May 25 and June 1, 2021.

23 There are numerous psychological studies discussing "Third Location Decompression" and reintegration after combat. Most of these stress the importance for teams that have lived and fought together needing an

opportunity to deal with their experiences post-combat in team settings. See for example Lieutenant-Commander Michael N. Sorsdahl, "Re-entry and Transition for Military Members: Phased Decompression Approach" (MDS Research Project, Canadian Forces College, 2011).

24 Lieutenant-Colonel Howie Nelson, interview by Wolf Riedel, Brian Reid and Kevin Smith, January 21 and 28, 2022.

25 Lieutenant-Colonel Andrew Nicholson, interview by Kevin Smith, May 3, 2022.

26 Ibid.

27 Master Warrant Officer (Retd) Paul Parsons and Lieutenant-Colonel Steve Gallagher, interview by Kevin Smith, May 25 and June 1, 2021.

28 Ibid.

29 Ibid., Paraphrasing Master Gunner Kevin Smith.

30 Colonel (Retd) Ian Hope, interview by Brian Reid, Wolf Riedel and Kevin Smith, May 28, and June 10, 2021.

31 *The Canadian Gunner 2006* 41a (February 2007): 7.

CHAPTER 17 - TASK FORCE 3-06: THE ROAD TO HIGH READINESS

1 Major Greg Ivey, interview by Brian Reid, August 7, 2008.

2 Master Warrant Officer Bob Montague, interview by Brian Reid, July 23, 2008 and email to Brian Reid, July 31, 2008.

3 Ibid.

4 Major-General (Retd)Tim Grant and Lieutenant-Colonel Tom Bradley, interview by Wolf Riedel and Kevin Smith, June 27, 2023. Grant was attending a medals parade for Hope's returning battalion also attended by General Hillier and Lieutenant-General Leslie, the army's commander. He was advised he would be commanding a later rotation in Afghanistan but instead was assigned to the one that started a mere two months later.

5 Colonel (Retd) Peter Williams, message to Wolf Riedel, June 11, 2023, Technically, the Regional Command (South) area of operations also included the provinces of Nimruz and Daykundi. However, during AEGIS's tour there were no Coalition or ISAF forces permanently stationed in either of those two provinces.

6 Lieutenant-Colonel (Retd) Caleb Walker, interview by Wolf Riedel, Mark Zuehlke and Kevin Smith, September 6, 2023.

7 Chief Warrant Officer Rod Gallant, interview by Wolf Riedel, March 20, 2023.

8 Captain Roger Pierce, email to Brian Reid, undated.

9 Chief Warrant Officer Rod Gallant, interview by Wolf Riedel, March 20, 2023.

10 In The Royal Canadian Regiment, C Company is referred to as Charles

Company.

11 Major-General (Retd)Tim Grant and Lieutenant-Colonel Tom Bradley, interview by Wolf Riedel and Kevin Smith, June 27, 2023. An initial concept was that Canada would merely keep a National Command Element in place, but as the size of the mission grew in late 2006 and as General Hillier could see that there was a possibility of brigade level operations in Kandahar, the headquarters started to acquire more capabilities.

12 Lieutenant-Colonel Tim Spears, emails to Wolf Riedel, 12 and 24 June, 2023.

13 Major-General (Retd) Simon Hetherington, email to Wolf Riedel, June 30, 2023.

14 Bombardier NB Sylvester, "TF 3-06 PRT in Afghanistan," *The Quadrant* 23, no. 2 (Fall 2007): 14.

15 T.F.J .Leveridge, *Sagem CU-161 Sperwer Canadian Armed Forces Serial 16101* (Ottawa: Canadian Aviation and Space Museum Ottawa Museum, 2013), 12.

16 Colonel Bob Gunn, Fielding Plan - M777 Lightweight 155mm Towed Howitzer (LWTH) System, file 00001017-11025-1 (DLR 2), March 2006.

17 While the Americans were adapting their own version of a Digital Fire Control System for the M777 adapted from their M109s, the system was not compatible with the Canadian way of doing fire missions. When Australia acquired their M777s with American DFCS they had to adapt to the American procedures. Ken Whitnall, email to Wolf Riedel, March 10, 2022.

18 Selex, "FSP 1147 M777 Gun Management System Operator Information Issue 1," 2006.

19 Captain (Retd) Lorne Doucet and Captain (Retd) (Master Gunner) Kevin Smith, interviewed by Wolf Riedel, May 25, 2023.

20 Ibid.

21 Captain Michael John Reekie, "Ma'sum Ghar by Night," in *In Their Own Words: Canadian Stories of Valour and Bravery in Afghanistan 2001-2007*, ed. Craig Mantle et al (Kingston: Canadian Defence Academy Press Kingston, 2013), 163.

22 Colonel (Retd) Greg Ivey, Chief Warrant Officer (Retd) Bob Montague and Lieutenant-Colonel Ian Plummer, interview by Brian Reid, Wolf Riedel and Kevin Smith, September 21, 2021. per Ivey ??

23 Lieutenant-Colonel Tim Spears, interview by Brian Reid, Wolf Riedel and Kevin Smith, March 23, 2022.

24 Lieutenant-General (Retd) Omer Lavoie, interview by Wolf Riedel, May 16, 2023.

25 The Intelligence, Surveillance, Target Acquisition, and Reconnaissance Squadron comprised a reconnaissance troop from the Royal Canadian

Dragoons and the 1ˢᵗ Battalion's Reconnaissance Platoon and Sniper Section.

26 Captain Piers Pappin, email to Brian Reid, June 26, 2013.

27 Ibid.

28 Lieutenant-General (Retd) Omer Lavoie, interview by Wolf Riedel, May 16, 2023.

29 Lieutenant-Colonel Tim Spears, interview by Brian Reid, Wolf Riedel and Kevin Smith, March 23, 2022.

30 Colonel (Retd) Greg Ivey, Chief Warrant Officer (Retd) Bob Montague and Lieutenant-Colonel Ian Plummer, interview by Brian Reid, Wolf Riedel and Kevin Smith, September 21, 2021.

31 Department of National Defence, Chief Review Services, *Evaluation of CF/DND Participation in the Kandahar Provincial Reconstruction Team* (Ottawa: DND, December 2007), 16.

32 Major-General (Retd) Simon Hetherington, email to Wolf Riedel, June 30, 2023.

33 Lieutenant-Colonel Tim Spears, interview by Brian Reid, Wolf Riedel and Kevin Smith, March 9, 11, 23 and 25, 2022.

34 Lieutenant-General (Retd) Omer Lavoie, interview by Wolf Riedel, May 16, 2023.

35 Colonel (Retd) Greg Ivey, Chief Warrant Officer (Retd) Bob Montague and Lieutenant-Colonel Ian Plummer, interview by Brian Reid, Wolf Riedel and Kevin Smith, September 21, 2021.

36 Lieutenant-Colonel (Retd) Caleb Walker, interview by Wolf Riedel, Mark Zuehlke and Kevin Smith, September 6, 2023.

CHAPTER 18 - THE NEW KIDS ON THE BLOCK

1   Carter Malkasian, *The American War in Afghanistan: A History* (New York: Oxford University Press, 2021), 133.

2   Ibid.

3   Ibid., 130.

4   Ibid., 130

5   Ibid., 154-155.

6   Major Greg Ivey, Untitled paper provided to Brian Reid at interview, August 7, 2008, 5-6.

7   Chief Warrant Officer Rodney Gallant, interview by Wolf Riedel, March 20, 22 and 29, 2023.

8   Captain Mark Adkins, interview by Wolf Riedel, March 21, 2023.

9   Colonel (Retd) Peter Williams, message to Wolf Riedel, June 30, 2023.

10 General David Richards, *Taking Command: The Autobiography* (London:

Headline Publishing Group, 2014), 215.

11 Major-General (Retd) Simon Hetherington, email to Wolf Riedel, June 30, 2023.

12 Major-General (Ret'd) David Fraser and Brian Hanington, *Operation Medusa: The Furious Battle that Saved Afghanistan* (Toronto: McClelland and Stewart, 2018), 91. Also Major-General (Retd) David Fraser, interview by Wolf Riedel, March 16, 2023.

13 Colonel (Retd) Peter Williams, message to Wolf Riedel, June 30, 2023.

14 Fraser and Hanington, *Operation Medusa*, 111-112.

15 The commanders of Combined Task Force-76, Canadian Expeditionary Force Command and the Chief of Defence Staff respectively.

16 Fraser and Hanington, *Operation Medusa*, 98.

17 Colonel Bernd Horn, *No Lack of Courage, Operation Medusa, Afghanistan* (Toronto: Dundurn Press, 2010), 29.

18 Ibid.

19 Major Greg Ivey, Untitled paper provided to Brian Reid at interview, August 7, 2008, 3.

20 Ibid.

21 Lieutenant-Colonel (Retd) Caleb Walker, interview by Wolf Riedel, Mark Zuehlke and Kevin Smith, September 6, 2023.

22 Lieutenant-Colonel Tim Spears, email to Wolf Riedel, June 12, 2023.

23 Lieutenant-Colonel Tim Spears, interview by Brian Reid, Wolf Riedel and Kevin Smith, March 9, 11, 23 and 25, 2022.

24 Ibid., There are several ways of classifying the stages of an insurgency. The Central Intelligence Agency adopted four: 1. Pre-insurgency - leadership arises and organizations formed; 2. Incipient conflict - first use of violence; 3. Open insurgency - openly challenging authority and seizing control of territory through sophisticated and widespread violence; and 4. Resolution - through negotiated settlement or either government or insurgent victory. Sam W. Lauber et al, *Understanding States of Resistance: Pocket Guide* (Fort Bragg, NC: US Army Special Operations Command, 2019), 16-17.

25 Major-General (Retd) David Fraser, message to Wolf Riedel October 6, 2023. Not that much of the Taliban force had moved across the Arghandab River into Zhari.

26 Brigadier-General Steve Hunter, interview by Mark Zuehlke, Wolf Riedel and Kevin Smith, September 12, 2023.

27 Lieutenant-Colonel Tim Spears, interview by Brian Reid, Wolf Riedel and Kevin Smith, March 9, 11, 23 and 25, 2022.

28 Major-General (Retd) David Fraser, interview by Wolf Riedel, March 16, 2023.

29 Ibid.

30 Lieutenant-Colonel Ian Hope, *Dancing With the Dushman: Command Imperatives For The Counter-Insurgency Fight in Afghanistan* (Kingston: Canadian Defence Academy Press, 2008), 98-99.

31 Lieutenant-Colonel Tim Spears, interview by Brian Reid, Wolf Riedel and Kevin Smith, March 9, 11, 23 and 25, 2022.

32 Ibid.

33 Ibid.

34 Hope, *Dancing With the Dushman*, 138-9 and Lieutenant-General (Retd) OmerLavoie interview by Wolf Riedel, May 16, 2023.

35 Lieutenant-Colonel Steve Gallagher, email to Wolf Riedel, May 18, 2023.

36 Ibid.

37 Hope, *Dancing With the Dushman*, 138-140.

38 Captain Michael John Reekie, "Ma'sum Ghar by Night," in *In Their Own Words: Canadian Stories of Valour and Bravery in Afghanistan 2001-2007*, ed. Craig Leslie Mantle *et al* (Kingston: Canadian Defence Academy Press, 2013), 171.

39 Fraser and Hanington, *Operation Medusa*, 122.

40 Lieutenant-General (Retd) Omer Lavoie, interview by Wolf Riedel, May 16, 2023.

41 Ibid.

42 Colonel John Conrad, *What the Thunder Said: Reflections of a Canadian Officer in Kandahar* (Toronto: Dundurn Press, 2009), 130.

43 For a fuller discussion of these issues see Conrad, *What the Thunder Said*, "Chapter 7 Task Force ORION", 61-64.

44 Lieutenant-Colonel (Retd) Todd Scharlach, email to Kevin Smith, May 31, 2021. - emphasis is Scharlach's.

45 Ibid.

46 Task Force ORION after-action PowerPoint presentation, undated.

47 Conrad, *What the Thunder Said*, 63.

CHAPTER 19 · TRANSFER OF COMMAND AUTHORITY

1 Major-General (Ret'd) David Fraser and Brian Hanington, *Operation Medusa: The Furious Battle that Saved Afghanistan* (Toronto: McClelland and Stewart, 2018), 126-127.

2 Edmund Degen et al, *Modern War in an Ancient Land: The United States Army in Afghanistan 2001-2014 Vol II* (Washington: Center of Military History, United States Army, 2021), 94.

3 While A Company took over from Task Force ORION's B Company which was primarily equipped with the lightly armoured G-Wagons, it was in the process

of being converted to light armoured vehicles and already had about seven of them. See Captain Michael John Reekie, "Ma'sum Ghar by Night," in *In Their Own Words: Canadian Stories of Valour and Bravery in Afghanistan 2001-2007*, ed. Craig Leslie Mantle et al (Kingston: Canadian Defence Academy Press, 2013), 170.

4   Colonel Bernd Horn, *No Lack of Courage, Operation Medusa, Afghanistan* (Toronto: Dundurn Press, 2010), 50-51. See also Captain Reekie, "Ma'sum Ghar by Night," 161-189.

5   Major Greg Ivey, Untitled paper provided to Brian Reid at Interview, August 7, 2008, 8.

6   Degen, *Modern War in an Ancient Land Vol II*, 94. It should be noted that the numbers vary greatly from report to report.

7   Lieutenant-Colonel Steve Gallagher, interview by Brian Reid, Wolf Riedel and Kevin Smith, May 17, 18 and 19, 2021.

8   Ibid.

9   Ibid.

10   A small laptop computer capable of receiving video feeds from an aircraft's targeting pod.

11   A Type I control is where the forward air controller can see both the target and the attacking aircraft; a Type II the forward air controller can neither see the target nor the aircraft but is receiving targeting information from some forward resource such as a scout; a Type III control has the controller unable to see the aircraft, or the target, and all targeting data must be cleared through the supported commander's battle staff.

12   Major Greg Ivey, Untitled paper provided to Brian Reid at interview, August 7, 2008, 9.

13   Chief Warrant Officer Rodney Gallant, interview by Wolf Riedel, March 20, 22 and 29, 2023.

14   Major Greg Ivey, Untitled paper provided to Brian Reid at interview, August 7, 2008, 11.

15   Lieutenant-Colonel Ryan Stimpson, email to Wolf Riedel, June 27, 2023.

16   Major Greg Ivey, email to Brian Reid, October 7, 2010.

17   Major Greg Ivey, Untitled paper provided to Brian Reid at interview, August 7, 2008, 8.

18   Estimates of the numbers involved and killed vary greatly.

19   Major Greg Ivey, email to Brian Reid, October 7, 2010.

20   Lieutenant-General (Retd) Omer Lavoie, interview by Wolf Riedel, May 16, 2023.

21   Captain Chris Purdy, interview by Bernd Horn, October 17, 2006, quoted in

Horn, *No Lack of Courage*, 26.

22 Lieutenant-General (Retd) Omer Lavoie, interview by Wolf Riedel, May 16, 2023.

23 Ibid.

24 Major Greg Ivey, email to Brian Reid, October 7, 2010.

25 Lieutenant-Colonel (Retd) Todd Scharlach, email to Kevin Smith, May 31, 2021.

26 Lieutenant-General (Retd) Omer Lavoie, interview by Wolf Riedel, May 16, 2023.

27 Conrad, *What the Thunder Said,* 136. 25mm ammunition was also an issue. The timings of the meeting and the start of MEDUSA as of August 19, do not line up with the information provided by other sources.

28 Fraser and Hanington, *Operation Medusa*, 112.

29 Lieutenant-Colonel Ian Plummer, interview by Wolf Riedel, April 13 and 19, 2023.

30 Fraser and Hanington, *Operation Medusa*, 128. Fraser considers Buchanan as one of the most capable leaders he ever had the privilege of working with. Major-General (Retd) David Fraser, message to Wolf Riedel, October 6, 2023.

31 Horn, *No Lack of Courage*, 42.

32 Observation Post Log G23 TF 3-06, August 8, 2006 to February 12, 2007, entry for August 23, 2006.

33 Master Bombardier Lucas Cunningham, email to Brigadier-General (Retd) Ernest Beno, September 27, 2010. The mission is calculated as a normal illumination mission, except that the height of burst is lowered to a few hundred metres above the target. When the fuze functions, the canister is ejected and then follows the trajectory to impact in the target area before the parachute can deploy fully. The canister burning on the ground provides an intense thermal source for the attacking aircraft to use to guide his bomb to the target.

34 Ibid.

35 Major Greg Ivey, Untitled paper provided to Brian Reid at interview, August 7, 2008, 14.

36 All information of this mission, save and except the Cunningham quotes come from the Major Greg Ivey, Untitled paper provided to Brian Reid at interview, August 7, 2008, 13-14.

37 Chief Warrant Officer Rodney Gallant, interview by Wolf Riedel, March 20, 22 and 29, 2023.

38 Major Greg Ivey, Untitled paper provided to Brian Reid at interview, August 7, 2008, 15.

39 Chief Warrant Officer Rodney Gallant, interview by Wolf Riedel, March 20, 22

and 29, 2023.

40 Major Greg Ivey, Untitled paper provided to Brian Reid at interview, August 7, 2008, 15.

41 Colonel (Retd) Peter Williams, interview by Wolf Riedel, Brian Reid and Kevin Smith, June 16, 2021.

42 Chief Warrant Officer Rodney Gallant, interview by Wolf Riedel, March 20, 22 and 29, 2023.

43 Lieutenant-Colonel (Retd) Caleb Walker, interview by Wolf Riedel, Mark Zuehlke and Kevin Smith, September 6, 2023.

44 Lieutenant-Colonel (Retd) Todd Scharlach, email to Kevin Smith, May 31, 2021.

45 Lieutenant-Colonel (Retd) Todd Scharlach, email to Kevin Smith, May 31, 2021. J3 is Joint Operations, J4 is Joint Logistics.

46 Ibid.

CHAPTER 20 - OPERATION MEDUSA: SEPTEMBER 2-5, 2006

1 Colonel (Retd) Tim Bishop, interview by Wolf Riedel, Brian Reid and Kevin Smith, July 26 and August 2, 2021. It was a lesson learned from the August 3, 2006 situation.

2 Lieutenant-General (Retd) Omer Lavoie, interview by Wolf Riedel, May 16, 2023.

3 Ibid.

4 1st Battalion, 3rd Special Forces Group (Airborne), Fort Bragg, North Carolina—Note that in 2006 deployed Special Forces battalion headquarters were officially referred to as Forward Operating Bases e.g. FOB 31. In 2007 the term changed to Special Operations Task Force e.g. SOTF 31, however at the time of Operation MEDUSA the unit was generally referred to as Task Force 31.

5 Major Rusty Bradley and Kevin Mauer, *Lions of Kandahar: The Story of a Fight Against all Odds* (New York: BantamBooks, 2015), 69.

6 Edmund Degen and Mark Reardon, *Modern War in an Ancient Land: The United States Army in Afghanistan 2001-2014 Vol II* (Washington: Center of Military History, United States Army, 2021), 95.

7 Lieutenant-Colonel Tim Spears, interview by Brian Reid, Wolf Riedel and Kevin Smith, March 9, 11, 23 and 25, 2022.

8 Colonel Bernd Horn, *No Lack of Courage, Operation Medusa, Afghanistan* (Toronto: Dundurn Press, 2010), 49.

9 Major Greg Ivey, interview with Bernd Horn, October 17, 2006 as quoted in Horn *No Lack of Courage*, 45.

10 Ibid.

11 Fraser and Hanington, *Operation Medusa*, 98-100.

12 Major-General (Retd) Tim Grant and Lieutenant-Colonel Tom Bradley, interview by Wolf Riedel and Kevin Smith, June 27, 2023.

13 Lieutenant-Colonel Ian Plummer, Interview by Wolf Riedel, April 13, 2023.

14 Horn, No Lack of Courage, 45.

15 Ibid.

16 Fraser and Hanington, *Operation Medusa*, 143.

17 Horn, *No Lack of Courage*, 47.

18 Ibid., 41.

19 Ibid., 31.

20 Lieutenant-General (Retd) Omer Lavoie, interview by Wolf Riedel, May 16, 2023.

21 Ibid.

22 Major-General (Retd) David Fraser, interview by Wolf Riedel, March 16, 2023.

23 Fraser and Hanington, *Operation Medusa*, 130.

24 Major-General (Retd) David Fraser, interview by Wolf Riedel, March 16, 2023.

25 Ibid. But see Fraser and Hanington, *Operation Medusa*, 159-160 where he indicates that it was only on the afternoon of September 3, 2006 that he was advised by Bishop that there was a shortage.

26 Note that Major-General Freakley did not take on the role of ISAF Deputy Commander Security Operations until October 5, 2006 when Regional Command (East) came under ISAF. Brian Neumann and Colin J. Williams, *The U.S. Army in Afghanistan Operation Enduring Freedom May 2005 - January 2009* (Washington: Center of Military History, 2020), 35.

27 Lieutenant-Colonel Shane Schreiber, interview by Bernd Horn, October 18, 2006 as quoted in Horn *No Lack of Courage*, 49.

28 Colonel (Retd) Tim Bishop, interview by Wolf Riedel, Brian Reid and Kevin Smith, July 26 and August 2, 2021.

29 Captain Chris Purdy, interview by Bernd Horn, October 17, 2006 as quoted in Horn, *No Lack of Courage*, 59.

30 There are two books that support this, by way of confidential sources. Horn, *No Lack of Courage*, 64 and Adam Day, *Witness to War: Reporting on Afghanistan 2004-2009* (Kingston: Canadian Defence Academy Press, 2010), 175-6.

31 Colonel (Retd) Greg Ivey, Chief Warrant Officer (Retd) Bob Montague and Lieutenant-Colonel Ian Plummer interview by Brian Reid, Wolf Riedel and Kevin Smith, September 21, 2021.

32 Lieutenant-Colonel Tim Spears, interview by Brian Reid, Wolf Riedel and Kevin Smith, March 9, 11, 23 and 25, 2022.

33 Major Mark Gasparotto, *Clearing the Way: Combat Engineers in Kandahar* (London: Ardith Publishing, 2010), 37.

34 Ibid., 39-40.

35 Observation Post Log G23 TF 3-06, August 8, 2006 to February 12, 2007 entry for September 3, 2006.

36 Major Greg Ivey, interview by Bernd Horn, October 17, 2006 as quoted in Horn, No Lack of Courage, 50-51.

37 Observation Post Log G23 TF 3-06, August 8, 2006 to February 12, 2007 entry for September 3, 2006.

38 Ibid.

39 Ibid.

40 Major Greg Ivey, interview by Bernd Horn, October 17, 2006 as quoted in Horn, *No Lack of Courage*, 56.

41 Captain Ian Plummer, undated interview (approximately 2010-12) in support of the Clearing the Way project.

42 Lieutenant-Colonel Tim Spears, interview by Brian Reid, Wolf Riedel and Kevin Smith, March 9, 11, 23 and 25, 2022.

43 Horn, *No Lack of Courage*, 41.

44 Ibid., 43.

45 Major Greg Ivey, email to Lieutenant-Colonel Scott Johnson, September 20, 2006.

46 Observation Post Log G23 TF 3-06, August 8, 2006 to February 12, 2007, entry for September 4 - 8, 2006.

47 Department of National Defence, "Board of Inquiry Minutes of Proceedings, A10-A Friendly Fire Incident 4 September 2006, Panjwayi District, Afghanistan," (Declassified and redacted)," (Ottawa: Department of National Defence, 15 December 2006), 51/89 - 55/89.

48 Ibid., 5/89.

49 Ibid., 54/89 - 55/89.

50 Lieutenant-Colonel Tim Spears, email to Wolf Riedel, June 12, 2023.

51 Lieutenant-General (Retd) Stuart Beare, email to Brigadier-General (Retd) Ernie Beno and Wolf Riedel, September 4, 2013.

52 Ibid.

53 Bradley and Mauer, *Lions of Kandahar*, 202.

54 Fraser and Hanington, *Operation Medusa*, 167.

55 Colonel (Retd) Tim Bishop, interview by Wolf Riedel, Brian Reid and Kevin Smith, July 26 and August 2, 2021.

56 Lieutenant-General (Retd) Omer Lavoie, interview by Wolf Riedel, May 16, 2023.

57 Major Trevor Cadieu, "Canadian Armour in Afghanistan," *Canadian Army Journal* 10, no. 4 (Winter 2008): 7.

58 Peter Kasurak, *Canada's Mechanized Infantry: The Evolution of a Combat Arm, 1920-2012* (Vancouver: UBC Press, 2020), 200. The Direct Fire Unit was an experimental organization based on three systems: The Mobile Gun System, The Multi-Mission Effects vehicle and the TOW Under Armour vehicle.

59 Lieutenant-Colonel (Retired) Perry Wells, "The Leopard Tank Replacement Project," *Canadian Army Journal* 19, no. 2 (2021): 60; See also Fraser and Hanington, *Operation Medusa*, 176.

60 Horn, *No Lack of Courage*, 46.

61 Kenneth Finlayson and Alan Meyer, "Operation Medusa," *Veritas Journal of Army Special Operations History* 3, no. 4 (2007): 2. (Note. This article contains several fact and date errors).

62 Lieutenant-Colonel (Retd) Caleb Walker, interview by Wolf Riedel, Mark Zuehlke and Kevin Smith, September 6, 2023.

63 Colonel (Retd) Greg Ivey, Chief Warrant Officer (Retd) Bob Montague and Lieutenant-Colonel Ian Plummer, interview by Brian Reid, Wolf Riedel and Kevin Smith, September 21, 2021.

CHAPTER 21 - OPERATION MEDUSA: SEPTEMBER 6 - 17, 2006

1 Major Mark Gasparotto, *Clearing the Way: Combat Engineers in Kandahar* (London: Ardith Publishing, 2010), 54.

2 Lieutenant-Colonel Ian Plummer, interview by Wolf Riedel, April 13 and 19, 2023.

3 Ibid.

4 Major Greg Ivey, email to Lieutenant-Colonel Scott Johnson, September 20, 2006.

5 Lieutenant-Colonel Ian Plummer, interview by Wolf Riedel, April, 13 and 19 2023.

6 Observation Post Log G23 TF 3-06, August 8, 2006 to February 12, 2007, entries for September 9-11, 2006.

7 Major Greg Ivey, interview by Bernd Horn, October 17, 2006 as quoted in Colonel Bernd Horn, *No Lack of Courage, Operation Medusa, Afghanistan* (Toronto: Dundurn Press, 2010), 56.

8 On May 23, 2012, Lieutenant-General Stuart Beare presented the 1st Battalion of the 3rd Special Forces Group (Airborne) with the first ever award of the Commander-in-Chief's Unit Commendation to a non-Canadian unit for its service on Operation MEDUSA.

9 Observation Post Log G23 TF 3-06, August 8, 2006 to February 12, 2007,

entry for September 13, 2006.

10 Major Greg Ivey, email to Lieutenant-Colonel Scott Johnson, September 20, 2006.

11 Major Greg Ivey, email to Lieutenant-Colonel Scott Johnson, September 20, 2006.

12 Musgrave originally joined the battery as part of the miniature unmanned aerial vehicle troop but was transferred to the quartermaster stores after technical difficulties with the aircraft developed.

13 Warrant Officer (Retd) Rick Cameron, interview by Brian Reid and Kevin Smith, April 14, 2022.

14 Ibid.

15 Master Warrant Officer Bob Montague, interview with Brian Reid, July 23, 2008.

16 Chief Warrant Officer (Retd) Bob Montague, email to Wolf Riedel, June 30, 2023.

17 The purpose of a registration mission is to determine, by shooting, the corrections required to map bearing and range to compensate for the total effects of non-standard conditions, i.e. weather, equipment, ammunition and survey errors.

18 Major Greg Ivey, Untitled paper provided to Brian Reid at interview, August 7, 2008, 26.

19 Ibid., 27.

20 Ibid., 26.

21 Ibid., 27.

22 Captain (Retd) (Master Gunner) Kevin Smith, email to Wolf Riedel, April 29, 2023.

23 Captain (Retd) (Master Gunner) Kevin Smith, email to Wolf Riedel, April 30, 2023.

24 Ibid.

25 Ibid., and Major Greg Ivey, email to Lieutenant-Colonel Scott Johnson, September 20, 2006.

26 Captain (Retd) (Master Gunner) Kevin Smith, email to Wolf Riedel, April 30, 2023.

27 Major-General (Ret'd) David Fraser and Brian Hanington, *Operation Medusa: The Furious Battle that Saved Afghanistan* (Toronto: McClelland and Stewart, 2018), 152.

28 Lieutenant-Colonel Omer Lavoie, interview by Bernd Horn, October 10, 2006 as cited in Horn, *No Lack of Courage*, 76.

29 Fraser and Hanington, *Operation Medusa*, 177.

30 Colonel (Retd) Greg Ivey, email to Brian Reid, February 8, 2022.

31 Carl Forsberg, *Afghanistan Report 3: The Taliban Campaign for Kandahar* (Washington: Institute for the Study of War, 2009), 27.

32 Major Greg Ivey, email to Lieutenant-Colonel Scott Johnson, September 20, 2006.

33 Captain Ian Plummer, email to Brian Reid, undated.

34 "Suicide bomber kills 4 Canadian Soldiers," CBC News, Last Updated September 18, 2006.

35 Carter Malkasian, *The American War in Afghanistan: A History* (New York: Oxford University Press, 2021), 152-154

CHAPTER 22 · CONSOLIDATION

1   Chief Warrant Officer Rod Gallant, interview by Wolf Riedel, March 20, 22 and 29, 2023.

2   Captain (Retd) Ken Whitnall, email to Riedel, April 2, 2022.

3   Warrant Officer Justin Clarke, interview by Wolf Riedel, May 15, 2023.

4   Lieutenant-Colonel (Retd) Caleb Walker, interview by Wolf Riedel, Mark Zuehlke and Kevin Smith, September 6, 2023.

5   Ibid.

6   Ibid.

7   Ibid.

8   Major Renald Dufour, "The Future of the Royal Regiment" PowerPoint presentation for Artillery Working Group, October 3-4, 2006.

9   Ibid., See also *The Canadian Gunner 2006* 41a (February 2007): 15 and Captain (Retd) (Master Gunner) Kevin Smith, email to Wolf Riedel, May 11, 2023.

10 US Letter of Offer and Acceptance CN-P-LIA, September 26, 2006.

11 With the exception of the 105mm C3s designated for avalanche control under Operation PALACHI.

12 Dufour, "The Future of the Royal Regiment," slides 7, 9 & 10.

13 Ibid., Slide 12.

14 Ibid.

15 Ibid., In its simplest form, a small unmanned aerial vehicle (UAV) is a class of aircraft that falls between the army operated miniature UAV Skylark (contemplated for employment at the company and below level) and the RCAF operated tactical UAV Sperwer (contemplated at the brigade group level). That would envision the small UAV as a battalion or battle group resource.

16 Major Renald Dufour, Briefing Note for Chief of Land Staff, October 26, 2006.

17 Dufour, "The Future of the Royal Regiment", Notes to slide 55.

18 Brigadier-General (Retd) and Assistant Deputy Minister (Material) (Retd)

Dan Ross, interviewed by Wolf Riedel, Brian Reid and Kevin Smith, May 5, 2021.

19 House of Commons, Standing Committee on National Defence, *Minutes of Proceedings and Evidence*, no. 38, Thursday, 22 February 2007, time 1025-1030.

20 Department of National Defence, Land Operations 2021: Adaptive Dispersed Operations—The Force Employment Concept for Canada's Army of Tomorrow, ed. Major Andrew Godfrey (Kingston: Directorate of Land Concepts and Design, 2007).

21 As an example, see Major Hart, DAD 6-3 PowerPoint Presentation "Command CDR Orientation Briefing to the Arty WG", October 3, 2006 to define effective command and command support structures for land operations.

22 For a discussion see Major Sean Hackett, "Modularity and the Canadian Army: Dispersion, Command, and Building the Sum of all Parts," (MDS Research project, Canadian Forces College, 2007). The army would go so far as to designate and organize the 2nd Battalion, The Royal Canadian Regiment in Gagetown as an experimental optimized battle group for several years.

23 Dufour, "The Future of the Royal Regiment," Notes to slide 55.

24 Edmund Degen and Mark Reardon, *Modern War in an Ancient Land: The United States Army in Afghanistan 2001-2014 Vol II* (Washington: Center of Military History, United States Army, 2021), 114.

25 Observation Post Log G23 TF 3-06, 8 August, 2006 to 12 February, 2007.

26 Ibid.

27 Colonel (Retd) Greg Ivey, email to Brian Reid, February 12, 2022.

28 For a detailed account of the battle see Colonel Bernd Horn, "Defence on Strong Point Centre-14 October 2006," *Canadian Military Journal* 8, No. 2 (Spring 2007): 11.

29 Colonel (Retd) Greg Ivey, email to Brian Reid, February 13, 2022.

30 Major Mark Gasparotto, ed. *Clearing the Way: Combat Engineers in Kandahar* (London: Ardith Publishing, 2010), 97.

31 The award had been criticized by many who believe that he should have received the highest award, the Victoria Cross. At the time of writing there is an active campaign to have the award upgraded.

32 Observation Post Log G23 TF 3-06, 8 August, 2006 to February 12, 2007 entry for October 14, 2006.

33 Captain (Retd) (Master Gunner) Kevin Smith, email to Wolf Riedel, April 5, 2023.

34 Chief Warrant Officer Rodney Gallant, interview by Wolf Riedel, March 20, 22 and 29, 2023.

35 Observation Post Log G23 TF 3-06, August 8, 2006 to February 12, 2007.

36 Captain (Retd) Lorne Doucet, and Captain (Master Gunner) (Retd) Kevin Smith, interview by Wolf Riedel, May 25, 2023 and Chief Warrant Officer Rodney Gallant, interview by Wolf Riedel, March 20, 22 and 29, 2023.

37 Harvey Goldman, "LWH M777 Towed Artillery Digitization" (June 12, 2007) Accessed May 26, 2023. https://ndiastorage.blob.core.usgovcloudapi.net/ndia/2007/armaments/Goldman.pdf.

38 Gasparotto, *Clearing the Way*, 101.

39 Major-General (Retd) Tim Grant and Lieutenant-Colonel Tom Bradley, interview by Wolf Riedel and Kevin Smith, June 27, 2023.

40 Rob Baker, TF AEGIS PowerPoint "Multi-national Brigade Airspace Coordination", undated. See also TF AEGIS, TF ORION, TF 3-06, TF 1-07 Powerpoint "2006-2007 TFK ASCC Ops", undated.

41 Lieutenant-Colonel Rouleau would subsequently become the commander of Canadian Special Operations Forces Command, Canadian Joint Operations Command and would retire in the rank of Lieutenant-General as Vice Chief of the Defence Staff.

42 Lieutenant-General (Retd) Mike Rouleau, interview by Wolf Riedel, Mark Zuehlke, and Kevin Smith, April 25, 2023 .

43 John Geddes, "Canadian Forces in Afghanistan Focus on Reconstruction" *The Canadian Encyclopedia*, Last edited December 14th, 2013 accessed on June 28, 2023, https://www.thecanadianencyclopedia.ca/en/article/canadian-forces-in-afghanistan-focus-on-reconstruction

44 Major-General (Retd) Tim Grant and Lieutenant-Colonel Tom Bradley, interview by Wolf Riedel and Kevin Smith, June 27, 2023.

45 Master Bombardier Lucas Cunningham, email to Brigadier-General (Retd) Ernest Beno, September 27, 2010.

46 Chief Warrant Officer(Retd) Bob Montague, interview by Brian Reid, July 23, 2008.

47 Observation Post Log G23 TF 3-06, August 8, 2006 to February 12, 2007, entry for October 27, 2006.

48 Chief Warrant Officer Montague, (Retd) Bob, interview by Brian Reid, July 23, 2008.

CHAPTER 23 - OPERATION BAAZ TSUKA: OUTREACH

1 Joseph T. Jockel, *Canada and The Netherlands in Afghanistan* (Kingston: Centre for International and Defence Policy, Queen's University, 2014), 59.

2 Lieutenant-Colonel Donald Bolduc, interview by Dr Kenneth Finlayson, January 31, 2008, quoted in Kenneth Finlayson, "Operation BAAZ TSUKA: Task Force 31 Returns to the Panjwayi" *Veritas Journal of Army Special*

Operations History 4, no. 1 (2008): 16-17.

3 François D'Alançon, "Afghanistan: le général van Loon veut réduire l'audience des talibans," *La Croix* November 19, 2006. (translated from French)

4 Ibid.

5 Colonel Bernd Horn, *No Lack of Courage, Operation Medusa, Afghanistan* (Toronto: Dundurn Press, 2010), 107.

6 Ibid.

7 Finlayson, "Operation BAAZ TSUKA", 18.

8 Lieutenant-General (Retd) Omer Lavoie, interview by Wolf Riedel, May 16, 2023.

9 Major-General (Retd) Tim Grant and Lieutenant-Colonel Tom Bradley, interview by Wolf Riedel and Kevin Smith, June 27, 2023.

10 A "check bearing" is a drill done after extended pauses in firing, for example overnight, to confirm parallelism for all the guns.

11 Lieutenant-Colonel(Retd)Caleb Walker, interview by Wolf Riedel, Mark Zuehlke and Kevin Smith, September 6, 2023.

12 Observation Post Log G23 TF 3-06, August 8, 2006 to February 12, 2007, entry for 13 December 2006.

13 Finlayson, "Operation BAAZ TSUKA", 17.

14 Michael Smith, "Taliban leader 'killed' after RAF tracks phone' *TimesOnline* December 24, 2006. See also Bill Roggio, "Taliban Commander Mullah Akhtar Usmani Killed in Airstrike," *Long War Journal* (December 23, 2006).

15 Ibid.

16 Observation Post Log G23 TF 3-06, August 8, 2006 to February 12, 2007, entry for December 20, 2006.

17 Ibid.

18 Toronto Star, January 7, 2007.

19 Major-General (Retd) Simon Hetherington, email to Wolf Riedel, June 30, 2023.

20 Ibid.

21 Observation Post Log G23 TF 3-06, August 8, 2006 to February 12, 2007, entry for 20 December 2006.

22 Ibid.

23 Finlayson, "Operation BAAZ TSUKA", 19.

24 Ibid.

25 Ibid.

26 Major Mark Gasparotto, ed *Clearing the Way: Combat Engineers in Kandahar* (London: Ardith Publishing, 2010), 132 and 135.

27 Events would demonstrate that Monroe was an extremely capable NCO.

28 Observation Post Log G22 TF 3-06, July 31, 2006 to February 7, 2007, entry for December 17, 2006; Major Ian Plummer, emails to Brian Reid, June 19 - 20, 2013.

29 Observation Post Log G22 TF 3-06, July 31, 2006 to February 7, 2007, entries for 21 - 29 December, 2006.

30 Major Ian Plummer, emails to Brian Reid, June 19 - 20, 2013.

31 Captain Piers Pappin, email to Brian Reid, June 20, 2013.

32 Major Ian Plummer, email to Brian Reid, June 20 2013.

33 Ibid.

34 Observation Post Log G23 TF 3-06, August 8, 2006 to February 12, 2007, entry for 29 December 2006.

35 Major Ian Plummer, email to Brian Reid, June 19, 2013.

36 Sergeant Byron Sheppard, email to Reid Jun 20, 2013.

37 Major Ian Plummer, email to Brian Reid, June 20, 2013; Observation Post Log G23 TF 3-06, August 8, 2006 to February 12, 2007, entry for 29 December 2006, and Lieutenant-Colonel Ian Plummer, email to Wolf Riedel, June 30, 2023 .

38 Major Ian Plummer, email to Brian Reid, June 19, 2013.

39 Ibid.

40 Lieutenant-Colonel Ian Plummer, interview by Wolf Riedel, April 13 and 19, 2023.

41 Captain (Retd) (Master Gunner) Kevin Smith, message to Wolf Riedel, June 22, 2023. Many ROVERs were distributed by the USAF in what could be called "tailgate deals" after the A10 incident. They were simply handed out in the field with basic training to facilitate allies controlling US aircraft. Canada would subsequently obtain their own through the Unforecasted Operational Requirement process.

42 T.F.J. Leveridge, *Sagem CU-161 Sperwer Canadian Armed Forces Serial 16101* (Ottawa: Canadian Aviation and Space Museum Ottawa Museum, 2013), 12-15.

43 Lieutenant-General (Retd) Omer Lavoie, interview by Wolf Riedel, May 16, 2023.

44 Master Warrant Officer (Master Gunner) Tony Tullet, interview by Wolf Riedel and Kevin Smith, October 20, 2021.

45 Colonel (Retd) Greg Ivey, and Chief Warrant Officer (Retd) Bob Montague, interview by Wolf Riedel and Kevin Smith, September 27, 2021.

46 Major Greg Ivey, Untitled paper provided to Brian Reid at Interview August 7,2008, 28 and Colonel Greg Ivey, message to Wolf Riedel, June 18th, 2023.

47 Lieutenant-General (Retd) Omer Lavoie, interview by Wolf Riedel, May 16,

2023.

48   Lieutenant-Colonel Ian Plummer, interview by Wolf Riedel, April 13 and 19, 2023.

49   Gasparotto, *Clearing the Way*, 135; Major Greg Ivey, email to Brian Reid 10 July 2010.

50   Major Greg Ivey, email to Brian Reid, October 7, 2010.

51   Master Warrant Officer Bob Montague, interview by Brian Reid, July 23, 2008.

52   Kevin Bannister, Facebook, January 29, 2019.

53   Their FOO, Captain Jeff Francis would be killed by an IED along with five others from the Princess Patricia's Canadian Light Infantry on July 4, 2007.

54   Lieutenant-Colonel Ian Plummer, interview by Wolf Riedel, April 13 and 19, 2023, Lieutenant-Colonel Ian Plummer, email to Wolf Riedel, June 30, 2023,

55   Chief Warrant Officer Rodney Gallant, interview by Wolf Riedel, March 20, 22 and 29, 2023. "Left seat/right seat" refers to both the outgoing member and the incoming one working together with the outgoing one in charge until it's agreed to pass the function on to the incoming one.

56   Warrant Officer Justin Clarke, interview by Wolf Riedel, May 15, 2023.

57   Ibid. With only six gun batteries in the artillery and a battery rotating every six months, many gunners would deploy again on later tours. And begin training for that deployment shortly after returning home.

58   Chief Warrant Officer Rodney Gallant, interview by Wolf Riedel, March 20, 22 and 29, 2023.

59   Lieutenant-Colonel Ian Plummer, interview by Wolf Riedel, April 13 and 19, 2023, Lieutenant-Colonel Ian Plummer, email to Wolf Riedel, June 30, 2023.

60   The incoming commanding officer of 3rd Battalion of the Princess Patricia's Canadian Light Infantry went so far as to convene a new series of honour boards to handle the issue.

61   Major Greg Ivey, email to Brian Reid, November 10, 2010.

62   Ibid.

63   Ibid.

64   Ibid.

65   Operation MEDUSA is often referred to as the 2nd Battle of Panjwayi while Operation ZAHAR on May 17, 2006 is referred to as the 1st Battle of Panjwayi (see for example Wikipedia). Strangely enough, neither was fought in Panjwayi. In 2004 President Kharzai readjusted Panjwayi and some other districts' borders so that the area north of the Arghandab River became Zhari District.

66   Horn, *No Lack of Courage*, 66.

67   Colonel (Retd) Peter Williams, message to Wolf Riedel, June 12, 2023.

68   Major-General (Retd) Simon Hetherington, email to Wolf Riedel, June 30,

2023.

69 Squadron Leader Dave Marsh, Spokesman Regional Command (South) as quoted in Lobjakas, Ahto "Afghanistan: NATO Downplays 'Conventional' Threat in South" Radio Free Europe January 23, 2007 https://www.rferl.org/a/1074237.html accessed June 3, 2023.

70 Lieutenant-General (Retd) Omer Lavoie, interview by Wolf Riedel, May 16, 2023.

71 Major Greg Ivey and Major Dan Bobbit, PowerPoint presentation "Fire Support in Kandahar Province The Canadian Experience", undated, Slide 12.

EPILOGUE

1 See for example J.L. Granatstein and Lieutenant-General (Ret'd) Charles Belzile, *The Special Commission on the Restructuring of the Reserves: Ten Years Later* (Calgary: Canadian Defence & Foreign Affairs Institute, September 2005), 11-12.

2 Carter Malkasian, *The American War in Afghanistan: A History* (New York: Oxford University Press, 2021), 155.

3 Ibid., 155-156.

4 Ibid.

5 Ibid.

SELECT BIBLIOGRAPHY

GOVERNMENT DOCUMENTS

Canada. Department of National Defence. B-GL-371-003/FP-001 *Field Artillery Operational Procedures*. Ottawa: Department of National Defence, August 27, 2000.

Canada. Department of National Defence. *Canadian Army, Advancing With Purpose: The Army Strategy*. Kingston: Department of National Defence, May 2002.

Canada. Department of National Defence. Sandy Babcock. "Canadian Network Enabled Operations Initiative." Ottawa: Department of National Defence, June 2004.

Department of National Defence. B-GL-381-001/TS-000 *Operational Training, Training Safety*. Ottawa: DND, September 24, 2004.

Canada. Department of National Defence. C-74-315-H00/TA-000 *Ammunition for 105 mm Howitzer*. Ottawa: Department of National Defence, September 24, 2004.

Canada. Department of National Defence. *Canada's International Policy Statement: A Role of Pride and Influence in the World – Defence*. Ottawa: Department of National Defence, 2005.

Canada. Department of National Defence. Lieutenant-General Marc Caron. "3185-1(LFDI 2) Implementation Directive Transformation of Field Artillery" July 20, 2005.

Canada. Department of National Defence. Synopsis Sheet (Effective Project Approval) Lightweight 155mm Towed Howitzer Project 00001017." Ottawa: Department of National Defence, August 2005.

Canada. Department of National Defence. "Draft Introduction Plan M777

Lightweight 155MM Towed Howitzer (LWTH) System." Ottawa: Department of National Defence, November 2005.

Canada. Department of National Defence. Major Steve Gallagher. "3350-1 Artillery Tactical Recce Report." Shilo, MB: Department of National Defence, 4 November 2005.

Canada. Department of National Defence. Major Steve Gallagher. "3350-1(BC A) Artillery Tactical Recce Report." Shilo, MB: Department of National Defence, 5 November 2005.

Canada. Department of National Defence. Brigadier-General Stuart Beare. "Land Force Doctrine and Training System Headquarters, 4500-1 (ATA) Training Directive – M777 Lightweight Towed Howitzer." Kingston, ON: Department of National Defence, 29 November 2005.

Canada. Department of National Defence. Colonel Bob Gunn. "00001017-11025-1 (DLR 2) Fielding Plan - M777 Lightweight 155mm Towed Howitzer (LWTH) System." Ottawa: Department of National Defence, March 2006.

Canada. Department of National Defence. Lieutenant-Colonel Ian Hope. "TF ORION 3350-3 (ALLO), Task Force Orion - Fire Support, Initial Theatre Lesson Report." Kandahar: Department of National Defence, 26 March 2006.

Canada. Department of National Defence. Major Mason. Stalker. "TF ORION – Warning Order for Op BRAVO CORRIDOR (Frag O 93)." Kandahar: Department of National Defence, July 29, 2006.

Canada. Department of National Defence. Major Mason Stalker. "TF ORION - Frag O 93 - Op BRAVO CORRIDOR - FINAL SUMMARY" August 5, 2006.

Canada. Department of National Defence. Brigadier-General David Fraser," CFT AEGIS 3350-1 (Comd) "Authority to Fire and Indirect Safe Distances." Kandahar?? August 13, 2006.

Canada. Department of National Defence. Captain MP Williams. RCAS 4500-4-1 (IG) Sep 2006. "Instructor in Gunnery Report Exercise DELTA ARCHER / REDLEG ARCHER II." Gagetown, NB: Department of National Defence, September 2006.

Canada. Department of National Defence. Major Renald Dufour. "Briefing Note for Chief of Land Staff. Ottawa: Department of National Defence, 26 October 2006.

Canada. Department of National Defence. "Board of Inquiry Minutes of Proceedings, A-10A Friendly Fire Incident 4 September 2006, Panjwayi District, Afghanistan." (Declassified and redacted). Ottawa: Department of National Defence, 15 December 2006.

Canada. Department of National Defence. *Land Operations 2021: Adaptive Dispersed Operations—The Force Employment Concept for Canada's Army of*

Tomorrow, edited by Major Andrew Godfrey. Kingston: Directorate of Land Concepts and Design, 2007.

Canada. Department of National Defence. Lieutenant-General J.C.M. Gauthier. "CEFCOM 1080-1 (DComd), CEFCOM Review of BOI Report on the Action at FOB ROBINSON, Afghanistan, 28/29 Mar 2006 (redacted)." Ottawa: Department of National Defence, 8 March 2007.

Canada. Department of National Defence. Chief Review Services. *Evaluation of CF/DND Participation in the Kandahar Provincial Reconstruction Team*. Ottawa: DND, December 2007.

Department of National Defence. The Mention in Dispatches 1991-2016. Ottawa: Department of National Defence, 2016, 118. https://www.canada.ca/content/dam/themes/defence/caf/militaryhistory/dhh/honours/mention-in-dispatches.pdf.

Department of National Defence. "United Nations Protection Force (UNPROFOR)" (Ottawa: DND, last modified December 11, 2018), Accessed May 7, 2021. https://www.canada.ca/en/department-national-defence/services/military-history/history-heritage/past-operations/europe/canengbat-mandarin-harmony-cavalier-medusa-panorama.html.

Canada. Department of National Defence. *Advancing With Purpose: The Canadian Army Modernization Strategy*.4th ed. Kingston: Department of National Defence, December 2020.

Canada. Department of Public Works and Government Services. Branker, Sandi, Public Works and Government Services Canada, Canadian Embassy Washington (Letter of Request (Restate) LOR-CN-P-P-082306-01", August 23. 2006.

Canada. House of Commons. Standing Committee on National Defence and Veterans' Affairs. *Minutes of Proceedings and Evidence,* Wednesday, 4 December 2002, 1540-1545.

Canada. House of Commons. Standing Committee on National Defence. *Minutes of Proceedings and Evidence*, no. 38, Thursday 22 February 2007.

Canada. Senate of Canada. Lieutenant-Colonel Pat Stogran Testimony. *Debates of the Senate (Hansard)* no. 18. Tuesday, 19 November, 2002. 1430.

Canada. Senate of Canada. Standing Senate Committee on National Security and Defence. *Canadian Security Guide Book 2005 An Update of Security Problems in Search of Solutions*. Ottawa: Senate, December 2004.

Godefroy, Major Andrew B. "Transformation and the Army of Tomorrow" In B-GL-310-001/AF-001 *Toward Land Operations 2021: Studies in Support of the Army of Tomorrow Force Employment Concept*, edited by Major Andrew B.

Godefroy and Mr. Peter Gizewski, 3-1-3-10. Kingston: Department of National Defence, Directorate of Land Concepts and Design, 2009.

United Nations. *United Nations Security Council Resolution 1368 S/Res/1368 (2001)*. New York: United Nations Security Council, 12 September 2001. http://unscr.com/en/resolutions/doc/1368.

United Nations. *United Nations Security Council Resolution 1373 S/Res/1373 (2001)*. New York: United Nations Security Council, 28 September 2001. http://unscr.com/en/resolutions/doc/1373.

United Nations. *United Nations Security Council Resolution 1386 S/Res/1386 (2001)*. New York: United Nations Security Council, 20 December 2001. http://unscr.com/en/resolutions/doc/1386.

United States. United States General Accounting Office. *Military Transformation: Realistic Deployment Timelines Needed For Army Stryker Brigades*. Washington: GAO, June 30, 2003.

United States. Department of Defence. United States Army FM 3-09.32 *JFIRE Multi-service Procedures for the Joint Application of Firepower*. Fort Monroe: US Army Training and Doctrine Command, October 2004.

United States. Special Inspector General for Afghanistan Reconstruction. *Reconstructing the Afghan National Defense and Security Forces: Lessons from the US Experience in Afghanistan*. Arlington, VA: SIGAR, September 2017.

US Letter of Offer and Acceptance CN-P-LIA, September 26, 2006

BOOKS AND PUBLICATIONS

Bercuson, David J. and J.L. Granatstein with Nancy Pearson Mackie. *Lessons learned? What Canada Should learn From Afghanistan*. Calgary: Canadian Defence & Foreign Affairs Institute, 2011.

Blatchford, Christie. *Fifteen Days*. Toronto: Doubleday Canada, 2007.

Blumenstock, Lieutenant-Commander Paul. "Canada's Strategic Dilemma: Changing World Conditions and the Need for Organizational Reform of Defence." MDS Research Project, Canadian Forces College, 2012.

Boileau, John. "Canadian Peacekeepers in the Balkans," *The Canadian Encyclopedia 2019*. Accessed May 14, 2021. https://www.thecanadianencyclopedia.ca/en/article/canadian-peacekeepers-in-the-balkans. Note that Canada is still committed to Kosovo under Operation KOBALT in 2021

Bradley, Major Rusty and Kevin Mauer. *Lions of Kandahar: The Story of a Fight Against all Odds*. New York: Bantam Books, 2015.

Conrad, Colonel John. *What the Thunder Said: Reflections of a Canadian Officer in Kandahar*. Toronto: Dundurn Press, 2009.

Day, Adam. *Witness to War: Reporting on Afghanistan 2004-2009.* Kingston: Canadian Defence Academy Press, 2010.

Degen, Edmund and Mark Reardon. *Modern War in an Ancient Land: The United States Army in Afghanistan 2001-2014 Vol I.* Washington: Center of Military History, United States Army, 2021.

Degen, Edmund and Mark Reardon. *Modern War in an Ancient Land: The United States Army in Afghanistan 2001-2014 Vol II.* Washington: Center of Military History, United States Army, 2021.

Denine, Michael Thomas Victor. "Dwindling Options." In *In Their Own Words: Canadian Stories of Valour and Bravery in Afghanistan 2001-2007,* edited by Craig Leslie Mantle, CPO2 Paul Pellerin (Ret'd), Tom Douglas, Justin Wright and Melanie Denis, 81-102. Kingston: Canadian Defence Academy Press, 2013.

Forsberg, Carl. *Afghanistan Report 3: The Taliban Campaign for Kandahar.* Washington: Institute for the Study of War, 2009.

Fraser, Major-General (Ret'd) David and Brian Hanington. *Operation Medusa: The Furious Battle that Saved Afghanistan.* Toronto: McClelland and Stewart, 2018.

Gasparotto, Major Mark. Ed *Clearing the Way: Combat Engineers in Kandahar.* London: Ardith Publishing, 2010.

Geddes, John. "Canadian Forces in Afghanistan Focus on Reconstruction." *The Canadian Encyclopedia,* Last edited December 14, 2013. accessed on June 28, 2023, https://www.thecanadianencyclopedia.ca/en/article/canadian-forces-in-afghanistan-focus-on-reconstruction.

Goldman, Harvey. "LWH M777 Towed Artillery Digitization" National Defense Industry Association Armaments Technology and Firepower Symposium June 12, 2007. Accessed May 26, 2023. https://ndiastorage.blob.core.usgovcloudapi.net/ndia/2007/armaments/Goldman.pdf.

Granatstein J.L. and Lieutenant-General (Retd) Charles Belzile. *The Special Commission on the Restructuring of the Reserves: Ten Years Later.* Calgary: Canadian Defence & Foreign Affairs Institute, September 2005.

Hackett, Major Sean. "Modularity and the Canadian Army: Dispersion, Command, and Building the Sum of all Parts." MDS Research Project, Canadian Forces College, 2007.

Harding, Christopher Lorne. "Helping a Buddy...Under Fire." In *In Their Own Words: Canadian Stories of Valour and Bravery in Afghanistan 2001-2007,* edited by Craig Leslie Mantle, CPO2 Paul Pellerin (Ret'd), Tom Douglas, Justin Wright and Melanie Denis, 103-123. Kingston: Canadian Defence Academy Press, 2013.

Hillier, General Rick. *A Soldier First: Bullets, Bureaucrats and the Politics of War.* Toronto: HarperCollins, 2015.

Hope, Lieutenant-Colonel Ian. *Dancing With the Dushman: Command Imperatives For The Counter-Insurgency Fight in Afghanistan.* Kingston: Canadian Defence Academy Press, 2008.

Horn, Colonel Bernd. *No Lack of Courage, Operation Medusa, Afghanistan.* Toronto: Dundurn Press, 2010.

Horn, Colonel Bernd. *No Ordinary Men: Special Operations Forces Missions in Afghanistan.* Toronto: Dundurn Press, 2016.

Institute for the Study of War. "Regional Command South." Washington, DC: Institute for the Study of War, n.d. Accessed February 4, 2023, https://www. understandingwar.org/region/regional-command-south-0.

Jeffery, Lieutenant-General (Retired) Michael K. *Inside Canadian Forces Transformation: Institutional Leadership as a Catalyst for Change.* Kingston: Canadian Defence Academy Press, 2009.

Jockel, Joseph T. *Canada and The Netherlands in Afghanistan.* Kingston: Centre for International and Defence Policy, Queen's University, 2014.

Kasurak, Peter. *Canada's Mechanized Infantry: The Evolution of a Combat Arm, 1920-2012.* Vancouver: UBC Press, 2020.

Lagsse, Philippe. "Specialization and the Canadian Forces," *Occasional paper No. 40* (Ottawa: Norman Paterson School of International Affairs, Carleton University, 2003), 5-6. Accessed June 6, 2021. https://www3.carleton.ca/csds/ docs/occasional_papers/npsia-40.pdf.

Lauber, W. Sam, Steven Babin, Katharine Burnett, Jonathon Cosgrove, Catherine Kane and Theodore Plettner. *Understanding States of Resistance: Pocket Guide.* Fort Bragg, NC: US Army Special Operations Command, 2019.

Leveridge T.F.J. *Sagem CU-161 Sperwer Canadian Armed Forces Serial 16101.* Ottawa: Canadian Aviation and Space Museum, 2013.

Macdonald, Sergeant William Kenneth. "Pinned Down, Not Defeated." In *In Their Own Words: Canadian Stories of Valour and Bravery in Afghanistan 2001-2007,* edited by Craig Leslie Mantle, CPO2 (Retd) Paul Pellerin, Tom Douglas, Justin Wright and Melanie Denis, 125-159. Kingston: Canadian Defence Academy Press, 2013.

Malkasian, Carter. *The American War in Afghanistan: A History.* New York: Oxford University Press, 2021.

Maloney, Sean M. *Fighting for Afghanistan: A Rogue Historian at War.* Annapolis: Naval Institute Press, 2011

Maloney, Sean. "RCAC History: Ch 19" A Brave New World 1990-2000 (draft)." In *The Royal Canadian Armoured Corps: An Illustrated History,* edited by John

Marteinson and Michael R. McNorgan, Accessed June 12, 2021, http://www.seanmmaloney.com/old/pdfs/Ch19RCAC.pdf.

Maloney, Sean M. *The Canadian Army in Afghanistan Volume 1: A Nation Under Fire, 2001-2006.* Ottawa: Army Publication Office, 2022.

Mantle, Craig, CPO2 (Retd) Paul Pellerin, Tom Douglas, Justin Wright and Melanie Denis. Editors. *In Their Own Words: Canadian Stories of Valour and Bravery in Afghanistan 2001-2007.* Kingston: Canadian Defence Academy Press, 2013.

McNabb, John. "Chemical and Biological Threats against Public Water Systems." In *Weapons of Mass Destruction and Terrorism,* edited by James J. F. Forest and Russel D. Howard, 338-364. New York: McGraw-Hill Education, 2012.

Mitchell, G.D. (With B.A. Reid & W. Simcock). *RCHA – Right of the Line; An Anecdotal History of the Royal Canadian Horse Artillery From 1871.* Ottawa: RCHA History Committee, 1971.

Naylor, Sean. *Not A Good Day to Die: The Untold Story of Operation Anaconda.* New York: Berkley Publishing Group, 2005.

Naylor, Sean. *Relentless Strike: The Secret History of Joint Special Operations Command.* New York: St Martin's Press, 2015.

Neumann, Brian and Colin J. Williams. *The U.S. Army in Afghanistan Operation Enduring Freedom May 2005 - January 2009.* Washington: Center of Military History, 2020.

Ochmanek, David, Peter A. Wilson, Brenna Allen, John Speed Meyers and Carter C. Price. U.S. *Military Capabilities and Forces for a Dangerous World: Rethinking the U.S. Approach to Force Planning.* Santa Monica: RAND Corporation, 2017.

Pigott, Peter. *Canada in Afghanistan: The War So Far.* Toronto: Dundurn Press, 2007.

Pocock, Charlie, Jim Gordon, Jerry Allen, and Charlie Heidel. *A Brief History of Forward Air Controlling.* Polson: FAC Association, 2008.

Reekie, Captain Michael John. "Ma'sum Ghar by Night." *In Their Own Words: Canadian Stories of Valour and Bravery in Afghanistan 2001-2007,* edited by Craig Leslie Mantle, CPO2 Paul Pellerin (Ret'd), Tom Douglas, Justin Wright and Melanie Denis, 161-189. Kingston: Canadian Defence Academy Press, 2013.

Richards, General David. *Taking Command: The Autobiography.* London: Headline Publishing Group, 2014.

Sorsdahl, Lieutenant-Commander Michael N. "Re-entry and Transition for Military Members: Phased Decompression Approach." MDS Research Project, Canadian Forces College, 2011.

The Royal Regiment of Canadian Artillery. *Standing Orders Volume I History,*

Organization and Heritage. Shilo: Royal Canadian Artillery Association, May 26, 2021.

Taylor, Scott and Brian Nolan. *Tested Mettle: Canada's Peacekeepers at War.* Toronto: Esprit de Corps Books, 1998.

Teeple, Nancy. *Canada in Afghanistan: 2001-2010 A Military Chronology.* Kingston: Defence R&D Canada, 2010.

Thruelsen, Peter. *From Soldier to Civilian: Disarmament, Demobilization, Reintegration in Afghanistan,* DIIS Report 2006:7 Copenhagen: Danish Institute for International Studies, 2006.

Tootal, Colonel Stuart. *Danger Close: The True Story of Helmand from the Leader of 3 Para.* London: John Murray Publishers, 2009. (Kindle edition location 404)?

Vick Alan, David Oretsky, Bruce Pirnie and Seth Jones. *The Stryker Brigade Combat Team: Rethinking Strategic Responsiveness and Assessing Deployment Options.* Santa Monica, CA: RAND Project Air Force, 2002.

Watling, Jack. *The Future of Fires, Maximizing the UK's Tactical and Operational Firepower.* Occasional Paper. London: Royal United Services Institute, 2019.

Wright, Dr. Donald P., James R. Bird, Steven E. Clay, Peter W. Connors, Lieutenant-Colonel Scott C. Farquhar, Lynne Chandler Garcia and Dennis F Van Wey. *A Different Kind of War: The United States Army in Operation ENDURING FREEDOM (OEF): October 2001–September 2005.* Fort Leavenworth: Combat Studies Institute Press, 2010.

JOURNALS

Buchanan, Captain D.C. "Intelligence Surveillance Target Acquisition and Reconnaissance Coordination Centre IISTAR CC - Providing the Commander's Situational Awareness." *The Bulletin* 11, no. 1 (February 2005): 13-16.

Cadieu, Major Trevor. "Canadian Armour in Afghanistan," *Canadian Army Journal* 10, no. 4 (Winter 2008): 5-25.

Capstick, Colonel M.D. (Mike). "The Civil-Military Effort in Afghanistan: A Strategic Perspective," *Journal of Military and Strategic Studies* 10, no. 1 (Fall 2007): 1-27.

Chagon, Captain Michael. "Canadian Embedded Training Team." *The Bulletin* 10, no. 8 (December 2004): 6-14.

Charchuk, Captain Andrew. "'Contact Charlie' A Forward Observation Officer with Task Force Orion." *Canadian Army Journal* 10, no.2 (Summer 2007): 25-35.

Cossette, Master Warrant Officer D. "To Centralize or Not to Centralize:

Comments on the Reconnaissance Squadron Echelon Doctrine." *The Bulletin* 11, no. 7 (November 2005): 7.

Cross, Colonel Michael A. "Operation Mountain Lion: CJTF-76 in Afghanistan, Spring 2006." *Military Review* (January-February 2008): 22-29.

D'Alançon, François. "Afghanistan: le général van Loon veut réduire l'audience des talibans." *La Croix* (November 19, 2006). (translated from French).

Devlin, Brigadier-General Peter, "A Mid-Tour Update from the Commander KMNB - Op ATHENA Roto 0." *The Bulletin* 10, no. 2 (January 2004): 5-9.

Devlin, Brigadier-General Peter, "Canadian Soldiers Deploy to the Kabul Multi-National Brigade-July 2003." *The Bulletin* 10, no. 2 (January 2004): 1-5.

DiNicola, Captain Daniel C., Captain Leo F. Brennan III and Captain Bruce J. Carter. "Afghanistan: CJTF-76 Joint Fires Board in OEF 04-06." *Field Artillery* (March -April 2006): 34-37

Ellis, Colonel W.J. "Comd TFK End Tour Report - Operation Athena Roto 2: 9 Aug 04 - 10 Feb 05." *The Bulletin* 11, no. 2 (March 2005): 1-8.

Ettinger, Aaron and Jeffery Rice. "Hell is other people's schedules: Canada's limited-term military commitments, 2001-2015." *International Journal* 71, no. 3 (September 2016): 371-392.

Eyestone, Captain GR, and Lieutenant PDD Gilbert. "Athena Battery ISTAR Assets Deployed." *The Bulletin* 11, no. 5 (August 2005): 4-5.

Finlayson, Kenneth and Alan D. Meyer. "Operation Medusa." *Veritas Journal of Army Special Operations History* 3, no. 4 (2007): 1-13.

Finlayson, Kenneth. "Operation BAAZ TSUKA: Task Force 31 Returns to the Panjwayi." *Veritas Journal of Army Special Operations History* 4, no. 1 (2008): 15-24.

Fitzsimmons, Dan. "Canada, the North Atlantic Treaty Organization (NATO) and the International Security Assistance Force (ISAF) in Afghanistan." *International Journal* 68, no. 2, (June 2013): 305-313.

Fortin, Major Dany, with Major H Skaarup and Captain M.C.M. Bouchard. "The Challenges of a Multinational Headquarters - Kabul Multinational Brigade. *The Bulletin* 11, no. 3 (April 2005): 10-16.

Gagnon, Captain P. "UAVs in the Theatre of Operations." *The Bulletin* 11, no. 3 (April 2005): 17.

G Coy Deploys on Op Athena." *Pro Patria 2005* 87 (April 2006):16.

Ges, Lieutenant-Colonel Bertrand A. "3-319 AFAR TF Gun Devils: Providing FA Fires for Afghanistan and Maneuvering on the Enemy." *Field Artillery* (September-October 2006): 20-26.

Godefroy, Major Andrew B. "Chasing the Silver Bullet: The Evolution of Capability

Development in the Canadian Army." *Canadian Military Journal* 8, no. 2 (Spring 2007): 52-66.

Granatstein, J.L. "Fighting the Bean Counters." *Legion Magazine* (November 1, 2002). Fighting The Bean Counters - Legion Magazine

Grebstad, Captain David W. "The Role of Artillery in Afghanistan." *Canadian Army Journal* 10, no. 3 (Fall 2007): 13-26.

Harvey, Lieutenant-Colonel André. "Directorate of the Army Training Update: The Brigade Training Event: Managed Versus Operational Readiness." *Canadian Army Journal* 7, no.1 (Spring 2004): 6-12.

Hennessy, Dr Michael A. "Operation 'Assurance': Planning a Multi-National Force for Rwanda/Zaire." *Canadian Military Journal* 2, no. 2 (Spring 2001): 11-20.

Hillier, Lieutenant-General Rick. "Army Transformation: Punching Above Our Weight." *The Army Doctrine and Training Bulletin* 6, no. 3 (Fall/Winter 2003): 3-4.

Hobson, Sharon, "Plain Talk - Who Decides?" *Canadian Naval Review* 2, no. 2 (Summer 2006): 36-37.

Hope, Lieutenant-Colonel Ian, "Misunderstanding Mars and Minerva: The Canadian Army's Failure to Define an Operational Doctrine," *The Army Doctrine and Training Bulletin* 4, no. 4 (Winter 2001-2002): 16-35.

Horn, Colonel Bernd. "Defence on Strong Point Centre - 14 October 2006." *Canadian Military Journal* 8, no. 2 (Spring 2007): 7-18.

Jeffery, Lieutenant-General Mike "Doctrine Development in Canada's Army in the 1990s." *The Canadian Army Journal* 17, no. 1 (2016): 13-27.

Jeffery, Lieutenant-General (ret'd) Michael K. "Inside Canadian Forces Transformation." *Canadian Military Journal* 10, no. 2 (Spring 2009): 9-18.

KMNB in action," *ISAF Mirror* 5 (April 2004): 7.

Kulberg, Anssi, "Warlords and Governors in Today's Afghanistan," The Eurasian Politician (November 2002). http://users.jyu.fi/~aphamala/pe/2002/afgawhoswho.htm

Lambert, David, "Adapting the Canadian Army Organisation: 'Transformation' and the Enduring Nature of Warfare." *Security Challenges* 6, no. 1, (Autumn 2010): 43 - 70.

Lévesque, Captain P. "Combat Service Support (CSS)." *The Bulletin* 11, no. 7 (November 2005): 3-4.

Lewis, Lieutenant R.G. "A Bty prepared for Task Force Orion." *The Quadrant* 21, no.3 (Winter 2006): 9.

Little, Captain R.N.W. "Target Acquisition Coordination Centre-Lessons Learned for Both TUAV and CBTA Radar Introduction on Operations." *Canadian Army Journal* 7, no. 3-4 (Fall/Winter 2004): 67-73.

Little, Major Richard. "A Short History of Target Acquisition Artillery." *Canadian Army Journal* 11, no. 3 (Fall 2008): 43-53.

Maloney, Sean, "Purple Haze: Joint Planning in the Canadian Forces from Mobile Command to J-Staff, 1975-1991", *The Army Doctrine and Training Bulletin* 5, no. 4 (Winter 2002-2003): 57-72.

Maples, MGen Michael D. "Relevant and Ready: The FA Now and in the Future." *Field Artillery* (November-December 2003): 1-5.

McElroy, Robert. "Afghanistan Fire Support for Operation Anaconda." *Field Artillery* (September-October 2002): 5-9.

McInnes, Captain Matthew. "First Principles and the Generation of Armoured Fighting Power," *Canadian Army Journal* 17, no. 3 (2017): 83-113

Mitchell, Captain Joshua. "A Case for Howitzers in Afghanistan." *Field Artillery* (November-December 2003): 6-9.

Moon, Captain RC. "Colonel Commandant Visits A Battery." *The Quadrant* 22, no. 2 (Fall 2006): 10.

Moore, Captain Rory. "Experiences of a Junior Officer." *The Quadrant* 23, no. 1 (Summer 2007): 5.

Munger, Captain C. "Combat Service Support - Centralized or Decentralized - As Seen In The Context Of Op Athena Roto 1." *The Bulletin* 11, no. 7 (November 2005): 5-6.

Murphy, Major M.F. "Airspace Coordination in Operations." *The Bulletin* 11, no. 3 (April 2005): 1- 9.

Notaro, Major M.F. "Airspace Coordination in Afghanistan." *The Bulletin* 10, no. 6 (November 2004):1-7.

Plummer, Captain I. "Lessons Learned by the Op Athena Roto 0 TUAV Troop-Units Undergoing Training With Civilian Companies." *The Bulletin* 11, no. 4 (June 2005): 7-14.

Prochniak, Warrant Officer One Scott E. and Major Dennis W. Yates. "Counterfire in Afghanistan." *Field Artillery* (September-October 2002): 15-18.

Rivard, Captain Martin. "ISTAR Sensor Integration: A Non-melting Pot Option." *The Army Doctrine and Training Bulletin* 3, no. 3, (Fall 2000): 16-19.

Roggio, Bill. "Taliban Commander Mullah Akhtar Usmani Killed in Airstrike." *Long War Journal* (December 23, 2006) https://www.longwarjournal.org/archives/2006/12/taliban_commander_mu.php.

Romano, Major P.A. "The Land Force Intelligence, Surveillance, Target Acquisition, and Reconnaissance Project: A Primer for Our Readers." *The Army Doctrine and Training Bulletin* 6. no. 1 (Spring 2003): 7-9.

Schaub Jr., Gary, and Kristian Kristensen. "But who's flying the plane? Integrating

UAVs into the Canadian and Danish armed forces." *International Journal* 70, no. 2 (June 2015): 250-267.

Scott, Captain John C. "Sequencing For Future Success - Observation of Task Force Kabul Mission Draw-Down." *The Bulletin* 12, no. 1 (March 2006): 6-9.

Senft, Major D.J. "The Medium Gun System is Coming! ....Now What?" *The Army Doctrine and Training Bulletin* 6, no. 3 (Fall/Winter 2003): 26-32.

Shrum, Captain L.A. "Lessons Not Yet Learned - Tactical Airspace Operations in Afghanistan." *The Bulletin* 11, no. 8 (December 2005): 2-7.

Shrum, Captain L.A. "Transformation and Airspace Operations in Afghanistan." *Canadian Military Journal* 7, no. 4 (Autumn 2006): 15-24.

St. Louis, Michel-Henri. "The Strategic Advisory Team-Afghanistan - Part of The Comprehensive Approach to Stability Operations." *Canadian Military Journal* 9, no. 3 (Summer 2008): 58-67.

Stogran, Lieutenant-Colonel P. "Fledgling Swans Take Flight: The Third Battalion, Princess Patricia's Canadian Light Infantry in Afghanistan." *Canadian Army Journal* 7, no. 3-4 (Fall/Winter 2004): 14-21.

Stone, Major J. Craig. "An Examination of the Armoured Personnel Carrier Replacement Project." *Canadian Military Journal* 2, no. 3 (Summer 2001): 59-66.

Sylvester, Bombardier N.B., "TF 3-06 PRT in Afghanistan," *The Quadrant* 23, no. 2 (Fall 2007): 14.

The Canadian Gunner 2002 38, (June 2004). to *The Canadian Gunner 2006* 41a (February 2007).

The Patrician 53 (2001). to *The Patrician* 58 (2006).

The Strathconian (2001). to *The Strathconian* (2006).

Voith, Mike, "Military Readiness," The Army *Training and Doctrine Bulletin 4.2 (2001): 41.*

Wells, Lieutenant-Colonel (Retired) Perry. "The Leopard Tank Replacement Project," *Canadian Army Journal* 19.2, (2021): 60-69.

Whittier, Major D.W. "The Weight Behind Our Punch - SAS and the Cost of A Knowledge-Based Army." *The Bulletin* 12, no. 1 (March 2006): 2-5.

Williams, Lieutenant-Colonel P.J. "Effects Based Operations In Afghanistan." *The Quadrant* 22, No. 3 (Winter 2006): 10.

Williams, Peter J. "Being Effective in Snake Fighting - Lessons For The Canadian Forces in the Effects-Based Operations Era." *Canadian Military Journal* 10, no. 4 (Autumn 2009): 19-25.

NEWSPAPERS AND MEDIA

Associated Press. "Canada to nearly double troops in Afghanistan." *AP CTV*

News 14 February 2005. Accessed 10 June 2021. https://web.archive.org/web/20061004011130/http://www.ctv.ca/servlet/ArticleNews/story/CTVNews/1108317447589_3/?hub=Canada.

Baker, Darren. "M113A1 with AN/MPQ-501 Radar" *Armorama*. 8 January 2012. https://armorama.kitmaker.

Bronskill, Jim. "Canadian intelligence assessment of Saddam's Iraq got it right, new paper says," The Canadian Press, CBC. 23 August 2020. Canadian intelligence assessments of Saddam's Iraq got it right, new paper says | CBC News.

"Canada sending more troops to Afghanistan" CBC News, 17 May 2005. Accessed 21 February 2022. https://www.cbc.ca/news/canada/canada-sending-more-troops-to-afghanistan-1.559176.

Carlson, Lieutenant-General Bruce. "U.S. Air Force Verdict: Text of Decision, Approved Punishment—Schmidt Art 15." CBC News Online. 6 July 2004. Accessed December 7, 2022. https://web.archive.org/web/20040804021748/http://www.cbc.ca/news/background/friendlyfire/verdict.html.

Fiorino, Joseph. "Why Canada Really Didn't Go Into Iraq in 2003." NATO Association of Canada. 7 June 2015. accessed 7 February 2021.Why Canada Really Didn't Go To Iraq In 2003 – NAOC (natoassociation.ca)

Hawthorn, Tom. "Myles Mansell, stand easy." Globe and Mail. May 4, 2006, accessed 22 January 2023. https://www.theglobeandmail.com/news/national/myles-mansell-stand-easy/article708273/.

Khan, Adnan. "The View From Ambush Alley," MacLeans.ca. September 11, 2006, accessed 20 May 2021. https://archive.macleans.ca/article/2006/9/11/the-view-from-ambush-alley.

Pugliese, David. "The Myth Surrounding Canadian Leopard Tanks in Afghanistan," Ottawa Citizen. 27 May 2018.

Shiller, Bill. "The Road to Kandahar: How Did We Get There?" Toronto Star. 9 September 2006.

Smith, Michael. "Taliban leader 'killed' after RAF tracks phone.' TimesOnline. 24 December 2006.

Wastnage, Justin. "Denmark sells unwanted second-hand Sagem Sperwer Unmanned Aerial Vehicles to Canada at 10% of price." FlightGlobal. 1 September 2006.

APPENDIX A - IN MEMORIAM

A solemn promise from all the gunner's past, present, and future:
WE WILL REMEMBER THEM!
UBIQUE

Bombardier Myles Stanley John Mansell
Age 25
Victoria, British Columbia
August 5, 1980 to April 22, 2006
5th (British Columbia) Field Artillery Regiment, RCA, Victoria, British Columbia
Task Force AEGIS—Regional Command (South)

Lieutenant William Montague Turner
Age 45
Toronto, Ontario
April 13, 1961 to April 22, 2006
20th Field Artillery Regiment, RCA, Edmonton Alberta
Task Force ORION—Regional Command (South)

Captain Nichola Kathleen Sarah Goddard
Age 26
Maddang—Papua New Guinea
May 2, 1980 to May 17, 2006
1st Regiment, Royal Canadian Horse Artillery, Shilo, Manitoba
Task Force ORION—Regional Command (South)

Captain Jefferson Clifford Francis
Age 36
Oromocto, New Brunswick
November 11, 1970 to July 4, 2007
1ˢᵗ Regiment, Royal Canadian Horse Artillery, Shilo, Manitoba
Task Force 1-07—Regional Command (South)

Gunner Jonathan J.J. Dion
Age 27
Val d'Or, Quebec
January 10, 1980 to December 30, 2007
5ᵉ Regiment d'Artillerie légére du Canada, Valcartier, Quebec
Task Force 3-07—Regional Command (South)

Bombardier Jeremie Ouellet
Age 22
Matane, Quebec
March 25, 1985 to March 11, 2008
1ˢᵗ Regiment, Royal Canadian Horse Artillery, Shilo, Manitoba
Task Force 1-08—Regional Command (South)

Sergeant Kirk Garret Taylor
Age 28
Yarmouth, Nova Scotia
April 10, 1981 to December 30, 2009
84ᵗʰ Independent Field Battery, RCA, Yarmouth, Nova Scotia
Kandahar Provincial Reconstruction Team, Regional Command (South)

Bombardier Karl Manning
Age 31
Chicoutimi, Quebec
February 3, 1980 to May 27, 2011
5ᵉ Regiment d'Artillerie légére du Canada, Valcartier, Quebec
Task Force 3-10, Regional Command (South)

Appendix B - List of Donors

This book would not be possible without the kind and generous donations of the following people.

Veteran Level (Over $10,000)
HCol John Irving
HCol A. Britton Smith
Artillery Support Group Guelph

Fire Planning Level ($1,000 - $5,000)
BGen (Retd) Claude Archambault
LGen (Retd) Stuart Beare
BGen (Retd) Ernest Beno
Bruce Buchanan
Clearihue Family Foundation - HCol Mark Clearihue
HCol Stephen Gregory
Col (Retd) Robert Gunn
MGen (Retd) John A MacInnis
Maj (Retd) Robert Sears
Col (Retd) Charles Simonds
HCol Sir Cyril Woods
5th (British Columbia) Field Artillery Regiment
Fifth BC Artillery RCA Foundation
In memorium of Bdr. Myles Mansell

Fire For Effect Level ($500 - $1,000)
LCol (Retd) Murray Beare
HCol Barry Downs
HLCol Donald Foster
Darrin Langen

HLCol Brian Midwinter
Col (Retd) Conrad A Namiesniowski
BGen (Retd) David Patterson
LCol (Retd) Mike Walker
Col (Retd) Douglas Walton

ADJUSTING FIRE LEVEL (OTHER DONATIONS)

Jeff Austin
CWO (Retd) Jean Boivin
Col (Retd) JD Briscoe
Col (Retd) Michael Capstick
Maj (Retd) David Chaplin
Ronald Chassie
HLCol Jeannette Chau
Capt Maurice Rene de Cotret
LCol (Retd) Alain Boisvert
Linda Bossi
CWO (Retd) David Ferretti
CWO (Retd) John Flanagan
Greg Frank
Maj Brian Gendron-Houle
Sgt (Retd) Tippy Graham
Maj (Retd) Richard Gratton
Patrick Grundle
BGen (Retd) K. Hague
BGen (Retd) David Henley
George Hope
LCol (Retd) Neil Johnstone
Ozair Haq Kazi
Maj (Retd) Douglas Knight
LCol (Retd) Robert W Lockhart

Peter MacLean
CWO (Retd) William MacLean
Brent MacIntyre
Maj (Retd) Alan Mcintosh
Capt (Retd) Al Mills
Capt (Retd) Keith Orton
Lt Col (UK Retd) William Pender
LCol (Retd) Wayne Petersen
Scott Puillandre
John Redmond
Steven Reynolds
Maj (Retd) Ray Schell
Maj (Retd) Pascal Sevigny
LCol (Retd) Victor Skaarup
CWO (Retd) Lawrence Skinner
Col (Retd) Tim Sparling
Maj (Retd) Dr. Craig Stone
Bdr (Retd) David Targett
Capt (Retd) Garth Wigle
Col (Retd) PJ Williams
LCol (Retd) Scott Wisdahl
LCol (Retd) Frederick Wolanski
Kody Young

Appendix C - List of Interviews and Select Emails for Volume 1

Interviews

Adkins, Captain Mark, interview by Wolf Riedel, March 21, 2023.

Anderson, Brigadier-General (Retd) Dave interview by Wolf Riedel, January 30, 2023.

Bailey, Warrant Officer Doug, interview #1 by Kevin Smith, May 25 and 30, 2022.

Bartlett, Chief Warrant Officer (Retd) Rob, interview by Wolf Riedel February 28, 2021.

Bishop, Sergeant (Retd) Donnie, Lieutenant-Colonel Tyler Kennedy and Master Warrant Officer (Retd) Donnie Simpson, interview by Brian Reid and Kevin Smith, January 17, 2021.

Bishop, Colonel (Retd) Tim interview by Wolf Riedel, Brian Reid and Kevin Smith, July 26 and August 2, 2021.

Bolduc, Lieutenant-Colonel Donald interview by Dr Kenneth Finlayson, January 31, 2008.

Bounyarattanaphon, Sergeant Makthepharak, interview by Wolf Riedel and Kevin Smith, February 16, 2022.

Bradley, Lieutenant-Colonel Tom and Major-General (Retd) Tim Grant, interview by Wolf Riedel and Kevin Smith, June 27, 2023.

Brunelle, Major (Retd) Justin interview by Wolf Riedel and Kevin Smith, June 20, 2021.

Button, Sergeant Mark, interview by Wolf Riedel, May 13, 2023.

Cameron, Warrant Officer (Retd) Rick, interview by Brian Reid and Kevin Smith, April 14, 2022.

Capstick, Colonel (Retd) Mike, telephone interview by Wolf Riedel, November 17, 2021.

Causey, Lieutenant-Colonel Jennifer, interview by Wolf Riedel and Kevin Smith, March 8, 2021.

Causey, Lieutenant-Colonel Jennifer and Lieutenant-Colonel Patrick Pitt interview by Wolf Riedel and Kevin Smith, November 30, 2022.

Clark, Lieutenant-Colonel Iain, interview by Wolf Riedel and Kevin Smith, March 16, 2021.

Clarke, Warrant Officer Justin, interview by Wolf Riedel, May 15, 2023.

Claveau, Lieutenant-Colonel Jean-François, interview by Wolf Riedel and Kevin Smith, March 18, 2022.

Cunningham, Warrant Officer (Retd) Lucas, interview by Wolf Riedel, April 1, 2021.

Cyr, Captain (Retd) Darcy interview by Wolf Riedel, Brian Reid and Kevin Smith, August 9, 2021.

Doucet, Captain (Retd) Lorne and Captain (Master Gunner) (Retd) Kevin Smith, interview by Wolf Riedel, May 25, 2023.

Dupuis, Major (Retd) Ray, interview by Wolf Riedel and Kevin Smith, April 15, 2021.

Durant, Major Cory, interview by Mark Zuhlke, Wolf Riedel and Kevin Smith, December 15, 2022.

Fekete, Warrant Officer Robert, interview by Wolf Riedel and Kevin Smith, November 23, 2022.

Fillier, Captain (Retd) Ron, interview by Wolf Riedel and Kevin Smith, March 12, 2021.

Fortin, Major-General Danny, interview by Wolf Riedel and Kevin Smith, February 18, 2022.

Franken, Chief Warrant Officer (Retd) Dennis, interview by Wolf Riedel and Kevin Smith, March 21, 2021.

Fraser, Major-General (Retd) David, interview by Wolf Riedel, March 16, 2023.

French, Bombardier (Retd) Scott, interview by Wolf Riedel and Kevin Smith, February 17, 2021.

Gagne, Colonel Sylvaine interview by Wolf Riedel, Brian Reid, Mark Zuehlke and Kevin Smith, December 9 and 13, 2021

Gallagher, Debbie, interview by Wolf Riedel, Brian Reid and Kevin Smith, May 19, 2021.

Gallagher, Lieutenant-Colonel Steve, interview by Brian Reid, Wolf Riedel and Kevin Smith, May 17 and 18, 2021

Gallagher, Lieutenant-Colonel Steve and Master Warrant Officer (Retd) Paul Parsons, interview by Kevin Smith, May 25 and June 1, 2021.

Gallagher, Lieutenant-Colonel Steve interview by Wolf Riedel, February 10, 2023

Gallant, Chief Warrant Officer Rodney, interview by Wolf Riedel, March 20, 22 and 29, 2023.

Gauvin, Lieutenant-Colonel (Retd) Bart, interview by Wolf Riedel and Kevin Smith, February 4, 2021.

Gero, Master Warrant Officer (Retd) John, interview by Wolf Riedel, February 22, 2023.

Goodland, Master Warrant Officer (Retd) Dennis, interview by Brian Reid and Kevin Smith, March 13, 2021.

Grant, Major-General (Retd) Tim and Lieutenant-Colonel Tom Bradley, interview by Wolf Riedel and Kevin Smith, June 27, 2023.

Grebstad, Lieutenant-Colonel David, interview by Kevin Smith, January 31, 2021.

Gunn, Colonel (Retd) Bob, interview by Wolf Riedel and Kevin Smith, March 31, 2022.

Haire, Lieutenant-Colonel Kathy and Lieutenant-Colonel Sarah Heer, interview by Wolf Riedel, Kevin Smith, and Brian Reid, June 15, 2021.

Hammond, Colonel (Retd) Lee, interview by Wolf Riedel and Kevin Smith, February 25, 2022.

Harvey, Colonel Marie-Christine, written responses to questionnaire, January 5, 2022.

Heer, Lieutenant-Colonel Sarah and Lieutenant-Colonel Kathy Haire, interview by Wolf Riedel, Kevin Smith, and Brian Reid, June 15, 2021.

Herbert, Warrant Officer Ryan and Major Wayne Lundrigan, interview by Brian Reid and Kevin Smith, 24 January, 2021

Hope, Colonel (retd) Ian, interview by Brian Reid, Wolf Riedel and Kevin Smith, May 28, and June 10, 2021.

Hunter, Brigadier-General Steve, interviewed by Mark Zuehlke, Wolf Riedel and Kevin Smith, September 12, 2023.

Ivey, Major Greg, interview by Brian Reid, August 7, 2008.

Ivey, Colonel (Retd) Greg, Chief Warrant Officer (Retd) Bob Montague and Lieutenant-Colonel Ian Plummer interview by Brian Reid, Wolf Riedel and Kevin Smith, September 21, 2021.

Ivey, Colonel (Retd) Greg and Chief Warrant Officer (Retd) Bob Montague, interview by Wolf Riedel and Kevin Smith, September 27, 2021

Jeffery, Lieutenant-General (Retd) Mike interview by Wolf Riedel, November 8 and 16, 2022, and January 4 and 27, 2023.

Johnson, Captain Kevin, interview by Brian Reid and Kevin Smith, March 14, 2021.

Kennedy, Lieutenant-Colonel Tyler, Master Warrant Officer (Retd) Donnie Simpson and Sergeant (Retd) Donnie Bishop, interview by Brian Reid and Kevin Smith, January 17, 2021.

Lacroix, Colonel (Retd) Roch, interview by Wolf Riedel and Kevin Smith, September 6, 2022.

LaFortune, Colonel Marc, interview by Wolf Riedel and Kevin Smith, April 8 and 9, 2021.

Lanningan, Master Warrant Officer (Retd) John, interview by Mark Zuehlke and Kevin Smith, December 20, 2022.

Lavoie, Lieutenant-General (Retd) Omer interview by Wolf Riedel, May 16, 2023.

Leslie, Lieutenant-General (Retd) Andrew interview by Wolf Riedel and Kevin Smith, January 26, 2021.

Leslie, Lieutenant-General (Retd) Andrew, interview by Wolf Riedel, Brian Reid and Kevin Smith, May 6, 7 and 11, 2021.

Leslie, Lieutenant-General (Retd) Andrew interview by Wolf Riedel, Mark Zuehlke and Kevin Smith, June 9, 2023.

Little, Major Richard, interview by Wolf Riedel and Kevin Smith, February 6 and 9, and October 26, 2021.

Lundrigan, Major Wayne and Warrant Officer Ryan Herbert, interview by Brian Reid and Kevin Smith, 24 January, 2021.

MacInnis, Major-General (Retd) John Arch, interview by Wolf Riedel, Brian Reid and Kevin Smith, February 10, 2022.

MacLean, Warrant Officer Wayne, interview by Wolf Riedel and Kevin Smith, March 11, 2021.

Marvin, Lieutenant-Colonel Chris, interview by Wolf Riedel and Kevin Smith, April 16, 2021.

Matheson, Lieutenant-Colonel Dan, interview by Wolf Riedel and Kevin Smith, March 4, 2021.

Montague, Master Warrant Officer Bob, interview by Brian Reid, July 23, 2008.

Merson, Warrant Officer Steve, interview by Mark Zuehlke and Kevin Smith, April 25, 2023.

Montague, Chief Warrant Officer (Retd) Bob, Colonel (Retd) Greg Ivey and Lieutenant-Colonel Ian Plummer, interview by Brian Reid, Wolf Riedel and Kevin Smith, September 21, 2021.

Nelson, Lieutenant-Colonel Howie, interview by Wolf Riedel, Brian Reid and Kevin Smith, January 21 and 28, 2022.

Ng, Captain (Retd) Nat interview by Wolf Riedel and Kevin Smith, February 10, 2021.

Nicholson, Lieutenant-Colonel Andrew, interview by Kevin Smith, May 3, 2022.

Parsons, Master Warrant Officer (Retd) Paul and Lieutenant-Colonel Steve Gallagher interview by Kevin Smith, May 25 and June 1, 2021.

Patterson, Brigadier-General David interview by Mark Zuehlke, Wolf Riedel and Kevin Smith, November 20, 2022.

Pinard, Warrant Officer (Retd) G."Gabby", interview by Wolf Riedel and Kevin Smith, April 18, 2021.

Pitt, Lieutenant-Colonel Patrick and Lieutenant-Colonel Jennifer Causey, interview by Wolf Riedel and Kevin Smith, November 30, 2022

Plummer, Captain Ian, interview by Paul Culliton, February 2018.

Plummer, Lieutenant-Colonel Ian, Colonel (Retd) Greg Ivey and Chief Warrant Officer (Retd) Bob Montague, interview by Brian Reid, Wolf Riedel and Kevin Smith, September 21, 2021.

Plummer, Lieutenant-Colonel Ian, interview by Wolf Riedel, April 13 and 19, 2023.

Podolas, Major (Retd) Michael interview by Wolf Riedel, March 8, 2023.

Poss, Captain David and Master Warrant Officer (Retd) Donnie Simpson, interview by Brian Reid and Kevin Smith, December 30, 2020.

Purdy, Captain Chris, interview by Bernd Horn, October 17, 2006.

Rein, Sergeant Cory, interview by Wolf Riedel, February 16, 2023.

Rooney, Major (Retd) Rob interview by Wolf Riedel, Brian Reid and Kevin Smith, May 31 and June 4, 2021.

Ross, Brigadier-General (Retd) and Assistant Deputy Minister (Material) (Retd) Dan, interview by Wolf Riedel, Brian Reid and Kevin Smith May 5, 2021.

Rouleau, Lieutenant-General (Retd) Mike interview by Wolf Riedel, Mark Zuehlke, and Kevin Smith, April 25, 2023.

Simpson, Master Warrant Officer (Retd) Donnie and Captain Dave Poss, interview by Brian Reid and Kevin Smith, December 30, 2020.

Simpson, Master Warrant Officer (Retd) Donnie, Lieutenant-Colonel Tyler Kennedy and Sergeant (Retd) Donnie Bishop, interview by Brian Reid and Kevin Smith, January 17, 2021.

Skinner, Master Warrant Officer (retd) Andy, interview by Wolf Riedel and Kevin Smith, February 2, 2021.

Smith, Captain (Retd) (Master Gunner) Kevin and Captain (Retd) Lorne Doucet, interview by Wolf Riedel, May 25, 2023.

Snodgrass, Master Warrant Officer (Retd) Art, interview by Wolf Riedel and Kevin Smith, February 24, 2021.

Spears, Lieutenant-Colonel Tim, interview by Brian Reid, Wolf Riedel and Kevin Smith, March 9, 11, 23 and 25, 2022.

Stewart, Major (Retd) John, interview by Wolf Riedel, September 5 and 6, 2023.

Stogran, Colonel Patrick, interview by Angus Brown, August 1, 2006.

Sullivan, Colonel Mike, interview by Wolf Riedel and Kevin Smith, September 22, 2021.

Tremblay, Major-General (Retd) Eric, interview by Wolf Riedel, Mark Zuehlke, and Kevin Smith, December 2022, interview by Wolf Riedel September 15, 2023.

Tullet, Master Warrant Officer (Master Gunner) Tony, interview by Wolf Riedel and Kevin Smith, October 20, 2021.

Walker, Lieutenant-Colonel (Retd) Caleb, interview by Wolf Riedel, Mark Zuehlke and Kevin Smith, September 6, 2023.

Whitnall, Captain (Retd) Ken, interview by Wolf Riedel, Brian Reid and Kevin Smith, September 23 and 27, 2021.

Willcox, Warrant Officer (retd) Kerry, interview by Wolf Riedel and Kevin Smith, February 19, 2021.

Williams, Colonel (Retd) Peter interview by Wolf Riedel and Kevin Smith, January 19 and 29, 2021; by Wolf Riedel, Brian Reid and Kevin Smith, June 16, and December 17, 2021; by Wolf Riedel, March 4, 2023.

Wolanski, Lieutenant-Colonel Fred, interview by Brian Reid and Kevin Smith, December 29, 2020.

Young, Colonel (Retd) Tim, interview by Wolf Riedel and Kevin Smith, August 4, 2023.

EMAILS AND MESSAGES

Beare, Lieutenant-General (Retd) Stuart, email to Brigadier-General (Retd) Ernie Beno and Wolf Riedel, September 4, 2013.

Cunningham, Master Bombardier Lucas, email to Brigadier-General (Retd) Ernest Beno, September 27, 2010.

Duval, Colonel (Retd) Jean-François, email to Wolf Riedel, 20 September 2023.

Franken, Chief Warrant Officer (Retd) Dennis, email to Wolf Riedel, September 24, 2021.

Fraser, Major-General (Retd) David, message to Wolf Riedel, October 6, 2023.

Gallagher, Major Steve, email to Kevin Smith, May 17, 2007 and to Brian Reid, August 7, 2009.

Gallagher, Lieutenant-Colonel Steve, email to Brian Reid, January 13, 2021 and to Wolf Riedel, May 18, 2023.

Gobin, Major Jacques, email to Major Steve Gallagher, August, 5 2005.

Gunn, Colonel (Retd) Bob, emails to Wolf Riedel, April 4 and 12, 2022.

Hetherington, Major-General (Retd) Simon, email to Wolf Riedel, June 30, 2023.

Ivey, Major Greg, email to Lieutenant-Colonel Scott Johnson, September 20, 2006.

Ivey, Major Greg, email to Brian Reid, October 7, 2010 and November 10, 2010.

Ivey, Colonel (Retd) Greg, email to Brian Reid, February 8, 12 and 13, 2022.

Jeffery, Lieutenant-General (Retd) Mike, Email to Wolf Riedel, December 2, 2022 and January 4, 2023.

Johnson, Captain Kevin, email to Wolf Riedel December 14, 2022.

Kennedy, Major Tyler, email to Warrant Darcy Cyr "TF ORION FIRES" 1034 hours local, August 3, 2006.

Little, Major Richard, email to Wolf Riedel, December 14, 2021.

McDonald, Chief Warrant Officer and Master Gunner (Retd) Mike, email to Wolf Riedel, September 8, 2023.

Montague, Master Warrant Officer Bob, email to Brian Reid, July 31, 2008.

Montague, Chief Warrant Officer (Retd) Bob, email to Wolf Riedel, June 30, 2023.

Normand, Chief Warrant Officer Éric, email to Wolf Riedel January 17, 2022.

Notaro, Lieutenant-Colonel Mike, email to Wolf Riedel, May 31, 2021.

O'Donnell, Captain Robert, email to Brain Reid October 29, 2010 and February 11, 2011.

Pappin, Captain Piers email to Brian Reid, June 20 and 26, 2013.

Pierce, Captain Roger, email to Brian Reid, undated.

Pinard, Warrant Officer (Retd) G."Gabby", emessage to Kevin Smith, September 16, 2023.

Podolas, Major (Retd) Michael, message to Wolf Riedel, March 9, 2023.

Plummer, Captain Ian, email to Brian Reid December 29, 2006.

Plummer, Major Ian, emails to Brian Reid, June 19 and 20, 2013.

Plummer, Lieutenant-Colonel Ian, email to Wolf Riedel, June 30, 2023.

Scharlach, Lieutenant-Colonel (Retd) Todd, email to Kevin Smith, May 31, 2021.

Sheppard, Sergeant Byron, email to Brian Reid, June 20, 2013.

Smith, Captain (Retd) (Master Gunner) Kevin, emails to Brian Reid, August 9, 2018 and December 20, 2020.

Smith, Captain (Retd) (Master Gunner) Kevin, emails to Wolf Riedel, April 19, December 26, 2022, April 5, April 29, April 30, May 11, May 23 and June 22, 2023.

Spears, Lieutenant-Colonel Tim, Emails to Wolf Riedel, June 12 and 24, 2023.

Stimpson, Lieutenant-Colonel Ryan, email to Wolf Riedel, June 27, 2023.

Whitnall, Captain (Retd) Ken, email to Wolf Riedel, March 9 and 10, 2022.

Whitnall, Captain (Retd) Ken, email to Wolf Riedel, April 2, 2022.

Williams, Lieutenant-Colonel Peter, email to Major LP McGarry et al cc Major-General Andrew Leslie et al, February 20, 2006.

Williams, Colonel Peter, email to Brian Reid, January 20, 2011.

Williams, Colonel Peter, email to Brian Reid, September 3, 2021.

Williams, Colonel (Retd) Peter, messages to Wolf Riedel, June 11 and 12, 2023.

Willis, Lieutenant-Colonel Jim, email to Colonel Bob Gunn, September 1, 2005.

Willis, Lieutenant-Colonel Jim, email to Major Bruno Di Ilio, October 17, 2005.

Wolanski, Lieutenant-Colonel Fred, email to Wolf Riedel, December 12, 2022.

Young, Colonel (Retd) Tim, email to Wolf Riedel, March 1, 2022.

Young, Colonel (Retd) Tim, message to Wolf Riedel, March 16, 2023.

ACKNOWLEDGMENTS

With a Few Guns has its genesis in a meeting at the Brigadoon Inn in Oxford Mills in 2006, shortly before Brigadier-General (Retd) Ernie Beno became Colonel Commandant of the Royal Regiment of Canadian Artillery. He and the then president of the Royal Canadian Artillery Association, Lieutenant-Colonel (Retd) Jim Bryce, were there with Lieutenant-Colonel (Retd) Brian Reid. Their purpose was to explore the production of something in the nature of a memorial or souvenir book for those who had served and were currently serving in Afghanistan and to preserve a record of what happened for future historians. All three, being instructors in gunnery, immediately saw the need to document what the gunners were achieving with just a few guns at the time. They also wanted to tell the human side of this then unfolding story—the bravery, sacrifice, innovation, determination and professionalism of Canadian gunners.

These early discussions led to a formal proposal in 2007 for a book of roughly 70,000 words which received the cooperation and moral support of the then Director of Artillery, Colonel Rocky Lacroix, and the Royal Canadian Artillery Heritage Council. With a generous donation from the Artillery Support Group in Guelph, Brian Reid started to toil away gathering interviews and research on the ongoing mission. The intent was that the book would be published within a few years of the end of the mission. At the time no one expected that this would become Canada's longest war. As the war continued and turned into a training mission, Brian had taken on several other projects and, consequently, the book progressed only slowly...until 2020.

In the fall of 2020, General Ernie—as he's known throughout the Royal Regiment—revived the project and assembled a team. An advisory/steering committee—made up of Lieutenant-Generals (Retd) Andrew Leslie and Stu Beare, Major-General (Retd) Eric Tremblay, Brigadier-General (Retd) Dave Patterson, Lieutenant-Colonel Jen Causey, Chief Warrant Officer (Retd) and Master Gunner Mike McDonald, and Chief Warrant Officers (Retd) Dan Moyer and Jean

Boivin—agreed to help General Ernie in giving the project direction and focus. Lieutenant-Colonel (Retd) Bart Gauvin was brought on as the project manager and Colonel (Retd) Dave Marshall agreed to head up an editing team which eventually consisted of Colonels (Retd) Peter Williams and Tim Young and Major (Retd) Mike McNorgan. They not only pointed out the glaring spelling and grammar issues but also brought to bear their decades of experience in the regiment to point out issues that needed clarification, context or correction.

With the team in place, the Regimental Senate of the RCA was approached to "bless," endorse and support the writing of "With a Few Guns," with the eventual ownership to go to the Royal Canadian Artillery Association. The project was enthusiastically supported and many gunners came forward to share their stories.

That brings us to Captain (Retd) and Master Gunner Kevin Smith. There are two people in the artillery who seem to know everyone. General Ernie is one and Kevin is clearly the other. Kevin initially came on board to help out with research. This he did and he did it in spades. More importantly though, Kevin is the hub around which the project's interviews and writing spins. His extensive list of contacts proved to be the project's Rolodex. His tireless efforts in tracking people down and persuading them to agree to interviews is what kept the entire project humming. Moreover he participated in the majority of the interviews bringing with him the technical expertise that only a Master Gunner can have. The team's—and the Regiment's—debt to him for his work on this project is enormous.

Unfortunately, with time, one of our Cold Warriors, Brian Reid had to cut back his role due to failing health. Two authors were brought on to help Brian. My background as a gunner was from 1965 to 1981 when I left the regular force to pursue a career in law and became a reserve force legal officer. My years of legal research and writing factums and my post-retirement activities as an author of military-based mystery novels seemed to be enough to get me in the door and, coincidentally, help me to reconnect with the regimental family of gunners.

When I joined the team in the winter of 2020/21 it quickly became apparent that the original target of 70,000 words was quite inadequate to cover the rich topic. It became obvious that the book would need to be published in two volumes. Fortunately Mark Zuehlke, an award winning author and Canada's foremost popular military historian agreed to join the team in 2022. He brought with him not only his expertise but also a cheerful approach to the project that made him a pleasure to work with. Mark Zuehlke and I are indebted to Brian for the pioneering steps he took on the project, not least of which is coming up with the title of the book which, like all good titles, resonates on several levels.

With the project now moving in high gear, General Ernie put his considerable skills to work at making things happen. He ran an extensive fund raising campaign which was generously responded to by numerous individuals and agencies who are too numerous to mention in this short paragraph and are therefore listed in an annex. Many serving and former gunners and others responded to Kevin and General Ernie's entreaties to be interviewed for the project. Again, they are too numerous to mention here so the ones interviewed for Volume 1 have been listed in an annex. It goes without saying that the contributions which came so generously in funds, time and, most of all, their stories and photos is what made these books possible.

As the material came together, Major (Retd) Dr J. Craig Stone volunteered to review the footnotes and bibliography and eventually turned the tangle of my legal citation system into the proper Chicago-style required for a publication such as this. Major (Retd) Richard Gratton took on responsibilities for photos and production and Lieutenant-Colonel (Retd) Rory Fowler, a former legal officer, agreed to be the project's legal advisor. C. Stuart Daniel, whose maps grace over a hundred publications, signed on to become our cartographer. Their expertise and contribution to the project is greatly appreciated.

Thanks as well to Dr. Steve Harris—Chief Historian at the Directorate of History and Heritage—and Captain Scott McDowell, Sergeant Matthew Prowse and Corporal Justin Morowitz for their time and assistance in making various war diaries from the units involved available to us. Thanks also go out to Master Corporal Michael MacIsaac and Mrs. Janet LaCroix at the National Defence Image Library for their assistance in searching their extensive collections for photos and providing some of the images that bring so much of our gunners' stories to life.

Our team would also like to thank the staff at Double Dagger Books. The publisher, Phil Halton and publicist, James Leslie, and their team provided assistance and patience throughout the final production of this book.

Finally, a huge thank you to my wife Kathy without whose support and companionship over the last three years my work on this project would never have gotten off the ground much less completed.

Wolf Riedel
Southwest Ontario, October, 2023

About the Authors

Lieutenant-Colonel (Retd) Brian A. Reid, CD

Reid "BA of the RCA" joined the Canadian Army in 1957 as a gunner and was commissioned as an officer in 1961. He served in regimental, staff and liaison appointments in Canada, Europe and the United States during his long career. His last appointment, before his retirement as a Lieutenant-Colonel in 1994, was in the Joint Plans and Operations Staff at National Defence Headquarters in Ottawa.

Reid has written a number of works on Canadian military history. His book "No Holding Back: Operation Totalize, Normandy, August 1944" has met with critical praise. John Marteinson, former editor of Canadian Military Journal and teacher at the Royal Military College of Canada wrote: "This book should be in the library of every student of Canadian military history."

Books by Brian Reid:

No Holding Back: Operation Totalize, Normandy, August 1944
Named by the Enemy: A History of The Royal Winnipeg Rifles
Our Little Army in the Field: The Canadians in South Africa
Fighting For Canada: Seven Battles, 1758-1945 (chapters)
More Fighting for Canada: Five Battles, 1760-1944 (chapters)
RCHA - Right of the Line (co-author)
Canada at War and Peace II: A Millennium of Military Heritage (contributor)
Green On! Go! Canada's Airborne Gunners (co-author)

Colonel (Retd) Wolf Riedel, OMM, CD, KC

Wolf was born in Berlin, Germany and grew up in Toronto, Ontario. In 1965, while in high school, he started what would eventually become a forty-four year career with the army in both the reserve force and the regular force by enrolling as a gunner with the 7th Toronto Regiment, Royal Canadian Artillery. In 1969 he transfered to the regular force serving tours with the 2nd and 3rd Regiments, Royal Canadian Horse Artillery and 26th Field Regiment, Royal Canadian Artillery.

In 1982 he started a second career as a civil litigation lawyer and returned to the reserve force first as an infantry company commander and subsequently with the Office of the Judge Advocate General where, as a Colonel, he was appointed Senior Reserve Force Legal Advisor for the Canadian Forces. He is a life bencher with the Law Society of Manitoba, was a hearing officer with the Manitoba Human Rights Commission and was appointed a Queen's Counsel.

Wolf is now retired and has become an author when not dabbling with his model railroad. He and his wife Kathy make their home in southwestern Ontario.

Books by Wolf Riedel:

Unsustainable at Any Price: The Canadian Armed Forces in Crisis

The "Allies" series	*The "Mark Winters, CID" series*
The Inquiry	*The Bay*
The Trial	*The Gulf*
The Rivers	*The Coast*
	The Marina
	The Beach

Mark Zuehlke

Mark Zuehlke is an award-winning author generally considered to be Canada's foremost popular military historian. His Canadian Battle Series is the most exhaustive recounting of the battles and campaigns fought by any nation during World War II to have been written by a single author. In recognition of his contribution to popularizing Canadian history, Mark was awarded the 2014 Governor General's History Award for Popular Media: The Pierre Berton Award. In 2007, his For Honour's Sake: The War of 1812 and the Brokering of an Uneasy Peace won the Canadian Author's Association Lela Common Award for Canadian History. The Canadian Battle Series Holding Juno captured the City of Victoria Butler Book Prize in 2006.

Mark is also an award winning mystery writer, whose popular Elias McCann series has garnered much critical praise in Canada and abroad. Hands Like Clouds, the debut in this series, won the Crime Writer's of Canada's Arthur Ellis Award for the 2000 Best First Novel and the third installment, Sweep Lotus, was nominated for the 2004 Arthur Ellis Best Novel.

A regular contributor to Legion Magazine, Mark also does regular duty as a tour historian with the Canadian Battlefield Tour company, Liberation Tours Canada.

When not writing, this Victoria, British Columbia resident can often be found tinkering around the Garry oak studded property he shares with partner and fellow writer Frances Backhouse. He enjoys hiking, cycling, kayaking, travelling, and cooking.

Books by Mark Zuehlke include:

The Gallant Cause
The Canadian Military Atlas
For Honour's Sake
Brave Battalion
Ortona
The Liri Valley
The Gothic Line
Juno Beach
Holding Juno
Terrible Victory
Operation Husky
The Juno Beach Trilogy
On to Victory
Ortona Street Fight

Breakout from Juno
Assault on Juno
Tragedy at Dieppe
Forgotten Victory
Through Blood and Sweat
The Cinderella Campaign
The River Battles
Hands Like Clouds
Carry Tiger to Mountain
Sweep Lotus
Magazine Writing from the Boonies
Scoundrels, Dreamers & Second Sons
The Loxleys and the War of 1812
The Loxleys and Confederation

Index

Formations and Units

Canadian

82nd Airborne Division/Combined Joint Task Force-82, 57, 354
    4th Brigade/Task Force Fury, 354
101st Airborne Division, 21, 35
3rd Brigade/Task Force RAKKASAN, 21, 28, 33-35, 48, 50, 377
173rd Airborne Brigade Combat Team/Task Force BAYONET, 157, 171, 271
Combined Joint Task Force-76, 125, 133, 152, 157, 180, 192, 197, 216, 236, 272, 330
Combined Joint Task Force PHOENIX, 58, 86, 133, 172
Task Force GRIZZLY, 279, 310, 312, 315, 316
Task Force K-Bar, 30

Other
I German-Netherlands Corps, 58
1st Light Reconnaissance Squadron (DK), 238
3rd Battalion, Parachute Regiment (UK), 157, 181, 205, 238
3rd (UK) Division, 58
7th Parachute Regiment, RHA (UK), 207
29 Commando Regiment (UK), 83
12 Infanteriebataljon (NL), 343
13 Infanteriebataljon (NL), 157
101 Remotely Piloted vehicle Battery (NL), 81
141 Infantry Battalion (RO), 157
201st Corps (AFGH), 132, 133, 295
205th Corps (AFGH), 172, 295
341st Infantry Battalion "Rechinii Albi"(RO), 192
Household Cavalry (UK), 238
Kabul Multinational Brigade, 58, 62, 68, 78, 79, 84, 88, 89, 100, 116, 118, 119, 122, 125, 126, 129, 135, 139
Regional Command (Capital), 216
Regional Command (East), 171, 180, 192, 198, 286, 330, 354
Regional Command (North), 131, 216
Regional Command (South), 149, 151, 152, 157, 169, 170, 175-177, 180, 192, 214, 216, 219, 247, 251, 170, 271, 273, 279, 297, 308, 338, 342-344
Regional Command (West), 131, 137, 216
Royal Irish Regiment (UK), 238
Task Force 42 (UK), 310
Telemark Task Force (NO), 110

Operations

TABAR POLAD, 199, 200
TABAR ROGH, 199
TORII, 48
VIGILANT, 28
WHITE FOX, 47
YADGAR, 197
ZAHAR, 203

PLACES

NAMES

ABOVE: Just prior to Christmas 2001, C Battery conducted a mortar conversion course at CFB Shilo. This would be one of the few times snowmobiles were used, and it was only for an ammunition drop. Otherwise, they would move entirely by foot. (Kevin Johnson)
BELOW: Mortar training at Tarnak Farm, in Kandahar just prior to Operation HARPOON. The command post is in the centre using "plotting boards". (Kevin Johnson)

ABOVE: At Bagram airbase for Operation HARPOON, chalks assemble for final rucksack checks before waddling to the Chinooks. (Kevin Johnson)

BELOW: During Operation HARPOON, some enemy caves were found near the mortar base plate position. These were cleared by C Battery with the assistance of combat engineers. This photo quite possibly was taken during the "go right!" incident. (Kevin Johnson)

ABOVE: In preparation for deployment as 3 PPCLI's sniper detachment commander, Sergeant Johnson, top of photo, zeroes a C3 sniper rifle while his spotter assists using Vector binoculars. (Kevin Johnson)

BELOW: Canadian soldiers dismount from an American Chinook onto Tora Bora Mountain during Operation TORRI. The ruggedness of the terrain, and the incredible skills of the aircrew are quite evident. (SSgt Jeremy Lock)

ABOVE: Operation TORRI resupply being brought in via American Chinook. Mortar ammunition is already stacked near the right front of the aircraft. Note the blackened stumps from trees being blown down by special operations forces using detonating cord.(Dave Poss)
BELOW: A donkey—not the IR donkey—passes by a C Battery mortar detachment during Operation TORRI. (Dave Poss)

ABOVE: The "Gargoyles" of G31 during a quiet moment during Operation TORRI. (Don Simpson)
BELOW: Sergeant Johnson's sniper detachment and recce platoon assembling for Operation CHEROKEE SKY.(Kevin Johnson)

ABOVE: Gun position of 155 mm self-propelled M109 howitzers from E Battery, 2 RCHA, during a live fire phase of Exercise RESOLUTE WARRIOR in Wainwright, Alberta in 2003. The M109s would all be withdrawn from service over the next two years.(DND/Cpl Ronald Duchesene)

BELOW: F Battery's initial gun position at Camp WAREHOUSE was "shoehorned" into a corner, which is quite evident in this photo of a check bearing of the guns orientation being conducted. The tent structure to the left is a "penthouse" attached to the troop's command post vehicle. (Kathy Haire)

ABOVE: G31's light armoured vehicle at Observation Post SUMMIT, just before Christmas 2003. From this location, just north of Kabul, they would support the radars in the event of incoming indirect fire to Kabul. The position was shared with two Afghan soldiers who shared some good tea in exchange for some Canadian rations. (Wayne Maclean)

BELOW: ISTAR was an evolving concept in 2003. The capabilities of the artillery played a critical role in this. Pictured is an ARTHUR radar behind the members of the brigade's target acquisition coordination centre. The TACC managed both the radars, Sperwer and German UAVs. (Art Snodgrass)

ABOVE: F Battery's troops moved primarily by ground in unarmoured vehicles, such as the gun tractor variant of the medium logistic vehicle wheeled. Here an airmobile exercise is being performed with a German CH-53 Sea Stallion. A few veterans from E Battery (Para) helped revive a skill rarely practiced in Canada at this time. (Kathy Haire)

BELOW: The gun platforms at Camp JULIEN were eventually dug into shallow gun pits with bunkers for both the detachment and ammunition. (Kathy Haire)

ABOVE: Warrant Officer Art Snodgrass in France attending training on the Sperwer tactical UAV in 2003. (Art Snodgrass)

BELOW: F Battery's Bombardier Kevin Goddin loads a round into a 105mm LG1 howitzer for firing on a range near Kabul.(DND/ MCpl. Brian Walsh)

ABOVE: F Battery fires a 105mm high explosive extended range (HEER) round from Camp Warehouse in Kabul on a training exercise.(DND/MCpl Brian Walsh)
BELOW: Lieutenants Kathy Haire and Sarah Heer, in the troop command post's "penthouse", do a gross error check using a check map to verify firing data computed using the Indirect Fire Control Computer Software (IFCCS).(Kathy Haire)

ABOVE: Sperwer tactical unmanned aerial vehicle 161001 launches on its maiden flight from Camp JULIEN in Kabul, Afghanistan on November 6, 2003. (DND/Cpl Doug Farmer)

BELOW: While F Battery rarely fired from the camps they did deploy to a range to the east of Kabul for training to maintain their skill level, and as a show of force. (Kathy Haire)

ABOVE: G32's Captain Jennifer Causey adjusts fire from her light armoured vehicle during a practice shoot on St Barbara's Day, 2003. (Jennifer Causey)
BELOW: 5 RALC's G34 making its way through narrow, winding roads outside Kabul. (Eric Normand)

ABOVE: Members of the 5 RALC firing on a range near Kabul, Afghanistan while conducting live fire training with their LG1 howitzers. (DND/Cpl John Bradley)

BELOW: 5 RALC's Batterie Athéna, fires one of their LG1 howitzer at a firing range near Kabul, Afghanistan. While the battery had been formed around Batterie R, the inclusion of so many personnel from the regiment's other batteries caused its battery commander to adopt the name Athéna for the composite battery. (DND/Cpl John Bradley)

ABOVE: A Sperwer tactical unmanned aerial vehicle and its ground control station, operated primarily by 5 RALC's Batterie X personnel, is pictured at Camp JULIEN. (DND/ Cpl Doug Farmer)

BELOW: A member of Batterie Athéna directs a German Army CH-53G Sea Stallion helicopter to hook onto a gun during an airmobile exercise. Working with the helicopter, the gunners are practising airlifting their LG-1 howitzer and its ammunition. (DND/MCpl Yves Proteau)

ABOVE: A CH-53G transport helicopter from the German Army, prepares to lift an LG1 105mm howitzer while training with members of 5 RALC. A pallet of ammunition rigged for a sling load sits off to the side. (DND/Cpl John Bradley)

BELOW: As the army divested itself of 155mm M109 howitzers, 26 of them, pictured here in 2005, were temporarily retained in long term preservation in Montreal for the possible return to service post Afghanistan. By 2008, however, the decision was made to turn the remainder of the fleet into memorials. (Kevin Smith)

ABOVE: Twin 35mm Oerlikon anti-aircraft guns in storage in Montreal in 2005. Although these guns were identified for disposal, ironically a few were brought back into service in 2006 to assist American Forces studying counter rocket, mortar and UAV capabilities. By 2011 Canada had divested all of its air defence shooting capabilities. At front right is an M578 light recovery vehicle. One M578 had supported each six-gun M109 battery. (Kevin Smith)

BELOW: A gun detachment from 1 RCHA, rides in the back of a medium logistics vehicle wheeled towing a 105mm C3 howitzer along Red Route in the Wainwright training area on Exercise PHOENIX RAM in 2005. (DND/MCpl John Bradley)

ABOVE: A detachment from each of B Battery, 1 RCHA and F Battery, 2 RCHA conduct training with the new 155mm M777 lightweight towed howitzer at Fort Sill Oklahoma The gun represented a major leap in technology and its first use in an area of conflict was with Canadian gun detachments. The joint Canadian-American New Equipment Training Team, established at Fort Sill, also attended at CFB Shilo for the arrival of the M777 and the training of A Battery for its use in Afghanistan. (DND/MCpl Dennis Power)

ABOVE: A Skylark miniature unmanned aerial vehicle is being prepared for launch. In the background is its ground control station through which the operator, using a laptop, controls the aircraft and gathers data from its sensor pod. (Art Snodgrass)

BELOW: A Battery, 1 RCHA in Shilo in December of 2005 on Exercise TITANIUM GUNNER A Battery had very little time to train on the M777 or its heavy logistics vehicle wheeled gun tractors in Canada. Fortunately, time would allow for additional training on arrival in Afghanistan. (Cory Rein)

ABOVE:Master Bombardier Steve Merson of the Strategic Advisory Team-Afghanistan with his rescued battle-buddy, Whooh-Tan in downtown Kabul in 2005. (Steve Mercer)

ABOVE: A Battery's newly arrived M777s in the gun park at Kandahar Airfield. (Stephen Gallagher)
BELOW: A Battery moves cross country north of Kandahar Airfield towards Khakrez province in an area close to the "Bellybutton". This was an exercise as part of the relief in place with Task Force GUN DEVILS' Battery B of the 3rd Battalion, 319th Airborne Field Artillery Regiment. (Andrew Nicholson)

ABOVE: At Tarnak Farms, near the Kandahar Airfield, the first round from an 81mm mortar sends dirt flying as call sign 15A fires. The first round, a "bedding" round, pushes the base plate for the mortar tube into the ground. (DND/MCpl Ken Fenner)

BELOW: The relief in place with Battery B involved a joint shoot. This photo of Canada's A Battery, 1 RCHA captures the firing of the first round by an M777 in an any operational theatre. (Terry Degerness)

ABOVE: The relief in place practice shoot involved a fair of amount of fire, in this case the battery is firing in sequence from the right. This volume of fire surprised an enemy force that had been hiding near the impact area, and would eventually lead to a troops-in-contact event at the GUMBAD platoon house later in the day. (Terry Degerness)

BELOW: A flight of CU-161 Sperwer, tactical unmanned aerial vehicles, began keeping watch over South Afghanistan. Canadian artillery fly the plane from a mobile ground control station and operate the Sperwer's high-tech camera, side-by-side with 408 Tactical Helicopter Squadron's pilots. (DND/Sgt Carole Morissette)

ABOVE: A gun troop halts temporarily in a narrow defile and forms a cordon. Each gun troop was very limited in self protection capabilities. The limitations of the pintle-mounted machine gun on the Bison alone are easily seen. (Stephen Gallagher)

BELOW: An A Battery M777 is lifted a few feet at Kandahar Airfield to test the sling rigging. (DND/MCpl Doug Desrochers)

ABOVE: Members of A Battery 1 RCHA hook an M777 onto an American Chinook helicopter to do a practice lift of the gun to test its rigging. (DND/MCpl Doug Desrochers)

ABOVE: An A Battery 155mm M777 in action in support of American and Afghan forces at FOB ROBINSON in Helmand province. (Stephen Gallagher)
BELOW: Bombardier Corey Rein's Bison armoured detachment vehicle after having struck a mine outside FOB ROBINSON in Helmand. (Corey Rein)

ABOVE: A troop of M777's parked inside the FOB ROBINSON compound conducting maintenance on their guns. A Mercedes G-Wagon is parked to the right rear. (DND/Cpl Robin Mugridge)

ABOVE: The heavy logistics vehicle wheeled was used as the gun tractor for the M777. The absence of an echelon required that these vehicles be heavily overloaded with everything from personal kit to a basic load of ammunition for both the gun and the mortar. In the extreme heat, dust and terrain of Afghanistan these vehicles frequently had mechanical breakdowns such as this one from overheating. (Corey Rein)

BELOW: The inside of 15D's Bison armoured detachment carrier on the road. (Andrew Nicholson)

ABOVE: Gun positions at PB WILSON were close quarters with those of neighbouring units. The battle group's widely dispersed operations, presented numerous technical challenges. Here, we can see each of the troop's guns pointed in a different centre of arc. The mortars (not visible in picture) would cover yet a third. (Stephen Gallagher)

BELOW: An MQ-1 Predator unmanned aerial vehicle, seen here at Kandahar Airfield mounting AGM-114 Hellfire missiles, became one of the favoured reconnaissance and strike vehicles for use by Canadian forward observers and air controllers. (John A. MacInnis)

ABOVE: Gun troops frequently traveled alone without escort or additional security. As a result the reconnaissance party and the guns would move as a single group for protection purposes. Here, the guns have stopped at a rendezvous just off the gun position with the dismounted detachments deployed into overwatch positions while the reconnaissance party prepares the gun position for occupation. (John A. MAcInnis)

BELOW: B Troop fires a "last round" in honour of Captain Nichola Goddard. (Andrew Nicholson)

ABOVE: Task Force ORION moves back into Helmand under the cover of a massive sand storm. This time the operation was to support the British army under Operation HEWAD. B Troop can be seen in the second row of the leaguer. (Stephen Gallagher)
BELOW: The gun position at FOB MARTELLO in its early days. (Andrew Nicholson)

ABOVE: E Battery's G29 on the summit of the razor backed ridge of Ma'Sum Ghar where on August 19, 2006, G21, A Company of 1 RCR and Afghan police fought off a major assault by hundreds of Taliban. (Greg Ivey)

BELOW: The guns of E Battery had already been involved in weeks of shaping operations when they moved to an austere gun position for Operation MEDUSA. (Bob Montague)

ABOVE: The ammunition compound at Kandahar Airfield. At the time of this photo, Warrant Officer Rick Cameron and his tiny BQMS staff had already, by themselves, received, unpacked and prepared for transport by truck and air some 2,500 rounds to the battery. (Rick Cameron)

BELOW: At KAF, the BQMS staff would break down pallets of projectiles and propellant, build kicker pallets like these for Chinooks, repack them with a mix of projectiles, propellants and fuzes and load them on the helicopters. These pallets would be "kicked" out of the back of the Chinook near the gun position where they were unpacked and loaded onto a Bison for transport to the gun platforms. (Bob Montague)

ABOVE: New American M825A1 White Phosphorous projectiles on the gun platform. These proved superior to the type Canada had used previously and the Hexachlorethane type Canada was using at the time. (Greg Ivey)
BELOW: A field expedient shower set up next to a Bison during Operation MEDUSA about to be enjoyed by Warrant Officer Rod Gallant. (Bob Montague)

ABOVE: Dawn after a night of firing during Operation MEDUSA. Detachments are busy cleaning up their gun platforms from the night's activities and preparing for the next day while new ammunition is being dropped. (Bob Montague)

BELOW: Dutch 155mm self-propelled Panzerhaubitze 2000 from the 14e Afelding Veldartillerie deploy on E Battery's left flank on Operation MEDUSA. (Bob Montague)

ABOVE: Two American Black Hawk helicopters supported by an Apache overfly the gun position. (DND/Sgt Lou Penney)
BELOW: A detachment ramming a 155mm projectile into an M777. (Greg Ivey)

ABOVE: G21 taking a break after successfully clearing one of A company's objectives. (Greg Ivey)

BELOW: G23 setting up hasty observation post during the advance in the final days of Operation MEDUSA. (Greg Ivey)

ABOVE: Consolidation on Objective RUGBY next to the remnants of a grape drying hut. (Greg Ivey)
BELOW: Operation MEDUSA—End of Mission; Stand Easy. (Greg Ivey)

ABOVE: PB WILSON in the morning after the return of a company patrol. Gunners would "rack out" in the space between their armoured vehicles and HESCO barriers. (Bob Montague)

ABOVE: Skylark flying in support of operations on October 13th 2006 from what is now becoming FOB MA'SUM GHAR. The operator has a towel over his head and laptop to cut the sun's glare on the screen. The Arghandab River and Pashmul are visible in the distance. (Bob Montague)

ABOVE: Members of C Troop putting an American 120 mm mortar, belonging to Task Force 31, into operation. (Bob Montague)

BELOW: Running maintenance at Sperwan Ghar which too is being turned into an FOB. The hill is still occupied by elements of the American special forces hence the presence of the American flag. (Bob Montague)

ABOVE: M777 firing at Sperwan Ghar. (Bob Montague)
BELOW: Three weapons in use by C Troop at what is now FOB SPERWAN GHAR: the 155mm M777, a 120mm mortar, and in the pit, an 81mm mortar. (Bob Montague)

ABOVE: Photo taken from G29 as the battle group's tactical command group forms a cordon in response to an incident in a village. The vehicle at the near right is an RG-31 mine resistant vehicle. (Bob Montague)

BELOW: A Triple Seven at FOB SPERWAN GHAR with the new digital gun management system installed. The detachment commander's display unit can be seen on the tripod. Other components on the gun are still covered by plastic. (Bob Montague)

ABOVE: The interior of Strong Point West. The bearings marked on the walls are for the platoon's 60mm mortar. (Bob Montague)
BELOW: Both C and D Troops are now at FOB SPERWAN GHAR which continues to be developed. (Bob Montague)

ABOVE: At the going down of the sun...we will remember them. (Bob Montague)

DOUBLE‡DAGGER

— www.doubledagger.ca —

Double Dagger Books is Canada's only military-focused publisher. Conflict and warfare have shaped human history since before we began to record it. The earliest stories that we know of, passed on as oral tradition, speak of war, and more importantly, the essential elements of the human condition that are revealed under its pressure.

We are dedicated to publishing material that, while rooted in conflict, transcend the idea of "war" as merely a genre. Fiction, non-fiction, and stuff that defies categorization, we want to read it all.

Because if you want peace, study war.